T0181961

.NET 2.0 Interoperability Recipes

Recipes

A Problem-Solution Approach

Bruce Bukovics

Apress®

.NET 2.0 Interoperability Recipes: A Problem-Solution Approach

Copyright © 2006 by Bruce Bukovics

ISBN-13: 978-1-4842-2021-4

ISBN-10: 1-4842-2021-8

DOI 10.1007/978-1-4302-0145-8

9 8 7 6 5 4 3 2 1

Distributed to the book trade worldwide by Springer-Verlag New York, Inc., 233 Spring Street, 6th Floor, New York, NY 10013. Phone 1-800-SPRINGER, fax 201-348-4505, e-mail orders-ny@springer-sbm.com, or visit http://www.springeronline.com.

For information on translations, please contact Apress directly at 2560 Ninth Street, Suite 219, Berkeley, CA 94710. Phone 510-549-5930, fax 510-549-5939, e-mail info@apress.com, or visit http://www.apress.com.

The source code for this book is available to readers at http://www.apress.com in the Source Code section.

For my son, Brennen

Contents at a Glance

Contents

About the Author

BRUCE BUKOVICS has been a working developer for over 25 years. Over the last quarter-century he has designed and developed applications in such widely varying areas as banking, corporate finance, credit card processing, payroll processing, and retail automation.

He has firsthand developer experience with C, C++, Delphi, Visual Basic, C#, and Java, and rode the waves of technology as they drifted from mainframe to client/server to n-tier, from COM to COM+, and from web services to .NET Remoting and beyond.

He considers himself a pragmatic programmer. He doesn't stand on formality and doesn't do things a certain way just because they have always been done that way. He's willing to look at alternate or unorthodox solutions to a problem if that's what it takes.

Bruce is currently employed at Radiant Systems, Inc., in Alpharetta, Georgia, as a senior developer and architect in the central technology group.

About the Technical Reviewers

CHRISTOPHE NASARRE is a software architect for Business Objects, a company that develops desktop and web-based business intelligence solutions. During his spare time, Christophe writes articles for MSDN Magazine, MSDN/Longhorn, and ASP Today, and since 1996 he has reviewed books on Win32, COM, MFC, and .NET.

NICHOLAS PALDINO is a developer in the New York City area for Exis Consulting, Inc., a boutique software provider that offers software solutions in the fixed income space. Nicholas has also been awarded the Microsoft MVP award for the past four years for his frequent contributions in the `microsoft.public.dotnet.languages.csharp` newsgroup, where he submits anywhere between 100 and 500 posts a month. He also provides technical review services for a number of publishers.

Acknowledgments

First of all, I'd like to thank the entire team at Apress. You all worked very hard to make this book a reality. Thank you for an exceptional job and for making the process a smooth one. Special thanks go to Ewan Buckingham, who was my editor at Apress, and to Sofia Marchant, who kept things organized and on track. Thanks also go to Nicole LeClerc and Ellie Fountain for a great job copy editing and production editing, respectively, and for being so easy to work with.

I would especially like to thank Ralph Davis, who took on the role of development editor for the book. Ralph did a fantastic job handling this first-time author. Not only was he there to correct my mistakes, but also he questioned things that weren't clear and encouraged me to improve things that were. Ralph was my sounding board and voice of reason.

I would also like to thank my technical reviewers, Christophe Nasarre and Nicholas Paldino, who both did an amazing job. Their comments and suggestions helped to improve the accuracy and clarity of all of the recipes. Their efforts and attention to detail made this a much better book.

Thanks also go to John Osborn for believing in the initial idea for this book and championing it.

Finally, I'd like to thank my loving wife, Teresa, and son, Brennen, for being patient with me when I was working late, for understanding when I said I was busy, and for encouraging me when things didn't always go as planned. I love both of you very much. Brennen, I have time to play that game of chess now.

Introduction

It is difficult or impossible to immediately throw out all existing code and start over when a new technology arrives. That's the situation with Microsoft .NET. It represents a new and improved way of developing software for the Windows platform. And, given the chance, you would likely love to rewrite all of your existing code in the newer managed code environment that .NET provides.

However, you have that little problem known as legacy code. You may have C libraries, C++ class libraries, Visual Basic 6.0 COM components, or ATL COM components that you rely upon to run your applications. You may be using third-party libraries and COM components that represent a significant investment. You can't simply throw all of that away. Instead, you need to find a way to move forward with new .NET development while reusing existing pieces of tested, working code. You need a way to interoperate with the existing code until you have a chance to finally rewrite all of it in .NET (if ever).

Fortunately, Microsoft .NET provides a rich set of tools that allow you to do just that. These tools simplify the transition to an all-.NET environment, allowing you to replace a component here and a component there. The problem is that sometimes those tools are difficult to understand and use. And in many cases, Microsoft has provided more than one way to accomplish a particular interop task. Finding the appropriate tool for the task at hand can sometimes be a frustrating experience.

I wrote this book as a resource for other Windows developers who are transitioning from native Windows code to .NET managed code. My aim is to guide you past the infrequently used interop options and focus on those that you will use most often.

Intended Audience

This book is appropriate for any .NET developer who needs to interoperate between .NET code and non-.NET Windows code. You may be an experienced .NET developer who has never had the need to interoperate with native code before. Or you may be completely new to .NET and are just learning the languages and class libraries associated with .NET. In either case, this book is for you.

Most of the examples in this book are presented in both C# and Visual Basic .NET (VB.NET). You will be able to understand the examples as long as you know one of these languages. But this book isn't designed to teach you a language. Likewise, you should already be familiar with the basics of the .NET Framework Class Library (FCL). You don't have to be a guru, but you should at least know the basics.

Since the book is all about interop with existing code, the examples also typically use one or more native Windows languages. For example, the chapters covering the use of C-style functions use examples written in native C++ code. The chapter that focuses on the use of COM components presents Visual Basic 6.0 (VB6) and C++ ATL example components that are used by .NET client code. These same native languages are later used as client code when managed classes are exposed to COM.

While unmanaged code is used extensively in the examples, it is not the primary focus of this book. So if you know VB6 but don't know C++, that's OK—you'll still benefit from the examples. Most of the .NET code works the same way regardless of the unmanaged language used. If there are differences, they are noted in the examples.

Likewise, the chapters covering COM and COM+ assume that you are already familiar with these technologies. This is not a book about learning COM and COM+, but it will show you how to use COM and COM+ from .NET.

How This Book Is Organized

This book is organized into nine chapters, with each one focusing on a different aspect of Windows interoperability. The following sections provide a brief summary of the contents of each chapter.

Chapter 1: Using C-Style APIs

This chapter discusses the use of Platform Invocation Services (PInvoke) to access C-style functions from managed .NET code. It includes recipes that demonstrate how to declare and use unmanaged functions, change the calling convention and character set, handle errors and exceptions, and manage memory.

Chapter 2: C-Style APIs: Structures, Classes, and Arrays

This chapter is a logical continuation of Chapter 1 and covers topics that relate to user-defined types such as structures and classes. Recipes in this chapter cover passing structures, classes, and arrays between managed and unmanaged code; controlling the field alignment within a structure; and implementing field-level marshaling within a structure.

Chapter 3: Win32 API

This chapter covers the topics associated with using Win32 functions from managed .NET code. Recipes include accessing the ANSI or Unicode version of a function, retrieving Win32 error codes, handling callbacks, and passing handles and objects between managed and unmanaged code. The chapter also provides a recipe that illustrates how to replace a set of Win32 functions entirely with managed code.

Chapter 4: Using C++ Interop

The focus of this chapter is on using C++ to solve various interop problems. Recipes in this chapter include how to mix managed and unmanaged code in a project and within a single source file, how to use managed objects from unmanaged code, and how to marshal strings and structures with embedded pointers and callbacks. There is also a recipe that demonstrates the use of C++ as a custom COM wrapper.

Chapter 5: Using COM

All of the recipes in this chapter demonstrate some aspect of using COM components from managed .NET code. Recipes include importing and using a COM object, handling COM events, marshaling common COM data types, handling HRESULT codes, and providing error information.

Chapter 6: Exposing Managed Code to COM

The recipes in this chapter are the reciprocal of Chapter 5. They show you how to expose managed .NET code as COM components, suitable for use by any COM client. Recipes include exposing managed components to COM by defining your own interface, controlling COM identity and visibility, exposing managed events to COM, and handling HRESULT codes and managed exceptions.

Chapter 7: Marshaling to COM Clients

This chapter continues where Chapter 6 left off, focusing on a set of specific COM marshaling problems. Recipes include how to control parameter direction; how to marshal strings, arrays, Variants, and currency; and how to marshal classes and structures to COM clients.

Chapter 8: COM+ Enterprise Services

This chapter shows you how to make use of COM+ services from managed code. Recipes include developing a COM+ component in managed code, installing and registering the component, using just-in-time (JIT) activation, using object pooling, implementing role-based COM+ security, and writing Queued Components.

Chapter 9: COM+ Enterprise Services Transactions

The recipes in this chapter all focus on the use of COM+ transactions. The recipes demonstrate how to enable transactions, how to place a vote for a transaction, how to use the new .NET Framework 2.0 transactional code blocks, how to build your own resource manager, and how to use services without components.

Software Requirements

To run the examples in this book, you need some way to build and run C# or VB.NET code. The bare minimum for this is the .NET Framework SDK and a source code editor. While this minimal setup allows you to run the example code, many of the recipes show you how to use features of Visual Studio .NET 2005 to simplify the job of interop. Therefore, use of Visual Studio .NET 2005 is highly recommended.

All of the code in this book was originally developed using beta 2 and release candidate 1 of Visual Studio .NET 2005. It was subsequently checked using the final release to manufacturing (RTM) version.

All of the C++ unmanaged code used in the examples can be built with Visual Studio .NET 2005. You don't need the older 6.0 version of Visual C++ for this purpose. However, many of the COM examples use VB6. Since VB6 is a drastically different language than VB.NET, you'll need VB6 to build and run those examples.

CHAPTER 1

■ ■ ■

Using C-Style APIs

Platform Invocation Services (PInvoke or P/Invoke) is the part of the common language runtime (CLR) that enables managed .NET code to access unmanaged functions. The functions can be written in ordinary C or C++, and they are usually packaged as dynamic link libraries (DLLs). These are the same unmanaged functions that you know and love, as they are routinely used by your non-.NET applications to provide core business functionality. PInvoke allows you to reuse the functions you need now while you contemplate a future rewrite in a .NET language.

When boiled down to only the essential elements, the steps to using PInvoke to access unmanaged functions are as follows:

1. Identify the function that you need to call.

2. Declare the function in managed code and apply the attributes that PInvoke uses.

3. Call the function.

This is the essence of PInvoke, but along the way there will likely be several twists and turns. The complexity of PInvoke is directly related to the complexity of the unmanaged function you need to call.

If you are using Visual C++, you have a second option available to you for accessing unmanaged functions, one that no other .NET language supports. It's simply called C++ Interop. This C++ technology was previously called It Just Works, or IJW. It enables you to make calls to unmanaged code without the special function declarations or attributes required by PInvoke in other languages.

Interop marshaling (or just *marshaling*) is the process of passing data between managed and unmanaged memory during a call. Marshaling takes place when input parameters are passed to an unmanaged function, and when a result is returned from the call. Tasks performed by the marshaler include conversion of data between managed and unmanaged types, copying of the converted data between managed and unmanaged memory, and freeing memory at the conclusion of the call.

Most of the PInvoke classes and attributes can be found in the System.Runtime. InteropServices namespace. The documentation for this namespace is a good starting point when you are searching for just the right attribute or class for the task at hand.

This chapter focuses on the core topics related to the use of unmanaged functions from managed code. There are recipes that cover the process of identifying the function to call, then declaring and calling the function. Several recipes discuss the use of managed wrappers to encapsulate the unmanaged calls, with one version of a wrapper focusing on exception handling and another on security.

The performance implications of the data types used during interop are demonstrated in one recipe, while memory-management issues are discussed in another. In between all of this, there are recipes that cover calling conventions, renaming of functions, error handling, and string character-set issues.

The chapter concludes with a recipe that demonstrates how to dynamically call a function in a DLL.

One common use of PInvoke is to call Win32 API functions. The techniques described in this chapter are applicable to calling Win32 functions or calling your own functions. Additional information on calling Win32 functions is provided in Chapter 3.

1-1. Identifying the Unmanaged Function

Problem

You want to use an existing unmanaged function from managed code, and you think you've identified the DLL containing the function. However, you need a way to verify the presence and exact name of the function within the DLL.

Solution

Use the dumpbin.exe command-line utility to view the functions that have been exported from an unmanaged DLL. This utility is included with Visual Studio .NET as part of the Visual C++ set of tools. To run this utility against a DLL, follow these steps:

1. Open a Visual Studio .NET command prompt. You'll find a shortcut to this command prompt within the Visual Studio .NET Program Files tree structure off the Start menu. Opening this command prompt sets up the environment variables needed to access the Visual Studio .NET command-line tools.

2. Change to the directory containing the DLL that you wish to examine.

3. Execute the tool using a command in this format:

```
dumpbin /exports <dllname>
```

The output from this command lists the function names that have been exported from the named DLL. You can then use this list to confirm the presence and entry point of the function that you need to use.

As an example, you can execute dumpbin on one of the DLLs provided by Microsoft, such as kernel32.dll. This DLL is located in the System32 folder where Windows was installed. This DLL contains many of the Win32 functions, and the list of functions exported from it is very large.

To see the exports from kernel32.dll, you execute this command:

```
dumpbin /exports kernel32.dll
```

When you execute this command, you'll see a long scrolling list of functions. If you prefer, you can redirect the output to a file, like this:

```
dumpbin /exports kernel32.dll > MyList.txt
```

A partial list of the output from this command follows.

```
Dump of file kernel32.dll

File Type: DLL

  Section contains the following exports for KERNEL32.dll

    00000000 characteristics
    40B53BB8 time date stamp Wed May 26 20:52:08 2004
        0.00 version
           1 ordinal base
         829 number of functions
         829 number of names

    ordinal hint RVA      name

          1    0 00010E2C AddAtomA
          2    1 0000A977 AddAtomW
          3    2 00038EEC AddConsoleAliasA
          4    3 00038EB5 AddConsoleAliasW
          5    4 0003A0E2 AllocConsole
          6    5 0001EA71 AllocateUserPhysicalPages
          7    6 0001EE5C AreFileApisANSI
          8    7 00038608 AssignProcessToJobObject
```

Of course, depending on the version of Windows that you're running, this list may look different.

As shown in this partial listing, the exact name of each exported function is shown. Using this information, you can now easily verify the presence and exact entry point of a particular function.

How It Works

The dumpbin utility has been included with Visual C++ for several releases now, including Visual C++ 6.0 and Visual Studio .NET 2003 and 2005. It is designed to display information from a binary file that is in the 32-bit Common Object File Format (COFF). This can include libraries of COFF objects, executable files, and DLLs.

Note The dumpbin utility has a number of other command-line options, allowing you to further dissect any COFF binary. However, the /exports option works best for viewing functions that have been exported from an unmanaged DLL. Consult the MSDN documentation for the complete list of options.

In general, in order to use an unmanaged function, you'll need to identify a number of items related to the function, including the following:

- The entry point of the function itself

- The name of the DLL containing the function

- The signature of the function, including the number, type, and order of any calling arguments as well as any return value

- The calling convention of the function (i.e., StdCall, Cdecl)

- Memory management requirements (i.e., does the function allocate any memory that you are expected to free)

- Prerequisites for calling the function (i.e., do you need to first call other functions in order to set up some internal state)

Some of these items may be readily available, while others may take some amount of research on your part. The dumpbin utility can assist you with some of that research, helping you to locate the correct dynamic link library that contains a particular function and to verify the exact entry point name of the function (the first two items in the preceding list).

You may wonder why we need to verify the function name itself. After all, shouldn't the name of the function be obvious? You would think so, but that's not always the case. We need to make an important distinction between the function name declared within the C or C++ header file and the actual entry point that is exported from the DLL, since these are not always the same. When calling a function from managed code, we are concerned with only the actual entry point name exported from the DLL.

Many times, the header file will use a #define statement to provide a consistent alias name for a number of function entry points, varying the actual entry point based on compile-time options. The Win32 API is notorious for this, exposing either the wide (Unicode) or ANSI version of a function depending on your compile options. An example of this is shown in the sample output of this command, where you see AddAtomA and AddAtomW, the ANSI and Wide versions of AddAtom. When referencing this function from unmanaged C or C++ code, you'll usually just refer to AddAtom without the trailing letter. The correct version is defined behind the scenes based on your compile settings and preprocessor definitions (e.g., UNICODE). However, when referencing this function from managed code, you'll need to specify the actual entry point using the full name shown in the dumpbin listing.

Once we've identified the function entry point and DLL, we're still left with the other items in the list. Unfortunately, we don't have another utility that will help us with this research. Our best source for answering the remaining questions is the header file that declares the unmanaged function and any available documentation. The C or C++ header files can usually help us identify the calling arguments. We may also get lucky and find comments in the code that help answer the remaining questions.

Related Information

See recipe 3-1 (Accessing ANSI or Wide Functions).

1-2. Using the Function from Managed Code

Problem

You've identified the function you need to call, and now you want to use it from your managed code.

Solution

You need to declare the function within your managed code and add the DllImport attribute to the declaration.

Consider this rather trivial C function that you need to use:

```
//
// A trivial unmanaged function that we want to call
// from managed code
int AddSomeNumbers(int numOne, int numTwo)
{
    return numOne + numTwo;
}
```

The C header that declares this function looks like this:

```
extern "C" __declspec(dllexport)
    int AddSomeNumbers(int numOne, int numTwo);
```

An example of using this function from managed C# code follows.

```
using System;
using System.Runtime.InteropServices;
namespace ManagedClient
{
    /// <summary>
    /// sample c# client calling an unmanaged api
    /// </summary>
    class CSharpClient
    {
        //declare the unmanaged api
        [DllImport("FlatAPILib.DLL")]
        public static extern int AddSomeNumbers(
            int myNumA, int myNumB);

        /// <summary>
        /// The main entry point for the application.
        /// </summary>
        [STAThread]
        static void Main(string[] args)
```

```
        {
            //make the unmanaged call
            int result = AddSomeNumbers(1, 2);

            //show the result
            Console.WriteLine("Result from AddSomeNumbers = "
                + result.ToString());

            //wait for input
            Console.WriteLine("Press any key to exit");
            Console.Read();
        }
    }
}
```

Here is the result when this code is executed:

```
Result from AddSomeNumbers = 3
Press any key to exit
```

If you prefer Visual Basic .NET, here is an example of calling the same unmanaged function:

```
Imports System.Runtime.InteropServices   'needed for DllImport
Module VBClient

    'declare the unmanaged function
    <DllImport("FlatAPILib.dll")> _
    Public Function AddSomeNumbers( _
            ByVal numA As Integer, ByVal numB As Integer) _
        As Integer
    End Function

    Sub Main()
        Dim result As Integer = 0
        'call the unmanaged function
        result = AddSomeNumbers(1, 2)
        'show the results
        Console.WriteLine( _
            String.Format("Result from function is {0}", result))
        Console.Read()
    End Sub

End Module
```

The result from the Visual Basic .NET code looks like this:

```
Result from function is 3
```

How It Works

The DllImport attribute contains a number of optional properties that give you complete control over the way an unmanaged function is called. Many of these properties are discussed in other recipes in the first three chapters of this book. The preceding example illustrates the bare minimum that you'll need and makes a number of assumptions.

Any function that you call must be declared within your managed code. That's why the example contains this declaration:

```
public static extern int AddSomeNumbers(int myNumA, int myNumB);
```

This allows other managed code to reference this function. Note that we've declared the function with the extern modifier. This tells the compiler that this function is implemented externally and not to look for it within any managed code.

In this example, we've also declared the function as static. The compiler enforces this whenever the DllImport attribute is applied. This makes sense, since the function we're declaring isn't a method on an object instance.

Note In Visual Basic .NET, the Shared keyword is used to declare a static function. If you apply the DllImport attribute to a function that is declared within a class, the function must be declared with the Shared keyword. However, notice that the Visual Basic .NET example code shown here does not declare the AddSomeNumbers function as Shared. This works without the Shared keyword since the function is declared within a Visual Basic .NET module instead of a class.

Immediately above the function declaration, we add the DllImport attribute:

```
[DllImport("FlatAPILib.DLL")]
```

Within this attribute, we specify the full name of the unmanaged DLL that contains the function. We can omit the .DLL extension and enter the DllImport attribute like this, if preferred:

```
[DllImport("FlatAPILib")]
```

We haven't specified one of the optional DllImport properties, EntryPoint. This implies that the function name we've declared in our managed code must exactly match the name of the function that was exported from the DLL.

In this example, we've declared the unmanaged function as extern "C" in the C header file. This prevents the C++ compiler from mangling or decorating the function name. Since C++ allows function overloading, the compiler will normally use the function name, parameters, and return value to generate a unique name for the function. Declaring the function as extern "C" suppresses this behavior and provides us with an exported function with the name that we expect.

Also note that the parameter names used in the unmanaged and managed code do not need to match. The only requirement is that the exact number, order, and type of parameters match.

We haven't specified a calling convention in the DllImport attribute, so the default of Winapi is used. This uses the default calling convention for the platform. For most Windows platforms, this defaults to StdCall. For Windows CE, the default is Cdecl. The calling convention determines the order in which the parameters are passed and who cleans up the stack. The only requirement is that the calling convention specified in the DllImport attribute must match the convention used in your unmanaged code.

Once the function is declared, we can easily call it from our managed code as if it were just another static method in our class.

```
//make the unmanaged call
int result = AddSomeNumbers(1, 2);
```

Since we've declared this function as static within our managed code, we must call it as a member of the class rather than an object instance. We don't need to do anything special to translate the parameters or the return value between the managed and unmanaged code. In this case, we're dealing with only integers, which are represented the same way in both environments. This won't always be the case.

Related Information

See recipes 1-1 (Identifying the Unmanaged Function), 1-4 (Changing the Calling Convention), and 1-5 (Renaming a Function).

1-3. Simplifying Reuse of Unmanaged Functions

Problem

You have an unmanaged function that must be used in a number of places within your managed application. However, you would like to simplify the way your managed code calls this function by hiding most of the low-level details.

Solution

One way to enable easier reuse of unmanaged code is to develop a managed wrapper class. The wrapper is easily used by other managed classes and completely hides the details of calling the unmanaged function. In fact, it completely hides the fact that you are calling an unmanaged function.

Consider an example using this unmanaged function:

```
int GetCustomerStatus(char* customerId, int customerType)
{
    //code to look up the customer and return
    //a status goes here

    if (customerType == 2122)
    {
        return 1; //current
    }
```

```
    else if (strcmp(customerId, "bbbbbb") == 0)
    {
        return 3; //past due
    }

    return 0;
}
```

While this certainly isn't production-level code, the function implements just enough code to demonstrate the use of a wrapper.

The declaration of the function looks like this:

```
extern "C" __declspec(dllexport)
    int GetCustomerStatus(char* customerId, int customerType);
```

A C# managed wrapper for this function might look like this:

```
using System;
using System.Runtime.InteropServices;

namespace CustomerWrapperTest
{
    /// <summary>
    /// Defines customer status values returned
    /// returned from the unmanaged function
    /// </summary>
    enum CustomerStatus
    {
        Unknown        = 0,
        Current        = 1,
        Inactive       = 2,
        PastDue        = 3,
        InCollections  = 4
    }

    /// <summary>
    /// Defines the type of customer and is used
    /// by the unmanaged function to determine
    /// the database to search
    /// </summary>
    enum CustomerType
    {
        Individual    = 1001,
        Corporate     = 2122,
        Government    = 35,
        NonProfit     = 501
    }
```

```csharp
/// <summary>
/// Internal class containing any unmanaged
/// method declarations
/// </summary>
internal sealed class NativeMethods
{
    //declare the unmanaged api
    [DllImport("FlatAPILib.DLL")]
    public static extern int GetCustomerStatus(
        String customerId, int customerType);
}


/// <summary>
/// A managed wrapper for unmanaged customer functions
/// </summary>
class CustomerWrapper
{
    /// <summary>
    /// Returns customer status
    /// </summary>
    /// <param name="custType"></param>
    /// <param name="custId"></param>
    /// <returns></returns>
    public CustomerStatus
        GetCustomerStatus(CustomerType custType, String custId)
    {
        //convert enum values to those expected
        //by the unmanaged function. This eliminates
        //the need to pass magic numbers from
        //managed code. We can validate the enum
        //prior to calling the function.
        int customerTypeInt    = 0;
        if (Enum.IsDefined(typeof(CustomerType), custType))
        {
            customerTypeInt = (int)custType;
        }
        else
        {
            throw new ArgumentOutOfRangeException(
                String.Format(
                "Invalid CustomerType {0}", custType));
        }

        //make the function call
        int result = NativeMethods.GetCustomerStatus(
            custId, customerTypeInt);
```

```
        //we convert the integer result to our enum
        //to make the result clearer to other managed code
        if (Enum.IsDefined(typeof(CustomerStatus), result))
        {
            return (CustomerStatus)result;
        }
        else
        {
            return CustomerStatus.Unknown;
        }
    }
  }
}
```

A Visual Basic .NET version of this wrapper could be implemented like this:

```vbnet
Imports System
Imports System.Runtime.InteropServices

'define enum for status
Public Enum CustomerStatus
    Unknown = 0
    Current = 1
    Inactive = 2
    PastDue = 3
    InCollections = 4
End Enum

'define enum for cust type
Public Enum CustomerType
    Individual = 1001
    Corporate = 2122
    Government = 35
    NonProfit = 501
End Enum

Friend Class NativeMethods
    'declare the unmanaged api
    <DllImport("FlatAPILib.DLL")> _
    Public Shared Function GetCustomerStatus( _
        ByVal customerId As String, _
        ByVal customerType As Integer) As Integer
    End Function
End Class

Public Class CustomerWrapperVB
    'wrapper method
    Public Function GetCustomerStatus( _
```

```vbnet
            ByVal custType As CustomerType, _
            ByVal custId As String) As CustomerStatus

        Dim customerTypeInt As Integer = 0

        'validate the enum value passed in
        If (System.Enum.IsDefined( _
            GetType(CustomerType), custType)) Then
            customerTypeInt = custType
        Else
            Throw New ArgumentOutOfRangeException( _
                String.Format( _
                "Invalid CustomerType {0}", custType))
        End If

        'make the function call
        Dim result As Integer
        result = NativeMethods.GetCustomerStatus( _
            custId, customerTypeInt)
        'convert the result
        If (System.Enum.IsDefined( _
            GetType(CustomerStatus), result)) Then
            Return result
        Else
            Return CustomerStatus.Unknown
        End If
    End Function
End Class
```

In this example, we've chosen to declare the unmanaged function in a separate class named NativeMethods. This follows a Microsoft pattern that is checked by tools such as FxCop. Implementing things this way is certainly not a requirement. However, it does provide a subtle reminder that the function being called is unmanaged code and is possibly unsafe.

Code to execute the C# version of this wrapper looks like this:

```csharp
CustomerWrapper wrapper = new CustomerWrapper();
//call the wrapper and show the result
CustomerStatus status = wrapper.GetCustomerStatus(
    CustomerType.Corporate, "aaaaa");
Console.WriteLine(
    "Result status is " + status.ToString());

//call the wrapper and show the result
status = wrapper.GetCustomerStatus(
    CustomerType.Individual, "bbbbbb");
Console.WriteLine(
    "Result status is " + status.ToString());
```

When this code is executed, we see these results:

```
Result status is Current
Result status is PastDue
```

How It Works

Developing a wrapper for unmanaged code allows you to hide the details of calling an unmanaged function from other managed code. Other managed classes simply create an instance of your wrapper class and use it, without knowing or caring that it actually references an unmanaged function.

The idea of hiding low-level details using a wrapper isn't a new concept. However, this is an especially important technique to use when dealing with unmanaged code. The following are some of the benefits of this approach:

- A wrapper isolates the interop code to a single class. If the unmanaged function changes, you need to modify and test only the wrapper class. The remainder of your managed code isn't affected.

- A wrapper acts as a convenient place to logically group calls to related functions. In many cases, you may need to make calls to multiple functions that work together when executed in a prescribed sequence. Placing all of the related functions in a single wrapper allows you to execute multiple functions during a single method call.

- A wrapper provides you with a convenient place to normalize input and output parameters. This involves controlling the input/output parameters to and from the unmanaged function using enumerated types and type conversion logic. This allows you to reduce the spread of any "magic numbers" used by the unmanaged code.

- A wrapper provides a central place for memory-management code needed to call some functions. The example function (GetCustomerStatus) doesn't have any special memory-management requirements, but this won't always be the case.

- A wrapper can include any amount of validation prior to calling the unmanaged function. This is especially important when calling unmanaged functions that might be considered dangerous if passed incorrect values.

- A wrapper provides a place to check unmanaged return codes and translate these into results that are more meaningful to your managed code. This might include throwing exceptions when incorrect results are returned.

- Most important, a wrapper provides a better migration path away from the unmanaged function. Your other managed code is dependent on only the wrapper, not the unmanaged function. As your needs change, you can replace the unmanaged function call with new managed code called from the wrapper, without affecting the remainder of your application.

In the example wrapper, we've tried to control the input and output of the function by first defining enumerated types. These types define any "magic numbers" used by the function.

This greatly simplifies the use of this function for all other managed code. It allows us to write code that is much more descriptive and less error-prone. For example, consider this code:

```
if(status == CustomerStatus.PastDue)
```

or

```
if(status == 3)
```

Which code would you rather read? Which code is self-describing? Which code will be easier to modify years from now once the original developer has moved on to greener pastures?

The sample wrapper also uses an enumerated type for the custType input parameter. This allows you to validate the input value against a set of named values, eliminating the chance of passing an invalid magic number to the function. You won't have to wonder if a corporate customer is a type 2122 or a 2123, because you'll have an enum type that defines the acceptable values.

Related Information

See recipes 1-9 (Using C++ Interop As a Managed Wrapper) and 1-13 (Securing Access to Unmanaged Code).

1-4. Changing the Calling Convention

Problem

The unmanaged function you need to call does not use the default calling convention of StdCall.

Solution

Modify the managed function declaration to specify a different calling convention. Use the CallingConvention field of the DllImport attribute. For example, consider this unmanaged function declaration:

```
extern "C" __declspec(dllexport)
    int __cdecl AddSomeNumbers(int numOne, int numTwo);
```

To specify that this function should be invoked with the cdecl calling convention, you declare the function like this in C#:

```
[DllImport("FlatAPILib.DLL",
    CallingConvention=CallingConvention.Cdecl)]
public static extern int AddSomeNumbers(int myNumA, int myNumB);
```

The same declaration in a Visual Basic .NET module looks like this:

```
<DllImport("FlatAPILib.DLL", _
    CallingConvention:=CallingConvention.Cdecl)> _
Public Function AddSomeNumbers( _
    ByVal myNumA As Integer, ByVal myNumB As Integer) _
        As Integer
End Function
```

The possible calling convention values are as follows:

- StdCall

- Cdecl

- ThisCall

- Winapi

The default calling convention if not specified is Winapi. This uses the default calling convention for the platform. For most Windows platforms, this defaults to StdCall. For Windows CE, the default is Cdecl.

How It Works

The calling convention is important since it defines part of the contract between the unmanaged function and your managed code. In particular, the calling convention determines the party responsible for cleaning up the stack. Table 1-1 summarizes the possible choices, as defined in the CallingConvention enumeration.

Table 1-1. *CallingConvention Enumeration*

Calling Convention	Description
StdCall	The callee (the unmanaged function) cleans up the stack. Parameters are pushed on the stack from right to left (reverse order).
Cdecl	The caller (managed code) cleans up the stack. Parameters are pushed on the stack from right to left (reverse order). Since the caller performs the cleanup, this calling convention supports functions that accept a variable number of parameters.
Winapi	If this calling convention is specified, the default for the platform will be used. If run under Windows, StdCall will be used. However, if run under Windows CE .NET (the .NET Compact Framework), Cdecl will be used.
ThisCall	This calling convention is primarily used for interop with C++ class methods. It passes a pointer to the C++ object as the first parameter. It would not typically be used when calling flat functions.
FastCall	This calling convention makes an attempt to pass parameters in registers whenever possible. While this convention is available in the CallingConvention enumeration, it isn't supported in .NET. Therefore, you will never use it in your managed code.

One other aspect to the calling convention is that it controls the way functions are named as they are exported in unmanaged code. This is referred to as *name decoration*.

For example, if a function is defined as __stdcall and extern "C", it is decorated with a leading underscore (_), and the function name is followed by the at sign (@) and the number of bytes in the argument list (the total bytes of all parameters).

Using the AddSomeNumbers function shown in the example, the actual entry point for the function name would look something like this: _AddSomeNumbers@8. The magic number of 8 is used because we're passing two 4-byte integers, giving us a grand total of 8. This name can be confirmed by running the dumpbin utility on the sample DLL.

However, as long as the calling conventions specified by the unmanaged function and your managed code agree, you shouldn't have to worry about the differences in decorated names.

In the example, by specifying Cdecl as the CallingConvention in DllImport, .NET interop correctly matched the entry point names. On the other hand, if the function were defined in C as __stdcall, but we incorrectly defined it in managed code as CallingConvention.Cdecl, the names would not match. In this case, the function call would fail because it could not find the correct entry point.

Note For additional error information during debugging, you can enable the Managed Debugging Assistants included with Visual Studio .NET (by selecting Debug ➤ Exceptions). These agents provide lower-level details as to the cause of the problem during a debug session.

The best way to determine the calling convention used by a function is to examine the C/C++ header file. If there is no explicit calling convention specified for the function, it will default to the C/C++ project settings.

If the source for the function isn't available, or as a sanity check, you can examine the names exported from the DLL using the dumpbin utility. By viewing the names and knowing the rules for decorated names, you should be able to determine the calling convention for a function.

Related Information

See recipe 1-1 (Identifying the Unmanaged Function).

1-5. Renaming a Function

Problem

You need to change the name used within your managed code to reference an unmanaged function. This may be due to a naming conflict with another unmanaged function or managed method, to comply with internal naming standards, or for another reason.

Solution

The DllImport attribute allows you to optionally specify the entry point name of an unmanaged function. When an entry point name is specified, that name will be matched to the entry point exported from the DLL. You are then free to choose a different name of the function to be used by managed code.

Consider the C declaration for this simple unmanaged function:

```
int FunctionToRename(int valueOne)
```

Normally, you would use DllImport in your C# code to declare the function, like this:

```
[DllImport("FlatAPILib.DLL")]
public static extern int FunctionToRename(int anInt);
```

This means that PInvoke looks for the name FunctionToRename exported from the FlatAPILib.DLL. Using this declaration, your managed code references this function with the same name (FunctionToRename).

However, by adding the optional EntryPoint field to the DllImport attribute, you can effectively rename the function:

```
[DllImport("FlatAPILib.DLL", EntryPoint="FunctionToRename")]
public static extern int RenamedFunction(int anInt);
```

The declaration looks like this in Visual Basic .NET:

```
<DllImport("FlatAPILib.DLL", _
    EntryPoint:="FunctionToRename")> _
Public Function RenamedFunction( _
    ByVal anInt As Integer) As Integer
End Function
```

Once this is done, your managed code must reference the function with the new name of RenamedFunction. When the function call is made, the actual entry point name of FunctionToRename will be called.

How It Works

You might need to rename a function like this for a number of reasons, including the following:

- The function name conflicts with another function. Perhaps you are using multiple unmanaged libraries of functions, and the name has already been used in another library.

- The name conflicts with your internal naming standards.

- There are ANSI and wide (Unicode) versions of the same function and you need to specify which one to use.

- The function is written in such a way that it accepts untyped parameters. In order to add type safety to your managed code, you would like to declare the function multiple times using different data types and possibly different names. This would make the intent of the function clearer to anyone using it.

Note An alternative to renaming a function is to create a managed wrapper for it. Once this is done, any potential problems with the function name are eliminated since the only class referencing the function is the wrapper itself. The managed wrapper then exposes methods that conform to the internal standards and do not cause any naming conflicts. See recipe 1-2 (Using the Function from Managed Code).

A function might be written to accept any data type as an input parameter. Internally, the function will determine the type of parameter that was passed in and process it accordingly. As an example, consider a function that is defined like this:

```
int PolymorphicFunction(void* anyValue, int dataType)
```

This function accepts one parameter that is type void*, meaning that any data type can be passed to the function. However, when we use this function from our managed code, we would like to declare the function so that it is type-safe, accepting only valid types. To accomplish this, we can declare the same function multiple times in our code, each time using a different name but pointing to the same entry point.

■**Caution** This is certainly not the recommended way to implement this unmanaged function. This is simply a manufactured example that demonstrates one possible use of renaming a function. However, on occasion, you do need to interoperate with badly written unmanaged code such as this. This example demonstrates how you can use renaming, along with different method signatures, to apply some amount of type safety to the function.

Here is an example:

```
//first declaration of a function that accepts any type
[DllImport("FlatAPILib.DLL", EntryPoint="PolymorphicFunction")]
public static extern int FunctionWithInteger(
    ref int anInt, int type);

//second declaration of a function that accepts any type
[DllImport("FlatAPILib.DLL", EntryPoint="PolymorphicFunction")]
public static extern int FunctionWithChar(
    ref char aChar, int type);
```

In the example function, we might have discovered that it really accepts only two data types: an integer or a Unicode character. So as shown here, we declare the function twice, each time with a different name and accepting a different data type. In both declarations, the EntryPoint directs us to the same function within the unmanaged DLL.

■**Note** In this example, the first void* parameter is declared with the ref modifier. This is necessary since the example function is expecting a pointer to an integer or char, rather than the value itself.

With this in place, we can invoke the function with a small degree of type safety, knowing that we've declared the function to accept only the allowed data types. Exposing the function in this way prevents someone from passing an unacceptable data type. We can then call the function from C# using either one of our declared methods:

```
int myIntValue = 123;
FunctionWithInteger(ref myIntValue, 1);

char myCharValue = 'A';
FunctionWithChar(ref myCharValue, 2);
```

The function declaration in Visual Basic .NET looks like this:

```
<DllImport("FlatAPILib.DLL", _
    EntryPoint:="PolymorphicFunction")> _
Public Function FunctionWithInteger( _
    ByRef anInt As Integer, _
    ByVal type As Integer) As Integer
End Function

<DllImport("FlatAPILib.DLL", _
    EntryPoint:="PolymorphicFunction")> _
Public Function FunctionWithChar( _
    ByRef aChar As Char, _
    ByVal type As Integer) As Integer
End Function
```

And code to execute these functions looks like this:

```
Dim myIntValue As Integer = 123
Dim result As Integer = FunctionWithInteger( _
    myIntValue, 1)
Console.WriteLine("Result from FunctionWithInteger = " _
    + result.ToString())

Dim myCharValue As Char = "A"
result = FunctionWithChar( _
    myCharValue, 2)
Console.WriteLine("Result from FunctionWithChar = " _
    + result.ToString())
```

We could also create overloaded versions of the function with the same name rather than giving it two completely different names. The declarations could look like this:

```
//first overloaded version of a polymorphic function
[DllImport("FlatAPILib.DLL", EntryPoint="PolymorphicFunction")]
public static extern int OverloadedFunction(
    ref int anInt, int type);

//second overloaded version of a polymorphic function
[DllImport("FlatAPILib.DLL", EntryPoint="PolymorphicFunction")]
public static extern int OverloadedFunction(
    ref char aChar, int type);
```

The calls to this function would look like this:

```
char myCharValue = 'Z';
EntryPointTest.OverloadedFunction(ref myCharValue, 2);

int myIntValue = 456;
EntryPointTest.OverloadedFunction(ref myIntValue, 1);
```

Here is the declaration in Visual Basic .NET:

```
<DllImport("FlatAPILib.DLL", _
    EntryPoint:="PolymorphicFunction")> _
Public Function OverloadedFunction( _
    ByRef anInt As Integer, _
    ByVal type As Integer) As Integer
End Function

<DllImport("FlatAPILib.DLL", _
    EntryPoint:="PolymorphicFunction")> _
Public Function OverloadedFunction( _
    ByRef aChar As Char, _
    ByVal type As Integer) As Integer
End Function
```

And here is the code to execute the functions in Visual Basic .NET:

```
Dim myCharValue As Char = "Z"
Dim result As Integer = EntryPointTest.OverloadedFunction( _
    myCharValue, 2)
Console.WriteLine("Result from OverloadedFunction = " _
    + result.ToString())

Dim myIntValue As Integer = 456
result = EntryPointTest.OverloadedFunction( _
    myIntValue, 1)
Console.WriteLine("Result from OverloadedFunction = " _
    + result.ToString())
```

In either case, the idea is the same. We've taken a function that accepts any data type and added a small amount of type safety by defining it multiple times. This allows the compiler to perform some basic checking for us, preventing us from passing an unexpected data type.

Related Information

See recipes 1-3 (Simplifying Reuse of Unmanaged Functions) and 1-6 (Changing the Character Set Used for Strings).

1-6. Changing the Character Set Used for Strings

Problem

All .NET strings are Unicode strings, but some of the unmanaged functions you need to use expect ANSI strings, and others expect Unicode strings. You need a way to control how the strings are passed to each function.

Solution

The CharSet field of the DllImport attribute is used to specify how strings are marshaled between managed and unmanaged code. If you don't specify this field, the default is ANSI strings. Therefore, if the function you are calling expects char* strings (ANSI), either as an input parameter or a return value, you are not required to specify the CharSet field.

However, if the unmanaged function expects wide strings (wchar_t*, WCHAR), you will need to set the CharSet field when declaring the function.

■Note CharSet is also a field of the StructLayout attribute and serves the same purpose as described here, to control how strings are marshaled. Refer to recipe 2-4 (Controlling Field-Level Marshaling Within Structures) for more information about structures.

Consider this unmanaged function that concatenates two strings, returning the result in a third parameter:

```
void CombineAnsiStrings(char* stringA, char* stringB, char* result);
```

Since this function expects the default ANSI strings, you can declare the function without the CharSet field in C#:

```
[DllImport("FlatAPILib.DLL")]
public static extern void CombineAnsiStrings(string stringA,
    string stringB, StringBuilder result);
```

And shown here in Visual Basic .NET as a Shared member of a class named CharacterSetWrapper:

```
<DllImport("FlatAPILib.DLL")> _
Public Shared Sub CombineAnsiStrings( _
    ByVal stringA As String, _
    ByVal stringB As String, _
    ByVal result As StringBuilder)
End Sub
```

On the other hand, this function uses wide character strings:

```
void CombineUnicodeStrings(
    wchar_t* stringA, wchar_t* stringB, wchar_t* result);
```

When declaring this function in managed code, you are required to include the CharSet field in order to marshal the strings correctly as Unicode. Here is the declaration in C#:

```
[DllImport("FlatAPILib.DLL", CharSet=CharSet.Unicode)]
public static extern void CombineUnicodeStrings(string stringA,
    string stringB, StringBuilder result);
```

And here it is in Visual Basic .NET:

```
<DllImport("FlatAPILib.DLL", CharSet:=CharSet.Unicode)> _
Public Shared Sub CombineUnicodeStrings( _
    ByVal stringA As String, _
    ByVal stringB As String, _
    ByVal result As StringBuilder)
End Sub
```

Regardless of the way the function is declared, it is called the same way from your managed code:

```
StringBuilder result = new StringBuilder(300);
CharacterSetWrapper.CombineAnsiStrings("part1", "part2", result);
CharacterSetWrapper.CombineUnicodeStrings("part1", "part2", result);
```

In either case, you get back a Unicode string in the result parameter, since that's the encoding .NET uses for strings. PInvoke performs the necessary ANSI/Unicode conversions for you.

Note In the example shown here, we pass a StringBuilder instance as the third parameter. The unmanaged function uses this parameter as the output containing the concatenated strings. Since the .NET String class is immutable, it cannot be used for this parameter; the unmanaged code would be unable to update the parameter with the new string. Passing a StringBuilder solves the problem, since the underlying string buffer can be updated by the unmanaged code. However, we must remember to allocate the StringBuilder with a large enough internal buffer. Failure to allocate the StringBuilder or to use an insufficient buffer size will likely cause a failure within the unmanaged code. In the example code, we allocated the StringBuilder with a 300-byte internal buffer, which is sufficient for our purposes.

How It Works

The CharSet field of DllImport is also used in situations where you have two versions of the same function, one for ANSI strings and another for Unicode strings. This is often the case within the Win32 API where the same function is defined twice, once for each character set. However, this technique isn't limited to the Win32 API. You may need to reference a library of functions that follows this same practice, copying the naming conventions used in the Win32 API.

Consider these functions that are similar in purpose to the ones reviewed earlier:

```
void __cdecl CombineStringsW(
    wchar_t* stringA, wchar_t* stringB, wchar_t* result);
void __cdecl CombineStringsA(
    char* stringA, char* stringB, char* result);
```

The difference here is that the functions follow the ANSI/Unicode naming conventions used by the Win32 API. They also use the Cdecl calling convention instead of StdCall. The root function name is the same for each function. However, each name has a single character suffix that identifies the string type, either A for ANSI strings or W for wide (Unicode) strings.

By simply changing the CharSet field, we can control which one of these functions is referenced. This behavior is based on hard-wired rules within PInvoke.

Note Notice that we've defined these functions as __cdecl. If we instead used __stdcall, the compiler would have decorated the function names, changing them to _CombineStringsW@12 and _CombineStringsA@12. When function names are decorated like this, the rules described here regarding function name resolution based on the CharSet field don't apply. Only nondecorated function names with a suffix of A and W work as described here.

To demonstrate this behavior, we first declare two wrapper classes, one for each version of the function. We need to use a wrapper, rather than declaring the function inline, because we will be referring to this function using only the root name (CombineStrings), without the single-character suffix. We can't define the same function twice within the same class scope. In your code, you will likely choose to use one version over the other and use it consistently. In that case, feel free to define the function inline in your code.

Our first simple function wrapper looks like this:

```
class CharacterSetAnsiWrapper
{
    //declare the unmanaged api
    [DllImport("FlatAPILib.DLL", CharSet=CharSet.Ansi,
        CallingConvention = CallingConvention.Cdecl)]
    public static extern void CombineStrings(string stringA,
        string stringB, StringBuilder result);
}
```

Notice that we're declaring the function name as CombineStrings, without any character-set suffix, and we've specified CharSet.Ansi.

The Unicode function wrapper is similar:

```
class CharacterSetUnicodeWrapper
{
    //declare the unmanaged api
    [DllImport("FlatAPILib.DLL", CharSet=CharSet.Unicode,
        CallingConvention = CallingConvention.Cdecl)]
    public static extern void CombineStrings(string stringA,
        string stringB, StringBuilder result);
}
```

The only real difference here is that we've specified CharSet.Unicode instead of CharSet.Ansi.

The code to execute the functions looks like this:

```
StringBuilder result = new StringBuilder(300);

//this executes the CombineStringsA version of the function
CharacterSetAnsiWrapper.CombineStrings("part1", "part2", result);

//this executes the CombineStringsW version of the function
CharacterSetUnicodeWrapper.CombineStrings("part1", "part2", result);
```

Here are the wrappers shown in Visual Basic .NET:

```
Public Class CharacterSetAnsiWrapper
    <DllImport("FlatAPILib.DLL", CharSet:=CharSet.Ansi, _
        CallingConvention:=CallingConvention.Cdecl, _
        ExactSpelling:=False)> _
    Public Shared Sub CombineStrings( _
        ByVal stringA As String, _
        ByVal stringB As String, _
        ByVal result As StringBuilder)
    End Sub
End Class

Public Class CharacterSetUnicodeWrapper
    <DllImport("FlatAPILib.DLL", CharSet:=CharSet.Unicode, _
        CallingConvention:=CallingConvention.Cdecl, _
        ExactSpelling:=False)> _
    Public Shared Sub CombineStrings( _
        ByVal stringA As String, _
        ByVal stringB As String, _
        ByVal result As StringBuilder)
    End Sub
End Class
```

And here is the code to execute them in Visual Basic .NET:

```
Dim result As StringBuilder _
    = New StringBuilder(300)

'this executes the CombineStringsA version of the function
CharacterSetAnsiWrapper.CombineStrings( _
    "part1", "part2", result)

'this executes the CombineStringsW version of the function
CharacterSetUnicodeWrapper.CombineStrings( _
    "part1", "part2", result)
```

Even though we declared and executed a function named CombineStrings, PInvoke was able to execute the correct version based on the character set selected.

Be aware that the ExactSpelling field of the DllImport attribute also affects this automatic behavior based on the CharSet. As the name implies, if the ExactSpelling field is true, the function name you declare must exactly match the name of the unmanaged function. Setting ExactSpelling to false allows the automatic behavior just described.

The default for ExactSpelling varies by .NET language. C# and C++ default to false, while Visual Basic .NET defaults to true. If you want this behavior in Visual Basic .NET, you'll need to explicitly set ExactSpelling to false.

The rules that determine how the function name is ultimately resolved vary by the character set specified. If you specify CharSet.Ansi, PInvoke first searches for the root function name (CombineStrings in the example) and uses that if found. Otherwise, it searches for the A-terminated name (CombineStringsA) and uses that function if found.

If you specify CharSet.Unicode, the search order is reversed. PInvoke will first search for the W-terminated name (CombineStringsW) and use it first if found. It will search for and use the root name (CombineStrings) only if the wide version is missing.

Related Information

See recipes 1-3 (Simplifying Reuse of Unmanaged Functions) and 2-4 (Controlling Field-Level Marshaling Within Structures).

1-7. Using Data Types That Improve Performance

Problem

You're successfully using unmanaged functions from managed code, but you're concerned about the performance of each call and are looking for possible ways it could be improved.

Solution

One factor in the performance of PInvoke calls is the additional time spent marshaling all of the input and output parameters. As data is passed between managed and unmanaged code, it may require conversion of data types, as well as copying of values from one type of memory to another.

A simple way to reduce some of the overhead in PInvoke calls is to use data types that are represented the same way in the managed and unmanaged environments. Data types such as this are referred to as *blittable* types and do not require any conversion. Table 1-2 lists the available blittable types.

Table 1-2. *Blittable Types*

Type	Description
System.Sbyte	Signed 8-bit integer
System.Byte	Unsigned 8-bit integer
System.Int16	Signed 16-bit integer
System.UInt16	Unsigned 16-bit integer
System.Int32	Signed 32-bit integer
System.UInt32	Unsigned 32-bit integer
System.Int64	Signed 64-bit integer
System.UInt64	Unsigned 64-bit integer
System.Single	Single-precision floating point number
System.Double	Double-precision floating point number
System.IntPtr	Platform-specific signed pointer
System.UIntPtr	Platform-specific unsigned pointer

■**Note** The IntPtr and UIntPtr types are designed to be platform-specific. This means they are represented by a 32-bit integer on 32-bit platforms and by a 64-bit integer on 64-bit platforms. In either case,
they are designed to store a pointer or handle and come in very handy during interop with unmanaged code.

In addition to these simple types, single-dimensional arrays of these types are also considered blittable, as are structs made up of only these types.

If you restrict yourself to using these basic types, the overhead of data-type conversions
during each function call will be reduced. This may or may not noticeably improve overall
performance. That depends on a number of factors, including the amount and type of processing done within the unmanaged function and the number of times the function is called from
your application. If the function being called performs simple in-memory operations, then the
use of blittable types may make a noticeable difference. On the other hand, if the function makes
extensive use of system resources, accesses a database or other files, then the impact of blittable
types may not be as substantial.

■**Note** In many cases, you will not have the luxury of optimizing existing functions. After all, the reason you
are using an unmanaged function is that it has previously been developed and tested, either by you or someone else. As is always the case, if you change working code, even for a good reason such as optimization,
you risk breaking existing behavior. At a minimum, you will spend additional time testing your new code. You
should always weigh the additional costs associated with changing a working function against the possible
performance gains before deciding to change parameter data types.

How It Works

The lack of ambiguity in how they are marshaled is another characteristic of blittable types. A 32-bit signed integer is marshaled as a 32-bit signed integer. A single byte (8-bit unsigned integer) is marshaled as a byte. The decisions and subsequent conversions that the marshaler has to make are either reduced or eliminated.

There are several notable omissions from the list of blittable types, namely System.String, System.Boolean, and System.Char. These commonly used types are not blittable, either because they are represented differently in managed and unmanaged code or because they cannot be converted unambiguously.

For example, System.String could be marshaled to unmanaged code as an ANSI character array, a Unicode character array, or a BSTR. The PInvoke marshaler determines how the string will be converted based on the CharSet field of the DllImport attribute, or the optional MarshalAs attribute applied to the string parameter. System.Char follows similar rules for how it can be marshaled.

Likewise, the System.Boolean type could be marshaled as a 1-, 2-, or 4-byte integer value, depending on the attributes that you apply to the function declaration.

■**Note** The comments here concerning System.String, System.Char, and System.Boolean do not apply to the .NET Compact Framework. When running under the Compact Framework, these types are considered blittable. The System.String and System.Char types are marshaled as Unicode characters, and System.Boolean is marshaled as an 8-bit integer.

The following examples illustrate the potential performance gains using blittable types. We start with an unmanaged function implemented like this:

```
bool NonblittableFunction(char valueToTest)
{
    return (islower(valueToTest) != 0);
}
```

This function uses the C run-time library function islower that returns a nonzero result if the integer passed to it is an ANSI lowercase character. An uppercase ANSI character will return zero. It's a trivial function, but it does demonstrate the difference in performance when using blittable versus non-blittable parameters.

As written, this function uses non-blittable data types. The input parameter is a char, which is actually an 8-bit integer representing an ANSI character. Since it is defined as a char in the function signature, a conversion must take place when passing the value from the managed to unmanaged code.

Likewise, the bool returned as a result is non-blittable. The C/C++ reference describes a bool as a type that can have values of only true or false, but its size is undefined. A conversion will be necessary when returning the bool to managed code since a managed System.Boolean is actually a struct.

To test this function from managed C# code, we first declare it like this in the test class:

```
class BlittableTypesTest
{
    [DllImport("FlatAPILib.DLL")]
    public static extern bool NonblittableFunction(char valueToTest);
}
```

We then call the function repeatedly 100,000 times, and check the total elapsed time when the loop concludes. An execution count of 100,000 provides just enough of a test to actually measure the difference once we change data types. Smaller loops of perhaps 10,000 executions won't show a measurable difference because this function executes so quickly.

The C# code to execute the non-blittable version of the function looks like this:

```
const int numberOfCalls        = 100000;
bool result;

//create the StopWatch used for timings
Stopwatch stopWatch = new Stopwatch();

//test non-blittable function
stopWatch.Start();
for(int i = 0; i < numberOfCalls; i++)
{
    result = BlittableTypesTest.NonblittableFunction('a');
}
stopWatch.Stop();
Console.WriteLine(
    "{0} Nonblittable function calls: {1} milliseconds",
    numberOfCalls, stopWatch.ElapsedMilliseconds);
```

The code uses the Stopwatch class found in the System.Diagnostics namespace to time the results of the test.

When we run this test, the results typically look something like this, varying between 60 and 70 milliseconds:

```
100000 Nonblittable function calls: 70.1008 milliseconds
```

Of course, your results will likely be different based on your machine specifications.

While the code is passing the literal a as the character to test, remember that .NET characters are actual 16-bit Unicode characters. Therefore, each time we call this function, the interop marshaler must perform a conversion of this single character from Unicode (16-bit) to ANSI (8-bit). This unmanaged function is written to support only ANSI characters, so we're fine with this conversion. However, there is a performance price to pay for this conversion. In addition to data type conversions, the marshaler also has to copy non-blittable values from managed to unmanaged memory.

Upon return from the function, the unmanaged bool value is converted to the managed bool. Remember that a managed bool is actually an alias for the struct System.Boolean. It is not represented the same way as a simple C/C++ integer with a zero or nonzero value.

To see the difference blittable types make on the performance, we can rewrite the unmanaged function like this;

```
int BlittableFunction(__int8 valueToTest)
{
    return islower(valueToTest);
}
```

To improve performance using blittable types, we change the unmanaged function signature slightly. We start by changing the input parameter from a char to a __int8. This is a Microsoft-specific C++ type that represents an 8-bit integer—the same size as an ANSI char. The function is then changed to return an integer rather than a bool. The islower runtime function actually returns an integer, so we can return the result directly without any additional checks in the unmanaged code.

The declaration of this new function in managed code looks like this:

```
[DllImport("FlatAPILib.DLL")]
public static extern int BlittableFunction(byte valueToTest);
```

We then run the same test of 100,000 calls on this revised function:

```
const int numberOfCalls      = 100000;
bool result;

//create the StopWatch used for timings
Stopwatch stopWatch = new Stopwatch();

//test blittable function
stopWatch.Start();
for(int i = 0; i < numberOfCalls; i++)
{
    result = (BlittableTypesTest.BlittableFunction((byte)'a') != 0);
}
stopWatch.Stop();
Console.WriteLine(
    "{0} Blittable function calls:    {1} milliseconds",
    numberOfCalls, stopWatch.ElapsedMilliseconds);
```

Notice that we've moved the logic that checks the function result for a nonzero value into the managed code. Previously, the unmanaged code made this check and returned an unmanaged bool. The problem is that the unmanaged bool required additional marshaling into the managed bool. We avoid that marshaling overhead by performing that check in the managed code.

The result of this test is typically around 30 milliseconds on my machine.

```
100000 Blittable function calls:    30.0432 milliseconds
```

That makes the function call using blittable types twice as fast (give or take a few milliseconds).

For good measure, we can perform this same test entirely in unmanaged code. This will further demonstrate the overhead associated with the PInvoke calls. To do this, we write a new unmanaged function that performs the same loop 100,000 times. The function looks like this:

```
// function for blittable type testing
// used to execute test entirely in unmanaged code
void BlittableUnmanagedTest()
{
    const int numberOfCalls = 100000;
    bool result              = false;
    for(int i = 0; i < numberOfCalls; i++)
    {
        result = ::NonblittableFunction('a');
    }
}
```

Notice that the function executes the same NonblittableFunction unmanaged function that we tested previously. The difference is this time, our managed code calls this unmanaged function only once and we stay there, executing NonblittableFunction 100,000 times. No marshaling of parameters is required, so we should see the best possible performance.

We can declare this function in our C# code like this:

```
[DllImport("FlatAPILib.DLL")]
public static extern void BlittableUnmanagedTest();
```

In our managed code, we use the Stopwatch class to time the call just as before:

```
//perform the same test, done entirely in unmanaged code
stopWatch.Start();
BlittableTypesTest.BlittableUnmanagedTest();
stopWatch.Stop();
Console.WriteLine(
    "{0} Unmanaged only test:        {1} milliseconds",
    numberOfCalls, stopWatch.ElapsedMilliseconds);
```

The results are even better than the test from managed code using blittable types.

```
100000 Unmanaged only test:        10.0144 milliseconds
```

Finally, for a good comparison between managed and unmanaged code, we can perform this same test entirely in managed code, completely bypassing all interop issues. The C# code looks like this:

```
//test isLower done entirely in managed code
stopWatch.Start();
for (int i = 0; i < numberOfCalls; i++)
{
    result = Char.IsLower('a');
}
stopWatch.Stop();
Console.WriteLine(
    "{0} Managed only test:          {1} milliseconds",
    numberOfCalls, stopWatch.ElapsedMilliseconds);
```

As expected, we see results that are similar to the unmanaged test:

```
100000 Managed only test:          10.0144 milliseconds
```

After all of these tests, we're left with the results shown in Table 1-3, listed from best to worst. Please remember that your results for these tests will vary based on the exact configuration of your PC. The results you see may be different, but the relative differences in performance should be consistent with these results.

Table 1-3. *Blittable Test Results*

Test	Results
Managed code only; no interop	10 milliseconds
Unmanaged code only; a single interop call from managed to unmanaged	10 milliseconds
Individual interop calls using blittable types	30 milliseconds
Individual interop calls using non-blittable types	70 milliseconds

The conclusion we can draw from these tests are that interop between managed and unmanaged code always costs you some performance. However, using only blittable types for interop does provide measurable improvement.

An additional optimization occurs when using single-dimensional arrays of only blittable types. When using blittable types in an array, the memory isn't copied—it's pinned. *Pinning* means that the addresses of the passed values are temporarily locked to prohibit garbage collection. This prevents the value from being moved in memory during the lifetime of the function call. Because of the pinning of memory, the marshaler is able to pass the original parameter memory addresses directly to the unmanaged code. This results in much faster execution compared to a scenario where all of the individual values in an array are copied from one memory location to another.

Related Information

See recipes 1-6 (Changing the Character Set Used for Strings), 2-7 (Passing Simple Arrays), 2-8 (Handling String Arrays), and 2-9 (Passing Arrays of Structures).

1-8. Handling Errors from Unmanaged Functions

Problem

You need to know what kinds of errors are possible when calling an unmanaged function and how you should handle them in your managed code.

Solution

Normal success or failure results are usually returned from a function as the return value or as an out parameter. The result codes produced are a byproduct of the normal operation of the function. Either the requested operation worked or it didn't work. In either case, a well-written function will provide you with some indication of the result. The managed code that calls the function will normally check the result code to determine the appropriate steps to take based on the result.

On the other hand, unexpected error conditions are always possible when calling a function (unmanaged or managed). .NET provides a rich exception-handling mechanism for use in managed code. This same mechanism continues to work during interop calls to unmanaged code and allows you to catch exceptions thrown as a result of the interop call.

The basics of exception handling are the same for managed and unmanaged code. To catch an exception, you wrap the operations you wish to protect in a try/catch block. Here is an example in C#:

```csharp
try
{
    // managed or unmanaged calls go here
}
catch(Exception e)
{
    // handle the exception by logging the problem, retrying
    // the operation, etc.
}
finally
{
    // do any final cleanup and freeing of resources
}
```

The syntax is basically the same in Visual Basic .NET:

```vbnet
Try
    ' managed or unmanaged calls go here
Catch ex As Exception
    ' handle the exception by logging the problem, retrying
    ' the operation, etc.
Finally
    ' do any final cleanup and freeing of resources
End Try
```

■**Note** The code shown here catches the base Exception class, but you'll want to always catch the most specific set of exceptions possible. Catching the base Exception class is generally not a good idea.

You should routinely wrap your interop calls in a try/catch block, especially in cases where the function has a greater than normal chance of failure. For example, a function that relies on external resources such as files and databases or performs communication with external systems is more likely to fail than one that performs simple in-memory calculations. That said, in-memory calculations can fail due to memory and stack overflow, index out of range, null pointer, divide by zero, and overflow issues. So perhaps they aren't that safe after all.

How It Works

An unmanaged function can produce and report an error in two ways:

- Normal error or result codes are returned from the function.

- An unexpected condition occurs and an exception is thrown.

Most functions provide a reasonable mechanism to determine the success or failure of the function. This could take the form of an integer return value, with a zero indicating success and nonzero indicating failure (or vice versa). A function that performs some type of I/O might return a pointer or handle to a file if it is successful, or a null pointer if it has failed. Or you might be required to call a second function (i.e., GetLastError) to determine the success or failure of the prior function call.

Regardless of the mechanism used, unmanaged functions should provide a way to determine their success or failure. It is the responsibility of the managed code that makes the call to check the result from the function (in whatever way the function provides). However, this mechanism works only for error conditions that the function expects and successfully handles.

Exceptional or unexpected conditions often arise, and you need a mechanism to handle them. The DLL containing the unmanaged function may be missing. The wrong version of the DLL might have been deployed, and the function you are calling has changed or is missing. The function may attempt to reference files or directories that are missing. Calculations may result in an overflow or divide-by-zero condition. Low-memory conditions may cause problems during an unmanaged function call.

To make it easier to handle these exceptions, .NET interop does a good job of turning unmanaged errors into managed exceptions. As unhandled runtime errors are detected in the unmanaged code, the error is mapped to an appropriate managed exception that is then thrown. The managed code can then catch the exception and determine the best course of action.

The examples that follow will illustrate several scenarios where exceptions are thrown during interop calls.

In this first example, we will produce an exception by attempting to reference a missing or misnamed DLL. We start by declaring the unmanaged function like this:

```
//declare a nonexistent dll
[DllImport("TheMissingLibrary.DLL")]
public static extern int MissingDllFunction(int anInt);
```

We place the C# code to call this function within a try/catch block:

```
try
{
    int result = ErrorAndExceptionTest.MissingDllFunction(1001);
    Console.WriteLine(
        "Result from MissingDllFunction = {0}", result);
}
catch(DllNotFoundException e)
{
    Console.WriteLine(
        "DllNotFoundException from MissingDllFunction: {0}",
        e.Message);
}
```

When we run this test, we'll see this result:

```
DllNotFoundException from MissingDllFunction:
    Unable to load DLL 'TheMissingLibrary.DLL':
    The specified module could not be found.
    (Exception from HRESULT: 0x8007007E)
```

The DllNotFoundException that is thrown makes sense, since that's exactly the problem in this case.

Note In these examples, we're catching a particular exception, rather than the more general Exception class. It's usually best to catch the most specific exception type possible. Doing this allows you to handle the exception condition more appropriately based on the type of the exception. You will also want to avoid catching the general Exception class if you use tools that monitor Common Language Specification (CLS) compliance, such as FxCop (available free from Microsoft). By default, this tool will consider catching the Exception class a violation of best practices.

These examples are limited to a single exception type for each test, since we know the type of exception that we expect to receive. In live code, you would likely need to catch multiple exception types depending on the function you are calling. As is always the case, you do need to know a bit about the function in order to identify the ways that it can fail.

In this next example, we declare the correct DLL name for the function; however, the function name itself is incorrect:

```
//declare a bad entry point
[DllImport("FlatAPILib.DLL")]
public static extern int MissingFunction(int anInt);
```

As in the previous example, we place the calling code within a try/catch block:

```
//missing function entry point
try
{
    int result = ErrorAndExceptionTest.MissingFunction(1001);
    Console.WriteLine("Result from MissingFunction = {0}", result);
}
catch(DllNotFoundException e)
{
    Console.WriteLine(
        "DllNotFoundException from MissingFunction: {0}",
        e.Message);
}
catch(EntryPointNotFoundException e)
{
    Console.WriteLine(
        "EntryPointNotFoundException from MissingFunction: {0}",
        e.Message);
}
```

When the DLL name is correct (and the DLL is available for loading) but the function name (the entry point) is incorrect, we receive the EntryPointNotFoundException:

```
EntryPointNotFoundException from MissingFunction:
    Unable to find an entry point named MissingFunction
    in DLL FlatAPILib.DLL.
```

Notice that in this example, we included two catch statements: one for EntryPointNotFoundException and another for DllNotFoundException. In cases where more than one type of exception is possible, you'll need to catch each exception individually.

An easy mistake to make when using PInvoke is to incorrectly declare the function, specifying the wrong return data type or an incorrect number and type of input parameters. The next two examples illustrate the problem.

Here is the unmanaged declaration for the test function:

```
extern "C" __declspec(dllexport)
    int __stdcall AddSomeNumbers(int numOne, int numTwo);
```

The AddSomeNumbers function should be defined like this in C#:

```
[DllImport("FlatAPILib.DLL")]
public static extern int AddSomeNumbers(int numOne, int numTwo);
```

However, we incorrectly omit one of the input parameters and declare the function this way:

```
//incorrect number of parameters
[DllImport("FlatAPILib.DLL")]
public static extern int AddSomeNumbers(int numOne);
```

The code to test this incorrectly declared function looks like this:

```
//missing parameters
try
{
    //this generates an entry point exception since the
    //function signature doesn't match the one in the actual
    //unmanaged dll
    int result = ErrorAndExceptionTest.AddSomeNumbers(100);
    Console.WriteLine("Result from AddSomeNumbers = {0}", result);
}
catch(EntryPointNotFoundException e)
{
    Console.WriteLine(
        "EntryPointNotFoundException from AddSomeNumbers: {0}",
        e.Message);
}
```

The exception that is thrown is `EntryPointNotFoundException`:

```
EntryPointNotFoundException from AddSomeNumbers:
    Unable to find an entry point named AddSomeNumbers
    in DLL FlatAPILib.DLL.
```

You might have expected a different type of exception to be thrown, since a function with the specified name does exist in the DLL. However, the `EntryPointNotFoundException` does make the most sense, since we told PInvoke to look for a function named `AddSomeNumbers` that takes a single integer parameter and returns an integer. No such function exists with that exact signature; therefore, the entry point could not be found.

Remember that the calling convention comes into play when calling an unmanaged function. Notice that we've declared this unmanaged function as `__stdcall`. This means that the actual entry point for this function is exported from the DLL with a decorated name of `_AddSomeNumbers@8`. The trailing 8 represents the total number of bytes in the input parameters to the function. When we declared the function with only a single input parameter in managed code, this effectively tells the marshaler to look for a function with an entry point of `_AddSomeNumbers@4`. That's why the result is an `EntryPointNotFoundException`.

If instead we declare this function with the `__cdecl` convention, we receive a totally different result. With `__cdecl`, the exported entry point is `AddSomeNumbers` without any decoration. In this case, the marshaler successfully finds the entry point and makes the call to the unmanaged function, passing an uninitialized second parameter. The result will still be incorrect, since we are not passing the second parameter, but we won't necessarily receive an exception.

■**Note** For additional error information during debugging, you can enable the Managed Debugging Assistants included with Visual Studio .NET. These agents provide lower-level details as to the cause of the problem during a debug session. To use this feature, in Visual Studio .NET, select Debug ➤ Exceptions. From there, you can enable the Managed Debugging Assistants.

This next example also uses the AddSomeNumbers function, making a different type of mistake when it is declared:

```
//incorrect type of parameters
[DllImport("FlatAPILib.DLL" ,CharSet=CharSet.Unicode)]
public static extern int AddSomeNumbers(char charOne, int numTwo);
```

Here, we've declared the first parameter as a char rather than an integer. We run the test with this code:

```
//incorrect parameter type
try
{
    //this doesn't throw an exception. Instead, it uses the
    //unicode value of an 'A' (65) as an integer.
    int result = ErrorAndExceptionTest.AddSomeNumbers('A', 100);
    Console.WriteLine("Result from AddSomeNumbers = {0}", result);
}
catch(Exception e)
{
    Console.WriteLine("Exception from AddSomeNumbers: {0}",
        e.Message);
}
```

If you expected to see the same EntryPointNotFoundException, you might be surprised with the result. As the code comments indicate, this test doesn't throw any exception at all. Instead, the interop marshaler is able to make the most of what we've declared and find the matching function. How is it able to do this? Remember that the char that we've declared is actually a Unicode char (16-bit). PInvoke is able to pass the char to the unmanaged function as an integer.

The result is that the unmanaged function adds the decimal value for the character 'A' (65) to the other number we passed as a parameter (100), and returns a value of 165:

```
Result from AddSomeNumbers = 165
```

Not all mistakes end up as exceptions. More often than not, they end up as puzzling, incorrect results that require some investigation. In this case, it would have been easier to detect and correct the problem if we had received an exception.

In addition to these exceptions, the exception handling for unmanaged code also includes common runtime errors. For example, take the case of a simple divide-by-zero error. We would expect to receive a DivideByZeroException for this type of error in our managed code. To test this type of error in unmanaged code, we write a simple unmanaged function that divides the two numbers we pass in:

```
int DivideSomeNumbers(int numOne, int numTwo)
{
    return numOne / numTwo;
}
```

We declare it and test it like this in C# code:

```
[DllImport("FlatAPILib.DLL")]
public static extern int DivideSomeNumbers(int numOne, int numTwo);

try
{
    //cause an error in the unmanaged code by dividing by zero
    int result = ErrorAndExceptionTest.DivideSomeNumbers(1, 0);
    Console.WriteLine("Result from DivideSomeNumbers = {0}",
        result);
}
catch(DivideByZeroException e)
{
    Console.WriteLine(
        "DivideByZeroException from DivideSomeNumbers: {0}",
        e.Message);
}
```

As expected, we receive the same DivideByZeroException that we would have received from managed code:

```
DivideByZeroException from DivideSomeNumbers:
    Attempted to divide by zero.
```

We can also catch other common exceptions such as an AccessViolationException. The badly written unmanaged function that follows attempts to use an unallocated pointer:

```
int UnmanagedRuntimeError()
{
    //we force a problem below by using
    //these invalid pointers
    char* unAllocatedPointer    = NULL;
    char* sourcePointer         = NULL;
    //this should cause a problem
    strcpy(unAllocatedPointer, sourcePointer);

    return 0;
}
```

We declare and call the function like this:

```
[DllImport("FlatAPILib.DLL")]
public static extern int UnmanagedRuntimeError();

try
{
    int result = ErrorAndExceptionTest.UnmanagedRuntimeError();
    Console.WriteLine(
        "Result from UnmanagedRuntimeError = {0}", result);
}
catch(AccessViolationException e)
{
    Console.WriteLine(
        "Exception from UnmanagedRuntimeError: {0}", e.Message);
}
```

The intentional pointer problems we coded into this unmanaged function turn into an AccessViolationException in our C# code:

```
Exception from UnmanagedRuntimeError:
    Attempted to read or write protected memory.
    This is often an indication that other memory is corrupt.
```

Now, let's see what happens when the unmanaged code explicitly throws an exception rather than causing one to occur as a byproduct of some operation. To test this, we implement a function that doesn't do anything except throw an exception:

```
#include <exception> //needed for std::exception
int UnmanagedRuntimeException()
{
    //throw a standard library exception
    throw std::exception("My new exception");
}
```

The declaration and test in C# look like this:

```
[DllImport("FlatAPILib.DLL")]
public static extern int UnmanagedRuntimeException();

try
{
    //will always return a result code of x80004005 which is E_FAIL.
    //The same error code is returned for a structured
    //exception thrown via a call to RaiseException,
    //or for a simple C++ style throw statement.
    int result = ErrorAndExceptionTest.UnmanagedRuntimeException();
```

```
    Console.WriteLine("Result from UnmanagedRuntimeException = {0}",
        result);
}
catch(SEHException e)
{
    Console.WriteLine(
        "SEHException from UnmanagedRuntimeException: {0}: {1}",
            e.Message, e.ErrorCode);
}
```

An SEHException is thrown for any C++ exceptions, regardless of the style of exception thrown. If a structured exception (the older Microsoft-specific kind of exception handling used for C code) is thrown, the result is the same. The unmanaged function could have been written this way with the same SEHException being thrown:

```
#include <windows.h> //needed for RaiseException function
int UnmanagedRuntimeException()
{
    //throw a structured exception
    RaiseException(111, 0, 0, 0); //structured exception
}
```

Note When working to resolve a problem, it is often helpful to directly step into the code with a debugger. The Visual Studio debugger allows you to start debugging in your managed code and step directly into unmanaged functions, viewing the values of any parameters and watching as unmanaged code is executed. To enable unmanaged debugging, you need to set the Enable Unmanaged Debugging project property to true. This is a property of the managed project and can be found on the Debugging page of the project properties. If you don't check this check box, you will step over any unmanaged calls, rather than being able to step into them.

Related Information

See recipe 1-10 (Catching Unmanaged Exceptions with C++ Interop).

1-9. Using C++ Interop As a Managed Wrapper

Problem

Since most of your unmanaged code is either C or C++, you would like to try C++ Interop to reuse this code.

Solution

C++ Interop is actually the official name of a feature that is exclusive to Visual C++. While Visual C++ is able to make use of the DllImport attribute to declare and call unmanaged code, just like other managed languages, C++ Interop offers C++ developers an alternative.

Using C++ Interop can be as simple as writing standard, unmanaged C++ code. You include the header file for the function(s) you need to reference, and then, magically, you can make the call, even though you are calling into unmanaged code. There are no attributes required, no special function declarations, and no special procedures that you need to follow. You do need to include the lib associated with the function(s) in your C++ linker step, but that requirement is no different than unmanaged C++ code.

To illustrate this, consider this Visual C++ code that calls the AddSomeNumbers unmanaged function:

```
#include "FlatAPILib.h" //contains the unmanaged function declaration

int main()
{
    //call the unmanaged function using C++ Interop
    int result = AddSomeNumbers(100, 200);

    Console::WriteLine("Result from AddSomeNumbers = {0}",result);

    //wait for input
    Console::WriteLine("Press any key to exit");
    Console::Read();

    return 0;
}
```

We #include the FlatAPILib.h header file that declares the AddSomeNumbers function.

The project file must also include the FlatAPILib.lib in the linker step in order to resolve the reference to the function. We call AddSomeNumbers in the normal C++ way, without the DllImport attribute required by PInvoke. In fact, there is no visible indication that we are making an interop call from managed to unmanaged code. However, that is exactly what takes place when we call this function via C++ Interop.

If you are comfortable working in Visual C++, C++ Interop does simplify interop calls to many (but not all) C and C++ functions. And since Visual C++ is able to work with both managed and unmanaged code, it really is a very good interop tool.

To further simplify interop with unmanaged code, you can create small wrapper classes in Visual C++ that hide all of the code needed to call the functions. By doing so, you reap the potential benefits of using C++ Interop while allowing easy access to the wrapper from other managed languages (C# and Visual Basic .NET).

How It Works

One of the primary differences between C++ Interop and standard PInvoke (using the DllImport attribute) is that you are responsible for marshaling parameters when using C++ Interop.

In the AddSomeNumbers function example, the code to use C++ Interop is simple. We don't need any special marshaling code because the data types involved are blittable. This means they are represented the same way in the managed and unmanaged code, and conversion of data is not necessary.

On the other hand, if the function requires non-blittable types, you are required to handle the marshaling duties yourself, converting the input parameters prior to the call and the result upon conclusion of the call.

To illustrate the differences between C++ Interop and PInvoke, the following code executes two unmanaged functions, AddSomeNumbers and CombineStringsW. For comparison purposes, each function is called via PInvoke and C++ Interop. This example also demonstrates the concept of developing a small wrapper class in Visual C++ and using it from other managed languages like C# and Visual Basic .NET.

The unmanaged C++ functions for this test are defined like this:

```
extern "C" __declspec(dllexport)
    int __stdcall AddSomeNumbers(int numOne, int numTwo);
extern "C" __declspec(dllexport)
    void __cdecl CombineStringsW(wchar_t* stringA,
        wchar_t* stringB, wchar_t* result);
```

And implemented like this:

```
int __stdcall AddSomeNumbers(int numOne, int numTwo)
{
    return numOne + numTwo;
}


void __cdecl CombineStringsW(wchar_t* stringA,
    wchar_t* stringB, wchar_t* result)
{
    int bufLength = (int)wcslen(stringA)
        + (int)wcslen(stringB) + 100;
    wchar_t* tempResult = new wchar_t[bufLength];
    wcscpy_s(tempResult, bufLength, stringA);
    wcscat_s(tempResult, bufLength, stringB);
    wcscat_s(tempResult, bufLength,
        L" Another Unicode String ");
    wcscat_s(tempResult, bufLength, L"Unicode");
    wcscpy_s(result, bufLength, tempResult);
    delete [] tempResult;
}
```

We start by creating a Visual C++ DLL project named CppInteropWrappers. This project will contain our wrapper class. We need a project that supports the .NET CLR and is packaged as a DLL, since we will be referencing this assembly from other client projects. To do this in Visual Studio, we create a new C++ project using the CLR-Class Library template.

The wrapper class is declared in C++ header CppInteropTest.h and looks like this:

```
using namespace System;
using namespace System::Text;
using namespace System::Runtime::InteropServices;

namespace CppInteropWrappers
{
//declare unmanaged functions for PInvoke usage
[DllImport("FlatAPILib.DLL",
    CharSet=CharSet::Unicode, EntryPoint="CombineStringsW")]
extern void PInvokeCombineStrings(
    String^ stringA, String^ stringB, StringBuilder^ result);

[DllImport("FlatAPILib.DLL", EntryPoint="AddSomeNumbers")]
extern int PInvokeAddSomeNumbers(int numberA, int numberB);

//C++ wrapper for unmanaged function tests
public ref class CppInteropTest
{
public:
    int PInvokeAddNumbersTest(void);
    int CppInteropAddNumbersTest(void);
    String^ PInvokeStringsTest(void);
    String^ CppInteropStringsTest(void);
};

}
```

In this header file, we declare the CppInteropTest class (the wrapper) that includes the four test methods: two methods for each of the two unmanaged functions.

The declarations outside the class are used to declare the PInvoke versions of each method. Notice that we change the name of the function by specifying a different entry point name. This allows us to refer to the original function names for the C++ Interop tests and use these modified names for the PInvoke tests.

Here is the implementation of the C++ wrapper class:

```
#include "StdAfx.h"
#include ".\CppInteropTest.h"
#include "..\..\common\FlatAPILib\FlatAPILib.h"

namespace CppInteropWrappers
{
```

```
// execute AddSomeNumbers via PInvoke
int CppInteropTest::PInvokeAddNumbersTest(void)
{
    //call the unmanaged function using PInvoke
    return PInvokeAddSomeNumbers(100, 200);
}

// execute AddSomeNumbers via C++ Interop
int CppInteropTest::CppInteropAddNumbersTest(void)
{
    //call the unmanaged function using C++ Interop
    return AddSomeNumbers(100, 200);
}

//string test using standard PInvoke
String^ CppInteropTest::PInvokeStringsTest()
{
    //create a StringBuilder as an in/out buffer
    StringBuilder^ buf = gcnew StringBuilder(500);
    //call the function using PInvoke
    PInvokeCombineStrings(
        L"StringOne", L"StringTwo", buf);
    return buf->ToString();
}

//string test using C++ Interop
String^ CppInteropTest::CppInteropStringsTest()
{
    //allocate an unmanaged buffer
    wchar_t* buf = new wchar_t[500];
    //call the unmanaged function using C++ Interop
    CombineStringsW(L"StringOne", L"StringTwo", buf);
    //turn the result into a managed System::String
    String^ result = gcnew String(buf);
    //free the unmanaged buffer
    delete [] buf;
    return result;
}

}
```

Walking through the code, we see the PInvokeAddNumbersTest method that executes the AddSomeNumbers function via PInvoke. This is followed by the CppInteropAddNumbersTest method that executes the same function via C++ Interop. For this function, C++ Interop and PInvoke are just about a wash. PInvoke actually requires slightly more effort, since you need to declare the function and decorate it with the DllImport attribute.

Next are the two methods that call the CombineStringsW method. The PInvoke version is first, implemented in the PInvokeStringsTest method. To make this function call via PInvoke, we create a StringBuilder object to use as an output buffer, and then call the function. The output is returned in the StringBuilder that we return as a System.String.

The C++ Interop version implemented in CppInteropStringsTest is slightly more complicated. Remember that when calling a function via C++ Interop, you are responsible for marshaling of parameters, allocating and freeing memory, and other housekeeping duties.

Since CombineStringsW uses wide char arrays (Unicode strings), the method starts by allocating a wide char buffer. It then makes the call to the unmanaged function, passing wide char literals and the buffer. Upon return from the function call, we create a new System.String object using the results of the updated wide char buffer. Since we allocated the buffer, we need to make sure we delete it, freeing the memory.

Now that we've created a managed wrapper for these function calls, we need a client to exercise the code. Staying in the C++ world for a few more moments, we write a Visual C++ managed client that looks like this:

```cpp
//
//use the C++ wrapper object from C++
//
#include "stdafx.h"
using namespace System;
using namespace CppInteropWrappers;

int _tmain()
{
    int result          = 0;
    String^ resultString = String::Empty;

    //create the C++ wrapper object
    CppInteropTest^ testObj
        = gcnew CppInteropTest();

    //test numbers function using PInvoke
    result = testObj->PInvokeAddNumbersTest();
    Console::WriteLine(
        "Result from PInvokeAddNumbersTest = {0}",result);

    //test numbers function using C++ Interop
    result = testObj->CppInteropAddNumbersTest();
    Console::WriteLine(
        "Result from CppInteropAddNumbersTest = {0}", result);

    //test string function using PInvoke
    resultString = testObj->PInvokeStringsTest();
    Console::WriteLine(
        "Result from PInvokeStringsTest = {0}",
        resultString);
```

```
    //test string function using C++ Interop
    resultString = testObj->CppInteropStringsTest();
    Console::WriteLine(
        "Result from CppInteropStringsTest = {0}",
        resultString);

    //wait for input
    Console::WriteLine("Press any key to exit");
    Console::Read();

    return 0;
}
```

In order to use the assembly containing the wrapper class, we need to add an assembly reference to the project. This is done using the references property page for the project. We also add the using namespace CppInteropWrappers statement to simplify things. If we didn't do this, we would need to scope the CppInteropTest object name with the namespace. The DLL containing the unmanaged functions must also be accessible to the calling code. To do this, we need to add the directory where FlatAPILib.DLL is located to the PATH, or simply copy this DLL to the same location as our managed assemblies.

Walking through the code, we can see that an instance of the wrapper object is created. Once that is done, the code executes each of the test methods in turn, displaying the results on the console.

One advantage of using the Visual C++ wrapper is that we've effectively hidden the complexity of calling these unmanaged functions from all other managed code. The wrapper is free to invoke the functions using PInvoke or C++ Interop depending on the complexity of the function.

Since the wrapper is a managed object, we are able to access it from other .NET languages. Here is a Visual Basic .NET client that uses the same managed C++ wrapper:

```
Imports CppInteropWrappers

Module MainModule

    'use the C++ wrapper from VB.NET
    Sub Main()
        Dim result As Integer = 0
        Dim resultString As String

        'create the C++ wrapper object
        Dim testObj As CppInteropTest = New CppInteropTest

        'test numbers function using PInvoke
        result = testObj.PInvokeAddNumbersTest()
        Console.WriteLine(String.Format( _
            "Result from PInvokeAddNumbersTest is {0}", _
            result))
```

```
    'test numbers function using C++ Interop
    result = testObj.CppInteropAddNumbersTest()
    Console.WriteLine(String.Format( _
        "Result from CppInteropAddNumbersTest is {0}", _
        result))

    'test string function using PInvoke
    resultString = testObj.PInvokeStringsTest()
    Console.WriteLine(String.Format( _
        "Result from PInvokeStringsTest is {0}", _
        resultString))

    'test string function using C++ Interop
    resultString = testObj.CppInteropStringsTest()
    Console.WriteLine(String.Format( _
        "Result from CppInteropStringsTest is {0}", _
        resultString))

    'wait for input
    Console.Read()
  End Sub

End Module
```

The only difference between the managed C++ code and this Visual Basic .NET code is syntax. The objects and methods used are exactly the same. The Visual Basic .NET code doesn't know or care that the managed object it is using is actually written in C++, or that it is referencing several unmanaged functions.

Just for completeness, here is the implementation of the same client code in C#:

```
using System;
using CppInteropWrappers;

namespace CppInteropClientCSharp
{
    /// <summary>
    /// Use the CppInteropWrapper object from C#
    /// </summary>
    class CppInteropClient
    {
        /// <summary>
        /// The main entry point for the application.
        /// </summary>
        [STAThread]
        static void Main(string[] args)
        {
            int result              = 0;
            string resultString     = String.Empty;
```

```
                    //create an instance of the wrapper object
                    CppInteropTest testObj = new CppInteropTest();

                    //test numbers function using PInvoke
                    result = testObj.PInvokeAddNumbersTest();
                    Console.WriteLine(
                        "Result from PInvokeAddNumbersTest = {0}",
                        result);

                    //test numbers function using C++ Interop
                    result = testObj.CppInteropAddNumbersTest();
                    Console.WriteLine(
                        "Result from CppInteropAddNumbersTest = {0}",
                        result);

                    //test string function using PInvoke
                    resultString = testObj.PInvokeStringsTest();
                    Console.WriteLine(
                        "Result from PInvokeStringsTest = {0}",
                        resultString);

                    //test string function using C++ Interop
                    resultString = testObj.CppInteropStringsTest();
                    Console.WriteLine(
                        "Result from CppInteropStringsTest = {0}",
                        resultString);

                        //wait for input
                    Console.WriteLine("Press any key to exit");
                    Console.Read();
                }
            }
        }
```

Regardless of the managed client language (C++, Visual Basic .NET or C#), the results are the same when this client code is executed:

```
Result from PInvokeAddNumbersTest = 300
Result from CppInteropAddNumbersTest = 300
Result from PInvokeStringsTest
    = StringOneStringTwo Another Unicode String Unicode
Result from CppInteropStringsTest
    = StringOneStringTwo Another Unicode String Unicode
Press any key to exit
```

Clearly, placing the code that calls unmanaged functions in a small wrapper class has advantages. By doing this, you isolate the code that has intimate knowledge of how to call the unmanaged function. And you limit the exposure of marshaling, data-conversion, and memory-management code, keeping it private within the wrapper. This is especially important if you are using C++ Interop, since there will generally be more code written to perform the marshaling.

By far, the greatest advantage to managed wrappers is the ease of interoperability it facilitates with other .NET languages. As you've seen, any .NET language can very easily make use of the wrapper, without the special attributes and procedures associated with unmanaged interop.

As far as C++ Interop goes, it has its place in your arsenal of .NET weapons. But it is not an answer to all interop problems. It has a distinct set of advantages and disadvantages.

The following are the advantages of C++ Interop:

- You don't need to use DllImport statements. You reference the unmanaged functions using the standard C/C++ header files.

- C++ Interop is slightly faster than standard PInvoke. This is because you are controlling the marshaling of data and are able to see when memory is being allocated, data is being converted, and so on. You have unlimited opportunities to optimize the marshaling code since it is completely under your control.

- You can further optimize marshaling of data that may be used by multiple unmanaged functions. By marshaling the data once, you may be able to pass the same data to each function, eliminating the marshaling normally done for each function call.

And here are the disadvantages of C++ Interop:

- Did I already say that you have to do the marshaling? If the function requires anything other than blittable data types, you are responsible for all marshaling of data in both directions. The additional code required on your part might be significant compared to letting PInvoke do the work for you.

- Unless you wrap the C++ Interop calls in a managed wrapper, the marshaling code is generally inline with your business logic. In contrast, PInvoke hides the complexity of marshaling under the covers and allows you to concentrate on solving your business problems.

C++ Interop can be more efficient, but at the cost of increased complexity. As a guideline, use C++ Interop when the function uses simple blittable types, when you need greater control over how parameters are marshaled, or when highly optimized code is a primary requirement.

Related Information

See recipes 1-3 (Simplifying Reuse of Unmanaged Functions) and 1-7 (Using Data Types That Improve Performance).

1-10. Catching Unmanaged Exceptions with C++ Interop

Problem

The unmanaged C++ code you are calling throws an exception that you catch in your client code. However, the exception you receive does not contain any of the detail information from the original exception. You need a way to report the original error message from the unmanaged code.

Solution

When a runtime error is generated within unmanaged code, PInvoke does a good job of turning the error into a managed exception. For example, if you divide by zero within an unmanaged function, the managed client receives a DivideByZeroException. By catching these managed exceptions, it is an easy matter to handle the error condition.

The same level of detail is not provided when an unmanaged function explicitly throws an exception. Unmanaged exceptions that are thrown are marshaled as an SEHException (structured exception handler exception) that doesn't provide the original error message, error code or any other useful information.

One technique that can be used to obtain information from the original exception is to catch the unmanaged exception within managed C++ code. C++ Interop allows us to obtain more details about the original exception. The managed C++ code is then able to forward the additional information from the unmanaged exception to any managed clients.

To accomplish this, you need to protect the unmanaged function call within a C++ try/catch block. You can add as many catch blocks as needed for different types of unmanaged exceptions. The pattern for this code looks like this:

```
try
{
    //call the unmanaged function here
}
catch(int e)
{
    //handle a simple integer exception
}
catch(CustomUnmanagedException& e)
{
    //handle a custom exception
}
catch(SomeOtherUnmanagedException& e)
{
    //handle another custom exception
}
```

Even though the exceptions are unmanaged, the managed C++ code is able to catch and handle them.

How It Works

Catching unmanaged exceptions is another great reason to write small C++ wrappers around your managed functions. They provide you much better access to the underlying exception and are easily consumed by other .NET languages like Visual Basic .NET and C#.

The example that follows demonstrates the use of a small C++ wrapper that is able to catch unmanaged exceptions.

The unmanaged function that throws the exceptions is defined like this:

```
//function for testing of custom unmanaged exceptions
int ThrowUnmanagedExceptions(int type);
```

The function is implemented this way:

```
//function for testing of custom unmanaged exceptions
int ThrowUnmanagedExceptions(int type)
{
    //depending on the value passed in, we
    //throw a different type of exception
    if (type == 1)
    {
        //throw a simple error number
        throw 1234;
    }
    else if (type == 2)
    {
        //throw a custom exception
        throw UnmanagedException("My exception Message", 2001);
    }
    else if (type == 3)
    {
        //throw a standard C++ exception
        throw std::exception("My Std Exception Message");
    }
    //no exception to throw so we just return our
    //input parameter
    return type;
}
```

As you can see, the function really doesn't do anything useful. Its sole purpose in life is to throw exceptions that we can attempt to catch. Based on an integer we pass in as a parameter, it throws one of three types of exceptions. If it is passed anything other than a 1, 2, or 3, the function simply returns the input parameter as a result.

The UnmanagedException that is thrown accepts a message and error code in the constructor and is defined like this in FlatAPILib.h:

```
class UnmanagedException
{
public:
    UnmanagedException(void) {}
```

```
        ~UnmanagedException(void)
        {
            delete [] Message;
        }
        UnmanagedException(char* msg, int errorCode)
        {
            ErrorCode = errorCode;
            size_t bufLength = strlen(msg) + 1;
            Message   = new char[bufLength];
            strcpy_s(Message, bufLength, msg);
        }
        char* Message;
        int   ErrorCode;
    };
```

The managed C++ wrapper is defined this way in CppExceptionTestWrapper.h:

```
using namespace System;

namespace CppInteropWrappers
{

//define a C++ wrapper for exception handling
public ref class CppExceptionTestWrapper
{
public:
    //an enum used to translate result integers
    enum struct ResultDescEnum
    {
        ValueOne = 1,
        ValueTwo = 2,
        ValueThree = 3,
        ValueFour = 4
    };
    String^ RunExceptionTest(int exceptionType);
};

}
```

The only defined method is the one we will use to call the unmanaged function. We also define a managed enum named ResultDescEnum. We use this enum in the implementation of the wrapper to give the integer returned from the function a string description.

Here is the full implementation of the wrapper class:

```
#include "StdAfx.h"
#include ".\cppexceptiontestwrapper.h"

#include "..\..\common\FlatAPILib\FlatAPILib.h"
#include <exception>
```

```
namespace CppInteropWrappers
{

//catch exceptions thrown by unmanaged code
String^ CppExceptionTestWrapper::RunExceptionTest(
    int exceptionType)
{
    String^ result = String::Empty;
    int resultCode = 0;
    try
    {
        //call the unmanaged function using C++ Interop
        resultCode = ThrowUnmanagedExceptions(exceptionType);
        //no exceptions thrown so turn the result code into an enum
        ResultDescEnum resultEnum
            = (ResultDescEnum)resultCode;
        //get the description for the enum
        result = Enum::Format(
            ResultDescEnum::typeid, resultEnum, "G");
    }
    catch(int e)
    {
        //catch the integer exception
        result = e.ToString();
    }
    catch(UnmanagedException& e)
    {
        //catch the custom unmanaged exception
        result = String::Format(
            "{0}: {1}", gcnew String(e.Message), e.ErrorCode);
    }
    catch(std::exception& e)
    {
        //catch a standard C++ exception
        result = gcnew String(e.what());
    }
    return result;
}

}
```

When this method is called, we pass the integer directly to the unmanaged function. Since the function is capable of throwing three different types of exceptions, we catch all of them here.

For demonstration purposes only, we return a string to the caller for each exception that we catch. However, the primary purpose in writing a wrapper such as this is to actually handle the exception in some way. How you handle it obviously depends on what the function actually does and what type of exception is thrown.

Notice that we are calling the ThrowUnmanagedExceptions function using C++ Interop. This is a choice, not a requirement. We could have declared the function using a DllImport attribute and called it via PInvoke. In either case, the exception handling within the wrapper works the same.

A C# client that exercises this wrapper could be implemented this way:

```csharp
using System;
using CppInteropWrappers;

namespace ExceptionWrapperTestCSharp
{
    /// <summary>
    /// Use the CppExceptionTestWrapper object from C#
    /// </summary>
    class ExceptionWrapperTestCSharp
    {
        /// <summary>
        /// The main entry point for the application.
        /// </summary>
        [STAThread]
        static void Main(string[] args)
        {
            string resultString        = String.Empty;

            //create an instance of the wrapper object
            CppExceptionTestWrapper testObj
                = new CppExceptionTestWrapper();

            //test a simple integer exception
            resultString = testObj.RunExceptionTest(1);
            Console.WriteLine(
                "Result from RunExceptionTest 1 = {0}",
                resultString);

            //test a custom C++ exception
            resultString = testObj.RunExceptionTest(2);
            Console.WriteLine(
                "Result from RunExceptionTest 2 = {0}",
                resultString);

            //test a standard C++ exception
            resultString = testObj.RunExceptionTest(3);
            Console.WriteLine(
                "Result from RunExceptionTest 3 = {0}",
                resultString);
```

```
            //test string name for an enum
            resultString = testObj.RunExceptionTest(4);
            Console.WriteLine(
                "Result from RunExceptionTest 4 = {0}",
                resultString);

            //wait for input
            Console.WriteLine("Press any key to exit");
            Console.Read();
        }
    }
}
```

After creating an instance of the managed C++ wrapper, we call the exception test method multiple times. Each time, we pass a different magic number that will end up generating a different exception.

Running this test produces these results:

```
Result from RunExceptionTest 1 = 1234
Result from RunExceptionTest 2 = My exception Message: 2001
Result from RunExceptionTest 3 = My Std Exception Message
Result from RunExceptionTest 4 = ValueFour
```

Note that you are under no obligation to catch and handle exceptions entirely within the C++ wrapper. As the next example demonstrates, you can also use the wrapper class as a simple marshaling tool. With this approach, the managed C++ wrapper catches the unmanaged exceptions and immediately throws a new managed exception using the information from the original exception. This allows any .NET client to catch the managed exception and handle the exception as it sees fit.

To implement this, we first define a new managed exception class. In the example, we implement this in C++, but it could be done in any .NET language.

```
//managed exception thrown by the C++ wrapper
public ref class CppException
    : public ApplicationException
{
public:
    CppException(String^ message, int errorCode)
        : ApplicationException(message)
    {
        ErrorCode = errorCode;
    };
    int ErrorCode;
};
```

Note Notice that the exception derives from the standard .NET ApplicationException class. It has always been the documented Microsoft recommendation that all new exception classes that you define should derive from ApplicationException. However, as is always the case with these types of recommendations, there are dissenting views. It is now believed that while deriving from ApplicationException won't cause any harm, it also doesn't add any value. You should follow a convention that makes sense for your application and that follows your own internal standards.

We then modify the C++ wrapper to throw this new exception, populating it with data from each of the unmanaged exceptions that are caught:

```
//catch exceptions thrown by unmanaged code
String^ CppExceptionTestWrapper2::RunExceptionTest(
    int exceptionType)
{
    String^ result = String::Empty;
    int resultCode = 0;
    try
    {
        //call the unmanaged function using C++ Interop
        resultCode = ThrowUnmanagedExceptions(exceptionType);
        //no exceptions thrown so turn the result code into an enum
        ResultDescEnum resultEnum
            = (ResultDescEnum)resultCode;
        //get the description for the enum
        result = Enum::Format(
            ResultDescEnum::typeid, resultEnum, "G");
    }
    catch(int e)
    {
        throw gcnew CppException(e.ToString(), e);
    }
    catch(UnmanagedException& e)
    {
        throw gcnew CppException(
            gcnew String(e.Message), e.ErrorCode);
    }
    catch(std::exception& e)
    {
        throw gcnew CppException(gcnew String(e.what()), 0);
    }
    return result;
}
```

We changed the wrapper name to avoid any confusion with the original version. The only real differences between this version and the original wrapper are how we handle each exception. While the original version returned a string with the exception message, this version throws the new managed exception.

Sample C# code to test the wrapper looks like this:

```
//create an instance of the wrapper object
CppExceptionTestWrapper2 testObj2
    = new CppExceptionTestWrapper2();

try
{
    //test a simple integer exception
    testObj2.RunExceptionTest(1);
}
catch(CppException e)
{
    Console.WriteLine(
        "Exception thrown by RunExceptionTest 1 = {0}:{1} ",
        e.Message, e.ErrorCode);
}

try
{
    //test a custom C++ exception
    testObj2.RunExceptionTest(2);
}
catch(CppException e)
{
    Console.WriteLine(
        "Exception thrown by RunExceptionTest 2 = {0}:{1} ",
        e.Message, e.ErrorCode);
}

try
{
    //test a standard C++ exception
    testObj2.RunExceptionTest(3);
}
catch(CppException e)
{
    Console.WriteLine(
        "Exception thrown by RunExceptionTest 3 = {0}:{1} ",
        e.Message, e.ErrorCode);
}
```

```
try
{
    //test string name for an enum
    resultString = testObj2.RunExceptionTest(4);
    Console.WriteLine(
        "Result from RunExceptionTest 4 = {0}", resultString);
}
catch (CppException e)
{
    Console.WriteLine(
        "Exception thrown by RunExceptionTest 4 = {0}:{1} ",
        e.Message, e.ErrorCode);
}

//wait for input
Console.WriteLine("Press any key to exit");
Console.Read();
```

When executed, the results look like this:

```
Exception thrown by RunExceptionTest 1 = 1234:1234
Exception thrown by RunExceptionTest 2 = My exception Message:2001
Exception thrown by RunExceptionTest 3 = My Std Exception Message:0
Result from RunExceptionTest 4 = ValueFour
Press any key to exit
```

The results are similar to the execution of the original wrapper.

Regardless of the way you handle the exception, a C++ wrapper is the key that provides visibility into the unmanaged exception.

Related Information

See recipes 1-8 (Handling Errors from Unmanaged Functions) and 1-9 (Using C++ Interop As a Managed Wrapper).

1-11. Freeing Unmanaged Memory

Problem

You need to call an unmanaged function that allocates memory and returns the pointer to you. You know that you should free the memory that was allocated, but you are not sure how to accomplish that.

Solution

In situations where an unmanaged function hands you a pointer to unmanaged memory, you must determine the method used to allocate the memory. Only after the allocation method is determined are you able to choose the correct options for interop.

The interop marshaler assumes that unmanaged memory was allocated using the COM allocation method CoTaskMemAlloc. When a pointer to unmanaged memory is marshaled directly to a .NET type (such as System.String), the marshaler creates the .NET object (i.e., System.String) using a copy of the unmanaged data. Since the original data has been marshaled and is no longer needed, it then attempts to free the unmanaged memory using CoTaskMemFree.

If the unmanaged memory was originally allocated with CoTaskMemAlloc, everything works fine and the memory is freed during marshaling. However, if the unmanaged memory was allocated using the C runtime, the memory will not be deallocated, resulting in an unmanaged memory leak.

As an example, consider this unmanaged function:

```
wchar_t* ReturnUnmanagedString(const wchar_t* leftString,
    const wchar_t* rightString);
```

It is clear from the function declaration that the function returns a wchar_t pointer (a Unicode string). Since this is a return value, the memory is most likely allocated within the unmanaged function.

Normally, we would want to declare this function in managed code like this, allowing the marshaler to return the result directly as a System.String:

```
[DllImport("FlatAPILib.DLL", CharSet=CharSet.Unicode)]
public static extern string ReturnUnmanagedString(
    string leftString, string rightString);
```

This might work, but it depends entirely on how the unmanaged memory was allocated. The only way to determine the allocation method is to either consult the documentation for the function, or review the code itself.

If your research finds that the function uses the C runtime for allocation, all is not lost. Several options are available for dealing with the memory. One option is to rewrite the unmanaged function to use CoTaskMemAlloc to allocate the memory. While that simplifies the managed code, it does require changes to the function. Those changes will affect all other unmanaged code using the function.

Another option is to marshal the string pointer as a System.IntPtr rather than System.String. The IntPtr is a special type that, when marshaled, is passed back directly as the underlying unmanaged pointer, without any type conversion or copying of data.

To marshal the function in this way, you would revise the declaration to look like this:

```
[DllImport("FlatAPILib.DLL", CharSet=CharSet.Unicode)]
public static extern IntPtr ReturnUnmanagedString(string leftString,
    string rightString);
```

In your calling code, you would then need to convert the resulting `IntPtr` to a `System.String` yourself. The `Marshal` class (found in the `System.Runtime.InteropServices` namespace) contains static methods that allow you to easily do this. For example, the C# code to make this call and marshal the string might look like this:

```
IntPtr ptr = UnmanagedWrapper.ReturnUnmanagedString("aa", "bb");
String myString = Marshal.PtrToStringUni(ptr);
```

We now have the result string, but we haven't solved the problem of freeing the unmanaged memory. Memory allocated from the unmanaged heap must be freed from the unmanaged heap. This means we must write new unmanaged code to free the memory—it cannot be done from the managed side.

A simple way to accomplish this is to write a new unmanaged function that accepts a pointer and frees the memory. The function might look like this:

```
void FreeUnmanagedString(void* p)
{
    delete [] p;
}
```

This function would then be declared in managed code:

```
[DllImport("FlatAPILib.DLL")]
public static extern void FreeUnmanagedString(IntPtr stringPtr);
```

Once we have marshaled the pointer to a `System.String`, we would then call this new function, passing back the `IntPtr` that we originally received. Here is the revised code that makes this series of calls:

```
IntPtr ptr = UnmanagedWrapper.ReturnUnmanagedString("aa", "bb");
String myString = Marshal.PtrToStringUni(ptr);
//call unmanaged function that frees the memory
FreeUnmanagedString(ptr);
```

The call to the `FreeUnmanagedString` function provides the unmanaged code with an opportunity to free the memory that was allocated from the unmanaged heap. Adding the new unmanaged function is the least disruptive solution since it doesn't require any changes to working code.

How It Works

The examples that follow expand on the preceding ideas. They demonstrate the options available to you when an unmanaged function allocates memory and returns the pointer to managed code.

The first example starts with an unmanaged function that uses the C++ `new` operator to allocate memory for a result string:

```
//function that allocates unmanaged memory using CRT
wchar_t* ReturnUnmanagedString(const wchar_t* leftString,
    const wchar_t* rightString)
```

```
{
    size_t charCount = wcslen(leftString)
        + wcslen(rightString) + 1;
    wchar_t* result    = new wchar_t[charCount];
    StringCbCopyW(result, charCount * 2, leftString);
    StringCbCatW(result, charCount * 2, rightString);
    return result;
}
```

In this example, the C++ new keyword is used to perform the allocation. The rules discussed here also apply to the malloc function used in C code.

A first attempt at calling this function from managed code would be to declare the function like this:

```
[DllImport("FlatAPILib.DLL", CharSet=CharSet.Unicode)]
public static extern string ReturnUnmanagedString(string leftString,
    string rightString);
```

However, as mentioned earlier, this would cause problems since the marshaler would attempt a call to CoTaskMemFree to free the memory during the marshaling process. Since the memory clearly was not allocated using CoTaskMemAlloc, the call to free the memory would fail and a leak (or worse) would result.

To correct the situation without changing the way the unmanaged memory is allocated, we can marshal the resulting string as an IntPtr instead. This allows us to control the marshaling and freeing of memory within the managed code.

However, we will need to write a small, unmanaged function that we can call to free the memory. This is necessary since the managed code isn't able to free unmanaged memory—too many variables are involved. The managed code doesn't know which version of the C runtime was used to allocate the memory. It also doesn't know exactly which method (new or malloc) was used. For these reasons, the freeing of memory is best left to the unmanaged code.

The new unmanaged function that we write to free memory looks like this:

```
//free unmanaged memory that was previously allocated
void FreeUnmanagedString(void* p)
{
    delete [] p;
}
```

We now restate the C# declaration of the original function and add one for the new function:

```
[DllImport("FlatAPILib.DLL", CharSet=CharSet.Unicode)]
public static extern IntPtr ReturnUnmanagedString(string leftString,
    string rightString);
[DllImport("FlatAPILib.DLL")]
public static extern void FreeUnmanagedString(IntPtr stringPtr);
```

The only difference from the original function declaration is the return type of IntPtr instead of string. This allows the C# code to call the function like this:

```
string resultString    = String.Empty;
IntPtr stringPtr;
```

```
//handle an unmanaged string allocated by the C runtime
stringPtr = UnmanagedMemoryTest.ReturnUnmanagedString(
    "left", "right");

//marshal the IntPtr to a string
resultString = Marshal.PtrToStringUni(stringPtr);

//call the unmanaged function that frees the memory
FreeUnmanagedString(stringPtr);
Console.WriteLine("Result from ReturnUnmanagedString = {0}",
    resultString);
```

Here are the function declarations in Visual Basic .NET:

```
<DllImport("FlatAPILib.DLL", CharSet:=CharSet.Unicode)> _
Public Function ReturnUnmanagedString( _
    ByVal leftString As String, ByVal rightString As String) _
        As IntPtr
End Function

<DllImport("FlatAPILib.DLL")> _
Public Sub FreeUnmanagedString(ByVal stringPtr As IntPtr)
End Sub
```

And here is the Visual Basic .NET code that executes this function:

```
Dim resultString As String = String.Empty
Dim stringPtr As IntPtr = IntPtr.Zero

'handle an unmanaged string allocated by the C runtime
stringPtr = UnmanagedMemoryTest.ReturnUnmanagedString( _
    "left", "right")
resultString = Marshal.PtrToStringUni(stringPtr)
FreeUnmanagedString(stringPtr)
Console.WriteLine( _
    "Result from ReturnUnmanagedString = {0}", _
    resultString)
```

After the IntPtr is marshaled to a string, we call the new unmanaged function that frees the memory, passing the original IntPtr that we received. We have solved the problem, capturing the result as a String, and then freeing the unmanaged memory.

When this code is executed, we see these results:

```
Result from ReturnUnmanagedString = leftright
```

The alternative solution to this problem involves rewriting the unmanaged function that performs the memory allocation. In this rewrite, use CoTaskMemAlloc instead of the C++ new operator or the C runtime to allocate the memory for the string. As you will see, this allows us to easily marshal the string and perform memory cleanup within managed code.

However, the downside is that we are changing a working function simply to allow its use by managed code. And in the process, we will break other unmanaged code that currently uses the function.

Here is the rewritten function using CoTaskMemAlloc for memory allocation:

```
//function that allocates unmanaged memory using CoTaskMemAlloc
wchar_t* ReturnComAllocatedString(const wchar_t* leftString,
    const wchar_t* rightString)
{
    size_t byteCount
        = (wcslen(leftString) +
            wcslen(rightString) + 1) * 2;
    wchar_t* result
        = (wchar_t*)CoTaskMemAlloc(byteCount);
    StringCbCopyW(result, byteCount, leftString);
    StringCbCatW(result, byteCount, rightString);
    return result;
}
```

In our managed C# code, we declare and then call the function like this:

```
[DllImport("FlatAPILib.DLL", CharSet=CharSet.Unicode)]
public static extern IntPtr ReturnComAllocatedString(
    string leftString, string rightString);

string resultString        = String.Empty;
IntPtr stringPtr;

//handle an unmanaged string allocated by CoTaskMemAlloc
stringPtr = UnmanagedMemoryTest.ReturnComAllocatedString(
    "left", "right");

//marshal the pointer to a string
resultString = Marshal.PtrToStringUni(stringPtr);

//free the memory using CoTaskMemFree
Marshal.FreeCoTaskMem(stringPtr);
Console.WriteLine(
    "Result from ReturnComAllocatedString = {0}", resultString);
```

Code to do the same thing in Visual Basic .NET looks like this:

```
<DllImport("FlatAPILib.DLL", CharSet:=CharSet.Unicode)> _
Public Function ReturnComAllocatedString( _
    ByVal leftString As String, ByVal rightString As String) _
        As IntPtr
End Function
```

```
'handle an unmanaged string allocated by CoTaskMemAlloc
stringPtr = UnmanagedMemoryTest.ReturnComAllocatedString( _
    "left", "right")

resultString = Marshal.PtrToStringUni(stringPtr)
```

Marshal.FreeCoTaskMem(stringPtr)
```
Console.WriteLine( _
    "Result from ReturnComAllocatedString = {0}", _
    resultString)
```

The primary difference between this version of the function and the original is that we are freeing the memory within managed code. We don't need to write the new unmanaged function and call it to free memory. Instead, we use the FreeCoTaskMem static method of the Marshal class. Under the covers, this method calls CoTaskMemFree, which is the correct method to use when memory was allocated with CoTaskMemAlloc.

Once we've taken the giant leap of rewriting the unmanaged function to use CoTaskMemAlloc, we can actually simplify this even more. Remember that the marshaler, by default, will call CoTaskMemFree to free memory after the data has been marshaled. This is exactly what is accomplished manually in the preceding code. Therefore, we should now be able to let the marshaler handle everything for us. We can declare the function like this in C#, telling the marshaler to return a System.String instead of an IntPtr:

```
[DllImport("FlatAPILib.DLL", CharSet=CharSet.Unicode)]
public static extern string ReturnComAllocatedString(
    string leftString, string rightString);
```

We can then call the function like this:

```
//handle an unmanaged string allocated by CoTaskMemAlloc
//this time marshaled as a string
resultString = UnmanagedMemoryTest.ReturnComAllocatedString(
    "left", "right");
Console.WriteLine("Result from ReturnComAllocatedString = {0}",
    resultString);
```

The revised declaration and code implemented in Visual Basic .NET looks like this:

```
<DllImport("FlatAPILib.DLL", CharSet:=CharSet.Unicode)> _
Public Function ReturnComAllocatedString( _
    ByVal leftString As String, ByVal rightString As String) _
        As String
End Function

'handle an unmanaged string allocated by CoTaskMemAlloc
'this time marshaled as a string
resultString = _
    UnmanagedMemoryTest.ReturnComAllocatedString( _
    "left", "right")
```

```
Console.WriteLine( _
    "Result from ReturnComAllocatedString = {0}", _
    resultString)
```

The critical step in making all of this work is to first determine how the unmanaged memory was allocated. Once you identify the allocation method used, you can address the problem in a number of ways, using the solution that best fits your requirements.

1-12. Requesting Permission to Access Unmanaged Code

Problem

You have developed code that accesses unmanaged code, and it runs fine in your development environment. When you deploy the code to a production environment, it fails due to security exceptions. You need to know more about code access security and how it affects calls to unmanaged code.

Solution

.NET code access security affects your ability to access local or remote resources (such as files and directories), read environment variables, access databases, make socket connections, and so on. In addition, it affects your ability to call unmanaged code.

Assemblies, classes, or methods can declaratively request a particular permission using the SecurityPermissionAttribute or by using inline code that creates and uses an instance of the SecurityPermission class.

To request permission to call unmanaged code, use the UnmanagedCode flag of the SecurityPermission class or attribute. For example, we can request this permission for a class by applying the SecurityPermissionAttribute to the class, like this:

```
using System.Security.Permissions;

[SecurityPermission(SecurityAction.Demand,
    Flags=SecurityPermissionFlag.UnmanagedCode)]
class ClassThatCallsUnmanagedCode
{
    //call unmanaged code
}
```

We can also demand this permission explicitly using the SecurityPermission class, like this:

```
using System.Security;
using System.Security.Permissions;
```

```
class ClassThatCallsUnmanagedCode
{
    public void CallUnmanagedCode()
    {
        try
        {
            SecurityPermission permission = new SecurityPermission(
                SecurityPermissionFlag.UnmanagedCode);
            permission.Demand();

            //call unmanaged code
        }
        catch (SecurityException e)
        {
            //handle the exception if we do not have permission
        }
    }
}
```

Note Remember that demanding permission to execute unmanaged code is not the same as receiving that permission. The demand indicates to code access security that this bit of managed code requires the demanded permission to execute properly. If the code has the requested permission, execution continues; otherwise, a SecurityException is thrown.

Code access security is configured by the .NET Framework Configuration tool (available from the Windows Control Panel) or by caspol.exe (The Code Access Security Policy Tool). Caspol.exe is a command-line tool provided with the .NET Framework. The utility has a large number of options that can be used to adjust the security. Consult the Microsoft documentation for examples of using either of these tools to configure .NET security.

How It Works

Regardless of whether managed code demands a permission or not, code access security will enforce the security profile that applies to the assembly. The profile can be based on an explicit security configuration for the assembly or on the settings in effect for the zone where the assembly is executing. Based on the profile, code will be allowed to execute, or it may fail due to the lack of a needed permission.

If the security profile is automatically enforced, why do you need to demand permissions in your code? You do so because demanding a required permission is better than simply allowing your code to fail for a number of reasons. By explicitly demanding a permission (either with an attribute or inline in code), your code will never unexpectedly fail due to a problem with code access security. You will know in advance when a permission is missing. You can allow the code to fail gracefully, perhaps providing a more meaningful message to end users.

Demanding permissions up front permits your code to catch any potential security issues much sooner, perhaps during the initial class startup. Otherwise, you might be far into a lengthy process before your code determined that it cannot complete the process due to a permissions issue. Depending on the process, you might then encounter expensive cleanup or rollback operations to get back to a consistent state.

Even though the examples in this book access unmanaged code, they are allowed to execute because they run in the My Computer security zone. By default, this zone is assigned Full Trust, meaning that it is allowed to do just about anything. If you like, you can change the default setting to see the effect on the example code.

Caution If you change the code access security settings as described here, make sure you reset them to their original values when you have completed your testing. If you don't, you might experience problems executing your own .NET code.

To change the settings for the My Computer zone, follow these steps:

1. Open the Windows Control Panel and then the Administrative Tools folder.

2. Start the .NET Configuration tool.

3. Select Configure Code Access Security Policy.

4. Select Adjust Zone Security.

5. Select the scope of the changes you want to make, either for yourself or the entire computer.

6. Select the My Computer zone and lower the security level from Full Trust to one setting below that.

Now when you execute the example code from this book, the tests should fail due to a SecurityException.

Caution Remember to reset the security settings back to the original values.

When deploying code that executes unmanaged code, you will need to evaluate the overall security needs of the application. If it will be executing locally within the My Computer zone, you should be fine without any code access security changes. However, if your code is designed to execute within another environment, perhaps from ASP.NET, from a web service, or via remoting, you will need to grant the assembly permission to execute the unmanaged code. This can be accomplished by adjusting the permissions for the entire execution zone or individually for the assembly.

The SecurityPermission attribute and class both use a SecurityAction enumeration to determine the action you are requesting. Depending on your needs, you can demand (request) a permission, deny a permission, or assert that you have the permission.

The examples that follow illustrate possible uses of these security actions. For all of these examples, assume that we need to call an unmanaged function that is implemented like this:

```
//function for testing of security permissions
int GetStringLength(char* aString)
{
    //just return the length of the string
    return (int)strlen(aString);
}
```

We will develop three separate wrapper classes that call this function, each one illustrating a different security action.

The first wrapper demands the UnmanagedCode permission and is implemented like this:

```
[SecurityPermission(SecurityAction.Demand,
    Flags=SecurityPermissionFlag.UnmanagedCode)]
class UnmanagedCallsAllowed
{
    [DllImport("FlatAPILib.DLL")]
    private static extern int GetStringLength(string aString);

    /// <summary>
    /// Call the unmanaged function
    /// </summary>
    /// <param name="aString"></param>
    /// <returns></returns>
    public static int CallGetStringLength(string aString)
    {
        return GetStringLength(aString);
    }
}
```

The demand causes the .NET runtime to examine the permissions of all callers in the stack, verifying that the requested permission (UnmanagedCode) has been granted to each caller. If any caller in the stack does not have the permission, a SecurityException is thrown.

The second wrapper asserts the UnmanagedCode permission:

```
[SecurityPermission(SecurityAction.Assert,
    Flags=SecurityPermissionFlag.UnmanagedCode)]
class UnmanagedCallsAsserted
{
    [DllImport("FlatAPILib.DLL")]
    private static extern int GetStringLength(string aString);

    /// <summary>
    /// Call the unmanaged function
    /// </summary>
```

```
/// <param name="aString"></param>
/// <returns></returns>
public static int CallGetStringLength(string aString)
{
    return GetStringLength(aString);
}
}
```

The Assert enables you to use permissions that you have been granted by code access security, but your immediate callers may not have permission to use. When you assert a permission, you are taking responsibility for security, not relying on any calling code for security permissions. This is obviously a dangerous practice and should generally be avoided.

This scenario is possible if you package the wrapper classes that access unmanaged code in a separate library. If you use the wrapper library from code in another execution zone, such as downloaded code, you may need to use Assert. In this case, the downloaded code won't have the permission to call unmanaged code, but your called wrapper library will. Therefore, your wrapper code might need to assert the permission in order to execute successfully.

The final wrapper denies the UnmanagedCode permission:

```
[SecurityPermission(SecurityAction.Deny,
    Flags=SecurityPermissionFlag.UnmanagedCode)]
class UnmanagedCallsNotAllowed
{
    [DllImport("FlatAPILib.DLL")]
    private static extern int GetStringLength(string aString);

    /// <summary>
    /// Call the unmanaged function
    /// </summary>
    /// <param name="aString"></param>
    /// <returns></returns>
    public static int CallGetStringLength(string aString)
    {
        return GetStringLength(aString);
    }
}
```

Deny will effectively revoke the permission from the current code as well as all downstream code that is called. The exception is that any code downstream that asserts the permission will not be affected by the Deny.

Note The concept of explicitly denying unmanaged code permission to a wrapper class designed to call unmanaged code doesn't make sense. You obviously wouldn't want to use Deny on a wrapper for unmanaged functions. However, Deny is very useful in other classes where you want to prohibit access to resources in order to remove potential security issues. The Deny action is used here merely as an example to demonstrate the results when Deny is used.

We can then write C# code to exercise all of these wrappers and view the results:

```csharp
static void Main(string[] args)
{
    int result;

    //call the wrapper that is allowed access to unmanaged code
    try
    {
        result = UnmanagedCallsAllowed.CallGetStringLength("abcde");
        Console.WriteLine(
            "Result from CallGetStringLength Allowed = {0}", result);
    }
    catch(SecurityException e)
    {
        Console.WriteLine(
            "Exception from CallGetStringLength Allowed = {0}",
            e.Message);
    }

    //call the wrapper that has been denied access to unmanaged code
    try
    {
        result = UnmanagedCallsNotAllowed.CallGetStringLength("abcde");
        Console.WriteLine(
            "Result from CallGetStringLength Not Allowed = {0}",
            result);
    }
    catch(SecurityException e)
    {
        Console.WriteLine(
            "Exception from CallGetStringLength Not Allowed = {0}",
            e.Message);
    }

    //remove the unmanaged code permission
    SecurityPermission permission
        = new SecurityPermission(SecurityPermissionFlag.UnmanagedCode);
    permission.Deny();

    //call the wrapper that is allowed access to unmanaged code
    try
    {
        result = UnmanagedCallsAllowed.CallGetStringLength("abcde");
        Console.WriteLine(
            "Result from CallGetStringLength Allowed = {0}",
            result);
    }
```

```
catch(SecurityException e)
{
    Console.WriteLine(
        "Exception from CallGetStringLength Allowed = {0}",
        e.Message);
}

//call the wrapper that asserts that
//it is allowed to access unmanaged code
try
{
    result = UnmanagedCallsAsserted.CallGetStringLength("abcde");
    Console.WriteLine(
        "Result from CallGetStringLength Asserted = {0}",
        result);
}
catch(SecurityException e)
{
    Console.WriteLine(
        "Exception from CallGetStringLength Asserted = {0}",
        e.Message);
}

//wait for input
Console.WriteLine("Press any key to exit");
Console.Read();
}
```

When we execute this code, we receive these results:

```
Result from CallGetStringLength Allowed = 5
Exception from CallGetStringLength Not Allowed
    = Request for the permission of type
        'System.Security.Permissions.SecurityPermission,
        mscorlib, Version=2.0.0.0, Culture=neutral,
        PublicKeyToken=b77a5c561934e089' failed.
Exception from CallGetStringLength Allowed = Request failed.
Result from CallGetStringLength Asserted = 5
Press any key to exit
```

Scanning through the results, we see that the wrapper that demanded the permission executed normally as expected. The wrapper that was denied the permission threw a SecurityException.

In the mainline code, we then created an instance of the SecurityPermission class and denied the UnmanagedCode permission by invoking its Deny method. Now when we execute the wrapper that demands the permission again, it also fails with a SecurityException. This makes sense, since we just denied ourselves the permission to execute unmanaged code. Finally, we execute the wrapper that asserts the UnmanagedCode permission. In this case, the wrapper executes successfully, even though we denied the permission. This is consistent with the way Assert works.

It is also possible to refuse permissions that have been granted to an assembly. This is an important technique that can help to make your code more secure and less prone to security vulnerabilities.

Your code will always be granted all permissions that are included in the appropriate security policy. The extra permissions really don't cause any immediate harm, but having a limited number of permissions could prevent future security issues. Allowing your code to inherit permissions that it doesn't need and doesn't use could increase the chances of its being used in a malicious way, perhaps for a purpose that wasn't originally intended.

For these reasons, it is a good idea to restrict permissions at the assembly level if they are not needed. Because of the inherent security risk with unmanaged code, you should consider refusing permission to execute unmanaged code unless you actually need it.

The refusal can be done easily by adding a SecurityPermissionAttribute to the C# AssemblyInfo.cs file like this:

```
[assembly:SecurityPermission(SecurityAction.RequestRefuse,
    Flags=SecurityPermissionFlag.UnmanagedCode)]
```

This will prevent access to unmanaged code from any classes in the assembly.

1-13. Securing Access to Unmanaged Code

Problem

As you use unmanaged functions, you are concerned about the potential security risks associated with unmanaged code. You want to mitigate the risks by controlling and limiting access to the unmanaged code.

Solution

In the .NET world, all unmanaged code is a security risk. The unmanaged code doesn't use code access security, isn't necessarily type-safe, and is generally unlimited in what it is allowed to do.

When using unmanaged code that may be considered dangerous, you should give special attention to security. The technique used most often to limit the risk is to write a managed security wrapper for the unmanaged code.

In addition to encapsulating the code needed to call the unmanaged function, the wrapper can act as a secure, trusted interface to other managed code. The wrapper can validate input parameters to ensure they are within an acceptable range. It can check for the length of values and buffers, eliminating potential buffer overruns when calling the unmanaged code. It can demand the necessary code access security prior to calling the function. In general, the wrapper is the trusted gatekeeper to the unmanaged code. Calling code must pass all tests imposed by the wrapper before the unmanaged call is allowed to take place.

Writing a secure wrapper is a straightforward task. After reviewing the unmanaged function that you want to wrap, you develop a managed class that makes the call to the function. However, prior to the unmanaged call, any number of validation checks can take place. Since the purpose of the wrapper is to prevent a security breach, you should look for ways that the unmanaged function can be misused. You should try to be as thorough as possible, ensuring that the caller is authorized to make the call and that any input parameters are in line with your expectations.

If an unmanaged function can be used in a number of different ways, you can use the wrapper to limit how it is used. You can place restrictions on the function, allowing only those operations that you consider safe.

Once a secure wrapper is developed, it is available for use from other .NET code. Since the wrapper has effectively hidden the details of calling the unmanaged function, the calling code is unconcerned with the security issues.

How It Works

To demonstrate the use of a secure wrapper, consider this unmanaged function:

```
char* ProcessTestFile(const char* fullFilePath);
```

The function accepts a file name and performs some type of processing on the file. In a real-life function, the processing could involve any conceivable action against the file. In this example, we will simply read the contents of the file and return the results as a pointer to char. The test function is implemented like this in C++ code:

```
//function used for security wrapper testing
char* ProcessTestFile(const char* fullFilePath)
{
    HANDLE hFile;
    //open the file for reading
    hFile = CreateFile(fullFilePath,         // file to open
                    GENERIC_READ,            // open for reading
                    FILE_SHARE_READ,         // share for reading
                    NULL,                    // default security
                    OPEN_EXISTING,           // existing file only
                    FILE_ATTRIBUTE_NORMAL,   // normal file
                    NULL);                   // no attr. template

    if (hFile == INVALID_HANDLE_VALUE)
    {
        printf("Could not open file (error %d)\n", GetLastError());
        return 0;
    }

    BOOL bResult        = false;
    char* buffer        = new char[2049];
    DWORD nBytesToRead  = 2048;
    DWORD nBytesRead    = 0;

    //read from the file -- we expect that it will fit within
    //a single buffer
    bResult = ReadFile(hFile, (void*)buffer, nBytesToRead, &nBytesRead, NULL) ;
```

```
buffer[nBytesRead] = '\0';
//save the file contents as a string
char* result        = new char[nBytesRead + 1];
strcpy_s(result, nBytesRead +1, (char*)buffer);
//free the original buffer
delete [] buffer;

//close the file
CloseHandle(hFile);

return result;
}
```

Since the function returns a pointer to memory that it allocates, we need a way to free that memory from unmanaged code. Therefore, we will use this function to free the memory after it has been marshaled.

```
void FreeUnmanagedString(void* p)
{
    delete [] p;
}
```

Note The example wrapper that follows is one of many possible ways to implement a secure environment for unmanaged functions. Likely, you would implement it differently depending on your exact needs. The example should serve only as a demonstration of the kinds of security and validation checks that you can perform prior to making an unmanaged call. It's not meant to be an exhaustive demonstration of security as it relates to file-handling routines.

Here is a sample C# implementation of a secure wrapper for this function:

```
using System;
using System.IO;
using System.Runtime.InteropServices;
using System.Security;
using System.Security.Permissions;

namespace SecurityWrapperTest
{
    /// <summary>
    /// Custom exception thrown by the FileProcessWrapper
    /// </summary>
    public class FileProcessException : ApplicationException
    {
        public FileProcessException(
            string msg, Exception innerException)
              : base(msg, innerException)
```

```
        {
        }
}

/// <summary>
/// Managed wrapper for the ProcessTestFile unmanaged function
/// </summary>
internal class FileProcessWrapper
{
    [DllImport("FlatAPILib.DLL", CharSet=CharSet.Ansi)]
    private static extern IntPtr ProcessTestFile(
        string fullFilePath);

    [DllImport("FlatAPILib.DLL")]
    private static extern void FreeUnmanagedString(IntPtr p);

    /// <summary>
    /// Invoke the unmanaged function
    /// </summary>
    /// <param name="filePath"></param>
    /// <returns></returns>
    public static string ProcessFile(string filePath)
    {
        //set up permissions that we need
        PermissionSet pSet = new PermissionSet(
            PermissionState.None);
        //restrict IO to only a single known directory
        pSet.AddPermission(new FileIOPermission(
            FileIOPermissionAccess.Read |
          FileIOPermissionAccess.PathDiscovery,
                @"c:\InteropTest"));
        //add permission to execute unmanaged code
        pSet.AddPermission(new SecurityPermission(
            SecurityPermissionFlag.UnmanagedCode));
        //make these permissions exclusive,
        //denying access to other directories
        pSet.PermitOnly();

        String result        = String.Empty;
        IntPtr stringPtr      = IntPtr.Zero;

        //file path validation
        if (filePath == null)
        {
            throw new NullReferenceException(
            "filePath is required");
        }
```

```
if (filePath.Length == 0)
{
    throw new FileProcessException(
        "filePath length must be greater than 0", null);
}

//get the directory name
string dirName = Path.GetDirectoryName(filePath);
//validate the directory
if (dirName.Length > 0)
{
    if (!Directory.Exists(dirName))
    {
        throw new FileProcessException(String.Format(
            "Directory {0} does not exist", dirName),null);
    }
}

//validate the file
if (!File.Exists(filePath))
{
    throw new FileProcessException(
        String.Format(
        "File {0} does not exist", filePath),null);
}

try
{
    //call the unmanaged function
    stringPtr = ProcessTestFile(filePath);
    if (stringPtr != IntPtr.Zero)
    {
        //marshal the returned pointer to a string
        result = Marshal.PtrToStringAnsi(stringPtr);
    }
}
finally
{
    if (stringPtr != IntPtr.Zero)
    {
        //free the memory from unmanaged code
        FreeUnmanagedString(stringPtr);
    }
}

return result;
```

```
        }
    }
}
```

The Visual Basic .NET implementation of the wrapper looks like this:

```vbnet
Imports System
Imports System.IO
Imports System.Runtime.InteropServices
Imports System.Security
Imports System.Security.Permissions

Module SecurityWrapperTest

    ''' <summary>
    ''' Custom exception thrown by the FileProcessWrapper
    ''' </summary>
    ''' <remarks></remarks>
    Public Class FileProcessException
        Inherits ApplicationException
        Public Sub New(ByVal msg As String, _
            ByVal innerException As Exception)
            MyBase.New(msg, innerException)
        End Sub
    End Class

    ''' <summary>
    ''' Managed wrapper for the ProcessTestFile unmanaged function
    ''' </summary>
    ''' <remarks></remarks>
    Friend Class FileProcessWrapper
        <DllImport("FlatAPILib.DLL", CharSet:=CharSet.Ansi)> _
        Private Shared Function ProcessTestFile( _
            ByVal fullFilePath As String) _
                As IntPtr
        End Function

        <DllImport("FlatAPILib.DLL")> _
        Private Shared Sub FreeUnmanagedString(ByVal p As IntPtr)
        End Sub

        ''' <summary>
        ''' Invoke the unmanaged function
        ''' </summary>
        ''' <param name="filePath"></param>
        ''' <returns></returns>
        ''' <remarks></remarks>
        Public Shared Function ProcessFile( _
```

```vbnet
ByVal filePath As String) _
    As String

'set up permissions that we need
Dim pSet As PermissionSet _
    = New PermissionSet(PermissionState.None)
'restrict IO to only a single known directory
pSet.AddPermission(New FileIOPermission( _
    FileIOPermissionAccess.Read _
    Or FileIOPermissionAccess.PathDiscovery, _
    "c:\InteropTest"))
'add permission to execute unmanaged code
pSet.AddPermission(New SecurityPermission( _
    SecurityPermissionFlag.UnmanagedCode))
'make these permissions exclusive,
'denying access to other directories
pSet.PermitOnly()

Dim result As String = String.Empty
Dim stringPtr As IntPtr = IntPtr.Zero

'file path validation
If filePath = Nothing Then
    Throw New NullReferenceException( _
    "filePath is required")
End If
If filePath.Length = 0 Then
    Throw New FileProcessException( _
    "filePath length must be greater than 0", _
    Nothing)
End If

'get the directory name
Dim dirName As String _
    = Path.GetDirectoryName(filePath)
'validate the directory
If dirName.Length > 0 Then
    If Not Directory.Exists(dirName) Then
        Throw New FileProcessException( _
            String.Format( _
            "Directory {0} does not exist", _
            dirName), Nothing)
    End If
End If

'validate the file
If Not File.Exists(filePath) Then
    Throw New FileProcessException( _
```

```
                    String.Format( _
                    "File {0} does not exist", filePath), _
                    Nothing)
            End If

            Try
                'call the unmanaged function
                stringPtr = ProcessTestFile(filePath)
                If Not stringPtr = IntPtr.Zero Then
                    'marshal the returned pointer to a string
                    result = Marshal.PtrToStringAnsi(stringPtr)
                End If
            Finally
                If Not stringPtr = IntPtr.Zero Then
                    'free the memory from unmanaged code
                    FreeUnmanagedString(stringPtr)
                End If
            End Try

            Return result
        End Function
    End Class

End Module
```

This code implements a number of security-related features.

Starting with the class declaration for FileProcessWrapper, we have declared the class in C# using the internal access modifier:

```
internal class FileProcessWrapper
```

This access modifier restricts the use of this class to the current assembly only. Managed classes that are packaged in other assemblies are prohibited from referencing this class. This is a simple way to limit the access to the unmanaged function, since we presumably trust the other code in the same assembly. While this works in the example code, it obviously would cause issues if you were developing a library of managed code that was to be used by multiple applications.

After declaring the unmanaged functions that the code will call, we reach the heart of the wrapper, the static ProcessFile method. The first task in this method is to establish our requirements for code access security using this code:

```
//set up permissions that we need
PermissionSet pSet = new PermissionSet(PermissionState.None);
//restrict IO to only a single known directory
pSet.AddPermission(new FileIOPermission(
    FileIOPermissionAccess.Read | FileIOPermissionAccess.PathDiscovery,
        @"c:\InteropTest"));
//add permission to execute unmanaged code
pSet.AddPermission(new SecurityPermission(
```

```
    SecurityPermissionFlag.UnmanagedCode));
//make these permissions exclusive, denying access to other directories
pSet.PermitOnly();
```

In this code, we add two permissions to a PermissionSet object. The PermissionSet simply allows us to set up two independent permission objects but act on them as a group (using the PermitOnly method).

We first add a FileIOPermission object, specifying that we want Read and PathDiscovery access for a single directory, C:\InteropTest. We then add the permission object for UnmanagedCode that we will need in order to access the unmanaged functions.

Once the permissions are added to the set, we call the PermitOnly method of the PermissionSet object. PermitOnly effectively denies all permissions except for those that we have specified in the set. In this case, that means we will be permitted to access unmanaged code and to read from the C:\InteropTest directory.

Note This example uses the .NET permission classes to perform some of the security checks. This is not a strict requirement but merely done as a demonstration. Instead, you can choose to perform all of the security checks in your own code and not use the code access security classes at all.

If the managed code attempts to read from another directory, a SecurityException will be thrown. Likewise, if we attempt to write to a file (instead of reading it) in the proper directory, an exception is thrown. If the managed code attempts anything else—such as accessing the registry, opening a socket connection, or reading environment variables—an exception is thrown. With these few lines, we have already restricted much of what the managed code is allowed to do. Now that our operational boundaries have been set using code access security, we can execute a series of checks in managed code prior to calling the unmanaged function.

The wrapper now performs several validation tasks. Starting with basic validation of input parameters, it verifies the presence of the file path input parameter. This is the type of simple validation that we would rather handle here in managed code instead of blindly passing parameters to the unmanaged function.

The individual parts of the full file path are now validated, checking the existence of the directory and the requested file. In this sample code, we assume that the file already exists prior to calling the function. That may not be a realistic assumption, but it works well enough for demonstration purposes.

During validation, we throw a custom FileProcessException object if any errors are detected. This simplifies any calling code, allowing it to catch a single exception regardless of the type of validation error encountered.

If the input parameters appear to be in order, we finally make the call to the unmanaged function. Since the memory for the returned string is allocated in unmanaged code, we marshal the returned pointer as an IntPtr. This allows us to marshal the result to a String ourselves and later free the memory.

In order to free the memory, we call the FreeUnmanagedString function, passing it the IntPtr that we received from the original function. Notice that we do this within a finally block. In the event an exception is thrown, we want to be assured that memory was properly freed.

This wrapper now allows us to easily invoke the unmanaged function. C# code to test the wrapper could be implemented like this:

```csharp
[STAThread]
static void Main(string[] args)
{

    //save the test file to be read later
    DirectoryInfo dirInfo   = new DirectoryInfo(@"c:\InteropTest");
    if (!dirInfo.Exists)
    {
        dirInfo.Create();
    }
    StreamWriter writer      = new StreamWriter(
        @"c:\InteropTest\SecurityWrapperTestFile.txt");
    writer.WriteLine("The Contents of SecurityWrapperTestFile.txt");
    writer.Flush();
    writer.Close();

    string result;

    //call the wrapper
    try
    {
        result = FileProcessWrapper.ProcessFile(
            @"c:\InteropTest\SecurityWrapperTestFile.txt");
        Console.WriteLine("Result from ProcessFile = {0}", result);
    }
    catch(FileProcessException e)
    {
        Console.WriteLine(
            "Exception from ProcessFile = {0}", e.Message);
    }

    //wait for input
    Console.WriteLine("Press any key to exit");
    Console.Read();
}
```

Prior to testing the wrapper itself, test data is written to the expected file. The Visual Basic .NET code to test the wrapper is implemented like this:

```vbnet
Sub Main()
    'save the test file to be read later
    Dim dirInfo As DirectoryInfo _
        = New DirectoryInfo("c:\InteropTest")
    If Not dirInfo.Exists Then
        dirInfo.Create()
    End If
```

```
    Dim writer As StreamWriter = New StreamWriter( _
        "c:\InteropTest\SecurityWrapperTestFile.txt")
    writer.WriteLine( _
        "The Contents of SecurityWrapperTestFile.txt")
    writer.Flush()
    writer.Close()

    Dim result As String

    'call the wrapper
    Try
        result = FileProcessWrapper.ProcessFile( _
            "c:\InteropTest\SecurityWrapperTestFile.txt")
        Console.WriteLine( _
            "Result from ProcessFile = {0}", result)
    Catch ex As FileProcessException
        Console.WriteLine( _
            "Exception from ProcessFile = {0}", ex.Message)
    End Try

    'clean up the test file when we are done
    Dim fileInfo As FileInfo = New FileInfo( _
        "c:\InteropTest\SecurityWrapperTestFile.txt")
    If fileInfo.Exists Then
        fileInfo.Delete()
    End If
    If dirInfo.Exists Then
        dirInfo.Delete()
    End If

    'wait for input
    Console.WriteLine("Press any key to exit")
    Console.Read()
End Sub
```

When the code is executed, the results look like this:

```
Result from ProcessFile =
    The Contents of SecurityWrapperTestFile.txt
Press any key to exit
```

Related Information

See recipes 1-3 (Simplifying Reuse of Unmanaged Functions), 1-11 (Freeing Unmanaged Memory), and 1-12 (Requesting Permission to Access Unmanaged Code).

1-14. Calling Functions Dynamically

Problem

You would like to dynamically load a function in a DLL rather than using the static DllImport mechanism. Is that possible?

Solution

If you declare an unmanaged function using the DllImport attribute, you specify the name of the DLL with the attribute. That means the call to that function is static. It is bound directly to that particular DLL.

Instead of using DllImport, you can also dynamically load an unmanaged DLL and execute a function in the DLL. To do this, you make use of the Win32 functions LoadLibrary and GetProcAddress. You also define the function you want to call as a delegate instead of declaring it with DllImport.

The steps to call a function dynamically are as follows:

1. Define a delegate for the unmanaged function.

2. Load the DLL using the LoadLibrary Win32 function.

3. Get the address of the function using the GetProcAddress Win32 function.

4. Marshal the function address to the delegate using GetDelegateForFunctionPointer method of the Marshal class.

5. Call the function using the delegate.

How It Works

In the following example, we want to dynamically call a function that is defined like this:

```
extern "C" __declspec(dllexport)
int __cdecl DynamicallyAddSomeNumbers(
    int numOne, int numTwo);
```

Notice that this example function specifies extern "C" and uses the __cdecl calling convention. By doing this, we avoid the function name decoration that would normally take place with other calling conventions. If we used __stdcall instead, the function name would be decorated as _DynamicallyAddSomeNumber@8. We would then need to specify this decorated name in the GetProcAddress function to call the function. Using __cdecl allows us to use the much simpler function name of DynamicallyAddSomeNumbers without any decoration.

Note Remember that we can always use the dumpbin.exe utility to view the exact names of any functions that have been exported from a DLL. See recipe 1-1 (Identifying the Unmanaged Function) for more information.

The function is implemented like this and is built into library FlatAPILib.DLL:

```
int __cdecl DynamicallyAddSomeNumbers(int numOne, int numTwo)
{
    return numOne + numTwo;
}
```

The code that follows shows how to dynamically call this function in C#:

```csharp
using System;
using System.IO;
using System.Runtime.InteropServices;

namespace DynamicLoading
{
    class DynamicLoadingTest
    {
        [DllImport("kernel32.dll")]
        private static extern IntPtr LoadLibrary(string dllName);

        [DllImport("kernel32.dll")]
        private static extern IntPtr GetProcAddress(
            IntPtr hModule, string procName);

        //managed delegate for the function call
        [UnmanagedFunctionPointer(CallingConvention.Cdecl)]
        private delegate int AddSomeNumbers(
            int myNumA, int myNumB);

        static void Main(string[] args)
        {
            try
            {
                //dynamically load the dll
                IntPtr dll = LoadLibrary("FlatAPILib.DLL");
                if (dll == IntPtr.Zero)
                {
                    throw new FileNotFoundException(
                        "Unable to load FlatAPILib.DLL");
                }

                //get the address of the function we need
                IntPtr funcAddr = GetProcAddress(
                    dll, "DynamicallyAddSomeNumbers");
                if (funcAddr == IntPtr.Zero)
                {
                    throw new ApplicationException(
                        "Unable to get address to function");
                }
```

```
        //marshal the function pointer to a delegate
        AddSomeNumbers asn = (AddSomeNumbers)
            Marshal.GetDelegateForFunctionPointer(
                funcAddr,
                typeof(AddSomeNumbers));
        //make the unmanaged call using the delegate
        int result = asn(1, 2);

        //show the result
        Console.WriteLine(
            "Result from DynamicallyAddSomeNumbers = "
            + result.ToString());
    }
    catch (Exception e)
    {
        Console.WriteLine(
            "Exception dynamically calling function: {0}",
            e.Message);
    }

    //wait for input
    Console.WriteLine("Press any key to exit");
    Console.Read();
    }
  }
}
```

After declaring the Win32 functions LoadLibrary and GetProcAddress, the delegate for the function is defined. The parameters to the delegate, as well as the return type, must exactly match the unmanaged function that we want to call. The delegate name doesn't matter. For this example, the delegate is named AddSomeNumbers.

The UnmanagedFunctionPointer attribute has also been applied to the delegate. Since the delegate will be used to call our unmanaged function, CallingConvention.Cdecl is specified to indicate that the unmanaged function uses the __cdecl calling convention. The UnmanagedFunctionPointer attribute is new to .NET Framework 2.0 and can be found in the System.Runtime.InteropServices namespace.

Walking through the code, we see that the DLL is first loaded using LoadLibrary. Using the pointer returned from that function, GetProcAddress is called. The result from that function is a pointer to the requested function in the DLL.

The GetDelegateForFunctionPointer static method of the Marshal class is then used to marshal this pointer to an instance of the delegate. Using the delegate, we are then able to call the function dynamically.

When this code is executed, we see these results:

```
Result from DynamicallyAddSomeNumbers = 3
Press any key to exit
```

▓**Note** One potential problem with dynamically calling a function is that the function name we pass to GetProcAddress must exactly match the name that was exported from the DLL. If the name was decorated because of the calling convention, the exact decorated name must be specified for GetProcAddress. When DllImport is used instead, the name is derived based on the CallingConvention field that is specified. In this case, PInvoke takes care of decorating the function names for us.

Related Information

See recipes 1-1 (Identifying the Unmanaged Function) and 1-2 (Using the Function from Managed Code).

CHAPTER 2

■ ■ ■

C-Style APIs: Structures, Classes, and Arrays

Classes and structures allow you to create your own custom data types. Whether they are C++ or C# structs and classes, or Visual Basic .NET structures and classes, you can define complex types and implement business logic that would otherwise be either impossible or cumbersome. Custom data types free you from the restrictions of simple integers, floats, and doubles. Without the ability to define custom types, a developer's life would indeed be dull.

Likewise, arrays are an important tool for any developer. They allow you to operate on sets of like data rather than individual variables.

It is fitting then that this chapter is devoted to the handling of classes, structures, and arrays in Windows Interop. As it does for built-in data types, .NET provides the facilities you need to pass classes, structures, and arrays between managed and unmanaged code.

Structures used by both managed and unmanaged code are defined twice, once for each environment. In order to allow structures to pass successfully between the two environments, the layout of the structures must agree. This doesn't mean that all available fields must be defined in both places, since there are ways to define partial structures.

The first few recipes in this chapter show you how to use structures (C++/C# `structs`, Visual Basic .NET `Structures`) with PInvoke. Although structures are more limited than classes, and therefore not as widely used, they clearly illustrate all the necessary techniques for passing programmer-defined types. To complete the discussion, passing classes instead of structures is demonstrated in another recipe.

This chapter includes a number of recipes that demonstrate different ways to define and pass structures. Fields in a structure can use a sequential layout, or the position of each field can be individually controlled. Structures can be allocated in managed code and passed to unmanaged code, or vice versa.

One recipe demonstrates how to specify the way each field in a structure should be marshaled, while another discusses how to allocate and free memory for individual fields in a structure.

The chapter ends with recipes that focus on passing arrays of data between managed and unmanaged code. Simple arrays using built-in types are discussed, followed by arrays of strings and finally arrays of structures. Throughout the chapter, the use of the directional attributes (`In` and `Out`) is demonstrated.

2-1. Passing Structures

Problem

The unmanaged function you need to call requires a structure rather than individual fields to be passed. You need to know how to define and pass structures between managed and unmanaged code.

Solution

An unmanaged function that requires a structure has its own definition of the structure that it will use. Managed code that calls the function will need to supply an equivalent definition in managed code, allowing any managed code to reference the individual fields in the structure. The key to marshaling structures is properly aligning the structure definitions in managed and unmanaged code.

For example, consider this simple unmanaged function:

```
//function for structure passing
void ProcessStruct1(UnmanagedStruct1* aStruct)
{
    if (aStruct != NULL)
    {
        aStruct->UmCount   = 1;
        aStruct->UmDelta   = 2;
        aStruct->UmPercent = 1.4567;
    }
}
```

The structure UnmanagedStruct1 is defined like this in unmanaged code:

```
struct UnmanagedStruct1
{
    int    UmCount;
    char   UmTypeIndicator;
    int    UmDelta;
    double UmPercent;
};
```

In order to call this function from managed code, you need to define a managed structure that has the same memory layout as this structure. The implementation in C# might look like this:

```
//struct is properly aligned with unmanaged struct
public struct ManagedStruct1
{
    public int    maCount;
    byte          maUnused;
    public int    maDelta;
    public double maPercent;
}
```

While the names of the individual fields in the structure may differ, the type and size of each field is the same. The sequence of fields is also the same, allowing you to use the default marshaling provided for structures.

The C# code that calls this unmanaged function is implemented in this way:

```
class StructurePassingTest
{
    [DllImport("FlatAPIStructLib.DLL")]
    public static extern void ProcessStruct1(
        ref ManagedStruct1 aStruct);

    /// <summary>
    /// The main entry point for the application.
    /// </summary>
    [STAThread]
    static void Main(string[] args)
    {
        //create an instance of the struct
        ManagedStruct1 struct1  = new ManagedStruct1();
        struct1.maCount         = 12345;
        struct1.maDelta         = 45678;
        struct1.maPercent       = 5.4321;
        //call the unmanaged function
        ProcessStruct1(ref struct1);
        //show the results
        Console.WriteLine("ProcessStruct1 results: {0}, {1}, {2}",
            struct1.maCount, struct1.maDelta, struct1.maPercent);

        //wait for input
        Console.WriteLine("Press any key to exit");
        Console.Read();
    }
}
```

When we run the code, we receive these results:

```
ProcessStruct1 results: 1, 2, 1.4567
Press any key to exit
```

This works because the structure definitions in managed and unmanaged code are essentially the same. Specifically, the size, data type, and sequence of the individual fields in the structure are the same.

Note Notice that the unmanaged function expects to be passed a pointer to a structure that has been allocated by the caller of the function. It then uses the pointer to reference the individual fields of the structure.

Since the managed code is the caller of the function, it must create the structure (allocating the memory for it in managed code) and pass the structure by reference to the function. The unmanaged code will receive this as a pointer to the memory that was allocated.

The equivalent Visual Basic .NET code to run this same test could be implemented like this:

```
Imports System.Runtime.InteropServices  'needed for DllImport
Module StructurePassingVBClient

    Public Structure ManagedStruct1
        Public maCount As Integer
        Public maUnused As Byte
        Public maDelta As Integer
        Public maPercent As Double
    End Structure

    <DllImport("FlatAPIStructLib.DLL")> _
    Public Sub ProcessStruct1(ByRef aStruct As ManagedStruct1)
    End Sub

    Sub Main()
        'allocate the structure
        Dim struct1 As ManagedStruct1 = New ManagedStruct1
        struct1.maCount = 12345
        struct1.maDelta = 45678
        struct1.maPercent = 5.4321
        'call the unmanaged function that fills the struct
        ProcessStruct1(struct1)
        'show the results
        Console.WriteLine("ProcessStruct1 results: {0}, {1}, {2}", _
            struct1.maCount, struct1.maDelta, struct1.maPercent)
        'wait for input
        Console.WriteLine("Press any key to exit")
        Console.Read()
    End Sub

End Module
```

How It Works

The StructLayout attribute is provided to control the way structures are marshaled. The attribute is optional and is not necessary as long as the managed and unmanaged structure definitions agree.

StructLayout provides a number of fields that you can use to modify structure marshaling. Among them are the LayoutKind and Pack fields.

LayoutKind is an enumeration that determines the method used to control layout of the individual fields within the structure. The default value for a structure when the StructLayout attribute is omitted is LayoutKind.Sequential. This instructs the marshaler to assume that the individual fields of the structure should be laid out in the sequence in which they are defined. This default value works for the preceding example since the structures are defined with the same field sequence and each field is the same size in memory.

The managed structure used previously could have been defined this way with the same result:

```
[StructLayout(LayoutKind.Sequential)]
public struct ManagedStruct1
{
    public int     maCount;
    byte           maUnused;
    public int     maDelta;
    public double  maPercent;
}
```

The other possible value for LayoutKind is Explicit. When this value is used, you take complete control of the structure, specifying the exact offset of each field in memory. Use of this option is discussed in recipe 2-3 (Specifying the Exact Layout of a Structure).

The Pack field of the StructLayout attribute determines the alignment of the individual fields in the structure and is used only when LayoutKind.Sequential is specified. Depending on the pack size specified, individual fields may be internally aligned in a way that you would not expect.

Fields within a structure are always aligned on a boundary. That boundary is the smaller of a multiple of the pack size, or a multiple of the field size. If the pack size is not specified, the default is 8. This corresponds to the C++ default of 8 used within Visual C++ for unmanaged code.

Using the example structure, a default pack size of 8 would result in an internal representation like this:

```
struct UnmanagedStruct1
{
    int    UmCount;           <- Offset 0
    char   UmTypeIndicator;   <- Offset 4
    int    UmDelta;           <- Offset 8  (not 5 as expected)
    double UmPercent;         <- Offset 16 (not 12 as expected)
};
```

Since the default pack size is 8 for managed and unmanaged code, the marshaler took care of this little alignment detail. However, if the unmanaged code used a different pack size, we would need to adjust the managed definition of the structure to match. As an example, this unmanaged struct explicitly sets the pack size to 1:

```
#pragma pack(1)
//struct aligned on 1 byte boundary
struct UnmanagedStruct2
{
    int    UmCount;
    char   UmTypeIndicator;
    int    UmDelta;
    double UmPercent;
};
#pragma pack() //reset pack size to default
```

If we need to pass a managed version of this structure to a function, we would set the Pack field of the StructLayout attribute. A working managed definition of this structure looks like this:

```
//struct is aligned on 1 byte packing boundary
[StructLayout(LayoutKind.Sequential, Pack = 1)]
public struct ManagedStruct2
{
    public int     maCount;
    byte           maUnused;
    public int     maDelta;
    public double  maPercent;
}
```

Failure to correctly match the pack size between managed and unmanaged structs will result in incorrect (or at best unpredictable) results.

Related Information

See recipe 2-3 (Specifying the Exact Layout of a Structure).

2-2. Returning a Structure from Unmanaged Code

Problem

An unmanaged function returns a structure rather than receiving one from the caller. You need to know how to receive the structure in managed code and to free the memory that was allocated.

Solution

When an unmanaged function expects to receive a pointer to a structure, the managed code is in charge. You allocate a managed structure in managed code and then pass it to the function for its own use.

However, structures that are allocated within unmanaged code and returned to the caller must be handled differently. Since unmanaged memory is allocated within the function, it must be freed by the caller (the managed code) when it is no longer needed.

The solution is to return the pointer to the structure as an IntPtr and marshal this to the structure within managed code. You can then pass the returned IntPtr back to another unmanaged function to free the memory.

Consider this unmanaged function:

```
ReturnedUnmanagedStruct* ReturnAStruct(void)
{
    //allocate the struct using C++ new keyword
    ReturnedUnmanagedStruct* pResult = new ReturnedUnmanagedStruct();
    pResult->Hours      = 1;
    pResult->Minutes    = 59;
    pResult->Seconds    = 11;
    return pResult;
}
```

The function allocates memory for a structure using the C++ new keyword, populates the structure, and returns it to the caller as a pointer. The structure is defined like this:

```
struct ReturnedUnmanagedStruct
{
    int    Hours;
    int    Minutes;
    int    Seconds;
};
```

We also need an unmanaged function that we can call to free the memory that was previously allocated. This simple function is implemented like this:

```
void FreeAStruct(ReturnedUnmanagedStruct* pStruct)
{
    if (pStruct != NULL)
    {
        delete pStruct;
    }
}
```

We can successfully call this function from managed C# code if we handle the returned pointer as an IntPtr like this:

```
using System;
using System.Runtime.InteropServices;

/// <summary>
/// Returning of structures from unmanaged code
/// </summary>
class StructureReturningTest
{
```

```csharp
[DllImport("FlatAPIStructLib.DLL")]
public static extern IntPtr ReturnAStruct();

[DllImport("FlatAPIStructLib.DLL")]
public static extern void FreeAStruct(IntPtr structPtr);

/// <summary>
/// The main entry point for the application.
/// </summary>
[STAThread]
static void Main(string[] args)
{
    //call the unmanaged function returning a struct
    IntPtr structPtr = ReturnAStruct();
    //marshal the returned pointer to a struct
    ReturnedManagedStruct aStruct
        = (ReturnedManagedStruct)Marshal.PtrToStructure(
            structPtr, typeof(ReturnedManagedStruct));
    //free the memory for the unmanaged struct
    FreeAStruct(structPtr);
    //show the results
    Console.WriteLine("ReturnAStruct results: {0}, {1}, {2}",
        aStruct.Hours, aStruct.Minutes, aStruct.Seconds);

    //wait for input
    Console.WriteLine("Press any key to exit");
    Console.Read();
}
}
```

We define the managed version of the structure this way, matching the layout defined in unmanaged code:

```csharp
public struct ReturnedManagedStruct
{
    public int      Hours;
    public int      Minutes;
    public int      Seconds;
}
```

Looking through the code, we see that the unmanaged function is declared as returning an IntPtr. When we make the call to the function, we are able to use the Marshal.PtrToStructure static method to marshal the IntPtr to the managed version of the structure. This copies (and converts if necessary) the data that the IntPtr points to. Using the IntPtr, we then call the unmanaged FreeAStruct method that frees the memory, avoiding a memory leak.

A Visual Basic .NET version of this code looks like this:

```vbnet
Imports System
Imports System.Runtime.InteropServices
```

```vb
Module StructureReturningTest

    Public Structure ReturnedManagedStruct
        Public Hours As Integer
        Public Minutes As Integer
        Public Seconds As Integer
    End Structure

    <DllImport("FlatAPIStructLib.DLL")> _
    Public Function ReturnAStruct() As IntPtr
    End Function

    <DllImport("FlatAPIStructLib.DLL")> _
    Public Sub FreeAStruct(ByVal structPtr As IntPtr)
    End Sub

    Sub Main()
        'call the unmanaged function returning a struct
        Dim structPtr As IntPtr = ReturnAStruct()
        'marshal the returned pointer to a struct
        Dim aStruct As ReturnedManagedStruct _
            = Marshal.PtrToStructure( _
                structPtr, GetType(ReturnedManagedStruct))
        'free the memory for the unmanaged struct
        FreeAStruct(structPtr)
        'show the results
        Console.WriteLine( _
            "ReturnAStruct results: {0}, {1}, {2}", _
            aStruct.Hours, aStruct.Minutes, aStruct.Seconds)

        'wait for input
        Console.WriteLine("Press any key to exit")
        Console.Read()

    End Sub

End Module
```

When this code is executed, the results are exactly the same as those for the C# version.

How It Works

As an alternative to calling a second unmanaged function to free memory, we can modify the original function to use CoTaskMemAlloc instead of new. Once we do this, we are able to free the memory from managed code using the Marshal class.

For example, the function discussed previously could be rewritten this way:

```
ReturnedUnmanagedStruct* ReturnCoMemStruct(void)
{
    //allocate the struct using CoTaskMemAlloc
```

```
    ReturnedUnmanagedStruct* pResult =
        (ReturnedUnmanagedStruct*)CoTaskMemAlloc(
            sizeof(ReturnedUnmanagedStruct));
    pResult->Hours        = 1;
    pResult->Minutes      = 59;
    pResult->Seconds      = 11;
    return pResult;
}
```

The only substantial difference between this and the original version is the use of CoTaskMemAlloc to allocate the structure. CoTaskMemAlloc allocates memory that we can free directly from managed code.

The managed code to call this revised function looks like this in C#:

```
[DllImport("FlatAPIStructLib.DLL")]
public static extern IntPtr ReturnCoMemStruct();

//call the unmanaged function returning a CoTaskMemAlloc struct
IntPtr structPtr = ReturnCoMemStruct();
//marshal the returned pointer to a struct
ReturnedManagedStruct bStruct
    = (ReturnedManagedStruct)Marshal.PtrToStructure(
        structPtr, typeof(ReturnedManagedStruct));
//free the CoTaskMemAlloc memory
Marshal.FreeCoTaskMem(structPtr);
//show the results
Console.WriteLine("ReturnCoMemStruct results: {0}, {1}, {2}",
    bStruct.Hours, bStruct.Minutes, bStruct.Seconds);
```

It is implemented like this in Visual Basic .NET:

```
<DllImport("FlatAPIStructLib.DLL")> _
Public Function ReturnCoMemStruct() As IntPtr
End Function


'call the unmanaged function
'returning a CoTaskMemAlloc struct
structPtr = ReturnCoMemStruct()
'marshal the returned pointer to a struct
Dim bStruct As ReturnedManagedStruct _
    = Marshal.PtrToStructure( _
        structPtr, GetType(ReturnedManagedStruct))
'free the CoTaskMemAlloc memory
Marshal.FreeCoTaskMem(structPtr)
'show the results
Console.WriteLine( _
    "ReturnCoMemStruct results: {0}, {1}, {2}", _
    bStruct.Hours, bStruct.Minutes, bStruct.Seconds)
```

Using CoTaskMemAlloc doesn't eliminate our responsibility to free the memory. However, we can easily take care of that duty using the static FreeCoTaskMem method of the Marshal class.

The output from the tests shows that regardless of the memory allocation method, we get the same results:

```
ReturnAStruct results: 1, 59, 11
ReturnCoMemStruct results: 1, 59, 11
Press any key to exit
```

Related Information

See recipes 2-1 (Passing Structures) and 1-11 (Freeing Unmanaged Memory).

2-3. Specifying the Exact Layout of a Structure

Problem

An unmanaged function requires a large structure as an input parameter; however, you are concerned with only one or two fields in the structure. You need a way to pass a partially defined structure to the function.

Solution

The StructLayout attribute can be applied to the managed version of a structure to control the overall approach used to marshal the structure. By specifying LayoutKind.Explicit in the attribute constructor, you take complete control of how the structure is marshaled to unmanaged code. Use of the FieldOffset attribute on each field in the structure is required to indicate the exact position within the structure.

For example, consider this unmanaged structure that defines a number of fields:

```
#pragma pack(1)
//structure for account info retrieval
struct UnmanagedAccountStruct
{
    int     AccountId;          //4 bytes
    int     AccountStatus;      //4 bytes
    short   AccountAgingMethod; //2 bytes
    short   AccountType;        //2 bytes
    int     RegionId;           //4 bytes
    double  CurrentBalance;     //8 bytes
    double  PastDueBalance;     //8 bytes
    int     SalesRepId;         //4 bytes
    char*   AccountName;        //4 bytes
    char*   Address1;           //4 bytes
    char*   Address2;           //4 bytes
    char*   City;               //4 bytes
    char*   State;              //4 bytes
    int     PostalCode;         //4 bytes
    double  LastPurchaseAmt;    //8 bytes
};
#pragma pack() //reset pack size to default
```

The total size of this unmanaged structure is 68 bytes.

We may not need to use all of these fields in our managed code. Alternatively, multiple unmanaged functions may each populate only a subset of the fields.

Note In this example, the pack boundary size is set to 1. The pack size determines the layout of individual fields, placing fields internally on a multiple of the specified boundary or a multiple of the field size.

For this example, we choose a pack size of 1 simply to make the calculation of field offsets more obvious. In the real world, other pack sizes are likely, and the calculation of the actual field offset may become much more difficult.

Using the StructLayout and FieldOffset attributes, we can define a managed version of this structure in C# that contains only the fields that concern us:

```
//partial structure definition
[StructLayout(LayoutKind.Explicit)]
public struct AccountBalanceStruct
{
    [FieldOffset(0)]    public int     AccountId;
    [FieldOffset(16)]   public double  CurrentBalance;
    [FieldOffset(24)]   public double  PastDueBalance;
    [FieldOffset(60)]   public double  LastPurchaseAmt;
}
```

Here is the same structure in Visual Basic .NET:

```
'partial structure definition
<StructLayout(LayoutKind.Explicit)> _
Public Structure AccountBalanceStruct
    <FieldOffset(0)> Public AccountId As Integer
    <FieldOffset(16)> Public CurrentBalance As Double
    <FieldOffset(24)> Public PastDueBalance As Double
    <FieldOffset(60)> Public LastPurchaseAmt As Double
End Structure
```

The use of LayoutKind.Explicit informs the marshaler that we will be specifying FieldOffset attributes for each field in the structure.

The FieldOffset attribute specifies the offset of the field from the beginning of the unmanaged structure, not the managed structure. If we calculated the offsets of each field correctly, the fields should correspond to the unmanaged structure.

How It Works

To complete the example started previously, we can implement an unmanaged function that uses a portion of this structure. The C++ code looks like this:

```
void RetrieveAccountBalances(int accountId,
    UnmanagedAccountStruct* pAccount)
```

```
{
    //return selected account fields
    if (pAccount != NULL)
    {
        pAccount->AccountId        = accountId;
        pAccount->AccountType      = sizeof(char*);
        pAccount->CurrentBalance   = 500.00;
        pAccount->PastDueBalance   = 350.00;
        pAccount->LastPurchaseAmt  = 10.95;
    }
}
```

The function expects an integer to identify the account ID and a pointer to the unmanaged struct defined previously. Presumably, the function would access a database or other data store to retrieve account information (those minor details don't affect this example). A subset of fields within the structure is then populated, making the values available to the calling code.

The complete C# implementation of code that accesses this function looks like this:

```
using System;
using System.Runtime.InteropServices;

namespace StructureExactLayoutTest
{
    //partial structure definition
    [StructLayout(LayoutKind.Explicit)]
    public struct AccountBalanceStruct
    {
        [FieldOffset(0)]    public int      AccountId;
        [FieldOffset(16)]   public double   CurrentBalance;
        [FieldOffset(24)]   public double   PastDueBalance;
        [FieldOffset(60)]   public double   LastPurchaseAmt;
    }

    /// <summary>
    /// Passing of structures between managed and unmanaged code
    /// </summary>
    class StructureExactLayoutTest
    {
        [DllImport("FlatAPIStructLib.DLL")]
        public static extern void RetrieveAccountBalances(
            int accountId, ref AccountBalanceStruct account);

        /// <summary>
        /// The main entry point for the application.
        /// </summary>
        [STAThread]
        static void Main(string[] args)
```

```
            {
                //uses a partially defined managed structure
                AccountBalanceStruct account = new AccountBalanceStruct();
                //make the unmanaged function call
                RetrieveAccountBalances(1001, ref account);
                //show the results
                Console.WriteLine(
                    "RetrieveAccountBalances results: {0}, {1}, {2}, {3}",
                        account.AccountId, account.CurrentBalance,
                        account.PastDueBalance, account.LastPurchaseAmt);

                    //wait for input
                Console.WriteLine("Press any key to exit");
                Console.Read();
            }
        }
}
```

The Visual Basic .NET implementation looks like this:

```
Imports System
Imports System.Runtime.InteropServices

''' <summary>
''' Passing of structures between managed and unmanaged code
''' </summary>
''' <remarks></remarks>
Module StructureExactLayoutTest

    'partial structure definition
    <StructLayout(LayoutKind.Explicit)> _
    Public Structure AccountBalanceStruct
        <FieldOffset(0)> Public AccountId As Integer
        <FieldOffset(16)> Public CurrentBalance As Double
        <FieldOffset(24)> Public PastDueBalance As Double
        <FieldOffset(60)> Public LastPurchaseAmt As Double
    End Structure

    <DllImport("FlatAPIStructLib.DLL")> _
    Public Sub RetrieveAccountBalances( _
        ByVal accountId As Integer, _
        ByRef account As AccountBalanceStruct)
    End Sub

    Sub Main()
        'uses a partially defined managed structure
        Dim account As AccountBalanceStruct _
            = New AccountBalanceStruct()
        'make the unmanaged function call
```

```
        RetrieveAccountBalances(1001, account)
        'show the results
        Console.WriteLine( _
            "RetrieveAccountBalances results: {0}, {1}, {2}, {3}", _
            account.AccountId, account.CurrentBalance, _
            account.PastDueBalance, account.LastPurchaseAmt)

        'wait for input
        Console.WriteLine("Press any key to exit")
        Console.Read()
    End Sub

End Module
```

Regardless of the language used, we see these results when the code is executed:

```
RetrieveAccountBalances results: 1001, 500, 350, 10.95
Press any key to exit
```

In this example, the managed version of the structure (AccountBalanceStruct) does not define all of the fields in the unmanaged version. However, notice that it does define the last field named LastPurchaseAmt at field offset 60. Since this final field has a size of 8 bytes, the overall size of the managed structure is the same as the unmanaged version: 68 bytes. The field with the largest FieldOffset determines the overall size of the structure.

The unmanaged code will thus receive a structure that has been initialized to the full length of 68 bytes. All memory in the unmanaged structure is first cleared. Fields that are not defined in the managed structure are seen as zeros in the unmanaged code. The values of all fields that are defined in the managed structure are marshaled to the unmanaged version.

We must be careful when defining the managed version of a structure. If we omit the last field in a structure, the unmanaged function will receive a structure that has not been completely initialized.

We can illustrate this behavior using this unmanaged function:

```
double RevisePurchaseAmt(UnmanagedAccountStruct* pAccount,
    double purchaseAmt)
{
    double lastPurchaseAmt;
    //revise the LastPurchaseAmt
    if (pAccount != NULL)
    {
        //save the LastPurchaseAmt
        lastPurchaseAmt = pAccount->LastPurchaseAmt;
        //update with the new amount
        pAccount->LastPurchaseAmt = purchaseAmt;
    }
    return lastPurchaseAmt;
}
```

This example uses the same UnmanagedAccountStruct used in the last example. The function is passed a pointer to this structure along with a double. The LastPurchaseAmt field in the structure is updated with the value that is passed to the function. The original value of the LastPurchaseAmt field is the return value of the function.

In the C# code, we define a version of the structure that deliberately omits the final LastPurchaseAmt field:

```
[StructLayout(LayoutKind.Explicit)]
public struct AccountBalanceStructShort
{
    [FieldOffset(0)]      public int        AccountId;
    [FieldOffset(16)]     public double     CurrentBalance;
    [FieldOffset(24)]     public double     PastDueBalance;

    //LastPurchaseAmt field is omitted
}
```

The C# declaration of the function that uses this managed structure looks like this:

```
[DllImport("FlatAPIStructLib.DLL")]
public static extern double RevisePurchaseAmt(
    ref AccountBalanceStructShort account,
    double purchaseAmt);
```

The code to test this function looks like this:

```
AccountBalanceStructShort accountShort
    = new AccountBalanceStructShort();
double lastPurchaseAmt
    = RevisePurchaseAmt(ref accountShort, 249.95);
Console.WriteLine(
    "RevisePurchaseAmt results: {0}",
    lastPurchaseAmt);
```

Since we create a new instance of the structure before we pass it to the function, we would expect to receive a return value of zero. The LastPurchaseAmt field that is returned from the function isn't defined in the managed version of the structure, so it should have a value of zero, right? Wrong. When we execute this code using the debugger, we see something similar to these results (the exact results shown on your machine may be different):

```
RevisePurchaseAmt results: 5.34315632523118E-315
```

Because the managed structure defined is shorter than the expected length of the unmanaged structure, the unmanaged code received memory that wasn't completely initialized. In this case, the LastPurchaseAmt field at the very end of the structure contains garbage.

■ **Note** It's interesting to note that we see these results only when we run the code under the Visual Studio .NET debugger. When we execute the same code outside of the debugger, the fields appear to be initialized.

In this function we are simply returning the value of this field. Really bad things would happen if the function actually used this field for something useful—perhaps for some type of calculation.

The StructLayout attribute has an optional Size field that corrects this problem. If Size is specified, it extends the memory that is passed to unmanaged code beyond the actual size of the defined fields. The Size field can only increase the total size of the structure; it cannot be used to make it smaller. Therefore, Size must be equal to or greater than the total size of the structure based on the defined fields.

To see the use of the Size field, we can modify the C# structure to look like this:

```
//partial structure definition
[StructLayout(LayoutKind.Explicit, Size = 68)]
public struct AccountBalanceStructSize
{
    [FieldOffset(0)]     public int       AccountId;
    [FieldOffset(16)]    public double    CurrentBalance;
    [FieldOffset(24)]    public double    PastDueBalance;

    //LastPurchaseAmt field is omitted
}
```

This structure uses the Size field to indicate that a total of 68 bytes of memory should be initialized and passed to unmanaged code. Notice that the structure is renamed to avoid confusion with the last example.

We now declare the unmanaged function again, this time using the revised structure:

```
[DllImport("FlatAPIStructLib.DLL",
    EntryPoint = "RevisePurchaseAmt")]
public static extern double RevisePurchaseAmtFull(
    ref AccountBalanceStructSize account,
    double purchaseAmt);
```

The revised C# code to use this version of the structure looks like this:

```
AccountBalanceStructSize accountWithSize
    = new AccountBalanceStructSize();
double lastPurchaseAmt
    = RevisePurchaseAmtFull(ref accountWithSize, 249.95);
Console.WriteLine(
    "RevisePurchaseAmtFull results: {0}",
    lastPurchaseAmt);
```

This time when we execute the code, we see the expected results:

```
RevisePurchaseAmtFull results: 0
```

Because of this behavior, it's actually a good idea to always include the Size field when you use LayoutKind.Explicit, especially for a structure that is only partially defined. The Size field isn't required, but including it will help to avoid potential problems like this.

Related Information

See recipe 2-1 (Passing Structures).

2-4. Controlling Field-Level Marshaling Within Structures

Problem

You need to pass a structure to unmanaged code that includes strings of multiple types. Some of the strings are defined as ANSI strings while others are Unicode. The CharSet field of the DllImport attribute won't do the trick, since it affects all strings in the function call, not individual fields within a structure.

Solution

When using structures, you can apply the MarshalAs attribute to control how individual fields in the structure are marshaled. The MarshalAs attribute is applied to those fields that require nondefault marshaling behavior.

The MarshalAs attribute allows you to specify the unmanaged type that is mapped to the managed field during marshaling. While you are free to apply this attribute to every field of every structure, in practice you only need it in cases where the data type conversion is ambiguous.

For example, a managed System.String can be marshaled in a number of ways, either as an ANSI string, a Unicode string, or a COM BSTR. Likewise, a System.Boolean could be marshaled as a C++-style bool (1 byte) or a Win32 BOOL (a 4-byte integer). In cases such as this, you may need to apply the MarshalAs attribute.

For example, this unmanaged structure contains a number of fields that demonstrate this problem:

```
struct UnmanagedAmbiguousStruct
{
    char*    AnsiString;
    wchar_t* WideString;
    BOOL     Win32Boolean;      //4 bytes
    bool     CStyleBoolean;     //1 byte
    unsigned short ShortInteger;
};
```

We have deliberately created a problem for ourselves by including both types of string and Boolean fields.

A managed version of this structure could be implemented like this in C#:

```
[StructLayout(LayoutKind.Sequential)]
struct ManagedAmbiguousStruct
{
    [MarshalAs(UnmanagedType.LPStr)]  public string AnsiString;
    [MarshalAs(UnmanagedType.LPWStr)] public string WideString;
    [MarshalAs(UnmanagedType.Bool)]   public bool   Win32Boolean;
```

```
    [MarshalAs(UnmanagedType.I1)]      public bool   CStyleBoolean;
    public ushort   ShortInteger;
};
```

Here is the same structure in Visual Basic .NET:

```
<StructLayout(LayoutKind.Sequential)> _
Public Structure ManagedAmbiguousStruct
    <MarshalAs(UnmanagedType.LPStr)> _
    Public AnsiString As String
    <MarshalAs(UnmanagedType.LPWStr)> _
    Public WideString As String
    <MarshalAs(UnmanagedType.Bool)> _
    Public Win32Boolean As Boolean
    <MarshalAs(UnmanagedType.I1)> _
    Public CStyleBoolean As Boolean
    Public ShortInteger As UShort
End Structure
```

By applying the MarshalAs attribute to each field, we remove the ambiguity. The marshaler now has explicit instructions from us as to how we want these fields converted to unmanaged values.

Note The MarshalAs attribute supports a large number of unmanaged data types. This example illustrates the use of attribute values that modify string and Boolean fields. Please consult the Microsoft documentation for a complete list of available unmanaged types.

How It Works

As demonstrated in this example structure, use of the MarshalAs attribute is not an all-or-nothing matter. You are free to mix and match the use of the attribute as needed, applying it only in cases where it is truly required. In the example, the ShortInteger field does not use the MarshalAs attribute; instead, it uses the default marshaling.

Furthermore, we could simplify the example structure slightly if we want to totally rely upon default marshaling behavior. The default marshaling for a string is to an ANSI string, and the default for a Boolean is to a 4-byte integer (Win32 BOOL). Therefore, we can omit the MarshalAs attributes from those fields without any adverse affect. The revised structure could look like this:

```
[StructLayout(LayoutKind.Sequential)]
struct ManagedAmbiguousStruct
{
    public string   AnsiString;
    [MarshalAs(UnmanagedType.LPWStr)] public string   WideString;
    public bool     Win32Boolean;
    [MarshalAs(UnmanagedType.I1)]     public bool   CStyleBoolean;
    public ushort   ShortInteger;
};
```

However, there is a benefit to being explicit, and in this case the inclusion of the MarshalAs attribute on the fields makes it clearer how things will be marshaled.

To illustrate the use of this structure, we can implement an unmanaged function that uses it:

```
int UseAmbiguousStruct(UnmanagedAmbiguousStruct aStruct)
{
    int result = 0;
    result += (int)strlen(aStruct.AnsiString);
    result += (int)wcslen(aStruct.WideString);
    if (aStruct.CStyleBoolean)
    {
        result++;
    }
    if (aStruct.Win32Boolean)
    {
        result++;
    }
    result += aStruct.ShortInteger;

    return result;
}
```

For testing purposes only, the function retrieves the length of each string and checks the value of each Boolean field. An integer with the results is returned.

The complete C# code to execute this function is implemented in this way:

```
using System;
using System.Runtime.InteropServices;

namespace StructureMarshalAsTest
{
    [StructLayout(LayoutKind.Sequential)]
    struct ManagedAmbiguousStruct
    {
        [MarshalAs(UnmanagedType.LPStr)]
        public string    AnsiString;
        [MarshalAs(UnmanagedType.LPWStr)]
        public string    WideString;
        [MarshalAs(UnmanagedType.Bool)]
        public bool      Win32Boolean;
        [MarshalAs(UnmanagedType.I1)]
        public bool      CStyleBoolean;
        public ushort    ShortInteger;
    };
```

```csharp
/// <summary>
/// Passing of structures between managed and unmanaged code
/// </summary>
class StructureMarshalAsTest
{
    [DllImport("FlatAPIStructLib.DLL")]
    public static extern int UseAmbiguousStruct(
        ManagedAmbiguousStruct aStruct);

    /// <summary>
    /// The main entry point for the application.
    /// </summary>
    [STAThread]
    static void Main(string[] args)
    {
        ManagedAmbiguousStruct mStruct
            = new ManagedAmbiguousStruct();
        mStruct.AnsiString      = "ansistring";
        mStruct.WideString      = "widestring";
        mStruct.CStyleBoolean   = true;
        mStruct.Win32Boolean    = true;
        mStruct.ShortInteger    = 5;

        int result = UseAmbiguousStruct(mStruct);

        //show the results
        Console.WriteLine("UseAmbiguousStruct results: {0}",
            result);

        //wait for input
        Console.WriteLine("Press any key to exit");
        Console.Read();
    }
}
}
```

The Visual Basic .NET implementation looks like this:

```vbnet
Imports System
Imports System.Runtime.InteropServices

Module StructureMarshalAsTest

    <StructLayout(LayoutKind.Sequential)> _
    Public Structure ManagedAmbiguousStruct
```

```vbnet
        <MarshalAs(UnmanagedType.LPStr)> _
        Public AnsiString As String
        <MarshalAs(UnmanagedType.LPWStr)> _
        Public WideString As String
        <MarshalAs(UnmanagedType.Bool)> _
        Public Win32Boolean As Boolean
        <MarshalAs(UnmanagedType.I1)> _
        Public CStyleBoolean As Boolean
        Public ShortInteger As UShort
    End Structure

    <DllImport("FlatAPIStructLib.DLL")> _
    Public Function UseAmbiguousStruct( _
        ByVal aStruct As ManagedAmbiguousStruct) _
        As Integer
    End Function

    Sub Main()
        Dim mStruct As ManagedAmbiguousStruct _
            = New ManagedAmbiguousStruct()
        mStruct.AnsiString = "ansistring"
        mStruct.WideString = "widestring"
        mStruct.CStyleBoolean = True
        mStruct.Win32Boolean = True
        mStruct.ShortInteger = 5

        Dim result As Integer = UseAmbiguousStruct(mStruct)

        'show the results
        Console.WriteLine( _
            "UseAmbiguousStruct results: {0}", result)

        'wait for input
        Console.WriteLine("Press any key to exit")
        Console.Read()
    End Sub

End Module
```

It should be noted that the StructLayout attribute and the DllImport attribute both contain a CharSet field. The purpose of this field is to specify the way strings are marshaled to unmanaged code. The StructLayout.CharSet field controls string marshaling for the structure, while DllImport.CharSet affects all strings in the function call.

However, the CharSet field won't solve the problem created here. If we were to rely upon the CharSet field, it would affect all strings in the structure. The problem at hand is the use of both types of strings within the same structure. The CharSet field is not the correct solution to this problem, but it might be useful in other scenarios.

DEBUGGING ENTRYPOINTNOTFOUNDEXCEPTION

When first working with structures, it is not uncommon to receive an EntryPointNotFoundException during testing. While this exception may appear to indicate an incorrect DLL or function name, the root cause is more typically an incorrectly defined structure.

If a structure is one of the input or output arguments for a function, depending on the calling convention, it forms part of the function signature. For example, if the UseAmbiguousStruct method uses the __stdcall calling convention, it is exported from the unmanaged DLL with a decorated entry point of _UseAmbiguousStruct@16. The 16 in this case represents the expected number of bytes in the structure passed as an argument. The number of bytes in the structure is affected by the packing size and the order of fields in the structure. PInvoke uses the size of the managed structure to determine the decorated entry point name for the call. If the managed and unmanaged versions of the structure do not match, PInvoke won't necessarily tell you that the structures don't match. Instead, PInvoke will inform you that no entry point using the parameters that you have defined (the incorrect structure) can be found.

If you have decorated individual fields in the structure with the MarshalAs attribute, the attribute settings should be reviewed along with the data types of the structure fields. The MarshalAs attribute does affect the PInvoke view of the function signature, and an incorrect MarshalAs attribute may be the root cause of the problem.

For example, we might incorrectly define the structure used in the example code like this:

```
[StructLayout(LayoutKind.Sequential)]
struct ManagedAmbiguousStruct
{
    public ushort ShortInteger;
    [MarshalAs(UnmanagedType.LPStr)]
    public string AnsiString;
    [MarshalAs(UnmanagedType.LPWStr)]
    public string WideString;
    [MarshalAs(UnmanagedType.Bool)]
    public bool Win32Boolean;
    [MarshalAs(UnmanagedType.I1)]
    public bool CStyleBoolean;

};
```

This incorrectly places the ShortInteger field at the beginning of the structure. If we make this change and run the sample code again, an EntryPointNotFoundException will be thrown with this message: "Unable to find an entry point named 'UseAmbiguousStruct' in DLL 'FlatAPIStructLib.DLL'".

After comparing the two versions of the structure and correcting any errors, the exception should be eliminated. If the function uses __cdecl instead of __stdcall, we would receive a different result. The entry point would be found and the call would occur. However, since the managed and unmanaged structures do not agree, the unmanaged function would receive and act upon incorrect data.

Related Information

See recipe 1-6 (Changing the Character Set Used for Strings).

2-5. Allocating Memory Within Structures

Problem

An unmanaged function that you need to call uses a structure containing a number of string fields. The function fills the structure with string values, allocating the unmanaged memory for each string. You need to know how to marshal the strings and free the memory.

Solution

When unmanaged code allocates memory, it must be freed. By definition, unmanaged code allocates unmanaged memory that is not part of the garbage-collected heap used by .NET languages. You can't simply wait for it to be garbage-collected, since that will never occur.

Depending on the mechanism used to allocate the memory, it can be freed in one of two ways:

1. If the memory is allocated from COM memory using CoTaskMemAlloc, the memory can be freed from managed code.

2. If the memory is allocated using any other unmanaged method (e.g., the new keyword in C++, malloc in C), it must be freed from unmanaged code, using an additional unmanaged function call.

■**Note** The example code in this recipe demonstrates the use of memory allocated with CoTaskMemAlloc. For examples of dealing with memory allocated by the C runtime, please refer to the recipes listed in the "Related Information" section.

By way of example, this unmanaged version of a structure defines a number of string fields:

```
#pragma pack(1)
//structure for account info retrieval
struct UnmanagedAccountStruct
{
    int    AccountId;          //4 bytes
    int    AccountStatus;      //4 bytes
    short  AccountAgingMethod; //2 bytes
    short  AccountType;        //2 bytes
    int    RegionId;           //4 bytes
    double CurrentBalance;     //8 bytes
    double PastDueBalance;     //8 bytes
    int    SalesRepId;         //4 bytes
    char*  AccountName;        //4 bytes
    char*  Address1;           //4 bytes
    char*  Address2;           //4 bytes
```

```
    char*  City;              //4 bytes
    char*  State;             //4 bytes
    int    PostalCode;        //4 bytes
    double LastPurchaseAmt;   //8 bytes
};
#pragma pack() //reset pack size to default
```

The unmanaged function that populates the string fields might be implemented like this:

```
void RetrieveAccountProfile(int accountId,
    UnmanagedAccountStruct* pAccount)
{
    //return selected account fields
    if (pAccount != NULL)
    {
        //allocate memory needed for strings
        pAccount->AccountName  = (char*)CoTaskMemAlloc(255);
        pAccount->Address1     = (char*)CoTaskMemAlloc(255);
        pAccount->Address2     = (char*)CoTaskMemAlloc(255);
        pAccount->City         = (char*)CoTaskMemAlloc(255);
        pAccount->State        = (char*)CoTaskMemAlloc(255);

        //populate fields with data
        pAccount->AccountId        = accountId;
        strcpy_s(pAccount->AccountName, 255, "Account Name");
        strcpy_s(pAccount->Address1, 255, "Address line 1");
        strcpy_s(pAccount->Address2, 255, "Address line 2");
        strcpy_s(pAccount->City, 255, "City name");
        strcpy_s(pAccount->State, 255, "Full state name");
        pAccount->PostalCode       = 12345;
    }
}
```

Since the memory for each string field is allocated using CoTaskMemAlloc, we should be able to marshal these strings and free the memory entirely from managed code. Because we are concerned with only a subset of the entire structure (just the string fields), the managed version of this structure looks like this in C#:

```
[StructLayout(LayoutKind.Explicit)]
public struct AccountBalanceStruct
{
    [FieldOffset(0)]     public int     AccountId;
    [FieldOffset(36)]    public string  AccountName;
    [FieldOffset(40)]    public string  Address1;
    [FieldOffset(44)]    public string  Address2;
    [FieldOffset(48)]    public string  City;
    [FieldOffset(52)]    public string  State;
    [FieldOffset(56)]    public int     PostalCode;
}
```

In this structure, we define only the fields that we need, ignoring the other fields in the structure. We identify the exact position of each field in the structure using the FieldOffset attribute.

When an unmanaged field is marshaled, the marshaler will call CoTaskMemFree to deallocate the memory after the field value has been copied. However, this will work only if the memory was allocated using CoTaskMemAlloc. Because the example function does allocate memory this way, we are allowed to declare the string fields as System.String and let the marshaler handle the dirty work. The PInvoke marshaler will be able to correctly marshal these values and free the memory without any manual intervention from us.

The function is declared this way in C#:

```
[DllImport("FlatAPIStructLib.DLL")]
public static extern void RetrieveAccountProfile(
    int accountId, ref AccountBalanceStruct account);
```

Notice that the structure is passed to the function by reference instead of by value. This is necessary since the function expects a pointer to the structure.

Here is the C# code to execute this function:

```
//create the struct
AccountBalanceStruct account = new AccountBalanceStruct();

//make the unmanaged function call, marshaling
//the strings as System.String
RetrieveAccountProfile(1001, ref account);

//show the results
Console.WriteLine(
    "RetrieveAccountProfile results: {0},{1},{2},{3},{4},{5}",
    account.AccountId, account.AccountName, account.Address1,
    account.Address2, account.State, account.PostalCode);
```

Visual Basic .NET code that executes this function can be implemented like this:

```
Imports System
Imports System.Runtime.InteropServices

Module StructureStringsTest

    'partial structure definition
    <StructLayout(LayoutKind.Explicit)> _
    Public Structure AccountBalanceStruct
        <FieldOffset(0)> Public AccountId As Integer
        <FieldOffset(36)> Public AccountName As String
        <FieldOffset(40)> Public Address1 As String
        <FieldOffset(44)> Public Address2 As String
        <FieldOffset(48)> Public City As String
        <FieldOffset(52)> Public State As String
        <FieldOffset(56)> Public PostalCode As Integer
    End Structure
```

```
<DllImport("FlatAPIStructLib.DLL")> _
Public Sub RetrieveAccountProfile( _
    ByVal accountId As Integer, _
    ByRef account As AccountBalanceStruct)
End Sub

Sub Main()
    'create the struct
    Dim account As AccountBalanceStruct _
        = New AccountBalanceStruct()
    'make the unmanaged function call, marshaling
    'the strings as System.String
    RetrieveAccountProfile(1001, account)

    'show the results
    Console.WriteLine( _
        "RetrieveAccountProfile results: " _
        + "{0},{1},{2},{3},{4},{5}", _
        account.AccountId, account.AccountName, _
        account.Address1, account.Address2, _
        account.State, account.PostalCode)

End Sub

End Module
```

How It Works

To better understand how all of this works under the covers, we can rewrite the managed code that calls this function and handle the marshaling and memory duties ourselves.

We start by creating a new managed version of the structure, changing it to look like this:

```
[StructLayout(LayoutKind.Explicit)]
public struct AccountBalanceStructRaw
{
    [FieldOffset(0)]     public int      AccountId;
    [FieldOffset(36)]    public IntPtr   AccountName;
    [FieldOffset(40)]    public IntPtr   Address1;
    [FieldOffset(44)]    public IntPtr   Address2;
    [FieldOffset(48)]    public IntPtr   City;
    [FieldOffset(52)]    public IntPtr   State;
    [FieldOffset(56)]    public int      PostalCode;
}
```

The only change we made is to declare the string fields as System.IntPtr instead of System.String. Using IntPtr will provide us with a raw pointer that will be used to marshal each string field and subsequently free the memory.

We add a second function declaration that points to the original unmanaged function but uses this revised structure:

```
[DllImport("FlatAPIStructLib.DLL",
    EntryPoint="RetrieveAccountProfile")]
public static extern void RetrieveAccountProfileRaw(
    int accountId, ref AccountBalanceStructRaw account);
```

The new C# code to execute the function looks like this:

```
AccountBalanceStructRaw accountRaw = new AccountBalanceStructRaw();

//make the unmanaged function call
RetrieveAccountProfileRaw(1001, ref accountRaw);

//marshal the pointers to strings
String accountName = Marshal.PtrToStringAnsi(accountRaw.AccountName);
String address1 = Marshal.PtrToStringAnsi(accountRaw.Address1);
String address2 = Marshal.PtrToStringAnsi(accountRaw.Address2);
String city = Marshal.PtrToStringAnsi(accountRaw.City);
String state = Marshal.PtrToStringAnsi(accountRaw.State);

//free the memory
Marshal.FreeCoTaskMem(accountRaw.AccountName);
Marshal.FreeCoTaskMem(accountRaw.Address1);
Marshal.FreeCoTaskMem(accountRaw.Address2);
Marshal.FreeCoTaskMem(accountRaw.City);
Marshal.FreeCoTaskMem(accountRaw.State);

//show the results
Console.WriteLine(
    "RetrieveAccountProfileRaw results: {0},{1},{2},{3},{4},{5}",
    accountRaw.AccountId, accountName, address1,
    address2, state, accountRaw.PostalCode);
```

The Visual Basic .NET version of this code looks like this:

```
Imports System
Imports System.Runtime.InteropServices

Module StructureStringsTest

    'partial structure definition
    <StructLayout(LayoutKind.Explicit)> _
    Public Structure AccountBalanceStructRaw
        <FieldOffset(0)> Public AccountId As Integer
        <FieldOffset(36)> Public AccountName As IntPtr
        <FieldOffset(40)> Public Address1 As IntPtr
        <FieldOffset(44)> Public Address2 As IntPtr
        <FieldOffset(48)> Public City As IntPtr
```

```vbnet
    <FieldOffset(52)> Public State As IntPtr
    <FieldOffset(56)> Public PostalCode As Integer
End Structure

<DllImport("FlatAPIStructLib.DLL", _
    EntryPoint:="RetrieveAccountProfile")> _
Public Sub RetrieveAccountProfileRaw( _
    ByVal accountId As Integer, _
    ByRef account As AccountBalanceStructRaw)
End Sub

Sub Main()
    'raw version where we do the marshaling and freeing.
    'Should provide the same results as above where
    'we let PInvoke do the work
    Dim accountRaw As AccountBalanceStructRaw _
        = New AccountBalanceStructRaw()
    'make the unmanaged function call
    RetrieveAccountProfileRaw(1001, accountRaw)
    'marshal the pointers to strings
    Dim accountName As String _
        = Marshal.PtrToStringAnsi(accountRaw.AccountName)
    Dim address1 As String _
        = Marshal.PtrToStringAnsi(accountRaw.Address1)
    Dim address2 As String _
        = Marshal.PtrToStringAnsi(accountRaw.Address2)
    Dim city As String _
        = Marshal.PtrToStringAnsi(accountRaw.City)
    Dim state As String _
    = Marshal.PtrToStringAnsi(accountRaw.State)
    'free the memory
    Marshal.FreeCoTaskMem(accountRaw.AccountName)
    Marshal.FreeCoTaskMem(accountRaw.Address1)
    Marshal.FreeCoTaskMem(accountRaw.Address2)
    Marshal.FreeCoTaskMem(accountRaw.City)
    Marshal.FreeCoTaskMem(accountRaw.State)

    'show the results
    Console.WriteLine( _
        "RetrieveAccountProfileRaw results: " _
        + "{0},{1},{2},{3},{4},{5}", _
        account.AccountId, accountName, _
        address1, address2, _
        state, account.PostalCode)

    'wait for input
    Console.WriteLine("Press any key to exit")
    Console.Read()
```

```
    End Sub

End Module
```

Clearly, this version of the calling code represents a substantial increase in code size and complexity compared to the original. The goal in presenting this code is not to promote it as a better solution than the original code; instead, it is presented here to illustrate the tasks normally handled by the marshaler.

All of the steps that we've coded are necessary and must be done each time this function is called. The string pointers that are returned must be used to retrieve the unmanaged string values and copy them to System.String variables. Once the values are copied, the pointers must be used to free the memory. We can choose to either allow the marshaler to handle these duties or perform the necessary steps in the application code.

Regardless of the method used to call the function (or the language), the end results are the same:

```
RetrieveAccountProfile results:
    1001,Account Name,Address line 1,Address line 2,
    Full state name,12345
RetrieveAccountProfileRaw results:
    1001,Account Name,Address line 1,Address line 2,
    Full state name,12345
```

Related Information

See recipes 2-3 (Specifying the Exact Layout of a Structure), 2-2 (Returning a Structure from Unmanaged Code), and 1-11 (Freeing Unmanaged Memory).

2-6. Passing Classes to Unmanaged Code

Problem

Although the unmanaged function you need to call expects to be passed a structure, you would prefer to define and pass an instance of a managed class.

Solution

Passing a class instance to a function is very similar to passing a structure. You have the same options available to you to control its field layout in memory. This includes use of the StructLayout, FieldOffset, and MarshalAs attributes that are discussed in other recipes. However, there are subtle differences in passing a class to unmanaged code.

Structures are value types and by default are passed as an input-only parameter to unmanaged code. If the function needs to update fields within the structure, you can pass it by reference instead of by value. The function receives a pointer to the structure that can be used to reference the individual fields.

Managed classes, on the other hand, are reference types. You would expect that they are passed to unmanaged code by reference and would be updatable by the called function.

However, this is not always the case. When you add the StructLayout attribute to a class, it is no longer marshaled according to the rules for a reference type, but is instead considered a *formatted class*, which is a class marshaled to unmanaged code as if it were a simple structure.

Note In order to pass a managed class to unmanaged code that expects a structure, you must decorate the class with the StructLayout attribute. This instructs the marshaler to handle the managed class according to the normal rules for marshaling structures.

By default, when an instance of a formatted class is marshaled to an unmanaged function, it is passed as an input-only parameter. The function can locally update the fields in the structure, but the modified values are not marshaled back to the caller. This default behavior is for performance reasons; it eliminates the need to copy values back to the calling code and is consistent with the rules for simple structures.

In order to see any changes made to a class instance, you need to apply the In and Out attributes to the function declaration. This takes the following form:

```
[DllImport("MyUnmanagedLib.DLL")]
public static extern bool MyFunction ( [In, Out] ManagedClass obj);
```

If your intent is to pass the class instance as input-only, you can omit the In and Out attributes.

As is the case when passing structures, the layout of the class that is passed to the function must match the expected layout. The managed version of the class can be decorated with OffsetOf and MarshalAs attributes if necessary to align the definitions and control how individual fields are marshaled.

As an example, consider this unmanaged structure:

```
struct UnmanagedItemStruct
{
    int    ItemId;
    char*  ItemDesc;
    long   CategoryCode;
    double UnitPrice;
    int    TaxCategoryId;
};
```

An unmanaged function that uses this structure could be implemented like this:

```
bool LookupItemDetail(UnmanagedItemStruct* itemStruct)
{
    if (itemStruct == NULL)
    {
        return false;
    }

    //look up item and fill the struct
    itemStruct->CategoryCode    = 10012002;
```

```
    itemStruct->TaxCategoryId   = 9988;
    itemStruct->UnitPrice       = 5.49;
    itemStruct->ItemDesc        = (char*)CoTaskMemAlloc(255);
    strcpy_s(itemStruct->ItemDesc, 255, "item description");
    return true;
}
```

The function expects a pointer to the structure, using it to populate the individual fields. We use CoTaskMemAlloc to allocate string memory so the PInvoke marshaler can automatically marshal and deallocate the string.

To call this function using a C# class instance rather than a struct, we need to first implement the class:

```
[StructLayout(LayoutKind.Sequential)]
public class ManagedItem
{
    private int    m_ItemId;
    private string m_ItemDesc;
    private long   m_CategoryCode;
    private double m_UnitPrice;
    private int    m_TaxCategoryId;

    public ManagedItem()
    {
        m_ItemDesc = String.Empty;
    }

    public int ItemId
    {
        get{return m_ItemId;}
        set{m_ItemId = value;}
    }
    public string ItemDesc
    {
        get{return m_ItemDesc;}
        set{m_ItemDesc = value;}
    }
    public long CategoryCode
    {
        get{return m_CategoryCode;}
        set{m_CategoryCode = value;}
    }
    public double UnitPrice
    {
        get{return m_UnitPrice;}
        set{m_UnitPrice = value;}
    }
    public int TaxCategoryId
    {
```

```
        get{return m_TaxCategoryId;}
        set{m_TaxCategoryId = value;}
    }
}
```

We define the individual fields using the same sequence and data types as expected by the unmanaged structure. LayoutKind.Sequential has been specified for the StructLayout attribute to tell the marshaler that the member variables of the class are already in the expected sequence. The presence of the StructLayout attribute informs the marshaler that this is a formatted class.

We declare the actual variables as private and dress up the class with public accessor properties for each variable. Since this is a full-fledged class, we could have added any number of public or private methods without affecting our ability to pass the class to unmanaged code as a structure.

All member variables are marshaled to unmanaged code, even if they are declared as private. Unlike serialization, marshaling does not require public access to the variables. The presence or absence of an accessor property does not affect marshaling.

To pass an instance of this class to the function, we need to declare the function, adding the In and Out attributes:

```
[DllImport("FlatAPIStructLib.DLL")]
public static extern bool LookupItemDetail(
    [In, Out] ManagedItem item);
```

Finally, the C# code to make the function call looks like this:

```
//pass a class object as an [In,Out]
ManagedItem item = new ManagedItem();
item.ItemId       = 111;

//call the unmanaged function using [In,Out]
bool result = LookupItemDetail(item);

//show the results
Console.WriteLine(
    "LookupItemDetail results: {0},{1},{2},{3},{4}",
    item.ItemId, item.ItemDesc, item.TaxCategoryId,
    item.CategoryCode, item.UnitPrice);
```

The Visual Basic .NET version of this code looks like this:

```
Imports System
Imports System.Runtime.InteropServices

Module StructureClassesTest

    <StructLayout(LayoutKind.Sequential)> _
    Public Class ManagedItem
        Private m_ItemId As Integer
        Private m_ItemDesc As String = String.Empty
```

```vb
Private m_CategoryCode As Long
Private m_UnitPrice As Double
Private m_TaxCategoryId As Integer

Public Property ItemId()
    Get
        Return m_ItemId
    End Get
    Set(ByVal value)
        m_ItemId = value
    End Set
End Property

Public Property ItemDesc()
    Get
        Return m_ItemDesc
    End Get
    Set(ByVal value)
        m_ItemDesc = value
    End Set
End Property

Public Property CategoryCode()
    Get
        Return m_CategoryCode
    End Get
    Set(ByVal value)
        m_CategoryCode = value
    End Set
End Property

Public Property UnitPrice()
    Get
        Return m_UnitPrice
    End Get
    Set(ByVal value)
        m_UnitPrice = value
    End Set
End Property

Public Property TaxCategoryId()
    Get
        Return m_TaxCategoryId
    End Get
    Set(ByVal value)
        m_TaxCategoryId = value
    End Set
End Property
```

```
    End Class

    <DllImport("FlatAPIStructLib.DLL")> _
    Public Function LookupItemDetail( _
        <[In](), Out()> ByVal item As ManagedItem) _
        As Boolean
    End Function

    Sub Main()
        'pass a class object as an [In,Out]
        Dim item As ManagedItem = New ManagedItem()
        item.ItemId = 111

        'call the unmanaged function using [In,Out]
        Dim result As Boolean = LookupItemDetail(item)

        'show the results
        Console.WriteLine( _
            "LookupItemDetail results: {0},{1},{2},{3},{4}", _
            item.ItemId, item.ItemDesc, item.TaxCategoryId, _
            item.CategoryCode, item.UnitPrice)

        'wait for input
        Console.WriteLine("Press any key to exit")
        Console.Read()
    End Sub

End Module
```

Regardless of the language used, the test results look like this, proving that the function was able to successfully return updated values:

```
LookupItemDetail results: 111,item description,9988,10012002,5.49
```

If the Out attribute is removed from the function declaration, the changes made by the function would not be visible to the caller. Likewise, if the In attribute is removed, any values set by the managed code will not be marshaled to the unmanaged function.

How It Works

Once you understand the basics of passing classes instead of structures, several variations are available to you.

For example, instead of receiving a pointer to a structure, the unmanaged code might expect a C++ reference (e.g., MyStruct& aStruct). The unmanaged C++ code might look like this:

```
bool LookupItemDetailCPPRef(UnmanagedItemStruct& itemStruct)
{
    //look up item and fill the struct
```

```
itemStruct.CategoryCode    = 10012002;
itemStruct.TaxCategoryId   = 9988;
itemStruct.UnitPrice       = 5.49;
itemStruct.ItemDesc        = (char*)CoTaskMemAlloc(255);
strcpy_s(itemStruct.ItemDesc, 255, "item description");
return true;
}
```

This change to the function does not require any changes to the managed code. The function would be declared and called in exactly the same way:

```
[DllImport("FlatAPIStructLib.DLL")]
public static extern bool LookupItemDetailCPPRef(
    [In, Out] ManagedItem item);
```

Since you are free to use either structures or classes in your managed code, it makes sense that the unmanaged code can do likewise. Instead of defining and using a struct, the unmanaged function could be rewritten to use this unmanaged class:

```
class UnmanagedItemClass
{
public:
    UnmanagedItemClass(void);
    ~UnmanagedItemClass(void);
    int    ItemId;
    char*  ItemDesc;
    long   CategoryCode;
    double UnitPrice;
    int    TaxCategoryId;
};
```

The C++ function would then look like this:

```
bool LookupItemDetailClass(UnmanagedItemClass* item)
{
    if (item == 0)
    {
        return false;
    }

    //look up item and fill the struct
    item->CategoryCode    = 10012002;
    item->TaxCategoryId   = 9988;
    item->UnitPrice       = 5.49;
    item->ItemDesc        = (char*)CoTaskMemAlloc(255);
    strcpy_s(item->ItemDesc, 255, "item description");
    return true;
}
```

Once again, no changes are required to the managed code. The managed declaration for this function looks like this and is called in exactly the same way as prior examples:

```
[DllImport("FlatAPIStructLib.DLL")]
public static extern bool LookupItemDetailClass(
    [In, Out] ManagedItem item);
```

There is one exception to the visibility rules when passing class instances. Normally, unless you add the In and Out attributes to the function declaration, changes made to the class instance are not visible to the caller. However, if the class is made up entirely of blittable fields, changes are visible to the caller even without the Out attribute. This is possible since classes (and structures) composed of only blittable fields are pinned in memory and directly referenced by the called function. No copying of data takes place and the original managed data is referenced by the called function.

This unmanaged structure contains only blittable data types:

```
struct UnmanagedItemStructBlit
{
    int    ItemId;
    int    TaxCategoryId;
    double UnitPrice;
    long   CategoryCode;
};
```

When used in this function, the changes are visible to the calling code even if the In and Out attributes are omitted:

```
bool LookupItemDetailBlit(UnmanagedItemStructBlit* itemStruct)
{
    if (itemStruct == NULL)
    {
        return false;
    }

    //look up item and fill the struct
    itemStruct->CategoryCode    = 10012002;
    itemStruct->TaxCategoryId    = 9988;
    itemStruct->UnitPrice        = 5.49;
    return true;
}
```

The managed blittable class passed to this function looks like this:

```
[StructLayout(LayoutKind.Sequential)]
public class ManagedItemBlit
{
    private int    m_ItemId;
    private int    m_TaxCategoryId;
    private double m_UnitPrice;
    private long   m_CategoryCode;
```

```
        public ManagedItemBlit()
        {
        }

        public int ItemId
        {
            get{return m_ItemId;}
            set{m_ItemId = value;}
        }
        public long CategoryCode
        {
            get{return m_CategoryCode;}
            set{m_CategoryCode = value;}
        }
        public double UnitPrice
        {

            get{return m_UnitPrice;}
            set{m_UnitPrice = value;}
        }
        public int TaxCategoryId
        {
            get{return m_TaxCategoryId;}
            set{m_TaxCategoryId = value;}
        }
    }
}
```

Here is the C# code to declare and call this function:

```
[DllImport("FlatAPIStructLib.DLL")]
public static extern bool LookupItemDetailBlit(ManagedItemBlit item);

//pass a blittable class to unmanaged function. Because
//the class contains only blittable fields, it is updatable
//by the unmanaged function even if we omit the [In,Out]
ManagedItemBlit itemBlit = new ManagedItemBlit();
itemBlit.ItemId        = 111;

//call the unmanaged function
bool result = LookupItemDetailBlit(itemBlit);

//show the results
Console.WriteLine(
    "LookupItemDetailBlit results: {0},{1},{2},{3}",
    itemBlit.ItemId, itemBlit.TaxCategoryId,
    itemBlit.CategoryCode, itemBlit.UnitPrice);
```

When we run this code, we see the following results, proving that changes made during the function call are visible to the caller:

```
LookupItemDetailBlit results: 111,9988,10012002,5.49
```

One final point. We saw earlier that a class (a reference type) is seen by unmanaged code as a pointer or C++ reference to a structure when it is marshaled as a formatted class. If we pass an instance of a formatted class by reference, how is that used in unmanaged code? It is seen as a pointer to a pointer. Consider this revised C# code that now passes a class by reference:

```
[DllImport("FlatAPIStructLib.DLL")]
public static extern bool LookupItemDetailByRef( ref ManagedItem item);

//pass a class instance by ref
ManagedItem item = new ManagedItem();
item.ItemId      = 111;

//call the unmanaged function passing the class by ref
result = LookupItemDetailByRef(ref item);

//show the results
Console.WriteLine(
    "LookupItemDetailByRef results: {0},{1},{2},{3},{4}",
    item.ItemId, item.ItemDesc, item.TaxCategoryId,
    item.CategoryCode, item.UnitPrice);
```

Note When passing a class instance by reference, you are not required to add the In and Out attributes.

In order to use the class instance passed by reference, the function needs to be rewritten like this:

```
bool LookupItemDetailByRef(UnmanagedItemStruct** ppItemStruct)
{
    if (ppItemStruct == NULL)
    {
        return false;
    }

    //lookup item and fill the struct
    (*ppItemStruct)->CategoryCode    = 10012002;
    (*ppItemStruct)->TaxCategoryId   = 9988;
    (*ppItemStruct)->UnitPrice       = 5.49;
    (*ppItemStruct)->ItemDesc        = (char*)CoTaskMemAlloc(255);
    strcpy_s((*ppItemStruct)->ItemDesc, 255, "item description");
    return true;
}
```

While this code isn't as straightforward as the prior examples, it does work. When you see that a function expects a pointer to a pointer to a struct (or class), you should be prepared to pass a class by reference.

Related Information

See recipes 2-1 (Passing Structures), 2-3 (Specifying the Exact Layout of a Structure), 2-4 (Controlling Field-Level Marshaling Within Structures), and 1-7 (Using Data Types That Improve Performance).

2-7. Passing Simple Arrays

Problem

You need to pass an array of variables to unmanaged functions. In some cases, the array is read-only; at other times, the function will update elements in the array.

Solution

Arrays are reference types and are normally passed within managed code as In/Out parameters. This behavior permits the called code to update elements within the array.

When arrays are passed to unmanaged code, the rules change. By default, arrays are passed to an unmanaged function as In only, meaning any changes made to array elements by the function are not visible to the calling code. This default behavior can be modified by adding the In and Out directional attributes to the function declaration.

Other than these special rules, passing arrays between managed and unmanaged code is a straightforward task. For example, this unmanaged function accepts an ANSI character array and counts the number of characters that are lowercase:

```
int CountLowerCaseChars(char charArray[], int arraySize)
{
    int result = 0;
    for(int i = 0; i < arraySize; i++)
    {
        if (islower(charArray[i]))
        {
            result++;
        }
    }
    return result;
}
```

We can declare this array in managed code like this in C#:

```
[DllImport("FlatAPIStructLib.DLL")]
public static extern int CountLowerCaseChars(
    char[] chars, int size);
```

■**Note** A char in .NET is always stored internally as a Unicode character. The default PInvoke behavior is to marshal chars to unmanaged code as ANSI characters. It is because of this default behavior that these examples are able to work correctly.

If necessary, we can override this behavior by specifying CharSet=CharSet.Unicode in the DllImport attribute, or by adding the MarshalAs attribute to the char[] parameter.

The C# code to test this function could be implemented this way:

```csharp
//create and populate an array of characters
char[] chars = new char[5];
chars[0]    = 'A';
chars[1]    = 'b';
chars[2]    = 'c';
chars[3]    = 'D';
chars[4]    = 'e';

//execute the function
int lcCharCount = CountLowerCaseChars(chars, chars.Length);
//show the results
Console.WriteLine("CountLowerCaseChars results: {0}", lcCharCount);
```

Here is the equivalent Visual Basic .NET code:

```vbnet
<DllImport("FlatAPIStructLib.DLL")> _
Public Function CountLowerCaseChars( _
    ByVal chars() As Char, _
    ByVal arraySize As Integer) _
    As Integer
End Function

'create and populate an array of characters
Dim chars(4) As Char
chars(0) = "A"
chars(1) = "b"
chars(2) = "c"
chars(3) = "D"
chars(4) = "e"
Dim lcCharCount As Integer _
    = CountLowerCaseChars(chars, chars.Length)
Console.WriteLine( _
    "CountLowerCaseChars results: {0}", lcCharCount)
```

When we execute the code, we see these results:

```
CountLowerCaseChars results: 3
```

Passing an array that will be updated by the called function is almost as simple. We only need to add the In and Out attributes to the function declaration to make it work. Consider this unmanaged function that changes lowercase characters to uppercase. The original char is replaced with the updated value.

```
int ChangeLowerCaseChars(char charArray[], int arraySize)
{
    int result = 0;
    for(int i = 0; i < arraySize; i++)
    {
        if (islower(charArray[i]))
        {
            //change the char to uppercase
            charArray[i] = toupper(charArray[i]);
            result++;
        }
    }
    return result;
}
```

We declare this function with the In and Out attributes, informing the marshaler that we want to see any changes made to the array by the called function:

```
[DllImport("FlatAPIStructLib.DLL")]
public static extern int ChangeLowerCaseChars(
    [In, Out] char[] chars, int size);
```

The call to this function looks exactly like the call to the read-only function:

```
//create an array of characters
char[] chars = new char[5];
chars[0]    = 'A';
chars[1]    = 'b';
chars[2]    = 'c';
chars[3]    = 'D';
chars[4]    = 'e';

//update the array
int lcCharCount = ChangeLowerCaseChars(chars, chars.Length);

//view the results
Console.WriteLine(
    "ChangeLowerCaseChars results: {0},{1},{2},{3},{4}",
    chars[0],chars[1],chars[2],chars[3],chars[4]);
```

The Visual Basic .NET code is implemented like this:

```
<DllImport("FlatAPIStructLib.DLL")> _
Public Function ChangeLowerCaseChars( _
    <[In](), Out()> ByVal chars() As Char, _
```

```
      ByVal arraySize As Integer) _
      As Integer
End Function

'update an array of characters
Dim chars(4) As Char
chars(0) = "A"
chars(1) = "b"
chars(2) = "c"
chars(3) = "D"
chars(4) = "e"
Dim lcCharCount As Integer _
      = ChangeLowerCaseChars(chars, chars.Length)
Console.WriteLine( _
      "ChangeLowerCaseChars results: {0},{1},{2},{3},{4}", _
      chars(0), chars(1), chars(2), chars(3), chars(4))
```

Regardless of the language used, we see that the array has been successfully updated:

```
ChangeLowerCaseChars results: A,B,C,D,E
```

How It Works

When dealing with an array of a blittable type (short, int, long, etc.), the visibility rule for arrays just discussed doesn't apply. Blittable types are represented the same way in managed and unmanaged code, therefore the marshaler will try to optimize performance whenever they are used.

In the case of arrays of a blittable type, the marshaler will pin the managed memory during the function call (preventing it from being moved during garbage collection) and will pass the original array instead of a copy. This improves performance, but has the side effect of allowing unmanaged code to update elements of the array—even when we don't include the In and Out attributes.

To illustrate this, we can use this unmanaged function:

```
int UpdateIntArrayElements(int pArray[], int arraySize)
{
    int result = 0;
    for(int i = 0; i < arraySize; i++)
    {
        //modify the original element
        pArray[i] += pArray[i];
        result += pArray[i];
    }
    return result;
}
```

The function accepts an array of integers (a blittable data type), updating each element by doubling the original value.

We declare the function without the In/Out attributes, which would normally prevent us from seeing any changes made to the array by the function:

```
[DllImport("FlatAPIStructLib.DLL")]
public static extern int UpdateIntArrayElements(
    int[] array, int size);
```

The C# code to execute the function looks like this:

```
int[] intArray     = new int[10];
//setup array with values of 0,1,2,3...
for(int i = 0; i < intArray.Length; i++)
{
    intArray[i]    = i;
}
//this will update the array
//since it contains a blittable type
int intArrayCount = UpdateIntArrayElements(
    intArray, intArray.Length);
Console.WriteLine(
    "UpdateIntArrayElements results: {0},{1},{2},{3},{4}",
    intArray[0],intArray[1],intArray[2],intArray[3],intArray[4]);
```

When we display the first few elements in the array, we expect to see the original values of 0, 1, 2, 3, and 4. We see this instead:

```
UpdateIntArrayElements results: 0,2,4,6,8
```

Clearly the unmanaged function has updated the read-only array. The message is clear: be mindful of blittable types since they have their own set of rules. When the PInvoke marshaler optimizes the performance for blittable types, there may be unexpected side effects.

Related Information

Please see recipe 1-7 (Using Data Types That Improve Performance).

2-8. Handling String Arrays

Problem

You need to work with arrays of strings, passing them to an unmanaged function or receiving a string array constructed within unmanaged code.

Solution

The concepts used in handling string arrays are similar to other data types. By default, arrays passed to unmanaged code are In only. This means that any changes made to the array by the called function will not be marshaled back to the managed caller. In order to marshal back updates to the original string elements, the Out attribute must be added to the function decla-ration. If the array contains initial values that the unmanaged function needs to read, the In attribute is also required.

The other concern with arrays of strings (and strings in general) is the allocation of mem-ory. Since the nature of strings is that they vary in length (unlike blittable data types that have a fixed size), the unmanaged code may need to free or allocate memory. As long as the allocation is done in a .NET-friendly way (such as using CoTaskMemAlloc), the memory can be successfully marshaled and freed within managed code.

This example function updates the elements of a string array, changing each string to uppercase:

```
void StringArrayToUpper(char* strings[], int size)
{
    //change all string elements to all uppercase
    for(int i = 0; i < size; i++)
    {
        //convert the string to uppercase
        int stringLen = (int)strlen(strings[i]);
        //save the pointer to the original string
        char* oldString = strings[i];

        //allocate new memory for the string
        strings[i] = (char*)CoTaskMemAlloc(stringLen + 1);

        //convert to uppercase while we copy into
        //the new string
        for(int j = 0; j < stringLen; j++)
        {
            strings[i][j] = toupper(oldString[j]);
        }
        strings[i][stringLen] = '\0';

        //free the original string memory
        CoTaskMemFree(oldString);
    }
}
```

Notice that since the function is passed a set of existing strings, the memory for each string must be freed. CoTaskMemFree and CoTaskMemAlloc are used for memory management, since those are the functions used internally by the marshaler. The memory allocated using CoTaskMemAlloc can be freed automatically during the marshaling process.

The function definition in C# looks like this:

```
[DllImport("FlatAPIStructLib.DLL")]
public static extern void StringArrayToUpper(
    [In,Out] string[] strings, int size);
```

Since we want to see any updates to the string array that we pass to the function, we include the [In, Out] attributes. The unmanaged function assumes that each element of the string array has been allocated prior to the function call. The C# code to create the array and execute the function looks like this:

```
//pass an array of strings to unmanaged code
string[] strings        = new string[3];
strings[0]              = "sTringOne";
strings[1]              = "stringTWO";
strings[2]              = "STRINGthree";
//call the unmanaged function to update the strings
StringArrayToUpper(strings, strings.Length);
Console.WriteLine(
    "StringArrayToUpper results: {0},{1},{2}",
    strings[0], strings[1], strings[2]);
```

The Visual Basic .NET code to use this function looks like this:

```
<DllImport("FlatAPIStructLib.DLL")> _
Public Sub StringArrayToUpper( _
    <[In](), Out()> ByVal strings() As String, _
    ByVal size As Integer)
End Sub

'pass an array of strings to unmanaged code
Dim strings(2) As String
strings(0) = "sTringOne"
strings(1) = "stringTWO"
strings(2) = "STRINGthree"
'call the unmanaged function to update the strings
StringArrayToUpper(strings, strings.Length)
Console.WriteLine( _
    "StringArrayToUpper results: {0},{1},{2}", _
    strings(0), strings(1), strings(2))
```

The results show that the changes made during the function call are visible to the managed code:

```
StringArrayToUpper results: STRINGONE,STRINGTWO,STRINGTHREE
```

Note In this example, the unmanaged function assumes that the string array contains ANSI strings. This example works because the default marshaling behavior for strings is to assume the strings are ANSI rather than Unicode.

If the function expected Unicode strings, we would need to either include the CharSet field of the DllImport attribute or add the MarshalAs attribute to the string array parameter.

How It Works

Another possible scenario is to allocate an array of empty string buffers and pass them to an unmanaged function to be filled. Here is an example of an unmanaged function that expects a set of empty buffers:

```
void FillStringArray(char* strings[], int size, int maxStringSize)
{
    //update array elements with strings.
    //no need to allocate new memory since we
    //have been passed allocated buffers

    char* resultStrings[] = {"One","Two","Three","Four"};

    for(int i = 0; i < size; i++)
    {
        if ((int)strlen(resultStrings[i]) < maxStringSize)
        {
            strcpy_s(strings[i], maxStringSize,
                resultStrings[i]);
        }
    }
}
```

When calling this function, we want to allocate the memory to capture the unmanaged strings and pass a raw array of pointers to the function. To do this, we start by declaring the function with an array of IntPtr like this:

```
[DllImport("FlatAPIStructLib.DLL")]
public static extern void FillStringArray(
    IntPtr[] buffers, int size, int maxStringSize);
```

The array of IntPtr does not require the [In,Out] attributes since IntPtr is a special data type that is passed between managed and unmanaged code as a pointer.

The C# code to execute this function follows:

```
//allocate buffers for use by the function
IntPtr[] buffers        = new IntPtr[3];
const int maxSize       = 255;
for(int i = 0; i < buffers.Length; i++)
{
    //allocate memory for each element
    buffers[i]          = Marshal.AllocCoTaskMem(maxSize);
}
//call the function to fill the buffers
FillStringArray(buffers, buffers.Length, maxSize);

//marshal the IntPtrs to strings
string[] strings = new String[buffers.Length];
for(int i = 0; i < buffers.Length; i++)
```

```
{
    strings[i] = Marshal.PtrToStringAnsi(buffers[i]);
    //free the memory we allocated
    Marshal.FreeCoTaskMem(buffers[i]);
}
//show the results
Console.WriteLine(
    "FillStringArray results: {0},{1},{2}",
    strings[0], strings[1], strings[2]);
```

The Visual Basic .NET implementation looks like this:

```
<DllImport("FlatAPIStructLib.DLL")> _
Public Sub FillStringArray( _
    ByVal buffers() As IntPtr, _
    ByVal size As Integer, ByVal maxStringSize As Integer)
End Sub


'allocate buffers for use by the function
Dim buffers(2) As IntPtr
Const maxSize As Integer = 255
Dim i As Integer
For i = 0 To buffers.Length - 1
    buffers(i) = Marshal.AllocCoTaskMem(maxSize)
Next


'call the function to fill the buffers
FillStringArray(buffers, buffers.Length, maxSize)
'marshal the IntPtrs to strings
Dim resultStrings(2) As String
For i = 0 To buffers.Length - 1
    resultStrings(i) = Marshal.PtrToStringAnsi(buffers(i))
    'free the memory we allocated
    Marshal.FreeCoTaskMem(buffers(i))
Next


'show the results
Console.WriteLine( _
    "FillStringArray results: {0},{1},{2}", _
    resultStrings(0), resultStrings(1), resultStrings(2))
```

Notice that since we allocated the memory for each string buffer, we are also responsible for freeing the memory once we have finished with it.

When we run the code, we see these results:

```
FillStringArray results: One,Two,Three
```

Finally, it is certainly possible to reverse things and allow the unmanaged function to allocate and populate the string array. In this case, we won't know the size of the array in advance and will have to rely upon the unmanaged function to provide its size.

Note While the code in this example works, it isn't the most efficient solution. In particular, it does a good bit of allocating and copying of memory, which will likely reduce performance.

This example is presented here to demonstrate how to implement the approach, but not necessarily to recommend it. If we compare the code in this section to the previous examples, we will quickly conclude that it's much easier to simply allocate the string array in managed code and pass it to the function.

An unmanaged function that allocates and populates a string array might be implemented as follows:

```
int AllocateAndReturnStringArray(void** strArray)
{
    int const elementCount = 7;
    int bytesToAllocate   = sizeof(char*) * elementCount;

    //allocate memory for the array
    char** pTempArray = (char**)CoTaskMemAlloc(bytesToAllocate);
    //fill each element of the new array
    for(int i = 0; i < elementCount; i++)
    {
        //allocate memory for the array element
        pTempArray[i] = (char*)CoTaskMemAlloc(255);
        //populate the element
        sprintf_s(pTempArray[i], 255, "element value %i", i);
    }
    //pass the new array back as the result
    *strArray = pTempArray;

    return elementCount;
}
```

Reading through the code, we see that after calculating the size of the array that it will return, memory for the array is allocated. This is memory to hold the array itself, not the individual string elements of the array. While filling the array elements, memory is allocated for each element, and the string is populated with a value. Finally, the entire array is passed back as the only function argument, and the count of array elements is returned as the value of the function.

We can then declare this function in managed code like this:

```
[DllImport("FlatAPIStructLib.DLL")]
public static extern int AllocateAndReturnStringArray(
    ref IntPtr array);
```

Just like the last example, we pass an IntPtr to the function, but this time we pass it by reference. Doing so equates to the void** expected by the function.

We then test the function in C# like this:

```
//return an array allocated within the unmanaged function
IntPtr arrayPtr = IntPtr.Zero;

//call the function that allocates and fills the array.
//we don't know the size of the array until the
//function returns.
int returnCount = AllocateAndReturnStringArray(ref arrayPtr);

//using the returned ptr to get pointers to each element
IntPtr[] arrayPtrs = new IntPtr[returnCount];
Marshal.Copy(arrayPtr, arrayPtrs, 0, returnCount);

//marshal each element pointer to a string
string[] strings = new string[returnCount];
for(int i = 0; i < returnCount; i++)
{
    strings[i] = Marshal.PtrToStringAnsi(arrayPtrs[i]);
    //free memory for the array element
    Marshal.FreeCoTaskMem(arrayPtrs[i]);
}
//free the entire array
Marshal.FreeCoTaskMem(arrayPtr);

//show the results
Console.WriteLine(
    "AllocateAndReturnStringArray: {0}, {1},{2}",
    returnCount, strings[0], strings[returnCount-1]);
```

After calling the function, we should have a single pointer to the strings that were allocated during the function call. As we saw in the unmanaged code, this pointer is actually an array of pointers to the strings.

Since we will want to reference each element in the array, we need to convert this single pointer to an array of pointers. We do this with the Marshal.Copy method, which populates our pointer array. Using the array of pointers, we can now marshal each string and then free the memory addressed by each pointer. Finally, we free the original pointer that we received.

The results look like this:

```
AllocateAndReturnStringArray: 7, element value 0,element value 6
```

Related Information

See recipes 2-7 (Passing Simple Arrays) and 1-6 (Changing the Character Set Used for Strings).

2-9. Passing Arrays of Structures

Problem

You need to pass an array of structures between managed and unmanaged code. What are the differences between structures and built-in types when used in arrays?

Solution

Since .NET Interop supports structures and arrays, it makes sense that the combination is also supported. Passing arrays of structures is fundamentally the same as passing arrays of other types. Like arrays of strings, you need to be concerned with the allocation and deallocation of memory.

With structures, the memory management issues are compounded since you have to allocate memory for each instance of the structure within the array, as well as any fields within the structure. For example, if a structure contains one or more string fields, each string must be allocated and subsequently deallocated.

■**Note** While this recipe illustrates arrays of structures, arrays of objects (class instances) work the same way. The same considerations discussed here apply equally to structures and classes.

To illustrate the use of an array of structures, consider this unmanaged structure:

```
struct UnmanagedAcctSummary
{
    int      AccountId;
    wchar_t* FirstName;
    wchar_t* LastName;
    double   CurrentBalance;
};
```

This simple structure contains a couple of blittable types (the int and the double), but also has two wide-string (Unicode) fields. If we were simply passing a single instance of this structure between managed and unmanaged code, we would immediately be concerned with the memory issues for these string fields. When we intend to pass an array of this structure, those issues are still present. Each instance of this structure within the array will require some code (either managed or unmanaged) to allocate memory for the string fields.

An unmanaged function that fills this structure is as follows:

```
void RetrieveAccountSummaries(
    UnmanagedAcctSummary summaries[], int size)
{
    for(int i = 0; i < size; i++)
    {
        //populate fields in the summary structure
```

```
        int acctId = summaries[i].AccountId;
        int stringSize = 255 * sizeof(wchar_t);
        summaries[i].FirstName
            = (wchar_t*)CoTaskMemAlloc(stringSize);
        summaries[i].LastName
            = (wchar_t*)CoTaskMemAlloc(stringSize);
        swprintf_s(summaries[i].FirstName, 255,
            L"First%i", acctId);
        swprintf_s(summaries[i].LastName, 255,
            L"Last%i", acctId);
        summaries[i].CurrentBalance = acctId * 3.14;
    }
}
```

The function uses CoTaskMemAlloc to allocate memory for each Unicode string. Doing this allows us to simplify the marshaling within the managed code since the PInvoke marshaler is able to handle this memory.

To call this function from C#, we start by defining the managed version of the structure:

```
[StructLayout(LayoutKind.Sequential, CharSet=CharSet.Unicode)]
public struct ManagedAcctSummary
{
    public int      AccountId;
    public string   FirstName;
    public string   LastName;
    public double   CurrentBalance;
};
```

The LayoutKind of Sequential is specified to indicate that the fields within the structure should be marshaled in the sequence shown in the structure definition. Since the default marshaling for strings is ANSI, we need to specify CharSet.Unicode in order to marshal the strings as Unicode.

We then declare the function in C# like this:

```
[DllImport("FlatAPIStructLib.DLL")]
public static extern void RetrieveAccountSummaries(
    [In, Out] ManagedAcctSummary[] summaries, int size);
```

We specify the [In,Out] attributes for the array since we want any changes made during the function call to be visible to the caller.

The C# code to execute this function is implemented in this way:

```
//allocate and populate an array of structs
ManagedAcctSummary[] summaries = new ManagedAcctSummary[5];
for(int i = 0; i < summaries.Length; i++)
{
    summaries[i].AccountId = i + 1001;
}
```

```
//call the unmanaged function to fill the array
RetrieveAccountSummaries(summaries, summaries.Length);

//show the results
for(int i = 0; i < summaries.Length; i++)
{
    Console.WriteLine(
        "RetrieveAccountSummaries: {0},{1},{2},{3}",
        summaries[i].AccountId, summaries[i].CurrentBalance,
        summaries[i].FirstName, summaries[i].LastName);
}
```

Walking through the code, we see that we first allocate the array. We then populate the AccountId field in each instance of the structure to be used as a key field by the function. After calling the function, we show the results of each array element.

Notice that we did not need to free the memory for each string field in the structure. Since the unmanaged function used CoTaskMemAlloc to allocate the memory, the marshaler was able to use CoTaskMemFree to free it. This was done automatically during the marshaling process after the string values were copied to the System.String fields in the structure.

Executing the code returns this result:

```
RetrieveAccountSummaries: 1001,3143.14,First1001,Last1001
RetrieveAccountSummaries: 1002,3146.28,First1002,Last1002
RetrieveAccountSummaries: 1003,3149.42,First1003,Last1003
RetrieveAccountSummaries: 1004,3152.56,First1004,Last1004
RetrieveAccountSummaries: 1005,3155.7,First1005,Last1005
```

How It Works

A Visual Basic .NET version of code to call this function follows:

```
Imports System.Runtime.InteropServices   'needed for DllImport
Module ArraysStructureVBClient

    <StructLayout(LayoutKind.Sequential, CharSet:=CharSet.Unicode)> _
    Public Structure ManagedAcctSummary
        Public AccountId As Integer
        Public FirstName As String
        Public LastName As String
        Public CurrentBalance As Double
    End Structure

    <DllImport("FlatAPIStructLib.DLL")> _
    Public Sub RetrieveAccountSummaries( _
        <[In](), Out()> ByVal summaries As ManagedAcctSummary(), _
            ByVal size As Integer)
    End Sub
```

```
Sub Main()
    'allocate and populate the array of structs
    Dim summaries(4) As ManagedAcctSummary
    Dim i As Integer
    For i = 0 To (summaries.Length - 1)
        summaries(i).AccountId = i + 1001
    Next

    'call the unmanaged function to fill the array
    RetrieveAccountSummaries(summaries, summaries.Length)

    'show the results
    For i = 0 To (summaries.Length - 1)
        Console.WriteLine( _
            "RetrieveAccountSummaries: {0},{1},{2},{3}", _
            summaries(i).AccountId, summaries(i).CurrentBalance, _
            summaries(i).FirstName, summaries(i).LastName)
    Next

    'wait for input
    Console.WriteLine("Press any key to exit")
    Console.Read()
End Sub

End Module
```

While the syntax is different than C#, the overall structure and intent of the code is the same.

■Note Since In is a Visual Basic .NET keyword, a special syntax is required when specifying the short version of the InAttribute (In without the Attribute suffix). As in the example just shown, we need to place left and right brackets around the attribute like this: <[In](), Out()>. Failure to do so will result in a build error.

Related Information

See recipes 2-1 (Passing Structures), 2-5 (Allocating Memory Within Structures), and 2-8 (Handling String Arrays).

CHAPTER 3

■ ■ ■

Win32 API

Calling a Win32 function is really no different from calling any other unmanaged function. You declare the function using `DllImport` and make the call. It really should be that simple.

What complicates things with Win32 is that it comes with its own set of baggage that must be brought along for the ride. The recipes in this chapter are designed to review and handle some of that baggage.

Many Win32 functions are implemented in ANSI and Unicode versions. The first recipe in the chapter describes the process of choosing the correct version to execute. Win32 has its own mechanism for retrieving error codes, and a recipe is devoted to this subject. Callbacks are a technique used by Win32 functions and are covered in another recipe. The Win32 API makes use of handles for just about everything (or so it seems), and two recipes cover how these handles should be used and passed.

An annoying aspect of Win32 is the use of its own set of data types. Most of the functions are declared in the API reference with Win32-specific types that must be translated into integral types. Similarly, Win32 functions use a seemingly endless list of constant values that are used as calling or return values. This chapter includes a recipe for each of these subjects.

The chapter concludes with a recipe on replacing Win32 calls with native .NET classes and methods. Interop with your own unmanaged functions may be necessary, but interop with Microsoft's Win32 functions shouldn't be. Moving away from Win32 has its benefits and should be considered when suitable .NET replacements are available.

3-1. Accessing ANSI or Wide Functions

Problem

Many of the Win32 API functions are available in either ANSI or Unicode versions. You need to designate which version is called.

Solution

Most Win32 functions that use or return a string are available in ANSI or Unicode versions. This also applies to functions using a character rather than a full string. For each version, the root function name is the same, but each function name has a single character suffix that identifies the string or character type. A is appended for ANSI and W for wide (Unicode).

As an example, the Win32 API reference says that the GetComputerName function is available in ANSI and Unicode versions. This means two GetComputerName functions have actually been implemented: GetComputerNameA is the ANSI version and GetComputerNameW is the wide (Unicode) version.

When calling this function from managed code, you need a way to determine the version that is executed. You control this with the CharSet field of the DllImport attribute. By simply changing the CharSet field, you can control which one of these functions is referenced. This behavior is based on hard-wired rules within PInvoke.

The default if you do not specify this field is ANSI. Therefore, this C# declaration of GetComputerName will result in a call to GetComputerNameA, the ANSI version:

```
[DllImport("kernel32.DLL")]
public static extern bool GetComputerName(
    StringBuilder computerName, ref int size);
```

We are passing a StringBuilder here rather than a System.String, since the function requires a preallocated buffer that it will fill with the computer name. The size argument is passed as a ref since it is updated with the number of bytes copied to the string buffer.

We can execute the default version of this function using this C# code:

```
StringBuilder buf   = new StringBuilder(255);
int size            = buf.Capacity;
GetComputerName(buf, ref size);
Console.WriteLine("GetComputerNameDefault: {0}, {1}",
    buf.ToString(), size);
```

The results on my machine look like this (obviously, your machine name should be different):

```
GetComputerNameDefault: VIVALDI, 7
```

If we want to call the Unicode version of this function, all we have to do is declare it like this in C#:

```
[DllImport("kernel32.DLL", CharSet=CharSet.Unicode)]
public static extern bool GetComputerName(
    StringBuilder computerName, ref int size);
```

Note In order to call the Unicode version of this function on Windows Me/98/95, the optional Microsoft Layer for Unicode must be installed.

The code to execute this version looks exactly the same, except for the change we made to the description:

```
StringBuilder buf   = new StringBuilder(255);
int size            = buf.Capacity;
GetComputerName(buf, ref size);
Console.WriteLine("GetComputerNameUnicode: {0}, {1}",
    buf.ToString(), size);
```

The declaration of GetComputerName using the Unicode version looks like this in Visual Basic .NET (VB.NET):

```
<DllImport("kernel32.DLL", _
    CharSet:=CharSet.Unicode, ExactSpelling:=False)> _
Public Shared Function GetComputerName( _
    ByVal computerName As StringBuilder, _
    ByRef size As Integer) As Boolean
End Function
```

> **Note** In VB.NET, the Shared keyword is used to declare a static function. If you apply the DllImport attribute to a function that is declared within a class, the function must be declared with the Shared keyword. However, if the function is declared within a VB.NET module instead of a class, the Shared keyword is not appropriate.

And here is the VB.NET code to execute this function:

```
Dim buf As StringBuilder = New StringBuilder(255)
Dim size As Integer = buf.Capacity
GetComputerName(buf, size)
Console.WriteLine("GetComputerNameUnicode: {0}, {1}", _
    buf.ToString(), size)
```

Notice that for the VB.NET version we set ExactSpelling to False. This is needed so VB.NET will correctly use either the ANSI or the Unicode version. This is discussed in detail later in this recipe.

Regardless of the language used, the results look like this:

```
GetComputerNameUnicode: VIVALDI, 7
```

> **Note** Remember that all strings in .NET are actually Unicode. That is why we should see no difference when we examine the results of an ANSI or Unicode function call. The resulting string that has been marshaled to the managed code is always Unicode.

How It Works

If you don't like to rely upon defaults, you can explicitly set the CharSet to Ansi like this:

```
[DllImport("kernel32.DLL", CharSet=CharSet.Ansi)]
public static extern bool GetComputerName(
    StringBuilder computerName, ref int size);
```

Again, the results are the same as the prior examples.

You also don't need to rely upon the automatic behavior that will call either the ANSI or Unicode version of a function. You can easily specify the entry point yourself, completely bypassing the automatic PInvoke logic. Here is an example where we specify the Unicode version of GetComputerName directly using the EntryPoint field:

```
[DllImport("kernel32.DLL",
    EntryPoint="GetComputerNameW", CharSet=CharSet.Unicode)]
public static extern bool GetComputerName(
    StringBuilder computerName, ref int size);
```

Notice that we also need to specify the Charset.Unicode value. Failure to do this will result in a call to the Unicode version of the function with the string marshaled as ANSI. In other words, we shouldn't do something like this:

```
//this is an incorrect function declaration since
//we specify the unicode version yet marshal
//the strings as Ansi
[DllImport("kernel32.DLL",
    EntryPoint="GetComputerNameW", CharSet=CharSet.Ansi)]
public static extern bool GetComputerName(
    StringBuilder computerName, ref int size);
```

When this code is executed, the results will look strange:

```
GetComputerNameMismatch: V, 7
```

We've told PInvoke to marshal any strings as ANSI, but we are explicitly calling the Unicode version of the function. Therefore, we see only the first character of the computer name. The Win32 function is returning a Unicode string that uses 2 bytes to represent each character. For the English string that we are returning, the second byte of each Unicode character is a \0. Since we told the marshaler that this is an ANSI string, it treats the second byte of the first character as a null terminator.

The CharSet field of DllImport also supports a value of CharSet=CharSet.Auto. This tells PInvoke to adjust the marshaling behavior depending on the version of the operating system. For Windows NT, 2000, XP, and Server 2003, strings will be marshaled as Unicode. This means the W version of the function will be called. When run under Windows 98 or ME, the ANSI version is used. Here is an example that uses CharSet.Auto:

```
//defaults to Unicode for NT, XP, 2000 and 2003,
//ANSI for 95 and ME
[DllImport("kernel32.DLL", CharSet=CharSet.Auto)]
public static extern bool GetComputerName(
    StringBuilder computerName, ref int size);
```

When executed on my XP machine, the Unicode version of the function is called. Again, the results look the same when executed.

```
GetComputerNameAuto: VIVALDI, 7
```

While all of these examples returned a string, the same rules apply when passing a string to a Win32 function. As an example, the following C# code declares the CreateDirectory function using the default string marshaling (ANSI):

```
[DllImport("kernel32.DLL")]
public static extern bool CreateDirectory(
    string dirName, IntPtr securityAttrs);
```

The code to execute CreateDirectory looks like this:

```
//create a directory
bool result = CreateDirectory(@"C:\MyTestDirectory", IntPtr.Zero);
Console.WriteLine("CreateDirectoryDefault: {0}", result);
//delete the directory now that we're done
Cleanup();
```

We don't want to leave test folders around once we're done with them, so we execute this Cleanup method:

```
public static void Cleanup()
{
    DirectoryInfo dir = new DirectoryInfo(@"C:\MyTestDirectory");
    if (dir.Exists)
    {
        Console.WriteLine("Directory {0} exists", dir.FullName);
        dir.Delete();
    }
}
```

We could have implemented this as a call to the Win32 RemoveDirectory function, but we chose to use the .NET System.IO.DirectoryInfo object instead. The .NET System.IO.Directory class also has static methods that allow us to remove a directory.

Note If you are developing new code, it makes sense to look for .NET alternatives instead of continuing to use Win32. The final recipe of this chapter discusses replacing Win32 calls with .NET equivalents.

When this code is executed, these are the results:

```
CreateDirectoryDefault: True
Directory C:\MyTestDirectory exists
```

If you want to execute the Unicode version of CreateDirectory, simply change the function declaration to look like this:

```
[DllImport("kernel32.DLL", CharSet=CharSet.Unicode)]
public static extern bool CreateDirectory(
    string dirName, IntPtr securityAttrs);
```

The results look the same when this version is executed.

Similar VB.NET code to call CreateDirectory is implemented like this:

```
Public Class CreateDirectoryUnicode
    <DllImport("kernel32.DLL", _
        CharSet:=CharSet.Unicode, ExactSpelling:=False)> _
    Public Shared Function CreateDirectory( _
        ByVal dirName As String, ByVal securityAttrs As IntPtr) _
        As Boolean
    End Function

    Public Shared Sub Test()
        Dim result As Boolean _
            = CreateDirectory("C:\MyTestDirectory", IntPtr.Zero)
        Console.WriteLine("CreateDirectoryUnicode: {0}", result)
        Cleanup()

    End Sub

    Private Shared Sub Cleanup()
        Dim dir As DirectoryInfo _
            = New DirectoryInfo("C:\MyTestDirectory")
        If dir.Exists Then
            Console.WriteLine("Directory {0} exists", dir.FullName)
            dir.Delete()
        End If

    End Sub
End Class
```

The code is executed by calling the static Test method of the class like this:

```
Sub Main()

    CreateDirectoryUnicode.Test()

End Sub
```

The results look the same as the C# version.

Be aware that the ExactSpelling field of the DllImport attribute also affects this automatic behavior based on the CharSet. As the name implies, if the ExactSpelling field is true, the function name you declare must exactly match the name of the unmanaged function. Therefore, a value of true for ExactSpelling disables the automatic behavior based on CharSet. Setting ExactSpelling to false allows the automatic behavior just described.

The default for ExactSpelling varies by .NET language. C# and C++ default to false, while VB.NET defaults to true. If you want this behavior in VB.NET, you'll need to explicitly set ExactSpelling to false.

The search sequence used to resolve the function name also varies based on the character set you specify. If you specify CharSet.Ansi, PInvoke first searches for the root function name (without a suffix) and uses that if found. Otherwise, it searches for the ANSI name (the root name suffixed with A) and uses that function if found.

If you specify CharSet.Unicode, the search order is reversed. PInvoke will first search for the Unicode name (the root name suffixed with W) and use it first if found. It will search for and use the root name only if the wide version is missing.

Note Since all .NET strings are stored internally as Unicode, you will receive a slight performance boost when calling the Unicode version of an API function. The reason is simple: no ANSI to Unicode conversions are needed. The Unicode string is returned and used directly from the unmanaged code without a character-set conversion.

How do you identify a Win32 function that is available in ANSI and Unicode versions? As a general rule, most functions that include or return a string or a character will be available in both versions. One clue is the use of LPTSTR or LPCTSTR in the function declaration in the Win32 header files. These data types were designed to change character set depending on the presence or absence of the _UNICODE preprocessor directive in your C/C++ project. Therefore, if these types are present in a function declaration, the function will be available in both versions.

The ultimate authority on any function is the Win32 API reference. It will tell you if the function is supported in ANSI and Unicode versions. The dumpbin utility can also help to discover ANSI and Unicode versions of a function. By executing this utility on a Win32 DLL, you'll see a list of all exported functions.

Related Information

See recipes 3-2 (Retrieving the Win32 Error Code), 1-6 (Changing the Character Set Used for Strings), 1-1 (Identifying the Unmanaged Function), and 3-7 (Marshaling Win32 Types).

3-2. Retrieving the Win32 Error Code

Problem

A call to a Win32 function is failing due to an error. Normally in unmanaged code, you would call the GetLastError function to retrieve the error and diagnose the problem. You want to find the equivalent way to obtain the Win32 error code during .NET interop calls.

Solution

Retrieving the last Win32 error code is a two-step process. First, you need to set an additional property in the DllImport attribute when declaring the function. By setting the SetLastError field to true, you instruct PInvoke to save the error code from the last API call. Second, after the called API fails, you use the static GetLastWin32Error method of the Marshal class to retrieve the error code.

For example, consider this C# call to the DeleteFile Win32 function:

```
//attempt to delete a file that doesn't exist
DeleteFile("TestFileNotThere");
```

If the call fails (as it should in this case), we can call the Marshal.GetLastWin32Error method to retrieve the Win32 error code like this:

```
Console.WriteLine("DeleteFile last error code: {0}",
    Marshal.GetLastWin32Error());
```

However, this will only work if we include the SetLastError field in the DllImport function declaration like this:

```
//save the last error, and use the wide version
[DllImport("kernel32.DLL", CharSet = CharSet.Unicode,
    SetLastError = true)]
public static extern
    bool DeleteFile(string fileName);
```

When we execute DeleteFile for a nonexistent file, we see these results:

```
DeleteFile last error code: 2
```

This is the correct error code since 2 is defined as ERROR_FILE_NOT_FOUND in the Win32 documentation. Since we set SetLastError to true, PInvoke saved the value from the GetLastError API function, making it available to us via Marshal.GetLastWin32Error.

If we declare the function like this, without the SetLastError field, we will be unable to get a meaningful error code:

```
//do not save the error code
[DllImport("kernel32.DLL", CharSet=CharSet.Unicode)]
public static extern
    bool DeleteFile(string fileName);
```

Calling Marshal.GetLastWin32Error in this case will give us an unpredictable result. We'll get a number returned, but it will not be the correct error code. The reason is that we have not instructed PInvoke to save the last error code from the Win32 call.

How It Works

Once you have obtained the last Win32 error code, you can use the Win32Exception class to look up a descriptive message for the error. It is not necessary to use PInvoke to call the Win32 FormatMessage function to look up the message. The constructor for this exception takes the error code that you retrieved like this:

```
//turn the win32 error into an exception
throw new Win32Exception(lastError);
```

When you throw this exception, any code that catches it will have access to a descriptive message for the Win32 error. We can rewrite the preceding code to not only retrieve the error code, but also throw the exception and show the results:

```
try
{
    //attempt to delete a file that doesn't exist
    DeleteFile("TestFileNotThere");
    //returns system error code 2: ERROR_FILE_NOT_FOUND
    //"The system cannot find the file specified"
    int lastError = Marshal.GetLastWin32Error();
    Console.WriteLine("DeleteFile last error code: {0}", lastError);

    //turn the win32 error into an exception
    throw new Win32Exception(lastError);
}
catch(Win32Exception e)
{
    Console.WriteLine(
        "DeleteFile last error message: {0}", e.Message);
}
```

Normally, you wouldn't throw and catch an exception like this within the same code block, but this works to demonstrate the results of the Win32Exception class. As an alternative, you can use one of the other constructors for this exception class that accept an error code. By doing this, you can simply construct a Win32Exception object and reference the Message property to obtain the description for the error.

Note You can actually simplify this code even more. The Win32Exception class has a default constructor that doesn't require any parameters. If you use this constructor, Win32Exception will make the call to Marshal.GetLastWin32Error for you.

When we execute this code, we now see these results:

```
DeleteFile last error code: 2
DeleteFile last error message:
    The system cannot find the file specified
```

Here is similar Visual Basic .NET (VB.NET) code that calls the DeleteFile function twice. The first time the SetLastError field is set to true, while it is false for the second call:

```
Imports System.Runtime.InteropServices
Imports System.ComponentModel

''' <summary>
''' Return the error code from a Win32 API call
''' </summary>
''' <remarks></remarks>
Module Win32ErrorTest
```

```vb
'save the last error, and use the wide version
<DllImport("kernel32.DLL", CharSet:=CharSet.Unicode, _
    SetLastError:=True)> _
Public Function DeleteFile( _
    <MarshalAs(UnmanagedType.LPWStr)> _
    ByVal fileName As String) _
    As Boolean
End Function

'do not save the last error
<DllImport("kernel32.DLL", EntryPoint:="DeleteFile", _
    CharSet:=CharSet.Unicode)> _
Public Function DeleteFileNoError( _
    ByVal fileName As String) _
    As Boolean
End Function

Sub Main()

    Try
        'attempt to delete a file that doesn't exist
        DeleteFile("TestFileNotThere")
        'returns system error code 2: ERROR_FILE_NOT_FOUND
        '"The system cannot find the file specified"
        Dim lastError As Integer _
            = Marshal.GetLastWin32Error()
        Console.WriteLine( _
            "DeleteFile last error code: {0}", lastError)

        'turn the win32 error into an exception
        Throw New Win32Exception(lastError)

    Catch ex As Exception
        Console.WriteLine( _
            "DeleteFile last error message: {0}", ex.Message)
    End Try

    'execute the same test,
    'without the SetLastError property
    DeleteFileNoError("TestFileNotThere")
    Console.WriteLine( _
        "DeleteFileNoError last error code: {0}", _
        Marshal.GetLastWin32Error())
```

```
    'wait for input
    Console.WriteLine("Press any key to exit")
    Console.Read()

  End Sub

End Module
```

When this code is executed, the results look like this:

```
DeleteFile last error code: 2
DeleteFile last error message:
  The system cannot find the file specified
DeleteFileNoError last error code: 1004
Press any key to exit
```

Notice that the second call to DeleteFile returns a value of 1004. Since the SetLastError field was not set, this is not the real error code.

Marshal.GetLastWin32Error will retrieve the same error that you would normally obtain by calling the Win32 GetLastError function. However, calling the GetLastError function yourself is not safe using PInvoke. Since .NET is free to make Win32 calls under the covers, it is possible that your PInvoke call to GetLastError would return the error from an internal .NET call rather than your last PInvoked function.

The .NET solution is to save the last error code from each of your PInvoke calls and to provide the static Marshal.GetLastWin32Error method to retrieve the saved error. Since there is additional overhead necessary to save the error codes in this way, .NET provides you with the SetLastError field to control this behavior. If you don't need to check the last error code, you can omit the property from the DllImport declaration. Doing this should improve performance, but don't expect the improvement to be noticeable.

However, even if you don't use Marshal.GetLastWin32Error to check the last error code, you should still check the results of each Win32 call for failure. How you do that depends on the function you're calling. You'll need to check the Win32 documentation for the function to find out how to determine success or failure.

Note C# and managed C++ code require the use of the DllImport attribute to PInvoke a function. When using these languages, the default for the SetLastError field is false.

When a DllImport attribute is used in VB.NET, the default for this field is also false. However, VB.NET also supports the older style Declare statement to declare unmanaged functions. If you use the Declare statement, the default behavior is to set the last error code for you. This provides you the same effect as if you coded a DllImport attribute with SetLastError set to true. When using this older Visual Basic syntax, you can still reference the Err.LastDllError property to obtain the error code.

3-3. Handling Callbacks

Problem

A number of Win32 functions require callbacks. How do you handle callbacks from unmanaged functions?

Solution

Callbacks are the general mechanism that permits a called function to invoke another function specified by the caller. This technique is typically used where the called function must return an unknown amount of repeating data to the caller.

Note Callbacks are discussed in this chapter since they are a technique used by a number of Win32 functions. They also can be used by non-Win32 functions. Therefore, the techniques discussed here apply equally whenever callbacks are required.

In the unmanaged world, callbacks are implemented using function pointers. When the original function is called, one of the calling arguments is a pointer to another function. When the called function wishes to invoke the callback, it uses the function pointer it was passed to reference the caller's function. In this sense, the original function *calls back* into the caller.

In the .NET world, callbacks from unmanaged code are handled as delegates. Delegates serve the same basic purpose as callbacks, but are object-oriented and type-safe. If you have ever handled a .NET event, you have used delegates.

To illustrate how to handle a callback from a Win32 API, consider the following example in C# that calls the EnumDateFormatsEx function. This function uses a callback to provide the caller with a list of available date formats.

After consulting the Win32 documentation for this function, we determine that this function requires a callback that takes a string and integer and returns a bool. This callback function is given the name EnumDateFormatsProcEx in the API documentation. We start by declaring a delegate for this callback function in C# like this:

```
//define the delegate for the callback
public delegate bool EnumDateFormatsProcEx(
    string dateFormat, int calId);
```

The actual Win32 function declaration looks like this:

```
[DllImport("kernel32.DLL", SetLastError = true)]
public static extern bool EnumDateFormatsEx(
    EnumDateFormatsProcEx callBackProc, int LCID, ulong flags);
```

Notice that one of the calling arguments is the callback delegate.

The Win32 documentation states that the flags argument must be one of several defined constants. Instead of passing a meaningless magic number, we define these constants in our code:

```
//constants used for date formats
private const int DATE_SHORTDATE    = 0x00000001;  //short date
private const int DATE_LONGDATE     = 0x00000002;  //long date
private const int DATE_YEARMONTH    = 0x00000008;  //year month
```

How did we get the values used for each constant? The easiest (and most accurate) way is to look in the Windows header file where the function is declared. The documentation for the function should identify the header. If no header is listed, we can search all of the Windows header files. We found these constants defined in Winnls.h and translated them into valid C# code.

Since the function will be calling back into our C# code, we need to implement the callback method that will be referenced. It must match the signature of the EnumDateFormatsProcEx delegate just defined. The implementation looks like this:

```
//callback method
static public bool EnumDateFormatsCallback(
    string dateFormat, int calId)
{
    Console.WriteLine(
        "CalId: {0}, Date Format: {1}", calId, dateFormat);
    return true;
}
```

The method simply prints out the date format that was passed to it by the Win32 function and returns true. The Win32 documentation states that if false is returned, the callback won't be called again. Since we want to see the complete list of available date formats (and to demonstrate callbacks), we return true.

Finally, we make the Win32 function call like this:

```
//call the function, passing a delegate for the callback
EnumDateFormatsEx(
    EnumDateFormatsCallback,
    Thread.CurrentThread.CurrentCulture.LCID,
    DATE_LONGDATE);

//wait for input
Console.WriteLine("Press any key to exit");
Console.Read();
```

When making the call, a delegate that points to the EnumDateFormatsCallback method is created and passed as an argument. We also pass one of the date format constants that we defined, along with the locale ID from the current thread.

When executed, the results look like this using the regional settings on my machine:

```
CalId: 1, Date Format: dddd, MMMM dd, yyyy
CalId: 1, Date Format: MMMM dd, yyyy
CalId: 1, Date Format: dddd, dd MMMM, yyyy
CalId: 1, Date Format: dd MMMM, yyyy
Press any key to exit
```

In this case, one call to the Win32 function generated four calls to the callback, each one printing a line in the results.

A Visual Basic .NET (VB.NET) implementation calling the same Win32 API looks like this:

```
Imports System.Runtime.InteropServices
Imports System.Threading

Module Win32CallbackTestVB

    'constants used for date formats
    Private Const DATE_SHORTDATE As Integer = &H1 ' short date
    Private Const DATE_LONGDATE As Integer = &H2  ' long date
    Private Const DATE_YEARMONTH As Integer = &H8 ' year month

    'define the delegate for the callback
    Public Delegate Function EnumDateFormatsProcEx( _
        ByVal dateFormat As String, ByVal calId As Integer) As Boolean

    <DllImport("kernel32.DLL", SetLastError:=True)> _
    Public Function EnumDateFormatsEx( _
        ByVal callBackProc As EnumDateFormatsProcEx, _
            ByVal LCID As Integer, ByVal flags As Long) As Boolean
    End Function

    Sub Main()
        'call the function, passing a delegate for the callback
        EnumDateFormatsEx( _
            AddressOf EnumDateFormatsCallback, _
            Thread.CurrentThread.CurrentCulture.LCID, _
            DATE_SHORTDATE)

        'wait for input
        Console.WriteLine("Press any key to exit")
        Console.Read()
    End Sub

    'callback function
    Function EnumDateFormatsCallback(ByVal dateFormat As String, _
            ByVal calId As Integer) As Boolean
        Console.WriteLine( _
            "CalId: {0}, Date Format: {1}", calId, dateFormat)
        Return True
    End Function

End Module
```

Just to see the difference, we pass DATE_SHORTDATE instead of DATE_LONGDATE to the function. The results look like this using my regional settings:

```
CalId: 1, Date Format: M/d/yyyy
CalId: 1, Date Format: M/d/yy
CalId: 1, Date Format: MM/dd/yy
CalId: 1, Date Format: MM/dd/yyyy
CalId: 1, Date Format: yy/MM/dd
CalId: 1, Date Format: yyyy-MM-dd
CalId: 1, Date Format: dd-MMM-yy
Press any key to exit
```

How It Works

As is the case with many of the Win32 API calls, EnumDateFormatsEx is implemented in both ANSI and Unicode versions. Since the default marshaling for strings is ANSI, the examples just shown execute the ANSI version (EnumDateFormatsExA).

If we instead want to use the Unicode version of this function, we need to declare the function like this:

```
[DllImport("kernel32.DLL", SetLastError = true,
    CharSet=CharSet.Unicode)]
public static extern bool EnumDateFormatsEx(
    EnumDateFormatsProcEx callBackProc, int LCID, ulong flags);
```

The addition of the CharSet field will cause the marshaler to reference EnumDateFormatsExW rather than EnumDateFormatsExA. However, when we now run the test, we see these unexpected results:

```
CalId: 1, Date Format: d
CalId: 1, Date Format: M
CalId: 1, Date Format: d
CalId: 1, Date Format: d
Press any key to exit
```

What's going on here? The problem is that we now have a mismatch of character sets between the function call and the callback. We're calling the Unicode version of the function, but the default behavior for marshaling the string in the callback function is ANSI. EnumDateFormatsExW is passing Unicode strings to the callback function, but we've told the marshaler to assume they are ANSI.

The Win32 callback is returning a Unicode string that uses 2 bytes to represent each character. The second byte of these Unicode characters is a \0. Since we defaulted to ANSI, and the marshaler thinks this is an ANSI string, it treats the second byte of the first character as a null terminator.

To correct this, we need to add the MarshalAs attribute to the delegate like this:

```
//This delegate is correct for the Unicode
//version of EnumDateFormatsEx.
public delegate bool EnumDateFormatsProcEx(
    [MarshalAs(UnmanagedType.LPWStr)]string dateFormat, int calId);
```

Now when this code is executed, we get the correct results:

```
CalId: 1, Date Format: dddd, MMMM dd, yyyy
CalId: 1, Date Format: MMMM dd, yyyy
CalId: 1, Date Format: dddd, dd MMMM, yyyy
CalId: 1, Date Format: dd MMMM, yyyy
Press any key to exit
```

An alternative solution is to apply the UnmanagedFunctionPointer attribute to the delegate like this:

```
[UnmanagedFunctionPointer(CallingConvention.Winapi,
    CharSet=CharSet.Unicode)]
public delegate bool EnumDateFormatsProcEx(
    string dateFormat, int calId);
```

By specifying CharSet.Unicode as an argument to this attribute, we instruct the marshaler to handle the string field as Unicode. This attribute is new to the .NET Framework 2.0 and can be found in the System.Runtime.InteropServices namespace.

Related Information

See recipe 3-1 (Accessing ANSI or Wide Functions).

3-4. Using Windows Constants

Problem

Many of the Win32 API functions accept or return constants that are defined in various Windows header files. How do you define and use these constants in .NET code?

Solution

The Windows API reference lists only the named constants that a particular function uses; it doesn't list the underlying values for these constants. That makes sense from the perspective of C or C++ developers, since they will be directly referencing the Windows header files that define the constant values. However, this practice makes it more difficult for .NET developers trying to use a Win32 API. Since our code doesn't reference the Windows header files directly, we need to manually look up the values for the constants and declare them in our managed code.

There are really only two sources for the constant values:

- The Windows header files that ship with Visual Studio .NET (or a subsequent Platform SDK). In almost all cases, the Win32 documentation identifies the header where the function is declared.

- An Internet search for the constant values.

The only reason to go with the second option is if you don't have access to the header files. Or, perhaps you find it quicker and easier to search the Internet rather than your desktop. Otherwise, the ultimate authority for a value is the Windows header files. You can use the search-in-files feature of Visual Studio to look for the constant definition and then translate those values to your particular .NET language. Alternatively, you can use any desktop search engine of your choosing.

For example, consider the GetDriveType Win32 function. It accepts a string path and returns an unsigned integer that identifies the type of drive. The problem is that the documentation identifies the unsigned int return values as shown in Table 3-1.

Table 3-1. *Win32 Drive Types*

DRIVE_UNKNOWN	The drive type cannot be determined.
DRIVE_NO_ROOT_DIR	The root path is invalid (e.g., no volume is mounted at the path).
DRIVE_REMOVABLE	The drive is a type that has removable media (e.g., a floppy drive or removable hard disk).
DRIVE_FIXED	The drive is a type that cannot be removed (e.g., a fixed hard drive).
DRIVE_REMOTE	The drive is a remote (network) drive.
DRIVE_CDROM	The drive is a CD-ROM drive.
DRIVE_RAMDISK	The drive is a RAM disk.

There is no mention at all of the underlying values for each of these constants. To find the real values, we open up the header file listed in the Win32 documentation for this function. In this case, these named constants are defined in WinBase.h. If no header file is listed in the documentation, we can search all of the Windows header files for one of the named constants to identify the header.

In WinBase.h, we find that these constants are defined like this:

```
#define DRIVE_UNKNOWN      0
#define DRIVE_NO_ROOT_DIR  1
#define DRIVE_REMOVABLE    2
#define DRIVE_FIXED        3
#define DRIVE_REMOTE       4
#define DRIVE_CDROM        5
#define DRIVE_RAMDISK      6
```

Armed with this information, we can define these constants in C# code like this:

```
private const uint DRIVE_UNKNOWN      = 0;
private const uint DRIVE_NO_ROOT_DIR  = 1;
private const uint DRIVE_REMOVABLE    = 2;
private const uint DRIVE_FIXED        = 3;
private const uint DRIVE_REMOTE       = 4;
private const uint DRIVE_CDROM        = 5;
private const uint DRIVE_RAMDISK      = 6;
```

Once defined, these constants can be used like any other C# constant. In this example, after calling the GetDriveType function, we return a string description depending on the returned value:

```
class DriveInfo
{
    //Get Drive Type
    [DllImport("kernel32.DLL")]
    private static extern uint GetDriveType(string rootPath);

    private const uint DRIVE_UNKNOWN     = 0;
    private const uint DRIVE_NO_ROOT_DIR = 1;
    private const uint DRIVE_REMOVABLE   = 2;
    private const uint DRIVE_FIXED       = 3;
    private const uint DRIVE_REMOTE      = 4;
    private const uint DRIVE_CDROM       = 5;
    private const uint DRIVE_RAMDISK     = 6;

    public static string GetDriveTypeDescription(string rootPath)
    {
        string result           = "unknown";
        //call the Win32 API to get the type code
        uint driveType          = GetDriveType(rootPath);
        //turn the type code into a description
        switch(driveType)
        {
            case DRIVE_UNKNOWN:
                result          = "Unknown";
                break;
            case DRIVE_NO_ROOT_DIR:
                result          = "No root dir";
                break;
            case DRIVE_REMOVABLE:
                result          = "Removable";
                break;
            case DRIVE_FIXED:
                result          = "Fixed";
                break;
            case DRIVE_REMOTE:
                result          = "Remote";
                break;
            case DRIVE_CDROM:
                result          = "CDRom";
                break;
            case DRIVE_RAMDISK:
                result          = "RamDisk";
                break;
            default:
```

```
            break;
        }
        return result;
    }
}
```

We execute this wrapper method like this:

```
string driveTypeDesc = DriveInfo.GetDriveTypeDescription(@"c:\");
Console.WriteLine(@"GetDriveType for C: {0}", driveTypeDesc);

driveTypeDesc = DriveInfo.GetDriveTypeDescription(@"D:\");
Console.WriteLine(@"GetDriveType for D: {0}", driveTypeDesc);
```

When the code is executed, the results look like this on my machine (your results might be different):

```
GetDriveType for C: Fixed
GetDriveType for D: CDRom
```

How It Works

Since most of the constants used by Windows are integral types like integers or unsigned integers, we can also define the constants as an enum within our code. This has the advantage of allowing us to use some of the built-in support from the Enum class.

For example, we could rewrite the wrapper class for the GetDriveType function presented earlier like this:

```
class DriveInfoEnum
{
    //Get Drive Type
    [DllImport("kernel32.DLL")]
    private static extern uint GetDriveType(string rootPath);

    private enum DriveType : uint
    {
        Unknown          = 0,
        NoRootDir        = 1,
        Removable        = 2,
        Fixed            = 3,
        Remote           = 4,
        CDRom            = 5,
        RamDisk          = 6
    }

    public static string GetDriveTypeDescription(string rootPath)
    {
        string result        = "unknown";
        //call the Win32 API to get the type code
```

```
        uint driveType              = GetDriveType(rootPath);
        //turn the type code into a description
        if (Enum.IsDefined(typeof(DriveType), driveType))
        {
            result  = ((DriveType)driveType).ToString();
        }
        return result;
    }
}
```

Obviously, we had to write much less code since we rely upon the Enum class to handle much of the grunt work for us. However, to make the descriptions meaningful, we need to use a meaningful name for each element of the enumeration.

The code to execute the wrapper method looks the same:

```
string driveTypeDesc = DriveInfoEnum.GetDriveTypeDescription(@"c:\");
Console.WriteLine(@"GetDriveType Enum for C: {0}", driveTypeDesc);

driveTypeDesc = DriveInfoEnum.GetDriveTypeDescription(@"D:\");
Console.WriteLine(@"GetDriveType Enum for D: {0}", driveTypeDesc);
```

When we execute this code, we get the same results:

```
GetDriveType Enum for C: Fixed
GetDriveType Enum for D: CDRom
```

Constants are also used as input parameters to many Win32 functions. Take the CreateFile function as an example. Checking the API reference, we find that this one function takes seven input parameters, and four of them are defined with a list of constants. Some of these may be combined using a bitwise OR.

One possible implementation of a wrapper for CreateFile might look like this in C#:

```
/// <summary>
/// A wrapper for the CreateFile Win32 API
/// </summary>
class CreateFileHelper
{
    /* from WinNT.h
    #define FILE_SHARE_READ             0x00000001
    #define FILE_SHARE_WRITE            0x00000002
    #define FILE_SHARE_DELETE           0x00000004
    */
    [Flags]
    public enum FileShareMode : uint
    {
        FILE_SHARE_READ             = 0x00000001,
        FILE_SHARE_WRITE            = 0x00000002,
        FILE_SHARE_DELETE           = 0x00000004
    }
```

```
/* from WinNT.h
#define FILE_ATTRIBUTE_READONLY              0x00000001
#define FILE_ATTRIBUTE_HIDDEN                0x00000002
#define FILE_ATTRIBUTE_SYSTEM                0x00000004
#define FILE_ATTRIBUTE_DIRECTORY             0x00000010
#define FILE_ATTRIBUTE_ARCHIVE               0x00000020
#define FILE_ATTRIBUTE_DEVICE                0x00000040
#define FILE_ATTRIBUTE_NORMAL                0x00000080
#define FILE_ATTRIBUTE_TEMPORARY             0x00000100
#define FILE_ATTRIBUTE_SPARSE_FILE           0x00000200
#define FILE_ATTRIBUTE_REPARSE_POINT         0x00000400
#define FILE_ATTRIBUTE_COMPRESSED            0x00000800
#define FILE_ATTRIBUTE_OFFLINE               0x00001000
#define FILE_ATTRIBUTE_NOT_CONTENT_INDEXED   0x00002000
#define FILE_ATTRIBUTE_ENCRYPTED             0x00004000
*/
[Flags]
public enum FileAttribute : uint
{
    FILE_ATTRIBUTE_READONLY            = 0x00000001,
    FILE_ATTRIBUTE_HIDDEN             = 0x00000002,
    FILE_ATTRIBUTE_SYSTEM             = 0x00000004,
    FILE_ATTRIBUTE_DIRECTORY          = 0x00000010,
    FILE_ATTRIBUTE_ARCHIVE            = 0x00000020,
    FILE_ATTRIBUTE_DEVICE             = 0x00000040,
    FILE_ATTRIBUTE_NORMAL             = 0x00000080,
    FILE_ATTRIBUTE_TEMPORARY          = 0x00000100,
    FILE_ATTRIBUTE_SPARSE_FILE        = 0x00000200,
    FILE_ATTRIBUTE_REPARSE_POINT      = 0x00000400,
    FILE_ATTRIBUTE_COMPRESSED         = 0x00000800,
    FILE_ATTRIBUTE_OFFLINE            = 0x00001000,
    FILE_ATTRIBUTE_NOT_CONTENT_INDEXED = 0x00002000,
    FILE_ATTRIBUTE_ENCRYPTED          = 0x00004000
}


/* from WinBase.h
#define CREATE_NEW        1
#define CREATE_ALWAYS     2
#define OPEN_EXISTING     3
#define OPEN_ALWAYS       4
#define TRUNCATE_EXISTING 5
*/
public enum CreationDisposition : uint
{
    CREATE_NEW       = 1,
    CREATE_ALWAYS    = 2,
    OPEN_EXISTING    = 3,
    OPEN_ALWAYS      = 4,
```

```csharp
        TRUNCATE_EXISTING   = 5
}

private const int INVALID_HANDLE_VALUE = -1;

[DllImport("kernel32.DLL", SetLastError=true)]
    private static extern IntPtr CreateFile(
    string fileName,
    uint desiredAccess,
    FileShareMode shareMode,
    IntPtr securityAttributes,
    CreationDisposition creationDisposition,
    FileAttribute flags,
    IntPtr templateHandle);

[DllImport("kernel32.DLL", SetLastError = true)]
private static extern void CloseHandle(IntPtr handle);

public static bool CreateFile(
    string fileName, FileShareMode shareMode,
    FileAttribute attributes, CreationDisposition disposition)
{
    //validate FileShareMode
    uint sumFileShare = 0;
    foreach(uint value in
        Enum.GetValues(typeof(FileShareMode)))
    {
        sumFileShare += value;
    }
    if (((uint)shareMode & sumFileShare) != (uint)shareMode)
    {
        throw new ArgumentException("Invalid FileShareMode");
    }

    //validate CreationDisposition
    if (!Enum.IsDefined(typeof(CreationDisposition),
        disposition))
    {
        throw new ArgumentException(
            "Invalid CreationDisposition");
    }

    //validate FileAttribute
    uint sumFileAttribute = 0;
    foreach (uint value in
        Enum.GetValues(typeof(FileAttribute)))
    {
```

```
            sumFileAttribute += value;
        }
        if (((uint)attributes & sumFileAttribute)
            != (uint)attributes)
        {
            throw new ArgumentException("Invalid FileAttribute");
        }

        IntPtr fileHandle = CreateFile(
            fileName, 0, shareMode, IntPtr.Zero,
            disposition, attributes, IntPtr.Zero);
        if (fileHandle.ToInt32() == INVALID_HANDLE_VALUE)
        {
            int lastErrorCode = Marshal.GetLastWin32Error();
            throw new Win32Exception(lastErrorCode);
        }
        else
        {
            CloseHandle(fileHandle);
            return true;
        }
    }
}
```

This wrapper doesn't do much other than create a file. Most of the work in making this call is actually defining all of the constants. Once that is done, it's a relatively simple matter to make the call.

Note This example uses an `IntPtr` to work with the file handle. A better alternative is to use the new classes derived from `SafeHandle` that were introduced in .NET 2.0. This is discussed in the next recipe.

Each one of the constants defined in the API reference required a search of the headers. Once they were found, we copied the constants directly from the Windows header into the C# code as a comment. This serves as a point of reference when converting these constants to .NET code. Later we can look back at these comments and see how each constant was originally defined by Microsoft.

Note In this example code, we've chosen to declare the Win32 functions in the class that actually uses them. However, there is a Microsoft pattern that recommends placing all such declarations in a separate class named `NativeMethods`. This wrapper class would then reference static methods of the `NativeMethods` class to execute the Win32 functions.

If you use a tool such as FxCop to check your adherence to standards, you will want to follow the `NativeMethods` pattern instead of the example code shown here.

Sample code that executes this wrapper looks like this:

```
CreateFileHelper.CreateFile(
    @"TestCreateFileAPI.txt",
    (CreateFileHelper.FileShareMode.FILE_SHARE_READ |
        CreateFileHelper.FileShareMode.FILE_SHARE_WRITE),
    (CreateFileHelper.FileAttribute.FILE_ATTRIBUTE_ENCRYPTED |
        CreateFileHelper.FileAttribute.FILE_ATTRIBUTE_READONLY),
    CreateFileHelper.CreationDisposition.OPEN_ALWAYS);
```

When calling the wrapper method, we pass the enum values that were defined within the wrapper. While this doesn't prevent us from passing an invalid value, it does help during code development since we can use Visual Studio IntelliSense to see the list of available values. And it does allow us to validate the enum values prior to their use, as shown in the example code.

The definition and use of Win32 constants can be done the same way in Visual Basic .NET (VB.NET). You have the option of defining individual constants or Enum types. The following example shows the CreateFile wrapper implemented in VB.NET:

```
Class CreateFileHelperVB
    'declare emums
    <Flags()> _
    Public Enum FileShareMode As UInteger
        FILE_SHARE_READ = &H1
        FILE_SHARE_WRITE = &H2
        FILE_SHARE_DELETE = &H4
    End Enum

    <Flags()> _
    Public Enum FileAttribute As UInteger
        FILE_ATTRIBUTE_READONLY = &H1
        FILE_ATTRIBUTE_HIDDEN = &H2
        FILE_ATTRIBUTE_SYSTEM = &H4
        FILE_ATTRIBUTE_DIRECTORY = &H10
        FILE_ATTRIBUTE_ARCHIVE = &H20
        FILE_ATTRIBUTE_DEVICE = &H40
        FILE_ATTRIBUTE_NORMAL = &H80
        FILE_ATTRIBUTE_TEMPORARY = &H100
        FILE_ATTRIBUTE_SPARSE_FILE = &H200
        FILE_ATTRIBUTE_REPARSE_POINT = &H400
        FILE_ATTRIBUTE_COMPRESSED = &H800
        FILE_ATTRIBUTE_OFFLINE = &H1000
        FILE_ATTRIBUTE_NOT_CONTENT_INDEXED = &H2000
        FILE_ATTRIBUTE_ENCRYPTED = &H4000
    End Enum

    Public Enum CreationDisposition As UInteger
        CREATE_NEW = 1
        CREATE_ALWAYS = 2
```

```vb
    OPEN_EXISTING = 3
    OPEN_ALWAYS = 4
    TRUNCATE_EXISTING = 5
End Enum

Const INVALID_HANDLE_VALUE As Integer = -1

<DllImport("kernel32.DLL", SetLastError:=True)> _
Shared Function CreateFile( _
    ByVal fileName As String, _
    ByVal desiredAccess As Integer, _
    ByVal shareMode As FileShareMode, _
    ByVal securityAttributes As IntPtr, _
    ByVal creationDisposition As CreationDisposition, _
    ByVal flags As FileAttribute, _
    ByVal templateHandle As IntPtr) As IntPtr
End Function

<DllImport("kernel32.DLL", SetLastError:=True)> _
Shared Sub CloseHandle(ByVal handle As IntPtr)
End Sub

'Call the CreateFile API function
Public Shared Function CreateFile(ByVal fileName As String, _
        ByVal shareMode As FileShareMode, _
        ByVal attributes As FileAttribute, _
        ByVal disposition As CreationDisposition) _
        As Boolean

    'validate FileShareMode
    Dim sumFileShare As UInteger = 0
    For Each value As UInteger _
        In System.Enum.GetValues(GetType(FileShareMode))
        sumFileShare += value
    Next value
    If Not (shareMode And sumFileShare) = shareMode Then
        Throw New ArgumentException("Invalid FileShareMode")
    End If

    'validate CreationDisposition
    If Not System.Enum.IsDefined( _
        GetType(CreationDisposition), disposition) Then
        Throw New ArgumentException( _
            "Invalid CreationDisposition")
    End If
```

```
        'validate FileAttribute
        Dim sumFileAttribute As UInteger = 0
        For Each value As UInteger _
            In System.Enum.GetValues(GetType(FileAttribute))
            sumFileAttribute += value
        Next value
        If Not (attributes And sumFileAttribute) = attributes Then
            Throw New ArgumentException("Invalid FileAttribute")
        End If

        Dim fileHandle As IntPtr
        'make the call
        fileHandle = CreateFile( _
            fileName, 0, shareMode, IntPtr.Zero, _
            disposition, attributes, IntPtr.Zero)

        'check the result
        If (fileHandle.ToInt32() = INVALID_HANDLE_VALUE) Then
            Dim lastErrorCode As Integer _
                = Marshal.GetLastWin32Error()
            Throw New Win32Exception(lastErrorCode)
        Else
            CloseHandle(fileHandle)
            Return True
        End If

    End Function

End Class
```

The VB.NET code that executes this wrapper looks like this:

```
CreateFileHelperVB.CreateFile( _
    "TestCreateFileAPI.txt", _
    (CreateFileHelperVB.FileShareMode.FILE_SHARE_READ Or _
        CreateFileHelperVB.FileShareMode.FILE_SHARE_WRITE), _
    (CreateFileHelperVB.FileAttribute.FILE_ATTRIBUTE_ENCRYPTED Or _
        CreateFileHelperVB.FileAttribute.FILE_ATTRIBUTE_READONLY), _
    CreateFileHelperVB.CreationDisposition.OPEN_ALWAYS)
```

Related Information

See recipe 3-2 (Retrieving the Win32 Error Code).

3-5. Handling Handles

Problem

Many Win32 functions either return or accept a handle to an unmanaged resource such as a file. You need to know how to use these handles in managed code.

Solution

A SafeHandle class was introduced in .NET 2.0. The purpose of this class is to provide a secure way to work with handles in managed code. The SafeHandle class itself is abstract, but there are classes derived from it that you can use.

For instance, SafeFileHandle is derived from the base SafeHandle class and is designed to work with file handles. It has additional properties that let us check the status of a file handle. It also knows how to close a file handle.

It is actually a reference-counting wrapper for a handle. The marshaler has intimate knowledge of the SafeHandle and knows that it has to increment its reference count when a handle is marshaled. When we indicate that we are done with the handle by calling the Close method, it will immediately close the handle for us as long as there are no other references to it.

Other derived classes can be developed that know how to deal with other handle types.

Note This recipe uses the SafeFileHandle as an example. Please refer to the documentation for the Microsoft.Win32.SafeHandles namespace for information on implementing other types of safe handles. Since SafeFileHandle is part of this namespace, you'll need to include it in your projects that use safe handles.

If a Win32 function returns a file handle, you can marshal it back to managed code as a SafeFileHandle. If you need to call another Win32 function that requires the handle, you simply pass the SafeFileHandle as a calling argument to the second function.

It is important to remember that when handles are created by unmanaged code, they should also be destroyed or freed by unmanaged code. Most Win32 handles can be destroyed by the CloseHandle function. However, when using a SafeFileHandle, we should use the Close method provided by the handle. This calls the CloseHandle API function for us when there are no more references to the handle. Since SafeFileHandle implements IDisposable, we can also choose to call Dispose instead of Close.

As an example, we'll look at the GetFileSize Win32 function. We pass it a handle to a file and it will return the size of the file, so right off the bat we know that in order to call this function we need a handle to a file. To obtain the handle, we can call the Win32 CreateFile function.

The implementation of a C# class to call CreateFile looks like this:

```
/// <summary>
/// A wrapper for the CreateFile Win32 API
/// </summary>
```

```
class CreateFileHelper
{
    [DllImport("kernel32.DLL", SetLastError=true)]
    private static extern SafeFileHandle CreateFile(
        string fileName,
        uint desiredAccess,
        uint shareMode,
        IntPtr securityAttributes,
        uint creationDisposition,
        uint flags,
        IntPtr templateHandle);

    /// <summary>
    /// Open a file for reading using the Win32
    /// CreateFile function
    /// </summary>
    /// <param name="fileName"></param>
    /// <returns></returns>
    public static SafeFileHandle OpenFileForReading(
        string fileName)
    {
        const uint FILE_SHARE_READ = 0x00000001;
        const uint OPEN_EXISTING   = 3;

        //call the Win32 API
        SafeFileHandle fileHandle = CreateFile(
            fileName, 0, FILE_SHARE_READ, IntPtr.Zero,
            OPEN_EXISTING, 0, IntPtr.Zero);
        if (fileHandle.IsInvalid)
        {
            int lastErrorCode = Marshal.GetLastWin32Error();
            throw new Win32Exception(lastErrorCode);
        }
        else
        {
            return fileHandle;
        }
    }
}
```

This class declares the CreateFile function that we will need to obtain a file handle. CreateFile returns a handle to a file, which we marshal as a SafeFileHandle.

Notice that we make use of the IsInvalid property of the SafeFileHandle. This takes the place of code that we would normally have to write to check for a –1 value in the file handle.

Since this wrapper is designed only as a way to open an existing file rather than a general-purpose CreateFile wrapper, we omit most of the constant definitions and only implement the values that we need.

The GetFileSize function is declared in C# like this:

```
[DllImport("kernel32.DLL", SetLastError=true)]
private static extern int GetFileSize(
    SafeFileHandle fileHandle,
    IntPtr fileSizeHigh);
```

The code to test these functions looks like this:

```
//create a test file in managed code so we
//can open and use it in unmanaged code.
using (StreamWriter writer = new StreamWriter("testfile.txt"))
{
    writer.WriteLine("this is a test line");
}


//
//open a file using the unmanaged CreateFile function
//and then use the handle to call GetFileSize.
//when the using block loses scope, the SafeFileHandle
//is closed. This will free the handle to the
//unmanaged resource (file).
//
using (SafeFileHandle fileHandle
    = CreateFileHelper.OpenFileForReading("testfile.txt"))
{
    //use the file handle to call the GetFileSize function
    Console.WriteLine("GetFileSize: {0}",
        GetFileSize(fileHandle, IntPtr.Zero));
}
```

We start our test by creating a test file that will be used to retrieve the file size. The OpenFileForReading method of our CreateFile class is executed and returns a SafeFileHandle to the file. Next, we pass this handle to the GetFileSize Win32 function that returns the size of the file. When the using block goes out of scope, the Dispose method is called on the SafeFileHandle. This indicates that we are done with this handle. If the internal reference count within the SafeFileHandle is zero, it will be closed using the CloseHandle Win32 function. In this example, we could have also called the Close method ourselves.

The internal reference count is automatically incremented when the SafeFileHandle is passed to a function via a PInvoke call. When the call returns it is decremented. If another thread is in the middle of a PInvoke call with this same handle, that would delay the closing of the handle. It is also possible to manually increment and decrement the count using the DangerousAddRef and DangerousRelease methods of SafeFileHandle. These methods are named this way for a reason and should be used with great care. Ultimately, the actual handle is closed when the last thread that is using the SafeFileHandle calls Dispose or Close on its reference at a time when the internal reference count is zero.

When the code is executed, the results look like this:

```
GetFileSize: 21
```

The file size of 21 is correct since we wrote a 19-byte ANSI string plus a carriage return and line feed.

Note In this example, we are able to marshal the handle as a `SafeFileHandle` since it is an opaque pointer. We don't need to know the actual value of the handle; we simply need to retrieve the handle from one API and pass it to another unmodified.

We also don't worry about object lifetimes or garbage collection. Since the handle was generated by a call to unmanaged code, we can be assured that it won't be garbage collected or otherwise destroyed between the two API calls.

Here is similar code implemented in Visual Basic .NET (VB.NET). First, the code that calls `CreateFile` is as follows:

```
Public Class CreateFileHelper

    <DllImport("kernel32.DLL", SetLastError:=True)> _
    Private Shared Function CreateFile( _
        ByVal fileName As String, _
        ByVal desiredAccess As UInteger, _
        ByVal sharedMode As UInteger, _
        ByVal securityAttributes As IntPtr, _
        ByVal creationDisposition As UInteger, _
        ByVal flags As UInteger, _
        ByVal templateHandle As IntPtr) _
            As SafeFileHandle
    End Function

    ''' <summary>
    ''' Open a file for reading using the Win32
    ''' </summary>
    ''' <param name="fileName"></param>
    ''' <returns></returns>
    ''' <remarks></remarks>
    Public Function OpenFileForReading( _
        ByVal fileName As String) _
            As SafeFileHandle
        Const FILE_SHARE_READ As UInteger = &H1
        Const OPEN_EXISTING As UInteger = 3

        'call the Win32 API
        'Dim fileHandle As IntPtr = CreateFile( _
        Dim fileHandle As SafeFileHandle = CreateFile( _
            fileName, 0, FILE_SHARE_READ, IntPtr.Zero, _
            OPEN_EXISTING, 0, IntPtr.Zero)
```

```
        If fileHandle.IsInvalid() Then
            Dim lastErrorCode As Integer _
                = Marshal.GetLastWin32Error()
            Throw New Win32Exception(lastErrorCode)
        Else
            Return fileHandle
        End If
    End Function

End Class
```

Here is the GetFileSize declaration in VB.NET:

```
<DllImport("kernel32.DLL", SetLastError:=True)> _
Public Function GetFileSize( _
    ByVal fileHandle As SafeFileHandle, _
    ByVal fileSizeHigh As IntPtr) As Integer
End Function
```

And here is the remainder of the code:

```
'create a test file in managed code so we
'can open and use it in unmanaged.
Using writer As StreamWriter _
    = New StreamWriter("testfile.txt")
    writer.WriteLine("this is a test line")
End Using


'open a file using the unmanaged CreateFile function
'and then use the handle to call GetFileSize
'
Dim helper As CreateFileHelper _
    = New CreateFileHelper()
Using fileHandle As SafeFileHandle _
    = helper.OpenFileForReading("testfile.txt")
    'use the file handle to call the GetFileSize function
    Console.WriteLine("GetFileSize: {0}", _
        GetFileSize(fileHandle, IntPtr.Zero))
End Using
```

When this code is executed, the results are exactly the same as the C# version.

How It Works

You can also create a file handle in managed code and pass it to an unmanaged API function.

To illustrate this, we can modify the code that calls GetFileSize previously discussed. Instead of calling the unmanaged CreateFile function to get a handle to a file, we open the file in managed code and use the managed handle.

The revised C# code looks like this:

```csharp
//
//open the file using managed code, then pass the
//SafeFileHandle from the FileStream to the
//unmanaged GetFileSize API
//
using(FileStream fileStream = new FileStream(
    "testfile.txt", FileMode.Open))
{
    Console.WriteLine("GetFileSize: {0}",
        GetFileSize(fileStream.SafeFileHandle, IntPtr.Zero));
}
```

And the same code implemented in VB.NET looks like this:

```vbnet
'
'open the file using managed code, then pass the
'SafeFileHandle from the FileStream to the
'unmanaged GetFileSize API
'
Using fileStream As FileStream _
    = New FileStream("testfile.txt", FileMode.Open)
    Console.WriteLine("GetFileSize: {0}", _
        GetFileSize( _
            fileStream.SafeFileHandle, IntPtr.Zero))
    fileStream.Close()
End Using
```

We open the file using a managed FileStream object and then use the SafeFileHandle property of the FileStream to obtain the SafeFileHandle. This safe handle is then passed to the unmanaged GetFileSize function. The unmanaged function sees only the actual handle.

When the code is executed, we see the same results as the prior version:

```
GetFileSize: 21
```

Related Information

See recipes 3-2 (Retrieving the Win32 Error Code) and 3-6 (Passing Managed Objects). Also refer to the MSDN documentation for the Microsoft.Win32.SafeHandles namespace for additional information.

3-6. Passing Managed Objects

Problem

You need to safely pass a managed object to a Win32 function.

Solution

Some Win32 functions allow you to pass any type of object to them. One example is the set of functions dealing with thread local storage. These functions allow you to allocate a storage slot, store something in it (an object, an array, or anything else), and then reference it later. Another example is a callback function that allows you to pass any type of object with the callback.

One potential problem when passing objects to unmanaged code is that .NET may attempt to garbage collect the object if it thinks there are no active references to it. You wouldn't want garbage collection to occur on an object that you still need. If the only references to the object are in unmanaged code, the garbage collector won't know about them.

Therefore, when passing a managed handle to unmanaged code, you must do something to prevent garbage collection. You can do this by wrapping the managed object in a GCHandle and then passing that handle to unmanaged code. The basic steps to use a GCHandle are as follows:

1. Allocate the GCHandle using the static Alloc method.

2. Pass the GCHandle to unmanaged code and use it as needed.

3. Free the GCHandle using the Free method when you are finished with it.

By wrapping an object in a GCHandle, you prevent garbage collection of that object until you call the Free method. This allows you to pass the managed object to unmanaged code without the worry of garbage collection during the unmanaged call.

If you forget to free a GCHandle using the Free method, it will never be garbage collected and that could eventually lead to memory-related performance problems.

How It Works

To illustrate passing an object with a GCHandle, the example that follows passes a managed object to the Win32 thread local storage functions.

Note The purpose of this example is not to demonstrate how to use thread local storage; instead, these functions are used because they conveniently allow passing of any type of object to a thread local storage memory slot. We could have used other Win32 APIs to demonstrate the use of a GCHandle. These techniques are also not limited to use with calling Win32 functions.

We start by declaring the Win32 functions that work with thread local storage:

```
[DllImport("kernel32.DLL")]
private static extern uint TlsAlloc();
```

```
[DllImport("kernel32.DLL")]
private static extern bool TlsFree(uint index);

[DllImport("kernel32.DLL")]
private static extern bool TlsSetValue(
    uint index, GCHandle gcObject);

[DllImport("kernel32.DLL")]
private static extern GCHandle TlsGetValue(uint index);
```

TlsAlloc and TlsFree are used to create and dispose of a memory slot. TlsSetValue and TlsGetValue are used to put an object into a slot or to retrieve it.

We need some type of managed object for this test, so we implement a simple one. This is the object that we will place into thread local storage using a GCHandle:

```
class GCHandleTestClass
{
    public int         field1;
    public int         field2;
    public string      field3;
}
```

To perform the test, we allocate a memory slot in thread local storage, hanging on to the index for later use. We then create and populate an instance of our test object:

```
//allocate a thread local storage slot
uint tlsIndex = TlsAlloc();

//create our managed test object
GCHandleTestClass testObj = new GCHandleTestClass();
testObj.field1 = 1;
testObj.field2 = 2;
testObj.field3 = "string3";
```

Next, we wrap the test object with a GCHandle and call the TlsSetValue method to place this object (the GCHandle) into thread local storage.

```
//put the test object into a GCHandle. This prevents
//the object from being garbage collected even
//when no managed code holds a reference to the object
GCHandle gch = GCHandle.Alloc(testObj);
//remove our reference to this object
testObj = null;
//request garbage collection now
GC.Collect();

//put the GCHandle into the thread local storage slot
TlsSetValue(tlsIndex, gch);
```

It is assumed that at this point some type of processing takes place using the object. We don't know what that processing is since it doesn't concern this discussion. All we care about is that our test object is safely in the hands of a GCHandle. It cannot be garbage collected until we explicitly free it.

The remainder of the test code looks like this:

```
//now retrieve the GCHandle from thread local storage
//and show the values
GCHandle gchRetrieved = TlsGetValue(tlsIndex);
GCHandleTestClass retrievedObj
    = gchRetrieved.Target as GCHandleTestClass;
if (retrievedObj != null)
{
    Console.WriteLine("Retrieved Test Obj: {0},{1},{2}",
        retrievedObj.field1, retrievedObj.field2,
        retrievedObj.field3);
}

//free the thread local storage
TlsFree(tlsIndex);

//release the GC handle
gch.Free();
```

We retrieve the object from thread local storage and display the values. Finally, we clean up by freeing the thread local storage memory slot and freeing the GCHandle.

It is very important to call Free on the GCHandle. If we don't do this, the underlying object won't be garbage collected. In this example, we do call Free on the GCHandle. However, when writing production code, you'll likely want to put this call to Free within a try/finally block to ensure that it is called even if an exception is thrown.

When this code is executed, the results look like this:

```
Retrieved Test Obj: 1,2,string3
```

In the preceding example, the GCHandle is used to prevent garbage collection of the managed object until Free is called on the handle. In addition, a GCHandle can optionally pin the memory until Free is called. Pinning an object in memory not only prevents garbage collection on that object, but also stops the object from being moved in memory. This is an advanced use of GCHandle, and we would only do this if the unmanaged code required a fixed pointer address for the object or memory that was allocated.

However, not all types can be pinned using a GCHandle. Only blittable types and arrays of blittable types can be used this way. For instance, since the GCHandleTestClass test class in the example contains a String field, it is not blittable and cannot be pinned in memory.

The C# code that follows demonstrates pinning an array of ints using GCHandle:

```
//allocate a thread local storage slot
uint tlsIndex = TlsAlloc();

//create our managed array that will go into the GCHandle
int[] blitArray = new int[3];
blitArray[0] = 123;
```

```
blitArray[1] = 456;
blitArray[2] = 789;

//pin the blittable array using a GCHandle
GCHandle gch = GCHandle.Alloc(blitArray,
    GCHandleType.Pinned);
//remove our reference to this object
blitArray = null;
//request garbage collection now
GC.Collect();

//put the GCHandle into the thread local storage slot
TlsSetValue(tlsIndex, gch);

//assume some unmanaged processing occurs here

//now retrieve the GCHandle from thread local storage
//and show the values
GCHandle gchRetrieved = TlsGetValue(tlsIndex);

int[] retrievedArray = (int[])gchRetrieved.Target;
if (retrievedArray != null)
{
    Console.WriteLine(
        "Retrieved Pinned Array: {0},{1},{2}",
        retrievedArray[0], retrievedArray[1],
        retrievedArray[2]);
}

//free the thread local storage
TlsFree(tlsIndex);

//release the GC handle; otherwise, it will be pinned forever
gch.Free();
```

The major difference here (apart from our use of a blittable array as a test object) is the inclusion of the GCHandleType.Pinned value passed to the Alloc method. This pins the object until Free is called.

Here are the results when we execute this test:

```
Retrieved Pinned Array: 123,456,789
```

Failure to free a pinned GCHandle is worse than failure to free a nonpinned GCHandle. If the pinned memory is never released, it can't be garbage collected or moved. The ability to move managed objects in memory is an important behavior of .NET.

Related Information

See recipe 3-5 (Handling Handles).

3-7. Marshaling Win32 Types

Problem

The Win32 API defines a number of special Windows types such as DWORD, HANDLE, and BOOL. How are these types marshaled when calling a Win32 function?

Solution

These special Windows types are nothing more than aliases for integral C or C++ types. For example, a BOOL is a typedef for long, and a DWORD is a typedef for unsigned long. The Windows API references these types when defining function parameters, return values, and members of structures.

By using these typedef names, the Windows developers have abstracted the underlying data type, making it easier to change the data type if the need arises. Most of these types are defined in the WTypes.h, WinNT.h, and WinDef.h header files.

The .NET marshaler doesn't perform any special magic with these types. In fact, it doesn't even have any special knowledge of them. Instead, it marshals data to and from Win32 functions using the underlying data types like ints, longs, chars, and wide chars.

The following table summarizes some of the commonly used Windows types. You can find the complete list of Windows data types in the MSDN topic "Windows Data Types."

Table 3-2. *Marshaling of Windows Data Types*

Windows Type	Unmanaged Type	Managed Type	Notes
BOOL	long	System.Int32	A 32-bit integer representing a Boolean value.
BOOLEAN	unsigned char	System.Byte	An 8-bit integer.
BYTE	unsigned char	System.Byte	An 8-bit integer.
CHAR	char	System.Char	A single ANSI character. ANSI is the default marshaling behavior for System.Char. However, you can also specify CharSet.Ansi to indicate ANSI marshaling of characters.
DOUBLE	double	System.Double	A 64-bit floating point.
DWORD	unsigned long	System.UInt32	An unsigned 32-bit integer.
FLOAT	float	System.Single	A 32-bit floating point.
HANDLE	void*	System.IntPtr	Marshaled as a 32- or 64-bit pointer depending on the operating system version.
HRESULT	long	System.Int32	A 32-bit integer.
INT	int	System.Int32	A 32-bit integer.
INT_PTR	int or __int64 depending on the operating system	System.IntPtr	A 32- or 64-bit integer depending on the operating system version.

Continued

Table 3-2. *Continued*

Windows Type	Unmanaged Type	Managed Type	Notes
LONG	long	System.Int32	A 32-bit integer. The Microsoft C++ implementation considers an int and long to be the same size.
LPCSTR	const char*	System.String	An ANSI string constant. The default marshaling for System.String is ANSI, but you can also specify CharSet.Ansi.
LPCTSTR	const char* or const wchar_t*	System.String	An ANSI or Unicode string constant depending on the version of the function invoked. If CharSet.Unicode is specified, the Unicode version is used; otherwise, the ANSI version is executed.
LPCWSTR	const wchar_t*	System.String	A Unicode string constant. You must specify that you want the string marshaled as Unicode by adding the CharSet.Unicode value.
LPSTR	char*	System.String or System.StringBuilder if the field is In/Out	An ANSI string. The default marshaling for System.String is ANSI but you can also specify CharSet.Ansi.
LPTSTR	char* or wchar_t*	System.String or System.StringBuilder if the field is In/Out	An ANSI or Unicode string depending on the version of the function invoked. If CharSet.Unicode is specified, the Unicode version is used; otherwise, the ANSI version is executed.
LPWSTR	wchar_t*	System.String or System.StringBuilder if the field is In/Out	A Unicode string. You must specify that you want the string marshaled as Unicode by adding the CharSet.Unicode value.
SHORT	short	System.Int16	A 16-bit integer.
TCHAR	wchar_t or char	System.Char	An ANSI or Unicode character depending on the version of the function invoked. If CharSet.Unicode is specified, the Unicode version is used; otherwise, the ANSI version is executed.
UINT	unsigned int	System.UInt32	An unsigned 32-bit integer.
ULONG	unsigned long	System.UInt32	An unsigned 32-bit integer.
WORD	unsigned short	System.UInt16	An unsigned 16-bit integer.

How It Works

The list of Windows types also includes a host of H* types (e.g., HFILE, HFONT, HBITMAP, and HWND). All of these equate to a HANDLE and could be marshaled as a System.IntPtr or as a class derived from SafeHandle. Handles may also require special handling such as the use of a GCHandle.

■Note Please refer to the "Related Information" section for other recipes that discuss the use of handles.

Prefixing a type with P usually means it is a pointer to the type. For example, PBYTE is a pointer to a BYTE, PCHAR is a pointer to a CHAR, etc. These pointer types should be marshaled by ref rather than by value so the Win32 function receives a pointer.

Characters and strings can be marshaled as either ANSI or Unicode. The default behavior is to marshal these as ANSI. To change this, you add the CharSet=CharSet.Unicode field to the DllImport attribute. When marshaling structures that contain characters or strings, you can add the CharSet field to the StructLayout attribute to control the character set used.

If individual string fields within a structure need to be marshaled differently from other structure fields, you can apply the MarshalAs attribute to individual fields. By specifying MarshalAs(UnmanagedType.LPWStr), you request Unicode marshaling. Use MarshalAs(UnmanagedType.LPStr) on a field to indicate ANSI marshaling of the string.

Related Information

See recipes 3-1 (Accessing ANSI or Wide Functions), 2-4 (Controlling Field-Level Marshaling Within Structures), 1-6 (Changing the Character Set Used for Strings), 1-7 (Using Data Types That Improve Performance), 3-5 (Handling Handles), and 3-6 (Passing Managed Objects).

3-8. Replacing Win32 Calls with .NET

Problem

Since PInvoke allows you to use all of your favorite Win32 APIs, why do you need to switch to .NET classes? Can't you continue to use Win32?

Solution

The short answer is that you don't *have* to switch. You *can* continue to use Win32 as long as it meets your needs. You *can* mix and match .NET and Win32 code, using PInvoke to call your favorite Win32 functions. However, there are good reasons to move to .NET, and most Win32 functions have a corresponding .NET replacement.

For instance, in order to call an unmanaged function through PInvoke, your code requires the UnmanagedCode security permission from code access security. If your code is executing as a local user, it usually has this permission. However, under other deployment scenarios, this permission may not be granted. For example, smart client applications deployed via the Web (no-touch and ClickOnce deployment) typically don't have this permission by default.

In addition, accessing unmanaged code is always a risk. Any number of things can go wrong when using PInvoke. For instance, you might incorrectly declare the function signature, causing a mismatch of parameters. There are also issues allocating and freeing memory and unmanaged resources.

To assist you, Microsoft provides an excellent document entitled "Microsoft Win32 to Microsoft .NET Framework API Map." This document is included with the MSDN library, and you can also view it on the MSDN web site. It provides a listing of Win32 functions by category to make it easier to find a function. For each function listed, a .NET replacement is listed.

For example, if you want to copy a file using Win32, you would reach for the CopyFile function. If you search for this function in the "Microsoft Win32 to Microsoft .NET Framework API Map" document, you would see the entry shown in Table 3-3.

Table 3-3. *CopyFile .NET Framework API Map*

Win32 Function	Description	.NET Framework API
CopyFile	Copies an existing file to a new file	Either of the following: System.IO.File.Copy System.IO.FileInfo.CopyTo

If you look up the information for the File class, you'll see that it does have a Copy method that copies a file. Similarly, the FileInfo class contains a CopyTo method that you can also use for the same purpose.

Armed with this information, you can use the .NET File or FileInfo class to perform the file copy. Congratulations! You have just eliminated one call to one Win32 API function. And you have learned how to use a small piece of the .NET Framework at the same time. Bring on the next function.

How It Works

Why would you want to continue using Win32 functions when .NET is available? There are really only two possible reasons:

- .NET does not supply a suitable replacement for a particular Win32 function.

- You're comfortable with the Win32 API and don't have the time to find and learn the .NET replacement for a function.

The .NET Framework Class Library provides replacements for most of the Win32 functions that you will need. There are some exceptions, but the chances are very good that there is a .NET class somewhere that will meet your needs.

That leaves comfort level. We all fall into routines where we use a tool just because it is a tool that we know. We've used it for years and may not like it very much, but it does the job and we instinctively know how to use it. It may not be the best tool for the job, but it does get the job done.

That describes Win32. Many of us have used it for years. We don't necessarily like it, but we know how to use it and it gets the job done. We might know that a better .NET replacement is available somewhere, but we haven't forced ourselves to look for it and learn to use it.

Here are a few advantages to leaving the old Win32 API behind and going with a pure .NET solution:

- *Garbage-collected managed memory*: .NET handles garbage collection, freeing us from the housekeeping duties of destroying memory that we allocate.

- *Type safety*: .NET methods are all very strongly typed. They typically don't just accept an integer or a pointer to void as an input parameter. They use enumerations, classes, and delegates.

- *Classes and methods instead of functions*: Win32 is a flat function-based API. It predates modern object-oriented APIs like the .NET Framework Class Library.

- *Consistency*: Win32 is inconsistent from one subsystem to another and from one function to another. One function might return a string, while another may require you to pass a pointer to a preallocated buffer. One function might fill an array, while another might use a callback. .NET has a clean design that is consistent from one class to the next. Once you learn how a few classes work, you'll be able to quickly apply what you've learned to the next set of classes.

- *Code access security*: Win32 is a security risk waiting to happen. There is no built-in security for any function. If you know how to call an API, you are free to do it. .NET implements code access security that monitors and controls what any piece of code is allowed to do.

- *Skills development*: You may need to say good-bye to the Win32 API eventually. Why not do it now and develop more marketable skills at the same time?

The process of moving from Win32 to .NET shouldn't be overwhelming, as long as you take it one function at a time. To illustrate this, the two examples that follow each perform the same file-based tasks. The first C# example calls various Win32 functions to do the real work. The second example replaces the Win32 calls with appropriate .NET classes and methods.

The examples are for demonstration purposes only. They both perform this set of actions:

1. Get the current directory.

2. Create a new subdirectory.

3. Open a new file in the subdirectory and write Unicode data to it.

4. Get the size of the newly written file.

5. Make a copy of the new file.

6. Get the size of the newly copied file.

7. Delete both of the files that were created.

8. Delete the new subdirectory.

Since the purpose of this chapter is to show interoperability with the Win32 API, the first example uses C# code to call the Win32 functions. It might have been easier to just write the entire series of Win32 calls in unmanaged C++ code, but that wouldn't demonstrate Win32 interop.

The Win32 example code looks like this:

```
//
//Win32 function declarations
//
[DllImport("kernel32.DLL", SetLastError=true,
    CharSet=CharSet.Unicode)]
private static extern int GetCurrentDirectory(
    int bufferLen, StringBuilder buffer);
```

```
[DllImport("kernel32.DLL", SetLastError=true,
    CharSet=CharSet.Unicode)]
private static extern bool CreateDirectory(
    string dirName, IntPtr securityAttrs);

[DllImport("kernel32.DLL", SetLastError=true,
    CharSet=CharSet.Unicode)]
private static extern bool RemoveDirectory(
    string dirName);

[DllImport("kernel32.DLL", SetLastError=true,
    CharSet=CharSet.Unicode)]
private static extern bool DeleteFile(
    string fileName);

[DllImport("kernel32.DLL", SetLastError=true,
    CharSet=CharSet.Unicode)]
private static extern IntPtr CreateFile(
    string fileName,
    uint desiredAccess,
    uint shareMode,
    IntPtr securityAttributes,
    uint creationDisposition,
    uint flags,
    IntPtr templateHandle);

[DllImport("kernel32.DLL", SetLastError=true,
    CharSet=CharSet.Unicode)]
private static extern bool WriteFile(
    IntPtr handle,
    byte[] buffer,
    uint bytesToWrite,
    ref uint bytesWritten,
    IntPtr pOverlapped);

[DllImport("kernel32.DLL", SetLastError=true)]
private static extern int GetFileSize(IntPtr fileHandle,
    IntPtr fileSizeHigh);

[DllImport("kernel32.DLL", SetLastError=true,
    CharSet=CharSet.Unicode)]
private static extern bool CopyFile(
    string existingFile, string newFile, bool exists);

[DllImport("kernel32.DLL", SetLastError=true)]
public static extern void CloseHandle(IntPtr handle);
```

```
public void ProcessFile()
{
    //define constants needed by the Win32 functions
    const int   INVALID_HANDLE_VALUE = -1;
    const uint FILE_SHARE_READ  = 0x00000001;
    const uint FILE_SHARE_WRITE = 0x00000002;
    const uint CREATE_ALWAYS    = 2;
    const uint OPEN_EXISTING    = 3;
    const uint FILE_ATTRIBUTE_NORMAL = 0x00000080;
    const uint GENERIC_WRITE    = 0x40000000;

    //get the current directory
    StringBuilder currDir   = new StringBuilder(255);
    int charsWritten
        = GetCurrentDirectory(currDir.Capacity, currDir);
    if (charsWritten == 0)
    {
        CheckLastResult();
    }

    //create a new subdirectory under the current one
    String newDir =
        Path.Combine(currDir.ToString(), "MyTestDir");
    if (!CreateDirectory(newDir, IntPtr.Zero))
    {
        CheckLastResult();
    }

    //declare file handles that we will use
    IntPtr fileHandle = IntPtr.Zero;
    IntPtr copiedFileHandle = IntPtr.Zero;

    //open a file for writing
    try
    {
        String fileName
            = Path.Combine(newDir, "MyTestFile.txt");
        fileHandle = CreateFile(
            fileName, GENERIC_WRITE,
            FILE_SHARE_READ | FILE_SHARE_WRITE,
            IntPtr.Zero, CREATE_ALWAYS,
            FILE_ATTRIBUTE_NORMAL, IntPtr.Zero);
        //check for invalid handle to see if this worked
        if (fileHandle.ToInt32() == INVALID_HANDLE_VALUE)
        {
            CheckLastResult();
        }
```

```csharp
//write data to the file
//Note:  Unicode files can be distinguished by the presence
//of the byte order mark (U+FEFF), which is represented
//as hexadecimal 0xFF 0xFE on little-endian platforms.
//we need to manually add these first 2 bytes to the
//file since Win32 doesn't do it for us.
String testData   = "this is the file test data";
int bytesNeeded
    = Encoding.Unicode.GetByteCount(testData) + 2;
byte[] testBytes  = new byte[bytesNeeded];
Encoding.Unicode.GetBytes(
    testData, 0, testData.Length, testBytes, 2);
//add the byte order mark as the first 2 bytes
testBytes[0]      = 0xFF;
testBytes[1]      = 0xFE;
//now write the byte array
uint bytesWritten = 0;
if (!WriteFile(fileHandle, testBytes,
    (uint)(testBytes.Length),
    ref bytesWritten, IntPtr.Zero))
{
    CheckLastResult();
}
Console.WriteLine(
    "Win32 Bytes written: {0}", bytesWritten);

//get the total file size
int fileSize = GetFileSize(fileHandle, IntPtr.Zero);
if (fileSize == 0)
{
    CheckLastResult();
}
Console.WriteLine("Win32 File size: {0}", fileSize);

//close the file handle
CloseHandle(fileHandle);
fileHandle = IntPtr.Zero;

//copy the file
String copiedFileName
    = Path.Combine(newDir,"MyCopiedFile.txt");
if (!CopyFile(fileName, copiedFileName, false))
{
    CheckLastResult();
}
```

```
        //check the file size of the newly copied file
        copiedFileHandle = CreateFile(
            fileName, 0, FILE_SHARE_READ,
            IntPtr.Zero, OPEN_EXISTING, 0, IntPtr.Zero);
        if (copiedFileHandle.ToInt32() == INVALID_HANDLE_VALUE)
        {
            CheckLastResult();
        }
        //use the new file handle to get the file size
        int copiedFileSize = GetFileSize(
            copiedFileHandle, IntPtr.Zero);
        if (copiedFileSize == 0)
        {
            CheckLastResult();
        }
        Console.WriteLine(
            "Win32 Copied File size: {0}", copiedFileSize);

        //close the copied file handle
        CloseHandle(copiedFileHandle);
        copiedFileHandle = IntPtr.Zero;

        //delete the original file
        if (!DeleteFile(fileName))
        {
            CheckLastResult();
        }

        //delete the copied file
        if (!DeleteFile(copiedFileName))
        {
            CheckLastResult();
        }

        //delete the directory
        if (!RemoveDirectory(newDir))
        {
            CheckLastResult();
        }
    }
    finally
    {
        //make sure all handles that we might have
        //opened are now closed
        if (fileHandle != IntPtr.Zero)
        {
            CloseHandle(fileHandle);
```

```
        }
        if (copiedFileHandle != IntPtr.Zero)
        {
            CloseHandle(copiedFileHandle);
        }
    }
}

/// <summary>
/// Check the last Win32 error
/// </summary>
private void CheckLastResult()
{
    int  lastResult = Marshal.GetLastWin32Error();
    //if we have a problem, throw an exception
    if (lastResult != 0)
    {
        throw new Win32Exception(lastResult);
    }
}
```

When we execute the ProcessFile method, we see these results:

```
Win32 Bytes written: 54
Win32 File size: 54
Win32 Copied File size: 54
```

The rewritten C# code that uses only native .NET classes and methods looks like this:

```
public void ProcessFile()
{
    //get the current directory
    String currDir        = Environment.CurrentDirectory;

    //create a new subdirectory under the current one
    DirectoryInfo currDirInfo
        = new DirectoryInfo(currDir);
    currDirInfo.CreateSubdirectory("MyTestDir");
    String newDir = Path.Combine(currDir, "MyTestDir");

    //open a file for writing
    //write data to the file
    String fileName
        = Path.Combine(newDir, "MyTestFile.txt");
    //create a StreamWriter that uses full Unicode encoding
    using (StreamWriter writer
        = new StreamWriter(fileName, false, Encoding.Unicode))
    {
```

```
        writer.NewLine = String.Empty;
        writer.Write("this is the file test data");
        writer.Flush(); //force a write immediately
        long bytesWritten = writer.BaseStream.Length;
        Console.WriteLine(".NET Bytes written: {0}", bytesWritten);
    }

    //get the total file size
    FileInfo fileInfo   = new FileInfo(fileName);
    long fileSize       = fileInfo.Length;
    Console.WriteLine(".NET File size: {0}", fileSize);

    //copy the file
    String copiedFileName
        = Path.Combine(newDir, "MyCopiedFile.txt");
    fileInfo.CopyTo(copiedFileName, true);

    //check the file size of the newly copied file
    fileInfo            = new FileInfo(copiedFileName);
    long copiedFileSize = fileInfo.Length;
    Console.WriteLine(
        ".NET Copied File size: {0}", copiedFileSize);

    //delete the original file
    File.Delete(fileName);

    //delete the copied file
    File.Delete(copiedFileName);

    //delete the directory
    Directory.Delete(newDir);
}
```

The same functionality implemented in Visual Basic .NET (VB.NET) looks like this:

```
Public Sub ProcessFile()
    'get the current directory
    Dim currDir As String _
        = Environment.CurrentDirectory
    'create a new subdirectory under the current one
    Dim currDirInfo As DirectoryInfo _
        = New DirectoryInfo(currDir)
    currDirInfo.CreateSubdirectory("MyTestDir")
    Dim newDir As String = Path.Combine(currDir, "MyTestDir")

    'open a file for writing
    'write data to the file
    Dim fileName As String _
        = Path.Combine(newDir, "MyTestFile.txt")
```

```vb
'create a StreamWriter that uses full Unicode encoding
Using writer As StreamWriter = New StreamWriter( _
    fileName, False, Encoding.Unicode)
    writer.NewLine = String.Empty
    writer.Write("this is the file test data")
    writer.Flush() 'force everything to be written
    Dim bytesWritten As Long = writer.BaseStream.Length
    writer.Close()
    Console.WriteLine( _
        ".NET Bytes written: {0}", bytesWritten)
End Using

'get the total file size
Dim fileInfo As FileInfo = New FileInfo(fileName)
Dim fileSize As Long = fileInfo.Length
Console.WriteLine(".NET File size: {0}", fileSize)

'copy the file
Dim copiedFileName As String _
    = Path.Combine(newDir, "MyCopiedFile.txt")
fileInfo.CopyTo(copiedFileName, True)

'check the file size of the newly copied file
fileInfo = New FileInfo(copiedFileName)
Dim copiedFileSize As Long = fileInfo.Length
Console.WriteLine( _
    ".NET Copied File size: {0}", copiedFileSize)

'delete the original file
File.Delete(fileName)

'delete the copied file
File.Delete(copiedFileName)

'delete the directory
Directory.Delete(newDir)

End Sub
```

Executing either .NET version of the ProcessFile method gives us the same expected results:

```
.NET Bytes written: 54
.NET File size: 54
.NET Copied File size: 54
```

If we compare the Win32 and C# versions side by side, we see a dramatic difference. Not only is the .NET code shorter (49 lines compared to 212), but it's also much simpler. We could describe it as trivial compared to the Win32 version.

Note It is interesting to note that the error checking in the Win32 example appears to be more complete than in the .NET code. After each Win32 call, we check the return value and, if necessary, execute the CheckLastResult method that retrieves the last Win32 error code. The .NET code does not do this type of checking after each action.

On the surface it may appear that the .NET code is not handling errors the same way. However, CheckLastResult throws an exception if an error is detected, effectively stopping further processing. This is also the default .NET behavior. If one of the .NET method calls has a major problem, it will throw an exception, stopping further processing. Therefore, the .NET implementation does provide the same level of error checking, without any additional code.

The Win32 example also shows that, in addition to detecting and throwing the appropriate exception ourselves, we also have to take care of disposing unmanaged resources such as handles.

Related Information

See recipes 3-2 (Retrieving the Win32 Error Code) and 3-4 (Using Windows Constants).

CHAPTER 4

■ ■ ■

Using C++ Interop

Like other .NET languages, C++ is capable of working with unmanaged code. C++ can use the same facilities available to other languages such as PInvoke. However, unlike other languages, C++ is in a unique position to interoperate with unmanaged C++ code. It does this at the source-code level by directly compiling and linking unmanaged C++ code. Other .NET languages cannot access C++ source directly, so they must use PInvoke to access unmanaged functions. This ability to directly interoperate with unmanaged C++ code is simply called *C++ Interop*. This C++ technology was previously called *It Just Works*, or *IJW*. C++ is the only .NET language that allows managed and unmanaged code to coexist within the same project.

C++ Interop uses a very simple mechanism to marshal data between managed and unmanaged code. Parameters are copied between the two environments without any data conversion. This provides the fastest possible marshaling of data, but it also requires that you perform your own data conversions when they are necessary.

In contrast, PInvoke provides robust parameter marshaling including data conversions, but this benefit comes at a performance and flexibility cost. In situations where you have access to the unmanaged C++ code, and performance is an important consideration, C++ Interop may be the right tool for the job.

Performing your own data marshaling is also a potential advantage. You have the opportunity to optimize the conversions based on your knowledge of how you use the data. You can cache parameters after they are converted because you know they will be used again in another method. You can implement shortcuts for the conversion process if they are available. And you can easily convert and marshal your own custom data types.

C++ Interop also provides better type safety than PInvoke. Since PInvoke relies upon your declarations of the unmanaged functions, there is always the possibility that you have incorrectly declared a function. C++ Interop compiles the C++ headers containing the declarations for the unmanaged classes, eliminating the possibility of mistyped parameters.

Since native C++ classes are capable of accessing COM components, it makes sense that C++ Interop also allows this. By accessing COM components directly from managed C++ wrappers, you can expose these components to other .NET languages. These wrappers, called Custom Runtime Callable Wrappers (CRCWs), eliminate the need to generate and reference COM interop libraries.

Why should you consider using C++ Interop instead of PInvoke? Generally, for the same reasons you would choose C++ instead of a higher-level language like C# or Visual Basic for any programming task. Native C++ provides a low-level, high-performance solution to every conceivable software problem. In a similar way, C++ Interop provides you with low-level, high-performance control of interop and data marshaling. It's the ultimate interop tool since it can tackle the most difficult interop challenges. But it does require additional work on your part since you are in total control of the interop process.

Consider using C++ Interop when you have access to the unmanaged C++ source and any of the following situations apply:

- You need the best possible performance when calling unmanaged code.

- You need to marshal custom data types that are difficult to handle with PInvoke.

- You need finer control over the way COM components are exposed to .NET.

- You want better type safety than PInvoke provides.

The first recipe in this chapter covers the basics of accessing unmanaged C++ classes. The chapter continues with recipes describing how to mix managed and unmanaged code, and how to detect attributes of a class at compile time. Another recipe shows how to reference and use managed objects from unmanaged code.

The next set of recipes covers how to marshal strings to unmanaged code, and how to work with structures that contain embedded pointers. Handling callbacks from unmanaged code is also discussed in another recipe.

The final recipe demonstrates how to create a managed C++ wrapper for a COM component.

PInvoke is not covered in this chapter, since it is addressed in other chapters. Only the features that are unique to C++ Interop are covered here.

C++ Interop builds upon the C++/CLI language syntax introduced in Visual Studio 2005. This new syntax replaces the Managed Extensions for C++ that were available with the original version of .NET. The original Managed Extensions were Microsoft-specific keywords that were added to the core C++ language. In contrast, the C++/CLI syntax has been submitted to the C++ standards body for inclusion into the language standard.

A brief review of key aspects of the syntax follows. If you are already well versed in the C++/CLI syntax, feel free to skip ahead to the first recipe.

First, a managed class or struct is identified by the ref or value keyword in the declaration. This is a managed reference class:

```
public ref class ManagedReferenceClass
{
public:
    void foo();
};
```

This is a managed struct:

```
public value struct ManagedStruct
{
};
```

A managed class or struct is visible to other .NET languages, just like a class you might implement in C# or VB.NET. The ref keyword here shouldn't be confused with the ref keyword used in C# when defining a parameter. In this context, ref means this is a *managed reference* type. When used in C#, ref means the parameter is passed *by reference*, allowing the called method to reference the original parameter rather than a copy.

If the ref or value keyword is missing, the class or struct is not managed. For example, this is an unmanaged class:

```
public class CUnmanagedClass
{
};
```

Unmanaged classes are not accessible from other .NET languages, but they can be used by other unmanaged C++ code.

To create an unmanaged object on the unmanaged heap, you still use the new keyword like this:

```
CUnmanagedClass* obj = new CUnmanagedClass();
```

When you are done with this object, you still need to free the unmanaged memory that you allocated like this:

```
delete [] obj;
```

In contrast, managed objects (ref or value keyword types) are allocated on a separate managed heap that is garbage collected. To do this allocation, you use the gcnew keyword like this:

```
ManagedReferenceClass^ obj = gcnew ManagedReferenceClass();
```

The ^ is used to declare a handle to a managed object. Because this object is created on the managed heap, it is automatically garbage collected, so you do not need to explicitly delete it.

To access a member of the object (a field, property, or method), you use the pointer-to-member operator (->) on the managed handle like this:

```
obj->foo();
```

4-1. Using C++ Classes

Problem

You have a number of unmanaged C++ class libraries that you would like to use from managed .NET code. How do you reuse these C++ classes?

Solution

C# and Visual Basic .NET (VB.NET) are unable to directly access unmanaged C++ code. PInvoke works well when accessing flat C-style functions, but doesn't allow you to expose entire classes. However, managed code written in Visual C++ is able to directly use these classes. This unique ability of Visual C++ is simply called C++ Interop. By creating a thin C++ wrapper around the unmanaged code, you can expose the functionality contained in the unmanaged classes, making them available to any managed language.

For example, consider this C++ class:

```
class CMyUnmanagedClass
{
```

```
public:
    CMyUnmanagedClass(void)  {};
    ~CMyUnmanagedClass(void) {};
    int foo(void)
    {
        return 1;
    }
};
```

To make this class available to the world beyond C++, you could implement a managed wrapper in C++ that exposes the methods of this class. The wrapper might look like this:

```
public ref class MyWrapper
{
public:
    MyWrapper (void)
    {
        pObj = new CMyUnmanagedClass();
    }
    ~MyWrapper (void)
    {
        delete pObj;
    }
    int foo(void)
    {
        //pass through to the unmanaged object
        return pObj->foo();
    }

private:
    CMyUnmanagedClass* pObj;
};
```

The ref keyword identifies this as a managed reference type. Thanks to the magic of C++ Interop, this wrapper class is able to seamlessly use the unmanaged C++ class. Once implemented, a wrapper such as this can be used by any .NET language. Of course, the wrapper must respect the rules of the Common Language Specification (CLS) in order to interoperate with other managed code.

Note C++ projects containing managed classes such as this must be compiled with the /clr option.

How It Works

Using C++ Interop to wrap unmanaged C++ classes like this has these advantages:

- No changes are required to the unmanaged code. This allows other unmanaged code to continue to use the classes without modification.

- The managed wrapper can be consumed just like any other managed class. This allows it to be used by all .NET languages including C#, VB.NET, and, of course, Visual C++.

- A wrapper allows you to control and refactor the public interface that you expose to managed code. You are free to create new methods, combining multiple method calls to the unmanaged class as you see fit. You can also hide functionality from managed code if it might pose a security risk.

- C++ Interop allows you to directly use C++ classes. PInvoke is designed to work with flat functions and is not capable of exposing and using the unmanaged class as an object.

- C++ Interop generally will provide better performance than using PInvoke to access a comparable flat function.

The example that follows illustrates this process of wrapping unmanaged C++ code in a managed class.

Note When using C++ Interop, you are responsible for marshaling all data between managed and unmanaged code. This is the primary difference between the use of C++ Interop and PInvoke. PInvoke handles much of the marshaling for you, but at the cost of performance. C++ Interop allows you to take full control over the marshaling of data. This allows you to add any performance optimizations that you feel are needed to convert and transfer the data.

The example presented here is very simple and does not require any special marshaling of data. Depending on the type of data that is passed between managed and unmanaged code, the marshaling code that you have to write might be much more complicated.

Here is an example header declaration for an unmanaged class:

```
#include "StdAfx.h"

namespace USharedLib
{
    class __declspec(dllexport) CUnmanaged
    {
    public:
        CUnmanaged(void);
        void AddNumber(int number);
        int GetTheResult();
    private:
        int m_Total;
    };
}
```

Here is the class implementation from the .cpp file:

```
#include "StdAfx.h"
#include "Unmanaged.h"

namespace USharedLib
{
    CUnmanaged::CUnmanaged(void)
    {
        m_Total      = 0;
    }

    //add to the internal integer
    void CUnmanaged::AddNumber(int number)
    {
        m_Total += number;
    }

    //retrieve the current total
    int CUnmanaged::GetTheResult()
    {
        return m_Total;
    }
}
```

Using the class, we can add numbers to a running total, and then call the GetTheResult method to retrieve the total. The class might be used like this from other unmanaged C++ code:

```
CUnmanaged obj;
obj.AddNumber(1);
obj.AddNumber(2);
int result = obj.GetTheResult();
```

To make this class available to all .NET languages, we can develop a thin C++ wrapper that contains an instance of this class. We have the choice of either exposing the same methods of this class one-for-one or modifying the public interface to suit our needs. We'll choose the latter, since we would like to perform the addition of numbers in fewer steps if possible.

The declaration of our managed wrapper looks like this:

```
#include "Unmanaged.h"

using namespace System;

namespace MClassLib
{
    //a managed wrapper for an unmanaged C++ class
    public ref class Managed
    {
```

```
    public:
        Managed(void);
        ~Managed(void);
        int AddTheNumbers(int numA, int numB);
    private:
        //pointer to the unmanaged object
        USharedLib::CUnmanaged*    m_pUnmanagedObj;
    };
}
```

First, notice that we declare the class with the ref keyword. This keyword identifies this as a managed class, meaning it is capable of being referenced from all .NET languages. Second, our wrapper declares a member variable containing a pointer to the unmanaged class. We'll populate this variable in the following constructor.

We implement the wrapper like this:

```
#include "StdAfx.h"
#include "Managed.h"

namespace MClassLib
{
    Managed::Managed(void)
    {
        //create an instance of the unmanaged class
        m_pUnmanagedObj
            = new USharedLib::CUnmanaged();
    }

    Managed::~Managed(void)
    {
        //delete the unmanaged memory we allocated
        delete m_pUnmanagedObj;
        m_pUnmanagedObj        = NULL;
    }

    int Managed::AddTheNumbers(int numA, int numB)
    {
        //call the methods of the unmanaged object
        m_pUnmanagedObj->AddNumber(numA);
        m_pUnmanagedObj->AddNumber(numB);
        return m_pUnmanagedObj->GetTheResult();
    }
}
```

The constructor is where we create an instance of the unmanaged class, saving the pointer in our member variable. We decide to simplify the public interface by exposing a single AddTheNumbers method. It calls the AddNumber and GetTheResult methods of the unmanaged object. We could have chosen to simply expose the same methods as the unmanaged class.

To use this class from managed code, we only need to reference the assembly containing the C++ wrapper and use it like any other managed class. For example, here is VB.NET code that uses this wrapper:

```
Module UseCPlusPlusTest

    Sub Main()
        'create the managed wrapper
        Using obj As New MClassLib.Managed()
            'call the managed method
            Dim result As Integer
            result = obj.AddTheNumbers(1, 2)
            Console.WriteLine( _
                "AddTheNumbers result: {0}", result)
        End Using

        'wait for input
        Console.WriteLine("Press any key to exit")
        Console.Read()
    End Sub

End Module
```

In this example code, we first create an instance of the wrapper class. We then call the AddTheNumbers method and display the results.

■Note Notice that our C++ wrapper implemented a destructor that deletes the unmanaged object. If a C++ destructor is defined for a reference class (ref keyword), it is converted into a Dispose method by the compiler and the class implements IDisposable. This allows us to use the Using syntax shown here to create a protected block of code. When we exit the Using block, the Dispose method is automatically called, freeing any resources used by the class. You can also explicitly call the Dispose method if you prefer.

Dispose is not called automatically when an object is garbage collected. If you don't call Dispose yourself or create the object within a Using block, it won't be called. If your class is holding any resources that must be released, you should ensure that Dispose is called.

When we execute this code, we see these results:

```
AddTheNumbers result: 3
Press any key to exit
```

Related Information

See recipe 4-2 (Mixing Managed and Unmanaged Code).

4-2. Mixing Managed and Unmanaged Code

Problem

Do you need to keep your managed and unmanaged C++ classes in separate projects? Is it possible to create a project that includes both types of classes?

Solution

Visual C++ provides a number of options to mix managed and unmanaged code. Depending on the compiler options chosen for a project, you are able to include both managed and unmanaged classes within a single project, or even within a single source file.

A fundamental requirement for writing any managed C++ code is the setting of the /clr compiler option. Several variations of this option are listed in Table 4-1, which appears in the "How It Works" section of this recipe. The /clr option by itself produces a *mixed assembly*, which is most useful when interoperating with unmanaged code.

When an assembly is mixed, it is capable of referencing and using managed code (including calls to the .NET Framework itself). It is also capable of being referenced by other .NET assemblies. The assembly is mixed in the sense that it can also contain unmanaged code that can be directly used by unmanaged C++ code in the traditional fashion. The /clr option enables the use of managed .NET classes, but does not require it, allowing you to mix managed and unmanaged code within the same project, keeping the two types of classes in separate source files. For example, a mixed project might include source files like this:

- Unmanaged.h, Unmanaged.cpp: Contain native C++ code

- MyDotNetClass.h, MyDotNetClass.cpp: Contain a managed C++ class

Unmanaged C++ projects are able to #include the Unmanaged.h header without any problems since it contains only native C++ code. However, the code in Unmanaged.h is invisible to .NET assemblies outside of Visual C++. If a class isn't managed, other .NET languages are unable to directly reference it.

If a native C++ project attempted to reference MyDotNetClass.h, it would produce compiler errors. The managed class declaration includes either the ref or value modifiers that are illegal syntax for an unmanaged C++ project. However, since MyDotNetClass.h declares a managed class, that class is visible to any other .NET project that references the mixed assembly. The reference to the managed class is done using .NET assembly references, not by directly using the C++ header file.

Code can also be mixed within a single source file using the managed and unmanaged #pragma preprocessor directives. These directives indicate that all code that follows will be either managed or unmanaged depending on the usage, for example:

```
#pragma unmanaged

void foo(void)
{
    //unmanaged function
}
```

#pragma managed

```
void bar(void)
{
    //managed function
}
```

You need to be careful to include only legal code after each #pragma. For example, you will receive compiler errors if you declare a managed class or reference part of the .NET Framework after the #pragma unmanaged directive.

These #pragma directives also limit the use of the source file. If the #pragma managed directive is used in a header file, then that header can be included only in projects that use the /clr compiler option. Including it in an unmanaged project will result in errors.

Note While this mixing and matching of code is permitted, it's generally not a great idea. A much cleaner approach is to move the managed and unmanaged code into separate source files that are compiled into the same project. This makes it easier to identify the portions of code that are managed and unmanaged. Keeping the managed and unmanaged code separate also allows you to continue using the unmanaged classes from other C++ projects.

How It Works

This first example demonstrates the use of mixed managed and unmanaged code packaged within the same project. In this example, we implement two classes, one managed and the other unmanaged. Each class is declared in a separate header file.

The project uses the /clr compiler option, which is necessary if we want to use any managed code. For our testing, the project is named MixedSharedLib. Both of the following header files are included in this project.

The managed class is in header MixedNumber.h and looks like this:

```
namespace MixedSharedLib
{
    public ref class MixedNumber
    {
    public:
        MixedNumber(void)  {}
        ~MixedNumber(void) {}
        int AddTheNumbers(int numA, int numB)
        {
            return numA + numB;
        }

    };
}
```

Notice that the class uses the ref modifier to indicate it is a garbage-collected, managed class.

An unmanaged class that performs the same functionality is implemented in MixedNativeNumber.h and looks like this:

```
namespace MixedSharedLib
{
    class __declspec(dllexport) CMixedNativeNumber
    {
    public:
        CMixedNativeNumber(void)  {}
        ~CMixedNativeNumber(void)  {}
        int AddTheNumbers(int numA, int numB);
    };

}
```

This class includes the __declspec(dllexport) attribute in order to export this class from the DLL, making it available to other native C++ code.

Note To keep this example code as simple as possible, we are directly including the __declspec(dllexport) here. However, the Visual Studio wizards for adding new C++ projects generate a sequence of #define statements that make importing and exporting functions easier.

For example, for this MixedSharedLib project, these #define statements were generated in the stdafx.h file:

```
#ifdef MixedSharedLib_EXPORTS
#define MixedSharedLib_API __declspec(dllexport)
#else
#define MixedSharedLib_API __declspec(dllimport)
#endif
```

To use these #define statements, you add MixedSharedLib_API instead of __declspec(dllexport) to your function declarations. This permits the use of the same header file for the project that exports the function as well as those that import it.

The implementation of the AddTheNumbers method in the .cpp file looks like this:

```
int CMixedNativeNumber::AddTheNumbers(int numA, int numB)
{
    return numA + numB;
}
```

Note We choose to put the implementation of the AddTheNumbers method in the .cpp file rather than including it inline here in the header. This demonstrates the traditional way that C++ class implementations are done. Only in rare cases can a class be fully implemented in the header. Most nontrivial classes are implemented in the .cpp file rather than the header. This approach also requires us to include the library containing the exported class when we include this header file.

After building the project, the following files are available for our use:

- MixedSharedLib.dll: The mixed assembly that can be referenced and used by managed or unmanaged projects

- MixedSharedLib.lib: The library of exported classes that can be included in the linker step of other unmanaged projects

Starting with the managed side of things, we can create a Visual Basic .NET (VB.NET) project to test the managed class. We implement the test code like this:

```
Dim obj As MixedSharedLib.MixedNumber
obj = New MixedSharedLib.MixedNumber()
Dim result As Integer _
    = obj.AddTheNumbers(111, 222)
Console.WriteLine("MixedNumber result: {0}", _
    result)
```

Prior to building this Visual Basic code, we make sure that we add a reference to the MixedSharedLib.dll assembly.

When we execute this test, the results look like this:

```
MixedNumber result: 333
```

Now that we've successfully used this mixed assembly from .NET code, we'll do the same thing from unmanaged code. We write this C++ code that uses the unmanaged class from our mixed assembly:

```
//test the mixed unmanaged/managed class
MixedSharedLib::CMixedNativeNumber obj;
int result = obj.AddTheNumbers(55, 66);

//show the results
_cprintf("Mixed assembly result: %i \r\n",
    result);
```

In order for this to build, we need to reference the header file with a #include "MixedNativeNumber.h" statement. We also need to add the MixedSharedLib.lib file to the linker input of this project.

When we execute this code, the results look like this:

Mixed assembly result: 121

The following example uses the #pragma directives to mix managed and unmanaged code within the same source file. We start by adding this code to the same MixedSharedLib project:

```
using namespace System;

namespace MixedSharedLib
{
    #pragma unmanaged

    //unmanaged helper function
    int ReturnHighest(int numA, int numB)
    {
        //return the higher number
        return (numA > numB ? numA : numB);
    }

    #pragma managed

    //managed class
    public ref class MixedWithHelper
    {
    public:
        MixedWithHelper(void) {}

        //find the length of the longest string
        int GetLongestStringLength(String^ paramA,
            String^ paramB, String^ paramC)
        {
            //use the unmanaged helper function
            int highest = ReturnHighest(
                paramA->Length, paramB->Length);
            highest = ReturnHighest(
                highest, paramC->Length);

            return highest;
        }
    };
}
```

After the first #pragma unmanaged directive, we implement a helper function that returns the greater of two numbers. We then implement the managed test class after the #pragma managed directive. Without this second directive, the compiler will flag the class with a number of errors, since we previously told it that the code was unmanaged.

The class is clearly managed since it includes the ref modifier and also uses the System. String class as a method parameter.

To test this class and its unmanaged helper, we write this VB.NET code:

```
Dim helperObj As MixedSharedLib.MixedWithHelper
helperObj = New MixedSharedLib.MixedWithHelper()
Dim length As Integer _
    = helperObj.GetLongestStringLength("aaa", "BBBB", "cc")
Console.WriteLine("Longest String Length {0}", _
    length)
```

When we run this code, we see these results:

```
Longest String Length 4
```

As mentioned earlier, the /clr compiler option has several variations. Each one applies a different set of restrictions on what you are allowed to code within a project. For interop between managed and unmanaged code, the /clr option that produces a mixed assembly is the most useful. Table 4-1 presents a summary of the available options.

Table 4-1. *lclr Compiler Options*

Option	Description	Notes
/clr	Mixed assembly	Produces an assembly that can contain managed and unmanaged code and data. The assembly is capable of being referenced from .NET code as well as linked into native C++ code.
/clr:pure	Managed-only assembly	Produces an assembly containing only managed code compiled to Microsoft Intermediate Language (MSIL). The assembly can be referenced from any .NET code, but cannot be used from native C++ code. The assembly is allowed to use unmanaged data types, but only managed functions and methods are allowed.
/clr:safe	Managed-only assembly enabled for code access security	Produces an assembly containing only managed code compiled to MSIL. This type of assembly can be checked at runtime to determine if it meets the security settings in effect. Use of any native data types and methods is prohibited. No interop features are allowed.
/clr:oldSyntax	Managed Extensions for C++	Enables the older Managed Extensions for C++ syntax that was used prior to Visual Studio 2005.

Related Information

See recipe 4-1 (Using C++ Classes).

4-3. Detecting Compile-Time Traits

Problem

When developing mixed assemblies containing managed and unmanaged code, it would be helpful to know if a type is managed or unmanaged. Is there a way to determine this within code? Can a class determine if it has been compiled within a mixed assembly?

Solution

The _MANAGED preprocessor macro can be used to write conditional code based on the presence or absence of the /clr compiler option, for example:

```
#ifdef _MANAGED
    //this code is compiled if /clr is set
#else
    //this code is compiled if /clr is not set
#endif
```

This code allows you to write one set of shared code that can be compiled in managed and native C++ environments. Only the code that is appropriate for each environment will be included when the source is compiled.

Visual C++ has built-in compiler support that helps you to determine various traits about a type. For example, this code checks the CMyClass class to determine if it is an unmanaged class or struct:

```
if (__is_class(CMyClass))
{
    //class is unmanaged so do something
}
```

This code checks if the type is a managed class:

```
if (__is_ref_class(CMyClass))
{
    //class is unmanaged so do something
}
```

A fairly large number of these built-in checks can be used to determine various traits of a type. Some other examples are as follows:

- __has_copy checks for a copy constructor.

- __is_abstract checks if the type is abstract.

- __is_delegate checks if the type is a delegate.

- __is_base_of determines if the type is derived from another specified type.

Note that all these checks begin with a double underscore. For the complete list, please consult the full Microsoft documentation.

Tip You can either search for any of the checks just shown in order to find the complete list or look for the MSDN topic "Compiler Support for Type Traits."

One important distinction is that these built-in checks provide compile-time support only. This means they will only work with types that can be fully resolved at compile time. You can't pass an instance of an object at runtime to one of these routines.

How It Works

The _MANAGED macro and the compile-time support for type traits obviously have limited use. You won't need to use them to develop most types of applications. However, if you are developing a set of class libraries that you want to share between managed and unmanaged code, they may be useful.

In the example code that follows, we implement code that conditionally compiles based on the presence or absence of the /clr option. While this is a manufactured example, it does demonstrate the possibilities that are available to us.

We start by writing this code:

```
namespace MixedSharedLib
{
    class CSharedUtility
    {
    public:

        //conditionally compiled code based on the presence
        //or absence of the /clr compiler option
        #ifdef _MANAGED
        static int GetStringLength(String^ stringToCheck)
        {
            return stringToCheck->Length;
        }
        #else
        static int GetStringLength(wchar_t* stringToCheck)
        {
            return (int)wcslen(stringToCheck);
        }
        #endif
    };
}
```

To make this code easier to test, we place it into a header file named SharedUtility.h. This allows us to include this header in both unmanaged and mixed C++ projects. The code implements a method that returns the length of a string. The method is implemented differently for the managed and unmanaged environments. Only one implementation will be compiled in any given project, depending on the setting of the /clr compiler option.

We can test this method with this unmanaged code:

```
#include <conio.h>
#include "SharedUtility.h"

using namespace MixedSharedLib;

int _tmain(int argc, _TCHAR* argv[])
{
    //call the non-clr version of the string length method
    int result = CSharedUtility::GetStringLength(L"abc");

    //show the results
    _cprintf("String length from Native call: %i \r\n",
        result);

    return 0;
}
```

This code is included in a project that does not specify the /clr compiler option. When the code executed, we see these results:

```
String length from Native call: 3
```

We can call this same method from a mixed project that does include the /clr option. Here is a managed class that uses this same method and also demonstrates the use of the compile-time type traits:

```
#include "MixedNumber.h"
#include "MixedNativeNumber.h"
#include "SharedUtility.h"

namespace MixedSharedLib
{
    public ref class TraitChecker
    {
    public:

        //determine if the type is a native c++ class
        static bool IsClass(int request)
        {
            bool result = false;
            switch(request)
            {
                case 1:
                    result = __is_class(MixedNumber);
                    break;
                case 2:
```

```
                    result = __is_class(CMixedNativeNumber);
                    break;
            }
            return result;
        }


        //determine if the type is a ref managed class
        static bool IsRefClass(int request)
        {
            bool result = false;
            switch(request)
            {
                case 1:
                    result = __is_ref_class(MixedNumber);
                    break;
                case 2:
                    result = __is_ref_class(CMixedNativeNumber);
                    break;
            }
            return result;
        }


        //has the /clr option been set?
        static String^ IsClrOptionSet(void)
        {
            #ifdef _MANAGED
                return "Clr option set";
            #else
                return "Native code only";
            #endif
        }


        //call the /clr version of the string length method
        static int GetStringLength(String^ str)
        {
            return CSharedUtility::GetStringLength(str);
        }
    };
}
```

In addition to calling the managed version of the GetStringLength method, we use __is_class to determine if a couple of classes are unmanaged. Likewise, we use __is_ref_class to determine if the same classes are managed. The MixedNumber and CMixedNativeNumber classes that we check were introduced in recipe 4-2 (Mixing Managed and Unmanaged Code).

Since this is a managed class, we can execute it from this Visual Basic .NET (VB.NET) code:

```
'check the traits of each class
Console.WriteLine( _
    "IsClass MixedNumber: {0}", _
    MixedSharedLib.TraitChecker.IsClass(1))
Console.WriteLine( _
    "IsClass CMixedNativeNumber: {0}", _
    MixedSharedLib.TraitChecker.IsClass(2))
Console.WriteLine( _
    "IsRefClass MixedNumber: {0}", _
    MixedSharedLib.TraitChecker.IsRefClass(1))
Console.WriteLine( _
    "IsRefClass CMixedNativeNumber: {0}", _
    MixedSharedLib.TraitChecker.IsRefClass(2))

'determine if the /clr option has been set
Console.WriteLine( _
    "IsClrOptionSet: {0}", _
    MixedSharedLib.TraitChecker.IsClrOptionSet())

'call the /clr version of the string length method
Console.WriteLine("GetStringLength {0}", _
    MixedSharedLib.TraitChecker.GetStringLength("abcdefg"))
```

Here are the results that we see when the test is executed:

```
IsClass MixedNumber: False
IsClass CMixedNativeNumber: True
IsRefClass MixedNumber: True
IsRefClass CMixedNativeNumber: False
IsClrOptionSet: Clr option set
GetStringLength 7
```

Related Information

See the MSDN topic "Compiler Support for Type Traits" and recipe 4-2 (Mixing Managed and Unmanaged Code).

4-4. Using Managed Objects from Unmanaged Code

Problem

Managed C++ code can use unmanaged code but does that work in reverse? Is there a way that unmanaged C++ code can use an instance of a managed object?

Solution

It is illegal for unmanaged code to directly hold a handle to a managed object. If the handle-to-object syntax is used (e.g., String^, MyClass^), a compiler error will result. However, this doesn't mean that you are unable to reference managed objects.

To reference a managed object, you need to convert the handle to the managed object into a pointer that the unmanaged code can hold and reference. You can do this using the static methods of the GCHandle structure.

To make this task easier, Microsoft provides the type-safe gcroot template. Under the covers, this template uses the static methods of GCHandle to convert the object reference to a void* handle. However, the real magic of gcroot is the way it provides seamless access to members of the underlying managed class.

As long as the gcroot is in scope, garbage collection of the managed object is prohibited. When the gcroot goes out of scope, the Free method of the GCHandle is called, permitting garbage collection to take place if there are no other references to the object.

To use this template, you declare a variable in unmanaged code like this:

```
gcroot<ManagedType^> myVariable;
```

You replace ManagedType with any managed type, including .NET Framework types such as System::String or types of your own creation.

Assume that ManagedType is defined like this:

```
public ref class ManagedType
{
public:
    void foo();
    int bar(int);
};
```

Using the gcroot variable just defined, you are able to reference the members of the ManagedType object using the overloaded -> operator like this:

```
myVariable->foo();
int result = myVariable->bar(123);
```

When using a GCHandle, it is important to free the underlying object reference when you have finished with it. Fortunately, gcroot takes care of this housekeeping for you, calling GCHandle::Free() when the variable goes out of scope.

How It Works

Using managed types from unmanaged code in this way provides an easier migration path for existing C++ code. For example, you might have a large set of unmanaged C++ classes that you need to use for the foreseeable future. You can't instantly rewrite all of them as managed code. However, you might want to slowly migrate bits and pieces of functionality to managed C++ classes, perhaps sharing them with other .NET languages. The gcroot template shown here enables the unmanaged classes to access the pieces that we refactor into managed code. It also allows you to use features of the .NET Framework that are not available in unmanaged code.

The example that follows illustrates the use of the gcroot template. As is always the case when using any managed code, we must set the /clr compiler option for the project. This produces a mixed assembly capable of supporting managed and unmanaged code.

We start with a managed class that is implemented like this in header file ManagedAccount.h:

```
using namespace System;

namespace MixedSharedLib
{
    //managed account class
    public ref class ManagedAccount
    {
    public:
        ManagedAccount(int acctNbr, double balance,
            String^ name)
        {
            m_AcctNumber = acctNbr;
            m_Balance    = balance;
            m_Name       = name;
        }

        property int AcctNumber
        {
            int get(){return m_AcctNumber;}
        }

        property String^ Name
        {
            String^ get(){return m_Name;}
            void set(String^ value)
            {
                m_Name = value;
            }
        }

        property double Balance
        {
            double get(){return m_Balance;}
            void set(double value)
            {
                m_Balance = value;
            }
        }

        property Boolean PastDue
        {
            Boolean get(){return m_PastDue;}
            void set(Boolean value)
```

```
            {
                m_PastDue = value;
            }
        }
    }

private:
    int     m_AcctNumber;
    String^ m_Name;
    double  m_Balance;
    Boolean m_PastDue;
};

}
```

This class is rather unremarkable. It defines four member variables along with properties to access them. The use of the ref modifier, the System::String type, and the property keyword all confirm that this is a managed class.

Now we *attempt* to implement an unmanaged class that makes use of gcroot to access this managed class.

Caution The following code does not compile as shown. Further modifications to the code are discussed shortly.

```
#include "ManagedAccount.h"
#include <gcroot.h>

#pragma unmanaged
namespace MixedSharedLib
{
    //unmanaged processing class
    class CNativeBalanceProcessor
    {
    public:
        void SetLateFee(double lateFee)
        {
            m_LateFee = lateFee;
        }

        void CalcNewBalance(gcroot<ManagedAccount^> acctObj)
        {
            //this will not compile due to error C3642
            if (acctObj->Balance > 500.00)
            {
                acctObj->Balance += m_LateFee;
```

```
                acctObj->PastDue  = true;
            }

        }

    private:
        double    m_LateFee;
    };
}
```

#pragma managed

We want the ability to create an instance of this unmanaged class and then pass ManagedAccount objects to the CalcNewBalance method. This method will modify the Balance and PastDue properties of the managed object if necessary.

We have the right idea, but this code doesn't compile. We receive the error "C3642 cannot call a function with __clrcall calling convention from unmanaged code" on all of the property references. The problem is that this class is implemented in a section of code marked with #pragma unmanaged.

Use of this #pragma causes the compiler to generate native C++ output (Common Object File Format or COFF) rather than Microsoft Intermediate Language (MSIL). Classes in a #pragma managed section of code are compiled to MSIL and use the __clrcall calling convention. Native C++ code (#pragma unmanaged) is incapable of calling into the __clrcall methods. We don't have a problem passing the object to this method, but do when we attempt to use it.

One solution is to remove the #pragma unmanaged from this code, causing it to be compiled to MSIL along with our fully managed class. Then the preceding code would work.

Another solution is to write a thin intermediate class that acts as an unmanaged wrapper for the managed class. This is the solution that we will demonstrate with the following code.

We implement our wrapper class like this, placing it in the same ManagedAccount.h header file as the ManagedAccount class that it wraps:

```
#include <gcroot.h>
using namespace System;

namespace MixedSharedLib
{
    //unmanaged wrapper for managed class
    public class CManagedAccountWrapper
    {
    public:
        CManagedAccountWrapper(gcroot<ManagedAccount^> obj)
        {
            m_Account = obj;
        }
        //property accessor methods
        double getBalance()
```

```
        {
            return m_Account->Balance;
        }
        void setBalance(double value)
        {
            m_Account->Balance = value;
        }
        void setPastDue(bool value)
        {
            m_Account->PastDue = value;
        }

    private:
        gcroot<ManagedAccount^> m_Account;
    };
}
```

This code doesn't include any #pragma directive, so by default it is compiled to MSIL along with our ManagedAccount class. However, this doesn't make it a managed class. It is still an unmanaged class in all respects. The only significant difference is that MSIL is generated.

The constructor takes a ManagedAccount object reference wrapped in a gcroot template. This allows the class to access the properties of ManagedAccount using the -> operator. Individual get or set methods are implemented for only those properties that we wish to expose to unmanaged code.

We can now revise our original unmanaged class to use this wrapper instead of ManagedAccount directly:

```
#include "ManagedAccount.h"

#pragma unmanaged
namespace MixedSharedLib
{
    //unmanaged processing class
    class CNativeBalanceProcessor
    {
    public:
        void SetLateFee(double lateFee)
        {
            m_LateFee = lateFee;
        }

        //use and modify properties of the managed object
        void CalcNewBalance(CManagedAccountWrapper acctObj)
        {
            //uses the wrapper to access the underlying
            //managed object
            if (acctObj.getBalance() > 500.00)
```

```
            {
                acctObj.setBalance(
                acctObj.getBalance() + m_LateFee);
                acctObj.setPastDue(true);
            }
        }

    private:
        double    m_LateFee;
    };
}
```

#pragma managed

Now this class compiles without any problems. We don't have to use gcroot in this class since CManagedAccountWrapper is itself an unmanaged class.

Here is the code that tests these classes:

```
//create the unmanaged processor class
CNativeBalanceProcessor processor;
processor.SetLateFee(1.95);

//create a managed account object
ManagedAccount^ account
    = gcnew ManagedAccount(1001, 501.99, "Account One");
//pass the managed obj to the unmanaged method
processor.CalcNewBalance(CManagedAccountWrapper(account));
_cprintf("Results for %i, %s is: %5.2f PastDue: %i \r\n",
    account->AcctNumber, account->Name,
    account->Balance, account->PastDue);

//try a second account object
account
    = gcnew ManagedAccount(2002, 499.95, "Another Acct");
processor.CalcNewBalance(CManagedAccountWrapper(account));
_cprintf("Results for %i, %s is: %5.2f PastDue: %i \r\n",
    account->AcctNumber, account->Name,
    account->Balance, account->PastDue);
```

We first create an instance of the CNativeBalanceProcessor class (unmanaged), and set the late fee to $1.95. Next, we create an instance of a ManagedAccount object (managed). The account is wrapped in a CManagedAccountWrapper (unmanaged using gcroot) and passed to the CalcNewBalance method. After displaying the results, we repeat the process with another managed account object.

When the code is executed, the results look like this:

```
Results for 1001, Account One is: 503.94 PastDue: 1
Results for 2002, Another Acct is: 499.95 PastDue: 0
```

Based on the results, it is clear that the properties of the managed object were both retrieved and updated by the unmanaged code.

■Note What exactly is the CManagedAccountWrapper class? It is within the section of code compiled as MSIL, but it isn't a value or ref managed class. What type of code can we include in such a class?

CManagedAccountWrapper is an unmanaged class, but it is capable of using managed classes, including .NET Framework classes. It can create instances of managed objects, but only within the scope of a method. It cannot hold a reference to a managed object as a member variable, unless it is wrapped as a gcroot.

As we've seen, CManagedAccountWrapper can be used by unmanaged code—even code compiled with the #pragma unmanaged directive. However, it cannot be used by other .NET languages at all. Even though it is compiled to MSIL, it is not a garbage-collected, managed class. To implement a managed class, we need to use the ref or value class modifiers.

Related Information

See recipe 4-2 (Mixing Managed and Unmanaged Code).

4-5. Marshaling Strings

Problem

C++ Interop requires you to handle all of the marshaling duties between managed and unmanaged code. You want to know if C++ Interop provides any shortcuts to assist with this marshaling.

Solution

.NET provides static methods in the Marshal class to assist with marshaling of string data. This includes methods such as PtrToStringUni and PtrToStringAnsi. These methods are available to all .NET languages including Visual C++.

However, Visual C++ provides another way to marshal strings that is not available to other languages. The header vcclr.h implements a method named PtrToStringChars. This method retrieves an interior pointer to the first character of a managed string. When this pointer is passed to unmanaged code, it works just like a native const pointer to wchar_t.

For example, consider the following unmanaged class, which uses wchar_t pointers:

```
#include <stdlib.h>
#include <string.h>

#pragma unmanaged
namespace MixedSharedLib
{
```

```
    //unmanaged utility class
    public class CStringUtility
    {
    public:
        //modify the string
        static wchar_t* ProcessString(
            const wchar_t* stringIn)
        {
            size_t bufSize = wcslen(stringIn) + 50;
            wchar_t* pResult = new wchar_t[bufSize];
            wcscpy_s(pResult, bufSize, stringIn);
            wcscat_s(pResult, bufSize, L"AddedString");
            return pResult;
        }
    };
}
#pragma managed
```

The code accepts a const wchar_t* as an input parameter, appends a literal to the string, and returns it.

Using the PtrToStringChars method, we can write managed code like this:

```
#include "StringUtility.h"
#include <vcclr.h>

using namespace System;
using namespace MixedSharedLib;

public ref class ManagedStrings
{
public:
    void ChangeTheString()
    {
        //get internal pointer to managed string
        pin_ptr<const wchar_t> pStr
            = PtrToStringChars(m_Target);
        //pass the pointer to the unmanaged method
        wchar_t* pNewStr
            = CStringUtility::ProcessString(pStr);
        //update the managed string with the result
        m_Target = gcnew String(pNewStr);
        //free the pointer to the new string
        delete [] pNewStr;
    }

    property String^ Target
    {
        String^ get() {return m_Target;}
```

```
        void set(String^ value) {m_Target = value;}
    }

private:
    String^ m_Target;
};
```

The code uses PtrToStringChars to obtain the interior pointer to a managed string object. It uses the pin_ptr keyword to pin the memory for the interior pointer. Pinning the memory prevents the string from being moved within the garbage-collected heap. When the pin_ptr goes out of scope, the memory is released from the pin and can be moved in memory if necessary.

The pinned pointer is then passed to the unmanaged ProcessString method. The result of that method call is a new string that is returned as a native wchar_t*. We then create a new System::String object that contains a copy of the returned wchar_t* string. Finally, we remember to free the memory for the native string that was returned.

Code to test all of this looks like this:

```
ManagedStrings^ obj = gcnew ManagedStrings();
obj->Target = "abcdef";
Console::WriteLine("String prior to call: {0}",
    obj->Target);

obj->ChangeTheString();

Console::WriteLine("String after call: {0}",
    obj->Target);
```

We get these results from executing the test:

```
String prior to call: abcdef
String after call: abcdefAddedString
```

How It Works

To marshal managed strings to ANSI, you need to use the static methods of the Marshal class. PtrToStringChars won't work in this situation.

Note PtrToStringChars works only when marshaling to wide (Unicode) strings. This makes sense, since the underlying string data held within a System::String object is Unicode. Since we're directly accessing this data via the interior pointer, no Unicode-to-ANSI conversions are possible.

The example that follows demonstrates how to marshal ANSI strings using the Marshal class. We start with the unmanaged method that accepts a char* instead of wchar_t*:

```
//the ansi version
static char* ProcessString(
    const char* stringIn)
{
    size_t bufSize = strlen(stringIn) + 50;
    char* pResult = new char[bufSize];
    strcpy_s(pResult, bufSize, stringIn);
    strcat_s(pResult, bufSize, "AddedANSIString");
    return pResult;
}
```

This method is added to the same unmanaged CStringUtility class just shown.

The managed method that calls the ANSI version of ProcessString is implemented like this:

```
using namespace System::Runtime::InteropServices;

void ChangeTheStringAnsi()
{
    //marshal the managed string to unmanaged Ansi
    IntPtr pStrPtr
        = Marshal::StringToHGlobalAnsi(m_Target);
    const char* pStr
        = static_cast<char*>(pStrPtr.ToPointer());
    //pass the pointer to the unmanaged method
    char* pNewStr
        = CStringUtility::ProcessString(pStr);
    //update the managed string with the result
    m_Target = gcnew String(pNewStr);
    //free the pointer to the new string
    delete [] pNewStr;
    //free our original marshaled string
    Marshal::FreeHGlobal(pStrPtr);
}
```

This method is added to the ManagedStrings class. Looking at the code, we see that it calls Marshal::StringToHGlobalAnsi to convert the System::String instance to an ANSI string. The result of this method is an IntPtr that is then cast to a char*. When we are done with the char pointer, we use Marshal::FreeHGlobal to free the memory that we allocated.

Here is the code used to test these methods:

```
ManagedStrings^ obj = gcnew ManagedStrings();
obj->Target = "abcdef";
Console::WriteLine("String prior to call: {0}",
    obj->Target);

obj->ChangeTheStringAnsi();

Console::WriteLine("String after Ansi call: {0}",
    obj->Target);
```

When the code is executed, the results look like this:

```
String prior to call: abcdef
String after Ansi call: abcdefAddedANSIString
```

4-6. Marshaling Structures and Embedded Pointers

Problem

You need to pass a C++ struct to an unmanaged method. Some of the fields in the struct are pointers. How do you allocate and pass this struct? How do you handle the pointers embedded within the struct?

Solution

There really is no difference in passing a C++ struct between unmanaged methods and passing it between managed and unmanaged code. C++ Interop allows seamless passing of structs. An instance of the struct can be created on the stack or on the unmanaged heap and passed to the unmanaged method.

When the struct contains pointers to data rather than the data itself, you must remember to perform the necessary memory allocations prior to calling the method. Of course, you have this same requirement when using the struct entirely within unmanaged code.

For a simple example, consider this unmanaged class along with the struct that it uses:

```cpp
#pragma unmanaged
namespace MixedSharedLib
{
    //unmanaged struct
    struct IntSummary
    {
        int*  intArray;       //pointer to int array
        int   arrayCount;
        long* sum;            //pointer to long
    };

    class CStructUtility
    {
    public:
        //use the unmanaged struct
        static void SumInts(IntSummary value)
        {
            long sum = 0;
            for(int i = 0; i < value.arrayCount; i++)
            {
                sum += value.intArray[i];
            }
```

```
            *(value.sum) = sum;
        }
    };
}
#pragma managed
```

The IntSummary struct contains two fields that are pointers to data. This means we need to allocate memory for these fields before passing the struct to the SumInts method. This method calculates a total of all elements in the array and returns it in the sum field.

The managed code to use this method looks like this:

```
//initialize the unmanaged struct
IntSummary intSum;
intSum.arrayCount   = 5;
intSum.intArray     = new int[intSum.arrayCount];
intSum.sum          = new long;
*intSum.sum         = 0;
for(int i = 0; i < intSum.arrayCount; i++)
{
    intSum.intArray[i]   = i;
}


//call the unmanaged method, passing the struct
CStructUtility::SumInts(intSum);
Console::WriteLine("Unmanaged sum of ints (stack) {0}",
    *(intSum.sum));
//free any memory that we allocated
delete [] intSum.intArray;
delete intSum.sum;
```

As shown in the preceding code, we create an instance of the IntSummary struct on the stack. We then initialize the fields in the struct, allocating memory for the pointer fields. Also note that after we have finished with the struct, we need to free any memory that we allocated. In this case, that includes the pointer fields in the struct, but not the struct itself.

When this code is executed, we see these results:

```
Unmanaged sum of ints (stack) 10
```

How It Works

To complete the example, we can rewrite the code such that the struct is allocated on the unmanaged heap instead of the stack. We can change the SumInts method to accept a pointer to the struct. The revised code looks like this:

```
static void SumInts(IntSummary* value)
{
    long sum = 0;
    for(int i = 0; i < value->arrayCount; i++)
    {
```

```
        sum += value->intArray[i];
    }
    *(value->sum) = sum;
}
```

Our managed code to test the method now allocates the struct on the unmanaged heap:

```
//initialize the unmanaged struct
IntSummary* pIntSum     = new IntSummary();
pIntSum->arrayCount     = 5;
pIntSum->intArray       = new int[pIntSum->arrayCount];
pIntSum->sum            = new long;
*(pIntSum->sum)         = 0;
for(int i = 0; i < pIntSum->arrayCount; i++)
{
    pIntSum->intArray[i]    = i;
}
```

```
//call the unmanaged method, passing the struct
CStructUtility::SumInts(pIntSum);
Console::WriteLine("Unmanaged sum of ints (heap)  {0}",
    *(pIntSum->sum));
//free any memory that we allocated
delete [] pIntSum->intArray;
delete pIntSum->sum;
delete pIntSum;
```

This test produces the expected results:

Unmanaged sum of ints (heap) 10

The major benefit in using C++ Interop is the reuse of the unmanaged C++ code. In this case, you can easily use the unmanaged C++ struct. You are not required to implement a matching version of the struct in managed code, as is necessary when using PInvoke.

However, although it isn't necessary in this case, it is possible to pass a managed version of the struct to this unmanaged method. To see how this is done, we can define the managed struct like this:

```
public value struct ManagedIntSummary
{
    int*  intArray;         //pointer to int array
    int   arrayCount;
    long* sum;              //pointer to long
};
```

We use a value struct here, but a ref struct would work the same way.

Since we will allocate this struct on the managed heap, we need to include additional code to marshal it to unmanaged memory. Our revised code now looks like this:

```
//initialize the managed struct
ManagedIntSummary^ pManIntSum
    = gcnew ManagedIntSummary();
pManIntSum->arrayCount  = 5;
pManIntSum->intArray    = new int[pManIntSum->arrayCount];
pManIntSum->sum         = new long;
*(pManIntSum->sum)      = 0;
for(int i = 0; i < pManIntSum->arrayCount; i++)
{
    pManIntSum->intArray[i]    = i;
}


//get a pointer for the managed struct
IntPtr pManPtr
    = Marshal::AllocHGlobal(sizeof(ManagedIntSummary));
Marshal::StructureToPtr(pManIntSum, pManPtr, true);
//cast to the unmanaged struct type
IntSummary* pUnmanagedPtr
    = static_cast<IntSummary*>(pManPtr.ToPointer());

//call the unmanaged method, passing the
//pointer to the managed struct
CStructUtility::SumInts(pUnmanagedPtr);
Console::WriteLine("Unmanaged sum of ints (managed) {0}",
    *(pManIntSum->sum));
//free any memory that we allocated
delete [] pManIntSum->intArray;
delete pManIntSum->sum;
Marshal::FreeHGlobal(pManPtr);
```

After creating an instance of the struct, we initialize the individual fields, including allocating memory for the pointers. Notice that even though this is a managed struct, the pointer fields that it contains are unmanaged. Therefore, we use the new keyword to allocate these pointers within the unmanaged heap. Using gcnew to allocate storage on the garbage-collected heap would be incorrect.

We then use the AllocHGlobal method of the Marshal class to allocate unmanaged memory large enough to hold a copy of our struct. The StructureToPtr method copies the managed structure to the unmanaged memory. After some necessary casting, we can call the unmanaged method.

When we have completed our work, we free the memory we allocated. The Marshal::FreeHGlobal method frees the memory that was allocated by AllocHGlobal.

An interesting point is that we are not using the Marshal::PtrToStructure method. Normally, we would need to execute this method to marshal the unmanaged structure back to managed memory. However, in this case, the only data that we care about is the sum field. Since that field was a pointer to memory allocated on the unmanaged heap, its location in memory hasn't changed due to the PtrToStructure call. We are able to reference the updated total using the original pointer in our managed struct.

When we execute this code, the results look like this:

```
Unmanaged sum of ints (managed) 10
```

Related Information

See recipes 4-4 (Using Managed Objects from Unmanaged Code) and 4-5 (Marshaling Strings).

4-7. Handling Callbacks with C++ Interop

Problem

An unmanaged C++ method you are using requires a callback function. You want to find out whether it is possible to perform a callback into managed C++ code, and, if so, how it is done.

Solution

Callbacks are the general mechanism that permits a called function to invoke another function specified by the caller. This technique is typically used where the called function must return an unknown amount of repeating data to the caller, or where the called function initiates an action that will complete at an unknown time in the future.

In the unmanaged world, callbacks are implemented using function pointers. In the .NET world, callbacks are handled as delegates. Delegates serve the same basic purpose as callbacks, but they are object-oriented and type-safe.

C++ Interop allows you to use either approach when handling callbacks from unmanaged code. The general approach that you use depends on a number of factors. To summarize the available options, you can handle a callback from an unmanaged method in either of these ways:

- Marshal a managed delegate to the unmanaged method.

- Implement a small, unmanaged wrapper class that handles the callback. This wrapper then forwards the callback to managed code.

To demonstrate the first option, consider this unmanaged class that uses a callback:

```
#include <wchar.h>

#pragma unmanaged
namespace MixedSharedLib
{
    //define the callback function using the project
    //default of __cdecl
    typedef void (*CallbackFunc)
        (long value, wchar_t* msg, int length);

    class CCallbackUtility
    {
    public:
```

```
        //method that does a callback
        void DoTheCallbacks(CallbackFunc pFunc)
        {
            if (pFunc)
            {
                for(int i = 0; i < 5; i++)
                {
                    wchar_t* pMsg = new wchar_t[20];
                    _swprintf_p(pMsg, 20, L"Msg #%i", i);
                    //do the callback to managed code
                    (*pFunc)(i, pMsg, (int)wcslen(pMsg));
                    delete [] pMsg;
                }
            }
        }
    };
}
#pragma managed
```

This class is implemented entirely in the header file CallbackUtility.h in a C++ project named MixedSharedLib. The project uses the default calling convention of Cdecl. The typedef named CallbackFunc defines the type of the callback function. As we can see, the function takes a long, a wchar_t*, and an int, and returns void. When the DoTheCallbacks method is called, a pointer to the callback function is passed in as the only argument. The code then executes the callback method a set number of times, each time passing the expected set of parameters.

To handle this callback from managed code, we implement a delegate and a managed class in C++ that are defined like this in a header file, CallbacksManaged.h:

```
using namespace System::Runtime::InteropServices;

//managed class that is used for unmanaged callbacks

//managed delegate
[UnmanagedFunctionPointer(CallingConvention::Cdecl)]
public delegate void CallbackDelegate(
    long value, wchar_t* msg, int length);

public ref class CallbackManaged
{
public:
    void DoCallTest(void);
private:
    //the target of the callbacks
    void ReturnTheAnswer(long value, wchar_t* msg, int length);
};
```

The delegate named CallbackDelegate uses the same set of parameters defined by the unmanaged typedef. Since the unmanaged function uses the Cdecl calling convention, we need to apply the UnmanagedFunctionPointer attribute to the delegate. When we set

CallingConvention::Cdecl for this attribute, C++ Interop uses a calling convention that correctly matches the unmanaged callback function.

The two methods of the managed class are implemented this way:

```
#include "CallbackUtility.h"
#include "CallbacksManaged.h"

using namespace System;
using namespace System::Runtime::InteropServices;
using namespace MixedSharedLib;

void CallbackManaged::DoCallTest(void)
{
    //create a managed delegate pointing to a method
    CallbackDelegate^ cbDelegate = gcnew CallbackDelegate(
        this, &CallbackManaged::ReturnTheAnswer);
    //prevent garbage collection of the delegate
    GCHandle gchDelegate = GCHandle::Alloc(cbDelegate);
    //marshal the delegate to a pointer
    IntPtr pFunc
        = Marshal::GetFunctionPointerForDelegate(cbDelegate);
    //cast the pointer to what the unmanaged method expects
    CallbackFunc cbFunc
        = static_cast<CallbackFunc>(pFunc.ToPointer());
    //create an instance of the unmanaged class
    CCallbackUtility umObj;
    //execute the unmanaged test method
    umObj.DoTheCallbacks(cbFunc);
    //allow garbage collection of the delegate
    gchDelegate.Free();
}

//the managed target of the callbacks
void CallbackManaged::ReturnTheAnswer(
    long value, wchar_t* msg, int length)
{
    Console::WriteLine(
        "Callback via Delegate: {0}, {1}, {2}",
        value, gcnew String(msg), length);
}
```

Walking through the DoCallTest method, we see how the callbacks are handled. We start by creating an instance of the delegate CallbackDelegate, using the address of the ReturnTheAnswer method. We allocate a GCHandle for the delegate to prevent it from being garbage collected during the unmanaged call.

The static GetFunctionPointerForDelegate method of the Marshal class is then used to convert the managed delegate to an unmanaged pointer. The pointer is then cast to the expected unmanaged type.

Finally, we are ready to call the DoTheCallbacks method of the CCallbackUtility object. The function pointer is passed as an argument to this method. Each time a callback from unmanaged code occurs, the ReturnTheAnswer method is executed. When the DoTheCallbacks returns, we remember to free the delegate from the GCHandle. This allows garbage collection to occur for the object.

We can now test this code like this:

```cpp
#include "CallbacksManaged.h"

using namespace System;

int _tmain(int argc, _TCHAR* argv[])
{
    CallbackManaged^ cbStdCall = gcnew CallbackManaged();
    cbStdCall->DoCallTest();

    return 0;
}
```

Here are the results:

```
Callback via Delegate: 0, Msg #0, 6
Callback via Delegate: 1, Msg #1, 6
Callback via Delegate: 2, Msg #2, 6
Callback via Delegate: 3, Msg #3, 6
Callback via Delegate: 4, Msg #4, 6
```

How It Works

The alternative approach is to simply let an unmanaged class handle the unmanaged callback (the second option listed in the previous section). The example code that follows demonstrates this approach using the same unmanaged callback function.

We now declare our managed class, as well as an unmanaged wrapper class that will handle the callback. The header file (CallbacksWrapper.h) looks like this:

```cpp
#include <gcroot.h>

//managed class that will handle the callback
public ref class CallbackManagedClass
{
public:
    //method to execute during a callback
    void ReturnTheAnswer(long value, wchar_t* msg, int length);
};

//unmanaged wrapper used to direct
//callbacks to CallbackManagedClass
public class CallbackWrapper
{
```

```
public:
    static void CallUnmanagedCode(
        gcroot<CallbackManagedClass^> obj);
    static void CallbackHandler(
        long value, wchar_t* msg, int length);
private:
    static gcroot<CallbackManagedClass^> s_ManagedObj;
};
```

And here is the implementation of the classes:

```
#include <gcroot.h>
#include "CallbackUtility.h"
#include "CallbacksWrapper.h"

using namespace System;
using namespace MixedSharedLib;

//
//methods used for wrapper testing
//

//method to execute during a callback
void CallbackManagedClass::ReturnTheAnswer(
    long value, wchar_t* msg, int length)
{
    Console::WriteLine(
        "Callback via Wrapper: {0}, {1}, {2}",
        value, gcnew String(msg), length);
}

//static instance of managed object
gcroot<CallbackManagedClass^> CallbackWrapper::s_ManagedObj;

void CallbackWrapper::CallUnmanagedCode(
    gcroot<CallbackManagedClass^> obj)
{
    //save the managed object
    s_ManagedObj = obj;
    //get the address of the unmanaged callback handler
    CallbackFunc cbFunc
        = static_cast<CallbackFunc>(CallbackHandler);
    //create the unmanaged obj and run the test
    CCallbackUtility umObj;
    umObj.DoTheCallbacks(cbFunc);
}
```

```
//the target of the callbacks
// - pass through to the managed object
void CallbackWrapper::CallbackHandler(
    long value, wchar_t* msg, int length)
{
    //call the method in the managed object
    s_ManagedObj->ReturnTheAnswer(value, msg, length);
}
```

The managed class CallbackManagedClass only has a single method, ReturnTheAnswer. This method is the ultimate target of the callback from unmanaged code.

The CallbackWrapper class is our unmanaged wrapper. The CallUnmanagedCode method is used to do the prep work for the callback and initiate the call to CCallbackUtility::DoTheCallbacks. We pass an instance of our managed class to this method, wrapping it in a gcroot template. The gcroot template allows unmanaged code such as this to reference and use a managed object. This object reference is saved in a static variable, making it available to the callback method.

The code then sets up the callback the old-fashioned way without a managed delegate. After casting, the address of the CallbackHandler method is passed directly to the unmanaged DoTheCallbacks method. Each time the callback is made, the CallbackHandler code is executed. It in turn calls the ReturnTheAnswer method of our managed object.

The code needed to test this looks like this:

```
CallbackManagedClass^ cbTest
    = gcnew CallbackManagedClass();
CallbackWrapper::CallUnmanagedCode(cbTest);
```

When we execute the code, we see these results:

```
Callback via Wrapper: 0, Msg #0, 6
Callback via Wrapper: 1, Msg #1, 6
Callback via Wrapper: 2, Msg #2, 6
Callback via Wrapper: 3, Msg #3, 6
Callback via Wrapper: 4, Msg #4, 6
```

This approach works due to the way the CallbackWrapper class is compiled. Since it isn't within a section of code controlled by a #pragma unmanaged directive, it is compiled to Microsoft Intermediate Language (MSIL) rather than the native C++ format (Common Object File Format, or COFF). This allows it to call the managed ReturnTheAnswer method even though it uses the __clrcall calling convention. And since the CallbackWrapper uses the default calling convention of the project (__cdecl), CCallbackUtility is capable of calling back into the wrapper.

As shown here, the best approach may not always involve doing things the .NET way. Even though we had to write an additional wrapper class, this second example is a viable and simple alternative.

Related Information

See recipes 4-4 (Using Managed Objects from Unmanaged Code), 4-2 (Mixing Managed and Unmanaged Code), and 3-3 (Handling Callbacks).

4-8. Using C++ As a Custom COM Wrapper

Problem

You have a number of COM components that you would like to use from .NET code. Since unmanaged C++ code can easily use these components, you need to know if the same holds true for managed C++. Does C++ Interop allow use of COM?

Solution

The usual way to use COM components from managed code is to generate a COM interop library. You do this by directly referencing the COM component in Visual Studio, or by executing the TlbImp utility.

Note Chapter 5 of this book focuses on the use of COM components from .NET. The use of a COM component is covered here since C++ Interop provides an alternative to the interop procedures covered in Chapter 5.

When an interop library is generated, a class called a Runtime Callable Wrapper (RCW) is created. This wrapper contains managed definitions for all interfaces and classes defined by the COM component or type library. Each RCW includes all of the properties and methods defined by the component. To use the COM component, the managed code creates an instance of the RCW and calls the methods of the COM object for you. The RCW acts as a proxy to the COM component, managing the reference counting for the COM object.

All of that works great, but C++ Interop provides an alternative. C++ Interop allows direct use of COM components from a managed class. This means you can write a small, managed C++ wrapper class that accesses the COM component. Since the wrapper is a managed class, it can be accessed from other .NET code without any special considerations. Microsoft calls this wrapper a *Custom* Runtime Callable Wrapper (CRCW).

As an example, here is a COM method implemented in a C++ Active Template Library (ATL) component:

```
#include "stdafx.h"
#include "DniComFromCppObj.h"
#include <comutil.h>

STDMETHODIMP CDniComFromCppObj::ModifyString(
    BSTR inParam, BSTR* outParam)
{
    _bstr_t workBSTR
        = _bstr_t(inParam) + _bstr_t(L"AddedThis");
    *outParam = workBSTR;
    return S_OK;
}
```

The method appends a literal to a BSTR that is passed as an input argument and returns the result. The IDL defines the COM interface like this:

```
interface IDniComFromCppObj : IDispatch{
    [id(1), helpstring("method ModifyString")]
    HRESULT ModifyString([in] BSTR inParam,
        [out,retval] BSTR* outParam);
};
```

Using C++ Interop, we can develop a managed wrapper this way:

```
//create a _com_ptr_t smart pointer for the com component
#import "DniComFromCpp.tlb" no_namespace

using namespace System;
using namespace System::Runtime::InteropServices;

namespace ComAccessLib
{
    //implement a managed wrapper for the COM component
    public ref class CppComWrapper
    {
    public:
        String^ ProcessString(String^ value)
        {
            String^ result    = String::Empty;
            //create an instance of the COM object
            IDniComFromCppObjPtr comObj(
                _uuidof(DniComFromCppObj));
            if (!comObj)
            {
                return L"Unable to create COM instance";
            }

            //marshal the System::String to a BSTR
            IntPtr pBSTR = Marshal::StringToBSTR(value);
            BSTR inBSTR
                = static_cast<BSTR>(pBSTR.ToPointer());
            //make the COM method call
            _bstr_t pResultBSTR
                = comObj->ModifyString(inBSTR);
            //cleanup
            Marshal::FreeBSTR(pBSTR);
            result
                = gcnew System::String((wchar_t*)pResultBSTR);
            return result;
        }
    };
}
```

There are a number of ways to use a COM component from C++. We could have used the native COM methods (e.g., CoCreateInstance), but we opted to use the _com_ptr_t smart pointer. The #import statement generates a customized smart pointer based on the type library of our component.

Walking through the code, we see that an instance of the COM object is created using the smart pointer. The static Marshal::StringToBSTR method is used to create a BSTR for the managed string parameter. After the call to the ModifyString COM method, we free the BSTR that we allocated and create a managed string for the result BSTR. The resultant BSTR does not require any cleanup since we used a _bstr_t smart pointer. It will perform cleanup as it goes out of scope.

Now that we have developed the managed wrapper, we can use it from any .NET language. Here is example Visual Basic .NET (VB.NET) code that uses this class:

```
Imports ComAccessLib

Module ComAccessTest
    Sub Main()
        Dim obj As CppComWrapper _
            = New CppComWrapper()
        Dim result As String _
            = obj.ProcessString("abc123")
        Console.WriteLine( _
            "Result from COM call: {0}", result)

        'wait for input
        Console.WriteLine("Press any key to exit")
        Console.Read()
    End Sub
End Module
```

The use of COM does not require us to use any special code here. In fact, as far as this code is concerned, we're simply using a managed class named CppComWrapper. The results look like this:

```
Result from COM call: abc123AddedThis
Press any key to exit
```

How It Works

Using a generated interop library and a standard RCW to access a COM component is very easy. However, this approach does have a few disadvantages:

- A separate interop assembly is generated that must be deployed with the application.

- Managed code is generated for all interfaces, classes, and types defined in the COM type library. If you are importing a fairly large COM component, this could result in a large interop library.

- Since all COM types are generated, it is difficult to restrict the use of functionality. If a property or method is defined in the COM component, it is available to anyone using the RCW.

- A generated interop library supports only a fixed set of standard data types. If you need to handle custom data types, custom marshaling is needed.

The alternative presented here using C++ Interop solves these issues and should be considered when referencing COM components.

Related Information

See recipes 5-1 (Using COM Components from .NET) and 5-2 (Importing a Type Library).

CHAPTER 5

■ ■ ■

Using COM

Prior to the introduction of .NET, Component Object Model (COM) was the recommended framework for Windows development. COM encourages the development of discrete, reusable components rather than massive, monolithic applications. Untold numbers of COM components have been developed using Visual Basic 6.0 (VB6), Active Template Library (ATL) for Visual C++, Delphi, and other development tools. Many applications (e.g., Microsoft Office) also expose interfaces via COM that allow you to extend and control them with your own code.

Given the popularity of COM, it's only natural that Microsoft provides good interoperability between COM and .NET. The focus of this chapter is using existing COM components from managed .NET code.

Some of the terminology used for COM development is confusing and not always intuitive, so a few definitions are in order. I've tried to use this terminology consistently throughout this chapter as well as in the other COM-related chapters of this book.

- A COM *interface* is the contract that contains a group of related COM methods or properties. The interface defines the methods or properties, but does not implement them. Each interface is identified by a unique ID.

- A COM *class* is the code that implements one or more COM interfaces. It contains the concrete implementation for the methods and properties of an interface. Each COM class is identified by a unique CLSID (a GUID). COM classes can also be identified by a ProgID, which is a string name associated with the class.

- A COM *component* is the binary package that contains the code for one or more COM classes and interfaces. Think of this as the entire COM DLL that must be deployed and registered on a computer before it can be used.

- A COM *type library* (type lib, typelib, or tlb) is a file that contains the definition of a COM component. This definition includes all interfaces and classes implemented in a component along with their IDs. The type library may be packaged as part of the component DLL, or it may be a separate .tlb file.

- A COM *object* is an active instance of a COM class.

In general, using a COM component from .NET managed code involves these steps:

1. Import a COM type library to produce an interop library. The interop library contains a managed proxy class called a Runtime Callable Wrapper (RCW) for each COM class and interface in the type library.

2. Reference the interop library from the managed project.

3. Create an instance of the RCW. This creates an active instance of the COM object.

4. Use methods or properties of the RCW instance.

5. When the RCW is garbage collected, the instance of the COM object is released.

This chapter starts by examining the basics of referencing and using COM components from .NET. Recipes describe how to reference components directly from Visual Studio .NET, or how to create interop libraries using the TlbImp utility. Handling of COM events in managed code is covered in another recipe. Several recipes are dedicated to COM data types and how they are marshaled, including handling of COM Variant and array data.

Extending a COM class in managed code is discussed in one recipe, while changing the apartment model is covered in another. Performance considerations and using late binding of COM objects each have a recipe. Creating a primary interop assembly and deploying an application that uses COM interop each have a recipe.

The chapter concludes with a series of recipes covering exception and error handling for COM interop.

5-1. Using COM Components from .NET

Problem

You have a COM component that you would like to call from .NET. What steps are needed to reference and use the component?

Solution

Using a COM component from .NET code is a three-step process:

1. Reference the COM component from your .NET project.

2. Create an instance of the COM object.

3. Use methods or properties of the object.

Prior to using a COM component, you need to establish a reference to it in your .NET project. This is similar to referencing another assembly or part of the .NET Framework Class Library. Once the component is referenced, you can create an instance of the COM class and use its methods and properties.

The easiest way to create a COM reference is to use the built-in Visual Studio .NET tools, as follows:

1. Select the .NET project that needs to use the COM component.

2. Select Add Reference from the context or Project menu.

3. When the Add Reference dialog appears, select the COM tab.

4. Locate the COM component name you need to reference and select OK.

Once you've performed these steps, the selected COM component is available for use in the current project.

Note The preceding steps assume that the COM component has been registered on your development machine. Only registered components can be referenced in this way.

Once a COM component is referenced, creating and using the component is really no different than using any other .NET class. You declare a variable of the correct type, create an instance of the type, and call methods and properties on the instance.

How It Works

For example, assume that we have a COM component that is defined like this:

```
// DniSimpleCom.idl : IDL source for DniSimpleCom
//
// This file will be processed by the MIDL tool to
// produce the type library (DniSimpleCom.tlb) and marshaling code.

import "oaidl.idl";
import "ocidl.idl";

[
    object,
    uuid(DBD8268F-2570-4991-9478-39DA8B32ECE5),
    dual,
    nonextensible,
    helpstring("IDniSimpleComObj Interface"),
    pointer_default(unique)
]
interface IDniSimpleComObj : IDispatch{
    [id(1), helpstring("method AddSomeNumbers")]
    HRESULT AddSomeNumbers(
        [in] int numA, [in] int numB, [out,retval] int* result);
};
[
```

```
    uuid(439068C7-4A28-47B9-B2DE-FA955C11259B),
    version(1.0),
    helpstring("DniSimpleCom 1.0 Type Library")
]
library DniSimpleComLib
{
    importlib("stdole2.tlb");
    [
        uuid(F004EC87-EFCE-4252-B595-069311963BBB),
        helpstring("DniSimpleComObj Class")
    ]
    coclass DniSimpleComObj
    {
        [default] interface IDniSimpleComObj;
    };
};
```

The Interface Definition Language (IDL) is shown as our definition since it allows us to focus on the declaration of the component without worrying about the implementation. It also provides us with all of the type names that we will be using from our client code. If you're interested in how this sample COM component was implemented, we review those details shortly.

The first step in using this component from .NET code is to reference the component. We do that by opening the Add Reference dialog and selecting the COM tab. We scroll down to where we find DniSimpleCom in the listing of available components and select it.

When we review the project references, we now see DniSimpleComLib listed. Notice that this is the name listed in the IDL as the library name for the component. This will also be the namespace associated with the COM component.

Note Unlike .NET components and non-COM libraries, COM components must be centrally registered in order to be used. All components regardless of origin must live in the same COM registry. This means you want to avoid name collisions with other components.

For this reason, the COM components used as examples in this book all start with Dni, which stands for "Dot Net Interop." In addition to avoiding collisions with other components, this naming scheme makes it easier to find these samples within the list of components. All like-named components will be together in the list.

After referencing the COM component, we can write C# code to use it:

```csharp
using System;

using DniSimpleComLib;  //reference the interop assembly

namespace SimpleComClientTest
{
    /// <summary>
```

```
/// Reference and use a simple COM object
/// </summary>
class SimpleComClientTest
{
    /// <summary>
    /// The main entry point for the application.
    /// </summary>
    [STAThread]
    static void Main(string[] args)
    {
        //define the component using the interface and
        //create an instance
        IDniSimpleComObj comObjInterface = new DniSimpleComObj();
        int result = comObjInterface.AddSomeNumbers(1, 2);
        Console.WriteLine(
          "Call Com Object, interface: {0}", result);

        //define using the object instead of the interface
        DniSimpleComObj comObj = new DniSimpleComObj();
        result = comObj.AddSomeNumbers(1, 2);
        Console.WriteLine("Call Com Object, class: {0}", result);

         //wait for input
        Console.WriteLine("Press any key to exit");
        Console.Read();
    }
}
}
```

Looking at the code, we see that we add a using statement for DniSimpleComLib. This namespace is generated for us when we reference the COM component and is needed to reference the COM types. If the using statement were omitted, we would need to prefix all of the COM types with DniSimpleComLib.

The sample code goes on to create an instance of the COM object and call the AddSomeNumbers method. We do this twice. The first time, the instance variable is declared as IDniSimpleComObj, using the name of the interface that we saw defined in the IDL. Since COM is all about interface-based programming, it makes sense to reference the interface rather than a concrete class implementation. The second time, we declare the variable as the COM class type DniSimpleComObj.

In either case, the results look the same when the code is executed:

```
Call Com Object, interface: 3
Call Com Object, class: 3
Press any key to exit
```

The Visual Basic .NET (VB.NET) code to use the same sample COM component could be implemented like this:

```
Imports DniSimpleComLib 'reference the interop assembly

Module SimpleComClientVBTest
    Sub Main()

        'create an instance of the COM object
        Dim comObj As IDniSimpleComObj = New DniSimpleComObj
        Dim result As Integer = comObj.AddSomeNumbers(1, 2)
        Console.WriteLine("VB Call Com Object: {0}", result)

        'wait for input
        Console.WriteLine("Press any key to exit")
        Console.Read()

    End Sub

End Module
```

This time we create the object only once, declaring the local variable as the IDniSimpleComObj interface. The results look the same as the C# version:

```
VB Call Com Object: 3
Press any key to exit
```

How are we able to use a COM component so simply from .NET? The answer is that .NET and Visual Studio are performing a bit of magic for us under the covers.

When using a COM component like this, .NET uses a proxy class called a Runtime Callable Wrapper or RCW. When we create an instance of DniSimpleComObj in the example code, we are creating an instance of this RCW proxy. The job of the RCW is to marshal the calls between the .NET caller and the real COM object. It also manages the reference counting that is so important to COM.

The RCW is a singleton object. The .NET runtime creates only a single instance of each RCW per process, regardless of how many managed references there are to it. The RCW manages the reference to the COM object by incrementing the COM reference count. When the RCW is garbage collected, it decrements the reference count to the real COM object. When the COM reference count reaches zero, the COM object is finally released. Because you can't control exactly when the RCW will be garbage collected, the releasing of the COM object is nondeterministic. You normally don't know exactly when it takes place.

It is also possible to manually release the reference to the COM object by calling the static ReleaseComObject method of the Marshal class. This class is in the System.Runtime. InteropServices namespace. Although calling the ReleaseComObject method is not required, you might want to do this if the COM object holds resources that must be released quickly. Or perhaps you are using multiple COM objects that must be released in a particular sequence. The following C# code demonstrates use of the ReleaseComObject method:

```
//create an instance of the COM object
IDniSimpleComObj comObjManualRelease = new DniSimpleComObj();
int result = comObjManualRelease.AddSomeNumbers(1, 2);
Console.WriteLine("Call Com Object, manual release: {0}", result);
//manually release the Com object reference
Marshal.ReleaseComObject(comObjManualRelease);
```

When you call `ReleaseComObject` on an object, it immediately decrements the COM reference count. Once you do this, the object can no longer be used anywhere within the process. If you attempt to use a method (or property) on the released object, you will get an `AccessViolationException`.

Each RCW is specific to a particular COM component. By referencing the COM component from your project, you actually instruct Visual Studio to create a COM interop assembly for you. That assembly contains the implementation of the RCW for the selected COM component.

For our example COM component, the interop assembly is named `Interop.DniSimpleComLib.dll` and is automatically produced when the component reference is made.

Note The interop assembly is required at runtime and must be deployed along with any other .NET assemblies. The COM component that is referenced must also be deployed and properly registered.

The RCW that is generated contains all of the type definitions that you need to use the COM component. Table 5-1 presents a recap of how things were mapped in our example.

Table 5-1. *RCW Type Name Mapping*

IDL Source	Generated RCW	Example
Library name	Namespace name	DniSimpleComLib
Interface name	An Interface type	IDniSimpleComObj
Coclass name	A Class type that implements the interface	DniSimpleComObj

The purpose of this chapter (and book) isn't to demonstrate how to build unmanaged COM components. We want to focus on how to interoperate with them. However, the implementation details for the sample COM component might be worthwhile to review. Therefore, what follows is a brief description of the process used to implement the sample COM component.

The component was implemented in C++ using ATL. This combination was chosen because it provides enough power to demonstrate just about anything you'd ever need to do with COM. It uses IDL and real interfaces, allowing us to do interface-based development. Visual Studio also supports ATL with a number of wizards that make development as easy as possible. And ATL is still supported in the latest version of Visual Studio .NET.

To create the sample COM component, follow these steps:

1. Select Add ➤ New Project.

2. Under project types, select Visual C++/ATL.

3. Select the ATL Project template and enter **DniSimpleCom** as the project name.

4. At the ATL Project Wizard dialog, keep the default of "Dynamic link library," but check the "Allow merging of proxy/stub code" option in the Application Settings section. When you click Finish, a new ATL project is generated.

5. Select Add Class for the new project. Under the ATL category, select the ATL Simple Object template and click the Add button.

6. At the wizard dialog, enter **DniSimpleComObj** as the short name. Leave all of the other options at their default values. When you click the Finish button, additional code is generated for the new COM object.

7. After switching to Class view, select the interface IDniSimpleComObj and then select Add Method. (Note: If all you see is Add Function, you've selected the wrong object.)

8. At the Add Method dialog, enter a method name of **AddSomeNumbers** and add the parameters that the method will use. The method takes two int parameters that are [In] and a result int* that is defined as [out,retval]. Note that you'll need to actually type **int*** since it's not available from the combo box. When you've entered everything, click the Finish button. This will add the method to the IDL, .h, and .cpp files.

9. If you navigate to the DniSimpleComObj.cpp file, you should see the template-generated AddSomeNumbers method. Modify the method to look like this:

```
STDMETHODIMP CDniSimpleComObj::AddSomeNumbers(int numA, int numB,
        int* result)
{
    *result = numA + numB;
    return S_OK;
}
```

Once you build the project, the COM component should be registered and available for testing from .NET.

Related Information

See recipe 5-2 (Importing a Type Library).

5-2. Importing a Type Library

Problem

You want to have more control over the import process when referencing a COM component. For example, you want to control the namespace that is assigned to the component when it is imported. Is there a way to do that?

Solution

If you need more control over the COM import process, you can use the command-line TlbImp.exe utility. This type library importer utility ships with the .NET Framework SDK (included with Visual Studio .NET) and provides a number of command-line options that let you control the way an interop assembly is generated.

The input to TlbImp is any file that contains a COM type library. The output is always an interop assembly. The interop assembly contains a Runtime Callable Wrapper (RCW) customized for the COM components defined in the type library.

Once this interop assembly is generated, you add a reference to it in any .NET projects that need access to the COM component. You can then create an instance of the COM component you are interested in using the RCW.

To create an interop assembly, you execute the utility like this:

```
TlbImp MyComComponent.dll
```

The output will be an interop assembly named MyComComponentLib.dll. The namespace used for the RCW will also be MyComComponentLib.

Note Visual Studio command-line utilities should be executed from a Visual Studio .NET command prompt. There is a shortcut for this within the Visual Studio .NET Program Files tree structure off of the Start menu. Opening this command prompt sets up the environment variables needed to access the Visual Studio .NET command-line tools. Once you open this command prompt, you should be able to change to the directory where your DLL is located and execute TlbImp.

Once the interop assembly is generated, you reference it in Visual Studio instead of the COM component directly. You do this by selecting the Add References project option and browsing to the interop assembly. You haven't made this a shared assembly and added it to the global assembly cache (GAC), so it won't be available from the .NET tab. You shouldn't use the COM tab of the References dialog since you don't want Visual Studio to re-create the interop assembly. Instead, you want to use the one that you generated with TlbImp.

How It Works

Adding a reference to a COM component directly from Visual Studio .NET is simple and allows you to quickly access the COM component. However, the price of this ease of use is flexibility. When Visual Studio generates the import library for your COM component, it does so using a set of default rules. Many times you can live with those defaults; other times you can't.

In those cases where you need more control, you can use TlbImp to generate the interop assembly with the options you need. You get the same result if you import a .tlb file (type library) instead of the component DLL. For example, importing this type library results in the same MyComComponentLib.dll described earlier:

```
TlbImp MyComComponent.tlb
```

This drives home the point that you are not importing an executable COM component. Instead you are importing the type library that defines the component.

If you want to change the name of the output file or the namespace, there are options to do that, for example:

```
tlbimp MyComComponent.dll /out:MyComComponent.Interop.dll
    /namespace:MyComComponent.Interop
```

As you might have guessed, this produces an interop assembly named MyComComponent.Interop.dll with a namespace of MyComComponent.Interop.

Using the /asmversion option, you can specify the version number for the interop assembly, for example:

```
TlbImp MyComComponent.dll /asmversion:1.2.3.4
```

You can also generate a strongly named interop assembly using the /keyfile option, for example:

```
TlbImp MyComComponent.dll /keyfile:Interop.MyComComponent.snk
```

This assumes that you've first created a strong-name key file named Interop.MyComComponent.snk using the sn.exe utility.

A number of other options are available. Please consult the MSDN documentation for the complete list.

The short examples that follow demonstrate the generation and use of an interop library. The examples use the same sample COM component from recipe 5-1. For the implementation details of this COM component, please refer to that recipe.

The first example generates an interop library using the default settings:

```
TlbImp DniSimpleCom.dll
```

The output is an assembly named DniSimpleComLib.dll with a namespace of DniSimpleComLib. A reference to this interop assembly is added to a client C# project by directly browsing to its location and selecting it. Once we've done this, we are able to create the COM object with this code:

```
DniSimpleComLib.IDniSimpleComObj comIObj
    = new DniSimpleComLib.DniSimpleComObj();
int result = comIObj.AddSomeNumbers(1, 2);
Console.WriteLine("Call Com Object: {0}: {1}",
    comIObj.GetType(), result);
```

We've used the fully qualified type names here to make it clear that these types come from the interop library, but you're free to add a using statement instead.

The execution results look like this:

```
Call Com Object: DniSimpleComLib.DniSimpleComObjClass: 3
```

This second example uses the same COM component but changes the namespace and assembly name:

```
tlbimp DniSimpleCom.dll /out: DniSimpleCom.Interop.dll
    /namespace:DniSimpleCom.Interop /verbose
```

The /verbose option provides additional details during the library creation, as shown here:

```
Resolved referenced file 'DniSimpleCom.dll'
    to file 'C:\src\DniSimpleCom.dll'.
Type 'DniSimpleComObj' imported.
Type 'IDniSimpleComObj' imported.
Type library imported to C:\src\DniSimpleCom.Interop.Dll
```

To use this library, we add a reference to DniSimpleCom.Interop.dll. The C# code to call the COM object looks like this:

```
DniSimpleCom.Interop.IDniSimpleComObj comIObjNs
    = new DniSimpleCom.Interop.DniSimpleComObj();
int result = comIObjNs.AddSomeNumbers(1, 2);
Console.WriteLine("Call Com Object: {0}: {1}",
    comIObjNs.GetType(), result);
```

When the code is executed, we see these results:

```
Call Com Object: DniSimpleCom.Interop.DniSimpleComObjClass: 3
```

TlbImp is also a valuable tool when using Visual Basic 6.0 (VB6) COM components. While you can directly reference these objects from Visual Studio's Add References option, using TlbImp to create an interop library solves one of the nagging problems with VB6 components.

The problem arises from the way VB6 components magically change their identity from one build to the next. This VB6 *feature* is called the Version Compatibility option. This option is set at the project properties page and by default is set to No Compatibility. This means that each time a VB6 COM component is built, a new set of class and interface GUIDs is assigned. If you use this option, the VB6 component is effectively brand-new each time it is built. The COM identity of the component has been altered. Any references to it from other projects (including .NET) are broken.

When adding a reference to a COM component directly from Visual Studio, a reference is made to that particular version of the component. The COM identifiers (GUID or ProgID) are stored as part of the reference. The .NET application will build and execute fine until the VB6 component is rebuilt. When that occurs, the .NET build will fail since it won't be able to find that exact version of the COM component. The COM reference is now broken and you need to manually remove the old reference and add it back again in order to successfully build.

VB6 also provides a Binary Compatibility setting for components. This option still changes the class and interface GUIDs, but it maintains the old set of IDs as well. The result is that you have a component with a growing set of alias COM IDs that all point to it. To maintain binary compatibility, you also need to save the last DLL that was built, checking it in to source control along with your source. Using this option is not the best solution to this problem.

A better solution is to use TlbImp to preprocess the VB6 COM component. By executing TlbImp as a prebuild step of the .NET project, you will always reference the latest version of the VB6 component. The .NET project references the interop library instead of the VB6 component directly, shielding it from COM identity changes.

To illustrate this, we can create a simple VB6 COM component and use it from .NET. We start by creating a new VB6 project, selecting ActiveX DLL as the project type. In our example, the project is called DniSimpleComVB and the default class module is DniSimpleComVBObj.

The single method that we add to the class module looks like this:

```
'implement a simple method for this VB6 COM object
Public Function AddSomeNumbers(ByVal numA As Long, _
        ByVal numB As Long) As Long
    'return the result
    AddSomeNumbers = numA + numB
End Function
```

The final VB6 step is to use the Make option from the File menu to build this component into a COM DLL that we can reference.

The next step in the process is to run the VB DLL through TlbImp to create the interop library. The command we use looks like this:

```
tlbimp.exe DniSimpleComVB.dll /out:Interop.DniSimpleComVB.dll /verbose
```

We specified the /verbose option in order to see additional details during the import process:

```
Resolved referenced file 'DniSimpleComVB.dll' to file
    'C:\code\bin\DniSimpleComVB.dll'.
Type '_DniSimpleComVBObj' imported.
Type 'DniSimpleComVBObj' imported.
Type library imported to C:\code\bin\Interop.DniSimpleComVB.dll
```

The C# project that uses this COM component requires a reference to the Interop. DniSimpleComVB.dll interop assembly that was just generated. Since the assembly is not in the GAC, the reference is added by directly browsing to the location of the assembly. We want to reference the interop assembly instead of the COM component directly. Once the reference is added, we can write C# code to execute the component like this:

```
using System;
using Interop.DniSimpleComVB;

namespace UsingInteropAssemblyTest
{
    /// <summary>
    /// Reference an interop assembly built using tlbimp.exe
    /// </summary>
    class UsingInteropAssemblyTest
    {
        /// <summary>
        /// The main entry point for the application.
        /// </summary>
        [STAThread]
        static void Main(string[] args)
        {
            //use a VB6 COM component
            DniSimpleComVBObj vbComObj = new DniSimpleComVBObj();
            int result = vbComObj.AddSomeNumbers(1, 2);
            Console.WriteLine("Call VB6 Com Object: {0}", result);
```

```
            //wait for input
            Console.WriteLine("Press any key to exit");
            Console.Read();
        }
    }
}
```

Similar code implemented in Visual Basic .NET (VB.NET) looks like this:

```
Imports Interop.DniSimpleComVB

Module UsingInteropAssemblyTest

    Sub Main()
        'use a VB6 COM component
        Dim vbComObj As DniSimpleComVBObj = New DniSimpleComVBObj()
        Dim result As Integer = vbComObj.AddSomeNumbers(1, 2)
        Console.WriteLine("Call VB6 Com Object: {0}", result)

        'wait for input
        Console.WriteLine("Press any key to exit")
        Console.Read()
    End Sub

End Module
```

Regardless of the .NET language used, when the code is executed, the results look like this:

```
Call VB6 Com Object: 3
Press any key to exit
```

Using this approach, we've insulated ourselves from the COM identity changes that occur each time the VB6 project is built.

Note It's a good idea to add the execution of the TlbImp utility to a build script or the prebuild step of the .NET project. Doing this ensures that the interop assembly will always reference the latest version of the VB6 component. The build steps have a set of built-in macros that allow you to execute a command-line utility, passing the project or assembly name as an argument.

If you want to execute TlbImp from the prebuild step of a .NET project, make sure you add the .NET Framework \SDK\bin directory to your path. Otherwise, the utility won't be found. As an alternative, you can start Visual Studio .NET from the command prompt rather than from the shortcut. To do this, open the Visual Studio .NET command prompt. Then type **devenv** and press Enter. This will start Visual Studio .NET, but the environment will have all of the proper paths to use any command-line Visual Studio utilities.

Related Information

See recipes 5-1 (Using COM Components from .NET) and 5-11 (Sharing an Interop Assembly). Also refer to the MSDN topics "TlbImp" and "Macros for Build Commands and Properties."

5-3. Handling COM Events

Problem

A COM component that you need to use fires an event that must be handled. How are COM events handled within .NET code?

Solution

Events fired from COM components are handled in .NET code as *delegates*. Delegates are the general mechanism within .NET used to reference a method and are used for .NET events and callbacks.

When a COM component that exposes an event is imported into an interop library, a delegate type is generated for each event. This is done regardless of the import method, either directly within Visual Studio .NET or using TlbImp.

After creating an instance of the COM object, the .NET code can subscribe to the event by creating an instance of the delegate type and passing it to the COM object. The exact syntax for assigning an event handler is different depending on the .NET language. The delegate references a local method in the .NET code that acts as the handler each time the event is fired.

As an example, consider this simple Visual Basic 6.0 (VB6) COM class:

```
'define an event that can be handled
Event OnDescChanged(ByVal newDesc As String, ByVal oldDesc As String)

Private m_Desc As String

'COM method that fires the event
Public Function ChangeDesc(ByVal newDesc As String)

    'fire the event to any subscribers
    RaiseEvent OnDescChanged(newDesc, m_Desc)
    'save the new value
    m_Desc = newDesc

End Function
```

The class exposes an event named OnDescChanged that passes two strings, an old and new description. There is a single method named ChangeDesc that accepts a single string. Each time ChangeDesc is called, it raises the OnDescChanged event, passing the previous description and the new value. We've named this class DniComEventsVBObj within a VB6 project named DniComEventsVB.

Using TlbImp, we create an interop library for this component and reference it from a .NET project. The TlbImp command line looks like this:

```
tlbimp.exe  DniComEventsVB.dll  /out:Interop.DniComEventsVB.dll
```

▋Note We use `TlbImp` rather than importing the COM component directly to avoid the VB6 COM identity issues. Using a separately generated import library isolates the .NET code from the COM identity changes each time the VB6 component is built.

In order to automate the import process, you can add the execution of `TlbImp` to the prebuild step of the managed project that uses the component. The same `TlbImp` command shown in the example can be added as a prebuild command without any modifications. Of course, this assumes that the component being imported (`DniComEventsVB.dll`) is in the same folder as your managed project. If it isn't, you can use one of the built-in Visual Studio macros available to the pre- and postbuild steps. For example, if you keep all of your COM components in the `\bin` folder under your solution folder, you could enter the command like this:

```
tlbimp.exe "$(SolutionDir)\bin\DniComEventsVB.dll"
  /out:Interop.DniComEventsVB.dll
```

Here you're using the `$(SolutionDir)` macro to identify the location of the solution folder. A number of other macros are provided by Visual Studio; use the one that makes the most sense depending on the organization of your source directory tree.

One potential problem is that command-line tools such as `TlbImp` are usually not found by Visual Studio pre- and postbuild steps. To remedy this, you can start Visual Studio a different way. Instead of using the shortcut to Visual Studio .NET, open up the Visual Studio Command Prompt instead. This is a Windows command prompt that sets all of the environment variables needed to run the .NET command-line tools. From the command prompt, simply enter **devenv** to start Visual Studio .NET. Now when you execute these prebuild steps, Visual Studio .NET is able to find the path to any .NET utility you need.

The C# code to handle the event and test the component looks like this:

```
using System;

using Interop.DniComEventsVB;     //the vb6 COM component

namespace EventHandling
{
    class EventHandlingTest
    {
        static void Main(string[] args)
        {
            //create the VB6 COM object
            DniComEventsVBObj comObj = new DniComEventsVBObj();

            //subscribe to the event
            comObj.OnDescChanged
                += new __DniComEventsVBObj_OnDescChangedEventHandler(
                    OnDescChangedHandler);
```

```
        //call the COM method that fires the event
        comObj.ChangeDesc("first");
        //call it again
        comObj.ChangeDesc("second");

        //wait for input
        Console.WriteLine("Press any key to exit");
        Console.Read();
    }


    /// <summary>
    /// Event handler for OnDescChanged COM event
    /// </summary>
    /// <param name="newDesc"></param>
    /// <param name="oldDesc"></param>
    static void OnDescChangedHandler(string newDesc,
        string oldDesc)
    {
        Console.WriteLine(
          "Received OnDescChanged event: Old:{0}, New:{1}",
              oldDesc, newDesc);
    }
  }
}
```

After adding a using statement for the interop library, we create an instance of the COM object. The OnDescChangedHandler method is the event handler implementation. A delegate is created for this event handler and registered with the OnDescChanged event of the COM object.

The typed delegate for the event was generated when we created the import library. For this COM component, the delegate is named __DniComEventsVBObj_OnDescChangedEventHandler. (Note the double underscore at the beginning of the generated name.)

When the code is executed, the output looks like this:

```
Received OnDescChanged event: Old:, New:first
Received OnDescChanged event: Old:first, New:second
Press any key to exit
```

How It Works

C# 2.0 supports a new way to handle delegates called *anonymous methods*. This feature allows you to implement the event-handling code inline rather than referring to a separate method. For example, the preceding C# example could be rewritten to use anonymous methods as follows:

```
//create the VB6 COM object
DniComEventsVBObj comObjAnn = new DniComEventsVBObj();

//subscribe to the event using a C# 2.0 anon delegate
comObjAnn.OnDescChanged
```

```
    += delegate(string newDesc, string oldDesc)
{
    Console.WriteLine(
        "Anonymous delegate for OnDescChanged: Old:{0}, New:{1}",
        oldDesc, newDesc);
};
//call the COM method that fires the event
comObjAnn.ChangeDesc("first");
//call it again
comObjAnn.ChangeDesc("second");
```

When the code is executed, the results look like this:

```
Anonymous delegate for OnDescChanged: Old:, New:first
Anonymous delegate for OnDescChanged: Old:first, New:second
Press any key to exit
```

Visual Basic .NET (VB.NET) uses a slightly different syntax to subscribe to events. Here is equivalent VB.NET code that uses the same COM component:

```
Imports Interop.DniComEventsVB

Module EventHandlingVBTest

    Sub Main()
        'create the VB6 COM object
        Dim comObj As DniComEventsVBObj = New DniComEventsVBObj()

        'create a delegate for the event handler
        Dim comDelegate As _
        __DniComEventsVBObj_OnDescChangedEventHandler _
            = New __DniComEventsVBObj_OnDescChangedEventHandler( _
                AddressOf OnDescChangedEventHandler)
        'subscribe to the event
        AddHandler comObj.OnDescChanged, comDelegate

        'call the COM method that fires the event
        comObj.ChangeDesc("VBfirst")
        'call it again
        comObj.ChangeDesc("VBsecond")

        'wait for input
        Console.WriteLine("Press any key to exit")
        Console.Read()
    End Sub

    Public Sub OnDescChangedEventHandler(ByVal newDesc As String, _
                ByVal oldDesc As String)
```

```
            Console.WriteLine( _
                "Received VB OnDescChanged event: Old:{0}, New:{1}", _
                oldDesc, newDesc)
        End Sub

End Module
```

When we execute the VB.NET code, we see these results:

```
Received VB OnDescChanged event: Old:, New:VBfirst
Received VB OnDescChanged event: Old:VBfirst, New:VBsecond
Press any key to exit
```

Regardless of the language used to implement the COM component, the handling of events within .NET code should work basically the same way. To illustrate this, we can implement this COM component in C++ using Active Template Library (ATL).

We can use the ATL wizards included in Visual Studio to build a COM component that supports connection points, using most of the generated code as is. However, we do need to define and implement the COM method that fires the event, and define the event itself.

What follows is the IDL for the component:

```
// DniComEvents.idl : IDL source for DniComEvents
//


// This file will be processed by the MIDL tool to
// produce the type library (DniComEvents.tlb)
// and marshaling code.

import "oaidl.idl";
import "ocidl.idl";


[
    object,
    uuid(04C62481-37D2-4BCA-B6DD-68583B0B67F7),
    dual,
    nonextensible,
    helpstring("IDniComEventsObj Interface"),
    pointer_default(unique)
]
interface IDniComEventsObj : IDispatch{
    [id(1), helpstring("method ChangeDesc")]
    HRESULT ChangeDesc([in] BSTR newDesc);
};
[
    uuid(01A8ECE7-34F8-4267-AC4A-EA2C6B93E089),
    version(1.0),
    helpstring("DniComEvents 1.0 Type Library")
]
```

```
library DniComEventsLib
{
    importlib("stdole2.tlb");
    [
        uuid(2C344C48-B0BF-487E-81B4-FC4860703993),
        helpstring("_IDniComEventsObjEvents Interface")
    ]
    dispinterface _IDniComEventsObjEvents
    {
        properties:
        methods:
        [id(1), helpstring("Desc changed event")]
        HRESULT OnDescChanged([in]BSTR newDesc, [in]BSTR oldDesc);
    };
    [
        uuid(D2B1D33B-FD3C-4822-9ABC-12786728C3B2),
        helpstring("DniComEventsObj Class")
    ]
    coclass DniComEventsObj
    {
        [default] interface IDniComEventsObj;
        [default, source] dispinterface _IDniComEventsObjEvents;
    };
};
```

The bolded lines show where ChangeDesc and OnDescChanged were added. OnDescChanged
was added to the _IDniComEventsObjEvents interface. We chose to have this interface added
for us by checking the Supports Connection Points option during the ATL wizard execution.

Once we manually add the OnDescChanged event to the IDL, we switch to Class view, select
the class for the COM object, and select Add Connection Point. This brings up a wizard dialog
where we choose the _IDniComEventsObjEvents interface to implement as a connection point.
This generates the following code for us automatically:

```
template<class T>
class CProxy_IDniComEventsObjEvents :
    public IConnectionPointImpl<T, &__uuidof(_IDniComEventsObjEvents)>
{
public:
    HRESULT Fire_OnDescChanged( BSTR newDesc,  BSTR oldDesc)
    {
        HRESULT hr = S_OK;
        T * pThis = static_cast<T *>(this);
        int cConnections = m_vec.GetSize();

        for (int iConnection = 0;
            iConnection < cConnections; iConnection++)
        {
            pThis->Lock();
            CComPtr<IUnknown> punkConnection
```

```
                    = m_vec.GetAt(iConnection);
            pThis->Unlock();

            IDispatch * pConnection
                = static_cast<IDispatch *>(punkConnection.p);

            if (pConnection)
            {
                CComVariant avarParams[2];
                avarParams[1] = newDesc;
                avarParams[1].vt = VT_BSTR;
                avarParams[0] = oldDesc;
                avarParams[0].vt = VT_BSTR;
                CComVariant varResult;

                DISPPARAMS params = { avarParams, NULL, 2, 0 };
                hr = pConnection->Invoke(1, IID_NULL,
                LOCALE_USER_DEFAULT, DISPATCH_METHOD,
                &params, &varResult, NULL, NULL);
            }
        }
        return hr;
    }
};
```

As the name implies, the `Fire_OnDescChanged` method that is generated for us is used to fire the event. Within the implementation of our `ChangeDesc` method, we can call this method to fire the event. The complete code for `ChangeDesc` looks like this:

```
STDMETHODIMP CDniComEventsObj::ChangeDesc(BSTR newDesc)
{
    //fire the event that notifies any subscribers of
    //the description change
    Fire_OnDescChanged(newDesc, m_LastDesc);

    //save the updated description
    m_LastDesc = newDesc;

    return S_OK;
}
```

To use this ATL COM component from .NET, we first add a reference to the COM component. Once that is done, the code to subscribe to the event and use the component is similar to using a VB6 COM component:

```
using System;

using DniComEventsLib;          //the C++ ATL COM component
```

```csharp
namespace EventHandling
{
    class EventHandlingTest
    {
        static void Main(string[] args)
        {
            //create the ATL COM component
            DniComEventsObj atlComObj = new DniComEventsObj();

            //subscribe to the event
            atlComObj.OnDescChanged
                += new _IDniComEventsObjEvents_OnDescChangedEventHandler(
                    OnDescChangedHandler);

            //call the COM method that fires the event
            atlComObj.ChangeDesc("ATLfirst");
            //call it again
            atlComObj.ChangeDesc("ATLsecond");

            //wait for input
            Console.WriteLine("Press any key to exit");
            Console.Read();
        }

        /// <summary>
        /// Event handler for OnDescChanged COM event
        /// </summary>
        /// <param name="newDesc"></param>
        /// <param name="oldDesc"></param>
        static void OnDescChangedHandler(string newDesc, string oldDesc)
        {
            Console.WriteLine(
                "Received OnDescChanged event: Old:{0}, New:{1}",
                    oldDesc, newDesc);
        }
    }
}
```

Notice that the type name generated for the delegate is different from the version that calls a VB6 component. When referencing an ATL component, the name defined in the IDL is used, while VB6 generates a name.

When the code executes, we see the expected results:

```
Received OnDescChanged event: Old:, New:ATLfirst
Received OnDescChanged event: Old:ATLfirst, New:ATLsecond
Press any key to exit
```

Related Information

See recipes 5-1 (Using COM Components from .NET) and 5-2 (Importing a Type Library).

5-4. Marshaling COM Data Types

Problem

COM uses standard data types such as int and long, but also defines its own data types such as BSTR, CURRENCY, and DATE. How are these data types marshaled between COM and managed code? How do you know what managed data types to use when calling a particular COM component?

Solution

The generated Runtime Callable Wrapper (RCW) contains a definition for all methods and properties exposed by a COM component. Each method and property is defined with managed data types that correspond to the COM data types.

Therefore, the data types to use are defined for you when you import the type library for a component. You generate the RCW by referencing the COM component directly from your .NET project, or by running the TlbImp utility.

Table 5-2 summarizes the most commonly used COM data types and shows how they are marshaled to managed types.

Table 5-2. *COM Data Type Marshaling*

COM Data Type	Managed Type	Description
bool	System.Int32	Boolean value
Boolean	System.SByte	8-bit signed integer
BSTR	System.String	Unicode string
byte	System.Byte	8-bit unsigned integer
char	System.SByte	8-bit signed integer
CURRENCY	System.Decimal	Currency value
DATE	System.DateTime	Date/time value
DECIMAL	System.Decimal	Decimal number
double	System.Double	64-bit float
float	System.Single	32-bit float
GUID	System.Guid	Globally unique ID
int	System.Int32	32-bit signed integer
long	System.Int32	32-bit signed integer
LPSTR	System.String	ANSI string marshaled as a Unicode string
LPWSTR	System.String	Unicode string
short	System.Int16	16-bit signed integer
unsigned char	System.Byte	8-bit unsigned integer

COM Data Type	Managed Type	Description
unsigned int	System.UInt32	32-bit unsigned integer
unsigned long	System.UInt32	32-bit unsigned integer
VARIANT_BOOL	System.Boolean	Boolean value

Note Conspicuously missing from this table are VARIANT and SAFEARRAY. These COM data types are discussed in later recipes.

How It Works

The job of mapping data types for a COM component is generally much easier than mapping a non-COM function called via PInvoke. When calling a non-COM function, you are responsible for the complete definition of the function. You need to determine the number of calling arguments along with the data type of each argument. Then you put all of that into a method declaration that is decorated with a DllImport attribute and hope you get it all right.

Thanks to the generation of the RCW from the COM type library, most of the hard work is done for you. You can use TlbImp to generate an import library, or reference a COM component directly from your .NET project in Visual Studio .NET. In either case, you end up with a type-safe wrapper class that correctly maps the data types for each method and property in the COM component.

The following example uses an ATL COM component to demonstrate how some of these data types are marshaled with managed code. The component defines a number of methods, with each one accepting and returning a particular data type. Here is the relevant part of the IDL containing the method definitions:

```
interface IDniDataTypesObj : IDispatch{
    [id(1), helpstring("method UseBool")]
    HRESULT UseBool([in] boolean inParam,
        [in, out] boolean* outParam);

    [id(2), helpstring("method UseVariantBool")]
    HRESULT UseVariantBool([in] VARIANT_BOOL inParam,
        [in,out] VARIANT_BOOL* outParam);

    [id(3), helpstring("method UseLong")]
    HRESULT UseLong([in] long inParam, [in,out] long* outParam);

    [id(4), helpstring("method UseDouble")]
    HRESULT UseDouble([in] double inParam,
        [in,out] double* outParam);

    [id(5), helpstring("method UseBSTR")]
    HRESULT UseBSTR([in] BSTR inParam, [in,out] BSTR* outParam);
```

```
    [id(6), helpstring("method UseDecimal")]
    HRESULT UseDecimal([in] DECIMAL inParam,
        [in,out] DECIMAL* outParam);

    [id(7), helpstring("method UseDate")]
    HRESULT UseDate([in] DATE inParam, [in,out] DATE* outParam);

    [id(8), helpstring("method UseCurrency")]
    HRESULT UseCurrency([in] CURRENCY inParam,
        [in,out] CURRENCY* outParam);

    [id(9), helpstring("method UseChar")]
    HRESULT UseChar([in] unsigned char inParam,
        [in,out] unsigned char* outParam);

    [id(10), helpstring("method UseLPSTR")]
    HRESULT UseLPSTR([in] LPSTR inParam, [in,out] LPSTR* outParam);

    [id(11), helpstring("method UseComCHAR")]
    HRESULT UseComCHAR([in] CHAR inParam, [in,out] CHAR* outParam);
};
```

The C++ code that implements this interface looks like this:

```
STDMETHODIMP CDniDataTypesObj::UseBool(boolean inParam,
    boolean* outParam)
{
    *outParam = inParam;
    return S_OK;
}

STDMETHODIMP CDniDataTypesObj::UseVariantBool(VARIANT_BOOL inParam,
    VARIANT_BOOL* outParam)
{
    *outParam = inParam;
    return S_OK;
}

STDMETHODIMP CDniDataTypesObj::UseLong(long inParam, long* outParam)
{
    *outParam = inParam;
    return S_OK;
}

STDMETHODIMP CDniDataTypesObj::UseDouble(double inParam,
    double* outParam)
{
    *outParam = inParam;
    return S_OK;
}
```

```
STDMETHODIMP CDniDataTypesObj::UseBSTR(BSTR inParam, BSTR* outParam)
{
    *outParam = inParam;
    return S_OK;
}


STDMETHODIMP CDniDataTypesObj::UseDecimal(DECIMAL inParam,
    DECIMAL* outParam)
{
    *outParam = inParam;
    return S_OK;
}


STDMETHODIMP CDniDataTypesObj::UseDate(DATE inParam, DATE* outParam)
{
    *outParam = inParam;
    return S_OK;
}


STDMETHODIMP CDniDataTypesObj::UseCurrency(CURRENCY inParam,
    CURRENCY* outParam)
{
    *outParam = inParam;
    return S_OK;
}


STDMETHODIMP CDniDataTypesObj::UseChar(unsigned char inParam,
    unsigned char* outParam)
{
    *outParam = inParam;
    return S_OK;
}


STDMETHODIMP CDniDataTypesObj::UseLPSTR(LPSTR inParam,
    LPSTR* outParam)
{
    *outParam = inParam;
    return S_OK;
}


STDMETHODIMP CDniDataTypesObj::UseComCHAR(CHAR inParam,
    CHAR* outParam)
{
    *outParam = inParam;
    return S_OK;
}
```

Admittedly, this is not very interesting code. Each method simply copies the input parameter to the output parameter. However, using this COM component, we will be able to see how each of these COM data types is mapped to a managed type.

The C# code to exercise this component looks like this:

```
using System;

using DniDataTypesLib;      //the RCW for the COM component

namespace ComDataTypes
{
    class ComDataTypesTest
    {
        static void Main(string[] args)
        {
            //create an instance of the COM object
            DniDataTypesObj comObj = new DniDataTypesObj();

            sbyte outUseBool     = 0;
            comObj.UseBool(1, ref outUseBool);
            Console.WriteLine("UseBoolean: {0}, {1}",
                outUseBool.GetType().Name, outUseBool);

            bool outUseVariantBool = false;
            comObj.UseVariantBool(true, ref outUseVariantBool);
            Console.WriteLine("UseVariantBool: {0}, {1}",
                outUseVariantBool.GetType().Name,
              outUseVariantBool);

            int outUseLong = 0;
            comObj.UseLong(123, ref outUseLong);
            Console.WriteLine("UseLong: {0}, {1}",
                outUseLong.GetType().Name, outUseLong);

            double outUseDouble = 0.0;
            comObj.UseDouble(45.67, ref outUseDouble);
            Console.WriteLine("UseDouble: {0}, {1}",
                outUseDouble.GetType().Name, outUseDouble);

            string outUseBSTR = "orig string out";
            comObj.UseBSTR("input string", ref outUseBSTR);
            Console.WriteLine("UseBSTR: {0}, {1}",
                outUseBSTR.GetType().Name, outUseBSTR);

            string outUseLPSTR = String.Empty;
            comObj.UseLPSTR("input string", ref outUseLPSTR);
            Console.WriteLine("UseLPSTR: {0}, {1}",
                outUseLPSTR.GetType().Name, outUseLPSTR);
```

```
            decimal outUseDecimal = 0;
            comObj.UseDecimal(9876.54m, ref outUseDecimal);
            Console.WriteLine("UseDecimal: {0}, {1}",
                outUseDecimal.GetType().Name, outUseDecimal);

            decimal outUseCurrency = 0;
            comObj.UseCurrency(9876.54m, ref outUseCurrency);
            Console.WriteLine("UseCurrency: {0}, {1}",
                outUseCurrency.GetType().Name, outUseCurrency);

            DateTime outUseDate = new DateTime();
            comObj.UseDate(new DateTime(2005,12,31),
                ref outUseDate);
            Console.WriteLine("UseDate: {0}, {1}",
                outUseDate.GetType().Name, outUseDate);

            byte outUseChar = (byte)0;
            comObj.UseChar((byte)'z', ref outUseChar);
            Console.WriteLine("UseChar: {0}, {1}",
                outUseChar.GetType().Name, outUseChar);

            sbyte outUseComChar = (sbyte)0;
            comObj.UseComCHAR((sbyte)'a', ref outUseComChar);
            Console.WriteLine("UseComChar: {0}, {1}",
                outUseComChar.GetType().Name, outUseComChar);

            //wait for input
            Console.WriteLine("Press any key to exit");
            Console.Read();
        }
    }
}
```

After creating an instance of the COM object, we test each method and display the results. For each data type test, we pass in an appropriate value and get the results passed back from the COM component in a variable. We display the data type associated with the variable as well as the value.

Here is the same set of test code implemented in Visual Basic .NET (VB.NET):

```
Imports DniDataTypesLib

Module ComDataTypesTest

    Sub Main()
        'create an instance of the COM object
        Dim comObj As DniDataTypesObj _
            = New DniDataTypesObj()
```

```
Dim outUseBool As SByte = 0
comObj.UseBool(1, outUseBool)
Console.WriteLine("UseBoolean: {0}, {1}", _
    outUseBool.GetType().Name, outUseBool)

Dim outUseVariantBool As Boolean = False
comObj.UseVariantBool(True, outUseVariantBool)
Console.WriteLine("UseVariantBool: {0}, {1}", _
    outUseVariantBool.GetType().Name, _
    outUseVariantBool)

Dim outUseLong As Integer = 0
comObj.UseLong(123, outUseLong)
Console.WriteLine("UseLong: {0}, {1}", _
    outUseLong.GetType().Name, outUseLong)

Dim outUseDouble As Double = 0.0
comObj.UseDouble(45.67, outUseDouble)
Console.WriteLine("UseDouble: {0}, {1}", _
    outUseDouble.GetType().Name, outUseDouble)

Dim outUseBSTR As String = "orig string out"
comObj.UseBSTR("input string", outUseBSTR)
Console.WriteLine("UseBSTR: {0}, {1}", _
    outUseBSTR.GetType().Name, outUseBSTR)

Dim outUseLPSTR As String = String.Empty
comObj.UseLPSTR("input string", outUseLPSTR)
Console.WriteLine("UseLPSTR: {0}, {1}", _
    outUseLPSTR.GetType().Name, outUseLPSTR)

Dim outUseDecimal As Decimal = 0
comObj.UseDecimal(9876.54D, outUseDecimal)
Console.WriteLine("UseDecimal: {0}, {1}", _
    outUseDecimal.GetType().Name, outUseDecimal)

Dim outUseCurrency As Decimal = 0
comObj.UseCurrency(9876.54D, outUseCurrency)
Console.WriteLine("UseCurrency: {0}, {1}", _
    outUseCurrency.GetType().Name, outUseCurrency)

Dim outUseDate As DateTime = New DateTime()
comObj.UseDate(New DateTime(2005, 12, 31), outUseDate)
Console.WriteLine("UseDate: {0}, {1}", _
    outUseDate.GetType().Name, outUseDate)
```

```
        Dim outUseChar As Byte = 0
        comObj.UseChar(CByte(122), outUseChar)
        Console.WriteLine("UseChar: {0}, {1}", _
            outUseChar.GetType().Name, outUseChar)

        Dim outUseComChar As SByte = 0
        comObj.UseComCHAR(CSByte(97), outUseComChar)
        Console.WriteLine("UseComChar: {0}, {1}", _
            outUseComChar.GetType().Name, outUseComChar)

        'wait for input
        Console.WriteLine("Press any key to exit")
        Console.Read()

    End Sub

End Module
```

Regardless of the language used, the results when we execute this code are the same:

```
UseBoolean: SByte, 1
UseVariantBool: Boolean, True
UseLong: Int32, 123
UseDouble: Double, 45.67
UseBSTR: String, input string
UseLPSTR: String, input string
UseDecimal: Decimal, 9876.54
UseCurrency: Decimal, 9876.54
UseDate: DateTime, 12/31/2005 12:00:00 AM
UseChar: Byte, 122
UseComChar: SByte, 97
Press any key to exit
```

Related Information

See recipes 5-1 (Using COM Components from .NET), 5-2 (Importing a Type Library), 5-5 (Marshaling COM Variants), and 5-6 (Marshaling COM Arrays).

5-5. Marshaling COM Variants

Problem

Many COM methods use the Variant data type. Since .NET doesn't support this data type, how is data marshaled to and from Variants?

Solution

Variants used within COM methods are marshaled as System.Object. This makes sense since a Variant can represent any type of data, just like a System.Object.

When data is passed to such a COM method, the underlying type of the data is used to set the correct Variant Type (VT_*) as it is marshaled to COM. Likewise, when a Variant is marshaled back to managed code, the Variant Type is used to determine the managed data type to create.

■ Note What is the difference between Variant and VARIANT (all caps)? Variant is the official name of this data type. VARIANT refers to the type definition that defines the Variant structure for C and C++ developers. Both versions of the name refer to the same thing.

Table 5-3 illustrates the conversion of data types to and from a Variant.

Table 5-3. *Variant Conversion Example*

Action	Original Type	Received Type
Value passed from .NET to COM	System.Int32	VARIANT, VT_I4
Value returned from COM to .NET	VARIANT, VT_I4	System.Int32

If you pass a simple integer to the COM method, it is marshaled as a VARIANT with the Variant Type set to VT_I4. This is the type that corresponds to a 32-bit signed integer.

When the same value is returned from a COM method, it starts out as a VARIANT with the Variant Type set to VT_I4. Based on the Variant Type and the underlying value, the marshaler determines that the managed code should receive a System.Int32.

Table 5-4 summarizes the data type conversions that take place when a COM method or property uses a VARIANT. When passing a managed type to a COM method, find the type in the Input Managed Type column. The second column identifies the Variant Type that will be set as the VARIANT is constructed for the COM method. The Output Managed Type column identifies the managed type that will be constructed as VARIANT values are returned to managed code.

Table 5-4. *Managed to VARIANT Type Conversion*

Input Managed Type	Variant Type	Output Managed Type
System.Array	VT_ARRAY	System.Array
System.Boolean	VT_BOOL	System.Boolean
System.String	VT_BSTR	System.String
CurrencyWrapper	VT_CY	System.Decimal
System.DateTime	VT_DATE	System.DateTime
System.Decimal	VT_DECIMAL	System.Decimal
null	VT_EMPTY	null
System.SByte	VT_I1	System.SByte
System.Int16	VT_I2	System.Int16

Input Managed Type	Variant Type	Output Managed Type
System.Int32	VT_I4	System.Int32
System.Int64	VT_I8	System.Int64
System.IntPtr	VT_INT	System.Int32
System.Single	VT_R4	System.Single
System.Double	VT_R8	System.Double
System.Byte	VT_UI1	System.Byte
System.UInt16	VT_UI2	System.UInt16
System.UInt32	VT_UI4	System.UInt32
System.UInt64	VT_UI8	System.UInt64
System.UIntPtr	VT_UINT	System.UInt32

How It Works

Variant is the universal data type made popular by its use in Visual Basic. It is a structure that can represent data of any type. While this type is not supported directly in .NET, we are able to marshal data to and from a Variant when calling a COM component.

To demonstrate the marshaling that takes place with Variants, we can use a simple COM method that accepts and returns a VARIANT. The C++ ATL implementation for such a method might look like this:

```
STDMETHODIMP CDniDataTypesObj::UseVariant(VARIANT inParam,
        VARIANT* outParam, BSTR* variantDesc)
{
    //return the input VARIANT in the outParam
    *outParam = inParam;

    //determine the type of variant passed in and
    //return a description for the type
    switch(inParam.vt)
    {
        case VT_BOOL:
            *variantDesc = (CComBSTR)"VT_BOOL";
            break;
        case VT_I4:
            *variantDesc = (CComBSTR)"VT_I4";
            break;
        case VT_I8:
            *variantDesc = (CComBSTR)"VT_I8";
            break;
        case VT_R8:
            *variantDesc = (CComBSTR)"VT_R8";
            break;
        case VT_BSTR:
            *variantDesc = (CComBSTR)"VT_BSTR";
            break;
```

```
                case VT_EMPTY:
                    *variantDesc = (CComBSTR)"VT_EMPTY";
                    break;
                case VT_NULL:
                    *variantDesc = (CComBSTR)"VT_NULL";
                    break;
                case VT_UNKNOWN:
                    *variantDesc = (CComBSTR)"VT_UNKNOWN";
                    break;
                case VT_RECORD:
                    *variantDesc = (CComBSTR)"VT_RECORD";
                    break;
                case VT_DECIMAL:
                    *variantDesc = (CComBSTR)"VT_DECIMAL";
                    break;
                case VT_DATE:
                    *variantDesc = (CComBSTR)"VT_DATE";
                    break;
                case VT_CY:
                    *variantDesc = (CComBSTR)"VT_CY";
                    break;
                case VT_ERROR:
                    *variantDesc = (CComBSTR)"VT_ERROR";
                    break;
                case VT_VOID:
                    *variantDesc = (CComBSTR)"VT_VOID";
                    break;
                case VT_INT:
                    *variantDesc = (CComBSTR)"VT_INT";
                    break;
                case VT_UINT:
                    *variantDesc = (CComBSTR)"VT_UINT";
                    break;
                case VT_UI4:
                    *variantDesc = (CComBSTR)"VT_UI4";
                    break;
                case VT_VARIANT:
                    *variantDesc = (CComBSTR)"VT_VARIANT";
                    break;
                case VT_PTR:
                    *variantDesc = (CComBSTR)"VT_PTR";
                    break;
                case VT_USERDEFINED:
                    *variantDesc = (CComBSTR)"VT_USERDEFINED";
                    break;
                case VT_ARRAY:
                    *variantDesc = (CComBSTR)"VT_ARRAY";
                    break;
```

```
        default:
            *variantDesc = (CComBSTR)"unknown type";
    }

    return S_OK;
}
```

The IDL for this component defines the method like this:

```
[id(1), helpstring("method UseVariant")]
HRESULT UseVariant([in] VARIANT inParam, [out] VARIANT* outParam,
    [out,retval] BSTR* variantDesc);
```

This method performs two tasks. First, it copies the input VARIANT into an output VARIANT. This allows us to see what happens to the same data as it is passed in and out of the COM method. Second, it passes back a description based on the Variant Type. This allows the calling code to see how the COM method sees the original data after it has been marshaled.

We can now write C# code that exercises this one method. The following code calls the method using different managed data types. After each call, we display the original data type, the returned data type, and the type description provided by the COM method. The test code looks like this:

```
using System;
using System.Runtime.InteropServices;

using DniDataTypesLib;

namespace ComVariants
{
    class ComVariantsTest
    {
        static void Main(string[] args)
        {
            //create an instance of the COM object
            DniDataTypesObj comObj = new DniDataTypesObj();
            string desc = string.Empty;

            //a variable used to return any VARIANT value
            Object result = null;

            Boolean testVariantBool   = true;
            desc = comObj.UseVariant(testVariantBool, out result);
            Console.WriteLine("Test Variant Bool: {0}, {1}, {2}",
                testVariantBool.GetType().Name,
                result.GetType().Name, desc);

            int testVariantInt = 123;
            desc = comObj.UseVariant(testVariantInt, out result);
            Console.WriteLine("Test Variant Int: {0}, {1}, {2}",
```

```
    testVariantInt.GetType().Name,
    result.GetType().Name, desc);

long testVariantLong = 123;
desc = comObj.UseVariant(testVariantLong, out result);
Console.WriteLine("Test Variant Long: {0}, {1}, {2}",
    testVariantLong.GetType().Name,
    result.GetType().Name, desc);

string testVariantString = "test string";
desc = comObj.UseVariant(testVariantString, out result);
Console.WriteLine("Test Variant String: {0}, {1}, {2}",
    testVariantString.GetType().Name,
    result.GetType().Name, desc);

object testVariantObject = new object();
desc = comObj.UseVariant(testVariantObject, out result);
Console.WriteLine("Test Variant Object: {0}, {1}, {2}",
    testVariantObject.GetType().Name,
    result.GetType().Name, desc);

object testVariantNull = null;
desc = comObj.UseVariant(testVariantNull, out result);
string returnType;
if (result == null)
{
    returnType = "null";
}
else
{
    returnType = result.GetType().Name;
}
Console.WriteLine("Test Variant Null: {0}, {1}, {2}",
    "null", returnType, desc);

double testVariantDouble = 123.45;
desc = comObj.UseVariant(testVariantDouble, out result);
Console.WriteLine("Test Variant Double: {0}, {1}, {2}",
    testVariantDouble.GetType().Name,
    result.GetType().Name, desc);

decimal testVariantDecimal = 123.45m;
desc = comObj.UseVariant(testVariantDecimal, out result);
Console.WriteLine("Test Variant Decimal: {0}, {1}, {2}",
    testVariantDecimal.GetType().Name,
    result.GetType().Name, desc);
```

```
DateTime testVariantDate = new DateTime(2005, 12, 31);
desc = comObj.UseVariant(testVariantDate, out result);
Console.WriteLine("Test Variant Date: {0}, {1}, {2}",
    testVariantDate.GetType().Name,
    result.GetType().Name, desc);

CurrencyWrapper testVariantCurrency
    = new CurrencyWrapper(123.45m);
desc = comObj.UseVariant(testVariantCurrency, out result);
Console.WriteLine("Test Variant Currency: {0}, {1}, {2}",
    testVariantCurrency.GetType().Name,
    result.GetType().Name, desc);

IntPtr testVariantIntPtr = IntPtr.Zero;
desc = comObj.UseVariant(testVariantIntPtr, out result);
Console.WriteLine("Test Variant IntPtr: {0}, {1}, {2}",
    testVariantIntPtr.GetType().Name,
    result.GetType().Name, desc);

//wait for input
Console.WriteLine("Press any key to exit");
Console.Read();

        }
    }
}
```

Since the output parameter is defined in the COM method as [out] VARIANT* outParam, we need to include the out modifier when calling the method from managed code. If the same parameter were defined as [in, out] VARIANT* outParam instead, we would pass the variable with the ref modifier. If the COM method expects a pointer to VARIANT, we must use either ref or out depending on the directional attributes for the method.

A Visual Basic .NET (VB.NET) implementation that performs the same tests looks like this:

```
Imports DniDataTypesLib
Imports System.Runtime.InteropServices

Module ComVariantsTest

    Sub Main()

        'create an instance of the COM object
        Dim comObj As DniDataTypesObj = New DniDataTypesObj()
        Dim desc As String = String.Empty

        'a variable used to return any VARIANT value
        Dim result As Object = Nothing
```

```vbnet
Dim testVariantBool As Boolean = True
desc = comObj.UseVariant(testVariantBool, result)
Console.WriteLine("Test Variant Bool: {0}, {1}, {2}", _
    testVariantBool.GetType().Name, _
    result.GetType().Name, desc)

Dim testVariantInt As Integer = 123
desc = comObj.UseVariant(testVariantInt, result)
Console.WriteLine("Test Variant Int: {0}, {1}, {2}", _
    testVariantInt.GetType().Name, _
    result.GetType().Name, desc)

Dim testVariantLong As Long = 123
desc = comObj.UseVariant(testVariantLong, result)
Console.WriteLine("Test Variant Long: {0}, {1}, {2}", _
    testVariantLong.GetType().Name, _
    result.GetType().Name, desc)

Dim testVariantString As String = "test string"
desc = comObj.UseVariant(testVariantString, result)
Console.WriteLine("Test Variant String: {0}, {1}, {2}", _
    testVariantString.GetType().Name, _
    result.GetType().Name, desc)

Dim testVariantObject As Object = New Object()
desc = comObj.UseVariant(testVariantObject, result)
Console.WriteLine("Test Variant Object: {0}, {1}, {2}", _
    testVariantObject.GetType().Name, _
    result.GetType().Name, desc)

Dim testVariantNull As Object = Nothing
desc = comObj.UseVariant(testVariantNull, result)
Dim returnType As String
If result = Nothing Then
    returnType = "null"
Else
    returnType = result.GetType().Name
End If
Console.WriteLine("Test Variant Null: {0}, {1}, {2}", _
    "null", returnType, desc)

Dim testVariantDouble As Double = 123.45
desc = comObj.UseVariant(testVariantDouble, result)
Console.WriteLine("Test Variant Double: {0}, {1}, {2}", _
    testVariantDouble.GetType().Name, _
    result.GetType().Name, desc)
```

```
        Dim testVariantDecimal As Decimal = 123.45D
        desc = comObj.UseVariant(testVariantDecimal, result)
        Console.WriteLine("Test Variant Decimal: {0}, {1}, {2}", _
            testVariantDecimal.GetType().Name, _
            result.GetType().Name, desc)

        Dim testVariantDate As DateTime = New DateTime(2005, 12, 31)
        desc = comObj.UseVariant(testVariantDate, result)
        Console.WriteLine("Test Variant Date: {0}, {1}, {2}", _
            testVariantDate.GetType().Name, _
            result.GetType().Name, desc)

        Dim testVariantCurrency As CurrencyWrapper _
            = New CurrencyWrapper(123.45D)
        desc = comObj.UseVariant(testVariantCurrency, result)
        Console.WriteLine("Test Variant Currency: {0}, {1}, {2}", _
            testVariantCurrency.GetType().Name, _
            result.GetType().Name, desc)

        Dim testVariantIntPtr As IntPtr = IntPtr.Zero
        desc = comObj.UseVariant(testVariantIntPtr, result)
        Console.WriteLine("Test Variant IntPtr: {0}, {1}, {2}", _
            testVariantIntPtr.GetType().Name, _
            result.GetType().Name, desc)

        'wait for input
        Console.WriteLine("Press any key to exit")
        Console.Read()

    End Sub

End Module
```

Regardless of the language used, when we execute this code, we see these results:

```
Test Variant Bool: Boolean, Boolean, VT_BOOL
Test Variant Int: Int32, Int32, VT_I4
Test Variant Long: Int64, Int64, VT_I8
Test Variant String: String, String, VT_BSTR
Test Variant Object: Object, Object, unknown type
Test Variant Null: null, null, VT_EMPTY
Test Variant Double: Double, Double, VT_R8
Test Variant Decimal: Decimal, Decimal, VT_DECIMAL
Test Variant Date: DateTime, DateTime, VT_DATE
Test Variant Currency: CurrencyWrapper, Decimal, VT_CY
Test Variant IntPtr: IntPtr, Int32, VT_INT
Press any key to exit
```

The results are generally what we expect, except for the last two tests. In these last two tests (currency and IntPtr), we receive back a different type from what we originally passed to the method. In all other tests, the original and received data types are the same.

The currency test required us to wrap the decimal value in a CurrencyWrapper class. This is a special class that tells the marshaler that the value should be converted to a VT_CY type VARIANT. If we didn't use this wrapper, the marshaler wouldn't have any way to distinguish a currency value (VT_CY) from a decimal value (VT_DECIMAL). We can see from the type description that the COM method did accurately receive a VT_CY value.

However, when this VARIANT is passed back to the managed code, the marshaler converts it to a System.Decimal. It doesn't convert it back to the original CurrencyWrapper since that wrapper doesn't add any value to the managed code. It is a one-way class that is needed only when passing currency values to COM.

Likewise, the System.IntPtr test returned the original value as System.Int32 rather than System.IntPtr. VT_INT represents a system-dependent integer, which is the same definition as a System.IntPtr. Therefore, a VT_INT should be returned as a System.IntPtr, but that's not how things currently work. Perhaps this will change in the future. Since I'm running a 32-bit operating system, I received a System.Int32. Presumably, on a 64-bit operating system we would see a System.Int64.

Related Information

See recipe 5-4 (Marshaling COM Data Types).

5-6. Marshaling COM Arrays

Problem

You have a COM component that uses a SAFEARRAY. How are arrays marshaled between COM and .NET?

Solution

Arrays passed to COM components are usually defined and implemented as a SAFEARRAY. This structure contains not only the array elements, but also additional fields that describe the array. Information such as the number of dimensions in the array and the number of elements in each dimension is included. This makes the SAFEARRAY suitable for marshaling between .NET and COM since it is self-describing.

When a COM method uses a SAFEARRAY, the marshaler can automatically handle the conversion to and from a normal managed array. No additional work is required on our part to pass the managed array.

For example, consider this COM method implemented in Visual Basic 6.0 (VB6):

```
'use a VB string array
Public Function UseArray(ByRef elements() As String) As String
    Dim result As String
    result = ""
    'add the array elements to the output string
```

```
    For i = 0 To UBound(elements)
        result = result + elements(i)
    Next i
    'return the new string
    UseArray = result
End Function
```

For our test, we package this method in a VB6 COM component named DniDataTypesVBObj. This method concatenates an undefined number of elements in a string array and passes back the result. How does the method determine the number of elements in the array? Under the covers, VB6 actually uses a SAFEARRAY.

To pass an array of strings from C# to this method, we can write code like this:

```
using System;

using Interop.DniDataTypesVB;

namespace ComSafeArrays
{
    class ComSafeArraysTest
    {
        static void Main(string[] args)
        {
            //test VB COM object with arrays
            DniDataTypesVBObj vbObj = new DniDataTypesVBObjClass();
            //create the test array of strings
            string[] vbArray = new string[3];
            vbArray[0] = "one";
            vbArray[1] = "two";
            vbArray[2] = "three";
            //make the call to the VB COM component
            string vbResult = vbObj.UseArray(ref vbArray);
            Console.WriteLine("VB Array: {0},{1},{2},{3}",
                vbArray[0], vbArray[1], vbArray[2], vbResult);

            //wait for input
            Console.WriteLine("Press any key to exit");
            Console.Read();
        }
    }
}
```

Here is similar code implemented in Visual Basic .NET (VB.NET):

```
Imports Interop.DniDataTypesVB

Module ComSafeArraysTest

    Sub Main()
```

```
        'test VB COM object with arrays
        Dim vbObj As DniDataTypesVBObj = New DniDataTypesVBObjClass()
        'create the test array of strings
        Dim vbArray(2) As String
        vbArray(0) = "one"
        vbArray(1) = "two"
        vbArray(2) = "three"
        'make the call to the VB COM component
        Dim vbResult As String = vbObj.UseArray(vbArray)
        Console.WriteLine("VB Array: {0},{1},{2},{3}", _
          vbArray(0), vbArray(1), vbArray(2), vbResult)

        'wait for input
        Console.WriteLine("Press any key to exit")
        Console.Read()
    End Sub

End Module
```

After creating an instance of the COM object, we create a test array of strings. The call to the UseArray method takes this string array directly without any conversion from us. The marshaler is able to convert this automatically into the SAFEARRAY expected by the COM method. When we execute this code, we see these results:

```
VB Array: one,two,three,onetwothree
Press any key to exit
```

Caution When referencing a VB6 COM component that uses an array, you may want to use TlbImp to create the interop library rather than referencing the component directly within Visual Studio. This is one case where the two methods of creating the interop library produce different results.

If you import the component directly, the VB6 array is typed as a System.Array. You would not be able to directly pass a string array to this method without additional work. In addition, the method signature is no longer type-safe, since the System.Array allows you to pass any data type in the array.

If you create an import library using TlbImp, the default settings will type the array according to the actual VB6 data type. For this example method, you would end up with the string array (string[]) used here. The TlbImp command line used for this sample component looks like this:

```
tlbimp.exe DniDataTypesVB.dll   /out:Interop.DniDataTypesVB.dll
```

How It Works

We can define and implement a similar COM method using C++ Active Template Library (ATL). The IDL for our example method looks like this:

```
[id(13), helpstring("method UseArray")]
HRESULT UseArray([in] SAFEARRAY(BSTR) inParam,
    [out,retval] BSTR* outParam);
```

The C++ implementation for the method looks like this:

```
STDMETHODIMP CDniDataTypesObj::UseArray(SAFEARRAY* inParam,
    BSTR* outParam)
{
    //process the elements of the safearray
    BSTR* pBstr;
    unsigned long i = 0;
    SafeArrayAccessData(inParam, (void**)&pBstr);
    _bstr_t buffer;

    //retrieve all elements of the array
    for (i = 0; i < inParam->rgsabound[0].cElements; i++)
    {
        buffer += _bstr_t(pBstr[i]);
    }

    //return the result string
    *outParam = buffer;
    SafeArrayUnaccessData(inParam);
    return S_OK;
}
```

Finally, the C# code to execute this version of the method looks like this:

```
using System;
using System.Runtime.InteropServices;

using DniDataTypesLib;

namespace ComSafeArrays
{
    class ComSafeArraysTest
    {
        static void Main(string[] args)
        {
            //create an instance of the COM object
            DniDataTypesObj comObj = new DniDataTypesObj();
            string desc = string.Empty;

            //pass an array in as a safearray
            string[] testSafeArray
                = new string[3] { "one", "two", "three" };
            Console.WriteLine("Input Array Before: {0}, {1}, {2}",
                testSafeArray[0], testSafeArray[1],
                testSafeArray[2]);
```

```
        //make the COM call passing the managed array
        desc = comObj.UseArray(testSafeArray);
        Console.WriteLine("UseArray results: {0}",    desc);

        //wait for input
        Console.WriteLine("Press any key to exit");
        Console.Read();
      }
    }
  }
}
```

Similar code implemented in VB.NET looks like this:

```
Imports DniDataTypesLib

Module ComSafeArraysTest

    Sub Main()

        'test C++ object with arrays
        'create an instance of the COM object
        Dim comObj As DniDataTypesObj = New DniDataTypesObj()
        Dim desc As String = String.Empty

        'pass an array in as a safearray
        Dim testSafeArray() As String = {"one", "two", "three"}
        Console.WriteLine("Input Array Before: {0}, {1}, {2}", _
            testSafeArray(0), testSafeArray(1), _
            testSafeArray(2))

        'make the COM call passing the managed array
        desc = comObj.UseArray(testSafeArray)
        Console.WriteLine("UseArray results: {0}", desc)

        'wait for input
        Console.WriteLine("Press any key to exit")
        Console.Read()
    End Sub

End Module
```

As was the case calling the VB6 component, we are able to pass a simple string array to the COM method without any problems. The results from this code are as follows:

```
Input Array Before: one, two, three
UseArray results: onetwothree
Press any key to exit
```

We can also update the passed-in array within the COM method and see the results in managed code. We can define a COM method to update the array like this:

```
[id(14), helpstring("method UpdateArray")]
HRESULT UpdateArray([in,out] SAFEARRAY(BSTR) inParam);
```

The C++ implementation of this method follows:

```
STDMETHODIMP CDniDataTypesObj::UpdateArray(SAFEARRAY* inParam)
{
    //updates the elements of the safearray
    BSTR* pBstr;
    unsigned long i = 0;
    SafeArrayAccessData(inParam, (void**)&pBstr);

    //change all elements of the array
    for (i = 0; i < inParam->rgsabound[0].cElements; i++)
    {
        _bstr_t buffer;
        buffer.Attach(pBstr[i]);
        buffer += "CHANGED";
        pBstr[i] = buffer.Detach();
    }
    SafeArrayUnaccessData(inParam);
    return S_OK;
}
```

The main difference in the method definition is that we've defined the SAFEARRAY as [in,out]. The C++ code adds the literal "CHANGED" to the end of each BSTR element in the array.

We can call this method from C# using this code:

```
using System;
using System.Runtime.InteropServices;

using DniDataTypesLib;

namespace ComSafeArrays
{
    class ComSafeArraysTest
    {
        static void Main(string[] args)
        {
            //create an instance of the COM object
            DniDataTypesObj comObj = new DniDataTypesObj();
            string desc = string.Empty;

            //update an array of strings within the COM component
            string[] testUpdateSafeArray
              = new string[3] { "one", "two", "three" };
```

```
            Console.WriteLine("Array Before: {0}, {1}, {2}",
                testUpdateSafeArray[0], testUpdateSafeArray[1],
                testUpdateSafeArray[2]);

            //make the COM call
            comObj.UpdateArray(testUpdateSafeArray);
            Console.WriteLine("Array After: {0}, {1}, {2}",
                testUpdateSafeArray[0], testUpdateSafeArray[1],
                testUpdateSafeArray[2]);

            //wait for input
            Console.WriteLine("Press any key to exit");
            Console.Read();
        }
    }
}
```

The VB.NET code to call the UpdateArray method looks like this:

```
Imports DniDataTypesLib

Module ComSafeArraysTest

    Sub Main()

        'test C++ object with arrays
        'create an instance of the COM object
        Dim comObj As DniDataTypesObj = New DniDataTypesObj()
        Dim desc As String = String.Empty

        'update an array of strings within the COM component
        Dim testUpdateSafeArray() As String = {"one", "two", "three"}
        Console.WriteLine("Array Before: {0}, {1}, {2}", _
            testUpdateSafeArray(0), testUpdateSafeArray(1), _
            testUpdateSafeArray(2))

        'make the COM call
        comObj.UpdateArray(testUpdateSafeArray)
        Console.WriteLine("Array After: {0}, {1}, {2}", _
            testUpdateSafeArray(0), testUpdateSafeArray(1), _
            testUpdateSafeArray(2))

        'wait for input
        Console.WriteLine("Press any key to exit")
        Console.Read()
    End Sub

End Module
```

We get these test results when we execute the code:

```
Array Before: one, two, three
Array After: oneCHANGED, twoCHANGED, threeCHANGED
Press any key to exit
```

C-style arrays that are not packaged as a SAFEARRAY can also be marshaled between .NET and COM. These arrays are less frequently used in COM since languages such as Visual Basic 6.0 (VB6) don't have much built-in support for them.

We can define a COM method that uses a C-style array like this:

```
[id(15), helpstring("method UseCStyleArray")]
HRESULT UseCStyleArray(
    [in, length_is(arraySize), size_is(arraySize)] long inParam[],
    [in] long arraySize, [in,out] BSTR* outParam);
```

Notice the inclusion of the length_is and size_is Microsoft Interface Definition Language (MIDL) attributes. These attributes are needed in order to provide COM with the size of the array that it must marshal. Here is the C++ implementation of this method:

```
STDMETHODIMP CDniDataTypesObj::UseCStyleArray(long inParam[],
    long arraySize, BSTR* outParam)
{
    //use a C-style array. Copy the input
    //values in the array into a BSTR and return it
    _bstr_t buffer;
    for(int i = 0; i < arraySize; i++)
    {
        buffer += _bstr_t(inParam[i]);
    }
    *outParam = buffer;

    return S_OK;
}
```

The output from this method is a concatenation of the strings in the input array. This C# code calls the COM method:

```
using System;
using System.Runtime.InteropServices;

using DniDataTypesLib;

namespace ComSafeArrays
{
    class ComSafeArraysTest
    {
        static void Main(string[] args)
        {
```

```
//create an instance of the COM object
DniDataTypesObj comObj = new DniDataTypesObj();
string desc = string.Empty;

//call a COM method that uses a C-style array instead
//of a safearray
int[] intArray = new int[3];
intArray[0] = 111;
intArray[1] = 222;
intArray[2] = 333;
string outParam = string.Empty;
//allocate unmanaged memory to pass the array
int memSize = Marshal.SizeOf(
    typeof(Int32)) * intArray.Length;
IntPtr arrayPtr = Marshal.AllocCoTaskMem(memSize);
//copy the array into the unmanaged memory
Marshal.Copy(intArray, 0, arrayPtr, intArray.Length);
//make the COM method call
comObj.UseCStyleArray(arrayPtr, intArray.Length,
    ref outParam);
//free the memory that we allocated
Marshal.FreeCoTaskMem(arrayPtr);
Console.WriteLine("C-Style Array: {0},{1},{2},{3}",
    intArray[0],intArray[1],intArray[2],outParam);

//wait for input
Console.WriteLine("Press any key to exit");
Console.Read();
        }
    }
}
```

Calling this method takes a bit more work on our part. After populating the array we want to pass to the COM method, we allocate unmanaged memory for the array using Marshal.AllocCoTaskMem. This allocates memory that COM is capable of using directly. We then copy the managed array into the allocated memory using Marshal.Copy. Now we are ready to make the COM call, and we do this by passing the IntPtr containing the address of the allocated memory. When the call completes, we remember to free the memory that we allocated using Marshal.FreeCoTaskMem.

When the code is executed, we get these results:

```
C-Style Array: 111,222,333,111222333
Press any key to exit
```

Related Information

See recipe 5-2 (Importing a Type Library).

5-7. Extending COM Classes

Problem

You need to execute additional logic before and after you call a set of COM methods. You would like to do this in a way that encapsulates this logic with the COM class itself. What is the best way to accomplish this?

Solution

Two options allow you to encapsulate additional logic with a COM class:

- Extend the managed proxy generated for the COM class, deriving a new class from it that contains the additional logic.

- Wrap the COM class in a new managed class that contains the additional logic.

This recipe covers the first option: extending the COM class to create a new class.

Note Please refer to the "Related Information" section for recipes that cover the creation of managed wrapper classes to encapsulate unmanaged calls. While the focus of these recipes is on non-COM functions, the ideas and techniques also apply to COM components.

The process of creating an import library for a COM component produces a Runtime Callable Wrapper (RCW). This is a class that acts as a proxy to the properties and methods of the COM component. Types are also generated for any interfaces that are defined in the COM component.

While the ultimate target of any properties or methods is the COM class, the RCW is a managed class. It behaves like a managed class, and as far as our code is concerned, it *is* a managed class. You are not allowed to extend the COM component itself from managed code, but you can extend the RCW.

You do this by implementing a new class that is derived from the RCW. For example, consider a Visual Basic 6.0 (VB6) COM class named MyVBComObj. When this COM type is imported into Visual Studio, an RCW class is generated with a name of MyVBComObjClass. In C#, you can derive your own class from the RCW like this:

```
public class MyExtendedClass : MyVBComObjClass
{
    //add code here
}
```

You are now able to add any additional code that you need to this class, including member variables, properties, or methods. When you need to call one of the COM methods, they are still available to you from the base RCW class.

Consumers of this COM component would then create an instance of your extended class rather than the generated RCW.

How It Works

The code that follows presents an example where an RCW is extended to provide additional functionality.

For this example, we start with a VB6 COM component named DniExtendComVB that contains a COM class named DniExtendComVBObj. Two methods have been implemented:

```
'look up an account ID based on a search type
Public Function AccountLookup(ByVal searchArg As String, _
        ByVal searchType As Long) As Long

    Dim acctId As Long
    'look up an account based on the search type
    acctId = 0
    If searchType = 1 Then
        'add name search code here
        acctId = 1001
    ElseIf searchType = 2 Then
        'add taxId search code here
        acctId = 2002
    ElseIf searchType = 3 Then
        'add address search code here
        acctId = 3003
    End If

    AccountLookup = acctId
End Function

'retrieve the current balance for an account
Public Function GetCurrentBalance( _
        ByVal acctId As Long) As Currency

    'add code to retrieve a balance here
    If acctId = 1001 Then
        GetCurrentBalance = 5432.11
    ElseIf acctId = 2002 Then
        GetCurrentBalance = 1.01
    ElseIf acctId = 3003 Then
        GetCurrentBalance = 5.95
    End If
End Function
```

The first method, AccountLookup, takes a string search argument and a search type integer. The purpose of the method is to search for an account using one of three different search types. It is the responsibility of the caller to provide a search argument and search type that correspond to each other. For our testing, we're returning fixed values based on the search type.

The second method, GetCurrentBalance, is passed an account ID integer and returns a currency amount representing the current balance for the account.

To use this COM class from managed code, we could import the component and call each method as we need it. However, there is an opportunity to improve on this by adding some managed code. Specifically, there is no validation performed within the AccountLookup method. It would be an improvement if we could perform the search without knowing the magic search type numbers of 1, 2, and 3. We would also like to validate that any search argument we pass corresponds to the search type we specify.

Additionally, we realize that each time we search for an account, we also need to retrieve the current balance. Therefore, we'd like to combine both of these COM method calls into a single managed method.

We start by generating an import library for the component using TlbImp. After referencing the import library in our C# code, we are able to derive a new class from the generated RCW. So far, our code looks like this:

```
using System;
using System.Text.RegularExpressions; //needed for RegEx

using Interop.DniExtendComVB; //the import library

namespace ExtendCom
{
    /// <summary>
    /// Extend a COM RCW
    /// </summary>
    public class ExtendedComClass : DniExtendComVBObjClass //RCW
    {
    }
}
```

The using statement for System.Text.RegularExpressions will be needed for code that we add next.

To eliminate the magic numbers for the search type, we define this enum:

```
/// <summary>
/// Define search types
/// </summary>
public enum SearchType
{
    Unknown = 0,
    Name = 1,
    TaxId = 2,
    Address = 3
}
```

This permits any managed consumers of this class to specify the search type using the enum rather than the magic numbers. Even though we are using this enum, it is still possible to pass in an invalid value for the search type. To guard against this, we add this private method to our ExtendedComClass to validate the search type:

```
/// <summary>
/// Validate the search type
/// </summary>
/// <param name="searchType"></param>
/// <returns></returns>
private SearchType ValidateSearchType(SearchType searchType)
{
    SearchType validSearchType = SearchType.Unknown;
    if (Enum.IsDefined(typeof(SearchType), searchType))
    {
        validSearchType = searchType;
    }
    else
    {
        throw new ApplicationException(String.Format(
            "Search type of {0} is invalid", searchType));
    }
    return validSearchType;
}
```

Later we'll see where we call this method. For this method and others to follow, we've chosen to simply throw an exception if something is wrong. Obviously, you can choose to handle error conditions more gracefully.

We also need a private method that will validate the search argument. This method should ensure that the search argument is valid for the specified search type. Here is the method that we add to our class:

```
/// <summary>
/// Validate the search argument based on the search type.
/// Throws an exception if the search argument is invalid.
/// </summary>
/// <param name="searchtype"></param>
/// <param name="searchArg"></param>
private void ValidateSearchArgument(SearchType searchType,
    string searchArg)
{
    //define regex strings used for validation
    const string TaxIdRegex
        = @"^(?!000)([0-6]\d{2}|7([0-6]\d|7[012]))"
        + @"([ -]?)(?!00)\d\d\3(?!0000)\d{4}$";
    const string NameRegex
        = @"^([a-zA-z\s]{4,50})$";
    const string AddressRegex
        = @"^[a-zA-Z\d]+(([\'\,\.\- #][a-zA-Z\d ])"
        + @"?[a-zA-Z\d]*[\.]*)*$";

    //validate the search argument based on the search type
    switch (searchType)
```

```
    {
        case SearchType.Name:
            if (!Regex.IsMatch(searchArg, NameRegex))
            {
                throw new ApplicationException(String.Format(
                    "Search argument of {0} is not a valid {1}",
                        searchArg, searchType));
            }
            break;
        case SearchType.TaxId:
            if (!Regex.IsMatch(searchArg, TaxIdRegex))
            {
                throw new ApplicationException(String.Format(
                    "Search argument of {0} is not a valid {1}",
                    searchArg, searchType));
            }
            break;
        case SearchType.Address:
            if (!Regex.IsMatch(searchArg, AddressRegex))
            {
                throw new ApplicationException(String.Format(
                    "Search argument of {0} is not a valid {1}",
                    searchArg, searchType));
            }
            break;

        default:
            break;
    }
}
```

Now that we've implemented a couple of private helper methods, it's time to add a public method that uses them. We've chosen to implement a method named AccountBalance that not only calls the COM AccountLookup method, but also calls GetCurrentBalance if the search was successful. The method looks like this:

```
public decimal AccountBalance(string searchArg,
    SearchType searchType)
{
    decimal result = 0;

    //validate the requested search type
    SearchType validSearchType
        = ValidateSearchType(searchType);

    //validate the search argument based on the search type
    ValidateSearchArgument(validSearchType, searchArg);
```

```
        try
        {
            //everything passes our tests, so make the COM call
            int acctId = base.AccountLookup(searchArg,
                (int)validSearchType);
            //check the result
            if (acctId == 0)
            {
                throw new ApplicationException(
                    String.Format("Account not found for {0} {1}",
                    searchType, searchArg));
            }

            //retrieve the current balance for the account
            result = base.GetCurrentBalance(acctId);
        }
        catch (Exception e)
        {
            throw new ApplicationException(
                "Exception thrown calling COM method", e);
        }

        return result;
    }
```

After executing the private validation methods, the code calls the COM AccountLookup method. Notice that we didn't need to create an instance of the COM RCW here. Remember that our class *is* the RCW since it is our base class.

If the search is successful, we call the COM GetCurrentBalance method and return the currency result to the caller.

Here is the code to test this new class:

```
/// <summary>
/// Test of an extended COM RCS class
/// </summary>
class ExtendComTest
{
    static void Main(string[] args)
    {
        //create an instance of the extended RCW
        ExtendedComClass comObj = new ExtendedComClass();

        decimal acctBal = 0m;
        acctBal = comObj.AccountBalance(
            "first last", SearchType.Name);
        Console.WriteLine("Balance by Name: {0}", acctBal);
        acctBal = comObj.AccountBalance(
            "123-45-6789", SearchType.TaxId);
```

```
        Console.WriteLine("Balance by Tax Id: {0}", acctBal);
        acctBal = comObj.AccountBalance(
            "1 main street", SearchType.Address);
        Console.WriteLine("Balance by Address: {0}", acctBal);

        //wait for input
        Console.WriteLine("Press any key to exit");
        Console.Read();
    }
}
```

Notice that we create an instance of our new extended class, not the original RCW. The results of this test look like this:

```
Balance by Name: 5432.11
Balance by Tax Id: 1.01
Balance by Address: 5.95
Press any key to exit
```

Here is the same functionality implemented in Visual Basic .NET (VB.NET) instead of C#:

```
Imports System
Imports System.Runtime.InteropServices
Imports System.Text.RegularExpressions

Imports Interop.DniExtendComVB

''' <summary>
''' Define search types
'''</summary>
Public Enum SearchType
    Unknown = 0
    Name = 1
    TaxId = 2
    Address = 3
End Enum

''' <summary>
''' Extend a COM RCW
''' </summary>
Public Class ExtendedComClass
    Inherits DniExtendComVBObjClass 'the RCW

    Public Function AccountBalance(ByVal searchArg As String, _
    ByVal searchType As SearchType) As Decimal

        Dim result As Decimal = 0
```

```vb
        'validate the requested search type
        Dim validSearchType As SearchType _
            = ValidateSearchType(searchType)

        'validate the search argument based on the search type
        ValidateSearchArgument(validSearchType, searchArg)

        Try
            'everything passes our tests, so make the COM call
            Dim acctId As Integer _
                = MyBase.AccountLookup(searchArg, validSearchType)
            'check the result
            If acctId = 0 Then
                Throw New ApplicationException( _
                    String.Format("Account not found for {0} {1}", _
                    searchType, searchArg))
            End If
            'retrieve the current balance for the account
            result = MyBase.GetCurrentBalance(acctId)

        Catch ex As Exception
            Throw New ApplicationException( _
                "Exception thrown calling COM method", ex)
        End Try

        Return result
    End Function


    ''' <summary>
    ''' Validate the search type
    ''' </summary>
    ''' <param name="searchType"></param>
    ''' <returns></returns>
    Private Function ValidateSearchType(ByVal searchType As SearchType) _
        As SearchType
        Dim validSearchType As SearchType _
            = ExtendComVB.SearchType.Unknown
        If [Enum].IsDefined(GetType(SearchType), searchType) Then
            validSearchType = searchType
        Else
            Throw New ApplicationException(String.Format( _
                "Search type of {0} is invalid", searchType))
        End If
        Return validSearchType
    End Function


    ''' <summary>
    ''' Validate the search argument based on the search type.
```

```vb.net
''' Throws an exception if the search argument is invalid.
''' </summary>
''' <param name="searchtype"></param>
''' <param name="searchArg"></param>
Private Sub ValidateSearchArgument(ByVal searchType As SearchType, _
        ByVal searchArg As String)
    'define regex strings used for validation
    Const TaxIdRegex As String _
        = "^(?!000)([0-6]\d{2}|7([0-6]\d|7[012]))" _
        + "([ -]?)(?!00)\d\d\3(?!0000)\d{4}$"
    Const NameRegex As String _
        = "^([a-zA-z\s]{4,50})$"
    Const AddressRegex As String _
        = "^[a-zA-Z\d]+((([\'\,\.\- #][a-zA-Z\d ])" _
        + "?[a-zA-Z\d]*[\.]*)*$"


    'validate the search argument based on the search type
    Select Case searchType
        Case ExtendComVB.SearchType.Name
            If Not Regex.IsMatch(searchArg, NameRegex) Then
                Throw New ApplicationException(String.Format( _
                    "Search argument of {0} is not a valid {1}", _
                    searchArg, searchType))
            End If
        Case ExtendComVB.SearchType.TaxId
            If Not Regex.IsMatch(searchArg, TaxIdRegex) Then
                Throw New ApplicationException(String.Format( _
                    "Search argument of {0} is not a valid {1}", _
                    searchArg, searchType))
            End If
        Case ExtendComVB.SearchType.Address
            If Not Regex.IsMatch(searchArg, AddressRegex) Then
                Throw New ApplicationException(String.Format( _
                    "Search argument of {0} is not a valid {1}", _
                    searchArg, searchType))
            End If
    End Select
End Sub

End Class
```

Code to execute this VB.NET class looks like this:

```vb.net
Module ExtendComTest

    Sub Main()
        'create an instance of the extended RCW
        Dim comObj As ExtendedComClass = New ExtendedComClass()
```

```
        Dim acctBal As Decimal = 0D
        acctBal = comObj.AccountBalance( _
            "first last", SearchType.Name)
        Console.WriteLine("Balance by Name: {0}", acctBal)
        acctBal = comObj.AccountBalance( _
            "123-45-6789", SearchType.TaxId)
        Console.WriteLine("Balance by Tax Id: {0}", acctBal)
        acctBal = comObj.AccountBalance( _
            "1 main street", SearchType.Address)
        Console.WriteLine("Balance by Address: {0}", acctBal)

        'wait for input
        Console.WriteLine("Press any key to exit")
        Console.Read()

    End Sub

End Module
```

We've added a good amount of code to the RCW. The end result is that we now have a class that provides some level of validation and combines multiple COM calls into a single method.

We could have implemented this as a managed class wrapper instead of deriving directly from the RCW. In that case, we would have developed a new managed class that internally created an instance of the unaltered COM RCW.

Ultimately, the implementation choice comes down to style. Do you prefer inheritance or containment? Which approach is a better fit with your existing classes? The good news is that the generated RCW gives you that choice.

Related Information

See recipes 5-1 (Using COM Components from .NET), 5-2 (Importing a Type Library), 1-3 (Simplifying Reuse of Unmanaged Functions), and 1-13 (Securing Access to Unmanaged Code).

5-8. Changing the Apartment Model

Problem

You have COM components that use different COM threading models. Most use a single-threaded apartment (STA), while others use the multithreaded apartment (MTA) model. How do you change the apartment threading model when making COM interop calls?

Solution

You can set the threading model within your managed code in one of two ways:

- Declaratively, using the STAThread or MTAThread attribute

- Procedurally, by calling the Thread.SetApartmentState method

The .NET runtime creates a COM apartment the first time any COM component is used by a managed thread. Once the apartment is initialized, the threading model cannot be changed.

The STAThread and MTAThread attributes are applied to the main method of the application. For example, use STAThread to create a single-threaded COM apartment:

```
[STAThread]
static void Main(string[] args)
{
}
```

Use MTAThread to create a multithreaded COM apartment:

```
[MTAThread]
static void Main(string[] args)
{
}
```

You can also use methods of the System.Threading.Thread class to set the COM apartment model. For example, the following sets the apartment model to an MTA:

```
Thread.CurrentThread.SetApartmentState(ApartmentState.MTA);
```

This sets an STA:

```
Thread.CurrentThread.SetApartmentState(ApartmentState.STA);
```

■**Caution** The call to SetApartmentState must be made prior to the first COM object being instantiated. SetApartmentState will throw an InvalidOperationException if the apartment model cannot be set, for example, if the code has already initialized the COM apartment by making a prior COM call. An exception is also thrown if the apartment model has already been set to a different type using the STAThread or MTAThread attribute.

You can use the Thread.TrySetApartmentState method instead if you want to avoid an exception. This method attempts to set the threading model but doesn't throw an exception if it fails.

How It Works

.NET doesn't use apartments but COM does. A COM apartment is a logical container that provides synchronization with resources. A COM object in an apartment can directly receive calls from any thread that has entered that apartment. To enter an apartment, the threading models must be compatible. An STA supports only a single thread, while an MTA contains one or more threads. Because of the multithreaded nature of an MTA, the COM object is responsible for ensuring that the code is thread-safe and properly protects the object's data members.

When the threading model for a COM object is compatible with the apartment created by the .NET runtime, the interop calls are made directly to the COM object. The COM and managed threads can both live in the same apartment. When the models are incompatible, an additional compatible apartment is created by COM and used as a proxy. The interop calls then use the proxy apartment to get to the COM object.

Any managed thread is capable of using COM objects of either type (STA or MTA). The difference is the potential overhead of creating and using the additional proxy apartment. For the best potential performance, we should try to select the managed apartment model that is compatible with the COM objects we will be using.

The C# code that follows demonstrates setting the apartment model:

```csharp
using System;
using System.Threading;

using DniThreadingLib;

namespace ComThreading
{
    class ComThreadingTest
    {
        /// <summary>
        /// The main entry point for the application.
        /// </summary>
        [STAThread]
        static void Main(string[] args)
        {
            Console.WriteLine("Original ApartmentState: {0}",
                Thread.CurrentThread.GetApartmentState());

            int result = 0;
            DniThreadingStaObj staObj
                = new DniThreadingStaObjClass();
            result = staObj.AddNumbers(1, 2);
            Console.WriteLine("STA Obj result: {0}, Threading: {1}",
                result, Thread.CurrentThread.GetApartmentState());

            //attempt a change to the apartment model
            //with SetApartmentState
            try
            {
                Thread.CurrentThread.SetApartmentState(
                    ApartmentState.MTA);
                Console.WriteLine(
                    "No Exception calling SetApartmentState");
            }
            catch (InvalidOperationException e)
            {
                Console.WriteLine(
                    "Exception calling SetApartmentState: {0}",
                    e.Message);
            }
```

```
//attempt a change to the apartment model
//with TrySetApartmentState
try
{
    bool changeStatus =
        Thread.CurrentThread.TrySetApartmentState(
            ApartmentState.MTA);
    Console.WriteLine(
        "TrySetApartmentState result {0}",
            changeStatus);
}
catch (InvalidOperationException e)
{
    Console.WriteLine(
        "Exception calling TrySetApartmentState: {0}",
        e.Message);
}

DniThreadingMtaObj mtaObj
    = new DniThreadingMtaObjClass();
result = mtaObj.AddNumbers(1, 2);
Console.WriteLine("MTA Obj result: {0}, Threading: {1}",
    result, Thread.CurrentThread.GetApartmentState());

//wait for input
Console.WriteLine("Press any key to exit");
Console.Read();
        }
    }
}
```

This managed code creates two different COM objects. DniThreadingStaObj is an Active Template Library (ATL) object implemented using an STA. DniThreadingMtaObj uses an MTA. Here's the IDL that defines the COM component with these classes:

```
import "oaidl.idl";
import "ocidl.idl";

[
    object,
    uuid(B09DA11F-8925-4F5C-B4C0-29B1C9A057D2),
    dual,
    nonextensible,
    helpstring("IDniThreadingStaObj Interface"),
    pointer_default(unique)
]
interface IDniThreadingStaObj : IDispatch{
    [id(1), helpstring("method AddNumbers")]
```

```
        HRESULT AddNumbers([in] long numA, [in] long numB,
            [out,retval] long* result);
};
[
    object,
    uuid(2F5E058B-5CE8-40D4-9205-75EF080C5985),
    dual,
    nonextensible,
    helpstring("IDniThreadingMtaObj Interface"),
    pointer_default(unique)
]
interface IDniThreadingMtaObj : IDispatch{
    [id(1), helpstring("method AddNumbers")]
    HRESULT AddNumbers([in] long numA, [in] long numB,
        [out,retval] long* result);
};
[
    uuid(18EBC191-70AF-4DA4-B47F-1ED1738F7FCB),
    version(1.0),
    helpstring("DniThreading 1.0 Type Library")
]
library DniThreadingLib
{
    importlib("stdole2.tlb");
    [
        uuid(56966392-3BDD-4B15-B4AD-32A0200D2E0C),
        helpstring("DniThreadingStaObj Class")
    ]
    coclass DniThreadingStaObj
    {
        [default] interface IDniThreadingStaObj;
    };
    [
        uuid(D3970753-9BA4-450D-9692-4D00457D8005),
        helpstring("DniThreadingMtaObj Class")
    ]
    coclass DniThreadingMtaObj
    {
        [default] interface IDniThreadingMtaObj;
    };
};
```

And here is the implementation of the AddNumbers method for each COM class:

```
STDMETHODIMP CDniThreadingStaObj::AddNumbers(
    long numA, long numB, long* result)
{
    *result = numA + numB;
    return S_OK;
}
STDMETHODIMP CDniThreadingMtaObj::AddNumbers(
    long numA, long numB, long* result)
{
    *result = numA + numB;
    return S_OK;
}
```

This test uses the STAThread attribute to set the threading model prior to the first COM call. The initial threading model is displayed using the Thread.GetApartmentState method. After calling the STA object, we use both SetApartmentState and TrySetApartmentState to change the model to MTA. Those calls will show us what happens when we try to change the model after the first COM call has occurred. Finally, we make the call to the MTA object.

When this code is executed, we get these results:

```
Original ApartmentState: STA
STA Obj result: 3, Threading: STA
Exception calling SetApartmentState:
    Failed to set the specified COM apartment state.
TrySetApartmentState result False
MTA Obj result: 3, Threading: STA
Press any key to exit
```

We see that the threading model is correctly set to STA. As expected, the call to SetApartmentState threw an exception, while the call to TrySetApartmentState did not. However, neither call succeeded since the final threading model displayed is still STA.

We can make a single-line change to this code to use the multithreading model. We replace the STAThread attribute with MTAThread and rebuild the project. Now when we execute the test, we see these results:

```
Original ApartmentState: MTA
STA Obj result: 3, Threading: MTA
No Exception calling SetApartmentState
TrySetApartmentState result True
MTA Obj result: 3, Threading: MTA
Press any key to exit
```

The apartment model is now correctly set to MTA and the calls to manually set the model execute without an exception.

5-9. Refactoring for Performance

Problem

You are concerned about the overhead of interop calls between managed code and COM objects. Are there changes you should consider making to the COM components to improve performance?

Solution

Each round-trip to a COM component incurs a performance price. Calling from managed code into COM (or vice versa) involves a transition between two different environments. They can work together, but they are not the same. For example, data types need to be converted if the data is not represented the same way in each environment. COM components also have apartment-threading issues that must be managed when the .NET runtime makes each COM call.

Each time a COM property is accessed, or a method is called, a round-trip is made between the two environments. Each and every round-trip has to address any data conversion, memory management, and threading issues. To optimize a COM component, you may need to modify the interface to reduce the round-trips. Performance will improve if you favor *chunky* interfaces over *chatty* ones.

An interface is considered chatty if it contains a number of methods or properties, with each performing only a single task. The client code must make multiple round-trips to the COM object to perform any meaningful work.

An interface is chunky if it allows you to perform some meaningful task in a single round-trip to the component. With a chunky interface, you are performing the same tasks, but with less interop overhead. Chunky interfaces typically include methods that require more than just a single argument.

For example, the COM object in use here would be considered chatty:

```
obj.AcctId        = 1234;
obj.Balance       = 500;
obj.StatusDesc    = "Really Past Due";
obj.SetPastDueStatus();
```

Each time we set a property, we are incurring the cost of a round-trip. To perform this simple operation, it takes four interop round-trips.

On the other hand, this COM object would be considered chunky:

```
obj.SetAcctPastDue(1234, 500, "Really Past Due");
```

We've accomplished the same task, but we require only a single trip to the COM object.

How It Works

The following example uses a Visual Basic 6.0 (VB6) COM component to demonstrate this refactoring. The original VB6 code looks like this:

```
'search for the account
Public Function SearchForAccount( _
```

```
                ByVal searchArg As String) As Long
        If searchArg = "accountKey" Then
            SearchForAccount = 1001
        Else
            SearchForAccount = 0
        End If
End Function


'retrieve the past due amount
Public Function GetPastDueBalance( _
            ByVal acctId As Long) As Currency
        If acctId = 1001 Then
            GetPastDueBalance = 123.45
        Else
            GetPastDueBalance = 0
        End If
End Function


'mark the account as delinquent
Public Function SetAccountDelinquent(ByVal acctId As Long)
        'add code to mark the account as delinquent
End Function
```

These three methods each perform a single task. The first method, SearchForAccount, returns an account ID based on a search argument. The second method, GetPastDueBalance, takes the account ID as an argument and returns a past-due balance. The third method, SetAccountDelinquent, takes an account ID and marks it as delinquent.

If we write C# code to use these methods, it might look like this:

```
DniComRefactorVBObj comObj = new DniComRefactorVBObjClass();
int acctId = comObj.SearchForAccount("accountKey");
if (acctId > 0)
{
    Decimal pastDueAmt = comObj.GetPastDueBalance(acctId);
    if (pastDueAmt > 100.00m)
    {
        comObj.SetAccountDelinquent(acctId);
    }
}
```

This code is simple enough and gets the job done. The problem is that it makes three separate round-trips to the COM object to perform this work. Why not refactor this code slightly to improve the performance? One way to do this is to move the managed logic we just executed to the COM component itself. By adding this new method, we've done just that:

```
'refactored method combining multiple methods
Public Function CheckAccountDelinquency( _
            ByVal searchArg As String, _
            ByVal limitAmt As Currency) As Boolean
```

```
    'set default result
    CheckAccountDelinquency = False

    'call the other methods locally rather
    'than across the COM boundary

    Dim acctId As Long
    Dim pastDueBal As Currency

    acctId = SearchForAccount(searchArg)
    If acctId > 0 Then
        pastDueBal = GetPastDueBalance(acctId)
        If pastDueBal > limitAmt Then
            SetAccountDelinquent (acctId)
            CheckAccountDelinquency = True
        End If
    End If
End Function
```

We now have a single COM method that performs the same work that we previously implemented in C#. The new C# code to execute this method looks like this:

```
DniComRefactorVBObj comObj = new DniComRefactorVBObjClass();
comObj.CheckAccountDelinquency("accountKey", 100.00m);
```

By moving this code into the COM component, we eliminate two of the round-trips from managed code, which does improve performance. The improvement may not be significant for a single call, but it will quickly add up if you repeatedly execute these methods.

If you are unable to modify the source for the COM component, you can develop a new COM component that acts as a wrapper for the target component. This new wrapper component would make the calls to the target COM component for you instead of making them directly from managed code. This isn't as beneficial as adding a method to the original COM component, but it should still provide better performance than making multiple calls directly from managed code.

5-10. Creating a Late-Bound COM Object

Problem

Is there a way to do late binding of COM objects in .NET? Visual Basic 6.0 (VB6) allowed you to do this, creating an instance of a COM object declared as Object.

Solution

Yes, .NET supports late binding of COM objects. *Binding* is the processing of locating the implementation for a particular type. Early binding of COM objects resolves the COM reference at compile time. This is the binding used when you directly reference a COM component from Visual Studio or when you create an import library using TlbImp.

Late binding waits until runtime to look for the COM object. Most of the time, you use early binding, but occasionally you might need to use late binding to reference a COM component. This might be the case if you don't have access to the type library during development. Or you may need to programmatically determine the ProgID or CLSID of the COM object at runtime based on some variables.

To late-bind a COM object, you follow these steps:

1. Retrieve the Type for the object.

2. Create an instance of the object.

3. Call the methods.

The syntax used to accomplish late binding varies between the languages. Visual Basic .NET (VB.NET) supports a streamlined syntax to use late binding, so we'll consider it first. Here is the sample VB.NET code:

```
'Retrieve the Type for the COM object
Dim comType As Type
comType = Type.GetTypeFromProgID( _
    "DniComRefactorVB.DniComRefactorVBObj")

'create an instance of the COM object
Dim comObj As Object     'dim for late-binding
comObj = Activator.CreateInstance(comType)

Dim acctId As Integer
Dim pastDueAmt As Decimal
'execute the first COM method
acctId = comObj.SearchForAccount("accountKey")
If acctId > 0 Then
    'the second COM method
    pastDueAmt = comObj.GetPastDueBalance(acctId)
    If pastDueAmt > 100 Then
        'the third COM method
        comObj.SetAccountDelinquent(acctId)
    End If
End If
Console.WriteLine("Acct Id:{0}, PastDueAmt:{1}", _
    acctId, pastDueAmt)

'wait for input
Console.WriteLine("Press any key to exit")
Console.Read()
```

This example calls the same COM object we used in the last recipe.

The first step is to retrieve the Type for the COM object. To do this, we can use either the static GetTypeFromProgID or GetTypeFromCLSID method of the Type class. We choose to use GetTypeFromProgID, specifying the full ProgID for the COM component. The ProgID can specify either a version-independent name or one that identifies a specific version of the component.

If we wanted to specify a Guid instead, we could have used the GetTypeFromCLSID method:

```
comType = Type.GetTypeFromCLSID( _
    New Guid("{6E6F51E4-7387-4C07-970D-AD452DC6971D}"))
```

In either case, the Type object returned would be the same. Remember that if you are referencing a VB6 component, the Guid may change from build to build. For that reason, it's easier to use the ProgID.

Note If you are not sure what the full ProgID or CLSID is for a component, you can find this information using the OLE Object Viewer tool included with Visual Studio.

Once a Type is retrieved, we use the CreateInstance method of the Activator class to instantiate an object of the Type. Notice that the result of CreateInstance is a System.Object. It is not a strongly typed object based on the COM type library, since we never imported the type library.

Now that we have an instance of the COM object, we can call methods on that object. Since we've declared the variable holding the reference to the COM object as System.Object, we are able to call any method we need by simply specifying the name.

While this looks like normal .NET method syntax, it isn't. Remember, System.Object is not strongly typed to look like our COM object. It shouldn't allow us to invoke these methods without compile errors. But it does because of the special way that VB.NET handles System.Object. With System.Object, there is no compile-time checking of method names. It is up to us to verify the method names we use, since the compiler will not flag any errors. Any misspelled method names will be caught at runtime.

As we will see, C# does not support this same syntax. It is possible to perform late binding in C#, but the code is not as intuitive.

When we execute this code, we see these results:

```
Acct Id:1001, PastDueAmt:123.45
Press any key to exit
```

Note Setting Option Strict On will disable the ability to perform late binding using System.Object. When this option is turned on, the preceding code will not build due to errors.

How It Works

The syntax to perform the same type of late binding in C# is slightly more complicated. C# doesn't allow us to call undefined methods on the System.Object type the way VB.NET does. If we tried this in C#, our code wouldn't compile.

Here is the equivalent code implemented in C#:

```
//Retrieve the Type for the COM object
Type comType = Type.GetTypeFromProgID(
    "DniComRefactorVB.DniComRefactorVBObj");

//create an instance of the COM object
Object comObj = Activator.CreateInstance(comType);

//execute the first COM method
Int32 acctId = (Int32)comType.InvokeMember(
    "SearchForAccount", BindingFlags.InvokeMethod, null,
    comObj, new Object[] { "accountKey" });
Decimal pastDueAmt = 0;
if (acctId > 0)
{
    //execute the second COM method
    pastDueAmt = (Decimal)comType.InvokeMember(
        "GetPastDueBalance", BindingFlags.InvokeMethod,
        null, comObj, new Object[] { acctId });
    if (pastDueAmt > 100m)
    {
        //execute the third
        comType.InvokeMember(
            "SetAccountDelinquent",
            BindingFlags.InvokeMethod, null,
            comObj, new Object[] { acctId });
    }
}
Console.WriteLine("Acct Id:{0}, PastDueAmt:{1}",
    acctId, pastDueAmt);

Console.WriteLine("Press any key to exit");
Console.Read();
```

The C# code starts out the same way as the VB.NET code. We retrieve a Type object for the COM object, and then we pass that type to Activator.CreateInstance to create an instance of the COM object.

From this point forward, the code differs. To call a method in C#, we need to use the InvokeMember method on the Type object that we retrieved. There are a number of overloaded versions of this method. To use the one we chose, we pass the method name, a BindingFlags value, the COM object we created, and an array of parameters. We need to cast the return value to the type we expect since InvokeMember returns only a System.Object.

When we execute this code, the results look the same as the VB.NET example:

```
Acct Id:1001, PastDueAmt:123.45
Press any key to exit
```

These examples pass parameters only as input (by value, or [in]). If we need to pass a parameter that is updatable by the COM method ([in,out]), the code is slightly more complicated. The example C# code that follows uses the DniDataTypes COM component introduced in a prior recipe. It implements a number of methods that use [in,out] parameters, including the following UseLong method. This method is defined in IDL like this:

```
[id(3), helpstring("method UseLong")]
HRESULT UseLong([in] long inParam, [in,out] long* outParam);
```

It is implemented like this:

```
STDMETHODIMP CDniDataTypesObj::UseLong(long inParam, long* outParam)
{
    *outParam = inParam;
    return S_OK;
}
```

Here is the C# code needed to call this method with late binding:

```
//Retrieve the Type for the COM object
Type comType = Type.GetTypeFromProgID(
    "DniDataTypes.DniDataTypesObj");

//create an instance of the COM object
Object comObj = Activator.CreateInstance(comType);

//tell the marshaler that the 2nd parameter is by ref
ParameterModifier paramMod = new ParameterModifier(2);
paramMod[0] = false;
paramMod[1] = true;     //in/out ref param

//set our array of parameters
Object[] args = { 123, 0 };

//show the arguments prior to the call
Console.WriteLine(
    "Arguments prior to COM call - In:{0}, Out:{1}",
    args[0], args[1]);

//execute the COM method
Object result = comType.InvokeMember(
    "UseLong", BindingFlags.InvokeMethod, null,
    comObj, args,
    new ParameterModifier[] { paramMod },
    null, null);

//remember that the in/out param is in the array!
Console.WriteLine(
    "Late-bound in/out method - In:{0}, Out:{1}",
    args[0], args[1]);
```

```
Console.WriteLine("Press any key to exit");
Console.Read();
```

To tell the marshaler that our second parameter will be modified by the COM method, we need to use the `ParameterModifier` type. This type internally contains an array of `Boolean` values. Note that our `paramMod` variable is not an array of `ParameterModifier`. It is a single instance of this class. Each element in the internal array corresponds to an element in the argument array passed to the method. Element zero in this array corresponds to the first argument, element one corresponds to the second argument, and so forth. We set an element to `true` if the corresponding argument will be modified by the COM method. In our example, the second element is marked as `true` since it is an `[in,out]` parameter.

We now use a different overloaded version of `InvokeMember` that accepts an array of `ParameterModifier` objects. After calling the COM method, we see that the second element in the argument array has been successfully modified:

```
Arguments prior to COM call - In:123, Out:0
Late-bound in/out method - In:123, Out:123
Press any key to exit
```

When using this version of `InvokeMember`, we need to remember that the modified parameter is in the argument array, not in the original variable used to populate the array.

Related Information

See recipes 5-1 (Using COM Components from .NET), 5-2 (Importing a Type Library), 5-4 (Marshaling COM Data Types), and 5-9 (Refactoring for Performance).

5-11. Sharing an Interop Assembly

Problem

You have several applications that all use the same COM component. Is there a way to create a single interop library for the component and share it among all your .NET applications?

Solution

.NET assemblies can be deployed as private or shared assemblies. Private assemblies are deployed into the same directory tree as the assemblies that use them, either in the same directory or a subdirectory. They cannot be referenced by assemblies located in other folders. Shared assemblies go into the global assembly cache (GAC) and are available to all .NET assemblies regardless of their location.

A *primary interop assembly* is a special kind of assembly that goes into the GAC. Like a normal interop assembly generated from `TlbImp`, it contains the type definitions that correspond to a COM component. The difference is indicated by the name "primary interop assembly"; it is designed to be the primary mechanism to interoperate with that COM component. There can be only a single primary interop assembly for any given COM component. Since it resides in the GAC, it must also be signed with a strong name.

▮**Note** If you are using a vendor-supplied COM component, the vendor should supply a primary interop assembly that corresponds to the component. This assembly must be signed by the vendor and stands as the official .NET definition of the types in the COM component.

If you are working with components developed in-house, you have the option of generating your own primary interop assembly. You might want to do this if the COM component is used by multiple .NET assemblies that are deployed to different locations.

The steps to create a primary interop assembly are as follows:

1. Generate a strong-name key pair using the sn utility. The generated key file is used by TlbImp during generation of the assembly. This step can be omitted if you are using a public/private key pair that has already been generated. This is generally the case for software publishers that have an official public/private key pair.

2. Use TlbImp to generate the interop assembly. Additional parameters are needed to make the generated assembly a primary interop assembly.

3. Use RegAsm to register the assembly. This creates a link in the registry between the COM component and the interop assembly.

4. Use gacutil to add the assembly to the global assembly cache (GAC).

Even though a primary interop assembly exists for a COM component, you still reference the COM component in the same way within Visual Studio .NET. The difference is that Visual Studio will know that a primary interop assembly exists for the component. It will reference and use that assembly rather than generating a new interop library.

How It Works

Here is an example of a command file that performs all of the steps needed to generate a primary interop assembly. Prior to executing these commands, the COM component is built and registered. In this example, a Visual Basic 6.0 (VB6) component named DniComRefactorVB is used.

```
@echo off
@echo Create a primary interop assembly

rem ---generate the strong name key pair---
sn -k DniComRefactorVB.snk

rem ---create the primary interop assembly---
tlbimp DniComRefactorVB.Dll /primary
    /keyfile:DniComRefactorVB.snk
    /namespace:Bukovics.DniComRefactorVB.Interop
    /out:Bukovics.DniComRefactorVB.Interop.dll
    /asmversion:1.0.1.0 /verbose
```

```
rem ---register the assembly---
regasm Bukovics.DniComRefactorVB.Interop.dll

rem ---add the assembly to the GAC---
gacutil /if Bukovics.DniComRefactorVB.Interop.dll
```

Walking through the commands, we see that we first generate the strong-name key pair using the sn (strong name) utility. This is done first since the key pair file generated by this step is used as an input to the next step. We name the key pair DniComRefactorVB.snk to correspond with the COM component name. It is not a requirement to use the same name as the component, but it's a good idea to help keep things organized.

Next we come to the TlbImp step that generates the interop assembly.

Note The TlbImp command line just shown was separated into multiple lines in order to fit the formatting of this book. When executed, all options are specified on a single line.

A number of additional parameters are needed when generating a primary interop assembly. Here's a rundown of the parameters we used in this example:

- /primary: This causes the generated assembly to be a primary interop assembly.

- /keyfile: This is where we specify the name of the strong-name key pair file that we generated in the sn step. As an alternative, we could specify the /delaysign option if we need to delay the signing of the assembly. This is typically the case for software publishers that closely guard their official public/private key pair that they use for signing.

- /namespace: Since a primary interop assembly is loaded into the GAC, we want to assign it a unique namespace and output DLL name. One way to do this is to include the company name as part of the name. This reduces the chance that the name chosen will conflict with that of another assembly.

- /out: This specifies the name of the output assembly file. See the preceding note for /namespace.

- /asmversion: Anything loaded into the GAC must have a valid version number, so we assign it here. We can use this option to specify a version number that corresponds with the matching COM component.

The output from this step is the assembly Bukovics.DniComRefactorVB.Interop.dll. This is the primary interop assembly.

Note This example uses the sn utility to generate a strong-name key file. While this works, software publishers will want to sign their interop assemblies using their official public/private key pair. This key file is closely guarded and used only to sign software components that are officially verified by the publisher.

Next, we register this assembly using the regasm utility. Performing this step adds COM registration entries that associate the original COM component with this primary interop assembly. For this assembly, here are the registration entries that are generated. We don't need to do anything with these entries—they are included here for information only.

```
[HKEY_CLASSES_ROOT\CLSID\
    {6E6F51E4-7387-4C07-970D-AD452DC6971D}\InprocServer32]
"Class"="Bukovics.DniComRefactorVB.Interop.DniComRefactorVBObjClass"
"Assembly"="Bukovics.DniComRefactorVB.Interop, Version=1.0.1.0,
    Culture=neutral, PublicKeyToken=a4a9a92b57f097de"
"RuntimeVersion"="v2.0.50215"

[HKEY_CLASSES_ROOT\CLSID\
    {6E6F51E4-7387-4C07-970D-AD452DC6971D}\InprocServer32\1.0.1.0]
"Class"="Bukovics.DniComRefactorVB.Interop.DniComRefactorVBObjClass"
"Assembly"="Bukovics.DniComRefactorVB.Interop, Version=1.0.1.0,
    Culture=neutral, PublicKeyToken=a4a9a92b57f097de"
"RuntimeVersion"="v2.0.50215"

[HKEY_CLASSES_ROOT\TypeLib\
    {9BB4CC13-5FB0-46ED-8124-1B6C5E49210A}\1.0]
"PrimaryInteropAssemblyName"="Bukovics.DniComRefactorVB.Interop,
    Version=1.0.1.0, Culture=neutral,
    PublicKeyToken=a4a9a92b57f097de"
```

The last set of entries identifies our assembly as the primary interop assembly for this COM component. Visual Studio .NET will use these entries to determine if a primary interop assembly exists. If it does, Visual Studio .NET will use that assembly; otherwise, it will generate one.

The final step is to add our assembly to the GAC using gacutil.

To use this COM component in a project, we reference the original component, not the interop assembly. In this example, we reference DniComRefactorVB from the COM tab of the References dialog in Visual Studio. If we later check the properties for that reference, we will see that it is referencing our primary interop assembly instead of generating a new one.

Related Information

See recipes 5-2 (Importing a Type Library) and 5-9 (Refactoring for Performance).

5-12. Deploying Your Application

Problem

You have developed a .NET application that uses one or more COM components. Now it is time to deploy the application, and you need to know which COM and .NET components to distribute.

Solution

When it's time to deploy your finished application, you need to distribute all of the components (COM and .NET) that are needed to run the application. In addition to distributing the components, you must address some COM and .NET registration issues.

Note The details provided here are not meant to replace the need for a formal installation package. Most applications of even moderate complexity require a formal installation package. The installation package deploys the components in the proper folders and performs other registration and initial setup activities.

Visual Studio .NET includes several types of Setup and Deployment projects, which automate much of the work needed to produce an installation package. Many third-party applications are also available to assist with the authoring of an installation package.

The focus of this recipe is the identification of *what* needs to be done during deployment. How you ultimately accomplish this depends on the deployment tools that you have chosen to use.

These types of components must be distributed with the application:

- Application assemblies containing the application's business logic

- Any COM components that are used by the application

- Any interop assemblies that are used to reference the COM components

Along with distribution of the physical DLLs and EXEs, these deployment steps should also be executed:

- Register any COM components using regsvr32.

- Register any type libraries referenced by the COM or .NET components.

- Register any primary interop assemblies using regasm.

- Add any shared assemblies to the global assembly cache (GAC) using gacutil.

How It Works

As an example, consider a .NET assembly named MyApplication.dll that uses a COM component, MyCom.dll. The component MyCom.dll must be registered using regsvr32. The COM component can be deployed to the same folder as MyApplication.dll or any other folder. Since the component is referenced by COM via registry entries, the actual physical location doesn't matter.

The interop assembly that is used to reference MyCom.dll must also be distributed. If we reference the MyCom component directly from Visual Studio .NET, an interop assembly is generated for us. The name will be Interop.MyComLib.dll if the COM object is implemented as a C++ Active Template Library (ATL) component. When using a Visual Basic 6.0 (VB6) COM component, the name will be Interop.MyCom.dll. If we use TlbImp to generate the interop assembly, we have complete control over the assembly name using the /out parameter.

Regardless of the name of the interop assembly, it must be deployed where the .NET Framework can locate it from the application assembly. If we choose to deploy it as a private assembly, it must be deployed to the same location as the application assembly or in a sub-folder under the application assembly. We can optionally use an application configuration file to specify the location used to load a private assembly.

If we want to deploy the interop assembly as a shared assembly, it goes into the GAC. If we do this, it must have a strong name.

If we generated a primary interop assembly for MyCom.dll, it must be deployed to the GAC. In addition, we need to execute the regasm utility that registers the primary interop assembly with COM.

Related Information

See recipes 5-1 (Using COM Components from .NET), 5-2 (Importing a Type Library), and 5-11 (Sharing an Interop Assembly).

5-13. Converting HRESULTs to Exceptions

Problem

When a COM component returns an error HRESULT, how is that handled by .NET? How do you determine the original HRESULT value?

Solution

COM relies upon result codes (HRESULT) to determine success or failure of a call. .NET makes use of exceptions to indicate a failure rather than a result code. In keeping with this design, error HRESULT codes are marshaled to exceptions in managed code.

This means that any managed code that calls COM methods should be wrapped in a try/ catch block. Any exception thrown indicates an error HRESULT was returned from the COM call.

Table 5-5 shows the standard HRESULT to exception mappings. Any error HRESULT that is not mapped to a specific Exception class is mapped to COMException.

Table 5-5. *HRESULT to Exception Mapping*

HRESULT	.NET Exception Type
COR_E_APPLICATION	ApplicationException
COR_E_ARGUMENT	ArgumentException
COR_E_ARGUMENTOUTOFRANGE	ArgumentOutOfRangeException
COR_E_ARITHMETIC	ArithmeticException
COR_E_ARRAYTYPEMISMATCH	ArrayTypeMismatchException
COR_E_BADIMAGEFORMAT	BadImageFormatException
COR_E_COMEMULATE_ERROR	COMEmulateException
COR_E_CONTEXTMARSHAL	ContextMarshalException
COR_E_CORE	CoreException

HRESULT	.NET Exception Type
COR_E_DIRECTORYNOTFOUND	DirectoryNotFoundException
COR_E_DIVIDEBYZERO	DivideByZeroException
COR_E_DUPLICATEWAITOBJECT	DuplicateWaitObjectException
COR_E_ENDOFSTREAM	EndOfStreamException
COR_E_EXCEPTION	Exception
COR_E_EXECUTIONENGINE	ExecutionEngineException
COR_E_FIELDACCESS	FieldAccessException
COR_E_FORMAT	FormatException
COR_E_INDEXOUTOFRANGE	IndexOutOfRangeException
COR_E_INVALIDCOMOBJECT	InvalidComObjectException
COR_E_INVALIDFILTERCRITERIA	InvalidFilterCriteriaException
COR_E_INVALIDOLEVARIANTTYPE	InvalidOleVariantTypeException
COR_E_INVALIDOPERATION	InvalidOperationException
COR_E_IO	IOException
COR_E_MEMBERACCESS	MemberAccessException
COR_E_METHODACCESS	MethodAccessException
COR_E_MISSINGFIELD	MissingFieldException
COR_E_MISSINGMANIFESTRESOURCE	MissingManifestResourceException
COR_E_MISSINGMEMBER	MissingMemberException
COR_E_MISSINGMETHOD	MissingMethodException
COR_E_MULTICASTNOTSUPPORTED	MulticastNotSupportedException
COR_E_NOTFINITENUMBER	NotFiniteNumberException
COR_E_NOTSUPPORTED	NotSupportedException
COR_E_NULLREFERENCE	NullReferenceException
COR_E_OUTOFMEMORY	OutOfMemoryException
COR_E_OVERFLOW	OverflowException
COR_E_PATHTOOLONG	PathTooLongException
COR_E_RANK	RankException
COR_E_REFLECTIONTYPELOAD	ReflectionTypeLoadException
COR_E_REMOTING	RemotingException
COR_E_SAFEARRAYTYPEMISMATCH	SafeArrayTypeMismatchException
COR_E_SECURITY	SecurityException
COR_E_SERIALIZATION	SerializationException
COR_E_STACKOVERFLOW	StackOverflowException
COR_E_SYNCHRONIZATIONLOCK	SynchronizationLockException
COR_E_SYSTEM	SystemException
COR_E_TARGET	TargetException

Continued

Table 5-5. *Continued*

HRESULT	.NET Exception Type
COR_E_TARGETINVOCATION	TargetInvocationException
COR_E_TARGETPARAMCOUNT	TargetParameterCountException
COR_E_THREADABORTED	ThreadAbortException
COR_E_THREADINTERRUPTED	ThreadInterruptedException
COR_E_THREADSTATE	ThreadStateException
COR_E_THREADSTOP	ThreadStopException
COR_E_TYPEINITIALIZATION	TypeInitializationException
COR_E_TYPELOAD	TypeLoadException
COR_E_VERIFICATION	VerificationException
COR_E_VTABLECALLSNOTSUPPORTED	VTableCallsNotSupportedException
COR_E_WEAKREFERENCE	WeakReferenceException
E_INVALIDARG	ArgumentException
E_NOINTERFACE	InvalidCastException
E_NOTIMPL	NotImplementedException
E_OUTOFMEMORY	OutOfMemoryException
E_POINTER	NullReferenceException
ERROR_ARITHMETIC_OVERFLOW	ArithmeticException
ERROR_BAD_FORMAT	BadImageFormatException
ERROR_FILE_NOT_FOUND	FileNotFoundException
ERROR_FILENAME_EXCED_RANGE	PathTooLongException
ERROR_PATH_NOT_FOUND	DirectoryNotFoundException
ERROR_STACK_OVERFLOW	StackOverflowException
NTE_FAIL	CryptographicException

■**Note** The COR_E* exceptions were defined when .NET was first introduced and are defined in CorError.h. They are designed to provide a much larger set of HRESULT codes that are mapped to specific .NET exceptions.

How It Works

Each one of the .NET exceptions is associated with a particular HRESULT. If we need to know the HRESULT associated with a particular exception, we can obtain it using the static Marshal. GetHRForException method. This is demonstrated along with general HRESULT to exception mapping in the examples that follow.

This first example uses a C++ Active Template Library (ATL) COM component that contains this method:

```
STDMETHODIMP CDniComResultsObj::ProvideDifferentResults(
        long request)
{
```

```
HRESULT result    = S_OK;
switch(request)
{
    case 1:
        result    = E_INVALIDARG;
        break;
    case 2:
        result    = E_NOTIMPL;
        break;
    case 3:
        result    = E_OUTOFMEMORY;
        break;
    case 4:
        result    = COR_E_NOTSUPPORTED;
        break;
    case 5:
        result    = 0x80040301L;    //user-defined error
        break;

    default:
        break;
}

return result;
}
```

This method simply returns a different HRESULT depending on a request parameter. We can write .NET code that calls this method and displays the results in order to see the way HRESULT codes are mapped to specific exceptions. We start by writing a C# helper method that calls this COM method:

```
/// <summary>
/// Call the ATL COM object
/// </summary>
/// <param name="comObj"></param>
/// <param name="request"></param>
private static void MakeTheCall(DniComResultsObj comObj,
        int request)
{
    try
    {
        comObj.ProvideDifferentResults(request);
        Console.WriteLine(
            "No Exception for request: {0}", request);
    }
    catch (Exception e)
    {
        int hResult = Marshal.GetHRForException(e);
```

```
            Console.WriteLine(
                "Exception: request: {0}, type: {1}, HRESULT: {2:X}",
                request, e.GetType().Name, hResult);
        }
    }
```

If an exception is caught, we display the exception type, along with the underlying HRESULT. We call this method repeatedly with different request numbers to see the results:

```
//create an instance of the COM object
DniComResultsObj comObj = new DniComResultsObjClass();

//call the object with different requests
MakeTheCall(comObj, 0);
MakeTheCall(comObj, 1);
MakeTheCall(comObj, 2);
MakeTheCall(comObj, 3);
MakeTheCall(comObj, 4);
MakeTheCall(comObj, 5);
```

When the code is executed, the results look like this:

```
No Exception for request: 0
Exception: request: 1, type: ArgumentException,
    HRESULT: 80070057
Exception: request: 2, type: NotImplementedException,
    HRESULT: 80004001
Exception: request: 3, type: OutOfMemoryException,
    HRESULT: 8007000E
Exception: request: 4, type: NotSupportedException,
    HRESULT: 80131515
Exception: request: 5, type: COMException,
    HRESULT: 80040301
```

As expected, each one of the standard HRESULT codes returned from the COM method is mapped to a corresponding .NET exception. Our user-defined exception of 80040301 is mapped to the generic COMException.

We can implement similar code in Visual Basic .NET (VB.NET) like this:

```
Imports System
Imports System.Runtime.InteropServices
Imports DniComResultsLib

Module ComResultsTest

    Sub Main()
        'create an instance of the COM object
```

```
        Dim comObj As DniComResultsObj _
            = New DniComResultsObjClass()

        'call the object with different requests
        MakeTheCall(comObj, 0)
        MakeTheCall(comObj, 1)
        MakeTheCall(comObj, 2)
        MakeTheCall(comObj, 3)
        MakeTheCall(comObj, 4)
        MakeTheCall(comObj, 5)

        Console.WriteLine("Press any key to exit")
        Console.Read()

    End Sub

    Private Sub MakeTheCall(ByVal comObj As DniComResultsObj, _
        ByVal request As Integer)

        Try
            comObj.ProvideDifferentResults(request)
            Console.WriteLine( _
                "No Exception for request: {0}", request)
        Catch ex As Exception
            Dim hResult As Integer = Marshal.GetHRForException(ex)
            Console.WriteLine( _
             "Exception: request: {0}, type: {1}, HRESULT: {2:X}", _
                request, ex.GetType().Name, hResult)
        End Try
    End Sub

End Module
```

When this code is executed, the results are exactly the same as the C# version.

Visual Basic 6.0 (VB6) doesn't let us explicitly set the HRESULT the way C++ does, but it does provide a way to affect the result code that is returned. This VB6 code demonstrates returning different HRESULT codes:

```
Public Function ProvideDifferentResults( _
        ByVal resultType As Long)
    If resultType = 1 Then
        'pass back user-defined HRESULT
        Err.Raise vbObjectError + 514
    Else
        'use a standard Overflow HRESULT
        Err.Raise 6
    End If
End Function
```

To call this COM method, we implement a similar C# helper method:

```
private static void MakeTheCallVB(
        DniComResultsVBObj comObj, int request)
{
    try
    {
        //make the call
        comObj.ProvideDifferentResults(request);
        Console.WriteLine(
            "No Exception for request: {0}", request);
    }
    catch (Exception e)
    {
        //catch and display the exception
        int hResult = Marshal.GetHRForException(e);
        Console.WriteLine(
          "Exception: request: {0}, type: {1}, HRESULT: {2:X}",
          request, e.GetType().Name, hResult);
    }
}
```

We then call the method like this:

```
//create an instance of the VB COM object
DniComResultsVBObj comObj
    = new DniComResultsVBObjClass();

MakeTheCallVB(comObj, 1);
MakeTheCallVB(comObj, 2);
```

And the results look like this:

```
Exception: request: 1, type: COMException, HRESULT: 80040202
Exception: request: 2, type: OverflowException, HRESULT: 800A0006
```

5-14. Refactoring HRESULTs

Problem

Failure HRESULT codes are marshaled as managed exceptions, but what about success codes? How do you retrieve a success HRESULT code from a COM method?

Solution

Success HRESULT codes are thrown away by .NET marshaling. The marshaler assumes that you only care about HRESULT codes that signal an error. Those error codes are marshaled as a managed exception that you can catch and examine.

However, the meaning of an HRESULT is overloaded. It conveys success or failure, but also supports multiple success HRESULT codes. For example, S_OK and S_FALSE both indicate success and do not result in an exception. If a COM component is written to pass back either one of these codes, you must be able to examine the actual HRESULT code in your managed code.

There are two solutions to the problem:

- Modify the COM method to pass the HRESULT as an out or out,retval parameter.

- Manually modify the generated Intermediate Language (IL) for an interop assembly.

The first option has the disadvantage of requiring a change to the COM method, but it is the easiest to implement and will be discussed in this recipe.

Note The next recipe presents the second option, which involves editing the generated IL code.

Consider the definition of this COM method:

```
[id(2), helpstring("method GetTheResult")]
HRESULT GetTheResult([in] long request);
```

Like all good COM methods, it returns an HRESULT. But that result is hidden from us if the method returns a success code (e.g., S_OK, S_FALSE). The interop library generated for this COM component will contain a definition for this method that looks like this:

```
void GetTheResult(int request)
```

There's no sign of the HRESULT being returned here. To retrieve the actual success HRESULT, we need to refactor the method to pass the HRESULT as an out,retval parameter. The revised method definition might look like this:

```
[id(3), helpstring("method GetTheResultRefactored")]
HRESULT GetTheResultRefactored(
    [in] long request, [out,retval] HRESULT* hResult);
```

Note There can be only one [out,retval] parameter per COM method. Obviously, if you already have an [out,retval], you'll need to pass the HRESULT as an [out] instead. In either case, the approach outlined here will work.

The generated code for this method will now look like this:

```
int GetTheResultRefactored(int request)
```

The refactored COM method will need to set the [out,retval] hResult parameter to the proper HRESULT code prior to the return, for example:

```
STDMETHODIMP CMyComObj::GetTheResultRefactored(
        long request, HRESULT* hResult)
```

```
{
    //other code here

    HRESULT result = S_FALSE;
    //set the out parameter with the HRESULT
    *hResult      = result;
    return result;
}
```

In situations where we have the freedom to refactor the COM method, this is the easiest solution to the problem.

How It Works

The following is a complete example using the methods described previously. Here is the original implementation of the COM method prior to any refactoring:

```
STDMETHODIMP CDniComResultsObj::GetTheResult(long request)
{
    HRESULT result   = S_OK;
    switch(request)
    {
        case 1:
            result   = S_FALSE;
            break;
        case 2:
            result   = 0x00040301L;    //user-defined code
            break;
        case 3:
            result   = E_INVALIDARG;
            break;

        default:
            break;
    }

    return result;
}
```

It can return several different HRESULT codes based on a request parameter. The first two codes are success codes, and they will not result in an exception being thrown.

To exercise this method, we can write a C# helper method that looks like this:

```
private static void MakeTheCall(DniComResultsObj comObj,
        int request)
{
    try
    {
        comObj.GetTheResult(request);
        Console.WriteLine(
```

```
            "No Exception: request {0}", request);
    }
    catch (Exception e)
    {
        int hResult = Marshal.GetHRForException(e);
        Console.WriteLine(
            "Exception: request: {0}, type: {1}, HRESULT: {2:X}",
            request, e.GetType().Name, hResult);
    }
}
```

All we need to do now is to create an instance of this COM object and call the helper method with different request values:

```
//create an instance of the COM object
DniComResultsObj comObj = new DniComResultsObjClass();

//call the original method
MakeTheCall(comObj, 0);
MakeTheCall(comObj, 1);
MakeTheCall(comObj, 2);
MakeTheCall(comObj, 3);
```

When the code is executed, we see these results:

```
No Exception: request 0
No Exception: request 1
No Exception: request 2
Exception: request: 3, type: ArgumentException, HRESULT: 80070057
```

As shown in this example, we have no way to differentiate between any of the success HRESULT codes. We don't know if the COM method returned S_OK, S_FALSE, or our user-defined success code. We do receive an exception if an error HRESULT is returned.

As described earlier, we can refactor this COM method to return the HRESULT code as an [out,retval] parameter. The modified method looks like this:

```
STDMETHODIMP CDniComResultsObj::GetTheResultRefactored(
        long request, HRESULT* hResult)
{
    HRESULT result    = S_OK;
    switch(request)
    {
        case 1:
            result    = S_FALSE;
            break;
        case 2:
            result    = 0x00040301L;    //user-defined code
            break;
        case 3:
```

```
                result    = E_INVALIDARG;
                break;

            default:
                break;
        }

    //set the out parameter with the HRESULT
    *hResult    = result;

    return result;
}
```

We modify our C# wrapper to display the returned HRESULT:

```
private static void MakeTheRefactoredCall(DniComResultsObj comObj,
        int request)
{
    try
    {
        int hResult
            = comObj.GetTheResultRefactored(request);
        Console.WriteLine(
            "No Exception: request {0}, HRESULT: {1:X}",
                request, hResult);
    }
    catch (Exception e)
    {
        int hResult = Marshal.GetHRForException(e);
        Console.WriteLine(
            "Exception: request: {0}, type: {1}, HRESULT: {2:X}",
            request, e.GetType().Name, hResult);
    }
}
```

The code to execute the wrapper method looks like this:

```
//create an instance of the COM object
DniComResultsObj comObj = new DniComResultsObjClass();

//call the refactored method
MakeTheRefactoredCall(comObj, 0);
MakeTheRefactoredCall(comObj, 1);
MakeTheRefactoredCall(comObj, 2);
MakeTheRefactoredCall(comObj, 3);
```

When we run this test, we see different HRESULT values returned for each call:

```
No Exception: request 0, HRESULT: 0
No Exception: request 1, HRESULT: 1
```

```
No Exception: request 2, HRESULT: 40301
Exception: request: 3, type: ArgumentException, HRESULT: 80070057
```

■**Caution** Error HRESULT values have always been designed to signal some type of exceptional condition. However, this usage is not strictly enforced by COM. This lack of enforcement has led to the use of HRESULT codes for conditions that are not really an error. HRESULT values may be defined to indicate a status or other application-specific result.

Remember that each time an error HRESULT is returned from a COM method, it will be marshaled as an exception (either COMException or a more specific exception class). The throwing of these exceptions will degrade performance if the HRESULT is not really meant as an exception condition and is returned frequently. Use error HRESULT values wisely and only to signal actual error conditions.

Related Information

See recipes 5-13 (Converting HRESULTs to Exceptions) and 5-15 (Retrieving the HRESULT).

5-15. Retrieving the HRESULT

Problem

Your COM object returns multiple HRESULT success values, and you are unable to modify the COM method as described in the previous recipe. Is there another way to retrieve the HRESULT when an exception is not thrown?

Solution

Success HRESULT codes are thrown away by .NET marshaling. The marshaler assumes that we care only about HRESULT codes that signal an error. Those error codes are marshaled as a managed exception that you can catch and examine.

One way to retrieve the HRESULT from a COM method is to manually edit the Intermediate Language (IL) for a generated interop library. The changes that you make to the IL cause the COM method signature to be preserved, allowing you to examine the actual HRESULT.

■**Note** Recipe 5-14 covered changing an existing COM method in order to retrieve the HRESULT. This recipe is used in situations where you don't have the freedom to modify an existing COM method.

The steps needed to accomplish this are as follows:

1. Generate an interop library for the COM component using the TlbImp utility.

2. Use Ildasm to dump the IL for the assembly into an editable text file.

3. Modify the IL text file to preserve the signature of the COM method(s).

4. Use Ilasm to assemble the modified IL code into a new interop assembly.

5. Reference and use the revised interop assembly in a managed project.

How It Works

The following example demonstrates the steps needed to modify the IL for a COM component. The method we will modify is the same one used in the previous recipe. The COM method is defined like this:

```
[id(2), helpstring("method GetTheResult")]
HRESULT GetTheResult([in] long request);
```

The first step is to create an import library for this COM component. To do this, we use the TlbImp command-line utility like this:

```
tlbimp.exe  DniComResults.dll  /out:Interop.DniComResults.dll
```

This generates an interop library named Interop.DniComResults.dll. If we were to use this interop library as is, we would see that the COM method is defined like this:

```
void GetTheResult(int request)
```

The HRESULT is thrown away, making it impossible to check within managed code.

To remedy this situation, we extract the IL code for this interop assembly, make a few minor modifications, and then re-create the assembly.

To disassemble the interop assembly, we use the Ildasm command-line utility like this:

```
ildasm.exe Interop.DniComResults.dll /out:DniComResults.il
```

This generates a text file named DniComResults.il. Opening the file in Visual Studio, we search for the GetTheResult method in the IL code and see that it is defined like this:

```
instance void  GetTheResult([in] int32 'request')
    runtime managed internalcall
```

We need to modify this method so that it returns an int32 (the HRESULT) instead of void. We also need to add the preservesig attribute so that the original signature of the COM method is preserved. Our changes look like this:

```
instance int32 GetTheResult([in] int32 'request')
    runtime managed internalcall preservesig
```

Caution In the IL file, this method is defined twice: once for the COM interface and once for the method implementation within the COM class. We need to make the same change to both locations in order for this code to work correctly.

After saving the changes, we reassemble the IL into a new interop assembly. To do this, we use the Ilasm command-line utility like this:

```
ilasm.exe DniComResults.il /DLL /output:Interop.DniComResults.dll
```

The /DLL option is needed in order to generate a DLL instead of an EXE.

Once the new assembly is created, we add a reference to it within our managed project. The C# code to use this COM method looks like this:

```
private static void MakeTheCall(DniComResultsObj comObj,
        int request)
{
    try
    {
        int hr = comObj.GetTheResult(request);
        Console.WriteLine(
            "No Exception: request {0}, HRESULT {1:X}",
            request, hr);
    }
    catch (Exception e)
    {
        int hResult = Marshal.GetHRForException(e);
        Console.WriteLine(
            "Exception: request: {0}, type: {1}, HRESULT: {2:X}",
            request, e.GetType().Name, hResult);
    }
}
```

Just like the prior recipe, we implement a helper method that allows us to easily call this COM method multiple times. Notice that unlike the example shown in the last recipe, this version of GetTheResult returns an Int32 value. This is the HRESULT. We can execute this helper method using this code:

```
//create an instance of the COM object
DniComResultsObj comObj = new DniComResultsObjClass();

//call the original method
MakeTheCall(comObj, 0);
MakeTheCall(comObj, 1);
MakeTheCall(comObj, 2);
MakeTheCall(comObj, 3);
```

The results look like this:

```
No Exception: request 0, HRESULT 0
No Exception: request 1, HRESULT 1
No Exception: request 2, HRESULT 40301
No Exception: request 3, HRESULT 80070057
```

We now receive the actual HRESULT returned from the COM method. Also note that request 3 returns an error HRESULT that would normally be marshaled as an exception. However, after these changes, no exception is thrown. Instead, we now take full responsibility for checking the HRESULT after each call to this COM method.

■**Caution** The changes to the IL outlined in this recipe will disable the normal exception marshaling of error HRESULT values. If you modify the method as demonstrated here, your managed code will need to inspect the HRESULT to determine success or failure. An exception will no longer be thrown for error HRESULT values.

Related Information

See recipes 5-13 (Converting HRESULTs to Exceptions), 5-14 (Refactoring HRESULTs), and 5-2 (Importing a Type Library).

5-16. Providing Additional Error Information

Problem

You are receiving a managed exception when calling a COM method. However, the message associated with the exception doesn't provide a good description of the problem. Is there a way to provide a better error message to return with the exception?

Solution

A managed exception is thrown when an error HRESULT value is returned from a COM method. Each type of exception is associated with a default error message describing the exception. While these messages are helpful, they may not provide as much information as we would like to help resolve the problem.

Additional error information can be returned from a COM component via the IErrorInfo interface. By supporting IErrorInfo, a COM component declares that it is capable of providing additional error information. If IErrorInfo is supported, the additional error information is retrieved and used to populate the managed exception. IErrorInfo implementation is done differently depending on the language used.

If the COM component is developed in Visual Basic 6.0 (VB6), we can specify additional information using the Raise method of the Err object. This method is used to raise a runtime error. The error number raised is returned as an HRESULT. Any additional information that we provide such as a Source or Message is made available via IErrorInfo.

The minimal form of Err.Raise requires only an error number like this:

```
Err.Raise 449
```

If you want to provide additional error information, you can specify a message and source like this:

```
Err.Raise 449, "My Source", "My Error Message"
```

As is usually the case, more work is involved if the COM component is implemented in C++ Active Template Library (ATL). You first need to indicate that your component supports IErrorInfo. This is accomplished by adding the ISupportErrorInfo interface to your component. It is easy to add this support when you first add an ATL object to the component. All you need to do is check the box marked Support ISupportErrorInfo.

In your C++ code, you then call a series of COM housekeeping functions to provide the error information. CreateErrorInfo is first called to create an error object. Properties of this object are used to provide a descriptive error message and source for the error. The SetErrorInfo function is then called to set the error information object for the current thread to our error object.

Regardless of the COM language used, you don't need to make any changes to your managed code to take advantage of this additional information. Your managed code can immediately make use of the properties of the exception object such as Message and Source.

How It Works

This first example demonstrates how to provide error information from a Visual Basic 6.0 (VB6) COM component. The test COM method is implemented like this:

```
Public Function GenerateError(ByVal inParam As Long)

    Err.Clear

    If inParam = 1 Then
        Err.Raise 449    'argument
    ElseIf inParam = 2 Then
        Err.Raise 449, _
        "DniErrorInfoVB.DniErrorInfoVBObj", _
        "Value is x but should be y"
    ElseIf inParam = 3 Then
        Err.Raise &H80040301    'user-defined error
    ElseIf inParam = 4 Then
        Err.Raise &H80040301, _
        "DniErrorInfoVB.DniErrorInfoVBObj", _
        "My Error Message"
    End If


End Function
```

The method raises different errors depending on a request parameter. The same error is returned twice: once using the default description and a second time with additional error information that we provide.

The C# code to test this method looks like this:

```
static private void CallTheMethod(
    DniErrorInfoVBObj comObj, int request)
{
    try
    {
        comObj.GenerateError(request);
    }
    catch (Exception e)
    {
        Console.WriteLine("Exception: {0}, {1}, {2}",
```

```
                    e.GetType().Name,
                    e.Message,
                    e.Source);
        }
}
```

We call the method four times to see the difference in the source and error messages that are returned:

```
DniErrorInfoVBObj vbComObj
    = new DniErrorInfoVBObjClass();

CallTheMethod(vbComObj, 1);
CallTheMethod(vbComObj, 2);
CallTheMethod(vbComObj, 3);
CallTheMethod(vbComObj, 4);
```

The results of our test look like this:

```
Exception: ArgumentException,
    Argument not optional, DniErrorInfoVB
Exception: ArgumentException,
    Value is x but should be y, DniErrorInfoVB.DniErrorInfoVBObj
Exception: COMException,
    Automation error, DniErrorInfoVB
Exception: COMException,
    My Error Message, DniErrorInfoVB.DniErrorInfoVBObj
```

The C++ ATL implementation of a similar method looks like this:

```
STDMETHODIMP CDniErrorInfoObj::GenerateError(long inParam)
{
    HRESULT result    = S_OK;
    //set the HRESULT based on the request
    switch(inParam)
    {
        case 1:
            result    = E_INVALIDARG;
            break;
        case 2:
            result    = E_INVALIDARG;
            GenerateErrorInfo(_uuidof(IDniErrorInfoObj),
                "CDniErrorInfoObj::GenerateError",
                "Value is x but should be y");
            break;
        case 3:
            result    = 0x80040301L;    //user-defined error
            break;
```

```
        case 4:
            result    = 0x80040301L;    //user-defined error
            GenerateErrorInfo(_uuidof(IDniErrorInfoObj),
                "CDniErrorInfoObj::GenerateError",
                "My Error Message");
            break;

        default:
            break;
    }

    return result;
}
```

Since there are a number of steps needed to populate an error information object, we implement a helper method to handle that for us:

```
void CDniErrorInfoObj::GenerateErrorInfo(REFGUID rGUID,
        _bstr_t source, _bstr_t message)
{
    ICreateErrorInfo* pCreateInfo = NULL;
    IErrorInfo* pErrorInfo        = NULL;
    //create a generic error object
    CreateErrorInfo(&pCreateInfo);

    //set properties of the object
    pCreateInfo->SetGUID(rGUID);
    pCreateInfo->SetSource(source);
    pCreateInfo->SetDescription(message);

    //get the IErrorInfo interface for the error info object
    pCreateInfo->QueryInterface(
        IID_IErrorInfo, (void**)&pErrorInfo);

    //set the error object for the local thread
    SetErrorInfo(0,pErrorInfo);

    //release our COM objects
    pErrorInfo->Release();
    pCreateInfo->Release();
}
```

The C# code to test this COM component looks just like the code used to test our VB6 object. The only real difference is the object type used:

```
static private void CallTheMethod(
    DniErrorInfoObj comObj, int request)
{
```

```
    try
    {
        comObj.GenerateError(request);
    }
    catch (Exception e)
    {
        Console.WriteLine("Exception: {0}, {1}, {2}",
            e.GetType().Name,
            e.Message,
            e.Source);
    }
}
```

Here is the code that exercises this method:

```
DniErrorInfoObj comObj
    = new DniErrorInfoObjClass();

CallTheMethod(comObj, 1);
CallTheMethod(comObj, 2);
CallTheMethod(comObj, 3);
CallTheMethod(comObj, 4);
```

When we execute this test, we see these results:

```
Exception: ArgumentException,
    Value does not fall within the expected range.,
    Interop.DniErrorInfoLib
Exception: ArgumentException,
    Value is x but should be y,
    CDniErrorInfoObj::GenerateError
Exception: COMException,
    Exception from HRESULT: 0x80040301,
    Interop.DniErrorInfoLib
Exception: COMException,
    My Error Message,
    CDniErrorInfoObj::GenerateError
```

The additional error information should make it much easier to diagnose a runtime problem.

Related Information

See recipe 5-13 (Converting HRESULTs to Exceptions).

CHAPTER 6

■■■

Exposing Managed Code to COM

COM interop works in both directions. Chapter 5 covered the ability to use existing COM components from managed code. COM interop also provides the ability to expose managed code to COM clients. That is the focus of this chapter.

In its simplest form, exposing a managed class to COM involves setting a few project options to prepare the assembly for COM interop. When you build the project, Visual Studio .NET exports all public members of your managed class for use by COM. A COM type library (typelib) file (.tlb) is generated, containing the definitions for the COM interface and COM class (a coclass) that were exported. The assembly is also registered as a COM component.

At this point, any COM client written in a language such as Visual Basic 6.0 (VB6) or C++ can reference the managed COM component. The managed classes and interfaces that are exposed look just like ordinary COM types to client code. Instances of the COM object are created using the normal syntax. Properties and methods are referenced in the normal way. Reference counting works as expected for a COM object.

The .NET runtime performs this magic through the use of a COM Callable Wrapper (CCW). Since the COM client is unable to access the managed object directly, the CCW acts as a proxy. When a COM client creates an instance of the COM object that is exposed from managed code, the .NET runtime creates a CCW. The CCW handles the creation of the underlying managed object. The CCW is allocated in unmanaged memory and the managed object resides in the garbage-collected heap.

One and only one CCW is created for each managed object. Multiple COM clients can access the managed object through this single CCW. The CCW in turn manages the reference counting for the managed object. When the CCW detects that there are no COM references to it, it releases its reference on the managed object, allowing it to be garbage collected.

Of course, that is COM interop in its simplest form. The mechanism just described exposes all public members of a class to COM using something called a *class interface*. This interface type has a number of drawbacks, and it is not the recommended approach, as discussed in the first two recipes of this chapter.

You can (and should) design your own interfaces to expose to COM. Doing this provides you with complete control of your public API. You can control the type of interface exported to COM, and in doing so determine whether the component supports early or late binding. The use of your own interfaces is covered in the third recipe.

In addition to these major topics, this chapter includes recipes on controlling the COM identity and selectively hiding members of an interface or class. Another recipe discusses the options available for generation of a typelib as well as for registration of the assembly for use by COM. The exposing of managed events for use by a COM client is covered in another recipe. The chapter concludes with two recipes that demonstrate ways to return HRESULT values to the calling code.

6-1. Exposing .NET Classes Using Late Binding

Problem

You would like to expose your .NET classes to COM, using them from clients like Visual Basic 6.0 (VB6) or scripting code. What is the easiest way to do that?

Solution

.NET makes it easy to expose managed classes to COM clients. The basic steps to do this are as follows:

1. Implement the managed class in the .NET language of your choice.

2. Add optional attributes to the class to control how the class is exposed to COM.

3. Generate a typelib for the .NET component and register it for COM usage.

4. Use your .NET class via COM just like any other COM object.

Note Binding is the process of resolving references to a COM object's properties, events, and methods. There are two ways to bind a COM client to an object: late binding and early binding. Late binding resolves references to the object's members at runtime and is the focus of this recipe. Early binding resolves references to the object's members at compile time and is discussed in a subsequent recipe.

Before you begin these steps, you have one very important decision to make. Will you expose an entire managed class to COM, or do you want to define your own interface? Since COM is all about interface-based component development, the preferred approach is to define your own interface, which is covered in a subsequent recipe.

But .NET also supports exposing an entire class to COM. This recipe demonstrates the simplest way to expose managed classes to COM, using a class interface that is automatically generated for you.

Note Please be aware that using a class interface to expose classes to COM has a number of major limitations that are discussed shortly. This is not the preferred way to expose a managed class to COM, but it is covered here since it is a workable solution. If you decide to use class interfaces to interoperate with COM, make sure you understand and manage the potential problems with this approach.

As the name implies, a class interface is designed to expose an entire class to COM. This generated interface exposes all public fields, properties, methods, and events of the class. Any public fields are actually exposed as COM properties. For example, consider this class implemented in C#:

```
using System;

namespace DniNetSimpleNumbers
{
    /// <summary>
    /// Managed class exposed to COM clients using
    /// the default class interface
    /// </summary>
    public class DniNetSimpleNumbersDisp
    {
        public int AddSomeNumbers(int numA, int numB)
        {
            return numA + numB;
        }
    }
}
```

This class is in a class library project named DniNetSimpleNumbers.

On the surface, this is an unremarkable C# class. Without modifying the class at all, we can expose it to COM clients. To do this, we need to generate a typelib and register the assembly containing this class for COM interop.

Visual Studio can perform these generation and registration duties, as long as you enable the correct options within the project properties. For a C# or Visual Basic .NET project, you can right-click the project in Solution Explorer and select Properties. Once there, you need to set both of the following options:

- On the Application tab, click the Assembly Information button. This opens a modal dialog. On the dialog, check the "Make assembly COM-visible" option.

- On the Build tab, check the "Register for COM interop" option.

Enabling these options adds the ComVisible and Guid attributes to the AssemblyInfo.cs file for a C# project. For a VB.NET project the AssemblyInfo.vb file is updated.

Note Now when you build the project, you'll see that a typelib file (.tlb) is also produced. If you view the COM registry using the Oleview.exe utility, you'll see that the .NET component is also now registered as a COM server. To see the entries for your new COM component, expand the All Objects group and look for the component with the full name of DniNetSimpleNumbers.DniNetSimpleNumbersDisp. You can see that it is registered just like an ordinary unmanaged COM component; this allows it to be referenced from any COM client that needs to use it.

All we need to do now is write a simple COM client to access the component. To do this, we need to know the name of the COM class that was generated. The COM class name (the coclass in COM lingo) is the same as the C# class name, DniNetSimpleNumbersDisp. As shown in the following example code, the full name that is used when creating an instance of this class is prefixed with the namespace name (DniNetSimpleNumbers).

The generated class interface is the class name with a leading underscore (_). In this example, the interface name generated is _DniNetSimpleNumbersDisp. However, since we are using late binding, we don't actually reference the interface in the example client code.

Note Without adding any attributes to the class, an AutoDispatch class interface is generated. This is an interface derived from IDispatch, but it only supports late binding. This means that definitions of the properties and methods of the class are not included in the typelib, which prevents COM clients from relying upon the dispatch IDs of each property or method. Instead, the dispatch IDs are discovered at runtime when a method is executed. This also means that you won't be able to see all of the available methods and properties of the COM class using IntelliSense.

Here is the code for a simple Visual Basic 6.0 (VB6) client that uses this .NET component via COM:

```
Private Sub Form_Load()

    'create the .NET object using COM IDispatch
    Dim dispObj As Object
    Set dispObj = CreateObject( _
        "DniNetSimpleNumbers.DniNetSimpleNumbersDisp")
    'call the method and show the results
    Dim result As Integer
    result = dispObj.AddSomeNumbers(1, 2)
    Text1.Text = _
        "AddSomeNumbers result via COM IDispatch: " _
            + CStr(result)

    'free the COM reference
    Set dispObj = Nothing

End Sub
```

The sample VB6 project is a simple Windows application with a single form. This code is added to the Load event for the form so that it executes immediately. The form contains a single TextBox control in order to display the results.

Notice that we have defined the variable for the COM object as Object. We also use the CreateObject function to create the object instance, rather than the New keyword with a strongly typed variable.

To use a strongly typed variable, we would have had to add the component to the VB6 project using the References option. But to use this COM class, we don't need to do this. We can do all of this using only late binding.

When this code is executed, we see these results displayed in the text box:

```
AddSomeNumbers result via COM IDispatch: 3
```

All of this works exactly the same way if we expose a VB.NET class. For example, here is a VB.NET class that is equivalent to the C# example just shown:

```
Public Class DniNetSimpleNumbersVB

    Public Function AddSomeNumbers( _
        ByVal numA As Integer, ByVal numB As Integer) _
            As Integer
        Return numA + numB
    End Function

End Class
```

By setting the same project options to register the assembly for COM interop, we have exposed this class to COM. We can exercise this class from the same VB6 client code by simply changing the class name from DniNetSimpleNumbersDisp to DniNetSimpleNumbersVB.

How It Works

To expose a managed class to COM like this, the class must have a public default constructor. This is a constructor without any parameters. Unless you explicitly add a default constructor and make it private, or add your own parameterized constructor, you get one for free without actually specifying one in code. Without this constructor, you are unable to activate an instance of the class via COM. Of course, you can add other parameterized constructors to the class, but these are visible only to managed code and are not exposed to COM clients. The class must also be public and cannot be abstract. In other words, you must be able to create an instance of the class.

As long as you are able to live with the limitations of the generated class interface, this is a workable approach to COM interop. By setting a couple of project options, you are able to quickly expose your managed class to COM clients. The limitations include the following:

- This approach is safe only when using late binding as demonstrated here. It is possible to generate a class interface that supports early binding, but that exposes you to a number of potential problems. Using early binding with a class interface is discussed in detail in the next recipe.

> **■Note** Why are class interfaces problematic when using early binding? The main issue concerns the binding
> to the generated dispatch IDs and versioning of the COM class. If a COM client uses early binding, it is bound
> at compile time to the interface's physical layout via the dispatch IDs.
>
> Any change to the layout, such as adding or removing a property or method, could produce unexpected
> results. Unless all COM clients are rebuilt each time the managed class changes, it is possible that they
> could reference the wrong method or property. And since the generated interface would be constantly
> changing along with the class, the interface is no longer immutable. This breaks one of the fundamental
> rules of COM that interfaces are (or should be) immutable.

- By default, class interfaces expose all public members to COM. It is possible to override this with the optional `ComVisible` attribute. However, unless you want to automatically expose all new public members that you add to the class, you will need to add this attribute to each new member.

- Class interfaces also include all public members from their base classes. This means that the management of what is and isn't exposed to COM becomes more difficult. As managed classes up and down the hierarchy change, the class interface exposed to COM changes along with them. This may or may not be your intent.

- COM is all about interfaces. It is an interface-based component model. By allowing an entire class to be exposed to COM as one flat interface, you are relinquishing control of your public API. In doing so, you lose much of the granularity and usefulness that COM interfaces provide. Key concepts such as polymorphism become much more difficult to implement in COM without well-designed interfaces.

Related Information

See recipes 6-2 (Exposing .NET Classes Using Early Binding), 6-3 (Exposing .NET Classes with Interfaces), 6-5 (Controlling COM Visibility), and 6-6 (Preparing Assemblies for COM Interop).

6-2. Exposing .NET Classes Using Early Binding

Problem

You would like to expose your managed classes to COM clients, but prefer to use early binding for the best possible performance. What is the easiest way to accomplish this?

Solution

Binding is the process of resolving references to a COM object's properties, events, and methods. There are two ways to bind a COM client to an object: late binding and early binding. Late binding (discussed in the preceding recipe) resolves references to the object's members at runtime. Early binding (discussed in this recipe) resolves those member references at compile time. The compiled client code caches references to the dispatch IDs of the methods and properties. This allows the code to execute much faster, since it can directly access an individual method or property via a cached dispatch ID. In contrast, late-binding code must first determine if an object even supports the requested method or property. Only then can it access the member.

In most cases, early binding is the preferred binding mechanism because of the performance gains. However, early binding when using the automatically generated class interface can cause versioning problems. These issues are discussed shortly.

Note Although early binding is fully supported, Microsoft strongly discourages its use with class interfaces. Early binding is discussed here because it is one of the many available ways to expose managed code to COM clients. Before using this approach, you should fully understand and manage the potential versioning problems.

The preferred way to expose managed code to COM is to define your own interfaces rather than using the generated class interface. This approach is discussed in the next recipe.

The class interface is one that is automatically generated for you. It exposes all public members of a managed class, including all public fields, properties, methods, and events of the class. Public fields are exposed as COM properties. By default, an IDispatch class interface is generated without any member details. This only supports late binding. To create a class interface capable of supporting early binding, you need to add the ClassInterface attribute to the class.

For example, this C# class produces a class interface that supports either late or early binding (a dual interface):

```
using System;
using System.Runtime.InteropServices; //needed for attribute

namespace DniNetSimpleNumbersDual
{
    /// <summary>
    /// Managed class exposed to COM clients
    /// via dual interface
    /// </summary>
    [ClassInterface(ClassInterfaceType.AutoDual)]
    public class DniNetSimpleNumbersDual
    {
        public int AddSomeNumbers(int numA, int numB)
        {
            return numA + numB;
        }
    }
}
```

Before using this class from a COM client, you must first generate a typelib and register the assembly for use by COM.

Note The easiest way to generate a typelib for a managed assembly is to set project property options within Visual Studio .NET. For a C# or Visual Basic .NET project, you can right-click the project in Solution Explorer, select Properties, and set these options:

- On the Application tab, click the Assembly Information button. This opens a modal dialog. On the dialog, check the "Make assembly COM-visible" option.

- On the Build tab, check the "Register for COM interop" option.

Setting these options will also cause the assembly to be registered for use by COM during the build process.

Visual Basic 6.0 (VB6) client code to access this managed class via COM looks like this:

```
Private Sub Form_Load()
    'create an instance of the managed object via COM
    'using early binding.
    Dim comObj As _
        New DniNetSimpleNumbersDual.DniNetSimpleNumbersDual

    'call the method and show the results
    Dim result As Integer
    result = comObj.AddSomeNumbers(1, 2)
    Text1.Text = "Result via early binding is " + CStr(result)

    'free the COM reference
    Set comObj = Nothing
End Sub
```

This code executes immediately during the form load event. Notice that we use a strongly typed variable and the New keyword to create an instance of the COM object (the managed class). In order to do this, we need to add a reference to the COM component using the VB6 Project References menu item. When adding this reference, we see that our managed assembly appears in the list of available COM components, just like an ordinary component.

When this client code is executed, these results are displayed in a TextBox on the form:

Result via early binding is 3

We can also use this COM component from C++ code like this:

```
#include "stdafx.h"
#include <conio.h>
#include <objbase.h>
#import "mscorlib.tlb"
#import "DniNetSimpleNumbersDual.tlb" no_namespace
```

```
int _tmain(int argc, _TCHAR* argv[])
{
    CoInitializeEx(NULL, COINIT_APARTMENTTHREADED);

    //create an instance of the .NET object via COM
    _DniNetSimpleNumbersDualPtr
        comObj(__uuidof(DniNetSimpleNumbersDual));
    if (comObj)
    {
        //call the method and show the results
        int result = comObj->AddSomeNumbers(1, 2);
        _cprintf(
            "Result from C++ client code: %i \r\n",
            result);
        comObj.Release();
    }

    CoUninitialize();
    return 0;
}
```

The code uses the #import statement to process the typelib generated by Visual Studio .NET. This produces a smart pointer for the COM class and its interface. In this example, we declare a local variable using the interface smart pointer instead of the COM coclass.

Notice that we also #import "mscorlib.tlb". This is needed to resolve references to .NET types that are included in the generated typelib for our class.

When we run this code, we see the following result:

```
Result from C++ client code: 3
```

How It Works

To understand better what is generated for us, we can view the generated typelib from the DniNetSimpleNumbersDual class using a tool such as OleView, the OLE/COM Object Viewer (included with Visual Studio). If we review the Interface Definition Language (IDL) extracted from the typelib, we see this:

```
// Generated .IDL file (by the OLE/COM Object Viewer)
//
// typelib filename: DniNetSimpleNumbersDual.tlb

[
  uuid(92B77D66-04E9-4474-8D7E-8454A97D68FD),
  version(1.0),
  custom(90883F05-3D28-11D2-8F17-00A0C9A6186D,
    DniNetSimpleNumbersDual, Version=1.0.0.0,
    Culture=neutral, PublicKeyToken=null)
```

```
]
library DniNetSimpleNumbersDual
{
    // TLib :      // TLib : mscorlib.dll :
    importlib("mscorlib.tlb");
    // TLib : OLE Automation :
    importlib("stdole2.tlb");

    // Forward declare all types defined in this typelib
    interface _DniNetSimpleNumbersDual;

    [
      uuid(0723F3BD-0C1C-3247-A34D-12AE9DEDB8F7),
      version(1.0),
      custom(0F21F359-AB84-41E8-9A78-36D110E6D2F9,
      DniNetSimpleNumbersDual.DniNetSimpleNumbersDual)
    ]
    coclass DniNetSimpleNumbersDual {
        [default] interface _DniNetSimpleNumbersDual;
        interface _Object;
    };

    [
      odl,
      uuid(4FD21497-83AB-3AC4-9C58-49948A367669),
      hidden,
      dual,
      nonextensible,
      oleautomation,
      custom(0F21F359-AB84-41E8-9A78-36D110E6D2F9,
      DniNetSimpleNumbersDual.DniNetSimpleNumbersDual)

    ]
    interface _DniNetSimpleNumbersDual : IDispatch {
        [id(00000000), propget,
          custom(54FC8F55-38DE-4703-9C4E-250351302B1C, 1)]
        HRESULT ToString([out, retval] BSTR* pRetVal);
        [id(0x60020001)]
        HRESULT Equals(
                    [in] VARIANT obj,
                    [out, retval] VARIANT_BOOL* pRetVal);
        [id(0x60020002)]
        HRESULT GetHashCode([out, retval] long* pRetVal);
        [id(0x60020003)]
        HRESULT GetType([out, retval] _Type** pRetVal);
        [id(0x60020004)]
        HRESULT AddSomeNumbers(
```

```
                    [in] long numA,
                    [in] long numB,
                    [out, retval] long* pRetVal);
    };
};
```

This shows the generated interface named _DniNetSimpleNumbersDual (with the leading underscore). The coclass is the same name as our managed C# class (DniNetSimpleNumbersDual). Along with our AddSomeNumbers method, other standard members such as ToString and GetType are generated. These methods are associated with the base System.Object that all managed classes are derived from.

Using the ClassInterface attribute, we can also explicitly select a dispatch-only interface like this:

```
[ClassInterface(ClassInterfaceType.AutoDispatch)]
```

This produces an interface that is *only* capable of being used via late binding. This is the same as omitting the ClassInterface attribute completely.

As mentioned previously, Microsoft strongly discourages the use of early binding to generated class interfaces. Some of the potential problems are as follows:

- Early binding causes the COM client to cache the dispatch IDs of the class members. This means that the COM client is bound to the current set of dispatch IDs that were generated the last time the component was built. The physical layout of the members in the class affects the numbering of the dispatch IDs. The addition or removal of a public member of the class will cause the order of the dispatch IDs to change. In the best-case scenario, the client will receive an error when trying to access a member that no longer exists. In the worst-case scenario, the wrong method or property may be accessed.

- Since the class interface changes along with the public members of the class, it is a moving target. It is certainly not immutable, as all good COM interfaces are supposed to be. By supporting early binding, you give the false impression that clients binding to the interface can rely upon it as a contract with the COM object. But when the class changes, you end up breaking that contract.

- Each time the public members of the class change, a different COM identity is generated. This means that the Guids associated with the interface will be different from the last time the class was changed. This makes it difficult for client code to consistently bind to the component, forcing you to recompile all client code whenever the managed class changes. Normally, this would constitute a major annoyance, but in this case, if it prevents you from accessing an object using a stale version of an interface, it may actually be a good thing. Because of this *feature*, the potential problems mentioned earlier of accessing the wrong member become merely theoretical.

- Changes to base classes also flow through to the generated class interface. This greatly increases the opportunity to break all COM clients using the generated interface.

In summary, the recommended ways to expose a managed class to COM are as follows, listed in descending order of preference:

- Don't use the generated class interface; design and expose your own interfaces instead. This is considered in the next recipe.

- Use class interfaces with late binding only. This is slower than early binding, but it eliminates the COM versioning issues discussed here.

- Use class interfaces with early binding only when you must. This might be when you require the improved performance that early binding provides. But if performance is an issue, see the first option listed here instead and design your own interface!

Related Information

See recipes 6-1 (Exposing .NET Classes Using Late Binding), 6-3 (Exposing .NET Classes with Interfaces), 6-4 (Managing COM Identity), 6-6 (Preparing Assemblies for COM Interop), and 6-5 (Controlling COM Visibility).

6-3. Exposing .NET Classes with Interfaces

Problem

You want to control the public interface that is exposed to COM clients. How do you implement a COM interface in managed code?

Solution

Implementing your own interface is the best way to expose managed code to COM. It allows you to use early binding from COM clients for the best possible performance. It also eliminates the versioning and COM identity issues associated with the generated class interface. In addition, it is in the true spirit of COM, which emphasizes the importance of interface-based component development.

You expose a COM interface by implementing a managed interface. There's nothing special you must do to the interface, other than to make sure it is public.

For example, consider this C# code that defines an interface and a class that implements the interface:

```
using System;
using System.Runtime.InteropServices; //needed for attributes

namespace DniNetSimpleNumbersIFace
{
    /// <summary>
    /// An interface for classes that do addition
    /// </summary>
    public interface IAddNumbers
    {
        int AddSomeNumbers(int numA, int numB);
    }
```

```
[ClassInterface(ClassInterfaceType.None)]
public class DniNetSimpleNumbersIFace : IAddNumbers
{
    public int AddSomeNumbers(int numA, int numB)
    {
        return numA + numB;
    }
}
}
```

The IAddNumbers interface looks just like any other managed interface. It is the same interface that we might use from our managed client code. The DniNetSimpleNumbersIFace class implements this interface.

Notice that we add the ClassInterface attribute with a value of ClassInterfaceType.None to our class. Since we are providing our own interface, this prevents the class interface from being generated. While this isn't strictly necessary, it is good practice to prevent unintended use of the class interface.

Because the class interface is no longer included in the typelib, this means that the members that were previously exposed from the base Object class are no longer included in any of the published interfaces. This includes the methods ToString, Equals, GetHashCode, and GetType.

As is always the case, to use this class from a COM client, we must first generate a typelib and register the assembly for use by COM.

Note The easiest way to set up an assembly for COM interop is to set the appropriate project options within Visual Studio .NET. Please refer to recipe 6-1 (Exposing .NET Classes Using Late Binding) for instructions on how to set these options.

A C++ client that uses this interface and class via COM could be implemented like this:

```cpp
#include "stdafx.h"
#include <conio.h>
#include <objbase.h>
#import "mscorlib.tlb"
#import "DniNetSimpleNumbersIFace.tlb" no_namespace

int _tmain(int argc, _TCHAR* argv[])
{
    CoInitializeEx(NULL, COINIT_APARTMENTTHREADED);

    //create an instance of the .NET object via COM
    IAddNumbersPtr
        comObj(__uuidof(DniNetSimpleNumbersIFace));
    if (comObj)
    {
```

```
            //call the method and show the results
            int result = comObj->AddSomeNumbers(1, 2);
            _cprintf(
                "Result using interface via COM: %i \r\n",
                result);
            comObj.Release();
        }

    CoUninitialize();
    return 0;
}
```

We use the #import statement to process the typelib generated by Visual Studio .NET. This generates a smart pointer for the COM class and the interface. We define the local variable using the smart pointer for the interface, IAddNumbersPtr.

Notice that we also #import "mscorlib.tlb". This is needed to resolve references to .NET types that are included in the generated typelib for our class.

The results look like this when the code is executed:

```
Result using interface via COM: 3
```

The VB.NET version of the managed class and interface looks like this:

```
Imports System.Runtime.InteropServices

''' <summary>
''' An interface for classes that do addition
''' </summary>
''' <remarks></remarks>
Public Interface IAddNumbers
    Function AddSomeNumbers( _
        ByVal numA As Integer, ByVal numB As Integer) _
            As Integer
End Interface


<ClassInterface(ClassInterfaceType.None)> _
Public Class DniNetSimpleNumbersIFaceVB
    Implements IAddNumbers

    Public Function AddSomeNumbers( _
        ByVal numA As Integer, ByVal numB As Integer) _
            As Integer Implements IAddNumbers.AddSomeNumbers

        Return numA + numB

    End Function
End Class
```

By modifying the name of the typelib that we import and the coclass name, we can use this class from the same C++ client code:

```
#include "stdafx.h"
#include <conio.h>
#include <objbase.h>
#import "mscorlib.tlb"
#import "DniNetSimpleNumbersIFaceVB.tlb" no_namespace

int _tmain(int argc, _TCHAR* argv[])
{
    CoInitializeEx(NULL, COINIT_APARTMENTTHREADED);

    //create an instance of the .NET object via COM
    IAddNumbersPtr
        comObj(__uuidof(DniNetSimpleNumbersIFaceVB));
    if (comObj)
    {
        //call the method and show the results
        int result = comObj->AddSomeNumbers(1, 2);
        _cprintf(
            "Result using VB.NET interface via COM: %i \r\n",
            result);
        comObj.Release();
    }

    CoUninitialize();
    return 0;
}
```

The results look like this:

```
Result using VB.NET interface via COM: 3
```

How It Works

Be aware that when an interface changes, the COM identity (the Guid) for that interface also changes. This means that unless you rebuild all client code that uses the interface, things will suddenly stop working correctly. The client code will either fail completely, or worse, it will behave in an unpredictable way.

However, well-designed interfaces should be immutable. The real benefit of an interface is to provide a contract between client and server code. That contract remains in force as long as we don't modify the interface.

One way to avoid breaking the contract is to provide additional functionality by extending an interface rather than modifying it. The managed class can change to implement the enhanced version of the interface. Existing COM clients can continue to use the original interface without any problems. New COM client code can use the advanced functionality provided by the new interface.

To illustrate this, we can enhance the IAddNumbers interface and the DniNetSimpleNumbersIFace class presented at the beginning of this recipe. The revised code looks like this:

```csharp
using System;
using System.Runtime.InteropServices; //needed for attributes

namespace DniNetSimpleNumbersIFace
{
    /// <summary>
    /// An interface for classes that do addition
    /// </summary>
    public interface IAddNumbers
    {
        int AddSomeNumbers(int numA, int numB);
    }

    /// <summary>
    /// An interface for classes that do addition
    /// and subtraction
    /// </summary>
    public interface IAddSubtractNumbers : IAddNumbers
    {
        int SubtractSomeNumbers(int numA, int numB);
    }

    [ClassInterface(ClassInterfaceType.None)]
    public class DniNetSimpleNumbersIFace : IAddSubtractNumbers
    {
        public int AddSomeNumbers(int numA, int numB)
        {
            return numA + numB;
        }
        public int SubtractSomeNumbers(int numA, int numB)
        {
            return numA - numB;
        }

    }
}
```

Rather than modifying the existing IAddNumbers interface, we define a new IAddSubtractNumbers interface derived from IAddNumbers. This interface includes a new SubtractSomeNumbers method. We then change DniNetSimpleNumbersIFace to implement the new interface instead of IAddNumber. We could have explicitly left IAddNumbers in the implementation list, but we didn't need to. Remember, IAddSubtractNumbers is derived from IAddNumber, so it includes everything from the base interface. After adding an implementation for SubtractSomeNumbers, we're ready to write client code to test this new interface.

Here's the revised C++ code that tests the old and new interfaces:

```cpp
#include "stdafx.h"
#include <conio.h>
#include <objbase.h>
#import "mscorlib.tlb"
#import "DniNetSimpleNumbersIFace.tlb" no_namespace

int _tmain(int argc, _TCHAR* argv[])
{
    CoInitializeEx(NULL, COINIT_APARTMENTTHREADED);

    //create an instance of the .NET object via COM
    //using the original interface
    IAddNumbersPtr
        comObj(__uuidof(DniNetSimpleNumbersIFace));
    if (comObj)
    {
        //call the method and show the results
        int result = comObj->AddSomeNumbers(1, 2);
        _cprintf(
            "AddSomeNumbers using IAddNumbersPtr: %i \r\n",
            result);
    }

    //create a smart pointer for the new interface using
    //the COM object we already created
    IAddSubtractNumbersPtr subObj(comObj);
    if (subObj)
    {
        //call the new method and show the results
        int result = subObj->SubtractSomeNumbers(10, 6);
        _cprintf(
            "SubtractSomeNumbers using IAddSubtractNumbers: %i \r\n",
            result);
        subObj.Release();
    }

    if (comObj)
    {
        comObj.Release();
    }

    CoUninitialize();
    return 0;
}
```

The code starts by creating an instance of the COM object using a smart pointer to the original IAddNumbers interface. After using that pointer, we create a smart pointer for the new IAddSubtractNumbers interface using the original smart pointer variable. This constructor calls QueryInterface for the new interface.

When we execute this test code, we see these results:

```
AddSomeNumbers using IAddNumbersPtr: 3
SubtractSomeNumbers using IAddSubtractNumbers: 4
```

You may be wondering why we used both interfaces in this client code. After all, IAddSubtractNumbers includes both methods, right? Well, yes and no. In the managed code, IAddSubtractNumbers does include both methods (AddSomeNumbers and SubtractSomeNumbers). But when managed interfaces are exported to a typelib for COM, the hierarchy is flattened. This means COM clients see two individual interfaces, each one containing only the members defined for that interface.

If we use OleView to view the IDL generated for this assembly, we see two distinct interfaces and a coclass supporting both of them. Here is a partial listing of the IDL:

```
interface IAddNumbers : IDispatch {
    [id(0x60020000)]
    HRESULT AddSomeNumbers(
                    [in] long numA,
                    [in] long numB,
                    [out, retval] long* pRetVal);
};

interface IAddSubtractNumbers : IDispatch {
    [id(0x60020000)]
    HRESULT SubtractSomeNumbers(
                    [in] long numA,
                    [in] long numB,
                    [out, retval] long* pRetVal);
};

coclass DniNetSimpleNumbersIFace {
    interface _Object;
    [default] interface IAddSubtractNumbers;
    interface IAddNumbers;
};
```

Notice that both of these interfaces derive from IDispatch. This makes them dual interfaces, supporting early and late binding. This is the default interface type when interfaces are exported to COM, but the default can be changed using the InterfaceType attribute.

If we want the interface to support only early binding, we can apply the InterfaceType attribute like this:

```
[InterfaceType(ComInterfaceType.InterfaceIsIUnknown)]
public interface IAddSubtractNumbers : IAddNumbers
{
    int SubtractSomeNumbers(int numA, int numB);
}
```

Note When one interface derives from another one, it is important that they both declare the same value for the `InterfaceType` attribute. For instance, if a base interface is declared with `InterfaceIsIUnknown`, interfaces that derive from it should also use `InterfaceIsIUnknown`. The attribute value should be the same regardless of the `InterfaceType` settings used.

The generated IDL for this interface now shows that it is derived from IUnknown:

```
interface IAddSubtractNumbers : IUnknown {
    HRESULT _stdcall SubtractSomeNumbers(
                    [in] long numA,
                    [in] long numB,
                    [out, retval] long* pRetVal);
};
```

This change prevents COM clients from using late binding with this interface.
The other available option for the attribute is `InterfaceIsIDispatch`:

```
[InterfaceType(ComInterfaceType.InterfaceIsIDispatch)]
public interface IAddSubtractNumbers : IAddNumbers
{
    int SubtractSomeNumbers(int numA, int numB);
}
```

This produces a `dispinterface` that is usable only from late-bound clients:

```
dispinterface IAddSubtractNumbers {
    properties:
    methods:
        [id(0x60020000)]
        long SubtractSomeNumbers(
                    [in] long numA,
                    [in] long numB);
};
```

When previously examining the IDL, you may have noticed that the IAddSubtractNumbers interface is declared as the default interface:

```
coclass DniNetSimpleNumbersIFace {
    interface _Object;
    [default] interface IAddSubtractNumbers;
    interface IAddNumbers;
};
```

By default, when the coclass is exported, the first interface listed is the default interface. The interface marked as the default affects how this class is used from Visual Basic 6.0 (VB6) and scripting clients. VB6 performs special processing with the interface that is marked as default. It assumes that we always want to use the default interface, so it tries to help us a bit. It hides the name of this interface from us and automatically calls QueryInterface for the default interface when the object is created. Generally, scripting clients only work with the default interface.

If we want to determine which interface will be the default one, we can apply the ComDefaultInterface attribute to the class. For example, if we want the IAddNumbers interface to be the default instead of IAddSubtractNumbers, we can apply the attribute like this:

```
[ClassInterface(ClassInterfaceType.None)]
[ComDefaultInterface(typeof(IAddNumbers))]
public class DniNetSimpleNumbersIFace2 : IAddSubtractNumbers
{
    //details not shown
}
```

Now viewing the IDL using OleView confirms that IAddNumbers is the default interface:

```
coclass DniNetSimpleNumbersIFace2 {
    interface _Object;
    interface IAddSubtractNumbers;
    [default] interface IAddNumbers;
};
```

Related Information

See recipes 6-1 (Exposing .NET Classes Using Late Binding), 6-2 (Exposing .NET Classes Using Early Binding), 6-6 (Preparing Assemblies for COM Interop), and 6-4 (Managing COM Identity).

6-4. Managing COM Identity

Problem

Is there a way to control the Guids that are assigned to managed types when they are exported to COM?

Solution

COM uses Guids for just about everything. Each interface and coclass has its own Guid that acts as the unique ID for that type. These IDs might go by different names such as uuid (universally unique ID) or CLSID (class identifier).

Normally, these IDs are generated automatically for you when you export a typelib for an assembly. This is done by enabling the "Make assembly COM-visible" and "Register for COM interop" options for a .NET project.

In some cases you may prefer to assign these Guids yourself. For example, many times component vendors that produce a suite of controls or components will manually assign a sequential range of Guids to their COM components. This makes it easier to find all of their components in the system registry. There's no requirement to do this—it's simply their preference.

.NET allows you to manually assign Guids to your interfaces and classes using the Guid attribute. To assign a Guid, you add this attribute to the type like this:

```
[Guid("8A5B68A5-EF70-4607-BE36-732D5B4DE744")]
public interface IMyInterface
{
    void MyMethod();
}
```

This attribute can also be assigned to a class in the same way:

```
namespace MyNamespace
{
    [Guid("08B7F90F-2BCB-4ce1-A4CF-C5A66DB59164")]
    public class MyClass : IMyInterface
    {
        public void MyMethod()
        {
        }
    }
}
```

When these types are exported to COM, these Guids will be used instead of generating new ones. This attribute can also be applied to other types such as structs, enums, and delegates.

How do you generate the Guids? The easiest way is to use guidgen.exe utility that is included with Visual Studio .NET. By default, this utility is started from the Tools menu by selecting Create GUID. This utility produces Guids in several formats. For our purposes, choose Registry Format. This produces almost exactly what you need for the Guid attribute in a format that looks like this:

```
{83C68334-797D-4b51-9590-574E75F85376}
```

When pasting this into the Guid attribute, you only need to change the curly brackets to double quotes like this:

```
"83C68334-797D-4b51-9590-574E75F85376"
```

You can also use the command-line uuidgen.exe utility to generate IDs. This utility is handy if you want to generate a series of sequential Guids. For example, entering a command of uuidgen -x -n10 produces this series of Guids:

```
bd8f46b0-e517-11d9-b754-000e35fcf76e
bd8f46b1-e517-11d9-b754-000e35fcf76e
bd8f46b2-e517-11d9-b754-000e35fcf76e
bd8f46b3-e517-11d9-b754-000e35fcf76e
bd8f46b4-e517-11d9-b754-000e35fcf76e
bd8f46b5-e517-11d9-b754-000e35fcf76e
bd8f46b6-e517-11d9-b754-000e35fcf76e
bd8f46b7-e517-11d9-b754-000e35fcf76e
bd8f46b8-e517-11d9-b754-000e35fcf76e
bd8f46b9-e517-11d9-b754-000e35fcf76e
```

Now you have plenty of sequential Guids to assign to all of your types.

Using the ProgId attribute, you are able to override the default naming for the ProgId. This programmatic identifier is another key that is associated with the CLSID in the registry. It is another way to look up and use the COM class. For instance, the native COM function CLSIDFromProgId returns the CLSID based on a search for the ProgId.

The ProgId that is automatically generated is a combination of the namespace and class names. For example, here is the ProgId for the class just shown:

```
MyNamespace.MyClass
```

Most of the time, this is what you would have assigned to the class anyway and there is no need to modify it. But if you do want to assign it yourself, you can apply the ProgId attribute to the class like this:

```
namespace MyNamespace
{
    [Guid("08B7F90F-2BCB-4ce1-A4CF-C5A66DB59164")]
    [ProgId("CompanyName.MySpecialClassName")]
    public class MyClass : IMyInterface
    {
        public void MyMethod()
        {
        }
    }
}
```

The maximum size of a ProgId is 39 characters. If the combination of your namespace and class name exceeds this limit, you will need to manually provide your own ProgId using this attribute.

How It Works

According to the rules established for COM, the correct way to add new functionality to an existing COM component is to derive a new interface from the existing one. You can then add any new methods and properties to the new interface while still supporting the current one. If this rule is followed, there won't be a problem with the COM identity.

If you break this rule and change an interface, the COM identity (the Guid) *should* change. For instance, if you change the signature of an existing method or add a new one, you essentially have a new interface. This breaks the COM rules and is not the preferred approach, but it does happen.

Be aware that if you manually apply the Guid attribute as shown here, this prevents any automatic changing of the COM identity. If you make a change that *should* change the COM identity, you must remember to also manually change the Guid. This will break existing clients, but that is the expected behavior when the COM identity changes. At a minimum, the client code should require a recompile using the latest typelib. Depending on the extent of the changes, you may need to change client code.

If you change an interface and don't also change the Guid, you've broken two rules instead of one. Clients will still use the existing Guid and assume that the interface is the same. In this case, the change to the COM identity is a safeguard, preventing you from using a COM object with an interface that is out of date.

To see the effect of these attributes in action, we can compare the typelib that is generated with and without the attributes discussed here. The example that follows contains a managed interface and class that we want to make available to COM:

```
using System;
using System.Runtime.InteropServices;

namespace DniNetAttributes
{
    public interface IComAttributes
    {
        void Foo();
    }

    [ClassInterface(ClassInterfaceType.None)]
    public class DniNetAttributesObj : IComAttributes
    {
        public void Foo()
        {
        }
    }
}
```

If we extract the IDL from the generated typelib using OleView, we see this:

```
// typelib filename: DniNetAttributes.tlb

[
  uuid(096C67DF-48E2-426D-8276-F8A41AD67392),
  version(1.0),
  custom(90883F05-3D28-11D2-8F17-00A0C9A6186D,
  DniNetAttributes, Version=1.0.0.0,
  Culture=neutral, PublicKeyToken=null)
```

```
]
library DniNetAttributes
{
    // TLib :     // TLib : mscorlib.dll :
    {BED7F4EA-1A96-11D2-8F08-00A0C9A6186D}
    importlib("mscorlib.tlb");
    // TLib : OLE Automation :
    {00020430-0000-0000-C000-000000000046}
    importlib("stdole2.tlb");

    // Forward declare all types defined in this typelib
    interface IComAttributes;

    [
      odl,
      uuid(BB1C57CF-A8CC-304F-88B0-367A05757E32),
      version(1.0),
      dual,
      oleautomation,
      custom(0F21F359-AB84-41E8-9A78-36D110E6D2F9,
      DniNetAttributes.IComAttributes)

    ]
    interface IComAttributes : IDispatch {
        [id(0x60020000)]
        HRESULT Foo();
    };

    [
      uuid(4E348386-50E2-3EA0-9F14-AA508CCF6BF5),
      version(1.0),
      custom(0F21F359-AB84-41E8-9A78-36D110E6D2F9,
      DniNetAttributes.DniNetAttributesObj)
    ]
    coclass DniNetAttributesObj {
        interface _Object;
        [default] interface IComAttributes;
    };
};
```

If we view the registry settings for this component using OleView, we see that the ProgId is:

```
ProgId=DniNetAttributes.DniNetAttributesObj
```

The ProgId as well as all Guids have been generated for us.

Here is the revised class that includes attributes to set the Guid and ProgId:

```
using System;
using System.Runtime.InteropServices;
```

```
namespace DniNetAttributes
{
    [Guid("406DD97B-8C4F-4fd6-A6D4-6F71103184A3")]
    public interface IComAttributes
    {
        void Foo();
    }

    [Guid("E4B81256-1727-4a1e-99CF-2ECED97B43B4")]
    [ProgId("DniNetAttributes.DniNetAttributesModified")]
    [ClassInterface(ClassInterfaceType.None)]
    public class DniNetAttributesObj : IComAttributes
    {
        public void Foo()
        {
        }
    }
}
```

And here we have the revised IDL showing the Guids that we manually assigned:

```
// typelib filename: DniNetAttributes.tlb

[
  uuid(096C67DF-48E2-426D-8276-F8A41AD67392),
  version(1.0),
  custom(90883F05-3D28-11D2-8F17-00A0C9A6186D,
    DniNetAttributes, Version=1.0.0.0,
    Culture=neutral, PublicKeyToken=null)

]
library DniNetAttributes
{
    // TLib :       // TLib : mscorlib.dll :
    {BED7F4EA-1A96-11D2-8F08-00A0C9A6186D}
    importlib("mscorlib.tlb");
    // TLib : OLE Automation :
    {00020430-0000-0000-C000-000000000046}
    importlib("stdole2.tlb");

    // Forward declare all types defined in this typelib
    interface IComAttributes;

    [
      odl,
      uuid(406DD97B-8C4F-4FD6-A6D4-6F71103184A3),
      version(1.0),
      dual,
```

```
    oleautomation,
    custom(0F21F359-AB84-41E8-9A78-36D110E6D2F9,
    DniNetAttributes.IComAttributes)

]
interface IComAttributes : IDispatch {
    [id(0x60020000)]
    HRESULT Foo();
};

[
  uuid(E4B81256-1727-4A1E-99CF-2ECED97B43B4),
    version(1.0),
    custom(0F21F359-AB84-41E8-9A78-36D110E6D2F9,
    DniNetAttributes.DniNetAttributesObj)
]
coclass DniNetAttributesObj {
    interface _Object;
    [default] interface IComAttributes;
};
};
```

The ProgId in the registry is now changed to this, matching the value that we manually assigned:

```
ProgId=DniNetAttributes.DniNetAttributesModified
```

The same class and interface implemented in VB.NET look like this:

```
Imports System.Runtime.InteropServices

<Guid("299E5465-6ADC-4336-BB54-1F9BEBB311A2")> _
Public Interface IComAttributes
    Sub Foo()
End Interface

<Guid("7F28D289-E549-4e4d-8822-ADD7B8EFD5FF")> _
<ProgId("DniNetAttributesVB.DniNetAttributesModified")> _
<ClassInterface(ClassInterfaceType.None)> _
Public Class DniNetAttributesObj
    Implements IComAttributes

    Public Sub Foo() Implements IComAttributes.Foo
        'not implemented
    End Sub
End Class
```

We've changed the Guid values and the ProgId attribute values in order to avoid a collision with the C# version.

Related Information

See recipes 6-3 (Exposing .NET Classes with Interfaces) and 6-6 (Preparing Assemblies for
COM Interop).

6-5. Controlling COM Visibility

Problem

You have a managed interface that you want to use from COM clients. However, there are some
members of the interface that you want to hide from COM clients. Is there a way to do that?

Solution

When an interface is exposed to COM, all public members are included. Likewise, when a class
interface is generated for an entire class, all public members of the class are available to COM
clients.

To override this default behavior, you can apply the ComVisible attribute to individual
members of your types. For example, consider this simple C# interface and class:

```csharp
using System;
using System.Runtime.InteropServices;

namespace DniNetComVisibility
{
    public interface IComVisibility
    {
        void Method1();
        void Method2();
        int Property1 { get;set;}
        int Property2 { get;set;}
    }

    [ClassInterface(ClassInterfaceType.None)]
    public class DniNetComVisibilityObj : IComVisibility
    {
        public void Method1()
        {
        }

        public void Method2()
        {
        }

        public int Property1
        {
            get{return 0;}
```

```
        set{}
    }

    public int Property2
    {
        get{return 0;}
        set{}
    }

    protected void ProtectedMethod1()
    {
    }

    private void PrivateMethod1()
    {
    }

    }
}
```

If we register the project for COM interop and generate a typelib, all of the public members will be exported to COM. We can view the generated typelib using a tool such as OleView. Here is a partial list of the generated IDL for this class:

```
[
  odl,
  uuid(DADD8E8F-EB0D-3B5B-B0EB-54E130D482AC),
  version(1.0),
  dual,
  oleautomation,
  custom(0F21F359-AB84-41E8-9A78-36D110E6D2F9,
  DniNetComVisibility.IComVisibility)

]
interface IComVisibility : IDispatch {
    [id(0x60020000)]
    HRESULT Method1();
    [id(0x60020001)]
    HRESULT Method2();
    [id(0x60020002), propget]
    HRESULT Property1([out, retval] long* pRetVal);
    [id(0x60020002), propput]
    HRESULT Property1([in] long pRetVal);
    [id(0x60020004), propget]
    HRESULT Property2([out, retval] long* pRetVal);
    [id(0x60020004), propput]
    HRESULT Property2([in] long pRetVal);
};
```

```
[
  uuid(355E00DB-B359-354E-98EF-E1DEA0ED2003),
  version(1.0),
  custom(0F21F359-AB84-41E8-9A78-36D110E6D2F9,
  DniNetComVisibility.DniNetComVisibilityObj)
]
coclass DniNetComVisibilityObj {
    interface _Object;
    [default] interface IComVisibility;
};
```

As expected, all public methods and properties have been exported to the typelib and are available to COM clients.

If we want to selectively hide members of this interface, we can add the ComVisible attribute like this:

```
public interface IComVisibility
{
    [ComVisible(false)]
    void Method1();
    void Method2();
    [ComVisible(false)]
    int Property1 { get;set;}
    int Property2 { get;set;}
}
```

Now when we view the generated IDL, it looks like this:

```
[
  odl,
  uuid(F0A00FFE-4E24-35D0-8E20-0417807085DD),
  version(1.0),
  dual,
  oleautomation,
  custom(0F21F359-AB84-41E8-9A78-36D110E6D2F9,
  DniNetComVisibility.IComVisibility)

]
interface IComVisibility : IDispatch {
    [restricted] void Missing7();
    [id(0x60020001)]
    HRESULT Method2();
    [restricted] void Missing9();
    [restricted] void Missing10();
    [id(0x60020004), propget]
    HRESULT Property2([out, retval] long* pRetVal);
    [id(0x60020004), propput]
    HRESULT Property2([in] long pRetVal);
};
```

```
[
  uuid(355E00DB-B359-354E-98EF-E1DEA0ED2003),
  version(1.0),
  custom(0F21F359-AB84-41E8-9A78-36D110E6D2F9,
  DniNetComVisibility.DniNetComVisibilityObj)
]
coclass DniNetComVisibilityObj {
    interface _Object;
    [default] interface IComVisibility;
};
```

The two members that we wanted to hide have been removed from the typelib. There are placeholders for them, but they are marked restricted, preventing their use by COM clients. Since one of the members we are hiding is a property, there are actually two entries that are hidden: one for the property getter and another for the setter.

We can hide individual members in a similar fashion using Visual Basic .NET, as demonstrated with the following VB.NET code that implements the same class:

```
Imports System.Runtime.InteropServices

Public Interface IComVisibility
    <ComVisible(False)> _
    Sub Method1()
    Sub Method2()
    <ComVisible(False)> _
    Property Property1() As Integer
    Property Property2() As Integer
End Interface

<ClassInterface(ClassInterfaceType.None)> _
Public Class DniNetComVisibilityObj
    Implements IComVisibility

    Public Sub Method1() Implements IComVisibility.Method1

    End Sub

    Public Sub Method2() Implements IComVisibility.Method2

    End Sub

    Public Property Property1() As Integer _
            Implements IComVisibility.Property1
        Get
            Return 0
        End Get
        Set(ByVal value As Integer)
```

```
        End Set
    End Property

    Public Property Property2() As Integer _
            Implements IComVisibility.Property2
        Get
            Return 0
        End Get
        Set(ByVal value As Integer)

        End Set
    End Property

    Protected Sub ProtectedMethod1()

    End Sub

    Private Sub PrivateMethod()

    End Sub
End Class
```

Aside from the different generated Guids, the IDL for this class looks exactly the same as the C# class. The hidden members of the interface have been marked as restricted and are not available to clients.

How It Works

The ComVisible attribute can only be used to restrict access to a member. It cannot be used to make a member visible to COM that would not normally be available. For instance, you can't apply this attribute to a private method to magically make it public to COM clients.

Although the use of class interfaces is discouraged, you can use the ComVisible attribute to help control them. For example, this C# class is exposed to COM via an automatically generated class interface:

```
using System;
using System.Runtime.InteropServices;

namespace DniNetComVisibility
{
    [ClassInterface(ClassInterfaceType.AutoDual)]
    public class DniNetComVisibilityClassObj
    {
        public void Method1()
        {
        }
```

```csharp
        [ComVisible(false)]
        public void Method2()
        {
        }

        public int Property1
        {
            get{return 0;}
            set{}
        }

        [ComVisible(false)]
        public int Property2
        {
            get{return 0;}
            set{}
        }

        protected void ProtectedMethod1()
        {
        }

        private void PrivateMethod1()
        {
        }

    }
}
```

We have hidden Method2 and Property2 from COM so they should be excluded from the interface. When we view the IDL for the generated interface, we see the expected results:

```
[
  odl,
  uuid(36921BCA-34FA-382F-B746-5B5BB1896F27),
  hidden,
  dual,
  nonextensible,
  oleautomation,
  custom(0F21F359-AB84-41E8-9A78-36D110E6D2F9,
  DniNetComVisibility.DniNetComVisibilityClassObj)

]
interface _DniNetComVisibilityClassObj : IDispatch {
    [id(00000000), propget,
      custom(54FC8F55-38DE-4703-9C4E-250351302B1C, 1)]
    HRESULT ToString([out, retval] BSTR* pRetVal);
    [id(0x60020001)]
```

```
    HRESULT Equals(
                    [in] VARIANT obj,
                    [out, retval] VARIANT_BOOL* pRetVal);
    [id(0x60020002)]
    HRESULT GetHashCode([out, retval] long* pRetVal);
    [id(0x60020003)]
    HRESULT GetType([out, retval] _Type** pRetVal);
    [id(0x60020004)]
    HRESULT Method1();
    [id(0x60020005), propget]
    HRESULT Property1([out, retval] long* pRetVal);
    [id(0x60020005), propput]
    HRESULT Property1([in] long pRetVal);
};
```

In this case there are no restricted placeholders for the hidden members. Remember that a class interface is generated based on the public members of the class. Since we marked Method2 and Property2 as ComVisible(false), those members were simply omitted during the generation process. There was no need to include the restricted placeholders.

The ComVisible attribute can also be applied to an entire class to prevent it from being exported to a COM typelib. For example, this C# class would not be included in the typelib:

```
[ComVisible(false)]
public class DniNetComVisibilityClassBaseObj
{
    public void Method1()
    {
    }
}
```

However, there is a loophole with derived classes that might allow Method1 of this class to suddenly become visible to COM. If we derive a new class from this one, Method1 will become visible to COM clients even though the base class itself is hidden. For example, consider this derived class:

```
[ClassInterface(ClassInterfaceType.AutoDual)]
public class DniNetComVisibilityClassDerivedObj
    : DniNetComVisibilityClassBaseObj
{
    public void Method2()
    {
    }
}
```

When we view the IDL for the generated class interface, we are surprised to see this:

```
[
  odl,
  uuid(44B686C0-AE8D-3419-A26F-6C4FFC584B9B),
  hidden,
  dual,
```

```
    nonextensible,
    oleautomation,
    custom(0F21F359-AB84-41E8-9A78-36D110E6D2F9,
    DniNetComVisibility.DniNetComVisibilityClassDerivedObj)

]
interface _DniNetComVisibilityClassDerivedObj : IDispatch {
    [id(00000000), propget,
      custom(54FC8F55-38DE-4703-9C4E-250351302B1C, 1)]
    HRESULT ToString([out, retval] BSTR* pRetVal);
    [id(0x60020001)]
    HRESULT Equals(
                    [in] VARIANT obj,
                    [out, retval] VARIANT_BOOL* pRetVal);
    [id(0x60020002)]
    HRESULT GetHashCode([out, retval] long* pRetVal);
    [id(0x60020003)]
    HRESULT GetType([out, retval] _Type** pRetVal);
    [id(0x60020004)]
    HRESULT Method1();
    [id(0x60020005)]
    HRESULT Method2();
};
```

The invisible Method1 from the base class is now suddenly visible to clients. This is another good reason to avoid class interfaces and instead develop your own.

The only way to correct this problem is to explicitly add the ComVisible attribute to all public members of the base class. Here is the revised base class:

```
[ComVisible(false)]
public class DniNetComVisibilityClassBaseObj
{
    [ComVisible(false)]
    public void Method1()
    {
    }
}
```

And here is the revised IDL that was generated for the derived class:

```
[
  odl,
  uuid(19EAD6DB-218B-3225-B9DF-F5F68BDFE1E5),
  hidden,
  dual,
  nonextensible,
  oleautomation,
  custom(0F21F359-AB84-41E8-9A78-36D110E6D2F9,
  DniNetComVisibility.DniNetComVisibilityClassDerivedObj)
```

```
]
interface _DniNetComVisibilityClassDerivedObj : IDispatch {
    [id(00000000), propget,
      custom(54FC8F55-38DE-4703-9C4E-250351302B1C, 1)]
    HRESULT ToString([out, retval] BSTR* pRetVal);
    [id(0x60020001)]
    HRESULT Equals(
                    [in] VARIANT obj,
                    [out, retval] VARIANT_BOOL* pRetVal);
    [id(0x60020002)]
    HRESULT GetHashCode([out, retval] long* pRetVal);
    [id(0x60020003)]
    HRESULT GetType([out, retval] _Type** pRetVal);
    [id(0x60020004)]
    HRESULT Method2();
};
```

The invisible method is now finally invisible as we intended.

Related Information

See recipes 6-2 (Exposing .NET Classes Using Early Binding) and 6-3 (Exposing .NET Classes with Interfaces).

6-6. Preparing Assemblies for COM Interop

Problem

.NET assemblies must be registered in the system registry before they can be used by COM clients. Clients that use early binding also require a typelib containing the types that have been exported. What options are available for creation of the typelib and registration of the assembly?

Solution

Generation of the typelib can be done in any of these ways:

- Set the Visual Studio .NET project options to automatically generate the typelib each time the project is built. There are two options that affect the generation of a typelib: "Register for COM interop" on the Build tab and "Make assembly COM-visible" (available by clicking the Assembly Information button from the Application tab).

- Use the TlbExp.exe command-line utility to generate the typelib.

- Use the RegAsm.exe utility to register the assembly and optionally generate a typelib.

- Use the TypeLibConverter class to write your own code that produces a typelib. This class is located in the System.Runtime.InteropServices namespace.

The easiest way to produce a typelib is to set the project options in Visual Studio .NET. When you check the "Make assembly COM-visible" option, Visual Studio adds the `ComVisible(true)` attribute to the `AssemblyInfo.cs` (or `AssemblyInfo.vb`) file. By default, this exposes all types in the assembly to COM. You can override this behavior by adding the `ComVisible(false)` attribute to individual types to hide them from COM.

Alternatively, you can leave this project option unchecked and individually decorate the types that you wish to expose to COM with `ComVisible(true)`. In either case, one requirement to generate a typelib is that the assembly contains at least one type that is visible to COM. If you don't check the "Make assembly COM-visible" option, and you don't decorate individual types with the `ComVisible(true)` attribute, your project won't generate a typelib.

Once the project options are set, a typelib is produced in the output directory for the project each time it is built. You can then publish the generated typelib to a central location where COM clients can access it. This allows them to build against the typelib in order to use early binding to access the COM object.

Optionally, you can use `TlbExp.exe` to generate the typelib. This type-library exporter command-line utility ships with the .NET Framework SDK and is therefore included with Visual Studio .NET.

The utility has a number of options available, but the basic usage is as follows:

```
tlbexp <assemblyname>
```

This generates a typelib using the same name as the assembly but with a `.tlb` extension. For example, if you execute the following command, the utility generates a typelib named `DniNetComVisibility.tlb`:

```
tlbexp DniNetComVisibility.dll
```

Most of the time, this is the name you would have chosen for the typelib. If you want to specify a different output name, you can include the `/out` parameter like this:

```
tlbexp DniNetComVisibility.dll /out: DniNetComVisibility_v1.0_.tlb
```

When deploying an assembly that is to be referenced by COM clients, you must register the assembly for COM interop. This is done using the `RegAsm.exe` utility. `TlbExp.exe` is used only to produce a typelib; it is not capable of registering the assembly.

Since `RegAsm.exe` is used for deployment of assemblies on a target machine, it is included with the .NET runtime. The installation location is the version-specific `Microsoft.Net\Framework` directory under the Windows directory.

`RegAsm.exe` is also capable of producing a typelib at the same time that it registers the assembly. This is an option and it is your choice whether to use `RegAsm.exe` to perform only the registration or to also generate a typelib. The typelib produced from `RegAsm.exe` is the same as what `TlbExp.exe` produces.

To register an assembly using `RegAsm.exe`, you can enter a command in this format:

```
regasm <assemblyname>
```

For example:

```
regasm DniNetComVisibility.dll
```

To unregister the assembly, you add the /u option like this:

```
regasm /u DniNetComVisibility.dll
```

So far, this is similar in concept to the regsvr32.exe utility that is used to register or unregister native COM components (those that are not .NET components).

If you add the /tlb option, RegAsm.exe also produces a typelib file. For example, this command will register the assembly and produce a typelib file named DniNetComVisibility.tlb:

```
regasm /tlb DniNetComVisibility.dll
```

Optionally, you can specify a different output file name for the typelib like this:

```
regasm /tlb:MyTypelib.tlb DniNetComVisibility.dll
```

As another option, instead of registering the assembly, this utility can produce a .reg file containing all of the registration entries. For example, this command produces a file named DniNetComVisibility.reg:

```
regasm /regfile DniNetComVisibility.dll
```

The file can be imported into the registry on the target deployment machine using regedit or regedt32. The default action if you double-click a .reg file in Windows Explorer is to install it in the registry; you would do this instead of running RegAsm.exe on the target machine to register the assembly. If you use the /regfile option, you'll need to install your assembly into the global assembly cache (GAC) in order to allow COM clients to locate it. As an alternative, you can deploy the assembly to the same directory as the COM client.

How It Works

Just like our assemblies, typelibs have a version number that is embedded within them. By default, the version number of the exported typelib and the assembly are the same. More specifically, the typelib version is the first two nodes of the assembly version.

For example, this assembly version:

```
1 (major) 2 (minor) 3 (build) 4 (revision)
```

would generate a typelib version number like this:

```
1 (major) 2 (minor)
```

This works fine in most cases. But consider the case where you have two assembly builds that end up generating the same typelib version number:

```
1.2.25.1
```

```
1.2.50.2
```

Both of these assembly versions will generate the same typelib version of 1.2. If you want to avoid this, you can manually set the typelib version number using the `TypeLibVersion` attribute, which you can find in the `System.Runtime.InteropServices` namespace.

This attribute can be applied only at the entire assembly level, so it would normally be placed in the `AssemblyInfo.cs` or `AssemblyInfo.vb` file. The C# version looks like this:

```
[assembly: TypeLibVersion(2, 1)]
```

Adding this attribute allows you to have complete control of the typelib version number.

Related Information

See recipes 6-2 (Exposing .NET Classes Using Early Binding) and 6-3 (Exposing .NET Classes with Interfaces).

6-7. Exposing Managed Events to COM

Problem

You have a managed class that fires an event. Is it possible to expose a managed event to COM clients? If so, how is that accomplished?

Solution

.NET supports events using delegates. A delegate serves the same basic purpose as a function pointer in unmanaged code: it acts as a proxy for a method in another class. When managed code raises an event, any subscribers to that event are notified, receiving any data that is passed as arguments of the delegate.

COM supports events using an event *source* and an event *sink*. The source of the event is the COM component that will raise the event. COM clients that subscribe to a COM event act as the event sink. When the COM event source raises an event, the sink receives notification and can act upon any data passed with the event.

COM interop marries these two concepts by allowing COM clients to see managed events as COM event sources. When managed code raises an event, any COM clients that have subscribed to the COM event source (which is really the managed event) receive notification.

The steps to expose a managed event to COM clients are as follows:

1. Implement a managed delegate for the event.

2. Define a separate event-sink interface in managed code.

3. Add the `ComSourceInterfaces` attribute to the managed class acting as the event source. This attribute can be found in the `System.Runtime.InteropServices` namespace.

4. Declare the event as public in the managed class.

5. Add code to the managed class to raise the event when it is appropriate.

The example that follows illustrates these steps. This C# code implements a simple class that permits changes to a string variable. Each time the string is changed, an event is raised to notify any event subscribers of the change. The event passes the old and new values of the string as parameters.

We start by declaring a delegate for the event:

```
//the delegate for the event
[ComVisible(false)]
public delegate void DescChangedHandler(
    string newDesc, string oldDesc);
```

The delegate defines a method taking two strings as parameters. When we declare the event within our managed class, it will use this delegate as its type. Any event handlers that subscribe to the event must have the same method signature, accepting two strings as parameters.

Notice that we add the ComVisible(false) attribute to this delegate. The delegate itself is used only within managed code and does not need to be exported to COM. If we don't hide the delegate with this attribute, it will be included in the typelib even though it will never be used. To avoid any possible confusion, it's best to hide it from COM clients.

We next define an event-sink interface like this:

```
//an interface defining our event source
[InterfaceType(ComInterfaceType.InterfaceIsIDispatch)]
public interface IDescriptionNotifier
{
    //the method name here must match the event name
    //in our managed class and interface. The DispId
    //attribute is needed to prevent errors in VB6
    //when no event handler is assigned.
    [DispId(21)]
    void DescChanged(string newDesc, string oldDesc);
}
```

This interface is exported to COM and defines the event handler that a client must implement to handle an event. COM clients will use this interface instead of the managed delegate. We add the InterfaceTypeAttribute to set the interface type to InterfaceIsIDispatch. This attribute causes this interface to be exported as a dispinterface. This is the type that is fully supported by COM clients like Visual Basic 6.0 (VB6). If we use a different type of interface, such as a dual interface, the event will not be available to VB6 clients.

Please see the sidebar in the upcoming "How It Works" section concerning the need for the DispId attribute shown here. This is also needed here because of the way VB6 works.

Since we don't want to expose the managed class using the default class interface, we define our own. Here is the interface that defines the one and only method that is available to COM clients:

```
//an interface defining the members we want to expose
//to COM clients
[InterfaceType(ComInterfaceType.InterfaceIsIDispatch)]
public interface IDescriptionManager
{
```

```
        void ChangeDesc(string newDesc);
}
```

To be consistent, we also define this interface as InterfaceIsIDispatch. However, this is not a strict requirement in order for this to work. Unlike the event-sink interface that we just defined, any type of interface is permitted here.

The managed class that acts as the source of the event is implemented like this:

```
[ClassInterface(ClassInterfaceType.None)]
[ComSourceInterfaces(typeof(IDescriptionNotifier))]
public class DniNetComEventsObj : IDescriptionManager
{
    //event that COM clients can subscribe to
    public event DescChangedHandler DescChanged;

    //causes the event to be fired
    public void ChangeDesc(string newDesc)
    {
        if (DescChanged != null)
        {
            //fire the event if there are any subscribers
            DescChanged(newDesc, m_Desc);
        }
        m_Desc = newDesc;
    }

    private string m_Desc = "empty";
}
```

We suppress generation of the class interface by adding the ClassInterface attribute. We have no need for the class interface since we have defined our own interface that we want COM clients to use (IDescriptionManager).

The ComSourcesInterface attribute is critical to make all of this work. It identifies this class as the event source for the interface identified in the attribute constructor (IDescriptionNotifier). Also notice that the method name (DescChanged) defined in this interface exactly matches the name of the event in this class. This was not an accident—it is a requirement that the method and event names match.

Finally, we implement code in the ChangeDesc method to raise the DescChanged event each time the string is changed.

As always, we remember to set the project options to generate a typelib file and register the assembly for COM interop.

To test this event code, we write a small VB6 COM client. The steps needed to handle this event include the following:

1. Add the .NET/COM component just developed to the VB6 Project References.

2. Declare the variable for the COM object using the WithEvents keyword.

3. Select the event we want to handle from the drop-down list and implement the handler code.

Here is the VB6 implementation of a COM client:

```
'declare a variable for the com object withevents
Public WithEvents comObj As DniNetComEvents.DniNetComEventsObj


'event handler for the com object
Private Sub comObj_DescChanged( _
        ByVal newDesc As String, ByVal oldDesc As String)
    'display the event arguments
    Text1.Text = Text1.Text + "Old: " + oldDesc _
        + "  New: " + newDesc + vbCrLf
End Sub


Private Sub Form_Load()
    'create an instance of the COM object
    Set comObj = New DniNetComEvents.DniNetComEventsObj

    'call the change description method that should
    'fire the event
    comObj.ChangeDesc ("one")
    comObj.ChangeDesc ("two")
    comObj.ChangeDesc ("three")

    'free the COM reference
    Set comObj = Nothing
End Sub
```

As shown in this example code, the variable for the COM object must be declared WithEvents. This enables VB to act as an event sink for any events that may be defined for the COM object.

After selecting the DescChanged event from the drop-down list, we can add our own code to handle this event. In this example, we update a TextBox with the old and new strings that are passed as event parameters.

The remainder of the code in the Form_Load event creates an instance of the COM object and calls the ChangeDesc method a number of times to exercise the event handling code.

When this code is executed, we see this in the TextBox:

```
Old: empty  New: one
Old: one  New: two
Old: two  New: three
```

Clearly, the VB6 client is receiving the managed events.

Here is the equivalent managed code for the event source implemented in VB.NET:

```
Imports System.Runtime.InteropServices


<ComVisible(False)> _
Public Delegate Sub DescChangedHandler( _
    ByVal newDesc As String, ByVal oldDesc As String)
```

```vb
'an interface defining our event source
<InterfaceTypeAttribute(ComInterfaceType.InterfaceIsIDispatch)> _
Public Interface IDescriptionNotifier
    <DispId(21)> _
    Sub DescChanged(ByVal newDesc As String, _
        ByVal oldDesc As String)
End Interface

'an interface defining the members we want to expose
'to COM clients
<InterfaceTypeAttribute(ComInterfaceType.InterfaceIsIDispatch)> _
Public Interface IDescriptionManager
    Sub ChangeDesc(ByVal newDesc As String)
End Interface

<ClassInterface(ClassInterfaceType.None)> _
<ComSourceInterfaces(GetType(IDescriptionNotifier))> _
Public Class DniNetComEventsVBObj
    Implements IDescriptionManager

    'declare the event
    Public Event DescChanged As DescChangedHandler

    Public Sub ChangeDesc(ByVal newDesc As String) _
        Implements IDescriptionManager.ChangeDesc

        'raise the managed event
        RaiseEvent DescChanged(newDesc, m_Desc)
        m_Desc = newDesc

    End Sub

    Private m_Desc As String = "empty"

End Class
```

The same VB6 client code can be used to execute this VB.NET version. All that is required is to change the object name from this:

```
DniNetComEvents.DniNetComEventsObj
```

to this:

```
DniNetComEventsVB.DniNetComEventsVBObj
```

When this code is executed, the results displayed are exactly the same as the version using the C# object.

How It Works

It is possible for a class to support multiple event-sink interfaces. The ComSourceInterfaces attribute has overloaded constructors that accept multiple interfaces. However, using more than one event-sink interface may not be a great idea if your client code is VB6. VB6 only supports the WithEvents keyword for the single source interface marked as the default. Instead, it would be better to define a single interface containing all events you wish to publish to COM clients.

DISPID AND VISUAL BASIC 6.0

In this recipe's example, we added the DispId attribute to the event-handler method defined in the IDescriptionNotifier interface like this:

```
[DispId(21)]
void DescChanged(string newDesc, string oldDesc);
```

This is needed because of the way this dispinterface is used by Visual Basic 6.0. If you implement an event handler for all events defined in the interface, you won't have a problem. However, if any defined events are not handled in your VB6 code, you may receive a DISP_E_UNKNOWNNAME error (x80020006) when running your code. This can easily occur if you have a number of events defined, but need to handle only a few of them.

The error occurs when the VB runtime calls IDispatch.GetIDsOfNames. If no event handler is registered for an event, VB is unable to resolve the dispatch ID and the error is returned. However, by declaring our own dispatch ID in managed code using the DispId attribute, we eliminate the problem. The number 21 that was used for this DispId attribute has no special meaning. You can assign any dispatch ID as long as it is unique within the interface.

Personally, I would consider this a COM interop bug. But based on various newsgroup postings, this bug has existed for a number of years, going back to the original version of .NET. It doesn't appear that this behavior will change anytime soon.

A good rule of thumb is that if you are planning on consuming managed events from VB6, you should always define a DispId for each handler method.

Related Information

See recipes 6-3 (Exposing .NET Classes with Interfaces) and 6-5 (Controlling COM Visibility).

6-8. Providing HRESULTs for Exceptions

Problem

Since COM relies upon HRESULT codes to determine the success or failure of a call, how do you return these from managed code?

Solution

COM uses an HRESULT code to signal that a method succeeded or failed. The code not only signals that an error occurred, but also indicates the reason for the error. Microsoft has defined a series of codes that can be used for common errors, but developers are allowed to define their own set of codes.

HRESULT codes can also be used to signal varying degrees of success. For example, the code S_OK (zero) is usually returned when a method succeeds. But the code S_FALSE (1) has also been defined and is considered a success instead of a failure.

Managed code doesn't directly use HRESULT codes. Instead, when an error occurs, an exception is thrown. Each one of the standard exceptions is mapped to an HRESULT value. If an exception is thrown during a COM interop call, the HRESULT associated with the exception is marshaled back to the COM client instead of the exception.

■Note For more information about the standard mappings between managed exceptions and COM HRESULT codes, please refer to recipe 5-13.

Unless an exception is thrown within managed code, S_OK is returned to signal success. Multiple success values such as S_FALSE are not directly supported and are thrown away by the marshaler. However, the next recipe does demonstrate how to preserve a success HRESULT when this is necessary.

When you implement your own managed exceptions, you need to provide an appropriate HRESULT for COM clients. Microsoft provides an HResult property in the base Exception class. Since HResult is a protected property, you need to set it within the constructor of your exception class.

For example, consider this custom exception class:

```
public class CustomException : ApplicationException
{
    public CustomException(string msg)
        : base(msg)
    {
    }
}
```

■Note The examples in this chapter make use of the standard .NET System.ApplicationException class. It has always been the documented Microsoft recommendation that all new exception classes defined by us should derive from ApplicationException.

However, as is always the case with these types of recommendations, there are dissenting views. If you do a quick Internet search, you'll find that some people recommend that you derive your exceptions directly from the System.Exception class instead of System.ApplicationException. Others support the long-standing use of ApplicationException.

You should use a convention that makes sense for your application and follows your own internal standards.

The class derives from ApplicationException, but it doesn't set the HResult property. Therefore, it will inherit the HResult from the parent class. ApplicationException uses 0x80131600 (COR_E_APPLICATION), so that is the code that will be returned to COM clients if this exception is ever thrown.

Compare this with a revised exception class:

```
public class CustomExceptionWithHResult : ApplicationException
{
    public CustomExceptionWithHResult(string msg)
        : base(msg)
    {
        this.HResult = unchecked((int)0x80040301);
    }
}
```

This class correctly sets the HResult property with a user-defined value that uniquely identifies the error. If this exception is thrown during a COM interop call, the value 0x80040301 will be returned to the COM client. The unchecked keyword is required since we are setting the high-order bit of the 32-bit field. This exceeds the normal range for an integer. Without the unchecked keyword, an overflow exception would be thrown.

Note The HRESULT range reserved for user-defined errors is 0x80040200 to 0x8004FFFF. This corresponds to the general FACILITY_ITF range allocated to errors from an interface. You should not define your own errors outside of this range. According to Microsoft, everything outside of this range is under its control. For more information, please refer to the "Related Information" section for the MSDN reference that describes the format of an HRESULT.

How It Works

To demonstrate the results when these exceptions are thrown, we can implement a class in C# and export it for use by COM clients. The exceptions thrown are those just defined and are not repeated here. The remainder of the C# implementation looks like this:

```
public interface IExceptions
{
    void ThrowStandardException();
    void ThrowCustomException();
    void ThrowCustomExceptionWithHResult();
}

[ClassInterface(ClassInterfaceType.None)]
public class DniNetExceptionsObj : IExceptions
{
    public void ThrowStandardException()
    {
        throw new ApplicationException(
```

```
                    "This is an ApplicationException");
        }

    public void ThrowCustomException()
    {
        throw new CustomException("My custom exception message");
    }

    public void ThrowCustomExceptionWithHResult()
    {
        throw new CustomExceptionWithHResult(
            "My custom exception message with HResult");
    }
}
```

We've chosen to expose the IExceptions interface to COM instead of using the class interface. The test implementation has three methods:

- ThrowStandardException throws a standard ApplicationException.

- ThrowCustomException throws the CustomException shown previously.

- ThrowCustomExceptionWithHResult throws the version that provides a user-defined HResult.

Here is the complete VB.NET implementation of this class along with the exception classes and interface:

```
Imports System.Runtime.InteropServices

Public Class CustomException
    Inherits ApplicationException

    Public Sub New(ByVal msg As String)
        MyBase.New(msg)
    End Sub
End Class

Public Class CustomExceptionWithHResult
    Inherits ApplicationException

    Public Sub New(ByVal msg As String)
        MyBase.New(msg)
        Me.HResult = &H80040301
    End Sub
End Class

Public Interface IExceptions
    Sub ThrowStandardException()
    Sub ThrowCustomException()
```

```
    Sub ThrowCustomExceptionWithHResult()
End Interface

<ClassInterface(ClassInterfaceType.None)> _
Public Class DniNetExceptionsObj
    Implements IExceptions

    Public Sub ThrowStandardException() _
            Implements IExceptions.ThrowStandardException
        Throw New ApplicationException( _
            "This is an ApplicationException")
    End Sub

    Public Sub ThrowCustomException() _
            Implements IExceptions.ThrowCustomException
        Throw New CustomException( _
            "My custom exception message")
    End Sub

    Public Sub ThrowCustomExceptionWithHResult() _
            Implements IExceptions.ThrowCustomExceptionWithHResult
        Throw New CustomExceptionWithHResult( _
            "My custom exception message with HResult")
    End Sub

End Class
```

Here is Visual Basic 6.0 (VB6) client code to test this class. It uses the C# version but could easily execute the VB.NET version instead. To do this, just reference the VB.NET component instead of the C# version and change the full object name to correspond with the VB.NET version:

```
Private Sub Form_Load()
    Dim comObj As _
        New DniNetExceptions.DniNetExceptionsObj

    On Error Resume Next

    Call comObj.ThrowStandardException
    Call ShowError

    Call comObj.ThrowCustomException
    Call ShowError

    Call comObj.ThrowCustomExceptionWithHResult
    Call ShowError
End Sub
```

```
Private Sub ShowError()
    If Err.Number <> 0 Then
        Text1.Text = Text1.Text + _
            Hex(Err.Number) + " " + _
            Err.Description + _
            vbCrLf
    End If
    Err.Clear
End Sub
```

We use the On Error Resume Next statement since we want to see the results of each of these exceptions. If we didn't do this, the first exception would terminate the program.

When we execute this test code, we see these results shown in a TextBox on the form:

```
80131600 This is an ApplicationException
80131600 My custom exception message
80040301 My custom exception message with HResult
```

Related Information

See recipes 6-9 (Preserving Success HRESULTs) and 5-13 (Converting HRESULTs to Exceptions). Also refer to the MSDN topic "Structure of COM Error Codes" for a detailed description of the HRESULT format.

6-9. Preserving Success HRESULTs

Problem

You'd like to return multiple HRESULT success values such as S_OK and S_FALSE from a managed method. However, .NET doesn't seem to support any way to set and return a success HRESULT. Is there a way to do this?

Solution

COM interop doesn't provide a direct way to return a success HRESULT to a COM client. When managed code throws an exception, an error HRESULT is returned to the caller. The same does not hold true for success HRESULT codes such as S_FALSE or a custom success HRESULT. Success HRESULT values are simply thrown away when a managed method returns. And there is no direct mechanism to even set an HRESULT from managed code.

However, using the PreserveSig attribute, you can pass multiple success HRESULT values to the calling code. This attribute can be found in the System.Runtime.InteropServices namespace.

Without this attribute, the default behavior is to transform all managed methods to return an HRESULT and to not preserve the original method signature. For instance, consider this managed method:

```
string MyMethod(int paramA);
```

When exported to a COM typelib, this method will be defined like this:

```
HRESULT MyMethod([in] long paramA, [out, retval] BSTR* pRetVal);
```

The result string is turned into an [out,retval] and the actual return value is an HRESULT. This is a very typical signature for a COM method.

We can apply the PreserveSig attribute to the method like this:

```
[PreserveSig]
string MyMethod(int paramA);
```

When the method is exported to a typelib, it is defined like this, preserving the original method signature:

```
BSTR* MyMethod([in] long paramA);
```

Now that you know what the PreserveSig attribute does, how does it help you return an HRESULT? Instead of allowing the marshaler to provide an HRESULT, you can define a method that explicitly returns an HRESULT. If you add PreserveSig to the method, the signature of the method will not be transformed. You can then return an HRESULT using the method as you have defined it. You will be in control and the marshaler will not attempt to set the HRESULT automatically for you.

To demonstrate this, consider this interface implemented in C#:

```
public interface IPreserveSig
{
    void CopyString(string inParam, ref string outParam);

    [PreserveSig]
    [return: MarshalAs(UnmanagedType.Error)]
    int CopyStringPreserve(string inParam, ref string outParam);
}
```

The CopyString method uses the default marshaling. It accepts a string as the first parameter and a string passed by reference as the second. It doesn't have a return value that we have defined.

The CopyStringPreserve method is defined the same way except that it returns an integer. It also has two attributes, PreserveSig and MarshalAs. The MarshalAs attribute is applied to the return value (the integer) and forces it to be marshaled as UnmanagedType.Error. This means it will be marshaled as an HRESULT.

By examining the generated typelib for this interface, we see that these two methods have the same signature to COM clients:

```
interface IPreserveSig : IDispatch {
    [id(0x60020000)]
    HRESULT CopyString(
                    [in] BSTR inParam,
                    [in, out] BSTR* outParam);
    [id(0x60020001)]
    HRESULT CopyStringPreserve(
                    [in] BSTR inParam,
```

```
                    [in, out] BSTR* outParam);
};
```

We can now write a C# class that implements this interface:

```
[ClassInterface(ClassInterfaceType.None)]
public class DniNetPreserveSigObj : IPreserveSig
{
    public void CopyString(string inParam, ref string outParam)
    {
        outParam = inParam;
        if (inParam.Length == 0)
        {
            //try to throw an S_FALSE HRESULT
            Marshal.ThrowExceptionForHR(1);
        }
    }

    public int CopyStringPreserve(
        string inParam, ref string outParam)
    {
        outParam = inParam;
        if (inParam.Length == 0)
        {
            return 1;    //S_FALSE;
        }
        return 0;    //S_OK;
    }
}
```

Both methods attempt to do the same thing. If the length of the input string is zero, they try to return an HRESULT of 1 (S_FALSE). CopyString doesn't have any way to set the HRESULT, so it attempts to throw an exception for a value of 1. We will see that this doesn't work.

The CopyStringPreserve method has a handy integer return code that has been mapped to an HRESULT for COM clients. By returning either a zero (S_OK) or 1 (S_FALSE), we can set the HRESULT.

To see this code in action, we can implement a COM client that uses this class. We've chosen C++ for this since it allows us to easily save and inspect the HRESULT that is returned from each method call. Here is the C++ implementation:

```
#include "stdafx.h"
#include <conio.h>
#include <objbase.h>
#include <atlbase.h>
#import "mscorlib.tlb"
#import "DniNetPreserveSig.tlb" no_namespace
```

```
int _tmain(int argc, _TCHAR* argv[])
{
    CoInitializeEx(NULL, COINIT_APARTMENTTHREADED);

    //create an instance of the .NET object via COM
    IPreserveSigPtr
        comObj(__uuidof(DniNetPreserveSigObj));
    if (comObj)
    {
        HRESULT hr;
        CComBSTR result;

        hr = comObj->CopyString(L"test", &result);
        _cprintf(
            "CopyString with string: 0x%8.8x \r\n", hr);

        hr = comObj->CopyString(L"", &result);
        _cprintf(
            "CopyString with empty string: 0x%8.8x \r\n", hr);

        hr = comObj->CopyStringPreserve(L"test", &result);
        _cprintf(
            "CopyStringPreserve with string: 0x%8.8x \r\n", hr);

        hr = comObj->CopyStringPreserve(L"", &result);
        _cprintf(
            "CopyStringPreserve with empty string: 0x%8.8x \r\n", hr);
        comObj.Release();
    }

    CoUninitialize();

    return 0;
}
```

The code calls each of the methods twice: first with a valid string and then with a zero-length string. The second call to each method *should* produce an HRESULT of S_FALSE (1). However, from what we have learned, it is unlikely that the CopyString method will return anything other than zero.

When we execute the code, we see these results:

```
CopyString with string: 0x00000000
CopyString with empty string: 0x00000000
CopyStringPreserve with string: 0x00000000
CopyStringPreserve with empty string: 0x00000001
```

As expected, CopyString always returns S_OK (zero). Even when the code attempts to throw an exception for a value of 1, the success HRESULT is thrown away. However, the CopyStringPreserve method does successfully return either S_OK or S_FALSE.

How It Works

Be aware that when the PreserveSig attribute is applied to a method, you have assumed the responsibility for returning all HRESULT values. If your intent is to return an HRESULT, you need to define your method accordingly.

As we've seen, the method will not be transformed to return an HRESULT when it is exported to a typelib. This means that unless you define your method to return an integer as we did here, you will not be able to pass any HRESULT values to the caller. This includes any failure HRESULT values resulting from an exception.

If you define your method with an integer return value as shown here, HRESULT values resulting from an exception will be passed back to the caller without any manual intervention from you. But if you omit the integer return value when defining the method, any failures resulting from an exception will be hidden from the caller.

Related Information

See recipe 6-8 (Providing HRESULTs for Exceptions).

CHAPTER 7

Marshaling to COM Clients

This chapter continues the discussion started in Chapter 6 on exposing managed code to COM clients. The focus of this chapter is on marshaling of parameters.

Since the managed code acts as the publisher of new COM components, you are in a position to control the look and feel of the API that you expose to COM clients. You can define and implement your managed types any way you see fit and use them from managed code. But the decisions you make may affect the way COM client code is able to use your components. If there are multiple ways to define a parameter, you want to make decisions that will make it easy for COM clients to use your code. You don't want to unknowingly place obstacles in the way of these clients.

This chapter reviews some of the options available to you when defining your managed interfaces and classes. We will examine several categories of data types to see how we can control the way they are marshaled.

The chapter starts with a recipe discussing parameter direction and the things you can do to control it. Additional recipes cover the marshaling of strings, arrays, and Variants, all core data types that are used frequently in COM development. Marshaling of entire classes and structures is demonstrated in another recipe.

Several specialized subjects are discussed in other recipes. One recipe demonstrates how to marshal currency, while another looks at the handling of null strings. Finally, the chapter closes with a discussion of optional parameters.

7-1. Controlling Parameter Direction

Problem

How are the COM directional attributes (in, out, and retval) determined when managed code is exported to a COM type library (typelib)? How can you affect the flow of data into and out of managed code?

Solution

Native COM uses directional attributes in the Interface Definition Language (IDL, ODL, or MIDL) to determine how parameters are passed to a COM method. The attributes of in and out indicate the parameter direction. They signify that a parameter is an input into a method (in) or that changes made to a parameter are marshaled back to the caller (out). Combinations of attributes are also possible, such as in,out and the ever-popular out,retval. This last combination (out,retval) signifies that a parameter is the return value for a method.

When a typelib is generated for managed code, the way a parameter is passed to a method determines the direction. A parameter can be passed by value or by reference.

Table 7-1 summarizes how the directional attributes are determined.

Table 7-1. *COM Directional Attributes*

Parameter Usage	IDL Directional Attributes	Notes
Passed by value (byval in VB)	[in]	Callers do not see changes to a parameter.
Passed by reference (byref in VB, ref in C#)	[in,out]	Callers see changes made to a parameter.
Method return value	[out,retval]	The parameter is the result value for the method.
Out only (available in C# only)	[out]	The parameter is an output from the method, and initial values are not passed in from the caller.

No distinction is made between value and reference types when determining the directional attributes for COM interop. Both types of data are handled in the same way according to the rules stated in Table 7-1.

Making a conscious decision to pass parameters by value or by reference is really the only way to control parameter direction. If you want the caller to see changes made to a parameter, then it must be passed by reference or out (available in C# only). If a parameter is truly read-only and will not be updated by the managed code, pass it by value.

A set of optional In and Out attributes is available to fine-tune the direction of data. As the names suggest, these mark an individual calling parameter as input or output. You can also apply both attributes to allow a flow of data in both directions. These attributes are not used when calling a method from managed code; they are used only during COM interop.

Note You may be wondering why these directional attributes are sometimes shown as all lowercase ([in,out]) and other times with a leading capital ([In,Out]). Is there a difference between the two?

Yes, there is a difference. The attributes that are all lowercase are MIDL attributes. MIDL is a language that is used to define interfaces for COM. It uses a set of attributes that are always lowercase. The attributes that start with a capital letter are .NET attributes that are used within your managed code. In this case, the two sets of attributes have the same meaning, but they are different and are not interchangeable.

These attributes cannot be used to expand the flow of data; they can only restrict it. For instance, adding [In,Out] to a parameter that is passed by value will not suddenly allow the caller to see changes to the parameter. In order to see changes, you need to pass a parameter by reference or as out only. The [In,Out] attributes cannot override the default behavior that requires parameters to be passed by reference in order to see changes.

■**Note** As usual, there are exceptions to any rule. One exception to this rule is when you are passing arrays by value. By adding the [In,Out] attributes to an array passed by value, the caller is able to see any changes to the array. The topic of marshaling arrays is discussed in-depth in recipe 7-3 (Marshaling Arrays).

Marshaling of managed classes and structures is also covered in another recipe.

On the other hand, adding [In] to a parameter that is passed by reference does restrict the flow of data. In this case, even though the parameter is passed by reference, the caller does not see any changes made to the parameter. Why would you do this? Most of the time you won't need to. But you could add this attribute for a slight performance gain or if you want to hide parameter changes from COM clients only.

System.String is considered a reference type, but it is special because it is immutable. Once created, an instance of a System.String cannot be updated. Updates to a System.String variable cause the creation of a new immutable string. Because of this, System.String is marshaled like a value type even though it is a reference type. In order to see any changes to a String parameter, it must be passed as a by reference or out parameter (ByRef in VB; ref or out in C#).

■**Note** System.Text.StringBuilder is another special class that doesn't play by all of the rules. The caller is always able to see changes made to a StringBuilder parameter. This occurs regardless of whether it is passed by value or by reference.

How It Works

The following C# code demonstrates the differences in COM interop when parameters are passed in different ways. We also apply the [In,Out] attributes to illustrate the effect that they do or do not have.

We start by defining a number of test methods in an interface:

```
using System;
using System.Runtime.InteropServices;

public interface IDirectionTester
{
    void IntInOnly(int paramA, int paramB);
    void IntInAndOut(int paramA, [In,Out] int paramB);
    void IntByRef(int paramA, ref int paramB);
    void IntByRefInOnly(int paramA, [In] ref int paramB);
    void IntOut(int paramA, out int paramB);
    void StringsInOnly(string paramA, string paramB);
    void StringsInAndOut(string paramA, [In,Out] string paramB);
    void StringsByRef(string paramA, ref string paramB);
    void StringsByRefInOnly(string paramA,
        [In] ref string paramB);
```

```
    void StringsOut(string paramA, out string paramB);
    void DateTimeInOnly(DateTime paramA, DateTime paramB);
    void DateTimeInAndOut(DateTime paramA,
        [In,Out] DateTime paramB);
    void DateTimeByRef(DateTime paramA, ref DateTime paramB);
    void DateTimeByRefInOnly(DateTime paramA,
        [In] ref DateTime paramB);
    void DateTimeOut(DateTime paramA, out DateTime paramB);
}
```

This interface will be exported to the typelib and can be used by COM clients.

The interface defines a series of test methods, with three different types of parameters being passed. We pass a blittable data type (an integer), a reference type (a string), and a value type (the DateTime struct). We have five methods for each of these types, with each method passing the parameters in a slightly different way.

Note One combination that is absent from this test is an out-only parameter with an [In] attribute. Since this combination doesn't make any sense, the C# compiler correctly flags it as build error CS0036 if we try this. The error message is "An out parameter cannot have the '[In]' attribute".

This C# class implements the previously defined interface:

```
[ClassInterface(ClassInterfaceType.None)]
public class DniNetInOutObj : IDirectionTester
{
    //blittable type - by value
    public void IntInOnly(int paramA, int paramB)
    {
        paramB = paramA;
    }
    //blittable type - by value, with out attribute
    public void IntInAndOut(int paramA, int paramB)
    {
        paramB = paramA;
    }
    //blittable type - by ref
    public void IntByRef(int paramA, ref int paramB)
    {
        paramB = paramA;
    }
    //blittable type - by ref, with in attribute
    public void IntByRefInOnly(int paramA, ref int paramB)
    {
        paramB = paramA;
    }
```

```csharp
//blittable type - out
public void IntOut(int paramA, out int paramB)
{
    paramB = paramA;
}


//reference type - by value
public void StringsInOnly(string paramA, string paramB)
{
    paramB = paramA;
}
//reference type - by value, with out attribute
public void StringsInAndOut(string paramA, string paramB)
{
    paramB = paramA;
}
//reference type - by ref
public void StringsByRef(string paramA, ref string paramB)
{
    paramB = paramA;
}
//reference type - by ref, with in attribute
public void StringsByRefInOnly(
    string paramA, ref string paramB)
{
    paramB = paramA;
}
//reference type - out
public void StringsOut(string paramA, out string paramB)
{
    paramB = paramA;
}


//value type - by value
public void DateTimeInOnly(
    DateTime paramA, DateTime paramB)
{
    paramB = paramA;
}
//value type - by value, with out attribute
public void DateTimeInAndOut(
    DateTime paramA, DateTime paramB)
{
    paramB = paramA;
}
//value type - by ref
public void DateTimeByRef(
```

```
        DateTime paramA, ref DateTime paramB)
    {
        paramB = paramA;
    }
    //value type - by ref, with in attribute
    public void DateTimeByRefInOnly(
        DateTime paramA, ref DateTime paramB)
    {
        paramB = paramA;
    }
    //value type - out
    public void DateTimeOut(
        DateTime paramA, out DateTime paramB)
    {
        paramB = paramA;
    }

}
```

All of the methods work the same way, assigning the value from the first parameter to the second. The purpose of this test class is to see which methods actually return the changed parameter value to the caller.

■Note The easiest way to prepare an assembly for COM interop is to set the appropriate project options within Visual Studio .NET. Please refer to recipe 6-1 (Exposing .NET Classes Using Late Binding) for instructions on how to set these options. Once this is done, a typelib will be generated when the project is built. The resulting assembly will also be registered for use by COM clients.

You can examine the typelib with a tool like `OleView.exe` (included with Visual Studio .NET). This tool allows you to extract the IDL for the typelib to see how the COM directional attributes were generated. Here is a partial listing of the IDL:

```
[
  odl,
  uuid(75C5DFB6-3E13-3E50-B30D-F5B47B3B7749),
  version(1.0),
  dual,
  oleautomation,
  custom(0F21F359-AB84-41E8-9A78-36D110E6D2F9,
  DniNetInOut.IDirectionTester)

]
interface IDirectionTester : IDispatch {
    [id(0x60020000)]
    HRESULT IntInOnly(
```

```
                [in] long paramA,
                [in] long paramB);
[id(0x60020001)]
HRESULT IntInAndOut(
                [in] long paramA,
                [in, out] long paramB);
[id(0x60020002)]
HRESULT IntByRef(
                [in] long paramA,
                [in, out] long* paramB);
[id(0x60020003)]
HRESULT IntByRefInOnly(
                [in] long paramA,
                [in] long* paramB);
[id(0x60020004)]
HRESULT IntOut(
                [in] long paramA,
                [out] long* paramB);
[id(0x60020005)]
HRESULT StringsInOnly(
                [in] BSTR paramA,
                [in] BSTR paramB);
[id(0x60020006)]
HRESULT StringsInAndOut(
                [in] BSTR paramA,
                [in, out] BSTR paramB);
[id(0x60020007)]
HRESULT StringsByRef(
                [in] BSTR paramA,
                [in, out] BSTR* paramB);
[id(0x60020008)]
HRESULT StringsByRefInOnly(
                [in] BSTR paramA,
                [in] BSTR* paramB);
[id(0x60020009)]
HRESULT StringsOut(
                [in] BSTR paramA,
                [out] BSTR* paramB);
[id(0x6002000a)]
HRESULT DateTimeInOnly(
                [in] DATE paramA,
                [in] DATE paramB);
[id(0x6002000b)]
HRESULT DateTimeInAndOut(
                [in] DATE paramA,
                [in, out] DATE paramB);
[id(0x6002000c)]
HRESULT DateTimeByRef(
```

```
                      [in] DATE paramA,
                      [in, out] DATE* paramB);
    [id(0x6002000d)]
    HRESULT DateTimeByRefInOnly(
                      [in] DATE paramA,
                      [in] DATE* paramB);
    [id(0x6002000e)]
    HRESULT DateTimeOut(
                      [in] DATE paramA,
                      [out] DATE* paramB);
};


[
  uuid(2CA6A279-5F25-39AC-A593-7A99F87D5BF4),
  version(1.0),
  custom(0F21F359-AB84-41E8-9A78-36D110E6D2F9,
  DniNetInOut.DniNetInOutObj)
]
coclass DniNetInOutObj {
    interface _Object;
    [default] interface IDirectionTester;
};
```

Finally, we can write a Visual Basic 6.0 (VB6) client that uses the class via COM:

```
Private Sub Form_Load()
    Dim comObj As _
        New DniNetInOut.DniNetInOutObj

    Dim resultLong As Long
    Dim resultString As String
    Dim resultDate As Date

    'blittable type: long
    resultLong = 0
    Call comObj.IntInOnly(123, resultLong)
    Text1.Text = Text1.Text + _
        "IntInOnly: " + CStr(resultLong) + vbCrLf

    resultLong = 0
    Call comObj.IntInAndOut(123, resultLong)
    Text1.Text = Text1.Text + _
        "IntInAndOut: " + CStr(resultLong) + vbCrLf

    resultLong = 0
    Call comObj.IntByRef(123, resultLong)
    Text1.Text = Text1.Text + _
        "IntByRef: " + CStr(resultLong) + vbCrLf
```

```
resultLong = 0
Call comObj.IntByRefInOnly(123, resultLong)
Text1.Text = Text1.Text + _
    "IntByRefInOnly: " + CStr(resultLong) + vbCrLf


resultLong = 0
Call comObj.IntOut(123, resultLong)
Text1.Text = Text1.Text + _
    "IntOut: " + CStr(resultLong) + vbCrLf


'reference type: string
resultString = "unchanged"
Call comObj.StringsInOnly("changed", resultString)
Text1.Text = Text1.Text + _
    "StringsInOnly: " + resultString + vbCrLf


resultString = "unchanged"
Call comObj.StringsInAndOut("changed", resultString)
Text1.Text = Text1.Text + _
    "StringsInAndOut: " + resultString + vbCrLf


resultString = "unchanged"
Call comObj.StringsByRef("changed", resultString)
Text1.Text = Text1.Text + _
    "StringsByRef: " + resultString + vbCrLf


resultString = "unchanged"
Call comObj.StringsByRefInOnly("changed", resultString)
Text1.Text = Text1.Text + _
    "StringsByRefInOnly: " + resultString + vbCrLf


resultString = "unchanged"
Call comObj.StringsOut("changed", resultString)
Text1.Text = Text1.Text + _
    "StringsOut: " + resultString + vbCrLf


'value type: date
resultDate = "2005/01/01"
Call comObj.DateTimeInOnly("1969/07/20", resultDate)
Text1.Text = Text1.Text + _
    "DateTimeInOnly: " + CStr(resultDate) + vbCrLf


resultDate = "2005/01/01"
Call comObj.DateTimeInAndOut("1969/07/20", resultDate)
Text1.Text = Text1.Text + _
    "DateTimeInAndOut: " + CStr(resultDate) + vbCrLf
```

```
    resultDate = "2005/01/01"
    Call comObj.DateTimeByRef("1969/07/20", resultDate)
    Text1.Text = Text1.Text + _
        "DateTimeByRef: " + CStr(resultDate) + vbCrLf

    resultDate = "2005/01/01"
    Call comObj.DateTimeByRefInOnly("1969/07/20", resultDate)
    Text1.Text = Text1.Text + _
        "DateTimeByRefInOnly: " + CStr(resultDate) + vbCrLf

    resultDate = "2005/01/01"
    Call comObj.DateTimeOut("1969/07/20", resultDate)
    Text1.Text = Text1.Text + _
        "DateTimeOut: " + CStr(resultDate) + vbCrLf


    'free the COM reference
    Set comObj = Nothing
End Sub
```

In order to reference the DniNetInOut.DniNetInOutObj object in VB6, we need to first use the Project References menu option to add a reference to our COM component. After creating an instance of the COM object, each method is called and the results are displayed in a TextBox control. When we execute this test code, we see these results displayed in the TextBox:

```
IntInOnly: 0
IntInAndOut: 0
IntByRef: 123
IntByRefInOnly: 123
IntOut: 123
StringsInOnly: unchanged
StringsInAndOut: unchanged
StringsByRef: changed
StringsByRefInOnly: unchanged
StringsOut: changed
DateTimeInOnly: 1/1/2005
DateTimeInAndOut: 1/1/2005
DateTimeByRef: 7/20/1969
DateTimeByRefInOnly: 1/1/2005
DateTimeOut: 7/20/1969
```

As expected, passing a parameter by value (e.g., the IntInOnly method) prohibited us from seeing any changes to the parameter. Likewise, adding the [In,Out] attributes to the method (e.g., IntInAndOut) didn't make any difference. We still didn't see any changes.

Passing parameters by reference (e.g., IntByRef) and passing as out-only (e.g., IntOut) allowed us to see changes to the parameter.

Adding [In] to a parameter passed by reference should have restricted the flow of data back to the caller. This worked for the String and DateTime parameters, but it didn't work for the integer. We were still able to see changes made to the integer even with the [In] attribute. The reason?

An integer is a blittable type and the others are not. For performance reasons, blittable types are pinned in memory and directly used by the called method rather than being copied. We saw this same behavior when using PInvoke to access unmanaged code. Please refer to this recipe's "Related Information" section for recipes that provide additional information about the behavior of blittable types.

A Visual Basic .NET (VB.NET) implementation of the test class and interface follows. First, here is the interface defined in VB.NET:

```
Imports System.Runtime.InteropServices

Public Interface IDirectionTester
    Sub IntInOnly(ByVal paramA As Integer, _
        ByVal paramB As Integer)
    Sub IntInAndOut(ByVal paramA As Integer, _
        <[In](), Out()> ByVal paramB As Integer)
    Sub IntByRef(ByVal paramA As Integer, _
        ByRef paramB As Integer)
    Sub IntByRefInOnly(ByVal paramA As Integer, _
        <[In]()> ByRef paramB As Integer)
    Sub StringsInOnly(ByVal paramA As String, _
        ByVal paramB As String)
    Sub StringsInAndOut(ByVal paramA As String, _
        <[In](), Out()> ByVal paramB As String)
    Sub StringsByRef(ByVal paramA As String, _
        ByRef paramB As String)
    Sub StringsByRefInOnly(ByVal paramA As String, _
        <[In]()> ByRef paramB As String)
    Sub DateTimeInOnly(ByVal paramA As DateTime, _
        ByVal paramB As DateTime)
    Sub DateTimeInAndOut(ByVal paramA As DateTime, _
        <[In](), Out()> ByVal paramB As DateTime)
    Sub DateTimeByRef(ByVal paramA As DateTime, _
        ByRef paramB As DateTime)
    Sub DateTimeByRefInOnly(ByVal paramA As DateTime, _
        <[In]()> ByRef paramB As DateTime)
End Interface
```

Notice that when we specify the In attribute in VB.NET, we must place brackets around the attribute like this:

```
<[In]()>
```

This distinguishes the In attribute from the In VB.NET keyword. Without the brackets, the code will not compile.

In this version of the interface, we have also omitted three of the methods that were in the C# version:

- IntOut

- StringsOut

- DateTimeOut

This was necessary since VB.NET doesn't support the out keyword that the C# version of these methods used.

The VB.NET class that implements this interface looks like this:

```vb
<ClassInterface(ClassInterfaceType.None)> _
Public Class DniNetInOutObj
    Implements IDirectionTester

    Public Sub DateTimeByRef(ByVal paramA As Date, _
        ByRef paramB As Date) _
        Implements IDirectionTester.DateTimeByRef
        paramB = paramA
    End Sub

    Public Sub DateTimeByRefInOnly(ByVal paramA As Date, _
        ByRef paramB As Date) _
        Implements IDirectionTester.DateTimeByRefInOnly
        paramB = paramA
    End Sub

    Public Sub DateTimeInAndOut(ByVal paramA As Date, _
        ByVal paramB As Date) _
        Implements IDirectionTester.DateTimeInAndOut
        paramB = paramA
    End Sub

    Public Sub DateTimeInOnly(ByVal paramA As Date, _
        ByVal paramB As Date) _
        Implements IDirectionTester.DateTimeInOnly
        paramB = paramA
    End Sub

    Public Sub IntByRef(ByVal paramA As Integer, _
        ByRef paramB As Integer) _
        Implements IDirectionTester.IntByRef
        paramB = paramA
    End Sub

    Public Sub IntByRefInOnly(ByVal paramA As Integer, _
        ByRef paramB As Integer) _
```

```
        Implements IDirectionTester.IntByRefInOnly
        paramB = paramA
    End Sub

    Public Sub IntInAndOut(ByVal paramA As Integer, _
        ByVal paramB As Integer) _
        Implements IDirectionTester.IntInAndOut
        paramB = paramA
    End Sub

    Public Sub IntInOnly(ByVal paramA As Integer, _
        ByVal paramB As Integer) _
        Implements IDirectionTester.IntInOnly
        paramB = paramA
    End Sub

    Public Sub StringsByRef(ByVal paramA As String, _
        ByRef paramB As String) _
        Implements IDirectionTester.StringsByRef
        paramB = paramA
    End Sub

    Public Sub StringsByRefInOnly(ByVal paramA As String, _
        ByRef paramB As String) _
        Implements IDirectionTester.StringsByRefInOnly
        paramB = paramA
    End Sub

    Public Sub StringsInAndOut(ByVal paramA As String, _
        ByVal paramB As String) _
        Implements IDirectionTester.StringsInAndOut
        paramB = paramA
    End Sub

    Public Sub StringsInOnly(ByVal paramA As String, _
        ByVal paramB As String) _
        Implements IDirectionTester.StringsInOnly
        paramB = paramA
    End Sub
End Class
```

The same VB6 client code can be used to test the VB.NET version of the class with a few modifications. We need to add a reference to the DniNetInOutVB COM object instead of DniNetInOut and change the code that creates the COM object from this:

```
Dim comObj As _
    New DniNetInOut.DniNetInOutObj
```

to this:

```
Dim comObj As _
    New DniNetInOutVB.DniNetInOutObj
```

We also need to comment out or remove the code that executes the three omitted methods. Once these changes are made, we can execute the VB.NET version of the class and observe the same results.

Related Information

See recipes 7-3 (Marshaling Arrays), 7-7 (Marshaling Classes and Structures), 2-6 (Passing Classes to Unmanaged Code), and 1-7 (Using Data Types That Improve Performance).

7-2. Marshaling Strings

Problem

How are strings marshaled between managed code and COM clients? How can you control the default marshaling?

Solution

By default, parameters of type System.String are marshaled as a COM BSTR. This makes perfect sense since the BSTR is a core type that was specifically designed for use within COM applications. The System.String and BSTR types both also use Unicode to internally represent strings. Because of this, most COM components use a BSTR for strings. Therefore, most of the time you can use the default behavior and allow your System.String parameters to be marshaled as a BSTR.

When a typelib is generated, the COM directional attributes will change depending on how the string is passed to the method. For instance, a string may be passed to a method by value like this:

```
void ReadOnlyString(string myString);
```

In this case, the string parameter will be marshaled as an [in]BSTR like this:

```
HRESULT ReadOnlyString([in] BSTR myString);
```

On the other hand, a string can be passed by reference to a method like this:

```
void RefString(ref string myString);
```

For this method, the string will be passed as an [in,out]BSTR* like this:

```
HRESULT RefString([in,out] BSTR* myString);
```

Strings returned from a method like this:

```
string ReturnAString();
```

are marshaled as an [out,retval]BSTR* like this:

```
HRESULT ReturnAString([out,retval] BSTR* pRetVal);
```

Optionally, you can modify how strings are marshaled by applying the MarshalAs attribute. This attribute can be applied to individual parameters or to the return value for a method.

For example, this method accepts a string passed as a LPWSTR (a pointer to a Unicode character array) instead of a BSTR:

```
void UseRawString([MarshalAs(UnmanagedType.LPWStr)] string myString);
```

This method returns a string as a LPWSTR:

```
[return:MarshalAs(UnmanagedType.LPWStr)]string ReturnRawString();
```

■**Caution** Be careful when using the MarshalAs attribute. It is possible to return strings in a format that is not supported by all COM clients. For example, returning a string as an LPWSTR isn't directly supported from Visual Basic 6.0 (VB6). However, it is fully supported with C++ COM clients. Make sure the client languages that you plan to use fully support the data types you have chosen. Or better yet, when in doubt, just use the default behavior and marshal your strings as a BSTR.

The System.Text.StringBuilder type is an exception to several of the established rules. First of all, it is always passed as an [in,out] parameter, regardless of whether you pass it by value or by reference. Second, it is always marshaled as an LPWSTR, not a BSTR.

In addition, the caller is always responsible for allocation of the StringBuilder internal buffer. When a COM client calls a managed method that uses a StringBuilder as a parameter, the size of the buffer is established by the caller. By initializing the unmanaged variable that is marshaled into the StringBuilder, the client code is actually setting the buffer size.

How It Works

The example code that follows demonstrates several ways to marshal strings to COM.

We start by defining the interface that we will export to COM clients in C#:

```
using System;
using System.Text;
using System.Runtime.InteropServices;

public interface IStrings
{
    string ReturnBSTR(string paramA, string paramB);

    void InOutBSTR(string paramA, string paramB,
        ref string result);

    void OutBSTR(string paramA, string paramB,
        out string result);
```

```
    void InOutBuilder(string paramA, string paramB,
        StringBuilder result);

    //VB6 doesn't support the data types that follow.
    //but we can still access these methods from unmanaged C++

    [return: MarshalAs(UnmanagedType.LPWStr)]
    string ReturnLPWSTR(string paramA, string paramB);

    [return: MarshalAs(UnmanagedType.LPStr)]
    string ReturnLPSTR(string paramA, string paramB);

    [return: MarshalAs(UnmanagedType.LPWStr)]
    string PassAndReturnLPWSTR(
        [MarshalAs(UnmanagedType.LPWStr)] string paramA,
        [MarshalAs(UnmanagedType.LPWStr)] string paramB);
}
```

This interface defines a number of methods, with each one marshaling strings in a slightly different way. The first four methods use default marshaling and are usable by all COM clients, including VB6. The final three methods use the MarshalAs attribute to alter the default marshaling. The parameter types used are not supported by VB6, but can be used from a C++ client.

The C# class that implements this interface looks like this:

```
[ClassInterface(ClassInterfaceType.None)]
public class DniNetStringsObj : IStrings
{
    public string ReturnBSTR(string paramA, string paramB)
    {
        return paramA + paramB;
    }

    public void InOutBSTR(string paramA, string paramB,
        ref string result)
    {
        result = paramA + paramB;
    }

    public void OutBSTR(string paramA, string paramB,
        out string result)
    {
        result = paramA + paramB;
    }

    public void InOutBuilder(string paramA, string paramB,
        StringBuilder result)
    {
```

```
        //since the StringBuilder is passed to us with a
        //fixed buffer size, we need to make sure we
        //have sufficient capacity to hold the new string
        int newStringSize = paramA.Length + paramB.Length;
        //this throws an exception if insufficient capacity
        result.EnsureCapacity(newStringSize);

        //first remove the current string if any
        result.Remove(0, result.Length);
        //append the new strings
        result.Append(paramA);
        result.Append(paramB);
    }

    public string ReturnLPWSTR(string paramA, string paramB)
    {
        return paramA + paramB;
    }

    public string ReturnLPSTR(string paramA, string paramB)
    {
        return paramA + paramB;
    }

    public string PassAndReturnLPWSTR(string paramA,string paramB)
    {
        return paramA + paramB;
    }
}
```

All of the methods simply concatenate the two input strings and return the result. Notice that the method accepting a StringBuilder (InOutBuilder) does have some additional code. This code is needed because of the way StringBuilder objects are marshaled. See the discussion that follows on StringBuilder for more information.

Here is a simple VB6 client that uses this managed interface and class:

```
Private Sub Form_Load()
    Dim comObj As _
        New DniNetStrings.DniNetStringsObj

    Dim resultString As String

    'returning a BSTR
    resultString = comObj.ReturnBSTR("one", "two")
    Text1.Text = Text1.Text + _
        "ReturnBSTR: " + resultString + vbCrLf
```

```
        'update an in/out BSTR
        resultString = "unchanged"
        Call comObj.InOutBSTR("one", "two", resultString)
        Text1.Text = Text1.Text + _
            "InOutBSTR: " + resultString + vbCrLf

        'receive an out BSTR
        resultString = "unchanged"
        Call comObj.OutBSTR("one", "two", resultString)
        Text1.Text = Text1.Text + _
            "OutBSTR: " + resultString + vbCrLf

        'marshaled as a StringBuilder.
        'the resultString must have an initial size that is
        'large enough to hold the new string
        resultString = "unchanged"
        Call comObj.InOutBuilder("one", "two", resultString)
        Text1.Text = Text1.Text + _
            "InOutBuilder: " + resultString + vbCrLf

        'free the COM reference
        Set comObj = Nothing
End Sub
```

After creating an instance of the COM object, it calls the first four methods and displays the results in a TextBox on the form. As noted earlier, VB6 doesn't support the data types used in the last three methods.

When this code is executed, we see these results in the Textbox:

```
ReturnBSTR: onetwo
InOutBSTR: onetwo
OutBSTR: onetwo
InOutBuilder: onetwo
```

Similar client code implemented in C++ looks like this:

```
#include "stdafx.h"
#include <conio.h>
#include <objbase.h>
#include <atlbase.h>
#import "mscorlib.tlb"
#import "DniNetStrings.tlb" no_namespace

int _tmain(int argc, _TCHAR* argv[])
{
    ::CoInitializeEx(NULL, COINIT_APARTMENTTHREADED);

    //create an instance of the .NET object via COM
    IStringsPtr comObj(__uuidof(DniNetStringsObj));
```

```
if (comObj)
{
    //return a BSTR
    _bstr_t bstrResult
        = comObj->ReturnBSTR(L"one", L"two");
    _cprintf("ReturnBSTR: %S \r\n", (wchar_t*)bstrResult);

    //return a BSTR as an in/out
    CComBSTR cBstrResult = "unchanged";
    comObj->InOutBSTR(L"one", L"two", (BSTR*)&cBstrResult);
    _cprintf("InOutBSTR: %S \r\n", (wchar_t*)bstrResult);

    //return a BSTR as an out
    cBstrResult = "unchanged";
    comObj->OutBSTR(L"one", L"two", (BSTR*)&cBstrResult);
    _cprintf("OutBSTR: %S \r\n", (wchar_t*)bstrResult);

    //return a BSTR as an in/out StringBuilder
    wchar_t* pWideBuilder = new wchar_t[10];
    wcscpy_s(pWideBuilder,10,L"unchanged");
    comObj->InOutBuilder(L"one", L"two", pWideBuilder);
    _cprintf("InOutBuilder: %S \r\n", pWideBuilder);
    delete [] pWideBuilder;

    //return the string as a LPWSTR
    wchar_t* pWideResult
        = comObj->ReturnLPWSTR(L"one", L"two");
    _cprintf("ReturnLPWSTR: %S \r\n", pWideResult);
    //free the memory that was returned
    ::CoTaskMemFree(pWideResult);

    //return the string as an ANSI string (LPSTR)
    char* pAnsiResult
        = comObj->ReturnLPSTR(L"one", L"two");
    _cprintf("ReturnLPSTR: %s \r\n", pAnsiResult);
    //free the memory that was returned
    ::CoTaskMemFree(pAnsiResult);

    //pass and return strings as a LPWSTR
    pWideResult
        = comObj->PassAndReturnLPWSTR(L"one", L"two");
    _cprintf("PassAndReturnLPWSTR: %S \r\n", pWideResult);
    //free the memory that was returned
    ::CoTaskMemFree(pWideResult);
    comObj.Release();
}
```

```
    //cleanup
    ::CoUninitialize();

    return 0;
}
```

The results from the C++ client test look like this:

```
ReturnBSTR: onetwo
InOutBSTR: onetwo
OutBSTR: onetwo
InOutBuilder: onetwo
ReturnLPWSTR: onetwo
ReturnLPSTR: onetwo
PassAndReturnLPWSTR: onetwo
```

The C++ test is able to call the final three COM methods that use character arrays instead of a BSTR. Notice that for each of these methods (ReturnLPWSTR, ReturnLPSTR, and PassAndReturnLPWSTR), we make sure that we call CoTaskMemFree to free the memory that was allocated. The call to the managed code allocated the memory for the return values, but we are responsible for freeing it. We use CoTaskMemFree for this purpose since we know that this memory was allocated by COM.

As mentioned previously, a StringBuilder is always passed as an [in,out]LPWSTR. When we think about what a StringBuilder really is, this makes sense. Under the covers it is really a raw Unicode character buffer. We use a StringBuilder when we need to do a lot of string manipulation that would be costly using normal immutable strings.

When a StringBuilder is marshaled between managed code and COM, the memory for the raw buffer is pinned and passed directly between the two environments. That is why it is always marshaled as an LPWSTR, because the underlying buffer is being exposed to COM.

When we passed System.String parameters, we didn't worry about explicit allocation of the string. When using a StringBuilder, we do need to make sure the underlying Unicode buffer is correctly allocated when the StringBuilder is created. This allocation is always done by the caller. Then when the parameter is marshaled to the called method, the size of the buffer cannot be changed. The called method must use the buffer it was given without changing the size.

To better understand this, consider a managed class that calls a COM method. The managed code may pass a StringBuilder to the COM method. In this case, the managed code is responsible for allocating the StringBuilder and setting the initial capacity of the underlying buffer.

What happens when the situation is reversed (as it is here)? If a managed class is called by a COM client, who initializes the StringBuilder? The caller still does the allocation. The caller in this case is the COM client, not the managed code. To be safe, the managed code should verify that the buffer capacity of the StringBuilder has been correctly set before using it.

This explains why we need this client code when calling the InOutBuilder method:

```
//return a BSTR as an in/out StringBuilder
wchar_t* pWideBuilder = new wchar_t[10];
wcscpy_s(pWideBuilder,10,L"unchanged");
comObj->InOutBuilder(L"one", L"two", pWideBuilder);
_cprintf("InOutBuilder: %S \r\n", pWideBuilder);
delete [] pWideBuilder;
```

The InOutBuilder method expects a StringBuilder, and we indirectly allocate the buffer for the StringBuilder here in the client code. The pWideBuilder variable that we allocate to a size of ten characters is passed directly to the StringBuilder object. Our managed code only sees a StringBuilder with a capacity set to nine characters (subtract one character for the null terminator). It doesn't know (or care) that the buffer was allocated here in unmanaged code. As shown here, when allocating memory, we remember to free it when we are done.

The following is a Visual Basic .NET (VB.NET) implementation of the DniNetStringsObj class and interface. We start by defining the interface in VB.NET this way:

```
Imports System.Runtime.InteropServices
Imports System.Text

Public Interface IStringsVB
    Function ReturnBSTR(ByVal paramA As String, _
        ByVal paramB As String) As String

    Sub InOutBSTR(ByVal paramA As String, _
        ByVal paramB As String, ByRef result As String)

    Sub InOutBuilder(ByVal paramA As String, _
        ByVal paramB As String, ByVal result As StringBuilder)

    'VB6 doesn't support the data types that follow.
    'but we can still access these methods from C++ ATL

    Function ReturnLPWSTR(ByVal paramA As String, _
        ByVal paramB As String) _
            As <MarshalAs(UnmanagedType.LPWStr)> String

    Function ReturnLPSTR(ByVal paramA As String, _
        ByVal paramB As String) _
            As <MarshalAs(UnmanagedType.LPStr)> String

    Function PassAndReturnLPWSTR( _
        <MarshalAs(UnmanagedType.LPWStr)> ByVal paramA As String, _
        <MarshalAs(UnmanagedType.LPWStr)> ByVal paramB As String) _
            As <MarshalAs(UnmanagedType.LPWStr)> String
End Interface
```

We've had to omit the OutBSTR method since VB.NET doesn't support passing a parameter with the out keyword. We've also changed the interface name from IStrings to IStringsVB to avoid confusion with the C# version.

The VB.NET implementation of the class looks like this:

```
<ClassInterface(ClassInterfaceType.None)> _
Public Class DniNetStringsObjVB
    Implements IStringsVB

    Public Function ReturnBSTR(ByVal paramA As String, _
        ByVal paramB As String) As String _
            Implements IStringsVB.ReturnBSTR
        Return paramA + paramB
    End Function

    Public Sub InOutBSTR(ByVal paramA As String, _
        ByVal paramB As String, ByRef result As String) _
            Implements IStringsVB.InOutBSTR
        result = paramA + paramB
    End Sub

    Public Sub InOutBuilder(ByVal paramA As String, _
        ByVal paramB As String, _
        ByVal result As System.Text.StringBuilder) _
            Implements IStringsVB.InOutBuilder

        'since the StringBuilder is passed to us with a
        'fixed buffer size, we need to make sure we
        'have sufficient capacity to hold the new string
        Dim newStringSize As Integer _
            = paramA.Length + paramB.Length
        'this throws an exception if insufficient capacity
        result.EnsureCapacity(newStringSize)

        'first remove the current string if any
        result.Remove(0, result.Length)
        'append the new strings
        result.Append(paramA)
        result.Append(paramB)
    End Sub

    Public Function ReturnLPWSTR(ByVal paramA As String, _
        ByVal paramB As String) As String _
            Implements IStringsVB.ReturnLPWSTR
        Return paramA + paramB
    End Function
```

```
    Public Function ReturnLPSTR(ByVal paramA As String, _
        ByVal paramB As String) As String _
            Implements IStringsVB.ReturnLPSTR
        Return paramA + paramB
    End Function

    Public Function PassAndReturnLPWSTR(ByVal paramA As String, _
        ByVal paramB As String) As String _
            Implements IStringsVB.PassAndReturnLPWSTR
        Return paramA + paramB
    End Function

End Class
```

Just like the interface, we've changed the class name from DniNetStringsObj to DniNetStringsObjVB to avoid confusion with the C# version.

To test this from C++ code, we import the typelib like this:

```
#import "DniNetStringsVB.tlb" no_namespace //VB.NET version
```

and test the class with this code:

```
//create an instance of the .NET object via COM
IStringsVBPtr comObj(__uuidof(DniNetStringsObjVB));
if (comObj)
{
    //return a BSTR
    _bstr_t bstrResult
        = comObj->ReturnBSTR(L"one", L"two");
    _cprintf("ReturnBSTR: %S \r\n", (wchar_t*)bstrResult);

    //return a BSTR as an in/out
    CComBSTR cBstrResult = "unchanged";
    comObj->InOutBSTR(L"one", L"two", (BSTR*)&cBstrResult);
    _cprintf("InOutBSTR: %S \r\n", (wchar_t*)bstrResult);

    //return a BSTR as an in/out StringBuilder
    wchar_t* pWideBuilder = new wchar_t[10];
    wcscpy_s(pWideBuilder,10,L"unchanged");
    comObj->InOutBuilder(L"one", L"two", pWideBuilder);
    _cprintf("InOutBuilder: %S \r\n", pWideBuilder);
    delete [] pWideBuilder;

    //return the string as a LPWSTR
    wchar_t* pWideResult
        = comObj->ReturnLPWSTR(L"one", L"two");
    _cprintf("ReturnLPWSTR: %S \r\n", pWideResult);
    //free the memory that was returned
    ::CoTaskMemFree(pWideResult);
```

```
//return the string as an ANSI string (LPSTR)
char* pAnsiResult
    = comObj->ReturnLPSTR(L"one", L"two");
_cprintf("ReturnLPSTR: %s \r\n", pAnsiResult);
//free the memory that was returned
::CoTaskMemFree(pAnsiResult);

//pass and return strings as a LPWSTR
pWideResult
    = comObj->PassAndReturnLPWSTR(L"one", L"two");
_cprintf("PassAndReturnLPWSTR: %S \r\n", pWideResult);
//free the memory that was returned
::CoTaskMemFree(pWideResult);

comObj.Release();
}
```

When executed, the results are the same as the C# version of the class:

```
ReturnBSTR: onetwo
InOutBSTR: onetwo
InOutBuilder: onetwo
ReturnLPWSTR: onetwo
ReturnLPSTR: onetwo
PassAndReturnLPWSTR: onetwo
```

Related Information

See recipes 7-1 (Controlling Parameter Direction) and 7-6 (Marshaling Null Variant Strings).

7-3. Marshaling Arrays

Problem

How are arrays marshaled between managed code and COM clients? What options are available to control the default marshaling?

Solution

When a managed array is exposed to COM clients, it is marshaled by default as a safe array (the SAFEARRAY structure). This COM data type is a self-describing array. Not only does it contain the array data, but also it contains the upper and lower bounds of the array, the number of dimensions, and the data type of the array elements. Because of the self-describing nature of this data type, it is perfect for marshaling arrays between managed and unmanaged code.

In most cases, you can define your managed methods to use an array in the normal way without any special work on your part. No special attributes are required. Even though the array will be exposed as a safe array when the typelib is generated, your managed code can still use it as a normal managed array. You don't need to do anything special just because the array is being used via COM.

For example, this C# method accepts an array of integers as a calling parameter:

```
void UseAnArray(ref int[] elements);
```

The same method is defined in Visual Basic .NET (VB.NET) like this:

```
Sub UseAnArray(ByRef elements() As Integer)
```

Regardless of the language used, the IDL generated for this method looks like this:

```
HRESULT UseAnArray([in, out] SAFEARRAY(long)* elements);
```

Because you are passing the array by reference (ref), the [in,out] MIDL directional attributes were added for you. Passing the array by reference like this allows the caller to see any changes made by the managed code during the call.

Languages such as Visual Basic 6.0 (VB6) and C++ have good support for safe arrays. If using C++ as a COM client, you have to write a bit of code to create and work with the safe array. In the case of VB6, safe arrays are the native type of array for the language. Therefore, VB6 hides almost all of the grunt work needed to work with safe arrays. This makes VB6 a much easier language to use if you often use arrays.

But VB6 also has one big problem when it comes to safe arrays: it only allows you to pass safe arrays by reference instead of by value. Since passing an array by reference allows the called method to make changes to the elements in the array, this may not always be desirable. C++ does not have this limitation and allows you to pass a safe array either by value or by reference.

Even when an array is passed by reference, you can restrict the flow of data back to the caller by adding the [In] attribute to the parameter. For example, we can revise the definition of the UseAnArray method like this in C#:

```
void UseAnArray([In] ref int[] elements);
```

and like this in VB.NET:

```
Sub UseAnArray(<[In]()> ByRef elements() As Integer)
```

The revised IDL for this method looks like this:

```
HRESULT UseAnArray([in] SAFEARRAY(long)* elements);
```

The array is still passed by reference from the caller, but the absence of the [out] attribute prevents changes from being marshaled back to the client code.

If you do want to pass an array by value, you can declare the managed method like this in C#, without the ref keyword:

```
void UseAnArrayByValue(int[] elements);
```

and using ByVal instead of ByRef in VB.NET:

```
Sub UseAnArrayByValue(ByVal elements() As Integer)
```

This produces a method defined like this in the typelib:

```
HRESULT UseAnArrayByValue([in] SAFEARRAY(long) elements);
```

■**Caution** If you declare a method that expects an array to be passed by value, you will not be able to call that method from a VB6 COM client.

By default, any changes made to this by-value array will not be seen by the caller. You can modify this behavior by adding the [In,Out] attributes to the method definition. The revised method looks like this in C#:

```
void UseAnArrayByValue([In,Out] int[] elements);
```

and like this in VB.NET:

```
Sub UseAnArrayByValue(<[In](), Out()> ByVal elements() As Integer)
```

This produces a method defined like this in the typelib:

```
HRESULT UseAnArrayByValue([in,out] SAFEARRAY(long) elements);
```

Now any changes made to the array by the called method will be marshaled back to the caller, even though it was passed by value.

In addition to passing an array as a parameter, you can return it as the result of a method. Here is the C# definition of a method that returns an integer array:

```
int[] ReturnAnArray();
```

and the same method defined in VB.NET:

```
Function ReturnAnArray() As Integer()
```

The generated typelib contains this definition of the method:

```
HRESULT ReturnAnArray([out, retval] SAFEARRAY(long)* pRetVal);
```

How It Works

The example code that follows demonstrates some of the ways we can work with arrays.

We start by defining a managed interface in C#:

```
using System;
using System.Runtime.InteropServices;

public interface IArrays
{
    int[] ReturnIntArray();
    int SumIntArray(ref int[] elements);
    int UpdateIntArray(ref int[] elements);
    int UpdateIntArrayInOnly([In]ref int[] elements);
    int SumStringArray(ref string[] elements);
    int UpdateStringArray(ref string[] elements);
    int UpdateStringArrayInOnly([In]ref string[] elements);
```

```
    //the following methods pass an array by value
    //instead of by reference. Passing arrays by value
    //is not supported by VB6. However, these methods
    //can be used by other languages such as C++.
    int UpdateIntArrayByValue(int[] elements);
    int UpdateIntArrayByValueInOut([In, Out]int[] elements);
    int SumStringArrayByValue(string[] elements);
}
```

As indicated by the code comments, the last three methods are not supported by VB6. They all pass an array by value, and VB6 doesn't provide support for that. Those methods will be called from C++ test code only.

The C# class that follows implements this interface:

```
[ClassInterface(ClassInterfaceType.None)]
public class DniNetArraysObj : IArrays
{
    public int[] ReturnIntArray()
    {
        int[] result = new int[5];
        result[0] = 0;
        result[1] = 1;
        result[2] = 22;
        result[3] = 333;
        result[4] = 4444;
        return result;
    }

    public int SumIntArray(ref int[] elements)
    {
        int result = 0;
        foreach(int element in elements)
        {
            result += element;
        }
        return result;
    }

    public int UpdateIntArray(ref int[] elements)
    {
        int result = 0;
        for (int i = 0; i < elements.Length; i++)
        {
            //update each element by adding 1000
            elements[i] = elements[i] + 1000;
            result += elements[i];
        }
        return result;
    }
```

```
        public int UpdateIntArrayInOnly(ref int[] elements)
        {
            return UpdateIntArray(ref elements);
        }

        public int UpdateIntArrayByValue(int[] elements)
        {
            return UpdateIntArray(ref elements);
        }

        public int UpdateIntArrayByValueInOut(int[] elements)
        {
            return UpdateIntArray(ref elements);
        }

        public int SumStringArray(ref string[] elements)
        {
            int result = 0;
            foreach(string element in elements)
            {
                result += element.Length;
            }
            return result;
        }

        public int UpdateStringArray(ref string[] elements)
        {
            int result = 0;
            for (int i = 0; i < elements.Length; i++)
            {
                //append a literal to each string element
                elements[i] += "extra";
                result += elements[i].Length;
            }
            return result;
        }

        public int UpdateStringArrayInOnly(ref string[] elements)
        {
            return UpdateStringArray(ref elements);
        }

        public int SumStringArrayByValue(string[] elements)
        {
            int result = 0;
            foreach (string element in elements)
            {
```

```
                result += element.Length;
            }
        return result;
        }
    }
}
```

Before we look at any client code, let's quickly review the test methods. This will set the stage for the results that we should see.

- ReturnIntArray: This creates and populates an integer array and returns it to the caller. The caller should be able to see all of the elements in the array.

- SumIntArray: This method is passed an integer array by reference and it returns a sum of all elements in the array.

- UpdateIntArray: This method updates an integer array that is passed by reference. It adds 1,000 to each integer in the array to demonstrate an update. It also returns the sum of the updated values. The caller should see that each element has been changed.

- UpdateIntArrayInOnly: This is the same as UpdateIntArray, except we add the [In] attribute to restrict visibility to any changes made to the array. The caller should not see any changes made by the called method to the array. However, the sum of the updated values is still returned from the method.

- SumStringArray: This method is passed a string array by reference. It returns a total of all string lengths in the array.

- UpdateStringArray: This method updates a string array that is passed to it by reference. It updates each string by appending the literal "extra". The caller should see the changed strings in the array.

- UpdateStringArrayInOnly: This is just like UpdateStringArray, but the caller should not see any changes due to the [In] attribute.

- UpdateIntArrayByValue: This is the first of three methods that pass an array by value instead of by reference. The managed code attempts to add 1,000 to each integer element. However, the caller should not see any changes made to the array. This is the expected behavior for an array passed by value that marshals the data as input only.

- UpdateIntArrayByValueInOut: This method is just like UpdateIntArrayByValue, but it includes the [In,Out] attributes. This allows the caller to see the updates made to the array, even though it is passed by value.

- SumStringArrayByValue: This method demonstrates passing an array of strings by value. It returns the total length of all strings in the array.

Our first COM client is VB6. The COM method calls have been highlighted to make it easier to spot each test:

```
Private Sub Form_Load()
    Dim comObj As _
        New DniNetArrays.DniNetArraysObj
```

```
Dim arrayObj As Variant
'return an integer array
arrayObj = comObj.ReturnIntArray
Text1.Text = Text1.Text + _
    "ReturnIntArray results: " + vbCrLf
DisplayArray (arrayObj)

'pass an integer array
Dim longArray(4) As Long
longArray(0) = 0
longArray(1) = 1
longArray(2) = 2
longArray(3) = 3
longArray(4) = 4
Dim result As Integer
result = comObj.SumIntArray(longArray)
Text1.Text = Text1.Text + _
    "SumIntArray results: " + CStr(result) + vbCrLf

'attempts an update to integer array
result = comObj.UpdateIntArrayInOnly(longArray)
Text1.Text = Text1.Text + _
    "UpdateIntArrayInOnly results: " _
    + CStr(result) + vbCrLf
DisplayArray (longArray)

'update an integer array
result = comObj.UpdateIntArray(longArray)
Text1.Text = Text1.Text + _
    "UpdateIntArray results: " _
    + CStr(result) + vbCrLf
DisplayArray (longArray)

'pass a string array
Dim stringArray(2) As String
stringArray(0) = "one"
stringArray(1) = "two"
stringArray(2) = "three"
result = comObj.SumStringArray(stringArray)
Text1.Text = Text1.Text + _
    "SumStringArray results: " + CStr(result) + vbCrLf

'attempt to update a string array. Even though
'we are passing the array byref, we shouldn't see
'any changes since the method has the [In] attribute
result = comObj.UpdateStringArrayInOnly(stringArray)
Text1.Text = Text1.Text + _
```

```
            "UpdateStringArrayInOnly results: " _
            + CStr(result) + vbCrLf
    DisplayArray (stringArray)


    'update a string array
    result = comObj.UpdateStringArray(stringArray)
    Text1.Text = Text1.Text + _
        "UpdateStringArray results: " + CStr(result) + vbCrLf
    DisplayArray (stringArray)


    'free the COM reference
    Set comObj = Nothing
End Sub

Private Sub DisplayArray(arrayObj As Variant)
    Dim i As Integer
    For i = LBound(arrayObj) To UBound(arrayObj)
        Text1.Text = Text1.Text + _
            "Array Element: " + CStr(arrayObj(i)) + vbCrLf
    Next i
End Sub
```

■Caution VB6 is capable of optionally specifying the lower bounds for an array. This means that instead of always using a zero-based array, it is possible to start an array at a different lower bounds number. However, .NET doesn't support nonzero-based arrays. If you want to pass an array from a VB6 client to .NET code (via COM), the array must be zero-based.

Here are the complete results from this test:

```
ReturnIntArray results:
Array Element: 0
Array Element: 1
Array Element: 22
Array Element: 333
Array Element: 4444
SumIntArray results: 10
UpdateIntArrayInOnly results: 5010
Array Element: 0
Array Element: 1
Array Element: 2
Array Element: 3
Array Element: 4
UpdateIntArray results: 5010
Array Element: 1000
```

```
Array Element: 1001
Array Element: 1002
Array Element: 1003
Array Element: 1004
SumStringArray results: 11
UpdateStringArrayInOnly results: 26
Array Element: one
Array Element: two
Array Element: three
UpdateStringArray results: 26
Array Element: oneextra
Array Element: twoextra
Array Element: threeextra
```

The most interesting results are from the UpdateIntArrayInOnly and UpdateStringArrayInOnly methods (highlighted in the preceding results). Even though the arrays are passed by reference, the calling code doesn't see changes to the elements. This is due to the inclusion of the [In] attribute in managed code. The update methods that omit this attribute work as expected and the caller can see the changed array.

Next up we have C++ code to test the remaining methods that pass arrays by value. Once again, the COM method calls have been highlighted:

```
#include "stdafx.h"
#include <conio.h>
#include <objbase.h>
#include <atlbase.h>
#import "mscorlib.tlb"
#import "DniNetArrays.tlb" no_namespace

int _tmain(int argc, _TCHAR* argv[])
{
    ::CoInitializeEx(NULL, COINIT_APARTMENTTHREADED);

    //create an instance of the .NET object via COM
    IArraysPtr comObj(__uuidof(DniNetArraysObj));
    if (comObj)
    {
        UseStringArray(comObj);
        UseIntArray(comObj);
        comObj.Release();
    }

    //cleanup
    ::CoUninitialize();

    return 0;
}
```

```
void UseStringArray(IArraysPtr comObj)
{
    //create a safearray
    SAFEARRAY* pSafeArray;
    SAFEARRAYBOUND saBound[1];
    saBound[0].lLbound = 0;
    saBound[0].cElements = 3;
    pSafeArray = SafeArrayCreate(VT_BSTR, 1, saBound);

    //populate the elements in the array
    BSTR *pBSTR;
    SafeArrayAccessData(pSafeArray, (void HUGEP**)&pBSTR);
    pBSTR[0] = CComBSTR(L"one").Detach();
    pBSTR[1] = CComBSTR(L"two").Detach();
    pBSTR[2] = CComBSTR(L"three").Detach();
    SafeArrayUnaccessData(pSafeArray);

    //attempt to update the string array. We should not
    //see changes made to the array since the COM method
    //is marked with the [In] attribute
    int result = comObj->UpdateStringArrayInOnly(&pSafeArray);
    _cprintf("UpdateStringArrayInOnly: %i \r\n", result);
    DisplayStringArray(pSafeArray);

    //this should update the string array successfully
    result = comObj->UpdateStringArray(&pSafeArray);
    _cprintf("UpdateStringArray: %i \r\n", result);
    DisplayStringArray(pSafeArray);

    //pass the safearray by value instead of by reference
    result = comObj->SumStringArrayByValue(pSafeArray);
    _cprintf("SumStringArrayByValue: %i \r\n", result);

    //clean up the safe array
    SafeArrayDestroy(pSafeArray);
}

void DisplayStringArray(SAFEARRAY* pSafeArray)
{
    BSTR *pBSTR;
    SafeArrayAccessData(pSafeArray, (void **)&pBSTR);
    for(int i = 0; i < 3; i++)
    {
        _cprintf("BSTR element: %S \r\n", pBSTR[i]);
    }
    SafeArrayUnaccessData(pSafeArray);
}
```

```
void UseIntArray(IArraysPtr comObj)
{
    //create a safearray
    SAFEARRAY* pSafeArray;
    SAFEARRAYBOUND saBound[1];
    saBound[0].lLbound = 0;
    saBound[0].cElements = 3;
    pSafeArray = SafeArrayCreate(VT_I4, 1, saBound);

    //populate the elements in the array
    int *pInt;
    SafeArrayAccessData(pSafeArray, (void HUGEP**)&pInt);
    pInt[0] = 111;
    pInt[1] = 222;
    pInt[2] = 333;
    SafeArrayUnaccessData(pSafeArray);

    //attempt to update the integer array. We should not
    //see changes made to the array since the COM method
    //is marked with the [In] attribute
    int result = comObj->UpdateIntArrayInOnly(&pSafeArray);
    _cprintf("UpdateIntArrayInOnly: %i \r\n", result);
    DisplayIntArray(pSafeArray);

    //this should successfully update the array
    result = comObj->UpdateIntArray(&pSafeArray);
    _cprintf("UpdateIntArray: %i \r\n", result);
    DisplayIntArray(pSafeArray);

    //attempt to update the integer array passed by value.
    result = comObj->UpdateIntArrayByValue(pSafeArray);
    _cprintf("UpdateIntArrayByValue: %i \r\n", result);
    DisplayIntArray(pSafeArray);

    //attempt to update the integer array passed by value
    //but this time the method has the [In,Out] attributes added.
    result = comObj->UpdateIntArrayByValueInOut(pSafeArray);
    _cprintf("UpdateIntArrayByValueInOut: %i \r\n", result);
    DisplayIntArray(pSafeArray);

    //clean up the safe array
    SafeArrayDestroy(pSafeArray);
}

void DisplayIntArray(SAFEARRAY* pSafeArray)
{
    int* pInt;
```

```
    SafeArrayAccessData(pSafeArray, (void **)&pInt);
    for(int i = 0; i < 3; i++)
    {
        _cprintf("Int element: %i \r\n", pInt[i]);
    }
    SafeArrayUnaccessData(pSafeArray);
}
```

■**Note** In order for this example code to compile, you also need to declare the functions in the stdafx.h header like this:

```
void DisplayStringArray(SAFEARRAY* pSafeArray);
void DisplayIntArray(SAFEARRAY* pSafeArray);
void UseStringArray(IArraysPtr comObj);
void UseIntArray(IArraysPtr comObj);
```

If you don't do this, make sure the functions are defined prior to their use by other functions.

When this code is executed, we see these results:

```
UpdateStringArrayInOnly: 26
BSTR element: one
BSTR element: two
BSTR element: three
UpdateStringArray: 26
BSTR element: oneextra
BSTR element: twoextra
BSTR element: threeextra
SumStringArrayByValue: 26
UpdateIntArrayInOnly: 3666
Int element: 111
Int element: 222
Int element: 333
UpdateIntArray: 3666
Int element: 1111
Int element: 1222
Int element: 1333
UpdateIntArrayByValue: 6666
Int element: 1111
Int element: 1222
Int element: 1333
UpdateIntArrayByValueInOut: 6666
Int element: 2111
Int element: 2222
Int element: 2333
```

The last two methods (`UpdateIntArrayByValue` and `UpdateIntArrayByValueInOut`) illustrate what happens when we try to update an array passed by value. `UpdateIntArrayByValue` uses the default marshaling that does not permit the caller to see any changes to the array. `UpdateIntArrayByValueInOut` adds the `[In,Out]` attributes that enable the calling code to see the updates to the array.

Related Information

See recipe 7-1 (Controlling Parameter Direction).

7-4. Marshaling Variants

Problem

.NET doesn't provide native support for the COM Variant data type. Is it possible to pass a Variant as a parameter when calling managed code? How is a Variant marshaled between COM and managed code?

Solution

Parameters of type `System.Object` are exposed to COM clients as Variants. This makes sense since a `System.Object` can represent any .NET data type, just as a Variant does for COM. The generated typelib will use a `VARIANT` for any `System.Object` parameters or return values.

For example, this C# method uses and returns a `System.Object`:

```
Object MyObjectMethod(Object param);
```

Here is the same method defined in Visual Basic .NET (VB.NET):

```
Function MyObjectMethod(ByVal param As Object) As Object
```

Regardless of the language, when exported to a typelib for use by COM, the method is defined like this:

```
HRESULT MyObjectMethod(
    [in] VARIANT param, [out, retval] VARIANT* pRetVal);
```

Variants include a Variant Type (VT_*) that identifies the underlying data type. The interop marshaler automatically sets the Variant Type for you based on the actual data type that is used.

For example, a managed method may return a `System.Object` as the result value. This means the method can potentially return any data type. When the result value is marshaled back to the COM client code, the actual data type is used to set the Variant Type. If the method returns a `System.Int32`, then the Variant Type is set to VT_I4 (32-bit signed integer). If the method returns a `System.String`, the Variant Type is set to VT_BSTR. And so on.

When data flows in the other direction, the marshaler has to pass data of the correct type as the `System.Object` parameter. If the COM client passes a Variant with a Variant Type of VT_DATE, then the managed code will see a `System.DateTime` value passed as the `System.Object` parameter. If a VT_BSTR is passed, then a `System.String` is provided by the marshaler.

This marshaling behavior is automatic and in most cases produces exactly the results that you want.

Note Please refer to Chapter 5 for more information on marshaling Variants between COM and managed code. While Chapter 5 covers use of COM components from managed code, much of the material is also applicable when you are exposing managed code to COM clients. In particular, refer to recipe 5-5 (Marshaling COM Variants), which has a table that lists the default marshaling between managed and Variant types.

How It Works

This C# code illustrates the marshaling that takes place when passing Variants to managed methods. We start by implementing an interface and managed class:

```csharp
using System;
using System.Runtime.InteropServices;

namespace DniNetVariants
{
    public interface IVariants
    {
        string UseVariant(Object inParam, ref Object outParam);
    }

    [ClassInterface(ClassInterfaceType.None)]
    public class DniNetVariantsObj : IVariants
    {
        public string UseVariant(object inParam,
            ref object outParam)
        {
            //copy the input param to the output
            outParam = inParam;

            //return the type description
            return inParam.GetType().Name;
        }
    }
}
```

Here is the same class and interface implemented in VB.NET:

```vbnet
Imports System.Runtime.InteropServices

Public Interface IVariants
    Function UseVariant(ByVal inParam As Object, _
        ByRef outParam As Object) As String
End Interface

<ClassInterface(ClassInterfaceType.None)> _
Public Class DniNetVariantsObj
    Implements IVariants
```

```
     Public Function UseVariant(ByVal inParam As Object, _
         ByRef outParam As Object) As String _
             Implements IVariants.UseVariant
         'copy the input param to the output
         outParam = inParam

         'return the type description
         Return inParam.GetType().Name
     End Function
End Class
```

We define a single method named UseVariant. This method accepts two parameters of type System.Object and returns a System.String. Looking at the implementation of this method, we see that the first parameter is simply copied to the second. The descriptive managed type name of the first parameter is the return value. This allows us to see the data type that was passed as a Variant parameter as well as how the same data is marshaled back to the COM client.

We can now write a simple Visual Basic 6.0 (VB6) client to test this code. This code uses the C# version of the class, but it could be changed to use the VB.NET version by referencing that COM component.

```
Private comObj As _
        New DniNetVariants.DniNetVariantsObj

Private Sub Form_Load()

    Call CallUseVariant("a string", "string")
    Call CallUseVariant(123, "short")
    Call CallUseVariant(CLng(123), "long")
    Call CallUseVariant(123.45, "double")
    Call CallUseVariant(CSng(123.45), "single")
    Call CallUseVariant(CDec(123.45), "decimal")
    Call CallUseVariant(True, "boolean")
    Call CallUseVariant(CByte(11), "byte")
    Call CallUseVariant(CDate("1969-07-20"), "date")

    Dim stringArray(5) As String
    Call CallUseVariant(stringArray, "string array")

    Dim intArray(5) As Integer
    Call CallUseVariant(intArray, "integer array")

    Dim dateArray(5) As Date
    Call CallUseVariant(dateArray, "date array")

    'free the COM reference
    Set comObj = Nothing
End Sub
```

```
Private Sub CallUseVariant(testValue As Variant, _
        testDesc As String)
    Dim outParam As Variant
    Dim desc As String
    'call the managed method via COM
    desc = comObj.UseVariant(testValue, outParam)
    Text1.Text = Text1.Text + _
        "Test: " + testDesc + _
        ", Managed Type: " + desc + _
        ", Var Type: " + TypeName(outParam) _
        + vbCrLf
End Sub
```

The code repeatedly calls the UseVariant method of our managed object. Each call passes a different data type as a Variant. After each call, we display the managed type name that was returned and the type name of the Variant that was returned as the second parameter.

When we execute this test, we see these results displayed in the TextBox:

```
Test: string, Managed Type: String, Var Type: String
Test: short, Managed Type: Int16, Var Type: Integer
Test: long, Managed Type: Int32, Var Type: Long
Test: double, Managed Type: Double, Var Type: Double
Test: single, Managed Type: Single, Var Type: Single
Test: decimal, Managed Type: Decimal, Var Type: Decimal
Test: boolean, Managed Type: Boolean, Var Type: Boolean
Test: byte, Managed Type: Byte, Var Type: Byte
Test: date, Managed Type: DateTime, Var Type: Date
Test: string array, Managed Type: String[], Var Type: String()
Test: integer array, Managed Type: Int16[], Var Type: Integer()
Test: date array, Managed Type: DateTime[], Var Type: Date()
```

All of the tests return the expected results. For instance, when a string is passed as a Variant, the managed code receives a System.String. When this value is passed back to the client code, it receives a Variant with a type of VT_BSTR (string).

Notice that we are also able to pass different types of arrays as a Variant. For instance, we pass an array of Date that is received by managed code as an array of DateTime. When the same data is returned, the client receives a Variant containing an array of Date.

Note One Variant Type that is missing from this test is Currency. This COM type requires special handling. Please refer to recipe 7-5 (Marshaling Currency) for more information on marshaling currency data types.

Related Information

See recipes 5-5 (Marshaling COM Variants) and 7-5 (Marshaling Currency).

7-5. Marshaling Currency

Problem

COM supports both a CURRENCY and a DECIMAL data type. However, .NET supports only a System. Decimal to represent both types. How is COM CURRENCY data marshaled to and from managed code?

Solution

The default behavior is to marshal CURRENCY as a System.Decimal. The System.Decimal type has more than enough precision to handle any CURRENCY value. When a CURRENCY value is passed to managed code, it can work with the data as a System.Decimal without a problem.

When a System.Decimal is marshaled back to a COM client, it uses the DECIMAL COM type. This maintains the precision of the System.Decimal. However, in some cases, you may want to return the data as CURRENCY instead of DECIMAL. Perhaps you have other COM methods that use CURRENCY instead of DECIMAL.

To accomplish this, you can add the MarshalAs attribute to the managed method signature. For example, this method uses the default marshaling and returns the System.Decimal as DECIMAL:

```
Decimal GetDecimal();
```

If you add the MarshalAs attribute, you can return the result as CURRENCY instead:

```
[return: MarshalAs(UnmanagedType.Currency)]
Decimal GetDecimal();
```

The generated typelib contains this definition for the method:

```
HRESULT GetDecimal([out, retval] CURRENCY* pRetVal);
```

The UnmanagedType.Currency value can be used only on a System.Decimal parameter or return value.

What about Variant data? Is it possible to pass back a System.Decimal as a VARIANT with a type of VT_CY (currency)? Yes, you can use the CurrencyWrapper class to do this. This is a one-way class that is needed only when returning currency values to COM clients. This is a special class that tells the marshaler to convert the value to a VT_CY type VARIANT. If you didn't use this wrapper, the marshaler would return the value as a VT_DECIMAL type VARIANT.

You use the CurrencyWrapper by wrapping a System.Decimal in it before returning the value to the client, for example:

```
Object myVarObject = new CurrencyWrapper(myDecimal);
```

If myVarObject is passed back as a return value or parameter to a COM client, it will now be marshaled as a type VT_CY VARIANT.

How It Works

To demonstrate the handling of currency, we can implement an interface and test class in C# like this:

```
using System;
using System.Runtime.InteropServices;

namespace DniNetCurrency
{
    public interface ICurrency
    {
        string UseNativeVariant(
            Object inParam, ref Object outParam);

        string UseVariantCurrency(
            Object inParam, ref Object outParam);

        string UseDecimalCurrency(
            [MarshalAs(UnmanagedType.Currency)]
            Decimal inParam,
            [MarshalAs(UnmanagedType.Currency)]
            ref Decimal outParam);
    }

    [ClassInterface(ClassInterfaceType.None)]
    public class DniNetCurrencyObj : ICurrency
    {
        public string UseNativeVariant(
            Object inParam, ref Object outParam)
        {
            outParam = inParam;
            return inParam.GetType().Name;
        }

        public string UseVariantCurrency(
            Object inParam, ref Object outParam)
        {
            outParam = new CurrencyWrapper(inParam);
            return inParam.GetType().Name;
        }

        public string UseDecimalCurrency(
            Decimal inParam, ref Decimal outParam)
        {
            outParam = inParam;
            return inParam.GetType().Name;
        }
    }
}
```

We can implement the same class and interface in Visual Basic .NET (VB.NET) like this:

```vb
Imports System.Runtime.InteropServices

Public Interface ICurrency
    Function UseNativeVariant(ByVal inParam As Object, _
        ByRef outParam As Object) As String
    Function UseVariantCurrency(ByVal inParam As Object, _
        ByRef outParam As Object) As String
    Function UseDecimalCurrency( _
        <MarshalAs(UnmanagedType.Currency)> _
        ByVal inParam As Decimal, _
        <MarshalAs(UnmanagedType.Currency)> _
        ByRef outParam As Decimal) As String
End Interface

<ClassInterface(ClassInterfaceType.None)> _
Public Class DniNetCurrencyObj
    Implements ICurrency

    Public Function UseNativeVariant(ByVal inParam As Object, _
        ByRef outParam As Object) As String _
            Implements ICurrency.UseNativeVariant
        outParam = inParam
        Return inParam.GetType().Name
    End Function

    Public Function UseVariantCurrency(ByVal inParam As Object, _
        ByRef outParam As Object) As String _
            Implements ICurrency.UseVariantCurrency
        outParam = New CurrencyWrapper(inParam)
        Return inParam.GetType().Name
    End Function

    Public Function UseDecimalCurrency(ByVal inParam As Decimal, _
        ByRef outParam As Decimal) As String _
            Implements ICurrency.UseDecimalCurrency
        outParam = inParam
        Return inParam.GetType().Name
    End Function

End Class
```

We expose the ICurrency interface to COM clients. It defines three methods:

- UseNativeVariant: This method is used to pass a Variant containing a VT_CY (currency) to managed code. This will demonstrate the default marshaling.

- UseVariantCurrency: This method demonstrates the use of a CurrencyWrapper to return a VARIANT with a type of VT_CY instead of VT_DECIMAL.

- UseDecimalCurrency: This method uses the MarshalAs attribute to alter the default marshaling of a System.Decimal.

The Visual Basic 6.0 (VB6) code to test these methods looks like this:

```
Private comObj As _
        New DniNetCurrency.DniNetCurrencyObj

Private Sub Form_Load()

    Call CallUseVariant(CCur(123.45), "variant")
    Call CallUseVariantCurrency(CCur(123.45), "currency wrapper")
    Call CallUseDecimalCurrency(CCur(123.45), "decimal currency")

    'free the COM reference
    Set comObj = Nothing
End Sub

Private Sub CallUseVariant(testValue As Variant, _
        testDesc As String)
    Dim outParam As Variant
    Dim desc As String
    'call the managed method via com
    desc = comObj.UseNativeVariant(testValue, outParam)
    Text1.Text = Text1.Text + _
        "Test: " + testDesc + _
        ", Managed Type: " + desc + _
        ", Var Type: " + TypeName(outParam) _
        + vbCrLf
End Sub

Private Sub CallUseVariantCurrency(testValue As Variant, _
        testDesc As String)
    Dim outParam As Variant
    Dim desc As String
    'call the managed method that uses a CurrencyWrapper
    desc = comObj.UseVariantCurrency(testValue, outParam)
    Text1.Text = Text1.Text + _
        "Test: " + testDesc + _
        ", Managed Type: " + desc + _
        ", Var Type: " + TypeName(outParam) _
        + vbCrLf
End Sub
```

```
Private Sub CallUseDecimalCurrency(testValue As Variant, _
        testDesc As String)
    Dim outParam As Currency
    Dim desc As String
    'call the managed method that uses the decimal type
    'instead of a variant for currency
    desc = comObj.UseDecimalCurrency(testValue, outParam)
    Text1.Text = Text1.Text + _
        "Test: " + testDesc + _
        ", Managed Type: " + desc + _
        ", Var Type: " + TypeName(outParam) _
        + vbCrLf
End Sub
```

This code uses the C# version of the test class, but you can change it to use the VB.NET version instead. To do this, simply reference the VB.NET COM component instead of the C# version in the VB6 project. Then change the line that creates the COM object from this:

```
Private comObj As _
    New DniNetCurrency.DniNetCurrencyObj
```

to this:

```
Private comObj As _
    New DniNetCurrencyVB.DniNetCurrencyObj
```

When we execute this code, we see these results in the TextBox on the form:

```
Test: variant, Managed Type: Decimal, Var Type: Decimal
Test: currency wrapper, Managed Type: Decimal, Var Type: Currency
Test: decimal currency, Managed Type: Decimal, Var Type: Currency
```

When the UseNativeVariant method was called, the default marshaling turned the currency value into a System.Decimal. The Variant that was returned was of the type VT_DECIMAL.

The method that used the CurrencyWrapper (UseVariantCurrency) correctly returned a Variant with a type of VT_CURRENCY.

And the final method that passed Decimal parameters instead of Variants (UseDecimalCurrency) was also able to return a Currency data type.

Related Information

See recipe 7-4 (Marshaling Variants).

7-6. Marshaling Null Variant Strings

Problem

You have a managed method that returns a string as a Variant. What happens if the managed code returns a null instead of a string? What type of Variant will you receive? Will it still be a BSTR?

Solution

If a managed method returns a System.String, the result will be marshaled as a BSTR. If the result of the method is null, it is still marshaled as a BSTR. It will be a BSTR with a zero-length string, but it will be a BSTR.

If the method returns a System.Object instead, the rules are slightly different. The System. Object is returned to the COM client as a Variant. When a valid System.String object is returned, the Variant will be of type VT_BSTR and will contain the BSTR.

However, when a null is returned, it is marshaled as a Variant of type VT_EMPTY, not a VT_BSTR. This works, but isn't the most elegant solution. If there is any chance that a null may be returned, the client code will need to always check the Variant Type to determine if a real BSTR has been returned.

Fortunately, you can fix this situation in managed code using the BStrWrapper class. This class is designed to assist with marshaling of System.String objects to COM clients. When a BStrWrapper is returned instead of a System.String, it is always marshaled as a BSTR, even if its original value is null.

To use the wrapper, you pass the System.String value into the constructor. The BStrWrapper is then returned instead of the original System.String.

Note If you know you are returning a string, the best way to do so is to actually return a System.String. Doing so eliminates the need for the BStrWrapper class since the System.String is marshaled as a BSTR even for null values. The BStrWrapper is needed only if you want to marshal the string as a Variant by returning a System.Object.

How It Works

To demonstrate this solution, the C# code that follows defines several test methods:

```
using System;
using System.Runtime.InteropServices;

namespace DniNetBstrWrapper
{
    public interface IStringHelper
    {
        Object GetString();
        Object GetNullString();
```

```csharp
        Object GetNullStringWithWrapper();
        Object GetStringWithWrapper();
    }


    [ClassInterface(ClassInterfaceType.None)]
    public class DniNetBstrWrapperObj : IStringHelper
    {
        public object GetString()
        {
            return "MyString";
        }

        public object GetNullString()
        {
            return null;
        }

        public object GetNullStringWithWrapper()
        {
            return new BStrWrapper(null);
        }

        public object GetStringWithWrapper()
        {
            return new BStrWrapper("MyString");
        }
    }
}
```

All of the methods return a System.Object. The first two methods (GetString and GetNullString) return a valid string and a null without any wrapper. The last two methods (GetNullStringWithWrapper and GetStringWithWrapper) wrap the string or null in a BStrWrapper.

We can execute this code with the following Visual Basic 6.0 (VB6) client code:

```vb
Private Sub Form_Load()

    Dim comObj As _
        New DniNetBstrWrapper.DniNetBstrWrapperObj

    Dim result As Variant

    result = comObj.GetString()
    Text1.Text = Text1.Text + _
        " GetString Type Returned: " + TypeName(result) _
        + " ,Value: " + result + _
        vbCrLf
```

```
    result = comObj.GetNullString()
    Text1.Text = Text1.Text + _
        " GetNullString Type Returned: " + TypeName(result) _
        + " ,Value: " + result + _
        vbCrLf

    result = comObj.GetNullStringWithWrapper()
    Text1.Text = Text1.Text + _
        " GetNullStringWithWrapper Type Returned: " _
        + TypeName(result) _
        + " ,Value: " + result + _
        vbCrLf

    result = comObj.GetStringWithWrapper()
    Text1.Text = Text1.Text + _
        " GetStringWithWrapper Type Returned: " _
        + TypeName(result) _
        + " ,Value: " + result + _
        vbCrLf

    'free the COM reference
    Set comObj = Nothing
End Sub
```

After creating an instance of the COM object, each of the test methods is executed and the results are displayed. When we run this code, we see these results in the TextBox on the form:

```
GetString Type Returned: String ,Value: MyString
GetNullString Type Returned: Empty ,Value:
GetNullStringWithWrapper Type Returned: String ,Value:
GetStringWithWrapper Type Returned: String ,Value: MyString
```

The GetString method returns a valid string and we receive a Variant of type VT_BSTR. However, notice the results from the GetNullString method that returns a null instead of a string. The Variant we receive is of type VT_EMPTY instead of VT_BSTR.

When we execute the methods using the BStrWrapper (GetNullStringWithWrapper and GetStringWithWrapper), we always receive a Variant of type VT_BSTR. This occurs even when a null value is returned.

Using the BStrWrapper in this case simplifies the client code. We eliminate the need for the client code to always check the Variant Type before using the variable.

Related Information

See recipes 7-2 (Marshaling Strings) and 7-4 (Marshaling Variants).

7-7. Marshaling Classes and Structures

Problem

You need to pass a managed class or structure as one of your method parameters. How do you expose the class or structure to COM? How is a custom data type like this marshaled?

Solution

Managed classes and structures are simply types. If they are part of an assembly that is exported to COM, they will be exported along with all other types. There is really nothing special that you have to do in order to pass a class or structure as a parameter to a method.

Within the typelib, each class or structure has its own COM identity (a unique Guid). This enables COM clients to create instances of these types or reference them as they are passed to methods. In effect, they have now become custom COM types that are defined in the typelib.

In the case of classes, you can choose to expose them using the default class interface, or you can define your own interface that identifies the properties and methods of the class. The preferred way is to always define your own interface.

As an example, consider this managed interface that we want to expose to COM:

```
//define an interface for account services
public interface IAccountLookup
{
    IAccount RetrieveAccount(int acctId);
    void UpdateBalance(IAccount account);
}
```

Both defined methods use a custom type (an interface) named IAccount. Obviously, for these methods to work via COM, the COM client must know how an IAccount is defined. We need to define and export this type to our typelib.

Let's define the IAccount interface like this:

```
//define an interface to expose class properties
//to COM clients
public interface IAccount
{
    int AccountId        {get;}
    string AccountName   {get;}
    decimal Balance
    {
        //marshal the balance to COM as CURRENCY
        [return: MarshalAs(UnmanagedType.Currency)] get;
        //prohibit setting of balance property via COM
        [ComVisible(false)]
        set;
    }
}
```

The interface defines three properties. The first two are read-only, while the last one (Balance) is read and write. However, the setter has the ComVisible attribute set to false, which effectively makes this a read-only property as far as COM is concerned. But remember that the ComVisible attribute only affects the visibility via COM clients. Managed code is free to use this property as read and write. We will see why we went to this trouble in the code that follows.

Next, we develop a class that implements this IAccount interface:

```
//Implement an account class
[ComVisible(false)]
public class Account : IAccount
{
    private int         m_AccountId;
    private string      m_AccountName;
    private decimal     m_Balance;

    public int AccountId
    {
        get { return m_AccountId;}
        set { m_AccountId = value; }
    }

    public string AccountName
    {
        get { return m_AccountName; }
        set { m_AccountName = value; }
    }

    public decimal Balance
    {
        get { return m_Balance; }
        set { m_Balance = value; }
    }
}
```

We apply the ComVisible attribute to the Account class to hide it from COM. We do this because we want COM clients to access this object via the IAccount interface instead. Remember, the methods we defined in the IAccountLookup interface referred to the IAccount type, not this concrete Account class. This means we can use those methods with any type that implements IAccount. This provides us with additional flexibility, which is generally a good thing.

Finally, we can develop a class that implements the IAccountLookup interface like this:

```
//implement a class to provide account services
[ClassInterface(ClassInterfaceType.None)]
public class DniNetClassesObj : IAccountLookup
{
    public IAccount RetrieveAccount(int acctId)
    {
        Account result = null;
```

```
        if (acctId == 123)
        {
            result = new Account();
            result.AccountId = acctId;
            result.AccountName = "myAccount";
            result.Balance = 1009.95M;
        }
        return result;
    }

    public void UpdateBalance(IAccount account)
    {
        //update the balance
        if (account != null)
        {
            account.Balance += 500.00M;
        }
    }
}
```

The RetrieveAccount method returns an IAccount object (an instance of the Account class). The UpdateBalance method simply increases the balance of the passed-in object by 500.00. Since UpdateBalance receives an IAccount instead of an Account reference, we needed to allow updates to the Balance property via this interface. That's the reason we needed to include the setter property in the IAccount interface.

In this C# example, we declared the UpdateBalance method like this, passing the IAccount object by value:

```
void UpdateBalance(IAccount account);
```

Even though it is passed by value, IAccount is still a reference type. Because of this, the COM client code is allowed to see any changes made to the object by the managed code. We could have also passed IAccount by reference like this:

```
void UpdateBalance(ref IAccount account);
```

This would have produced the same results, although the generated IDL is slightly different. In either case, changes made to the object by managed code are marshaled back to the COM client. To demonstrate this, the following Visual Basic .NET (VB.NET) version of this example passes the IAccount object by reference.

After building the project, we can examine the typelib that was generated. Using OleView.exe, we see that the extracted IDL for the typelib looks like this:

```
[
  odl,
  uuid(9E42C392-75D1-3855-989F-3D214A741179),
  version(1.0),
  dual,
  oleautomation,
```

```
  custom(0F21F359-AB84-41E8-9A78-36D110E6D2F9,
  DniNetStructs.IAccount)


]
interface IAccount : IDispatch {
    [id(0x60020000), propget]
    HRESULT AccountId([out, retval] long* pRetVal);
    [id(0x60020001), propget]
    HRESULT AccountName([out, retval] BSTR* pRetVal);
    [id(0x60020002), propget]
    HRESULT Balance([out, retval] CURRENCY* pRetVal);
};


 [
  odl,
  uuid(E63C96F0-542D-3687-97EC-882F3AB221F5),
  version(1.0),
  dual,
  oleautomation,
  custom(0F21F359-AB84-41E8-9A78-36D110E6D2F9,
  DniNetStructs.IAccountLookup)


]
interface IAccountLookup : IDispatch {
    [id(0x60020000)]
    HRESULT RetrieveAccount(
                    [in] long acctId,
                    [out, retval] IAccount** pRetVal);
    [id(0x60020001)]
    HRESULT UpdateBalance([in] IAccount* Account);
};


[
  uuid(A79A7702-27CA-3224-ADFB-DC8CE34D44C6),
  version(1.0),
  custom(0F21F359-AB84-41E8-9A78-36D110E6D2F9,
  DniNetStructs.DniNetClassesObj)
]
coclass DniNetClassesObj {
    interface _Object;
    [default] interface IAccountLookup;
};
```

The typelib includes only those types that we want to expose to COM as our public interface (highlighted in the preceding IDL). We have the IAccount and IAccountLookup interfaces along with the DniNetClassesObj concrete class. The Account class is not in the typelib since we decorated it with ComVisible(false) to prevent direct access by COM clients.

Using these types, we can write a Visual Basic 6.0 (VB6) client:

```
Private Sub Form_Load()
    Call UseClass
End Sub

Private Sub UseClass()
    'create instance of COM object
    Dim comObj As _
        New DniNetStructs.DniNetClassesObj
    'define account object
    Dim account As DniNetStructs.IAccount

    'retrieve the account
    Set account = comObj.RetrieveAccount(123)
    Text1.Text = Text1.Text + _
        "RetrieveAccount - " _
        + " AccountId: " + CStr(account.AccountId) _
        + ", Name: " + account.AccountName _
        + ", Balance: " + CStr(account.Balance) _
        + vbCrLf

    'update the account balance
    Call comObj.UpdateBalance(account)
    Text1.Text = Text1.Text + _
        "UpdateBalance   - " _
        + " AccountId: " + CStr(account.AccountId) _
        + ", Name: " + account.AccountName _
        + ", Balance: " + CStr(account.Balance) _
        + vbCrLf

    'free the COM reference
    Set comObj = Nothing
End Sub
```

The code first calls the RetrieveAccount method, storing the result in a local variable that is of type DniNetStructs.IAccount. After the properties of that variable are displayed, the UpdateBalance method is called. The local IAccount variable is passed by reference, so we should see any changes made to the object. The updated properties are again displayed in a TextBox on the form.

When we execute this code, we see these results in the TextBox:

```
RetrieveAccount -  AccountId: 123, Name: myAccount, Balance: 1009.95
UpdateBalance   -  AccountId: 123, Name: myAccount, Balance: 1509.95
```

As this example has demonstrated, we have successfully exported and used custom managed types in COM.

We can implement the same functionality using VB.NET. However, as we will see, we need to make a few adjustments to the design to accomplish this. As we did with the C# code, we start by defining the IAccount interface:

```vbnet
Imports System.Runtime.InteropServices

'defines the public API for an account object
Public Interface IAccount
    Property AccountId() As Integer

    Property AccountName() As String

    Function GetBalance() As _
        <MarshalAs(UnmanagedType.Currency)> Decimal

    <ComVisible(False)> _
    Sub SetBalance(<MarshalAs(UnmanagedType.Currency)> _
        ByVal value As Decimal)
End Interface
```

This looks similar to the C# version of the interface, with the exception of the Balance property. The C# interface defined a property named Balance that had read/write access and was marshaled as Currency. However, we suppressed the write access to COM clients using ComVisible(false). This allowed us to update the property from managed code, but made it read-only to COM clients.

VB.NET doesn't allow us to accomplish the same thing using a property. In VB.NET, we can declare a property as ReadOnly or WriteOnly. But when declaring a property within an interface, we don't have an opportunity to place attributes on the individual Get and Set methods.

Because of this, we choose to forgo the use of a property and simply declare separate GetBalance and SetBalance methods. This allows us to apply the necessary attributes for marshaling as well as COM visibility to each method. We end up with the same functionality, but have to do a bit more work to get there.

Here is the Account class that implements this interface in VB.NET:

```vbnet
'defines an account class
<ComVisible(False)> _
Public Class Account
    Implements IAccount

    Private m_AccountId As Integer
    Private m_AccountName As String
    Private m_Balance As Decimal

    Public Property AccountId() As Integer _
        Implements IAccount.AccountId
        Get
            Return m_AccountId
        End Get
```

```vb
            Set(ByVal value As Integer)
                m_AccountId = value
            End Set
        End Property


        Public Property AccountName() As String _
            Implements IAccount.AccountName
            Get
                Return m_AccountName
            End Get
            Set(ByVal value As String)
                m_AccountName = value
            End Set
        End Property


        Public Function GetBalance() As Decimal _
            Implements IAccount.GetBalance
            Return m_Balance
        End Function


        Public Sub SetBalance(ByVal value As Decimal) _
            Implements IAccount.SetBalance
            m_Balance = value
        End Sub

End Class
```

Next we have the IAccountLookup interface in VB.NET and the class that implements it:

```vb
'define an interface for account services
Public Interface IAccountLookup
    Function RetrieveAccount(ByVal acctId As Integer) _
        As IAccount
    Sub UpdateBalance(ByRef account As IAccount)
End Interface


<ClassInterface(ClassInterfaceType.None)> _
Public Class DniNetClassesObj
    Implements IAccountLookup


    Public Function RetrieveAccount(ByVal acctId As Integer) _
        As IAccount Implements IAccountLookup.RetrieveAccount
        Dim result As Account = Nothing
        If acctId = 123 Then
            result = New Account()
            result.AccountId = acctId
            result.AccountName = "myAccount"
            result.SetBalance(1009.95D)
        End If
```

```
        Return result
    End Function

    Public Sub UpdateBalance(ByRef account As IAccount) _
        Implements IAccountLookup.UpdateBalance
        If Not account Is Nothing Then
            account.SetBalance(account.GetBalance() + 500D)
        End If
    End Sub
End Class
```

Notice that for this VB.NET example, we chose to pass the IAccount object by reference rather than by value. This is not required, but it demonstrates that we can pass reference types either way, and the client will still see updates to the object.

The same VB6 client code shown with the C# example can be used to exercise this code. To do this, we need to reference the VB.NET project instead of the C# project. We then replace this line:

```
Dim comObj As _
    New DniNetStructs.DniNetClassesObj
```

with this:

```
Dim comObj As _
    New DniNetStructsVB.DniNetClassesObj
```

When executed, the results are the same as the C# version.

How It Works

Like its big brother the class, a structure (C# struct) is exported to the typelib when an assembly is exported. Other than the normal differences that exist between a class and a struct in managed code, there are no substantial differences in using structs from COM.

The example that follows duplicates the Account object example shown previously using a struct instead of a class. Also, in contrast with the first example, which exposed everything as an interface instead of the actual classes, this example exposes the struct directly instead of via an interface.

We start with the definition of the struct itself:

```
//Implement an account struct
public struct AccountStruct
{
    public int          AccountId;

    [MarshalAs(UnmanagedType.BStr)]
    public string       AccountName;

    [MarshalAs(UnmanagedType.Currency)]
    public decimal      Balance;
}
```

We add the MarshalAs attribute to the AccountName and Balance in order to adjust the default marshaling.

We do use an interface to define the action methods available to COM clients. The interface looks like this:

```
//define an interface for account services
public interface IAccountStructLookup
{
    AccountStruct RetrieveAccount(int acctId);
    void UpdateBalance(ref AccountStruct account);
}
```

Notice that the interface uses the actual AccountStruct rather than the IAccount interface that we used in the previous example.

The C# class that implements this interface looks like this:

```
//implement a class to provide account services
//using an AccountStruct
[ClassInterface(ClassInterfaceType.None)]
public class DniNetStructsObj : IAccountStructLookup
{
    public AccountStruct RetrieveAccount(int acctId)
    {
        AccountStruct result = new AccountStruct();
        if (acctId == 123)
        {
            result.AccountId = acctId;
            result.AccountName = "myAccount";
            result.Balance = 1009.95M;
        }
        return result;
    }

    public void UpdateBalance(ref AccountStruct account)
    {
        //update the balance
        account.Balance += 500.00M;
    }
}
```

To test these methods using a struct, we can modify our existing VB6 code to include this new subroutine:

```
Private Sub UseStruct()
    'create instance of COM object that uses structs
    Dim comObj As _
        New DniNetStructs.DniNetStructsObj
    'define account object (struct)
    Dim account As DniNetStructs.AccountStruct
```

```
    'retrieve the account into the struct
    account = comObj.RetrieveAccount(123)
    Text1.Text = Text1.Text + _
        "RetrieveAccount - " _
        + " AccountId: " + CStr(account.AccountId) _
        + ", Name: " + account.AccountName _
        + ", Balance: " + CStr(account.Balance) _
        + vbCrLf

    'update the account balance in the struct
    Call comObj.UpdateBalance(account)
    Text1.Text = Text1.Text + _
        "UpdateBalance   - " _
        + " AccountId: " + CStr(account.AccountId) _
        + ", Name: " + account.AccountName _
        + ", Balance: " + CStr(account.Balance) _
        + vbCrLf

    'create our own instance of the struct
    Dim acctStruct As DniNetStructs.AccountStruct
    acctStruct.AccountId = 456
    acctStruct.AccountName = "new account"
    acctStruct.Balance = 100.21

    'update the account balance in the struct
    Call comObj.UpdateBalance(acctStruct)
    Text1.Text = Text1.Text + _
        "UpdateBalance   - " _
        + " AccountId: " + CStr(acctStruct.AccountId) _
        + ", Name: " + acctStruct.AccountName _
        + ", Balance: " + CStr(acctStruct.Balance) _
        + vbCrLf

    'free the COM reference
    Set comObj = Nothing
End Sub
```

And we also need to modify the Form_Load event handler to call this new routine:

```
Private Sub Form_Load()
    Call UseClass
    Call UseStruct
End Sub
```

When we execute this test, we see these additional results:

```
RetrieveAccount -  AccountId: 123, Name: myAccount, Balance: 1009.95
UpdateBalance   -  AccountId: 123, Name: myAccount, Balance: 1509.95
UpdateBalance   -  AccountId: 456, Name: new account, Balance: 600.21
```

The results are the same for the first two methods. Notice that we've added a third test. This last test uses an instance of the AccountStruct that we create ourselves in VB code like this:

```
'create our own instance of the struct
Dim acctStruct As DniNetStructs.AccountStruct
acctStruct.AccountId = 456
acctStruct.AccountName = "new account"
acctStruct.Balance = 100.21
```

This demonstrates that the AccountStruct is a normal COM type in every way. We were unable to do this in the original example because we exposed the IAccount interface rather than the concrete Account class.

Related Information

See recipes 6-3 (Exposing .NET Classes with Interfaces) and 6-5 (Controlling COM Visibility).

7-8. Passing Optional Parameters

Problem

Does COM interop support optional parameters when calling a method?

Solution

Visual Basic .NET (VB.NET) supports optional parameters natively using the Optional keyword. Adding this modifier to a parameter provides callers with a choice: they can choose to either pass or omit the parameter. If the parameter is omitted, the default value specified for the parameter is used.

For example, this VB.NET method specifies an optional parameter:

```
Public Function MyOptionalMethod( _
    ByVal desc As String, _
    Optional ByVal actionCode As Integer = 1001) _
        As Integer
End Function
```

When this method is exported to a COM typelib, the method is defined like this:

```
HRESULT MyOptionalMethod(
    [in] BSTR desc,
```

```
[in, optional, defaultvalue(1001)] long actionCode,
[out, retval] long* pRetVal);
```

The MIDL attributes optional and defaultvalue shown here allow COM clients to omit the actionCode parameter.

C# does not support optional parameters natively. However, starting with version 2.0 of the .NET Framework, you can provide the same effect using a combination of interop attributes. The Optional attribute (not to be confused with the VB.NET keyword) flags a parameter as optional for COM callers. The DefaultParameterValue attribute allows you to specify the default value if the parameter is omitted. By combining these attributes, you mimic what VB.NET supports in the language. Both of these attributes can be found in the System.Runtime.InteropServices namespace.

Note This technique for C# applies only to COM interop. These attributes have no effect on managed classes using the method. As far as managed clients are concerned, all parameters are required.

For example, you can declare the same method in C# like this:

```
public int MyOptionalMethod(
    string desc,
    [Optional, DefaultParameterValue(1001)]
    int actionCode)
```

When this is exported, the generated typelib contains an identical COM method with this definition:

```
HRESULT MyOptionalMethod(
    [in] BSTR desc,
    [in, optional, defaultvalue(1001)] long actionCode,
    [out, retval] long* pRetVal);
```

Regardless of the managed language used, COM clients are able to call this method with one or two parameters. If called with a single parameter, the second parameter will have a default value of 1001.

How It Works

The example code that follows demonstrates the use of optional parameters in VB.NET and C#.
    We start with example code in VB.NET:

```
Imports System.Runtime.InteropServices

Public Interface IOptional
    Function AddOptionalNumbers( _
            ByVal numA As Integer, _
            Optional ByVal numB As Integer = 1, _
            Optional ByVal numC As Integer = 2) _
```

```
            As Integer
End Interface

<ClassInterface(ClassInterfaceType.None)> _
Public Class DniNetOptionalVBOb
    Implements IOptional

    Public Function AddOptionalNumbers( _
        ByVal numA As Integer, _
        Optional ByVal numB As Integer = 1, _
        Optional ByVal numC As Integer = 2) _
        As Integer Implements IOptional.AddOptionalNumbers

        Return numA + numB + numC
    End Function
End Class
```

The IOptional interface defines the method that we wish to expose to COM clients. The AddOptionalNumbers method takes three integer parameters and returns an integer. The first parameter is required, while the second and third are optional and have default values of 1 and 2.

Generally it is better to define our own interface and expose it to COM rather than using a generated class interface. However, in this case doing things this way requires more work on our part. We need to define the default values in both the interface and the class that implements it.

Next, we write Visual Basic 6.0 (VB6) code to execute this method and display the results:

```
Private Sub Form_Load()
    Call TestVBOptional
End Sub

Private Sub TestVBOptional()
    'use the VB.NET COM object
    Dim comObj As DniNetOptionalVB.IOptional
    Set comObj = New DniNetOptionalVB.DniNetOptionalVBOb

    'try the method with and without optional parameters
    Dim result As Integer
    result = comObj.AddOptionalNumbers(100)
    Text1.Text = Text1.Text + _
        "One param: " + CStr(result) + vbCrLf

    result = comObj.AddOptionalNumbers(100, 1000)
    Text1.Text = Text1.Text + _
        "Two params: " + CStr(result) + vbCrLf
```

```
    result = comObj.AddOptionalNumbers(100, 1000, 5000)
    Text1.Text = Text1.Text + _
        "Three params: " + CStr(result) + vbCrLf

    Set comObj = Nothing
End Sub
```

The AddOptionalNumbers method is executed three times. Each time we pass a different number of parameters. When the code is executed, these results are displayed in a TextBox on the form:

```
One param: 103
Two params: 1102
Three params: 6100
```

Since the first call passed only a single parameter of 100, the default values of 1 and 2 were used for the other parameters, so the result of 103 is correct. Likewise, the other calls return the expected results.

The equivalent code implemented in C# looks like this:

```csharp
using System;
using System.Runtime.InteropServices;

namespace DniNetOptional
{
    public interface IOptional
    {
        int AddOptionalNumbers(int numA,
            [Optional, DefaultParameterValue(1)]
            int numB,
            [Optional, DefaultParameterValue(2)]
            int numC);
    }

    [ClassInterface(ClassInterfaceType.None)]
    public class DniNetOptionalObj : IOptional
    {
        public int AddOptionalNumbers(int numA,
            int numB, int numC)
        {
            return numA + numB + numC;
        }
    }
}
```

We can test the C# version of the code by adding the highlighted code to the VB6 client:

```
Private Sub Form_Load()
    Call TestVBOptional
    Call TestCSharpOptional   'added
End Sub

Private Sub TestCSharpOptional()
    'use the C# COM object
    Dim comObj As DniNetOptional.IOptional
    Set comObj = New DniNetOptional.DniNetOptionalObj

    'try the method with and without optional parameters
    Dim result As Integer
    result = comObj.AddOptionalNumbers(100)
    Text1.Text = Text1.Text + _
        "One param: " + CStr(result) + vbCrLf

    result = comObj.AddOptionalNumbers(100, 1000)
    Text1.Text = Text1.Text + _
        "Two params: " + CStr(result) + vbCrLf

    result = comObj.AddOptionalNumbers(100, 1000, 5000)
    Text1.Text = Text1.Text + _
        "Three params: " + CStr(result) + vbCrLf

    Set comObj = Nothing
End Sub
```

When this test is executed, we now see the results from both tests:

```
One param: 103
Two params: 1102
Three params: 6100
One param: 103
Two params: 1102
Three params: 6100
```

CHAPTER 8

■■■

COM+ Enterprise Services

COM+ is the Microsoft architecture that provides a centralized runtime environment for COM components. Designed to run components in a middle tier, it provides a number of services that are necessary when using COM components in an enterprise-scale application. .NET does not replace COM+ since it doesn't directly address these services.

At its core, COM+ is a hosting environment. Instead of activating a COM component in the same process as the client application, the component can be hosted by COM+ in a separate process. This allows you to use other performance-oriented features of COM+ such as just-in-time (JIT) activation and object pooling.

COM+ organizes components into *applications*, with each application hosting one or more related *components*. This allows you to logically group components together according to how they are used. The Component Services management tool (available from the Administrative Tools folder in the Control Panel) is available to administer and configure the applications and components. This is also where COM+ role-based security is managed for each application.

The feature most often associated with COM+ is automatic transactions. Because this is a key component of COM+, it merits its own chapter. Please refer to Chapter 9, which provides in-depth coverage of transactions.

.NET provides good support for COM+ components. It does this directly without using COM or PInvoke to access COM+ services. The terminology has changed slightly, with .NET calling these *serviced components* instead of COM+ components. And the broad category of services known as COM+ is now called *Enterprise Services*. But the COM+ concepts have not changed. Using .NET, you can develop a component in managed code, register it as a COM+ (serviced) component, and use it from COM or managed client code.

That last point is an interesting one. Traditional COM+ components are available only to COM clients. However, when a managed component is registered as a serviced component, it is also available to managed client code. This allows managed code to take full advantage of the available COM+ services.

In general, the classes that are used for COM+ support are located in the System. EnterpriseServices namespace. This namespace contains the ServicedComponent base class that your managed component classes must derive from. It also contains a large number of attributes that are used to determine which COM+ features each assembly, class, and method use.

Just as COM has its own unique terminology, COM+ uses a number of terms that I'll define here:

- A COM+ *component* is equivalent to a managed *class*. When managed code is registered with COM+, each class is considered a separate component.

- A COM+ *application* hosts one or more COM+ components. Each application has an activation type of either *library* or *server*. When managed code is registered with COM+, each *assembly* is associated with a single application. The classes defined within the assembly all live in the same application. It is possible to install multiple assemblies into the same application.

- A COM+ *library application* activates the component in the caller's process and is limited in its use of COM+ services.

- A COM+ *server application* activates components in its own process that is separate from the caller. This type of application fully utilizes the COM+ hosting environment and can support all COM+ services.

- A COM+ *context* is an environment that is created by COM+ where objects live after they are activated. Each context has a set of properties that determine the runtime characteristics of the component. Every COM+ component is activated into either a new or an existing context.

The chapter starts with coverage of the most basic way to expose a managed class to COM+. Following that, we discuss implementing a server application instead of a library application. Additional recipes cover the registration and installation of serviced components. An alternative to manual registration is described in the recipe on dynamic component registration.

Two important performance-oriented topics are discussed next. JIT activation and object pooling each have a recipe that demonstrates how to use these features.

Security-related topics are covered in the next set of recipes. One recipe demonstrates the use of private components, while two others cover role-based security.

The chapter concludes with a look at Queued Components and how to implement and use them from .NET.

8-1. Exposing Managed Code to COM+

Problem

What is the easiest way to register a managed component with COM+? Can it be used just like a normal COM+ object? What steps are necessary to accomplish this?

Solution

.NET allows you to develop managed code that you then register as a COM+ component. Once this is done, the component is capable of using the services provided by COM+, and it can be referenced from COM or managed clients.

In .NET terminology, a COM+ component is now called a *serviced component*.

The basic steps to create a serviced component are as follows:

1. Derive a managed class from the ServicedComponent class, which resides in the System. EnterpriseServices namespace.

2. Define the public API that you want to expose to clients through a managed interface.

3. Make the assembly COM-visible using the project settings.

4. Provide a strong name for the assembly and add it to the global assembly cache (GAC).

5. Register the assembly with Enterprise Services using the regsvcs.exe utility.

In order to work within Enterprise Services, a class must derive from ServicedComponent. This class provides the base methods needed to operate in this environment.

Since COM+ is built upon a COM foundation, it shares many of the same design concepts. For this reason, it makes sense to implement your classes and interfaces as if you were developing a COM component. You should explicitly define your own interface rather than using a generated class interface. This allows you to control the API that you publish to clients.

You also need to make the assembly COM-visible by setting the "Make assembly COM-visible" project option. This option is available from the Application tab of the project options; click the Assembly Information button to view this option. When this option is changed, the ComVisible attribute in the AssemblyInfo (.cs or .vb) file is set to either true or false, for example:

```
[assembly: ComVisible(true)]
```

To illustrate the steps needed to use COM+, consider this class and interface implemented in C#:

```
using System;
using System.Runtime.InteropServices;
using System.EnterpriseServices;

namespace DniScSimpleComponent
{
    public interface IAddNumbers
    {
        int AddSomeNumbers(int numA, int numB);
    }

    [ClassInterface(ClassInterfaceType.None)]
    public class DniScSimpleComponentObj
        : ServicedComponent, IAddNumbers
    {
        public int AddSomeNumbers(int numA, int numB)
        {
            return numA + numB;
        }
    }
}
```

The IAddNumbers interface defines the method that we want exposed to clients. We apply the ClassInterface attribute to the class in order to suppress automatic generation of the class interface. Notice that our class derives from ServicedComponent as required.

Next, we set the "Make assembly COM-visible" project option. This is needed if we want to register this assembly as a COM+ component.

■**Note** Since COM+ builds upon the functionality available in COM, you have the ability to actively manage the COM identity for your interfaces and classes. You accomplish this by applying the Guid and ProgId attributes to your types.

Another requirement is that the assembly must have a strong name. To do this, we need to generate a public/private key pair and assign the key file to the assembly.

■**Note** You can either manually generate the key pair for the strong name using the sn utility or simply set the project options that do this for you. The Signing tab of the project options allows you to create a strong name key file. After checking the "Sign the assembly" option, you can select <new> for "Choose a strong name key file". After you provide a name for the new key file, the key pair is generated, saved to the file, and assigned to the assembly.

After building the project, we add it to the GAC. We use the gacutil command-line utility to do this. Our command looks like this:

```
gacutil /i DniScSimpleComponent.dll
```

Finally, we register this assembly with COM+ services using the regsvcs command-line utility. This utility provides a number of options, but all of the defaults will work fine for this recipe. The command looks like this:

```
regsvcs DniScSimpleComponent.dll
```

This adds the assembly into a COM+ application using the same name as the assembly (DniScSimpleComponent). If the application already exists, the assembly is added to it. Otherwise, a new application is created. As a by-product of this command, a type library (typelib) file is generated for the assembly. This file can be used by COM clients to access the types that have been exported from the assembly.

Note The execution of gacutil and regsvcs can be done automatically from the postbuild step of the project. For instance, you can add these commands to the postbuild step:

```
gacutil /i $(TargetFileName)
regsvcs $(TargetFileName)
```

These commands make use of the built-in $(TargetFileName) macro provided by Visual Studio .NET. Visual Studio also provides a number of other macros.

To help keep the registry clean of unused typelibs, it's also a good idea to unregister the previous version of the assembly in the prebuild step of the project by adding the /u flag like this:

```
regsvcs /u $(TargetFileName)
```

One potential problem is that regsvcs isn't normally found by the Visual Studio postbuild steps because of its location under the .NET Framework runtime directory. To remedy this, you can start Visual Studio a different way. Instead of using the shortcut to Visual Studio .NET, open up the Visual Studio Command Prompt instead. This is a Windows command prompt that sets all of the environment variables needed to run the .NET command-line tools. From the command prompt, simply enter **devenv** to start Visual Studio .NET. Now when you execute these postbuild steps, Visual Studio .NET is able to find the path to any .NET utility that you need.

We can verify that a new application was created using the Component Services Management Console plug-in.

Note When working with COM+ services, you will often use the Component Services Management Console plug-in, which is available from the Administrative Tools folder of the Control Panel. This tool allows you to add, change, or delete COM+ applications; add components to an application; monitor the status of running components; manage role-based security; start and stop applications, and so on. Since you'll use this utility frequently, you'll likely want to add a shortcut to it.

We are now ready to use this component from client code. The following C# code creates an instance of this class and calls the AddSomeNumbers method:

```csharp
using System;
using DniScSimpleComponent;

namespace ScSimpleComponent
{
    class Program
    {
        static void Main(string[] args)
        {
            IAddNumbers obj
                = new DniScSimpleComponentObj();
            int result = obj.AddSomeNumbers(1, 2);
            Console.WriteLine(
                "AddSomeNumbers using COM+ Library: {0}",
                result);

            Console.Read();
        }
    }
}
```

The output we see on the console looks like this:

```
AddSomeNumbers using COM+ Library: 3
```

Of course, we can also choose to implement the COM+ component in Visual Basic .NET (VB.NET). Here is an equivalent implementation in VB.NET:

```vbnet
Imports System.Runtime.InteropServices
Imports System.EnterpriseServices

Public Interface IAddNumbers
    Function AddSomeNumbers(ByVal numA As Integer, _
        ByVal numB As Integer) As Integer
End Interface

<ClassInterface(ClassInterfaceType.None)> _
Public Class DniScSimpleComponentObj
    Inherits ServicedComponent
    Implements IAddNumbers

    Public Function AddSomeNumbers(ByVal numA As Integer, _
        ByVal numB As Integer) As Integer _
            Implements IAddNumbers.AddSomeNumbers
```

```
    Return numA + numB

  End Function
End Class
```

Running the client code against this component produces the same results.

How It Works

The client code to access this component looks just like normal managed code. But under the covers, DniScSimpleComponentObj is loaded via the COM+ library runtime using the COM+ application information, instead of directly from the assembly via the CLR class loader.

To prove this to ourselves, we can disable the COM+ application. To do this, we open up the Component Services plug-in, locate the DniScSimpleComponent application, and right-click the mouse to see the available options, one of which is Disable. If we select that option, no clients should be able to access the components in that application.

Note The Enable/Disable options mentioned here are not available under Windows 2000. In order to see these options, you must be running Windows XP or above.

This time when we execute the client code, we receive a ComException with this error message:

```
The component or application containing the component
has been disabled. (Exception from HRESULT: 0x80004027)
```

If we enable the application, everything works normally once again.

The component we implemented in this recipe was installed into the GAC as a shared assembly. We also used the regsvcs utility to register it with Enterprise Services. This is the most common and straightforward way to register a serviced component. However, .NET also supports dynamic registration, which does not require either of these steps. This type of registration is covered in recipe 8-4 (Registering Components Dynamically).

Part of the elegance of Enterprise Services is that it works the same way for managed and COM clients. To demonstrate this, here is Visual Basic 6.0 (VB6) code that accesses the same component using COM:

```
Private Sub Form_Load()
    Dim comObj As DniScSimpleComponent.IAddNumbers
    Set comObj = CreateObject( _
        "DniScSimpleComponent.DniScSimpleComponentObj")

    Dim result As Integer
    result = comObj.AddSomeNumbers(1, 2)
    Text1.Text = Text1.Text + _
        "AddSomeNumbers using COM+ Library: " _
```

```
        + CStr(result) _
        + vbCrLf

    'free the COM reference
    Set comObj = Nothing
End Sub
```

Prior to building this project, we need to add a COM reference to DniScSimpleComponent from the VB6 Project References dialog.

When we execute the code, we see the same results as before, shown in the TextBox on the form:

AddSomeNumbers using COM+ Library: 3

This is clearly a very simple example that doesn't really require COM+ (Enterprise) Services. But even this simple example illustrates some of the power of COM+.

At a minimum, it provides us with a central location for administration and control of our components. And any configuration is used by managed and COM clients alike. The recipes that follow demonstrate how to use various aspects of these services.

Related Information

See recipes 6-3 (Exposing .NET Classes with Interfaces) and 8-2 (Implementing a Server Application).

8-2. Implementing a Server Application

Problem

COM+ supports two kinds of applications: library and server. How do you implement a server application using managed code?

Solution

.NET provides support for both types of COM+ applications. The type of application is determined by the activation type COM+ setting, which can be set to either Library or Server. You can control the activation type to use for your managed code by applying the ApplicationActivation attribute to an assembly.

If an activation type of Library is used, the application components are activated within the client's process. This is the default if the ApplicationActivation attribute is omitted. If ActivationOption.Server is specified as the activation type, the components are activated in a dedicated process that is separate from the client.

For example, in C# this attribute looks like this:

```
[assembly: ApplicationActivation(ActivationOption.Server)]
```

An assembly that is built with this attribute will create a COM+ server application when it is registered via regsvcs.

To create a library application, you can either omit this attribute altogether or specify Library as the activation type like this:

```
[assembly: ApplicationActivation(ActivationOption.Library)]
```

This creates the same type of library application that we used in the previous recipe.

Note These attributes are applied to the entire assembly rather than to a single class or interface. Therefore, the best place for them in a project is in the AssemblyInfo.cs file (for C#) or AssemblyInfo.vb (for Visual Basic .NET [VB.NET]).

Since server applications run in their own process, they provide security-access capabilities that are not available to library applications. By default, the access security is enabled and will be enforced for all clients. For our purposes right now, we don't require this security, so we need to turn it off for the COM+ application. We do this using the ApplicationAccessControl attribute like this in C#:

```
[assembly: ApplicationAccessControl(false)]
```

Now when the assembly is registered, access security for the server application will be disabled. Using role-based security for COM+ applications is discussed in recipe 8-8 (Using Role-Based Security).

Without this attribute, you receive an UnauthorizedAccessException with this message when you attempt to use the component:

```
Access is denied.
(Exception from HRESULT: 0x80070005 (E_ACCESSDENIED))
```

By applying the ApplicationName attribute to your assembly, you can specify the name of the COM+ application to use during registration, for example:

```
[assembly: ApplicationName("DniServerApplication")]
```

When registered, the assembly will be added to an application named DniServerApplication. If that application doesn't already exist, it will first be created using the values from the assembly attributes. If the ApplicationName attribute is omitted, the assembly will be added to a COM+ application using the same name as the assembly.

Note Be aware that an assembly can be added to only one COM+ application at a time. If an assembly is already installed in a COM+ application and you now want to install it somewhere else, you must first remove it from the original COM+ application. Please refer to recipe 8-3 (Installing a Serviced Component) for more information on this subject.

You can also provide a description for the application like this:

```
[assembly: Description(".NET Interop Server Application")]
```

The description, along with all of the application properties, is available for viewing from the Component Services Management Console plug-in.

How It Works

We can demonstrate the use of a server application using a modified version of the code from the last recipe:

```
using System;
using System.Runtime.InteropServices;
using System.EnterpriseServices;

namespace DniScServerComponent
{
    [Description("Interface used to add numbers")]
    public interface IAddNumbers
    {
        int AddSomeNumbers(int numA, int numB);
    }

    [ClassInterface(ClassInterfaceType.None)]
    [Description("Add numbers server component")]
    public class DniScServerComponentObj
        : ServicedComponent, IAddNumbers
    {
        public int AddSomeNumbers(int numA, int numB)
        {
            return numA + numB;
        }
    }
}
```

The code is almost exactly the same as that used in the last recipe. We've changed only the project, namespace, and class names to avoid any confusion. We've also added a Description attribute to the interface and class. This will provide a description that is viewable from the Component Services Management Console plug-in.

The most important changes can be found in the AssemblyInfo.cs file where we added these attributes:

```
using System.EnterpriseServices;

[assembly: ApplicationActivation(ActivationOption.Server)]
[assembly: ApplicationAccessControl(false)]
[assembly: ApplicationName("DniServerApplication")]
[assembly: Description(".NET Interop Server Application")]
```

This will register the assembly into a COM+ server application named DniServerApplication that has access security disabled.

The C# client code is also similar to what we used when accessing a library component:

```
using System;
using DniScServerComponent;

namespace ScServerComponent
{
    class Program
    {
        static void Main(string[] args)
        {
            IAddNumbers obj
                = new DniScServerComponentObj();
            int result = obj.AddSomeNumbers(1, 2);
            Console.WriteLine(
                "AddSomeNumbers using COM+ Server App: {0}",
                result);

            Console.Read();
        }
    }
}
```

When we execute this client code, we see these results displayed on the console:

```
AddSomeNumbers using COM+ Server App: 3
```

As was the case with a library application, we can also access this component from a Visual Basic 6.0 (VB6) client like this:

```
Private Sub Form_Load()
    Dim comObj As DniScServerComponent.IAddNumbers
    Set comObj = CreateObject( _
        "DniScServerComponent.DniScServerComponentObj")

    Dim result As Integer
    result = comObj.AddSomeNumbers(1, 2)
    Text1.Text = Text1.Text + _
        "AddSomeNumbers using COM+ Server App: " _
        + CStr(result) _
        + vbCrLf

    'free the COM reference
    Set comObj = Nothing
End Sub
```

When the code is executed, these results are displayed in the TextBox on the form:

```
AddSomeNumbers using COM+ Server App: 3
```

The VB.NET implementation of the serviced component looks like this:

```
Imports System.Runtime.InteropServices
Imports System.EnterpriseServices

<Description("Interface used to add numbers")> _
Public Interface IAddNumbers
    Function AddSomeNumbers(ByVal numA As Integer, _
        ByVal numB As Integer) As Integer
End Interface

<ClassInterface(ClassInterfaceType.None)> _
<Description("Add numbers server component")> _
Public Class DniScServerComponentObj
    Inherits ServicedComponent
    Implements IAddNumbers

    Public Function AddSomeNumbers(ByVal numA As Integer, _
        ByVal numB As Integer) As Integer _
            Implements IAddNumbers.AddSomeNumbers

        Return numA + numB

    End Function
End Class
```

These entries should be added to the AssemblyInfo.vb file to register the assembly as a server application:

```
Imports System.EnterpriseServices

<Assembly: ApplicationActivation(ActivationOption.Server)>
<Assembly: ApplicationAccessControl(False)>
<Assembly: ApplicationName("DniServerApplication")>
<Assembly: Description(".NET Interop Server Application")>
```

The results are exactly the same when the Visual Basic .NET (VB.NET) version of the component is used.

TESTING SERVER APPLICATIONS

When testing a library component, the assembly was unloaded when the client process ended. However, a server component runs in a separate process that continues to run after the client process has ended. This is by design and is the most significant difference between the two types of COM+ applications.

This may cause confusing results during initial development and testing of a component. It's very common to make changes to your code, build the assembly, and then wonder why the test results are the same as the last test. This usually occurs when the server application is still running from a prior test. The old version of our assembly was already loaded and running, and is still being used by clients.

To remedy this, make sure you shut down any COM+ server applications prior to testing any source changes. This will ensure that the latest version of the assembly is loaded for each test. Of course, prior to shutting down the COM+ applications, make sure clients are not using the application.

You can also set the shutdown options for the application so that it shuts down more quickly. The default setting is to leave the application running for three minutes after its last use.

Related Information

See recipes 8-1 (Exposing Managed Code to COM+) and 8-8 (Using Role-Based Security).

8-3. Installing a Serviced Component

Problem

The regsvcs utility is used to register and install an assembly of serviced components with COM+. What command-line options are provided to control the way an assembly is installed?

Solution

The regsvcs command-line utility provides a number of options that you can use during the registration and installation of your assemblies. This utility ships with the .NET Framework and is therefore available on all machines that run .NET, not only those used for development. When executed, this utility performs these tasks:

- Creates the COM+ application if it doesn't already exist

- Adds the assembly to the application, applying any attributes specified within the assembly

- Adds all components in the assembly to the COM+ application

- Generates and registers a typelib for the assembly

The basic format of the command is this:

```
regsvcs <assemblyname>
```

When no other parameters are provided, the assembly will be registered according to any attributes that were built into the assembly. If a particular attribute was not provided, default values are used. For instance, consider this command line:

```
regsvcs MyAssembly.dll
```

If the MyAssembly project includes the ApplicationName assembly attribute, then the name specified for this attribute is used as the COM+ application name. If this attribute is omitted, then the default behavior is to use the assembly name as the COM+ application name. In this case, the assembly is added to an application named MyAssembly.

You can use the optional /appname parameter to override the default application name, for example:

```
regsvcs /appname:MyServerApplication MyAssembly.dll
```

Using this command line, the assembly is added to an application named MyServerApplication.

However, the /appname parameter cannot override an application name that is specified within an assembly using the ApplicationName attribute. If you include this attribute in your code, the application name is fixed and cannot be changed externally. If you do try to override the name using /appname, the parameter is ignored and the name specified in the attribute is used instead.

One of the other tasks performed by regsvcs is the generation and registration of a typelib. By default, a typelib file is generated and registered using the assembly name. For example, this command generates a typelib file named MyAssembly.tlb:

```
regsvcs MyAssembly.dll
```

You can optionally specify a different name for the typelib like this:

```
regsvcs /tlb:MyTypeLib.tlb MyAssembly.dll
```

You can also suppress generation of a new typelib and instead instruct regsvcs to use an existing typelib. You do this with the /extlb parameter:

```
regsvcs /extlb /tlb:MyTypeLib.tlb MyAssembly.dll
```

An error will occur if the typelib that you specify with the /tlb parameter cannot be read.

You can execute regsvcs for the same assembly more than once. You may even want to add it to a postbuild step for your Visual Studio project. As long as the assembly is added to the same COM+ application, you won't have a problem doing this.

If you change the name of the application used for an assembly, you need to uninstall the assembly from the current application first. An assembly cannot be added to an application if it is currently installed in another application.

To uninstall an assembly, you use the /u parameter like this:

```
regsvcs /u MyAssembly.dll
```

To uninstall an assembly, you must provide the assembly name and the application name. This command uses the rules discussed previously to determine the application name. If the application name was specified within the assembly using the ApplicationName attribute, the assembly is removed from that application. Otherwise, the default name based on the assembly name is used.

If you manually specified an application name using the /appname parameter, you need to supply the same name to uninstall the assembly:

```
regsvcs /u /appname:MyServerApplication MyAssembly.dll
```

When an assembly is uninstalled from an application, the application itself is removed if it doesn't contain any other components.

How It Works

The default behavior of regsvcs is to reconfigure an existing COM+ application. For example, you may install an assembly into an application and specify that the activation type is Server. If you then install a second assembly into the same application, the attributes of that assembly may cause the application to be reconfigured. If the second assembly uses an activation type of Library, the COM+ application is now reconfigured as a library application. This is probably not your intent! The last assembly installed wins.

To suppress this behavior, you can add the /noreconfig parameter. When this parameter is included, regsvcs will not reconfigure an existing application, for example:

```
regsvcs /noreconfig MyAssembly.dll
```

Now the first assembly that is installed into an application wins. If the application doesn't already exist, it will be created using the parameters from the first assembly installed into it.

If all of your assemblies use a consistent set of attribute values, this isn't a problem. Otherwise, you need to tightly control the order in which assemblies are installed into their respective applications.

Another solution is to prevent regsvcs from creating any new applications. When the /exapp parameter is used, regsvcs will assume that the application already exists. If it doesn't exist, an error will be produced and the installation will fail for that assembly. If the application does exist, the assembly is installed.

When using the /exapp parameter, you would need to manually create a COM+ application using the Component Services Management Console plug-in prior to installing any components. Using the Management Console plug-in, you are able to set all parameters associated with the COM+ application. Once you set the parameters, you know that the process of installing assemblies into the application won't change your settings.

The /exapp parameter would typically be used along with /noreconfig like this:

```
regsvcs /exapp /noreconfig MyAssembly.dll
```

This will install the assembly into an existing application only. As the assembly is installed, it will not be reconfigured based on the attributes of the assembly.

Related Information

See recipes 8-1 (Exposing Managed Code to COM+), 8-2 (Implementing a Server Application), and 8-4 (Registering Components Dynamically).

8-4. Registering Components Dynamically

Problem

Do you always have to add your serviced components to the GAC and register them using regsvcs? Is there a way to register and install these components without these manual steps?

Solution

As an alternative to manually installing a serviced component using regsvcs, .NET also supports *dynamic registration*. This technique allows you to deploy private assemblies into a directory and use them from managed code without any prior registration.

To use dynamic registration of a serviced component, you deploy the assembly to a directory along with any managed client code that references it. In order to find and load the assembly, the client must be located in the same directory. So far, this is the same way all private assemblies are used.

However, if a class is derived from the ServicedComponent base class, it is registered as a COM+ component the first time it is referenced. The attributes that have been applied to the assembly and the class determine the values to use during registration. If a particular attribute has not been applied within our code, default values are used.

The dynamic registration process executes these tasks:

- Creates a COM+ application if it doesn't already exist

- Reconfigures the COM+ application parameters if necessary

- Generates and registers a typelib file for the component

- Adds all ServicedComponent classes to the application

This registration occurs only the first time a component class is referenced. On subsequent calls, the COM+ application will exist and the component is already installed. If the assembly contains multiple ServicedComponent classes, they are all registered at the same time. The dynamic registration is not limited to the class being used.

For example, consider this managed class and interface that was first introduced in recipe 8-1 (Exposing Managed Code to COM+):

```
using System;
using System.Runtime.InteropServices;
using System.EnterpriseServices;
```

```
namespace DniScSimpleComponent
{
    public interface IAddNumbers
    {
        int AddSomeNumbers(int numA, int numB);
    }

    [ClassInterface(ClassInterfaceType.None)]
    public class DniScSimpleComponentObj
        : ServicedComponent, IAddNumbers
    {
        public int AddSomeNumbers(int numA, int numB)
        {
            return numA + numB;
        }
    }
}
```

In recipe 8-1, we manually added this assembly to the GAC and used regsvcs to register it with COM+. Using dynamic registration, we can simply copy this assembly (DniScSimpleComponent.dll) to a directory along with the assembly containing any client code.

The first time this class is referenced, the following actions take place automatically:

- A new COM+ application named DniScSimpleComponent is created if it doesn't already exist. This is the default name that is used since we didn't explicitly specify an application name in code using the ApplicationName attribute. The application will default to an activation type of Library since we didn't specify the ApplicationActivation attribute.

- A typelib file named DniScSimpleComponent.tlb is generated in the same directory as the assembly and registered.

- The component DniScSimpleComponentObj is installed into the new COM+ application.

There are no changes needed to the managed code to allow dynamic registration. However, since the assembly is not in the GAC, the client assembly must be in the same private directory.

As is always the case when working with COM or COM+, we must expose one or more types to COM in order for all of this to work. We can do this by setting the "Make assembly COM-visible" option for the entire project or by exposing individual types to COM using the ComVisible(true) attribute. Using dynamic registration does not change how we actually expose types to COM+. It also doesn't remove the requirement to apply a strong name to the assembly.

Consider this example code from recipe 8-2 (Implementing a Server Application):

```
using System;
using System.Runtime.InteropServices;
using System.EnterpriseServices;

[assembly: ApplicationActivation(ActivationOption.Server)]
[assembly: ApplicationAccessControl(false)]
[assembly: ApplicationName("DniServerApplication")]
[assembly: Description(".NET Interop Server Application")]
```

```
namespace DniScServerComponent
{
    [Description("Interface used to add numbers")]
    public interface IAddNumbers
    {
        int AddSomeNumbers(int numA, int numB);
    }

    [ClassInterface(ClassInterfaceType.None)]
    [Description("Add numbers server component")]
    public class DniScServerComponentObj
        : ServicedComponent, IAddNumbers
    {
        public int AddSomeNumbers(int numA, int numB)
        {
            return numA + numB;
        }
    }
}
```

This code provides additional information (in the form of attributes) that is used during dynamic registration. The first time this class is used, these actions take place:

- A COM+ application named DniServerApplication is created if it doesn't already exist. This is the name specified in the ApplicationName attribute. Since the ApplicationActivation attribute specifies an activation type of ActivationOption.Server, this is configured as a server application. Because of the ApplicationAccessControl attribute, access control security is turned off for the application.

- A typelib file named DniScServerComponent.tlb is generated in the same directory as the assembly and registered.

- The DniScServerComponentObj class is installed into the application.

If you plan on using dynamic registration, you should use the assembly- and class-level attributes to control the registration process.

How It Works

When you are using dynamic registration, you are using a private assembly. This means you don't need to place it in the GAC. Doing that would defeat the whole purpose of a private assembly. However, even though it does not go into the GAC, it does need to have a strong name. This means you need to generate an .snk file containing a strong-name key pair and assign it to the assembly.

Dynamically registered components can be used by managed and COM clients, but the initial call to the component must be made from a managed client. Only a managed client can trigger the dynamic-registration process. If a COM client is the first to use a component, it will receive an error that the component isn't registered.

If you use the component from a managed client, the dynamic registration will take place, and then COM clients will be able to use the component. This behavior makes dynamic registration more suitable for use by managed clients. If most of the clients will be unmanaged (COM), it is better to manually register the component instead of using dynamic registration.

When should you use dynamic registration? It's best used for ASP.NET, Web Form, and web services applications. These applications typically make use of private assemblies that are all located within a private folder. The folder is exposed via IIS, allowing client access to the application. In some cases, multiple versions of the same application are supported at the same time via different URLs. Placing all of the assemblies into the GAC would only complicate the deployment of an application like this. In this case, dynamic registration makes more sense.

One of the tasks performed during dynamic registration is the generation of a typelib file (.tlb). When this file is generated, it is also registered as the typelib for the component. It will be generated in the same directory as the assembly. You shouldn't delete or otherwise move the generated file.

If the application has an activation type of Server, the component will fail to load if the typelib file has been deleted or moved. Remember that you're dealing with a private assembly. You wouldn't move or delete the assembly itself once it is registered. You also shouldn't move or delete the generated typelib since it is now referenced by COM+.

Caution During dynamic registration, it is possible to reconfigure an existing COM+ application. For instance, if the first assembly registered for an application used an activation type of Library, a library application will be created. However, if another assembly that uses server activation is dynamically registered into the same application, the activation type of the application will change to Server. This is not likely what you intended.

To avoid this, you can use manual registration, which provides greater control over the registration process. Or you must coordinate all of the assembly attributes that affect registration. Make sure that all assemblies that will be installed into the same application use the same set of attribute values.

Related Information

See recipes 8-3 (Installing a Serviced Component), 8-1 (Exposing Managed Code to COM+), and 8-2 (Implementing a Server Application).

8-5. Activating Components Just-in-Time

Problem

COM+ supports just-in-time (JIT) activation to improve the use of resources on the server. Is this option supported from managed code? How do you implement a .NET component that uses JIT activation?

Solution

JIT activation is fully supported from managed code. The purpose of this type of activation is to allow server resources to be used more efficiently.

Normally, when a client application holds a reference to a server object, the object is active for the entire time that the reference is alive. If a client creates an instance of an object, uses a method or two, but continues to hold the object reference, this ties up precious server resources (memory).

JIT activation is capable of deactivating the server object between method calls. The client still holds a reference to a server object, but that original object is no longer active on the server. When the client calls a method on the object reference, a server object is reactivated just in time. All of this is done transparently to the client, who holds on to the original object reference.

To use JIT activation, you need to perform these tasks:

1. Add the JustInTimeActivation attribute to the managed class.

2. Design the methods of the class to be completely stateless, so they do not rely on any internal state that is preserved between method calls.

3. Upon completion of a method, indicate that the object can be deactivated.

The JustInTimeActivation attribute is applied to a C# class like this:

```
[JustInTimeActivation]
public class MyJITClass : ServicedComponent
{
}
```

Once this attribute is applied, JIT activation will be enabled when the component is installed into a COM+ application.

Note You can view the JIT activation setting for a component using the Component Services Management Console plug-in. After selecting a COM+ application, you can drill down into the list of components installed in the application. Each component has its own set of property pages. The JIT activation setting can be found on the activation page for a component.

Since a JIT object can be reactivated with each method call, you must design the methods to be completely stateless. You cannot rely upon any internal object state that was set by prior methods or properties. Each method is a stand-alone, stateless execution that must use only the parameters that are passed to it. Alternatively, a method is free to retrieve any state that has been persisted somewhere else, perhaps from a database.

This means you must make a conscious effort to design JIT components. Adding the JustInTimeActivation attribute to a class is just a small part of the effort. You really need to make the decision to use JIT activation early in the design and then implement the class using only stateless methods. You can't simply add the JustInTimeActivation late in development and hope that things work correctly.

A final requirement of a JIT method is to signal that the object can be deactivated. COM+ will deactivate an object based on the done property of its object context. By default, this is set to indicate that the object is *not done*. Therefore, unless you set this property, the object will continue to live and the JIT activation is not actually used.

■**Note** Don't look for the done property on a .NET class. It's actually a property of the COM+ context that provides the runtime environment for a COM+ component. In the Microsoft documentation, it is referred to as the *done property* or sometimes the *done bit*. .NET sets this property for you based on attributes such as AutoComplete.

.NET makes it simple to set the done state of an object. The easiest way to do this is by applying the AutoComplete attribute to a method like this:

```
[AutoComplete]
public void MyMethod()
{
}
```

When the method completes, the done property of the object context is set. Combining this with the JustInTimeActivation attribute for the class allows the object to be immediately deactivated when the method completes. The next time a client calls a method using the same object reference, a new object instance is activated.

■**Note** AutoComplete is also used when working with COM+ transactions. The topic of transactions is covered in Chapter 9.

How It Works

The following C# code illustrates the use of JIT activation. We start by defining a public API that clients can use with this interface:

```
public interface IJITMethods
{
    //stateful methods
    void AddNumber(int number);
    int GetTotal();

    //stateless methods
    int AddSomeNumbers(int numA, int numB);
}
```

Two sets of methods are defined. The AddNumber and GetTotal methods are designed to be stateful. Calling AddNumber will add a number to a running total. Calling GetTotal retrieves that total. On the other hand, the AddSomeNumbers method is designed to be stateless. It uses only the parameters passed to it and doesn't use or alter any member variables of the class.

Note As you will see later in this example, methods that use JIT activation do not work correctly if they maintain state between calls. A stateful method is used in this example only to demonstrate this; it is not meant as the recommended way to implement this method.

Next, we develop two classes that implement this interface. One does not use JIT activation, and the other does. The goal of this example is to see the difference that JIT activation makes on the state of an object between method calls.

Here is the non-JIT class implementation:

```
[ClassInterface(ClassInterfaceType.None)]
public class DniScNotJITObj
    : ServicedComponent, IJITMethods
{
    private int m_Number;

    public void AddNumber(int number)
    {
        m_Number += number;
    }

    public int GetTotal()
    {
        return m_Number;
    }

    public int AddSomeNumbers(int numA, int numB)
    {
        return numA + numB;
    }
}
```

and here is the JIT version:

```
[ClassInterface(ClassInterfaceType.None)]
[JustInTimeActivation]
public class DniScJITObj
    : ServicedComponent, IJITMethods
{
    private int m_Number;

    [AutoComplete]
    public void AddNumber(int number)
    {
        m_Number += number;
    }
```

```
[AutoComplete]
public int GetTotal()
{
    return m_Number;
}


[AutoComplete]
public int AddSomeNumbers(int numA, int numB)
{
    return numA + numB;
}
}
```

The only difference (other than class name) is the addition of the JustInTimeActivation and AutoComplete attributes as discussed earlier. Without the AutoComplete attribute, the object would not be considered done when the method returns. If it isn't done, then it won't be deactivated and the benefits of JIT activation won't be seen.

Note As an alternative to the AutoComplete attribute, the ContextUtil.DeactivateOnReturn property could have been set to true. For example, the AddNumber method could have been implemented like this with the same effect:

```
public void AddNumber(int number)
{
    m_Number += number;
    ContextUtil.DeactivateOnReturn = true;
}
```

If you manually set the DeactivateOnReturn property rather than using the AutoComplete attribute, you do need to worry about exception conditions. Using AutoComplete, the method will be deactivated even if an exception is thrown. If you are setting DeactivateOnReturn yourself, you'll need to use a try/catch/finally block of code to make sure the property is always set.

The assembly also contains these attributes:

```
uses System.EnterpriseServices;

[assembly: ApplicationActivation(ActivationOption.Server)]
[assembly: ApplicationAccessControl(false)]
[assembly: ApplicationName("DniServerApplication")]
[assembly: Description(".NET Interop Server Application")]
```

The ApplicationActivation attribute is included to set the activation type to Server. Since library components are activated within the caller's process, JIT activation only makes sense when used with Server activation.

Clearly, the AddNumber and GetTotal methods are not stateless. They rely upon the state of a member variable (m_Number). We should be able to observe a difference in the results between the JIT and non-JIT classes.

To see the difference that JIT activation makes, we use both of these classes with this client code:

```
class Program
{
    static void Main(string[] args)
    {
        IJITMethods obj    = new DniScNotJITObj();
        ExecuteMethods(obj, "Non-JIT component");

        obj    = new DniScJITObj();
        ExecuteMethods(obj, "JIT component");

        Console.Read();
    }

    static void ExecuteMethods(IJITMethods obj, string desc)
    {
        //add numbers the stateful way
        obj.AddNumber(1);
        obj.AddNumber(2);
        int result = obj.GetTotal();
        Console.WriteLine(
            "GetTotal result from {0}: {1}",
            desc, result);

        //add numbers statelessly
        result = obj.AddSomeNumbers(1, 2);
        Console.WriteLine(
            "AddSomeNumbers result from {0}: {1}",
            desc, result);
    }
}
```

The code tests each class in exactly the same way. The stateful methods are executed first, followed by the stateless method. When the code is executed, we see these results:

```
GetTotal result from Non-JIT component: 3
AddSomeNumbers result from Non-JIT component: 3
GetTotal result from JIT component: 0
AddSomeNumbers result from JIT component: 3
```

The results are exactly what we expected to see. Both the stateful and stateless methods of the non-JIT class work fine. The stateful methods of the JIT class do not work correctly. This is because JIT activation creates a new object instance for each method call. Any state that was modified between method calls is lost.

The Visual Basic .NET (VB.NET) implementation of these components follows. Here is the VB.NET version of the public interface:

```
Public Interface IJITMethods
    'stateful methods
    Sub AddNumber(ByVal number As Integer)
    Function GetTotal() As Integer

    'stateless metehods
    Function AddSomeNumbers(ByVal numA As Integer, _
        ByVal numB As Integer) As Integer
End Interface
```

Here is the version of the class that uses JIT activation:

```
Imports System.Runtime.InteropServices
Imports System.EnterpriseServices

<ClassInterface(ClassInterfaceType.None)> _
<JustInTimeActivation()> _
Public Class DniScJITObj
    Inherits ServicedComponent
    Implements IJITMethods

    Private m_Number As Integer

    <AutoComplete()> _
    Public Sub AddNumber(ByVal number As Integer) _
        Implements IJITMethods.AddNumber

        m_Number += number

    End Sub

    <AutoComplete()> _
    Public Function GetTotal() As Integer _
        Implements IJITMethods.GetTotal

        Return m_Number

    End Function

    <AutoComplete()> _
    Public Function AddSomeNumbers(ByVal numA As Integer, _
        ByVal numB As Integer) As Integer _
        Implements IJITMethods.AddSomeNumbers

        Return numA + numB

    End Function

End Class
```

Here is the version that does not use JIT activation:

```vb
Imports System.Runtime.InteropServices
Imports System.EnterpriseServices

<ClassInterface(ClassInterfaceType.None)> _
Public Class DniScNotJITObj
    Inherits ServicedComponent
    Implements IJITMethods

    Private m_Number As Integer

    Public Sub AddNumber(ByVal number As Integer) _
        Implements IJITMethods.AddNumber

        m_Number += number

    End Sub

    Public Function GetTotal() As Integer _
        Implements IJITMethods.GetTotal

        Return m_Number

    End Function

    Public Function AddSomeNumbers(ByVal numA As Integer, _
        ByVal numB As Integer) As Integer _
        Implements IJITMethods.AddSomeNumbers

        Return numA + numB

    End Function

End Class
```

The standard set of attributes must also be added to the AssemblyInfo.vb file:

```vb
Imports System.EnterpriseServices

<Assembly: ApplicationActivation(ActivationOption.Server)>
<Assembly: ApplicationAccessControl(False)>
<Assembly: ApplicationName("DniServerApplication")>
<Assembly: Description(".NET Interop Server Application")>
```

When the client code is run against these VB.NET components, we see the same results as the C# version.

JIT activation is not right for all components. But it is a tool that helps you to more efficiently use your server resources. This is most important in high-volume applications where a very large number of small atomic transactions are executed.

The real advantage of JIT activation is that it allows you to conserve resources on the server without drastically changing how you code the client. The client is allowed to create an instance of an object and hold on to that reference for as long as necessary. Without JIT activation, this would unnecessarily tie up server resources. But with JIT activation, the server resources are freed for you automatically.

JIT activation does not necessarily improve performance. On the contrary, there is actually a slight performance hit when the reactivation of an object occurs. But JIT activation does improve scalability by reducing resource usage on the server.

Related Information

See recipes 8-2 (Implementing a Server Application), 8-6 (Using Object Pooling), and 9-2 (Enabling Automatic Transactions).

8-6. Using Object Pooling

Problem

Does .NET provide support for COM+ object pooling? How do you write a managed class that can take advantage of object pooling?

Solution

Object pooling is a COM+ facility that maintains a pool of live objects that are available to serve client requests. As clients request an instance of one of these objects, it is retrieved from the pool and used. This can dramatically improve performance by eliminating the up-front costs of object creation and initialization for every method call.

The steps needed to take advantage of object pooling include the following:

1. Add the ObjectPooling attribute to the managed class.

2. Override the CanBePooled method of the base ServicedComponent class to always return true.

3. Design the methods so that they do not hold any client-specific state.

The ObjectPooling attribute is added at the class level like this:

```
[ObjectPooling(10,50)]
public class MyOPClass : ServicedComponent
{
}
```

A number of overrides for the ObjectPooling constructor can be used, depending on your needs. The one shown here sets the minimum and maximum number of pooled objects to 10 and 50, respectively. This means that when the COM+ application first starts, 10 copies of this object will be immediately created and placed into the pool. The number 50 specifies the maximum number of class instances that are allowed to exist at any one time.

As is always the case for a serviced component, your class must derive from ServicedComponent. This base class contains a protected method named CanBePooled that you must override if you want the class to use object pooling. This method is called by the .NET runtime to determine if it should place the object back into the pool.

To enable object pooling for a class, just override this method to return true:

```
protected override bool CanBePooled()
{
    //override the base method in order to allow
    //pooling of this object
    return true;
}
```

In this example, we always return true, indicating that all objects can be placed back into the pool. You may have a situation where some objects can be placed back into the pool and others cannot. In this case, you can make that determination here in the CanBePooled method, returning true for only those objects that you wish to place back into the pool.

The final requirement to use object pooling affects your class design. You must avoid maintaining any *client-specific* state within the object. This is slightly different from designing a class that is completely stateless. In fact, to really take advantage of object pooling, you want to use it with classes that are costly to construct and initialize. Typically, that occurs with classes that maintain some state.

For instance, a class might open a database connection, read and cache some frequently used data, read and parse configuration files, open sockets, create log files, and so on. All of these activities are good candidates for object pooling, since they can be performed during construction of the object and they are not client specific. As multiple clients use the objects in the pool over and over again, this type of state doesn't change.

As long as you don't maintain state that belongs to a single client, the pooled objects are usable by any client.

How It Works

When will you get the most benefit from object pooling? Consider using object pooling for classes that

- Are expensive to create and initialize

- Are used frequently by clients

- Have methods that execute quickly compared to the time needed to construct the object

- Hold and maintain limited resources such as database or socket connections

- Are initialized and configured using files

On the other hand, object pooling isn't an appropriate tool for classes that

- Are infrequently used

- Have no significant construction and initialization costs

- Have methods that take longer to execute than the time needed for object construction

If used properly and for the right kinds of classes, object pooling can have a positive impact on the performance and scalability of an application. To demonstrate this, the example that follows implements and uses a class that supports object pooling.

We start with the C# definition of the public interface that is exposed to clients:

```
public interface IObjectPoolingMethods
{
    int LookupKeyCode(string key);
}
```

The LookupKeyCode accepts a string key and returns an integer associated with the key. The premise of this test is that this key lookup method is used frequently by a number of clients. We want it to execute as quickly as possible.

The class that implements this interface looks like this in C#:

```
[ObjectPooling(30,100)]
[JustInTimeActivation]
[EventTrackingEnabled]
[ClassInterface(ClassInterfaceType.None)]
public class DniScObjectPoolingObj
    : ServicedComponent, IObjectPoolingMethods
{
    private Hashtable m_KeyCodes;

    public DniScObjectPoolingObj()
    {
        //simulate the cost of object construction.
        //this might represent the time needed to
        //retrieve and locally cache selected
        //values from a database or other source.
        System.Threading.Thread.Sleep(100);

        //build an in-memory cache of frequently
        //used data. In a live application, this
        //might be populated from a database query.
        m_KeyCodes = new Hashtable();
        m_KeyCodes.Add("AAA", 11111);
        m_KeyCodes.Add("BBB", 22222);
        m_KeyCodes.Add("CCC", 33333);
        m_KeyCodes.Add("DDD", 44444);
        m_KeyCodes.Add("EEE", 55555);
    }

    [AutoComplete]
    public int LookupKeyCode(string key)
    {
        int result = 0;
        if (m_KeyCodes.Contains(key))
        {
```

```
                    result = (int)m_KeyCodes[key];
                }
                else
                {
                    //not in the local cache, so we need to
                    //retrieve it from the database
                }
                return result;
            }


            protected override bool CanBePooled()
            {
                //override the base method in order to allow
                //pooling of this object
                return true;
            }
        }
    }
```

The ObjectPooling(30,100) attribute indicates that we want object pooling for this class. The minimum number of objects is set to 30 and the maximum is 100. Although it is not required, we also include the JustInTimeActivation attribute to use just-in-time (JIT) activation.

JIT activation enhances object pooling since it delays the actual activation of an object until a method is called. Without JIT activation, a round-trip between client and server takes place when the client code creates an instance of the object. This occurs before the first method is even called. With JIT activation, a round-trip isn't made until a method is actually called. This eliminates the round-trip between the client and server each time the client code constructs an object. It also reduces the time each pooled object is in use. With JIT activation, the object can be immediately deactivated at the completion of a method.

■**Note** We also add the EventTrackingEnabled attribute to the class. This attribute allows us to see real-time statistics for the component using the Component Services Management Console plug-in. To see the statistics, select the Components folder under the COM+ application and change to the Status view.

This attribute is completely optional, but it is helpful when using object pooling. It allows us to easily monitor the number of active objects, the number remaining in the pool, and so on. Without this attribute, none of these totals will be available.

We'll see the most dramatic performance improvement with object pooling if our class is fairly expensive to construct. To simulate this, our class constructor builds a Hashtable containing a set of string keys and their associated code numbers. We've also added a short delay to make the construction costs more realistic.

In a real application, you might load this data from a database, a configuration file, or an embedded string resource. You might need to make a call to an external system using a socket connection or even access a web service. The key point is that the construction of the object takes time and is the expense that you want to avoid with each method call.

The LookupKeyCode method is fairly simple. It uses the passed-in string as a lookup key to the Hashtable. If an entry is found, the integer from the Hashtable is returned. The AutoComplete attribute has been placed on this method. This allows JIT activation to deactivate the object as soon as the method completes. It also sets the done property of the COM+ object context. COM+ will deactivate an object only when the done property is set to true. Doing this allows the object to be placed back into the pool.

As discussed previously, we override the base CanBePooled method and always return true. Without this small bit of code, our objects will never be placed back into the pool.

The assembly also contains attributes that control how it is installed and registered into a COM+ server application:

```
[assembly: ApplicationActivation(ActivationOption.Server)]
[assembly: ApplicationAccessControl(false)]
[assembly: ApplicationName("DniServerApplication")]
[assembly: Description(".NET Interop Server Application")]
```

We want to simulate using this class from multiple clients. To do this, we implement a set of test classes that use multiple threads. Each thread repeatedly creates an object instance and calls the LookupKeyCode method.

We start with the implementation of a test wrapper:

```
using System;
using System.Threading;
using DniScObjectPooling;
using System.Diagnostics;

public class ObjectPoolingTest
{
    private Thread thread;

    public ObjectPoolingTest()
    {
        thread = new Thread(new ThreadStart(ThreadProc));
    }

    public void Test()
    {
        thread.Start();
    }

    public static void ThreadProc()
    {
        Stopwatch sw = new Stopwatch();
        sw.Start();
        for (int i = 0; i < 100; i++)
        {
            IObjectPoolingMethods obj
                = new DniScObjectPooling.DniScObjectPoolingObj();
            int keyCode = obj.LookupKeyCode("BBB");
        }
        sw.Stop();
```

```
        Console.WriteLine(
            "Elapsed time for thread: {0}ms",
            sw.ElapsedMilliseconds);
    }
}
```

This wrapper represents one execution thread (a client). Once we start the thread, the ThreadProc loops 100 times, creating an object instance and calling the LookupKeyCode each time through the loop. After the loop completes, we display the elapsed time for the test.

The code to use this test wrapper looks like this:

```
static void Main(string[] args)
{
    const int NumberOfThreads = 10;

    //create multiple test objects, each with
    //its own thread that calls the test method
    ObjectPoolingTest[] testObjs
        = new ObjectPoolingTest[NumberOfThreads];
    for (int i = 0; i < NumberOfThreads; i++)
    {
        testObjs[i] = new ObjectPoolingTest();
    }

    //start all tests
    for (int i = 0; i < NumberOfThreads; i++)
    {
        testObjs[i].Test();
    }

    Console.Read();
}
```

After creating 10 instances of the ObjectPoolingTest wrapper, we start all execution threads. At this point, we have 10 virtual clients running, each one repeatedly creating an object and calling the test method 100 times.

When the code is executed, we see these results:

```
Elapsed time for thread: 2248ms
Elapsed time for thread: 2284ms
Elapsed time for thread: 2290ms
Elapsed time for thread: 2357ms
Elapsed time for thread: 2343ms
Elapsed time for thread: 2388ms
Elapsed time for thread: 2390ms
Elapsed time for thread: 2366ms
Elapsed time for thread: 2373ms
Elapsed time for thread: 2400ms
```

This shows that the elapsed time for all of the threads to finish is about 2.4 seconds. Obviously, your elapsed time may be different due to your machine specifications.

To see the difference that object pooling makes, we can make a small change to our code and run the test again. Simply comment out (or remove) the ObjectPooling attribute like this:

```
// [ObjectPooling(30,100)]
```

Before running the test again, we need to rebuild the DniScObjectPooling project. We also need to make sure we shut down the COM+ application named DniServerApplication, which we can do using the Component Services Management Console plug-in.

Now when we run the test again *without* object pooling, we see these results:

```
Elapsed time for thread: 10360ms
Elapsed time for thread: 10402ms
Elapsed time for thread: 10384ms
Elapsed time for thread: 10424ms
Elapsed time for thread: 10433ms
Elapsed time for thread: 10450ms
Elapsed time for thread: 10498ms
Elapsed time for thread: 10517ms
Elapsed time for thread: 10539ms
Elapsed time for thread: 10558ms
```

Now we're looking at over 10 seconds elapsed time for all threads. That's significantly slower than the test using object pooling. In this manufactured example, object pooling does improve overall performance.

What follows is the implementation of the same object-pooling component in Visual Basic .NET (VB.NET). We start with the public interface:

```
Public Interface IObjectPoolingMethods
    Function LookupKeyCode(ByVal key As String) _
        As Integer
End Interface
```

Here is the class that implements this interface:

```
Imports System.Collections
Imports System.Runtime.InteropServices
Imports System.EnterpriseServices


<ObjectPooling(30, 100)> _
<JustInTimeActivation()> _
<EventTrackingEnabled()> _
<ClassInterface(ClassInterfaceType.None)> _
Public Class DniScObjectPoolingObj
    Inherits ServicedComponent
    Implements IObjectPoolingMethods


    Private m_KeyCodes As Hashtable
```

```vb
    Public Sub New()
        'simulate the cost of object construction.
        'this might represent the time needed to
        'retrieve and locally cache selected
        'values from a database or other source.
        System.Threading.Thread.Sleep(100)

        'build an in-memory cache of frequently
        'used data. In a live application, this
        'might be populated from a database query.
        m_KeyCodes = New Hashtable()
        m_KeyCodes.Add("AAA", 11111)
        m_KeyCodes.Add("BBB", 22222)
        m_KeyCodes.Add("CCC", 33333)
        m_KeyCodes.Add("DDD", 44444)
        m_KeyCodes.Add("EEE", 55555)
    End Sub


    <AutoComplete()> _
    Public Function LookupKeyCode(ByVal key As String) _
        As Integer _
        Implements IObjectPoolingMethods.LookupKeyCode

        Dim result As Integer = 0
        If m_KeyCodes.Contains(key) Then
            result = m_KeyCodes.Item(key)
        Else
            'not in the local cache, so we need to
            'retrieve it from the database
        End If
    End Function

    Protected Overrides Function CanBePooled() As Boolean
        'override the base method in order to allow
        'pooling of this object
        Return True
    End Function
End Class
```

The usual set of assembly-level attributes are added to the AssemblyInfo.vb file:

```vb
Imports System.EnterpriseServices

<Assembly: ApplicationActivation(ActivationOption.Server)>
<Assembly: ApplicationAccessControl(False)>
<Assembly: ApplicationName("DniServerApplication")>
<Assembly: Description(".NET Interop Server Application")>
```

The test results using the VB.NET component look exactly like those using the one written in C#.

■**Caution** When setting the minimum and maximum numbers on the ObjectPooling attribute, be aware that the maximum is a fixed size. If the pool reaches the maximum number of objects, additional requests for an object will wait until a pooled object becomes available.

The amount of time the client will wait is configurable and can be set using one of the overloaded constructors of the ObjectPooling attribute. If the wait time has expired and an object is still not available, the client will receive an exception.

The best way to fine-tune the size of the object pool is to monitor actual usage.

Related Information

See recipes 8-2 (Implementing a Server Application) and 8-5 (Activating Components Just-in-Time).

8-7. Implementing Private Components

Problem

You've implemented a managed component that should be used only by other components in the same COM+ application. You'd like to prevent it from being used directly by clients. Is there a way to do this?

Solution

By default, COM+ components are available to all clients, including managed and COM clients. However, one way to restrict access to a component is to mark it as private. This is done with the PrivateComponent attribute, for example:

```
[PrivateComponent]
public class MyPrivateClass : ServicedComponent
{
}
```

This is a class-level attribute that must be applied to each class that you wish to make private. Once the attribute is applied, the class is accessible only from other components in the same COM+ application. If an attempt is made to access the class from outside of the current application, an exception will be thrown.

Note Private components are a COM+ feature supported only in Windows XP and above (e.g., Windows Server 2003). It is not supported in Windows 2000. If you use this attribute, you will be limiting the versions of the operating system that your application supports.

You might want to use this attribute for classes that are designed to be internal helpers for other classes. Perhaps you have a set of classes that manage your database connectivity. You might want to restrict their use in this way, only allowing their use by other components that you've designed to safely use those classes.

Obviously, it is important to plan your COM+ applications carefully when using this attribute. If you install the private component into the wrong assembly, you will limit its usefulness.

How It Works

The example that follows demonstrates use of a private component. This C# code defines a public interface and a class that implements it:

```
public interface IAccountServices
{
    int FindAccount(string searchArg);
    void ChangeActiveStatus(int acctId, bool activeFlag);
}


[ClassInterface(ClassInterfaceType.None)]
[PrivateComponent]
public class DniScPrivateObj
    : ServicedComponent, IAccountServices
{
    public int FindAccount(string searchArg)
    {
        //return the account ID based on search arguments
        return 2001;
    }

    public void ChangeActiveStatus(int acctId, bool activeFlag)
    {
        //nothing implemented
    }
}
```

Note the use of the PrivateComponent attribute. We should not be able to access this class from outside of the COM+ application. The name and type of application is determined by these assembly-level attributes that we've added to the project:

```
[assembly: ApplicationActivation(ActivationOption.Server)]
[assembly: ApplicationAccessControl(false)]
[assembly: ApplicationName("DniServerApplication")]
[assembly: Description(".NET Interop Server Application")]
```

Here is our first attempt at using this class from a client application:

```
using System;
using DniScPrivateComponent;

static void Main(string[] args)
{
    //try the private object

    try
    {
        IAccountServices obj
            = new DniScPrivateObj();
        int acctId = obj.FindAccount("MyAccountName");
        Console.WriteLine(
            "FindAccount results: {0}", acctId);
    }
    catch (Exception e)
    {
        Console.WriteLine(
            "Exception accessing DniScPrivateObj: {0}",
            e.Message);
    }

    Console.Read();
}
```

When we run this test it should fail, since the component is marked private to all code outside of the application. Here are the results we receive:

```
Exception accessing DniScPrivateObj:
    Access is denied because the component is private.
    (Exception from HRESULT: 0x80110821)
```

Now let's try to use this component from another class in the same application. Here is a C# interface and class that does just that:

```
public interface IPublicAccountServices
{
    int UpdateAccountStatus(string searchArg);
}


[ClassInterface(ClassInterfaceType.None)]
public class DniScPublicObj
    : ServicedComponent, IPublicAccountServices
{
    public int UpdateAccountStatus(string searchArg)
    {
```

```
        int acctId = 0;
        DniScPrivateComponent.IAccountServices privateObj
            = new DniScPrivateComponent.DniScPrivateObj();

        acctId = privateObj.FindAccount(searchArg);
        if (acctId > 0)
        {
            privateObj.ChangeActiveStatus(acctId, false);
        }
        return acctId;
    }
}
```

We've designed this class to be the public API that clients can use. This is effectively a public wrapper for the private class, hiding the implementation details of how the private class is used. When the UpdateAccountStatus method is called, it creates an instance of the private class and uses it. Since both of these classes are installed into the same COM+ application, this call is allowed.

To test this, we can rewrite the client code to use this new class instead of the private one:

```
using System;
using DniScPrivateComponent;

static void Main(string[] args)
{
    //try the public object
    IPublicAccountServices publicObj
        = new DniScPublicObj();
    int updateAcctId
        = publicObj.UpdateAccountStatus("MyAccountName");
    Console.WriteLine(
        "UpdateAccountStatus results: {0}", updateAcctId);

    Console.Read();
}
```

This time when we execute the test code, we have a successful result:

```
UpdateAccountStatus results: 2001
```

Related Information

See recipes 8-2 (Implementing a Server Application), 8-3 (Installing a Serviced Component), and 8-8 (Using Role-Based Security).

8-8. Using Role-Based Security

Problem

Is it possible to use COM+ role-based security with managed components? How do you apply this type of security to your classes?

Solution

Components developed in .NET can use COM+ role-based security. Most of the work neces-sary to use COM+ security takes the form of adding attributes to your managed code. There are assembly-, class-, and method-level attributes that you apply to control how role-based security affects your components.

Note COM+ role-based security is the predecessor of the .NET role-based security. Although many of the concepts are the same, they are two distinct frameworks for managing security. In addition, .NET provides code access security, which is another entirely different approach.

If you are developing a new managed application and need security based on roles, go with the .NET system. It is the one based on objects that implement IPrincipal and IIdentity. If you need to integrate with an existing application that already uses COM+ role-based security, follow the guidelines outlined in this recipe.

COM+ role-based security uses a set of roles that you define for a COM+ application. The roles can represent any group you want, such as Manager, User, Administrator, SuperUser, Clerk, Cashier, and so on. Using the Component Services Management Console plug-in, you add system users or groups to each role. They can be either domain users and groups or local to the machine.

Within your code, you identify the role that a caller must have in order to execute the code. You can specify a role at the class (component) level or for each individual method. Multiple roles can be specified for each level if necessary.

At runtime, the caller's identity is used to determine the role(s) that they play. If they have the role required by the code, the call is allowed. Otherwise, an UnauthorizedAccessException is thrown.

The steps needed to implement this type of security include the following:

1. Enable access control at the assembly (application) level using the ApplicationAccessControl attribute.

2. Optionally specify one or more roles to add to the COM+ application using the SecurityRole attribute at the assembly level.

3. Enable access control at the class (component) level using the ComponentAccessControl attribute.

4. Add one or more roles to the class or to individual methods using the SecurityRole attribute.

5. Add the SecureMethod attribute to the class or to each method.

We'll use the following example C# code to demonstrate these steps.

We start by adding `ApplicationAccessControl` to our assembly. This attribute is used to enable or disable access control for the entire COM+ application. It has a number of optional parameters, but the most basic constructor that meets our needs looks like this:

```
[assembly: ApplicationAccessControl(true)]
```

This will enable access security for the application. As with all assembly-level attributes, it makes the most sense to place this in the `AssemblyInfo.cs` or `AssemblyInfo.vb` file of the project.

Next, we use the `SecurityRole` attribute to add roles to the application:

```
[assembly: SecurityRole("AppAdministrator")]
[assembly: SecurityRole("AppManager")]
[assembly: SecurityRole("AppUser", true)]
```

When entered at the assembly level as shown here, the role is simply added to the application. This does not imply that one of these roles is required for all of the components in the assembly. It simply sets up the roles within the application, allowing us to assign users or groups to each role. You can accomplish the same thing using the Component Services Management Console plug-in. Select the Roles folder under an application, right-click, and select New ➤ Role to enter a new role name.

Note Role names are not the same thing as system or domain group names. Roles exist only within the scope of a single COM+ application. When assigning users to a role, you can assign one of the system user groups or an individual user.

To avoid confusion, the example role names are prefixed with `App`. This makes it clear that `AppAdministrator` is not the same thing as the `Administrator` user, for example.

Note the alternate constructor used for the `AppUser` role:

```
[assembly: SecurityRole("AppUser", true)]
```

The second parameter (`true`) indicates that the role should be prepopulated with the Everyone system group. You would normally do this for roles that represent the lowest possible security level. This allows all users of the system to have access to classes or methods with the `AppUser` role.

Note The use of the `SecurityRole` attribute is completely optional at the assembly level. If you opt to omit it here, the application will be set up with the unique list of roles gathered from all classes and methods.

Why would you want to add roles at the assembly level? One reason might be if you are installing multiple assemblies into the same COM+ application. It's possible that some of the assemblies use only a subset of the available roles. As these assemblies are loaded, they will add only the roles that they actually use. If you add all roles at the assembly level, you will immediately have a complete list of roles. You can then begin the task of assigning users and groups to each role.

The remainder of the assembly-level attributes used for this project look like this:

```
[assembly: ApplicationActivation(ActivationOption.Server)]
[assembly: ApplicationName("DniRoleSecurityApplication")]
[assembly: Description(".NET Interop Server Application")]
```

Note Missing from the list of usual assembly-level attributes is ApplicationAccessControl(false). Most of the examples in this chapter include this attribute to disable security checks for the application. However, in this case, we do actually want the security checks. The default for a Server type application if we omit this attribute is to enable security checks.

Next we implement a managed interface and class. We add a number of attributes to the class itself to control security:

```
using System;
using System.EnterpriseServices;
using System.Runtime.InteropServices;

namespace DniScRoleSecurity
{
    public interface IRoleClassSecurity
    {
        int SecuredMethod(string paramA);
    }

    [ComponentAccessControl(true)]
    [SecureMethod]
    [SecurityRole("AppManager")]
    [ClassInterface(ClassInterfaceType.None)]
    public class DniScRoleClassSecurityObj
        : ServicedComponent, IRoleClassSecurity
    {
        public int SecuredMethod(string paramA)
        {
            return paramA.Length;
        }
    }
}
```

We add the ComponentAccessControl attribute to each class that uses COM+ access control. It is possible to enable the application for COM+ security, but have individual components that do not require security. That's why we have to explicitly enable security at both levels.

The SecurityRole attribute is added to the class. In this example, it indicates that the AppManager role is required to access this class. The SecureMethod attribute informs the .NET runtime that calls to this class must be made via our interface. If this attribute is omitted, there is a loophole that allows security to be bypassed. This is discussed further in an upcoming section.

The `IRoleClassSecurity` interface is the public interface that clients will use to access this class. It does not require any security-related attributes.

At this point we can build this project, add the assembly to the GAC, and use `regsvcs` to install the assembly into COM+. If we use the Component Services Management Console plug-in, we should now see that the `DniRoleSecurityApplication` application has been created. If we drill down into the properties of that application, we see that the "Enforce access checks for this application" option is enabled. This option can be found on the Security tab of the application properties.

When we expand the folders under this application, we see a Roles folder. Under it are separate folders for each of the roles that we defined (`AppAdministrator`, `AppManager`, and `AppUser`). Drilling down under each of these roles we find a Users folder. For the `AppAdministrator` and `AppManager` roles, the list of users is empty. For `AppUser`, we see that the Everyone group has been added.

Note A `Marshaler` role is automatically added to the application. This special Microsoft role is described in the "How It Works" section of this recipe.

We can now add individual users or groups to each of these roles. Adding a user to a role permits them to use components and methods that require that role. For instance, the class just shown requires the `AppManager` role.

To test this security, we can implement a C# client like this:

```
using System;
using DniScRoleSecurity;

namespace ScRoleSecurity
{
    class Program
    {
        static void Main(string[] args)
        {
            try
            {
                IRoleClassSecurity classObj
                    = new DniScRoleClassSecurityObj();
                CallClassSecurityObj(classObj);

            }
            catch (Exception e)
            {
                Console.WriteLine(
                    "Exception during creation: {0}",
                    e.Message);
            }
```

```
        Console.Read();
    }

    static void CallClassSecurityObj(IRoleClassSecurity obj)
    {
        try
        {
            int result = obj.SecuredMethod("abcdefg");
            Console.WriteLine(
                "Class security method result: {0}", result);
        }
        catch (Exception e)
        {
            Console.WriteLine(
                "Exception using secured class: {0}",
                e.Message);
        }
    }
}
}
```

Since the component we are using requires the AppManager role and that role has no users assigned to it, we should not be able to access the component. As expected, when we execute this test we see this System.UnauthorizedAccess exception:

```
Exception using secured class: Access is denied.
Exception from HRESULT: 0x80070005 (E_ACCESSDENIED))
```

To allow access, we can use the Component Services Management Console plug-in to add ourselves to the AppManager role. We can either explicitly add our own user, our group, Authenticated Users, Everyone—really any group defined on the Windows system that we want, as long as we are in the group that we add. We do this by selecting the Users folder under the AppManager role for the application. Once there, we can right-click and select New User.

Now when we rerun the test, we see this result:

```
Class security method result: 7
```

We've successfully implemented class-level role-based security.

How It Works

You can also apply the SecurityRole attribute to individual methods instead of to the entire class. This class demonstrates the use of method-level security and should be added to the same project as the previous class:

```
using System;
using System.EnterpriseServices;
using System.Runtime.InteropServices;
```

```
namespace DniScRoleSecurity
{
    public interface IRoleMethodSecurity
    {
        int SecuredMethod(string paramA);
        int UnsecuredMethod(string paramA);
    }

    [ComponentAccessControl(true)]
    [SecureMethod]
    [ClassInterface(ClassInterfaceType.None)]
    public class DniScRoleMethodSecurityObj
        : ServicedComponent, IRoleMethodSecurity
    {
        [SecurityRole("AppManager")]
        public int SecuredMethod(string paramA)
        {
            return paramA.Length;
        }

        [SecurityRole("AppUser", true)]
        public int UnsecuredMethod(string paramA)
        {
            return paramA.Length;
        }
    }
}
```

Just as we did with the last example, we apply the ComponentAccessControl and SecureMethod attributes to the class. However, this time we apply the SecurityRole attribute to each method. As shown in this example, doing so allows us to assign a different role to each method.

■**Note** We have defined our own interface (IRoleMethodSecurity), and the class implements this interface. Calling methods via an interface is required for method-level security.

To test this code, we can modify our client code to look like this:

```
using System;
using DniScRoleSecurity;

namespace ScRoleSecurity
{
    class Program
    {
        static void Main(string[] args)
```

```
    {
        try
        {
            IRoleClassSecurity classObj
                = new DniScRoleClassSecurityObj();
            CallClassSecurityObj(classObj);

            IRoleMethodSecurity obj
                = new DniScRoleMethodSecurityObj();
            CallUnsecuredMethod(obj);
            CallSecuredMethod(obj);

        }
        catch (Exception e)
        {
            Console.WriteLine(
                "Exception during creation: {0}",
                e.Message);
        }

        Console.Read();
    }

    static void CallClassSecurityObj(IRoleClassSecurity obj)
    {
        try
        {
            int result = obj.SecuredMethod("abcdefg");
            Console.WriteLine(
                "Class security method result: {0}", result);
        }
        catch (Exception e)
        {
            Console.WriteLine(
                "Exception using secured class: {0}",
                e.Message);
        }
    }

    static void CallSecuredMethod(IRoleMethodSecurity obj)
    {
        try
        {
            int result = obj.SecuredMethod("abcdefg");
            Console.WriteLine(
                "SecuredMethod result: {0}", result);
        }
```

```
            catch (Exception e)
            {
                Console.WriteLine(
                    "Exception calling SecuredMethod: {0}",
                    e.Message);
            }
        }

        static void CallUnsecuredMethod(IRoleMethodSecurity obj)
        {
            try
            {
                int result = obj.UnsecuredMethod("abcdefg");
                Console.WriteLine(
                    "UnsecuredMethod result: {0}", result);
            }
            catch (Exception e)
            {
                Console.WriteLine(
                    "Exception calling UnsecuredMethod: {0}",
                    e.Message);
            }
        }
    }
}
```

Before running this test, we remove the user or group assignment that we made to the AppManager role. When we run the test, we get these results:

```
Exception using secured class: Access is denied.
(Exception from HRESULT: 0x80070005 (E_ACCESSDENIED))
UnsecuredMethod result: 7
Exception calling SecuredMethod: Access is denied.
(Exception from HRESULT: 0x80070005 (E_ACCESSDENIED))
```

The call to UnsecuredMethod worked since it required role AppUser. This role is currently assigned the Everyone group, so any user can access this method. The call to SecuredMethod failed because it requires the AppManager role and it is once again empty.

If we add our user or group back to the AppManager role and run the test again, we now see that we have access to all methods:

```
Class security method result: 7
UnsecuredMethod result: 7
SecuredMethod result: 7
```

■**Caution** .NET allows you to add roles to individual methods as well as to the class at the same time. However, doing this is not a good idea. The role assigned to the class overrides method-level security. This is probably not what you want. Access security checks stop as soon as a user is verified to be in a valid role.

For example, if you apply the role Restricted to a method, you would assume that only users who have been added to that role have access to the method. But if the class itself has a role named Users applied to it, anyone in the Users role will be allowed to access all methods in the class.

The best advice is to strictly use either class-level or method-level security, but don't mix the two.

The ApplicationAccessControl attribute has additional properties that allow you to fine-tune the security for the component. One property that deserves your attention is AccessChecksLevel. This property determines when the access checks take place.

The possible values for this property are as follows:

- AccessChecksLevelOption.ApplicationComponent: Access checks are enabled at the application, component, and method level. This is the default value if this property is not set.

- AccessChecksLevelOption.Application: Access checks are performed only at the application level.

In the examples shown earlier, we included the ApplicationAccessControl attribute without any additional properties like this:

```
[assembly: ApplicationAccessControl(true)]
```

This means the default AccessChecksLevel of ApplicationComponent is used. This is required if we want to perform checks at either the class or method level (which we do).

We could have also applied an attribute like this:

```
[assembly: ApplicationAccessControl(true,
  AccessChecksLevel = AccessChecksLevelOption.Application)]
```

This removes the security checks for the class and individual methods. If SecurityRole attributes are applied to those elements, they are ignored. In most cases, you will want to use the default value and let COM+ perform access checks at all levels.

To enforce security, the SecureMethod attribute must also be added to the class. Optionally, it can be applied to each method, but adding it to the class applies it to all methods of the class.

The SecureMethod attribute is poorly documented and not intuitive. It instructs the runtime to always make calls to the class using your interface. If this attribute is omitted, the runtime is permitted to make the actual calls to your class using a Microsoft-defined interface named IRemoteDispatch instead of your interface. By including this attribute, you are informing the runtime that you want to enforce security that has been defined and to always use your interface instead of IRemoteDispatch.

A side effect of including the SecureMethod attribute is that an additional role named Marshaler is automatically added to the application. This is a role that the runtime requires for several interfaces exposed by the ServicedComponent base class. These interfaces are used by the runtime during COM+ interop. The following interfaces use this role:

- IDisposable

- IManagedObject

- IServicedComponentInfo

By adding the SecureMethod attribute, you've told the runtime that it must always use interfaces instead of IRemoteDispatch. That includes calls that the runtime needs to make in addition to your calls. The runtime must now use these interfaces rather than IRemoteDispatch. That's why the Marshaler role has been created. It provides you with an opportunity to specify a superset of all users that are authorized to use your component.

As a general rule, whenever you add a user or group to one of your defined roles, you should also add the same user or group to the Marshaler role. If you don't include all authorized users in this role, the runtime will be denied access to the interfaces that it needs.

Selectively adding users to the Marshaler role is not the same thing as adding the Everyone group. Adding the Everyone group would allow component access to any user on the system. Since you are implementing role-based security, you presumably have a smaller subset of users that should have access to the component. Users outside that group should be denied access.

Note Testing role-based security can be difficult. Normally, shutting down a COM+ application ensures that the next test uses the latest version of the component. However, that doesn't always seem to be the case when making changes to the security attributes. In particular, the roles that have been assigned to components or methods may not always be refreshed after making changes.

If you experience unexpected behavior when testing security, the best approach is to simply delete the COM+ application and start over. Running regsvcs again on the test assembly will re-create the application with the current settings.

Related Information

See recipes 8-2 (Implementing a Server Application), 8-3 (Installing a Serviced Component), and 8-9 (Performing Manual Security Checks).

8-9. Performing Manual Security Checks

Problem

In addition to the role-based security provided by COM+, is there a way to perform security checks manually within your code?

Solution

When COM+ role-based security is used, access to a class or method is controlled by COM+ rather than your managed code. The class, or the methods of the class, declare the security role that is required for access. This declaration is made by applying the SecurityRole attribute.

At runtime, if the client is identified as being in that role, access is granted. Otherwise, access is prohibited and an exception is thrown.

.NET also provides the SecurityCallContext and ContextUtil classes that allow you to perform your own security checks. You might need to do this if the security decisions you face are not simple cases of all-or-nothing access. You might want to always allow access to a method, but modify the processing within the method based on the caller's role.

For example, you might need to implement a method that retrieves account data. All users of your application may need access to this method. However, only managers should have access to a subset of the account data. Perhaps part of the account data is confidential, containing fields such as a tax ID number, password, and so forth. One way to implement this behavior is to check for the presence of a particular role within your code. If the caller is in the Managers role, you provide all data, including the confidential fields. Otherwise, you can encrypt or omit the confidential fields.

There is some overlap between the SecurityCallContext and ContextUtil classes. ContextUtil contains a number of properties and methods that are not related to security; however, it does contain some security-related members. As the name implies, SecurityCallContext is directly related to security for the current call. Either class will work equally well if you need to manually check security within your code.

To use SecurityCallContext, you first obtain an instance of it using the CurrentCall static property like this:

```
SecurityCallContext context
    = SecurityCallContext.CurrentCall;
```

To determine if security checks have been enabled, you access the IsSecurityEnabled property like this:

```
if (context.IsSecurityEnabled)
{

}
```

In order for role-based security to be considered enabled, it must be turned on at the application and component level.

To determine if the caller is in a particular role, you use the IsCallerInRole method like this:

```
if (context.IsCallerInRole("MyRoleToCheck"))
{
    //caller is authorized for the role
}
else
{
    //not authorized, so do something else
}
```

You can perform the same checks using ContextUtil. This determines if security checks are enabled:

```
if (ContextUtil.IsSecurityEnabled)
{
}
```

This determines if a caller is in a particular role:

```
if (ContextUtil.IsCallerInRole("AppManager"))
{
    //caller is authorized for the role
}
else
{
    //not authorized, so do something else
}
```

How It Works

One of the additional properties supported by SecurityCallContext is DirectCaller. This returns a SecurityIdentity object representing the immediate caller of the current method. Among other things, it contains an AccountName property with the name of the caller.

The use of these classes is demonstrated with this code:

```
using System;
using System.EnterpriseServices;
using System.Runtime.InteropServices;

[assembly: ApplicationActivation(ActivationOption.Server)]
[assembly: ApplicationAccessControl(true)]
[assembly: ApplicationName("DniRoleSecurityApplication")]
[assembly: Description(".NET Interop Server Application")]

//setup the roles within the COM+ application
[assembly: SecurityRole("AppAdministrator")]
[assembly: SecurityRole("AppManager")]
[assembly: SecurityRole("AppUser", true)]

namespace DniScSecurityChecks
{
    public interface ISecuredMethods
    {
        bool IsSecurityEnabled();
        bool IsSecurityEnabledAlt();
        bool ManualSecurityCheck();
        bool ManualSecurityCheckAlt();
        string GetCaller();
    }

    [ComponentAccessControl(true)]
    [SecureMethod]
    [SecurityRole("AppUser", true)]
    [ClassInterface(ClassInterfaceType.None)]
    public class DniScSecurityChecksObj
        : ServicedComponent, ISecuredMethods
```

```
{
    public bool IsSecurityEnabled()
    {
        SecurityCallContext context
            = SecurityCallContext.CurrentCall;
        return context.IsSecurityEnabled;
    }

    public bool IsSecurityEnabledAlt()
    {
        return ContextUtil.IsSecurityEnabled;
    }

    public bool ManualSecurityCheck()
    {
        SecurityCallContext context
            = SecurityCallContext.CurrentCall;
        return context.IsCallerInRole("AppManager");
    }

    public bool ManualSecurityCheckAlt()
    {
        return ContextUtil.IsCallerInRole("AppManager");
    }

    public string GetCaller()
    {
        SecurityCallContext context
            = SecurityCallContext.CurrentCall;
        SecurityIdentity identity = context.DirectCaller;
        return identity.AccountName;
    }
}
}
```

The ApplicationAccessControl attribute that is applied to the assembly enables security for the COM+ application. The SecurityRole attributes applied to the assembly simply set up the roles within the application. When entered at the assembly level like this, they do not actually control access.

At the class level, we add the ComponentAccessControl and SecurityRole attributes. ComponentAccessControl enables security for the component (the class). The SecurityRole attribute identifies the role that is required in order to access any of the methods in the class. The SecureMethod attribute informs the .NET runtime that calls to this class must be made via our interface.

In this example, we specify the AppUser role with the optional second parameter of true. The second parameter causes the Everyone user group to be added to the role automatically. We've created a role that automatically includes all users. Therefore, all the methods of this class are unrestricted and all users can call them.

Each method of the class uses either SecurityCallContext or ContextUtil to obtain information about the current caller and return it.

A C# client to use this class and display the results looks like this:

```csharp
using System;
using System.Runtime.InteropServices;
using DniScSecurityChecks;

namespace ScSecurityChecks
{
    class Program
    {
        static void Main(string[] args)
        {
            try
            {
                ISecuredMethods obj
                    = new DniScSecurityChecksObj();

                bool isSecurityEnabled = obj.IsSecurityEnabled();
                Console.WriteLine(
                    "IsSecurityEnabled: {0}", isSecurityEnabled);
                isSecurityEnabled = obj.IsSecurityEnabledAlt();
                Console.WriteLine(
                    "IsSecurityEnabledAlt: {0}",isSecurityEnabled);

                bool isInRole = obj.ManualSecurityCheck();
                Console.WriteLine(
                    "ManualSecurityCheck: {0}", isInRole);
                isInRole = obj.ManualSecurityCheckAlt();
                Console.WriteLine(
                    "ManualSecurityCheckAlt: {0}", isInRole);

                string caller = obj.GetCaller();
                Console.WriteLine(
                    "GetCaller: {0}", caller);
            }
            catch (Exception e)
            {
                Console.WriteLine(
                    "Exception: {0}",
                    e.Message);
            }

            Console.Read();
        }
    }
}
```

When I execute this test, I receive these results:

```
IsSecurityEnabled: True
IsSecurityEnabledAlt: True
ManualSecurityCheck: False
ManualSecurityCheckAlt: False
GetCaller: VIVALDI\bruce
```

Both of the calls to IsSecurityEnabled report that security is enabled. Both of the calls to IsCallerInRole correctly report that I am not in the AppManager role. And the AccountName property of the SecurityIdentity object correctly identifies me as the caller.

The SecurityCallContext class contains two properties that are similar: DirectCaller and OriginalCaller. The two may be different, and you may need to check one or the other depending on your intent. In the example code just shown, DirectCaller is used.

DirectCaller contains the identity used by the process that is directly calling our COM+ component. That may not be the same as OriginalCaller, which is the identity used by the original process that made the call. If the call passed between multiple processes (such as multiple Server COM+ applications that use different identities), these two properties could be different.

SecurityCallContext also supports a Callers property. This is a collection of SecurityIdentity objects that identify all callers along the route leading to your component.

Related Information

See recipe 8-8 (Using Role-Based Security).

8-10. Writing Managed Queued Components

Problem

Does .NET support Queued Components? What is involved in developing a managed Queued Component?

Solution

Queued Components (QCs) provide a way to execute components asynchronously. They are a COM+ feature that uses Microsoft Message Queuing (MSMQ) to record the instructions to execute a method of a component. When the queued message is played back, the component is activated and the method is executed.

This provides asynchronous execution of the method as well as persistence of the request. QCs can be used to provide a degree of scalability to an application. The use of the queue can level out the peaks and valleys during the day, allowing messages to remain in the queue until they can be processed. The client application appears to be more responsive since it can request asynchronous execution of a method and doesn't have to wait for the method to complete.

The steps needed to develop a QC include the following:

1. The assembly must have the `ApplicationQueuing` attribute to identify the COM+ application as supporting QCs.

2. The managed class must be derived from the `ServicedComponent` class and must be registered as a COM+ component in the normal way.

3. An interface must be developed that defines the methods available to clients. This is a normal managed interface, but it must follow a few rules that are described in this recipe's "How It Works" section.

4. The `InterfaceQueuing` attribute must be added to the interface.

5. A separate exception class should be developed that will handle the message if it is undeliverable.

6. The original class should include the `ExceptionClass` attribute to identify the class that handles an undeliverable message.

A client can follow these steps to create an instance of a QC and execute one of its methods:

1. Use the static `Marshal.BindToMoniker` method to create an object instance.

2. Call the method on the object using the public interface.

Taking these steps one at a time, we start with the `ApplicationQueuing` attribute. This is an assembly-level attribute that enables support for QCs within the COM+ application. Since this is an assembly-level attribute, it is normally placed in the `AssemblyInfo.cs` (or `.vb`) file. It has several optional parameters that are illustrated here in C#:

```
[assembly: ApplicationQueuing(Enabled = true,
    QueueListenerEnabled = true,
    MaxListenerThreads = 1)]
```

As the name implies, the `Enabled` property enables queuing for the COM+ application. The `QueueListenerEnabled` property is needed to enable the listener for the QCs. If this is not enabled, there won't be a COM+ process that retrieves messages from the queue and actually processes them.

The `MaxListenerThreads` determines the number of concurrent threads available to process queued messages. Setting this to a number greater than 1 will allow multiple instances of our QCs to execute at the same time. In this example, we set `MaxListenerThreads` to 1 because this example doesn't require any more than that. As we will see next, the example QC simply writes messages to a file. We wouldn't want a large number of threads all trying to write to the same file.

So in this application, a single listener thread is the appropriate number. If you are developing a high-performance component that accesses a database, then you may want to increase the number of listener threads. The number really depends on the kind of work that the component is performing as well as your needs.

Since we will be registering this assembly for use by COM+, we need these additional attributes entered at the assembly level:

```
[assembly: ApplicationAccessControl(false)]
[assembly: ApplicationName("DniQCApplication")]
```

```
[assembly: Description(".NET Interop Queued Component Application")]
[assembly: ApplicationActivation(ActivationOption.Server)]
```

The class that implements the QC must derive from the ServicedComponent class and must be registered as a COM+ component. Additionally, we must define our own interface with the methods that we wish to make public. A generated class interface won't work in this case. The interface requires the InterfaceQueuing attribute in order to identify it as a QC interface.

Here is the implementation of our class and interface in C#:

```csharp
using System;
using System.IO;
using System.Runtime.InteropServices;
using System.EnterpriseServices;

namespace DniScQueuedComponent
{
    [InterfaceQueuing]
    public interface IQueuedComponent
    {
        void LogMessage(string message);
    }

    [ExceptionClass("DniScQueuedComponent.DniScQCErrorObj")]
    [ClassInterface(ClassInterfaceType.None)]
    public class DniScQCObj
        : ServicedComponent, IQueuedComponent
    {
        public void LogMessage(string message)
        {
            //append the message to a file
            using (StreamWriter writer
                = new StreamWriter(@"c:\QCLog.txt", true))
            {
                writer.WriteLine(message);
                writer.Flush();
            }
        }
    }
}
```

With the exception of the InterfaceQueuing and ExceptionClass attributes, this looks just like any other COM+ component. To illustrate the use of a QC, the LogMessage method takes the string that is passed as a parameter and appends it to a file in the root directory called QCLog.txt.

The ExceptionClass attribute identifies the name of the class that will handle the queued message if it becomes undeliverable. The use of this exception class and attribute is optional but highly recommended. They provide a fallback mechanism in the event the original QC cannot process the message for some reason. The implementation of this exception class is shown in this recipe's "How It Works" section.

■**Note** Notice that the declaration of the ExceptionClass uses a string name of the class instead of the actual type. This means there is no direct compile-time reference between the two classes. The ExceptionClass attribute is used to update the COM+ settings during registration. It doesn't affect the building of the project.

For this reason, you can actually defer the development of the exception class. This allows you to refine the design and implementation of your QC class. Then, once the design is solid, you can develop the exception class. Just be sure to develop it prior to the final deployment of your application.

Now we can build the project, add it to the GAC, and register it with COM+ services using regsvcs.

■**Caution** It is at this point that you must have MSMQ installed on your machine. If you don't, you'll receive an error during registration:

```
EXEC : An unknown COM+ 1.0 catalog error occurred:
MSMQ is required for the requested operation and is not installed (Exception from
HRESULT: 0x80110602)
```

The client code needed to create an instance of this QC looks like this:

```
using System;
using System.Runtime.InteropServices;
using System.EnterpriseServices;

using DniScQueuedComponent;

namespace ScQueuedComponent
{
    class Program
    {
        static void Main(string[] args)
        {
            LogTheMessage("message one");
            LogTheMessage("message two");

            Console.WriteLine("Press any key to continue");
            Console.Read();
        }

        static void LogTheMessage(string message)
        {
            IQueuedComponent obj
                = Marshal.BindToMoniker(
```

```
        "queue:/new:DniScQueuedComponent.DniScQCObj")
        as IQueuedComponent;

    if (obj != null)
    {
        obj.LogMessage(message);
    }
  }
 }
}
```

The only really interesting code here is the way in which we create an instance of the QC. You need to use the static BindToMoniker method of the Marshal class to do this. A *moniker* is simply a unique name to identify the component. In the case of a QC, the moniker must always be in this format:

```
queue:/new:[Namespace.ClassName]
```

Replace [Namespace.ClassName] with the real namespace and class name.

Once an instance of the QC is created, the LogMessage method is called in the normal way. However, this does not execute the method immediately; instead, it places a message that will be processed asynchronously into the queue. When the message is processed, an instance of the component is created and the LogMessage method is executed.

When we run this test, we should see the two messages logged to the file C:\QCLog.txt. However, after waiting patiently, we don't see this file appear. Nothing is happening because the COM+ application isn't running. Normal COM+ server applications will automatically start up the first time a component in the application is instantiated. Not so with QC applications. They must be manually started.

To start the application, you open the Component Services Management Console plug-in, which you can find in the Administrative Tools folder of the Control Panel. Drilling down into the COM+ applications folder of the tool, we should see our application: DniQCApplication. This is the name we specified in the ApplicationName assembly attribute. After right-clicking this application, we can select the Start option. Once a QC application has been started, it will continue running until it is manually shut down.

After a very brief delay, we should see the C:\QCLog.txt file appear. If we open it, we'll see that the contents look like this:

```
message one
message two
```

What follows is the implementation of the same QC class and interface in Visual Basic .NET (VB.NET). This code is in a project named DniScQueuedComponentVB with a default namespace of the same name:

```
Imports System.IO
Imports System.Runtime.InteropServices
Imports System.EnterpriseServices
```

```vbnet
<InterfaceQueuing()> _
Public Interface IQueuedComponent
    Sub LogMessage(ByVal message As String)
End Interface

<ExceptionClass("DniScQueuedComponentVB.DniScQCErrorObj")> _
<ClassInterface(ClassInterfaceType.None)> _
Public Class DniScQCObj
    Inherits ServicedComponent
    Implements IQueuedComponent

    Public Sub LogMessage(ByVal message As String) _
        Implements IQueuedComponent.LogMessage

        Dim writer As StreamWriter _
            = New StreamWriter("c:\QCLog.txt", True)
        writer.WriteLine(message)
        writer.Flush()
        writer.Close()
    End Sub
End Class
```

The assembly-level attributes added to the AssemblyInfo.vb file look like this:

```vbnet
Imports System.EnterpriseServices

<assembly: ApplicationAccessControl(false)>
<assembly: ApplicationName("DniQCApplication")>
<assembly: Description(".NET Interop Queued Component Application")>
<assembly: ApplicationActivation(ActivationOption.Server)>
<Assembly: ApplicationQueuing(Enabled:=True, _
 QueueListenerEnabled:=True, _
 MaxListenerThreads:=1)>
```

Since the namespace is different from the C# version, we need to use a different moniker for the VB.NET version like this:

```
IQueuedComponent obj
    = Marshal.BindToMoniker(
    "queue:/new:DniScQueuedComponentVB.DniScQCObj")
    as IQueuedComponent;
```

When the VB.NET QC executes, the results are exactly the same as the C# version.

Note It is possible to mix queued and nonqueued components in the same COM+ application. However, while this is possible, it's better to keep QCs in a separate application. This provides you with the flexibility to start and stop the QC application without affecting other components.

How It Works

When designing the interface for a QC, you must follow a few rules. First, a method is not able to return a value. Second, any parameters must be input-only. This means that you can't pass a parameter using ref or out (C#), or ByRef (VB.NET).

The BindToMoniker method of the Marshal class uses the moniker that you provide to obtain an instance of the QC interface. As mentioned earlier, the basic format of the string moniker looks like this:

```
queue:/new:[Namespace.ClassName]
```

However, you can specify additional parameters within this moniker to control the instance creation, for example:

```
queue:ComputerName=MyServer/new:DniScQueuedComponent.DniScQCObj
```

This moniker includes the optional ComputerName parameter. This causes the QC to be created on the MyServer computer instead of the local machine. Of course, this assumes that the QC has been installed and configured on that machine.

This example adds the Priority parameter:

```
queue:Priority=7,ComputerName=MyServer
    /new:DniScQueuedComponent.DniScQCObj
```

This parameter adjusts the priority of this QC relative to others in the same queue. The range for Priority is from 0 to 7, so this example sets the priority of this component to the maximum. If not specified, the default is a priority of 3.

A number of other available parameters are documented in MSDN. Please refer to this recipe's "Related Information" section for the MSDN reference where QC monikers are documented.

Because of the asynchronous nature of QCs, we really can't count on a guaranteed execution order for our components. As we've just seen, it is possible to change the relative priority of each QC. That will affect the execution order. It is also possible to control the number of execution threads available to a QC using the ApplicationQueuing attribute. If there are multiple threads, we no longer have a single thread sequentially pulling messages off of the queue. The execution order is unpredictable.

In our example code, we included this attribute on the QC class:

```
[ExceptionClass("DniScQueuedComponent.DniScQCErrorObj")]
```

This specifies the class that handles the message if it is undeliverable to the original component. Here is the C# implementation of this exception class:

```csharp
using System;
using System.IO;
using System.Runtime.InteropServices;
using System.EnterpriseServices;

namespace DniScQueuedComponent
{
    [ClassInterface(ClassInterfaceType.None)]
    public class DniScQCErrorObj : ServicedComponent,
        IPlaybackControl, IQueuedComponent
```

```csharp
{
    public void LogMessage(string message)
    {
        //called if the message cannot be delivered
        //to the original component

        using (StreamWriter writer
            = new StreamWriter(@"c:\QCErrorLog.txt", true))
        {
            writer.WriteLine(message);
            writer.Flush();
        }
    }

    public void FinalClientRetry()
    {
        //notification of a delivery failure
        //on the client side.
    }

    public void FinalServerRetry()
    {
        //notification of a playback failure
        //on the server
    }
}
}
```

The VB.NET version of the exception class looks like this:

```vbnet
Imports System.IO
Imports System.Runtime.InteropServices
Imports System.EnterpriseServices

<ClassInterface(ClassInterfaceType.None)> _
Public Class DniScQCErrorObj
    Inherits ServicedComponent
    Implements IQueuedComponent
    Implements IPlaybackControl

    Public Sub LogMessage(ByVal message As String) _
        Implements IQueuedComponent.LogMessage

        'called if the message cannot be delivered
        'to the original component

        Dim writer As StreamWriter _
            = New StreamWriter("c:\QCErrorLog.txt", True)
```

```
        writer.WriteLine(message)
        writer.Flush()
        writer.Close()
    End Sub

    Public Sub FinalClientRetry() _
        Implements IPlaybackControl.FinalClientRetry

    End Sub

    Public Sub FinalServerRetry() _
        Implements IPlaybackControl.FinalServerRetry

    End Sub
End Class
```

The exception class is another class that you must implement if you want the ability to handle undeliverable messages. An exception class must implement your original interface (IQueuedComponent) as well as the IPlaybackControl interface.

It's a good idea to package the exception class in a separate COM+ application. This helps to isolate the exception-handling component from the original component. Doing this allows the exception component to be called even if there is a configuration problem with the original QC application. The exception class is the final resting place for a message if the original component cannot be executed for any reason.

In our example, we placed the exception class in a different project and used these assembly-level attributes. This installs the C# class into a separate COM+ application:

```
[assembly: ApplicationActivation(ActivationOption.Server)]
[assembly: ApplicationAccessControl(false)]
[assembly: ApplicationName("DniQCErrorsApplication")]
[assembly: Description(".NET Interop Queued Component Application")]
```

The VB.NET version of these assembly-level attributes looks like this:

```
Imports System.EnterpriseServices
<Assembly: ApplicationActivation(ActivationOption.Server)>
<Assembly: ApplicationAccessControl(False)>
<Assembly: ApplicationName("DniQCErrorsApplication")>
<Assembly: Description(".NET Interop Queued Component Application")>
```

When an error occurs during playback of the message (during activation and execution of the component), the message goes through a series of retry queues. The purpose of these multiple queues is to prevent a single bad message from poisoning the primary execution queue. This could occur if the queue contains messages that will never be successfully processed.

The queue names are all based on the COM+ application name. In our example, the application name is DniQCApplication. This means that the primary execution queue has the same name: DniQCApplication. The retry queues are all based on this name and are as follows:

- DniQCApplication_0

- DniQCApplication_1

- DniQCApplication_2

- DniQCApplication_3

- DniQCApplication_4

- DniQCApplication_deadqueue

After a failed message is retried a number of times in the primary queue, it is moved to the DniQCApplication_0 queue. Once there, the message is retried three times with 1-minute intervals between retries. If it still fails, it is moved to the _1 queue. Here it is retried three times with 2-minute intervals between retries. The process continues in a similar fashion through all of the queues. Each queue doubles the time between retries from the prior queue, going from 1 to 2 to 4 to 8 to 16 minutes between retries.

After 90 minutes or so, the message is considered dead and the exception class is finally called. In the case of a server-side error, the FinalServerRetry method is called to notify us that there are no more retries allowed for the message. The original method is then called on our exception class. That's the reason we need to implement the original interface. In our example, the LogMessage method is called and we log the message to a different file.

Using an exception class like this allows you to gracefully handle QC errors. Exactly how you handle the error is up to you and will greatly depend on the type of work done in the original component method.

Related Information

See the MSDN topic "Using the Queue Moniker" for details on the available moniker parameters for a QC. Also see the MSDN topic "Server-side Errors with COM+ Queued Components" for a description of the retry and error handling logic. See recipes 8-2 (Implementing a Server Application) and 8-3 (Installing a Serviced Component).

CHAPTER 9

■■■

COM+ Enterprise Services Transactions

The feature most often associated with COM+ is *automatic transactions*, which removes the necessity for component code to manually manage a logical unit of work (a transaction). Gone is the need for code that calls BeginTransaction on an individual SqlConnection instance. Gone is the code to explicitly call Commit or Rollback on a SqlTransaction object.

Instead, the component is enlisted into (or added to) an automatic transaction. When a method of a COM+ component is called, it receives a transaction that has already been started. If the method returns normally, the work (such as database updates) is committed. If an exception is thrown, a Rollback is executed.

Automatic transactions seamlessly work with different types of resource managers (databases, queues, etc.). This allows you to enlist multiple resources, such as multiple databases, in a single transaction. All updates to the resources will be committed or rolled back as a single unit of work. Multiple components can also work together within a single transaction, perhaps with each one performing an update to a different resource.

The *COM+ context* is a key ingredient when using automatic transactions. A COM+ context is an environment that is created by COM+ where objects live after they are activated. Each context has a set of properties that determine the runtime characteristics of the component. Every COM+ component is activated into either a new or existing context.

A COM+ context supports two separate but related flags that are used during transaction processing. The *consistent* flag is used to cast a vote to commit or abort the transaction. The *done* flag indicates that the component's vote is now final. Several recipes in this chapter demonstrate ways to indirectly set these context flags.

This chapter begins with a recipe that shows how to monitor and inspect the current state of the transaction. This is followed by a recipe that demonstrates how to enable transaction support for a managed class.

Each component that participates in a transaction is allowed to vote on the outcome of the transaction. Therefore, the ability to place a vote is critical and is covered in a series of three recipes. Automatic and manual voting is covered in the first two recipes. The third recipe demonstrates the effect that voting and transaction options have on a transaction when working with multiple components.

The transaction isolation level prevents a component from working with data that is in an intermediate state. Changing the transaction isolation level is covered in one recipe.

Two recipes cover the use of a new lightweight transactional model that was introduced in the .NET Framework 2.0. It provides an alternative to using ServicedComponent and COM+ when only transaction support is needed. The first of these recipes covers the use of transactional code blocks, while the other demonstrates how to write your own resource manager. The ability to develop a resource manager enables the use of transactions for tasks that traditionally do not use transactions.

The final recipe demonstrates the use of *services without components*. This feature allows you to use COM+ services such as transactions without the need to implement a COM+ component.

Note It is difficult to see the results of a transaction without the use of a resource manager such as a database or queue. Automatic transactions are created, used, and completed without your intervention. Trying to view a transaction is like trying to see the wind. You can only observe it based on the effect that it has on other things.

The examples in this chapter do not use SQL to demonstrate the use of transactions. This was a deliberate choice in order to keep the focus of this chapter on COM+ and transactions and to avoid turning this into a SQL recipe chapter. Instead, most of the example code uses a class to log the state of the transaction at the beginning and end of a method call. The first recipe in this chapter describes this class in detail. Much of the data logged should be the same when the tests are run on your computer. However, certain values that are logged will be different. In particular, transactions IDs and start times will certainly be different when the tests are run on your machine.

9-1. Monitoring Transaction Status

Problem

How can a method determine if there is an active transaction? Can you obtain any information about the transaction? Can you detect when the transaction has completed?

Solution

.NET provides the ContextUtil and Transaction classes that allow you to monitor transaction state. ContextUtil contains static methods that can be used directly, while the Transaction class is an object that represents the current transaction (if there is one).

Note The classes described in this recipe will provide meaningful information only when they are used within the called method of a COM+ component (a ServicedComponent). A transaction exists only during the call to a COM+ component. It cannot be directly monitored from outside of the component unless the caller is itself a COM+ component.

To determine if a transaction is active, you can check the IsInTransaction static method of the ContextUtil class, for example:

```
if (ContextUtil.IsInTransaction)
{
    //we have an active transaction
}
```

You can also check the static Transaction.Current property to determine if there is an active transaction. If a transaction exists, a Transaction object will be returned. Otherwise, null (nothing in Visual Basic .NET [VB.NET]) is returned if no transaction exists, for example:

```
if (Transaction.Current != null)
{
    //use the Transaction.Current object
}
else
{
    //no active transaction
}
```

■**Note** The Transaction class, along with other related classes, is packaged in the System. Transactions.dll assembly. The namespace for these classes is also System.Transactions. The classes in this namespace are primarily used with a new lightweight transaction model rather than the one implemented by COM+ services. However, as this recipe illustrates, some of these classes can be used with either transaction model.

By default, this assembly is not added to new projects. You'll need to add a reference to it if you use these classes.

Once you have a Transaction object (using Transaction.Current), you can inspect its properties to obtain additional details. The IsolationLevel property obtains the isolation level of the transaction (RepeatableRead, Serializable, etc.), for instance:

```
if (Transaction.Current != null)
{
    if (Transaction.Current.IsolationLevel
        == IsolationLevel.Serializable)
    {
    }
}
```

The Transaction object also has a TransactionInformation property that returns a TransactionInformation object. You can retrieve this object like this:

```
if (Transaction.Current != null)
{
    TransactionInformation info
        = Transaction.Current.TransactionInformation;
    //use properties of the info object
}
```

The TransactionInformation class contains these properties that you can examine:

- Status: This property contains one of the values defined by the TransactionStatus enum. The possible values are as follows:

  - Active: The transaction is still active. The final outcome of the transaction is unknown at this time.

  - Committed: The transaction completed successfully and all resource managers have committed their work.

  - Aborted: The transaction has failed and any work performed during the transaction has been rolled back.

  - InDoubt: The transaction status is unknown. This is due to the inability of the transaction coordinator (MSDTC) to contact one or more resource managers. This status is appropriate only if using distributed transactions.

- CreationTime: This is a DateTime containing the time when the transaction was created.

- LocalIdentifier: Each transaction has a unique identifier. This is a string representing that ID.

- DistributedIdentifier: This is a Guid that uniquely identifies the transaction if it has been promoted to a distributed transaction. This ID can be used by Microsoft Distributed Transaction Coordinator (MSDTC) to coordinate the transaction between multiple resource managers. In many cases, this identifier will not contain a valid Guid. To check this, you can compare this property to the Guid.Empty static field. As long as the transaction is used within a single application domain and uses only a single durable resource, it will remain local and will not be escalated to a distributed transaction. In this case, this ID will contain an empty Guid (all zeros).

The ContextUtil class also has a MyTransactionVote property. Each method that participates in a transaction is allowed to vote on its success or failure. This property represents the current vote for the current method. The possible values are defined by the TransactionVote enum and can be either Commit or Abort.

You can either inspect this property to see the current vote or set it to one of these values to manually place your vote.

Note The subject of voting on a transaction is covered in several recipes later in this chapter.

Finally, the Transaction class has one event named TransactionCompleted. If you subscribe to this event, you will be notified when the transaction completes. In this way, you will be able to determine the success or failure of the transaction.

You subscribe to the event using a delegate, just like any other .NET event, for example:

```
if (Transaction.Current != null)
{
    Transaction.Current.TransactionCompleted
        += new TransactionCompletedEventHandler(
            tran_TransactionCompleted);
}
```

The event handler looks like this:

```
private void tran_TransactionCompleted(object sender,
    TransactionEventArgs e)
{
    if (e.Transaction != null)
    {
        //do something with the e.Transaction
    }
}
```

The Transaction property passed with the TransactionEventArgs contains the Transaction that just completed. The sender of the event is also the same Transaction object. You can check any of the properties of the transaction that were just reviewed. In particular, you might need to check the Status property to determine success or failure.

How It Works

A working example using these classes is the TransactionLogger class that follows.

▓Note This class is used in the other recipes of this chapter to monitor the state of a transaction within various test methods.

The complete C# code looks like this:

```
using System;
using System.IO;
using System.EnterpriseServices;
using System.Transactions;

namespace TransactionLogging
{
    class TransactionLogger
    {
        private string m_TargetName = string.Empty;
```

```
/// <summary>
/// Constructor
/// </summary>
/// <param name="target"></param>
public TransactionLogger(object target)
{
    m_TargetName = target.GetType().Name;
    Log("------Starting method call------");
    if (Transaction.Current != null)
    {
        Transaction.Current.TransactionCompleted
            += new TransactionCompletedEventHandler(
                tran_TransactionCompleted);
    }

    LogTranDetails(Transaction.Current,
        "*Transaction at start of method:");
}

/// <summary>
/// Log details about a transaction
/// </summary>
/// <param name="tran"></param>
/// <param name="msg"></param>
public void LogTranDetails(Transaction tran, String msg)
{
    Log(msg);
    if (tran != null)
    {
        Log(" IsInTransaction: {0}",
            ContextUtil.IsInTransaction.ToString());
        if (ContextUtil.IsInTransaction)
        {
            Log(" MyTransactionVote: {0}",
                ContextUtil.MyTransactionVote.ToString());
        }
        Log(" IsolationLevel: {0}",
            tran.IsolationLevel.ToString());

        TransactionInformation info
            = tran.TransactionInformation;
        Log(" Tran start time: {0}",
            info.CreationTime.ToString("HH:mm:ss.ffff"));
        if (info.DistributedIdentifier != null)
        {
            Log(" DistId: {0}",
                info.DistributedIdentifier);
        }
```

```csharp
            Log(" TranId: {0}", info.LocalIdentifier);
            Log(" Tran Status: {0}", info.Status);
        }
        else
        {
            Log("***No current transaction***");
        }
    }

    /// <summary>
    /// Handler for the TransactionCompleted event
    /// </summary>
    /// <param name="sender"></param>
    /// <param name="e"></param>
    private void tran_TransactionCompleted(object sender,
        TransactionEventArgs e)
    {
        if (e.Transaction != null)
        {
            LogTranDetails(e.Transaction,
                "*Transaction at TransactionCompleted:");
        }
    }

    /// <summary>
    /// Log a message
    /// </summary>
    /// <param name="msg"></param>
    public void Log(string msg)
    {
        StreamWriter writer = new StreamWriter(
            string.Format(@"c:\{0}.txt", m_TargetName),
            true);

        writer.WriteLine("{0} {1} {2}",
            DateTime.Now.ToString("HH:mm:ss.ffff"),
            m_TargetName, msg);

        writer.Flush();
        writer.Close();
    }

    /// <summary>
    /// Log a formatted message
    /// </summary>
    /// <param name="msg"></param>
    /// <param name="args"></param>
```

```csharp
        public void Log(String msg, params Object[] args)
        {
            Log(String.Format(msg, args));
        }
    }
}
```

Here is the VB.NET implementation of the class:

```vbnet
Imports System.IO
Imports System.EnterpriseServices
Imports System.Transactions

Namespace TransactionLogging

    Public Class TransactionLogger
        Private m_TargetName As String = String.Empty

        ''' <summary>
        ''' Constructor
        ''' </summary>
        ''' <param name="target"></param>
        ''' <remarks></remarks>
        Public Sub New(ByVal target As Object)
            m_TargetName = target.GetType().Name
            Log("------Starting method call------")
            If Transaction.Current <> Nothing Then
                AddHandler Transaction.Current.TransactionCompleted, _
                    AddressOf tran_TransactionCompleted
            End If
            LogTranDetails(Transaction.Current, _
                "*Transaction at start of method:")

        End Sub

        ''' <summary>
        ''' Log details about a transaction
        ''' </summary>
        ''' <param name="tran"></param>
        ''' <param name="msg"></param>
        ''' <remarks></remarks>
        Public Sub LogTranDetails(ByVal tran As Transaction, _
            ByVal msg As String)
            Log(msg)
            If (tran <> Nothing) Then
                Log(" IsInTransaction: {0}", _
                    ContextUtil.IsInTransaction.ToString())
```

```
            If ContextUtil.IsInTransaction Then
                Log(" MyTransactionVote: {0}", _
                    ContextUtil.MyTransactionVote.ToString())
            End If
            Log(" IsolationLevel: {0}", _
                tran.IsolationLevel.ToString())

            Dim info As TransactionInformation _
                = tran.TransactionInformation
            Log(" Tran start time: {0}", _
                info.CreationTime.ToString("HH:mm:ss.ffff"))
            If info.DistributedIdentifier <> Nothing Then
                Log(" DistId: {0}", _
                    info.DistributedIdentifier)
            End If
            Log(" TranId: {0}", info.LocalIdentifier)
            Log(" Tran Status: {0}", info.Status)
        Else
            Log("***No current transaction***")
        End If

    End Sub


    ''' <summary>
    ''' Handler for the TransactionCompleted event
    ''' </summary>
    ''' <param name="sender"></param>
    ''' <param name="e"></param>
    ''' <remarks></remarks>
    Private Sub tran_TransactionCompleted(ByVal sender As Object, _
            ByVal e As TransactionEventArgs)
        If e.Transaction <> Nothing Then
            LogTranDetails(e.Transaction, _
                "*Transaction at TransactionCompleted:")
        End If
    End Sub


    ''' <summary>
    ''' Log a message
    ''' </summary>
    ''' <param name="msg"></param>
    ''' <remarks></remarks>
    Private Sub Log(ByVal msg As String)
        Dim writer As StreamWriter _
            = New StreamWriter( _
            String.Format("c:\{0}.vblog.txt", m_TargetName), _
                True)
```

```
        writer.WriteLine("{0} {1} {2}", _
            DateTime.Now.ToString("HH:mm:ss.ffff"), _
            m_TargetName, msg)

        writer.Flush()
        writer.Close()
    End Sub


    ''' <summary>
    ''' Log a formatted message
    ''' </summary>
    ''' <param name="msg"></param>
    ''' <param name="arg"></param>
    ''' <remarks></remarks>
    Public Sub Log(ByVal msg As String, ByVal arg As Object)
        Log(String.Format(msg, arg))
    End Sub


End Class


End Namespace
```

The class logs the state of the transaction at two points: immediately when the class is constructed and when the transaction completes. It subscribes to the TransactionCompleted event in order to receive notification of a completed transaction. To keep the logging simple, the class logs to a text file. The file name is based on the object type passed in the constructor. It could easily be changed to log to some other destination.

Each log message includes a timestamp and the object type name. This is the same type name that is used as the file name. This facilitates sorting and merging of log files in order to observe the sequence of the operations across components. As an alternative, you might want to modify this code to log all messages to a single file rather than one for each component.

To use this class, you simply create an instance of it at the beginning of a method. This is demonstrated with this sample C# code:

```
using System;
using System.Runtime.InteropServices;
using System.EnterpriseServices;

using TransactionLogging;

namespace DniScMonitor
{
    public interface ITranMonitor
    {
        void LogTransactionDetails();
    }
```

```
    [Transaction(TransactionOption.Required)]
    [ClassInterface(ClassInterfaceType.None)]
    public class DniScMonitorObj
        : ServicedComponent, ITranMonitor
    {
        public void LogTransactionDetails()
        {
            //create logging object that will record
            //the transaction state
            TransactionLogger logger
                = new TransactionLogger(this);
        }
    }
}
```

This test project also requires these assembly-level attributes that are added to the AssemblyInfo.cs file:

```
using System.EnterpriseServices;

[assembly: ApplicationActivation(ActivationOption.Server)]
[assembly: ApplicationAccessControl(false)]
[assembly: ApplicationName("DniTranApplication")]
[assembly: Description(".NET Interop Server Application")]
```

You also need to sign the assembly with a strong name and expose the implemented types to COM. The steps needed to accomplish this are outlined in recipe 8-1 (Exposing Managed Code to COM+).

Finally, you can test the logging class with some C# client code:

```
using System;
using System.Runtime.InteropServices;

using DniScMonitor;

namespace ScMonitor
{
    class Program
    {
        static void Main(string[] args)
        {
            ITranMonitor obj
                = new DniScMonitorObj();
            obj.LogTransactionDetails();

            Console.WriteLine("Press enter to continue...");
            Console.Read();
        }
    }
}
```

The log file resulting from this test is named DniScMonitorObj.txt and contains the following:

```
------Starting method call------
*Transaction at start of method:
 IsInTransaction: True
 MyTransactionVote: Commit
 IsolationLevel: Serializable
 Tran start time: 20:47:08.7918
 DistId: 00000000-0000-0000-0000-000000000000
 TranId: 7c3d1f3a-824e-4817-9fdf-3514780064ff:1
 Tran Status: Active
*Transaction at TransactionCompleted:
 IsInTransaction: False
 DniScMonitorObj  MyTransactionVote: Commit
 IsolationLevel: Serializable
 Tran start time: 20:47:08.7918
 DistId: 00000000-0000-0000-0000-000000000000
 TranId: 7c3d1f3a-824e-4817-9fdf-3514780064ff:1
 Tran Status: Committed
```

Note Actually, each line of the test file also includes a timestamp and the object type name. These fields allow you to sort and merge the log files from multiple components to see the sequence of operations across components. However, in order to fit the format of this book, those elements are not shown in the preceding example.

Some of the results shown here will certainly be different on your machine. In particular, the transaction IDs and start times will be different.

Here is a VB.NET example that uses the TransactionLogger class in a similar way:

```
Imports System.EnterpriseServices
Imports System.Transactions
Imports System.Runtime.InteropServices

Public Interface ITranMonitor
    Sub LogTransactionDetails()
End Interface

<Transaction(TransactionOption.Required)> _
<ClassInterface(ClassInterfaceType.None)> _
Public Class DniScMonitorObj
    Inherits ServicedComponent
    Implements ITranMonitor
```

```
    Public Sub LogTransactionDetails() _
        Implements ITranMonitor.LogTransactionDetails

        'create the logging class
        Dim logger As TransactionLogging.TransactionLogger _
            = New TransactionLogging.TransactionLogger(Me)

    End Sub
End Class
```

These assembly-level attributes are required and are added to the `AssemblyInfo.vb` file:

```
Imports System.EnterpriseServices

<Assembly: ApplicationActivation(ActivationOption.Server)>
<Assembly: ApplicationAccessControl(False)>
<Assembly: ApplicationName("DniTranApplication")>
<Assembly: Description(".NET Interop Server Application")>
```

Just like the C# example, the assembly must be signed with a strong name and you need to expose the types in the project to COM.

When executed by the client code, the logged results are consistent with the C# version.

Related Information

See recipes 9-2 (Enabling Automatic Transactions), 9-3 (Placing an Automatic Vote), 9-4 (Placing a Manual Vote), 9-6 (Controlling the Transaction Isolation Level), and 8-1 (Exposing Managed Code to COM+).

9-2. Enabling Automatic Transactions

Problem

How are automatic COM+ transactions enabled for a serviced component? What transaction options are available?

Solution

Automatic transactions are those that are created for you by COM+. When using this type of transaction, you don't explicitly control when the transaction begins or ends. You also don't explicitly commit or roll back your work. Instead, you vote on the outcome of the transaction. Based on your vote, and perhaps the vote from other components, the transaction is either committed or aborted (rolled back).

To enable this type of transaction, you apply the `Transaction` attribute to the class. The absence of this attribute means that automatic transactions are *disabled* for the class.

For example, this C# class uses automatic transactions:

```
[Transaction]
public class MyTransactionClass : ServicedComponent
{
}
```

The same class implemented in Visual Basic .NET (VB.NET) looks like this:

```
<Transaction()> _
Public Class MyTransactionClass
    Inherits ServicedComponent

End Class
```

The Transaction attribute constructor has an optional TransactionOption parameter that determines when a transaction is created or used. If the attribute is applied without specifying this option (as in the previous example), the default value is TransactionOption.Required. This will use a transaction if one already exists; otherwise, it will start a new transaction. Specifying TransactionOption.Required like this is equivalent to the C# class just shown:

```
[Transaction(TransactionOption.Required)]
public class MyTransactionClass : ServicedComponent
{
}
```

and implemented in VB.NET:

```
<Transaction(TransactionOption.Required)> _
Public Class MyTransactionClass
    Inherits ServicedComponent

End Class
```

Table 9-1 summarizes the available values for the TransactionOption parameter. The real power of automatic transactions is their ability to enlist multiple components and multiple resource managers (databases or queues) in a single transaction. Many of these transaction options are primarily designed to address these situations.

Table 9-1. *TransactionOption Values*

Value	Usage
Required	An automatic transaction will always be used. If one already exists when a method is called, it is used. The current method is enlisted in the active transaction. If no transaction exits, a new one is started.
RequiresNew	A new transaction is always started, regardless of the presence of an active transaction. This allows components to call one another to perform some unit of work and maintain separate transactions. When the called component returns from a method call, the new transaction is committed or rolled back independently of the caller's original transaction.
Supported	If a transaction exists, the called method will participate in the transaction; however, a transaction is not required. If a transaction doesn't already exist, the method will execute without a transaction.

Value	Usage
NotSupported	Always executes without a transaction. If one exists when a method is called, the component is placed into a separate context that does not use a transaction. Any work performed within a method is done outside the context of a transaction. The component does not vote or otherwise participate in the caller's transaction if one exists.
Disabled	The COM+ logic to determine which context to place the component in is disabled. This doesn't necessarily mean that transactions are disabled. It does mean that the component will always execute within the context of the caller regardless of the presence or absence of a transaction. If the caller is using a transaction, the component doesn't directly participate in the transaction by voting on the outcome. However, if the method accesses a resource manager such as a database or queue, the outcome of the caller's transaction will affect any updates made to the resource.

We can illustrate these values with a few examples. The following class always requires a new transaction. Even if the caller already has an active transaction, a new one is always created:

```
[Transaction(TransactionOption.RequiresNew)]
public class MyTransactionClass : ServicedComponent
{
}
```

The following class supports a transaction if one already exists, but it does not require one and will not cause one to be started:

```
[Transaction(TransactionOption.Supported)]
public class MyTransactionClass : ServicedComponent
{
}
```

The following class does not support transactions. If the caller has an active transaction, this object will be created in a different COM+ context:

```
[Transaction(TransactionOption.NotSupported)]
public class MyTransactionClass : ServicedComponent
{
}
```

How It Works

The C# code that follows demonstrates the use of the Transaction attribute with different TransactionOption values. The only real purpose of the code is to see the differences in transaction state when each value is used.

We start with a simple interface that defines a single test method:

```
using System;
using System.EnterpriseServices;
using System.Runtime.InteropServices;
using TransactionLogging;
```

```
namespace DniScTransaction
{
    public interface ITranMethods
    {
        string GetTranStatus();
    }
}
```

We now implement a number of classes that all implement this interface. All classes derive from ServicedComponent since that is required for a COM+ component. Each class uses a different TransactionOption value for the Transaction attribute. Here is the complete set of classes:

```
[ClassInterface(ClassInterfaceType.None)]
public class DniScTransactionNoneObj
    : ServicedComponent, ITranMethods
{
    public string GetTranStatus()
    {
        //log details about the transaction
        TransactionLogger log = new TransactionLogger(this);
        return ContextUtil.IsInTransaction.ToString();
    }
}


[Transaction]    //defaults to TransactionOption.Required
[ClassInterface(ClassInterfaceType.None)]
public class DniScTransactionDefaultObj
    : ServicedComponent, ITranMethods
{
    public string GetTranStatus()
    {
        //log details about the transaction
        TransactionLogger log = new TransactionLogger(this);
        return ContextUtil.IsInTransaction.ToString();
    }
}


[Transaction(TransactionOption.Required)]
[ClassInterface(ClassInterfaceType.None)]
public class DniScTransactionRequiredObj
    : ServicedComponent, ITranMethods
{
    public string GetTranStatus()
    {
        //log details about the transaction
        TransactionLogger log = new TransactionLogger(this);
        return ContextUtil.IsInTransaction.ToString();
```

```
        }
    }

[Transaction(TransactionOption.RequiresNew)]
[ClassInterface(ClassInterfaceType.None)]
public class DniScTransactionRequiresNewObj
    : ServicedComponent, ITranMethods
{
    public string GetTranStatus()
    {
        //log details about the transaction
        TransactionLogger log = new TransactionLogger(this);
        return ContextUtil.IsInTransaction.ToString();
    }
}

[Transaction(TransactionOption.Disabled)]
[ClassInterface(ClassInterfaceType.None)]
public class DniScTransactionDisabledObj
    : ServicedComponent, ITranMethods
{
    public string GetTranStatus()
    {
        //log details about the transaction
        TransactionLogger log = new TransactionLogger(this);
        return ContextUtil.IsInTransaction.ToString();
    }
}

[Transaction(TransactionOption.NotSupported)]
[ClassInterface(ClassInterfaceType.None)]
public class DniScTransactionNotSupportedObj
    : ServicedComponent, ITranMethods
{
    public string GetTranStatus()
    {
        //log details about the transaction
        TransactionLogger log = new TransactionLogger(this);
        return ContextUtil.IsInTransaction.ToString();
    }
}

[Transaction(TransactionOption.Supported)]
[ClassInterface(ClassInterfaceType.None)]
public class DniScTransactionSupportedObj
    : ServicedComponent, ITranMethods
```

```
{
    public string GetTranStatus()
    {
        //log details about the transaction
        TransactionLogger log = new TransactionLogger(this);
        return ContextUtil.IsInTransaction.ToString();
    }
}


/// <summary>
/// Pass-through to the Supports class. When called
/// from this class that requires a transaction,
/// the Supports class is able to use the transaction.
/// </summary>
[Transaction(TransactionOption.Required)]
[ClassInterface(ClassInterfaceType.None)]
public class DniScTransactionUsesSupportsObj
    : ServicedComponent, ITranMethods
{
    public string GetTranStatus()
    {
        //log details about the transaction
        TransactionLogger log = new TransactionLogger(this);

        //call the object that supports but does
        //not require a transaction
        DniScTransactionSupportedObj obj
            = new DniScTransactionSupportedObj();
        obj.GetTranStatus();

        return ContextUtil.IsInTransaction.ToString();
    }
}


/// <summary>
/// Pass-through to the RequiresNew class. When called
/// from this class that requires a transaction,
/// the RequiresNew class should start a new transaction.
/// </summary>
[Transaction(TransactionOption.Required)]
[ClassInterface(ClassInterfaceType.None)]
public class DniScTransactionUsesRequiresNewObj
    : ServicedComponent, ITranMethods
{
    public string GetTranStatus()
    {
        //log details about the transaction
        TransactionLogger log = new TransactionLogger(this);
```

```
        //call the object that requires a new transaction
        DniScTransactionRequiresNewObj obj
            = new DniScTransactionRequiresNewObj();
        obj.GetTranStatus();

        return ContextUtil.IsInTransaction.ToString();
    }
}
```

Declaring automatic transactions for a class is the easy part. Viewing the results of a transaction is more difficult. Automatic transactions are created, used, and completed without our intervention. That's what makes them automatic. Because of this, it is difficult to observe a transaction while it is in use. It is created prior to the start of a method, and it doesn't actually end until after the method returns. You can really only see the results of a transaction by observing the effect it has on resource managers such as a database or queue.

However, .NET does provide a number of properties and methods in the ContextUtil and Transaction classes to help you monitor a transaction. The ContextUtil.IsInTransaction property used in these classes is one of those properties. As the name implies, it returns true or false to indicate whether there is an active transaction.

The TransactionLogger class used in these classes was written to help us observe a transaction in action. It logs various properties of a transaction to a text file. It is the primary mechanism that we use to see the effect that different attributes have on transactions. It uses the classes provided by .NET to accomplish this.

Note The use of the .NET classes that allow us to monitor and inspect the transaction state is really a separate discussion. For this reason, the details of the TransactionLogger class are covered in the previous recipe.

The project also requires these assembly-level attributes that are added to the AssemblyInfo.cs file:

```
[assembly: ApplicationActivation(ActivationOption.Server)]
[assembly: ApplicationAccessControl(false)]
[assembly: ApplicationName("DniTranApplication")]
[assembly: Description(".NET Interop Server Application")]
```

After building the project, adding it to the GAC, and executing regsvcs to register it, you are ready to write a client to test it. Here is a simple console application in C# that does that:

```
using System;
using System.Runtime.InteropServices;
using System.EnterpriseServices;
using DniScTransaction;

namespace ScTransaction
{
```

```
class Program
{
    static void Main(string[] args)
    {
        ITranMethods obj;

        obj = new DniScTransactionNoneObj();
        ExecuteTranMethod(obj);

        obj = new DniScTransactionDefaultObj();
        ExecuteTranMethod(obj);

        obj = new DniScTransactionRequiredObj();
        ExecuteTranMethod(obj);

        obj = new DniScTransactionRequiresNewObj();
        ExecuteTranMethod(obj);

        obj = new DniScTransactionDisabledObj();
        ExecuteTranMethod(obj);

        obj = new DniScTransactionNotSupportedObj();
        ExecuteTranMethod(obj);

        obj = new DniScTransactionSupportedObj();
        ExecuteTranMethod(obj);

        obj = new DniScTransactionUsesSupportsObj();
        ExecuteTranMethod(obj);

        obj = new DniScTransactionUsesRequiresNewObj();
        ExecuteTranMethod(obj);

        Console.Read();
    }

    static void ExecuteTranMethod(ITranMethods obj)
    {
        string msg = obj.GetTranStatus();
        Console.WriteLine("{0}.GetTranStatus: {1}",
            obj.GetType().Name, msg);
    }
}
}
```

The client creates each object in turn and calls the GetTranStatus method. Here are the results that we receive when we run this test:

```
DniScTransactionNoneObj.GetTranStatus: False
DniScTransactionDefaultObj.GetTranStatus: True
DniScTransactionRequiredObj.GetTranStatus: True
DniScTransactionRequiresNewObj.GetTranStatus: True
DniScTransactionDisabledObj.GetTranStatus: False
DniScTransactionNotSupportedObj.GetTranStatus: False
DniScTransactionSupportedObj.GetTranStatus: False
DniScTransactionUsesSupportsObj.GetTranStatus: True
DniScTransactionUsesRequiresNewObj.GetTranStatus: True
```

These results return a simple `true` or `false` for each class. This indicates that the method does or doesn't have an active transaction.

Much more interesting results are generated by the `TransactionLogger` class. This class logs details about the transaction when the method is first entered and when the transaction completes. Each class logs these details to a separate file. What follows is a review of these logs for each class.

This is logged for the `DniScTransactionNoneObj` class:

```
------Starting method call------
*Transaction at start of method:
***No current transaction***
```

This log makes perfect sense since this class doesn't include the `Transaction` attribute. The default setting for transaction support is `Disabled` if the `Transaction` attribute is omitted. So in this case, there are no transaction details to log.

Here is the log for the `DniScTransactionDefaultObj` class that uses the `Transaction` attribute without specifying a `TransactionOption`:

```
------Starting method call------
*Transaction at start of method:
 IsInTransaction: True
 MyTransactionVote: Commit
 IsolationLevel: Serializable
 Tran start time: 16:01:48.7064
 DistId: 00000000-0000-0000-0000-000000000000
 TranId: c3cfb690-7094-4fed-a3ac-ada8d1fec8e9:1
 Tran Status: Active
*Transaction at TransactionCompleted:
 IsInTransaction: True
 MyTransactionVote: Commit
 IsolationLevel: Serializable
 Tran start time: 16:01:48.7064
 DistId: 00000000-0000-0000-0000-000000000000
 TranId: c3cfb690-7094-4fed-a3ac-ada8d1fec8e9:1
 Tran Status: Committed
```

Since this class uses a transaction, we have much more detail available thanks to the TransactionLogger class.

In addition to the IsInTransaction property, we also display the Tran Status of the transaction (Active, Committed), the IsolationLevel (Serializable), the MyTransactionVote property (Commit) and two unique transaction IDs. The DistId is the distributed transaction ID and the TranId is the local transaction ID. The DistId consists of zeros since the transaction was handled locally without being escalated to a distributed transaction. The Tran start time indicates when the transaction started. This information is displayed twice for each method: first at the start of the method and then again when the transaction is completed. In this example we see that we do have a transaction at the start of the method. It starts with a state of Active and ends up with a state of Committed when the transaction completes.

Specifying the Transaction attribute without a TransactionOption is the same as entering TransactionOption.Required. Here is the log for the DniScTransactionRequiredObj class that uses a Transaction attribute with an explicit TransactionOption.Required:

```
------Starting method call------
*Transaction at start of method:
 IsInTransaction: True
 MyTransactionVote: Commit
 IsolationLevel: Serializable
 Tran start time: 16:01:48.8165
 DistId: 00000000-0000-0000-0000-000000000000
 TranId: c3cfb690-7094-4fed-a3ac-ada8d1fec8e9:2
 Tran Status: Active
*Transaction at TransactionCompleted:
 IsInTransaction: True
 MyTransactionVote: Commit
 IsolationLevel: Serializable
 Tran start time: 16:01:48.8165
 DistId: 00000000-0000-0000-0000-000000000000
 TranId: c3cfb690-7094-4fed-a3ac-ada8d1fec8e9:2
 Tran Status: Committed
```

Just like the last class, we have an active transaction that is Committed upon completion of the method. Notice that the transaction ID is different from the prior object. As illustrated here, transaction IDs are unique. This will later help us to determine when a method uses a transaction that it has inherited and when it creates a new transaction.

Note Remember that the local TranId shown in the log is a string, not a Guid. On the other hand, the DistId that represents a distributed transaction is actually a Guid. For many of these tests, only the last node of the TranId number changes. For instance, if we compare this test to the prior one, we see that the two local TranId numbers are as follows:

```
TranId: c3cfb690-7094-4fed-a3ac-ada8d1fec8e9:1
TranId: c3cfb690-7094-4fed-a3ac-ada8d1fec8e9:2
```

They differ only based on the last number.

The log for the DniScTransactionRequiresNewObj class (not shown) looks almost exactly like the last log. The only difference is that different transaction IDs are used. This class applies a Transaction attribute with TransactionOption.RequiresNew. This will force the creation of a new transaction even when one already exists.

We can consider the following classes together since the results we see for them are exactly the same:

- DniScTransactionDisabledObj

- DniScTransactionNotSupportedObj

- DniScTransactionSupportedObj

They all show that a transaction is not active at the time of the method call:

```
------Starting method call------
*Transaction at start of method:
***No current transaction***
```

This is as we expected, since none of the TransactionOption values used for these classes result in the creation of a new transaction. The DniScTransactionSupportedObj class uses the TransactionOption.Supported value. This supports an active transaction, but doesn't force the creation of one if it doesn't already exist.

The DniScTransactionUsesSupportsObj class is interesting because it shows us what happens when one component calls another one with a different TransactionOption value. The class itself specifies TransactionOption.Required so we know that a transaction will be created. But during the method call, an instance of the DniScTransactionSupportedObj class is created and used.

The previous call that we made to DniScTransactionSupportedObj did not have an active transaction. This time, we are calling it from a method that already has an active transaction, so the results should look different. What will the transaction state be when there is an active transaction? Here are the merged logs for both of these classes (the caller and the called):

```
UsesSupportsObj ------Starting method call------
UsesSupportsObj *Transaction at start of method:
UsesSupportsObj  IsInTransaction: True
UsesSupportsObj  MyTransactionVote: Commit
UsesSupportsObj  IsolationLevel: Serializable
UsesSupportsObj  Tran start time: 16:01:48.9868
UsesSupportsObj  DistId: 00000000-0000-0000-0000-000000000000
UsesSupportsObj  TranId: c3cfb690-7094-4fed-a3ac-ada8d1fec8e9:4
UsesSupportsObj  Tran Status: Active
SupportedObj ------Starting method call------
SupportedObj *Transaction at start of method:
SupportedObj  IsInTransaction: True
SupportedObj  MyTransactionVote: Commit
SupportedObj  IsolationLevel: Serializable
SupportedObj  Tran start time: 16:01:48.9868
SupportedObj  DistId: 00000000-0000-0000-0000-000000000000
SupportedObj  TranId: c3cfb690-7094-4fed-a3ac-ada8d1fec8e9:4
SupportedObj  Tran Status: Active
UsesSupportsObj *Transaction at TransactionCompleted:
UsesSupportsObj  IsInTransaction: True
UsesSupportsObj  MyTransactionVote: Commit
UsesSupportsObj  IsolationLevel: Serializable
UsesSupportsObj  Tran start time: 16:01:48.9868
UsesSupportsObj  DistId: 00000000-0000-0000-0000-000000000000
UsesSupportsObj  TranId: c3cfb690-7094-4fed-a3ac-ada8d1fec8e9:4
UsesSupportsObj  Tran Status: Committed
SupportedObj *Transaction at TransactionCompleted:
SupportedObj  IsInTransaction: True
SupportedObj  MyTransactionVote: Commit
SupportedObj  IsolationLevel: Serializable
SupportedObj  Tran start time: 16:01:48.9868
SupportedObj  DistId: 00000000-0000-0000-0000-000000000000
SupportedObj  TranId: c3cfb690-7094-4fed-a3ac-ada8d1fec8e9:4
SupportedObj  Tran Status: Committed
```

The logs show us that the same active transaction is shared by both of these objects. The DniScTransactionUsesSupportsObj object starts with an active transaction. This time when the test method in the DniScTransactionSupportedObj object is called, it has an active transaction. By comparing the transaction IDs, we see this is the same transaction as the one used by the caller. The called component has enlisted itself with the transaction of the caller.

When the transaction completes, the completion event is logged for each class. The calling object (DniScTransactionUsesSupportsObj) is logged first, followed by the called object (DniScTransactionSupportedObj).

■**Note** Remember that there is really only one transaction used in this example; it isn't Committed twice. The event that notifies us that the transaction has been completed is being handled twice since we subscribed to it within two objects.

The DniScTransactionUsesRequiresNewObj class performs a similar test. It requires a transaction itself, and it calls the test method of the DniScTransactionRequiresNewObj class. This called class specifies TransactionOption.RequiresNew, so we should see that it creates a new transaction that is different from the one used by the caller. The merged logs for these two classes looks like this:

```
UsesRequiresNewObj ------Starting method call------
UsesRequiresNewObj *Transaction at start of method:
UsesRequiresNewObj  IsInTransaction: True
UsesRequiresNewObj  MyTransactionVote: Commit
UsesRequiresNewObj  IsolationLevel: Serializable
UsesRequiresNewObj  Tran start time: 16:01:49.1070
UsesRequiresNewObj  DistId: 00000000-0000-0000-0000-000000000000
UsesRequiresNewObj  TranId: c3cfb690-7094-4fed-a3ac-ada8d1fec8e9:5
UsesRequiresNewObj  Tran Status: Active
RequiresNewObj ------Starting method call------
RequiresNewObj *Transaction at start of method:
RequiresNewObj  IsInTransaction: True
RequiresNewObj  MyTransactionVote: Commit
RequiresNewObj  IsolationLevel: Serializable
RequiresNewObj  Tran start time: 16:01:49.1670
RequiresNewObj  DistId: 00000000-0000-0000-0000-000000000000
RequiresNewObj  TranId: c3cfb690-7094-4fed-a3ac-ada8d1fec8e9:6
RequiresNewObj  Tran Status: Active
UsesRequiresNewObj *Transaction at TransactionCompleted:
UsesRequiresNewObj  IsInTransaction: True
UsesRequiresNewObj  MyTransactionVote: Commit
UsesRequiresNewObj  IsolationLevel: Serializable
UsesRequiresNewObj  Tran start time: 16:01:49.1070
UsesRequiresNewObj  DistId: 00000000-0000-0000-0000-000000000000
UsesRequiresNewObj  TranId: c3cfb690-7094-4fed-a3ac-ada8d1fec8e9:5
UsesRequiresNewObj  Tran Status: Committed
RequiresNewObj *Transaction at TransactionCompleted:
RequiresNewObj  IsInTransaction: True
RequiresNewObj  MyTransactionVote: Commit
RequiresNewObj  IsolationLevel: Serializable
RequiresNewObj  Tran start time: 16:01:49.1670
RequiresNewObj  DistId: 00000000-0000-0000-0000-000000000000
RequiresNewObj  TranId: c3cfb690-7094-4fed-a3ac-ada8d1fec8e9:6
RequiresNewObj  Tran Status: Committed
```

As we saw in the prior example, the called object has an active transaction at the beginning of the method call. When the test method of the DniScTransactionUsesRequiresNewObj object is called, it also has an active transaction. However, if we compare the transaction ID for these two objects, we see that they are indeed different. This is what we expect to see, since the called object uses TransactionOption.RequiresNew. The log also shows that both transactions are committed.

Related Information

See recipes 9-3 (Placing an Automatic Vote), 9-4 (Placing a Manual Vote), 9-1 (Monitoring Transaction Status), and 8-1 (Exposing Managed Code to COM+).

9-3. Placing an Automatic Vote

Problem

What is the easiest way to handle voting for an automatic transaction?

Solution

All methods that are part of a transaction are required to place their vote on the success or failure of the transaction. Voting for an automatic transaction can be done automatically using the AutoComplete attribute. This is a method-level attribute that should be placed on methods that use transactions, for example:

```
[Transaction(TransactionOption.Required)]
public class MyTranClass : ServicedComponent
{
    [AutoComplete]
    public void DoSomeWork()
    {
        //perform some work using a database or queue

        //throw an exception if there is a problem

        //return normally if everything is ok
    }
}
```

The AutoComplete attribute causes a vote to be placed for you when the method returns. It enables these two built-in .NET rules to determine how to vote:

- If the method returns normally without throwing an exception, a vote to *complete* the transaction is placed.

- If an unhandled exception is thrown during the method call, a vote to *abort* the transaction is placed.

An alternate way to cast a vote to abort is to set the MyTransactionVote property of the ContextUtil class to Abort, for example:

```
if (thereIsAProblem)
{
    ContextUtil.MyTransactionVote    = TransactionVote.Abort;
}
```

This changes the vote that will be placed for you to Abort. You could use this alternate approach in situations where the code doesn't actually throw an exception but does need to abort the transaction.

How It Works

The following C# code demonstrates the use of the AutoComplete attribute. We start with the definition of an interface that clients will use:

```
using System;

namespace DniScVoting
{
    public enum RequestedResult
    {
        Success,
        VoteToAbort,
        ThrowException
    }

    public interface ITranMethods
    {
        void PerformWork(RequestedResult request);
    }
}
```

The ITranMethods interface defines a single PerformWork method. The method accepts a single parameter of type RequestedResult. This is an enum that identifies the type of result that we want the method to produce.

The plan for this test is to call the PerformWork method multiple times, requesting a different result each time. We can then observe the effect that each result has on the active transaction.

A C# class that implements this interface looks like this:

```
using System;
using System.EnterpriseServices;
using System.Runtime.InteropServices;

using TransactionLogging;

namespace DniScVoting
{
```

```
[Transaction(TransactionOption.Required)]
[ClassInterface(ClassInterfaceType.None)]
public class DniScAutoVoteObj
    : ServicedComponent, ITranMethods
{
    [AutoComplete]
    public void PerformWork(RequestedResult request)
    {
        //log the transaction
        TransactionLogger log
            = new TransactionLogger(this);

        //determine what kind of result was requested
        switch (request)
        {
            case RequestedResult.VoteToAbort:
                ContextUtil.MyTransactionVote
                    = TransactionVote.Abort;
                break;
            case RequestedResult.ThrowException:
                throw new ApplicationException(
                    "Transaction should be aborted");
            default:
                break;
        }
    }
}
}
```

Each time the PerformWork method is called, it will produce one of three different results: throw an exception, set the MyTransactionVote property to Abort, or allow the method to return without doing anything. This last result should be interpreted as a success and the transaction should be committed.

Note The TransactionLogger class that we construct within the method is used to log the transaction state. It is used only to help us observe the votes that are cast for the transaction. The details of this class are covered in recipe 9-1 (Monitoring Transaction Status).

The project also uses these assembly-level attributes that are applied to the AssemblyInfo.cs file:

```
[assembly: ApplicationActivation(ActivationOption.Server)]
[assembly: ApplicationAccessControl(false)]
[assembly: ApplicationName("DniTranApplication")]
[assembly: Description(".NET Interop Server Application")]
```

Here is the Visual Basic .NET (VB.NET) implementation of this class and interface. First, the enum and the interface are defined like this:

```
Public Enum RequestedResult
    Success
    VoteToAbort
    ThrowException
End Enum


Public Interface ITranMethods
    Sub PerformWork(ByVal request As RequestedResult)
End Interface
```

The class is implemented like this in VB.NET:

```
Imports System.Runtime.InteropServices
Imports System.EnterpriseServices

<Transaction(TransactionOption.Required)> _
<ClassInterface(ClassInterfaceType.None)> _
Public Class DniScAutoVoteObj
    Inherits ServicedComponent
    Implements ITranMethods

    <AutoComplete()> _
    Public Sub PerformWork(ByVal request As RequestedResult) _
            Implements ITranMethods.PerformWork
        'log the transaction
        Dim log As TransactionLogging.TransactionLogger _
            = New TransactionLogging.TransactionLogger(Me)

        'determine what kind of result was requested
        Select Case request
            Case RequestedResult.VoteToAbort
                ContextUtil.MyTransactionVote _
                    = TransactionVote.Abort
            Case RequestedResult.ThrowException
                Throw New ApplicationException( _
                    "Transaction should be aborted")
        End Select
    End Sub
End Class
```

And the assembly-level attributes that are added to the AssemblyInfo.vb file look like this:

```
Imports System.EnterpriseServices

<Assembly: ApplicationActivation(ActivationOption.Server)>
<Assembly: ApplicationAccessControl(False)>
```

```
<Assembly: ApplicationName("DniTranApplication")>
<Assembly: Description(".NET Interop Server Application")>
```

To test this code, we use a simple C# console application implemented like this:

```
using System;
using System.Runtime.InteropServices;

using DniScVoting;

namespace ScVoting
{
    class Program
    {
        static void Main(string[] args)
        {
            AutoVotingTest(RequestedResult.Success);
            AutoVotingTest(RequestedResult.ThrowException);
            AutoVotingTest(RequestedResult.VoteToAbort);

            Console.Read();
        }

        private static void AutoVotingTest(RequestedResult request)
        {
            try
            {
                ITranMethods obj
                    = new DniScAutoVoteObj();

                obj.PerformWork(request);
                Console.WriteLine(
                    "DniScAutoVoteObj with {0} completed",
                    request);

                //this keeps the log files tidy
                System.Threading.Thread.Sleep(200);
            }
            catch (Exception e)
            {
                Console.WriteLine(
                    "DniScAutoVoteObj with {0} Exception: {1}",
                        request, e.Message);
            }
        }
    }
}
```

An instance of the test object is created and the PerformWork method is called. This is done three times, once for each of the requested results.

▇Note The slight delay of Sleep(200) added at the end of each test is used only to keep the transaction log files in order. The TransactionLogger class writes to a single file with a name based on the component being tested. Therefore, each time we execute the PerformWork method, we're writing to the same file. Without this delay, it is possible to begin logging a new transaction while the class is still writing the completion event from the last transaction. Adding the delay provides the class with time to flush out any remaining lines of text.

This test application uses the C# version of the class. However, you could easily use the VB.NET version and receive the same results. To do this, you would need to reference the VB.NET project instead of the C# project. You would also need to change the using DniScVoting statement to using DniScVotingVB.

When this test is executed, the results we see look like this:

```
DniScAutoVoteObj with Success completed
DniScAutoVoteObj with ThrowException Exception:
    Transaction should be aborted
DniScAutoVoteObj with VoteToAbort completed
```

If we view the transaction log produced by the TransactionLogger class, we see the whole transaction story for each method call.

As expected, the call that passed RequestedResult.Success committed the transaction:

```
------Starting method call------
*Transaction at start of method:
 IsInTransaction: True
 MyTransactionVote: Commit
 IsolationLevel: Serializable
 Tran start time: 15:15:32.4164
 DistId: 00000000-0000-0000-0000-000000000000
 TranId: 384f3b63-ac1b-4c5c-87c2-613248d93a1d:1
 Tran Status: Active
*Transaction at TransactionCompleted:
 IsInTransaction: True
 MyTransactionVote: Commit
 IsolationLevel: Serializable
 Tran start time: 15:15:32.4164
 DistId: 00000000-0000-0000-0000-000000000000
 TranId: 384f3b63-ac1b-4c5c-87c2-613248d93a1d:1
 Tran Status: Committed
```

The call that passed RequestedResult.ThrowException resulted in an aborted transaction:

```
------Starting method call------
*Transaction at start of method:
 IsInTransaction: True
 MyTransactionVote: Commit
 IsolationLevel: Serializable
 Tran start time: 15:15:32.7369
 DistId: 00000000-0000-0000-0000-000000000000
 TranId: 384f3b63-ac1b-4c5c-87c2-613248d93a1d:2
 Tran Status: Active
*Transaction at TransactionCompleted:
 IsInTransaction: True
 MyTransactionVote: Commit
 IsolationLevel: Serializable
 Tran start time: 15:15:32.7369
 DistId: 00000000-0000-0000-0000-000000000000
 TranId: 384f3b63-ac1b-4c5c-87c2-613248d93a1d:2
 Tran Status: Aborted
```

The call passing RequestedResult.VoteToAbort also resulted in an aborted transaction:

```
------Starting method call------
*Transaction at start of method:
 IsInTransaction: True
 MyTransactionVote: Commit
 IsolationLevel: Serializable
 Tran start time: 15:15:33.0673
 DistId: 00000000-0000-0000-0000-000000000000
 TranId: 384f3b63-ac1b-4c5c-87c2-613248d93a1d:3
 Tran Status: Active
*Transaction at TransactionCompleted:
 IsInTransaction: True
 MyTransactionVote: Abort
 IsolationLevel: Serializable
 Tran start time: 15:15:33.0673
 DistId: 00000000-0000-0000-0000-000000000000
 TranId: 384f3b63-ac1b-4c5c-87c2-613248d93a1d:3
 Tran Status: Aborted
```

Notice that this last test (RequestedResult.VoteToAbort) correctly aborted the transaction, but the method didn't provide the caller with any indication that the abort took place. This highlights one import aspect of transactions: they do not replace a normal feedback mechanism for a method.

Any well-designed method should provide some feedback to the caller as to the success or failure of the method. This can be done by simply returning a result value or by throwing an exception. In the example, our test method doesn't provide this feedback. The caller doesn't know that the underlying transaction was aborted. The version that throws an exception does provide feedback when an abnormal condition occurs.

In this example, we have a single client application calling a single method of a COM+ component. The transaction will be committed or aborted based on the vote of that single method.

In the real world, components frequently use methods from other components. If the called methods also support transactions, they are enlisted in the current transaction. Each method is allowed to vote on the success or failure of the transaction. In order to commit a transaction, all methods must vote to commit. A single vote to abort is enough to throw away the entire transaction, rolling back any work performed by all of the components. This is not a situation where the majority rules—there can be no dissenting votes.

With multiple components voting in a transaction, how does COM+ know when the vote has ended? The votes are counted when the *transaction root* object is finished. The root is the component and method that originally caused the creation of a new transaction. It may call other components that in turn call other components, and so on. But the votes that have been cast are finally counted when the original method returns to its caller. Any components that are called during the lifetime of the transaction are called *interior* objects.

A COM+ context actually supports two separate but related flags. The *consistent* flag indicates that the object is in either a consistent or inconsistent state. When we vote to commit a transaction, this flag is set to indicate that everything is consistent.

The *done* flag determines if the object has completed its work and can be deactivated. Only when this is set to true will COM+ deactivate the object. During deactivation, it checks the consistent flag to determine the success or failure of the transaction.

The consistent flag is used to cast a vote to commit or abort the transaction. The done flag indicates that the component's vote is now final. Fortunately, when `AutoComplete` does the voting for us, it sets both of these flags. This allows the object to be immediately deactivated and its vote finalized.

It is possible to auto-complete transactions without the use of the `AutoComplete` attribute, although this is not recommended. By default, when a method starts, the vote is initialized to commit. If nothing occurs to change this vote, the method will end with a vote to commit. However, without the `AutoComplete` attribute, the done flag isn't set. This means the vote will not be cast immediately when a method returns. The transaction will eventually be committed, but it will have to wait until there are no references to the object and it is finally deactivated. This could take seconds or even longer depending on how long object references are held.

Related Information

See recipes 9-2 (Enabling Automatic Transactions), 9-1 (Monitoring Transaction Status), 9-4 (Placing a Manual Vote), and 9-5 (Defining a Unit of Work).

9-4. Placing a Manual Vote

Problem

Instead of using the `AutoComplete` attribute to place votes for a transaction, is there a way to do this manually?

Solution

.NET does provide a way to manually cast a vote for a transaction. It's generally easier to use the AutoComplete attribute and allow .NET to handle the details for you. However, it really comes down to style and preference. Either approach works fine.

To take control over transaction voting, you omit the AutoComplete attribute. Instead, you call the SetComplete and SetAbort static methods of the ContextUtil class, for example:

```
[Transaction(TransactionOption.Required)]
public class MyManualTranClass : ServicedComponent
{
    public void DoSomeWork()
    {
        //perform some work using a database or queue

        //set the transaction vote
        if (noProblems)
        {
            ContextUtil.SetComplete();
        }
        else
        {
            ContextUtil.SetAbort();
        }
    }
}
```

You call SetComplete if the work that was performed in the method should be committed. As the name implies, calling SetAbort instructs COM+ to abort the current transaction, rolling back all pending work that was part of the transaction.

Calling either of these methods sets the consistent and done flags within the COM+ context. The consistent flag is used to cast a vote to commit or abort the transaction. The done flag indicates that the component's vote is now final. Setting the done flag is important since it allows immediate deactivation of the object and completion of the transaction.

As an alternative to these methods, you can set properties that set each of these COM+ context flags individually. Setting the MyTransactionVote static property of the ContextUtil class sets the consistent flag. The DeactivateOnReturn property of this same class sets the done flag, for example:

```
[Transaction(TransactionOption.Required)]
public class MyManualTranClass : ServicedComponent
{
    public void DoSomeWork()
    {
        //perform some work using a database or queue

        //always set the done flag
        ContextUtil.DeactivateOnReturn = true;
```

```
        //set the transaction vote
        if (noProblems)
        {
            ContextUtil.MyTransactionVote
                = TransactionVote.Commit;
        }
        else
        {
            ContextUtil.MyTransactionVote
                = TransactionVote.Abort;
        }
    }
}
```

Regardless of the method that you choose to set a transaction vote, you must make sure that you always vote. In particular, you should watch out for exception conditions that may bypass the normal logic that casts a vote. Throwing an exception does not automatically vote to abort the transaction. Remember, without the AutoComplete attribute, you are handling all of the voting duties.

For this reason, it is often a good idea to set a default vote early in the method, perhaps immediately upon entry to the method. You can then override this default when you reach a point of success in the code. There is no problem with setting these properties or calling SetComplete or SetAbort multiple times. The last vote that is in effect when the method completes is the one that is applied. This is illustrated in the examples shown in the next section.

How It Works

The examples that follow illustrate ways to handle manual transaction voting. We use the same C# interface and enum that was defined in recipe 9-3 (Placing an Automatic Vote):

```
using System;

namespace DniScVoting
{
    public enum RequestedResult
    {
        Success,
        VoteToAbort,
        ThrowException
    }

    public interface ITranMethods
    {
        void PerformWork(RequestedResult request);
    }
}
```

The ITranMethods interface defines a single PerformWork method. The method accepts a single parameter of type RequestedResult. This is an enum that identifies the type of result that we want the method to produce.

Our test code will call the PerformWork method multiple times, requesting a different result each time. We can then observe the effect that each result has on the active transaction.

Here is a C# class that implements this interface and performs manual voting:

```csharp
using System;
using System.EnterpriseServices;
using System.Runtime.InteropServices;

using TransactionLogging;

namespace DniScVoting
{
    [Transaction(TransactionOption.Required)]
    [ClassInterface(ClassInterfaceType.None)]
    public class DniScSetManualVoteObj
        : ServicedComponent, ITranMethods
    {
        public void PerformWork(RequestedResult request)
        {
            //log the transaction
            TransactionLogger log
                = new TransactionLogger(this);

            ContextUtil.SetComplete();

            try
            {
                //determine what kind of result was requested
                switch (request)
                {
                    case RequestedResult.VoteToAbort:
                    case RequestedResult.ThrowException:
                        throw new ApplicationException(
                            "Transaction should be aborted");
                    default:
                        break;
                }

                //if we get this far,
                //the SetComplete vote will stand
            }
            catch (Exception e)
            {
                ContextUtil.SetAbort();
                throw e;
```

```
                }
            }
        }
}
```

Almost immediately upon entry to the method, we call SetComplete. We do this to provide a default vote. If the method returns without an exception condition, this is the vote that will apply.

For exceptions, we call SetAbort. We've chosen to put the bulk of the code within a try/catch block. This allows us to throw exceptions at any point in our code and handle the call to SetAbort in one central location where those exceptions are caught.

With this code, we've made the assumption that the method will complete normally and that we will only call SetAbort on exceptions. We could have just as easily reversed this assumption by immediately calling SetAbort at the start of the method. Then we would call SetComplete at the end of our normal processing logic if we reached that point.

It really comes down to preference. In either case, choose an approach and consistently use it throughout your code.

Note The TransactionLogger class that we construct within the method is used to log the transaction state. It is used only to help us observe the votes that are cast for the transaction. The details of this class are covered in recipe 9-1 (Monitoring Transaction Status).

The project also uses these assembly-level attributes that are applied to the AssemblyInfo.cs file:

```
[assembly: ApplicationActivation(ActivationOption.Server)]
[assembly: ApplicationAccessControl(false)]
[assembly: ApplicationName("DniTranApplication")]
[assembly: Description(".NET Interop Server Application")]
```

Here is the same class and interface implemented in Visual Basic .NET (VB.NET). First, we define the interface and enum:

```
Public Enum RequestedResult
    Success
    VoteToAbort
    ThrowException
End Enum


Public Interface ITranMethods
    Sub PerformWork(ByVal request As RequestedResult)
End Interface
```

We then implement this interface with a VB.NET class that performs manual voting:

```
Imports System.Runtime.InteropServices
Imports System.EnterpriseServices
Imports DniScVotingVB.TransactionLogging
```

```vbnet
<Transaction(TransactionOption.Required)> _
<ClassInterface(ClassInterfaceType.None)> _
Public Class DniScSetManualVoteObj
    Inherits ServicedComponent
    Implements ITranMethods

    Public Sub PerformWork(ByVal request As RequestedResult) _
            Implements ITranMethods.PerformWork
        'log the transaction
        Dim log As TransactionLogger _
            = New TransactionLogger(Me)

        'set the default vote prior to performing any work
        ContextUtil.SetComplete()

        Try
            'determine what kind of result was requested
            Select Case request
                Case RequestedResult.VoteToAbort, _
                    RequestedResult.ThrowException
                    Throw New ApplicationException( _
                        "Transaction should be aborted")
            End Select

            'if we get this far,
            'the SetComplete vote will stand

        Catch ex As Exception
            ContextUtil.SetAbort()
            Throw ex
        End Try

    End Sub
End Class
```

The necessary assembly-level attributes are also added to the AssemblyInfo.vb file:

```vbnet
Imports System.EnterpriseServices

<Assembly: ApplicationActivation(ActivationOption.Server)>
<Assembly: ApplicationAccessControl(False)>
<Assembly: ApplicationName("DniTranApplication")>
<Assembly: Description(".NET Interop Server Application")>
```

Our C# client code looks like this:

```csharp
using System;
using System.Runtime.InteropServices;
```

```csharp
using DniScVoting;

namespace ScVoting
{
    class Program
    {
        static void Main(string[] args)
        {
            SetManualVotingTest(RequestedResult.Success);
            SetManualVotingTest(RequestedResult.ThrowException);
            SetManualVotingTest(RequestedResult.VoteToAbort);

            Console.Read();
        }

        private static void SetManualVotingTest(RequestedResult request)
        {
            try
            {
                ITranMethods obj
                    = new DniScSetManualVoteObj();

                obj.PerformWork(request);
                Console.WriteLine(
                    "DniScSetManualVoteObj with {0} completed",
                    request);

                //this keeps the log files tidy
                System.Threading.Thread.Sleep(200);
            }
            catch (Exception e)
            {
                Console.WriteLine(
                    "DniScSetManualVoteObj with {0} Exception: {1}",
                        request, e.Message);
            }
        }
    }
}
```

As shown here, this application uses the C# version of our class. To use the VB.NET version instead, we only have to reference the VB.NET project instead of the C# project. The results are the same for the C# and VB.NET versions.

The code calls the test object three times, once with each requested result. The first call should commit the transaction, while the others should result in an aborted transaction. When we execute this code, we see these results:

```
DniScSetManualVoteObj with Success completed
DniScSetManualVoteObj with ThrowException Exception:
    Transaction should be aborted
DniScSetManualVoteObj with VoteToAbort Exception:
    Transaction should be aborted
```

If we review the transaction log file produced by the TransactionLogger class, we see that the first request committed the transaction:

```
------Starting method call------
*Transaction at start of method:
 IsInTransaction: True
 MyTransactionVote: Commit
 IsolationLevel: Serializable
 Tran start time: 19:02:32.9259
 DistId: 00000000-0000-0000-0000-000000000000
 TranId: 077abde2-e10c-4e06-9518-93b8efbc6287:15
 Tran Status: Active
*Transaction at TransactionCompleted:
 IsInTransaction: True
 MyTransactionVote: Commit
 IsolationLevel: Serializable
 Tran start time: 19:02:32.9259
 DistId: 00000000-0000-0000-0000-000000000000
 TranId: 077abde2-e10c-4e06-9518-93b8efbc6287:15
 Tran Status: Committed
```

The second method call aborted the transaction:

```
------Starting method call------
*Transaction at start of method:
 IsInTransaction: True
 MyTransactionVote: Commit
 IsolationLevel: Serializable
 Tran start time: 19:02:33.1763
 DistId: 00000000-0000-0000-0000-000000000000
 TranId: 077abde2-e10c-4e06-9518-93b8efbc6287:16
 Tran Status: Active
*Transaction at TransactionCompleted:
 IsInTransaction: True
 MyTransactionVote: Abort
 IsolationLevel: Serializable
 Tran start time: 19:02:33.1763
 DistId: 00000000-0000-0000-0000-000000000000
 TranId: 077abde2-e10c-4e06-9518-93b8efbc6287:16
 Tran Status: Aborted
```

And the third call also ended with an aborted transaction:

```
------Starting method call------
*Transaction at start of method:
 IsInTransaction: True
 MyTransactionVote: Commit
 IsolationLevel: Serializable
 Tran start time: 19:02:33.3165
 DistId: 00000000-0000-0000-0000-000000000000
 TranId: 077abde2-e10c-4e06-9518-93b8efbc6287:17
 Tran Status: Active
*Transaction at TransactionCompleted:
 IsInTransaction: True
 MyTransactionVote: Abort
 IsolationLevel: Serializable
 Tran start time: 19:02:33.3165
 DistId: 00000000-0000-0000-0000-000000000000
 TranId: 077abde2-e10c-4e06-9518-93b8efbc6287:17
 Tran Status: Aborted
```

As an alternative, we could have written the class this way in C#:

```csharp
using System;
using System.EnterpriseServices;
using System.Runtime.InteropServices;

using TransactionLogging;

namespace DniScVoting
{
    [Transaction(TransactionOption.Required)]
    [ClassInterface(ClassInterfaceType.None)]
    public class DniScSetManualVoteObj
        : ServicedComponent, ITranMethods
    {
        public void PerformWork(RequestedResult request)
        {
            //log the transaction
            TransactionLogger log
                = new TransactionLogger(this);

            //indicate that the object is done when
            //this method returns
            ContextUtil.DeactivateOnReturn = true;
```

```
//determine what kind of result was requested
switch (request)
{
    case RequestedResult.Success:
        ContextUtil.MyTransactionVote
            = TransactionVote.Commit;
        break;
    case RequestedResult.VoteToAbort:
        ContextUtil.MyTransactionVote
            = TransactionVote.Abort;
        break;
    case RequestedResult.ThrowException:
        //must still vote even though we
        //throw an exception
        ContextUtil.MyTransactionVote
            = TransactionVote.Abort;
        throw new ApplicationException(
            "Transaction should be aborted");
    default:
        break;
    }
}
}
}
```

This version sets the DeactivateOnReturn and MyTransactionVote static properties of the ContextUtil class instead of calling SetComplete and SetAbort.

This code produces similar results to the last test. When passed the RequestedResult.Success parameter, the transaction is committed. The other calls result in an aborted transaction.

Related Information

See recipes 9-3 (Placing an Automatic Vote), 9-2 (Enabling Automatic Transactions), and 9-1 (Monitoring Transaction Status).

9-5. Defining a Unit of Work

Problem

If multiple components use the same transaction, how do they affect one another? What happens when one component aborts the transaction? When is the transaction committed? Is there a way for a component to always use a separate transaction?

Solution

When a component calls a method in another component, it is possible that the two calls will use the same transaction. This all depends on the Transaction attribute settings that were applied to each class.

If they do use the same transaction, they will succeed or fail together. This is by design since they are participating in the same logical unit of work. Because this is the primary reason to use transactions, it is the behavior you would expect.

As each method returns control to the caller, a vote is cast for the transaction. The vote can be to complete the transaction or to abort it. For the completion to take place, the vote must be unanimous. If any method votes to abort the transaction, everything under the control of the transaction will be rolled back.

The called component will use the same transaction as the caller if they are placed into the same COM+ context. The context is an environment that is created by COM+ where objects live. Each context has a set of properties that determine the transaction state, among other things. Every COM+ component is activated into either a new or existing context. If the transaction attributes of the called component are compatible with the caller, they can live in the same context. This means they will share the same transaction.

The TransactionOption property of the Transaction attribute is one of the properties that determine if two components are compatible. Isolation level is another one.

Table 9-2 summarizes the compatibility between two components based on their TransactionOption settings. The calling object is the First Component while the called object is the Second Component. The assumption is that the First Component is the first COM+ component called by a client application.

Table 9-2. *TransactionOption Settings for Multiple Components*

First Component	Is Root?	Transaction	Second Component	Is Root?	Transaction
Required	Yes	New	Required	No	Shared
Required	Yes	New	RequiresNew	Yes	New
Required	Yes	New	Supported	No	Shared
Required	Yes	New	NotSupported		None
RequiresNew	Yes	New	Required	No	Shared
RequiresNew	Yes	New	RequiresNew	Yes	New
RequiresNew	Yes	New	Supported	No	Shared
RequiresNew	Yes	New	NotSupported		None
Supported		None	Required	Yes	New
Supported		None	RequiresNew	Yes	New
Supported		None	Supported		None
Supported		None	NotSupported		None
NotSupported		None	Required	Yes	New
NotSupported		None	RequiresNew	Yes	New
NotSupported		None	Supported		None
NotSupported		None	NotSupported		None

The possible values for the Transaction column are as follows:

- *None*: No transaction will be used.

- *New*: A new transaction will be created and used.

- *Shared*: The existing transaction will be shared by both components.

The final decision to complete or abort the transaction is made when the *root component* completes its work. The root component is the one that originated the transaction. Any other components that share the original transaction are called *interior objects*. The Is Root? columns in Table 9-2 identify the object that is the root of the transaction (if there is one).

For example, a client application may call a method of a component that requires a transaction. Let's call that component A. During the method call to A, a call is made to a method in another component (B) that uses the same transaction. When B returns, a vote is cast to complete the transaction.

But the transaction is not immediately completed since we are still in the middle of the A call. The A method may need to call other components or perform other work—all under the same transaction. Finally, when the A method completes, the transaction is completed. The A component was the root and B was the interior component.

Remember that automatic transactions do not replace a normal feedback mechanism for a method. Any well-designed method should provide some feedback to the caller as to the success or failure of the method. This can be done by simply returning a result value or by throwing an exception if there is a problem. The flow of control from one component to another is still entirely in the hands of the developer.

When the called component uses the `RequiresNew` option, a new transaction is always created. The called component has now created its own unit of work and has effectively become its own root transaction object.

How It Works

To demonstrate the behavior of multiple components, the code that follows implements three classes. The `DniScRootObj` class requires a transaction and will be the one called by a client application. Another class (`DniScCalledObj`) is called from this root and also requires a transaction. The final class (`DniScCalledNewObj`) uses the `RequiresNew` option for the `Transaction` attribute. This means it should always receive a separate transaction from the caller.

We start with a common interface in C# that is implemented by both called classes:

```
using System;

namespace DniScMultiComponents
{
    public interface ICalledComponent
    {
        bool PerformUpdate(bool succeed);
    }
}
```

The first called class is implemented like this in C#:

```
using System;
using System.EnterpriseServices;
using System.Runtime.InteropServices;

using TransactionLogging;

namespace DniScMultiComponents
{
    [Transaction(TransactionOption.Required)]
    [ClassInterface(ClassInterfaceType.None)]
    public class DniScCalledObj
        : ServicedComponent, ICalledComponent
    {
        public bool PerformUpdate(bool succeed)
        {
            //log the transaction
            TransactionLogger log
                = new TransactionLogger(this);

            //set the default vote
            ContextUtil.SetComplete();

            if (!succeed)
            {
                ContextUtil.SetAbort();
                throw new ApplicationException(
                    "Exception was requested");
            }
            return succeed;
        }
    }
}
```

The class uses the Required option for the Transaction attribute. This means it will use the transaction from the caller if one exists. The sole test method uses the TransactionLogger class that we developed in recipe 9-1 (Monitoring Transaction Status). The purpose of this class is to log the results shown shortly.

Based on the bool value that is passed as a parameter, the method either returns normally or throws an exception. The static SetComplete and SetAbort methods of the ContextUtil class are used to perform the voting.

The second called class is almost identical:

```
using System;
using System.EnterpriseServices;
using System.Runtime.InteropServices;

using TransactionLogging;
```

```
namespace DniScMultiComponents
{
    [Transaction(TransactionOption.RequiresNew)]
    [ClassInterface(ClassInterfaceType.None)]
    public class DniScCalledNewObj
        : ServicedComponent, ICalledComponent
    {
        public bool PerformUpdate(bool succeed)
        {
            //log the transaction
            TransactionLogger log
                = new TransactionLogger(this);

            //set the default vote
            ContextUtil.SetComplete();

            if (!succeed)
            {
                ContextUtil.SetAbort();
                throw new ApplicationException(
                    "Exception was requested");
            }
            return succeed;
        }
    }
}
```

Other than the class name, the only difference is the TransactionOption. Here we specify RequiresNew instead of Required. This means that a new transaction will always be created when this class is used.

The root class is fairly simple:

```
using System;
using System.EnterpriseServices;
using System.Runtime.InteropServices;

using TransactionLogging;

namespace DniScMultiComponents
{
    public interface IRootComponent
    {
        bool PerformUpdate(int testNumber);
    }

    [Transaction(TransactionOption.Required)]
    [ClassInterface(ClassInterfaceType.None)]
    public class DniScRootObj
```

```
    : ServicedComponent, IRootComponent
{
    public bool PerformUpdate(int testNumber)
    {
        //log the transaction
        TransactionLogger log
            = new TransactionLogger(this);

        //set the default vote
        ContextUtil.SetComplete();

        ICalledComponent calledObj;
        try
        {
            switch (testNumber)
            {
                //everything succeeds
                case (1):
                    calledObj = new DniScCalledObj();
                    calledObj.PerformUpdate(true);
                    break;

                //called component throws exception
                case (2):
                    calledObj = new DniScCalledObj();
                    calledObj.PerformUpdate(false);
                    break;

                //called obj RequiresNew - everything succeeds
                case (3):
                    calledObj = new DniScCalledNewObj();
                    calledObj.PerformUpdate(true);
                    break;

                //called obj RequiresNew - throws exception
                case (4):
                    calledObj = new DniScCalledNewObj();
                    calledObj.PerformUpdate(false);
                    break;

                default:
                    break;
            }
        }
        catch (Exception)
        {
```

```
                //we ignore any exceptions from the called object
                return false;
            }

        return true;
        }
    }
}
```

This class also requires a transaction. The bulk of the PerformUpdate method is a switch statement. Depending on the test number passed in as a parameter, one of the called objects is created and the test method called with either a true or false value. If we pass in false, the called object will throw an exception.

As is always the case with COM+ components, we need to include these assembly-level attributes. They are placed in the AssemblyInfo.cs file:

```
[assembly: ApplicationActivation(ActivationOption.Server)]
[assembly: ApplicationAccessControl(false)]
[assembly: ApplicationName("DniTranApplication")]
[assembly: Description(".NET Interop Server Application")]
```

Finally, we can write a console application that calls this root class:

```
using System;
using System.Runtime.InteropServices;

using DniScMultiComponents;

namespace ScMultiComponents
{
    class Program
    {
        static void Main(string[] args)
        {
            if (args.Length == 0)
            {
                //run all tests
                PerformTest(1);
                PerformTest(2);
                PerformTest(3);
                PerformTest(4);
            }
            else
            {
                //run a single test
```

```
        try
        {
            int testNumber = Int32.Parse(args[0]);
            PerformTest(testNumber);
        }
        catch
        {
            Console.WriteLine("Unable to parse argument");
        }
    }

    Console.WriteLine("Press enter to continue");
    Console.Read();
}

private static void PerformTest(int testNumber)
{
    try
    {
        IRootComponent obj = new DniScRootObj();
        obj.PerformUpdate(testNumber);

        Console.WriteLine(
            "DniScRootObj testNumber {0} completed",
                testNumber);

        //this keeps the log files tidy
        System.Threading.Thread.Sleep(200);
    }
    catch (Exception e)
    {
        Console.WriteLine(
            "DniScRootObj test:{0} Exception: {1}: {2}",
                testNumber, e.GetType().Name, e.Message);
    }
    }
}
}
```

This client code creates an instance of the root class (DniScRootObj) and calls the
PerformUpdate test method. For each test, a different magic number is passed in order to execute each test case.

We can now review each of the tests to see the results. The first two tests called use the
DniScCalledObj object, which specifies TransactionOption.Required. For the first test, the called
object returns normally so the transaction should be committed:

```
DniScRootObj ------Starting method call------
DniScRootObj *Transaction at start of method:
DniScRootObj  IsInTransaction: True
DniScRootObj  IsolationLevel: Serializable
DniScRootObj  MyTransactionVote: Commit
DniScRootObj  DistId: 00000000-0000-0000-0000-000000000000
DniScRootObj  Tran start time: 00:47:33.5783
DniScRootObj  TranId: d9aedd90-cef6-414e-940f-94b92268d774:3
DniScRootObj  Tran Status: Active
DniScCalledObj ------Starting method call------
DniScCalledObj  IsInTransaction: True
DniScCalledObj *Transaction at start of method:
DniScCalledObj  IsolationLevel: Serializable
DniScCalledObj  MyTransactionVote: Commit
DniScCalledObj  DistId: 00000000-0000-0000-0000-000000000000
DniScCalledObj  Tran start time: 00:47:33.5783
DniScCalledObj  TranId: d9aedd90-cef6-414e-940f-94b92268d774:3
DniScCalledObj  Tran Status: Active
DniScRootObj *Transaction at TransactionCompleted:
DniScRootObj  IsInTransaction: True
DniScRootObj  MyTransactionVote: Commit
DniScRootObj  IsolationLevel: Serializable
DniScRootObj  Tran start time: 00:47:33.5783
DniScRootObj  DistId: 00000000-0000-0000-0000-000000000000
DniScRootObj  TranId: d9aedd90-cef6-414e-940f-94b92268d774:3
DniScRootObj  Tran Status: Committed
DniScCalledObj *Transaction at TransactionCompleted:
DniScCalledObj  IsInTransaction: True
DniScCalledObj  MyTransactionVote: Commit
DniScCalledObj  IsolationLevel: Serializable
DniScCalledObj  Tran start time: 00:47:33.5783
DniScCalledObj  DistId: 00000000-0000-0000-0000-000000000000
DniScCalledObj  TranId: d9aedd90-cef6-414e-940f-94b92268d774:3
DniScCalledObj  Tran Status: Committed
```

This log (as well as the other logs that follow) has been sorted by time. This allows us to see what happened to each transaction along with the overall sequence of events.

The Tran Status shows that the transaction was successfully committed. By comparing the TranId used by the two components, we see that they both used the same transaction.

The next test uses the same objects, but instructs the called object to throw an exception. Here are the sorted results from this test:

```
DniScRootObj ------Starting method call------
DniScRootObj *Transaction at start of method:
DniScRootObj  IsInTransaction: True
DniScRootObj  MyTransactionVote: Commit
DniScRootObj  IsolationLevel: Serializable
DniScRootObj  Tran start time: 00:56:45.3717
DniScRootObj  DistId: 00000000-0000-0000-0000-000000000000
DniScRootObj  TranId: d9aedd90-cef6-414e-940f-94b92268d774:4
DniScRootObj  Tran Status: Active
DniScCalledObj ------Starting method call------
DniScCalledObj *Transaction at start of method:
DniScCalledObj  IsInTransaction: True
DniScCalledObj  MyTransactionVote: Commit
DniScCalledObj  IsolationLevel: Serializable
DniScCalledObj  Tran start time: 00:56:45.3717
DniScCalledObj  DistId: 00000000-0000-0000-0000-000000000000
DniScCalledObj  TranId: d9aedd90-cef6-414e-940f-94b92268d774:4
DniScCalledObj  Tran Status: Active
DniScRootObj *Transaction at TransactionCompleted:
DniScRootObj  IsInTransaction: True
DniScRootObj  MyTransactionVote: Commit
DniScRootObj  IsolationLevel: Serializable
DniScRootObj  Tran start time: 00:56:45.3717
DniScRootObj  DistId: 00000000-0000-0000-0000-000000000000
DniScRootObj  TranId: d9aedd90-cef6-414e-940f-94b92268d774:4
DniScRootObj  Tran Status: Aborted
DniScCalledObj *Transaction at TransactionCompleted:
DniScCalledObj  IsInTransaction: True
DniScCalledObj  MyTransactionVote: Commit
DniScCalledObj  IsolationLevel: Serializable
DniScCalledObj  DistId: 00000000-0000-0000-0000-000000000000
DniScCalledObj  Tran start time: 00:56:45.3717
DniScCalledObj  TranId: d9aedd90-cef6-414e-940f-94b92268d774:4
DniScCalledObj  Tran Status: Aborted
```

In this test, the transaction was aborted due to the called component throwing an exception. We also see that as in the previous test, the same transaction was used for both components.

Since the root transaction was aborted, the client application received this exception:

```
DniScRootObj test:2 Exception: COMException:
The root transaction wanted to commit, but transaction aborted
(Exception from HRESULT: 0x8004E002)
```

The final two tests call the DniScCalledNewObj class. This class uses RequiresNew for the Transaction attribute, so we should see a new transaction being used by the called object. The first test of this set should complete the transaction normally:

```
DniScRootObj ------Starting method call------
DniScRootObj *Transaction at start of method:
DniScRootObj  IsInTransaction: True
DniScRootObj  MyTransactionVote: Commit
DniScRootObj  IsolationLevel: Serializable
DniScRootObj  Tran start time: 01:16:26.7504
DniScRootObj  DistId: 00000000-0000-0000-0000-000000000000
DniScRootObj  TranId: d9aedd90-cef6-414e-940f-94b92268d774:5
DniScRootObj  Tran Status: Active
DniScCalledNewObj ------Starting method call------
DniScCalledNewObj *Transaction at start of method:
DniScCalledNewObj  IsInTransaction: True
DniScCalledNewObj  MyTransactionVote: Commit
DniScCalledNewObj  IsolationLevel: Serializable
DniScCalledNewObj  Tran start time: 01:16:26.8005
DniScCalledNewObj  DistId: 00000000-0000-0000-0000-000000000000
DniScCalledNewObj  TranId: d9aedd90-cef6-414e-940f-94b92268d774:6
DniScCalledNewObj  Tran Status: Active
DniScRootObj *Transaction at TransactionCompleted:
DniScRootObj  IsInTransaction: True
DniScRootObj  MyTransactionVote: Commit
DniScRootObj  IsolationLevel: Serializable
DniScRootObj  Tran start time: 01:16:26.7504
DniScRootObj  DistId: 00000000-0000-0000-0000-000000000000
DniScRootObj  TranId: d9aedd90-cef6-414e-940f-94b92268d774:5
DniScRootObj  Tran Status: Committed
DniScCalledNewObj *Transaction at TransactionCompleted:
DniScCalledNewObj  IsInTransaction: True
DniScCalledNewObj  MyTransactionVote: Commit
DniScCalledNewObj  IsolationLevel: Serializable
DniScCalledNewObj  Tran start time: 01:16:26.8005
DniScCalledNewObj  DistId: 00000000-0000-0000-0000-000000000000
DniScCalledNewObj  TranId: d9aedd90-cef6-414e-940f-94b92268d774:6
DniScCalledNewObj  Tran Status: Committed
```

As we expected, each component used a different transaction. This was due to the called class using RequiresNew. Each transaction was committed normally. The sequence of events in these logs shows that the transaction for the called object was not committed until after the root transaction. This occurs even though the called object used a separate transaction.

The final test instructs the called component to throw an exception. Here are the sorted logs for this test:

```
DniScRootObj ------Starting method call------
DniScRootObj *Transaction at start of method:
DniScRootObj  IsInTransaction: True
DniScRootObj  MyTransactionVote: Commit
DniScRootObj  IsolationLevel: Serializable
DniScRootObj  Tran start time: 01:20:33.2248
DniScRootObj  DistId: 00000000-0000-0000-0000-000000000000
DniScRootObj  TranId: d9aedd90-cef6-414e-940f-94b92268d774:7
DniScRootObj  Tran Status: Active
DniScCalledNewObj ------Starting method call------
DniScCalledNewObj *Transaction at start of method:
DniScCalledNewObj  IsInTransaction: True
DniScCalledNewObj  MyTransactionVote: Commit
DniScCalledNewObj  IsolationLevel: Serializable
DniScCalledNewObj  Tran start time: 01:20:33.2749
DniScCalledNewObj  DistId: 00000000-0000-0000-0000-000000000000
DniScCalledNewObj  TranId: d9aedd90-cef6-414e-940f-94b92268d774:8
DniScCalledNewObj  Tran Status: Active
DniScCalledNewObj *Transaction at TransactionCompleted:
DniScCalledNewObj  IsInTransaction: True
DniScCalledNewObj  MyTransactionVote: Abort
DniScCalledNewObj  IsolationLevel: Serializable
DniScCalledNewObj  Tran start time: 01:20:33.2749
DniScCalledNewObj  DistId: 00000000-0000-0000-0000-000000000000
DniScCalledNewObj  TranId: d9aedd90-cef6-414e-940f-94b92268d774:8
DniScCalledNewObj  Tran Status: Aborted
DniScRootObj *Transaction at TransactionCompleted:
DniScRootObj  IsInTransaction: True
DniScRootObj  MyTransactionVote: Commit
DniScRootObj  IsolationLevel: Serializable
DniScRootObj  Tran start time: 01:20:33.2248
DniScRootObj  DistId: 00000000-0000-0000-0000-000000000000
DniScRootObj  TranId: d9aedd90-cef6-414e-940f-94b92268d774:7
DniScRootObj  Tran Status: Committed
```

In this test, we still see that the called and root objects use different transactions. The called object throws an exception that aborts its transaction. However, the transaction for the calling object is successfully committed. Notice also that in this case, the called transaction is aborted immediately, prior to the commit of the root transaction.

Related Information

See recipes 9-2 (Enabling Automatic Transactions), 9-1 (Monitoring Transaction Status), 9-3 (Placing an Automatic Vote), and 9-4 (Placing a Manual Vote).

9-6. Controlling the Transaction Isolation Level

Problem

By default, COM+ transactions are isolated from each other using the Serializable isolation level. This prevents a component from working with data that is in an intermediate state, but it is also the most restrictive setting. Is there a way to change the isolation level used for a COM+ transaction?

Solution

Starting with version 1.5, COM+ supports multiple isolation levels. Previously, the default of Serializable was used and this setting was not configurable.

COM+ 1.5 is delivered with Windows XP and above. It is not supported on Windows 2000. If you choose to use the technique described here to change the isolation level, your components will not work under Windows 2000.

To change the isolation level, you add the optional Isolation property to the Transaction attribute, for example:

```
[Transaction(TransactionOption.Required,
    Isolation = TransactionIsolationLevel.RepeatableRead)]
public class MyIsolatedClass: ServicedComponent
{
}
```

Table 9-3 summarizes the possible values for the TransactionIsolationLevel enum.

Table 9-3. *TransactionIsolationLevel Values*

Value	Usage
Serializable	This the highest possible isolation level and the default if a value isn't specified. With this level, data that is read by the current transaction cannot be changed by another transaction. It is named "serializable" since it allows the current transaction to reread the original data prior to any changes and obtain the same results. To enforce this, inserts to the data by another transaction are also prohibited, which makes this level the most restrictive and potentially a source of performance issues. It typically can result in excessive locking within the database as well as timeouts while one transaction has to wait for another to complete.
	Even though this is the most restrictive isolation level, it is still appropriate for many applications. When an application is correctly designed with short-lived transactions updating a limited amount of data, Serializable provides a good balance between integrity and performance.
RepeatableRead	Like Serializable, this isolation level prevents changes to the same data by another transaction. However, inserts to the data are allowed by other transactions. The transaction is no longer serializable in the sense that a reread of data may result in additional rows. However, this option can improve performance by reducing locking and timeouts.

Value	Usage
ReadCommitted	This level prevents a transaction from reading data being updated by another uncommitted transaction. Once the second transaction commits the changes, the data can be read.
ReadUncommitted	This level allows reading of uncommitted data, otherwise known as *dirty reads*. It provides the greatest possible concurrency and performance; however, this comes at a very big cost. A transaction may be working with data that is in an intermediate state, making business decisions based on data that have not been committed.
Any	This level accepts any isolation level. This is particularly useful for called components since it allows them to support the isolation level of the calling component. When this is used for a root component (the first one in a transaction), Serializable is substituted as the isolation level.

How It Works

You are free to mix and match the isolation level between components. However, a called component must use an isolation level that is the same or lower than its caller. A called component is not allowed to increase the isolation level.

For example, a component at the root of a transaction might use RepeatableRead as the isolation level. If another component that it calls uses RepeatableRead or ReadCommitted, the call is allowed. However, if the called component specifies Serializable, an exception is thrown and the transaction is aborted. This is because the called component required a higher isolation level.

One solution is to specify Any as the isolation level for the called component. This allows it to work with the isolation level of the calling component, regardless of the level that is specified. The other solution is to specify RequiresNew for the called component. This forces it to create a new transaction, and that transaction is capable of using any isolation level that it specifies. Of course, the two components are no longer in the same logical unit of work.

When choosing an isolation level, you need to strike a balance between data integrity and performance. Using too high an isolation level (such as Serializable) for all components may impact performance. This level may lead to excessive locking of objects in the database. Lock escalation is also fairly typical, where larger and larger sets of data are locked during the life of a transaction. This is especially troublesome for long-running tasks. While objects in the database are locked, other transactions that use the same data have to wait. This leads to timeout conditions, retries, and other issues. Many of these problems can be avoided by designing the application correctly to avoid long-running transactions and by limiting the set of data updated in the transaction.

The other extreme (using a level of ReadUncommitted) for all components is also a problem. By reading uncommitted data, you've thrown away any chance of data integrity. Any decisions made within a component are suspect since they may have been made based on transient data.

The solution is to use the appropriate isolation level for the job. If you have a lot of short-running transactions that work against a fairly small set of data, go ahead and use Serializable or RepeatableRead. This will guarantee you data integrity with minimal cost in performance. If you have long-running transactions against a large set of data, you may need to reduce the isolation level to improve concurrency within the application. But do so only in those situations where it makes sense and the potential for data-integrity problems is minimal.

Related Information

See recipes 9-2 (Enabling Automatic Transactions) and 9-5 (Defining a Unit of Work).

9-7. Implementing Transactional Code Blocks

Problem

Is there a way to use automatic transactions outside of COM+? Can this be done without deriving from the ServicedComponent class?

Solution

In addition to the transaction support provided by EnterpriseServices and the ServicedComponent class, .NET also supports the TransactionScope class in the System. Transactions namespace. This class uses a lightweight, simplified, and flexible transaction model that offers an alternative to EnterpriseServices. It allows you to use transactions without deriving from ServicedComponent. In fact, you don't even need to register the class with COM+ at all.

Note The TransactionScope class and the lightweight transaction model associated with it were introduced with the .NET Framework 2.0.

You use TransactionScope like this:

```
public void MyMethod()
{
    using (TransactionScope scope = new TransactionScope())
    {
        //update a database, queue, or other resource manager

        //perform other updates, including other databases

        //indicate that the transaction should be committed
        scope.Complete();
    }
}
```

Any operations within the TransactionScope code block are grouped together in a single transaction. Any data providers that are used within the code block will enlist themselves in the transaction. An example of a data provider is the .NET Framework provider for SQL Server. Multiple data providers referencing multiple databases can all be enlisted within the same transaction.

When `Dispose` is called on the `TransactionScope`, the transaction is either completed or aborted. By default it is aborted. To complete it, you must call the `Complete` method on the `TransactionScope` object prior to `Dispose`. In this example we use the C# using statement, which calls `Dispose` at the end of the code block. Any exception that is thrown from within the transaction block will cause `Dispose` to be called immediately.

The interesting part of this lightweight transaction model is what you don't have to do. You don't have to derive from any special class. You don't have to register the assembly with COM+ or place it in the GAC. And you don't have to work with the myriad attributes required by `EnterpriseServices`. You simply write code within the transaction block and it is enlisted in a transaction.

How It Works

For automatic transaction support along with just-in-time (JIT) activation, object pooling, role-based security, and a runtime environment to host your components, use `EnterpriseServices` (COM+). `EnterpriseServices` provides valuable services that should still be used when they meet your needs.

However, if all you really need is a simple way to enlist multiple resources in a single transaction, this lighter-weight transaction model may provide just what you need in a much simpler way.

What problems does this model solve?

- You don't have to derive your classes from `ServicedComponent`. This is sometimes a problem with the `EnterpriseServices` transaction model since only single inheritance is supported. In some cases you may prefer to inherit functionality from another class.

- It eliminates the task of deploying your code as COM+ components. You don't have to create and manage COM+ applications. Your assemblies do not need to be strongly named and they don't have to go into the GAC.

- It provides control of the transaction within your code. This is the ultimate in flexibility, allowing you to group sections of code into a transaction as you see fit. The `EnterpriseServices` model controlled transactions at the component and method level. Multiple transactions within a single method call are not supported with `EnterpriseServices`.

- It fully supports distributed transactions that span multiple resource managers such as databases and queues. `EnterpriseServices` supports this, but direct ADO.NET does not. This makes it a good candidate for supplementing ADO.NET when multiple databases must be enlisted in a single transaction.

- When dealing with a single resource, it uses a lightweight transaction that is more efficient than a distributed transaction. If multiple resources are enlisted in the transaction, it is able to promote this lightweight transaction to a distributed transaction.

The `TransactionScope` class supports several options that control creation of a transaction. By setting the `TransactionScopeOption` value during construction, you can either use the current transaction (if there is one) or create a new one. For example, the use of the `RequiresNew` value will cause a new transaction to be created, even if one already exists:

```
using (TransactionScope scope = new TransactionScope(
    TransactionScopeOption.RequiresNew))
{
    //perform resource updates

    scope.Complete();
}
```

This option is useful if we are embedding TransactionScope blocks within other TransactionScope blocks. You can also use a TransactionScope block within a ServicedComponent method. In this case, using RequiresNew forces the creation of a new transaction instead of using the one inherited by the component.

If the TransactionScopeOption parameter is omitted, the default value is Required. This will use an existing transaction or create one if it doesn't exist.

The other available option for TransactionScopeOption is Suppress. The best example of using this option would be when you are embedding a TransactionScope block within a ServicedComponent method. Using Suppress will cause the block of code to execute as if a transaction didn't exist. The remainder of the code outside of the block will work within the transaction that was supplied to the component.

Another TransactionScope constructor accepts a TransactionOptions structure. This allows you to set the isolation level and transaction timeout, for example:

```
TransactionOptions options = new TransactionOptions();
options.IsolationLevel = IsolationLevel.RepeatableRead;
options.Timeout = new TimeSpan(0, 0, 30); //30 sec timeout
using (TransactionScope scope = new TransactionScope(
    TransactionScopeOption.Required, options))
{
    //perform resource updates

    scope.Complete();
}
```

The C# code that follows provides a simple example of using TransactionScope:

```
using System;
using System.Transactions;

using TransactionLogging;

namespace DniScTranScope
{
    public interface ILocalScope
    {
        void UseLocalScope(bool succeed);
    }

    public class DniScTranScopeObj : ILocalScope
    {
```

```csharp
public void UseLocalScope(bool succeed)
{
    TransactionScope scope = new TransactionScope();
    using (scope)
    {
        //log the state of the transaction
        TransactionLogger log
            = new TransactionLogger(this);

        //
        //update a database or other
        //resource manager here
        //

        if (succeed)
        {
            //signal that the transaction
            //should be committed
            scope.Complete();
        }
    }
}
```

As shown here, you need to reference the System.Transactions namespace since that's where the TransactionScope class is located. Remember to add this assembly to your project; it isn't included by default.

Based on the bool value passed to UseLocalScope, the method either calls the Complete method or omits the call. This allows us to see the results when a transaction completes or is aborted. The TransactionLogger class (discussed in recipe 9-1 [Monitoring Transaction Status]) is used here to log details of the transaction for us to see.

If we compare this code to other examples in this chapter, we see the simplicity of using TransactionScope. Gone are all of the EnterpriseServices and interop attributes such as Transaction, AutoComplete, ClassInterface, and the ServicedComponent class. We also don't need any of the assembly-level attributes that we usually add, such as ApplicationActivation, ApplicationAccessControl, and ApplicationName.

Here is a Visual Basic .NET (VB.NET) implementation of the same class and interface:

```vbnet
Imports System.Transactions
Imports DniScTranScopeVB.TransactionLogging

Public Interface ILocalScope
    Sub UseLocalScope(ByVal succeed As Boolean)
End Interface

Public Class DniScTranScopeObj
    Implements ILocalScope
```

```vb
Public Sub UseLocalScope(ByVal succeed As Boolean) _
    Implements ILocalScope.UseLocalScope

    'start the transaction scope
    Using scope As TransactionScope _
        = New TransactionScope()

        'log the transaction
        Dim log As TransactionLogger _
            = New TransactionLogger(Me)

        '
        'update a database or other
        'resource manager here
        '

        If succeed Then
            scope.Complete()
        End If
    End Using

End Sub
End Class
```

The client code to use the C# version of this class is implemented like this:

```csharp
using System;
using DniScTranScope;

namespace ScTranScope
{
    class Program
    {
        static void Main(string[] args)
        {
            ILocalScope obj
                = new DniScTranScopeObj();
            obj.UseLocalScope(true);
            obj.UseLocalScope(false);

            Console.WriteLine("Press enter to continue");
            Console.Read();
        }
    }
}
```

Once this is executed, we can review the transaction logs produced by the TransactionLogger class. The first call to UseLocalScope passed a value of true so the transaction was committed:

```
------Starting method call------
*Transaction at start of method:
 IsInTransaction: False
 IsolationLevel: Serializable
 Tran start time: 20:53:52.8300
 DistId: 00000000-0000-0000-0000-000000000000
 TranId: 63d517db-6548-4286-a961-41022ea376ff:1
 Tran Status: Active
*Transaction at TransactionCompleted:
 IsInTransaction: False
 IsolationLevel: Serializable
 Tran start time: 20:53:52.8300
 DistId: 00000000-0000-0000-0000-000000000000
 TranId: 63d517db-6548-4286-a961-41022ea376ff:1
 Tran Status: Committed
```

As always, the results when run on your machine will be different. Notice that we have a local transaction ID but not a distributed transaction ID. This is because TransactionScope always starts with a lightweight (more efficient) local transaction. It is capable of promoting this to a distributed transaction if and when it becomes necessary. This makes TransactionScope efficient for simple operations that involve only a single local resource.

The second call to UseLocalScope passed a value of false, so the Complete method is never called on the TransactionScope object. This causes the transaction to be aborted:

```
------Starting method call------
*Transaction at start of method:
 IsInTransaction: False
 IsolationLevel: Serializable
 Tran start time: 20:53:52.8300
 DistId: 00000000-0000-0000-0000-000000000000
 TranId: 63d517db-6548-4286-a961-41022ea376ff:2
 Tran Status: Active
*Transaction at TransactionCompleted:
 IsInTransaction: False
 IsolationLevel: Serializable
 Tran start time: 20:53:52.8300
 DistId: 00000000-0000-0000-0000-000000000000
 TranId: 63d517db-6548-4286-a961-41022ea376ff:2
 Tran Status: Aborted
```

Related Information

See recipes 9-2 (Enabling Automatic Transactions), 9-1 (Monitoring Transaction Status), 9-3 (Placing an Automatic Vote), 9-9 (Using Services Without Components), and 9-8 (Building Your Own Resource Manager).

9-8. Building Your Own Resource Manager

Problem

You'd like to use transactional code blocks with resources other than databases and queues. Are you limited to using only the standard resource managers? Is there a way to develop your own resource manager?

Solution

.NET provides a way to develop and use our own resource managers. Why would you want to do this? Perhaps you need to update an XML or text file. Or you need to make a web services call that updates an external application. Or you need to update a set of objects that reside in an in-memory cache. You can certainly perform all of these activities without writing a resource manager.

However, perhaps you want to perform these tasks within the scope of a transaction. You may need to coordinate these tasks with updates to other resources such as a database or queue. That's the problem that a custom resource manager solves. It allows you to enlist other custom activities within the logical unit of work called a transaction.

The steps needed to develop and use your own resource manager include the following:

- Develop a class that is capable of being managed. This is your resource class. The class may have the concept of committing and rolling back its state. Exactly how this is done will greatly depend on the purpose of the class. Or, the commit and rollback logic may reside in the resource manager.

- Develop a resource manager class that implements the IEnlistmentNotification interface. This class uses the resource class that was developed.

- Provide implementations for the methods of the IEnlistmentNotification interface such as Prepare, Commit, and Rollback. After this resource manager is enlisted in a transaction, these methods are called at specific times during the life of the transaction.

- The resource class should create an instance of its resource manager and enlist it in the current transaction. It should first determine if a transaction exists before attempting to do this.

- Use the resource class within the scope of a transaction. When the resource object is created or changed, its resource manager is enlisted in the transaction. When the transaction is completed, the resource manager is notified and the state of the resource can be committed or rolled back.

If you enlist a new activity within the scope of a transaction, it means that everything in the transaction either succeeds or fails. If any resources have been updated and a failure occurs elsewhere within the transaction, those resources must be rolled back. Likewise, if everything in the transaction succeeds, you need to commit any changes to the resource. How you define the commit and rollback is up to you; they are specific to the resource that you are managing.

For instance, if you have a resource that writes an XML file, rolling back the change may involve deleting the file. Or it may be restoring a prior version of the file. That would require you to create a backup of the file prior to any changes. Those decisions are up to you.

If you have a resource that calls a web service, rolling back the call itself isn't possible today, although enhanced web service APIs will support this in the future. However, you could logically roll back the effect of the call by invoking a different web service. To put it another way, if the first web service call debited an account, the rollback could perform a credit.

Consider the task of writing a string to a file. We can use this simple task to illustrate the use of a custom resource manager. We want the ability to enlist the changes we make to a file with an active transaction. This will allow the transaction to control whether to commit or roll back the file changes.

We can start with a class that handles the writing of string data to a file. This is our resource class. Here is the implementation in C#:

```csharp
using System;
using System.IO;
using System.Transactions;

namespace DniScResource
{
    /// <summary>
    /// Writes a file that can be under the control
    /// of a transaction
    /// </summary>
    public class CommittableFile : IDisposable
    {
        private string           m_FilePath;
        private string           m_TempFilePath;
        private StreamWriter     m_Writer;
        private bool             m_Completed;
        private bool             m_WriterOpen;

        public CommittableFile(string filepath)
        {
            //save the real file path
            m_FilePath = filepath;
            //create a temporary file path
            string path = Path.GetPathRoot(filepath);
            string tempFileOnly
                = Path.GetFileName(Path.GetTempFileName());
            m_TempFilePath = Path.Combine(path, tempFileOnly);
            //initially write to a temporary file
            m_Writer = new StreamWriter(m_TempFilePath);
            m_WriterOpen = true;

            if (Transaction.Current != null)
            {
```

```
            //create our resource manager and enlist
            //it in the current transaction
            FileResourceManager resourceMgr
                = new FileResourceManager(this);
            Transaction.Current.EnlistVolatile(
                resourceMgr, EnlistmentOptions.None);
        }
    }

    public void WriteString(string data)
    {
        m_Writer.Write(data);
        m_Writer.Flush();
    }

    public void Commit()
    {
        //close the temporary file
        CloseTempFile();
        //copy the temp file to the real file name
        File.Copy(m_TempFilePath, m_FilePath, true);
        //delete the temporary file
        File.Delete(m_TempFilePath);
        m_Completed = true;
    }

    public void Rollback()
    {
        //clean up any temporary and permanent files
        CloseTempFile();
        if (!m_Completed)
        {
            //delete the temporary file if it exists
            if (File.Exists(m_TempFilePath))
            {
                File.Delete(m_TempFilePath);
            }
        }
    }

    public void Dispose()
    {
        CloseTempFile();

        //if commit was never called, we do a rollback
        if (!m_Completed)
        {
            Rollback();
```

```
            }
        }

        private void CloseTempFile()
        {
            if (m_WriterOpen)
            {
                m_Writer.Close();
                m_WriterOpen = false;
            }
        }
    }
}
```

A requirement of this example is to allow commit and rollback logic for the file. The approach that we've taken with this class is to write data to a temporary file instead of the requested file. When a commit takes place, the temporary file is closed, copied to the requested file path, and finally deleted. If a rollback is necessary, we delete the temporary file.

To keep this example simple, we've made the assumption that the output file does not already exist. By making that assumption, we don't have to worry about backing up and restoring the original version of the file during a rollback. Instead, we can delete the temporary (uncommitted) file.

The constructor of our class is passed the full path to the output file that it should create. It uses the path from this parameter to build a temporary file name. A StreamWriter is opened using the name of the temporary file. All writes are made to this temporary file.

The constructor also includes the code to enlist this class in an existing transaction. This is where we create an instance of our resource manager class, FileResourceManager. We'll look at the details of this class next. After constructing the resource manager, we enlist it in the current transaction using the EnlistVolatile method. Notice that we do this only if there is an active transaction. This allows us to also use this class outside of a transaction.

The WriteString method is where we write a string to the open StreamWriter. The Commit and Rollback methods finalize the state of this file resource. The Commit method closes the temporary file and copies it to the permanent file path. The temporary file is then deleted. The Rollback method closes the temporary file and deletes it.

We've also implemented the IDisposable interface and its Dispose method for this class. This allows us to implement default behavior to clean up the temporary file if Commit is never called.

Now we can move on to the FileResourceManager class. This is our resource manager that is enlisted into the current transaction. Here is the C# implementation for this class:

```
using System;
using System.Transactions;

namespace DniScResource
{
    public class FileResourceManager : IEnlistmentNotification
    {
        private CommittableFile m_File;
```

```
        public FileResourceManager(CommittableFile file)
        {
            //save the file passed to us
            m_File = file;
        }

        public void Commit(Enlistment enlistment)
        {
            //commit our committable file object
            m_File.Commit();
            //indicate that everything committed ok
            enlistment.Done();
        }

        public void InDoubt(Enlistment enlistment)
        {
            //the transaction is in doubt because one or more
            //resource managers cannot be contacted
            Rollback(enlistment);
        }

        public void Prepare(PreparingEnlistment preparingEnlistment)
        {
            //called when we are about to commit.
            //indicate that everything is ok to commit.
            preparingEnlistment.Prepared();
        }

        public void Rollback(Enlistment enlistment)
        {
            //the transaction is rolling back. We need
            //to roll back our committable file object
            m_File.Rollback();
            enlistment.Done();
        }
    }
}
```

The class implements the IEnlistmentNotification interface. This is a requirement in order to enlist this class with a transaction. Other than the constructor, all of the methods shown in this class are defined by this interface.

The constructor is passed an instance of a CommittableFile object. This is the class that was just reviewed. It is passed as an argument to identify the resource that we are managing. The remainder of this class is fairly straightforward. The methods are called at specific times during the lifetime of the transaction.

The Prepare method is called just before the transaction is about to call Commit. By calling the Prepared method of the PreparingEnlistment object passed to us, we indicate that we are ready to commit the transaction.

For the Commit and Rollback methods, we simply call the corresponding method in the resource class. We also signal the completion of the commit or rollback by calling the Done method of the Enlistment object.

The InDoubt method is called only if the transaction is considered "in doubt." This occurs when the transaction coordinator is unable to contact one of the resource managers. In that case, we decided to simply Rollback any pending changes.

We can test our new classes with this C# console application:

```
using System;
using System.IO;
using System.Transactions;

using DniScResource;

namespace ScResourceManager
{
    class Program
    {
        static void Main(string[] args)
        {
            NoTranFileTest();
            FileTestCommit();
            FileTestRollback();
            TwoFileRollback();

            Console.WriteLine("Press enter to continue");
            Console.Read();
        }

        static void NoTranFileTest()
        {
            //use the file class without a transaction

            CommittableFile file
                = new CommittableFile(@"c:\DniTestFile0.txt");
            file.WriteString("write this text");
            file.Commit();

            Console.WriteLine(
                "NoTranFileTest file exists: {0}",
                    File.Exists(@"c:\DniTestFile0.txt"));
        }

        static void FileTestCommit()
        {
            //use the file class within a transaction
            //and successfully commit it
```

```
        TransactionScope scope = new TransactionScope();
        using (scope)
        {
            CommittableFile file
                = new CommittableFile(@"c:\DniTestFile1.txt");
            file.WriteString("write this text");
            scope.Complete();
        }

        Console.WriteLine(
            "FileTestCommit file exists: {0}",
                File.Exists(@"c:\DniTestFile1.txt"));
    }

    static void FileTestRollback()
    {
        //use the file class within a transaction
        //but cause it to be rolled back

        TransactionScope scope = new TransactionScope();
        using (scope)
        {
            CommittableFile file
                = new CommittableFile(@"c:\DniTestFile2.txt");
            file.WriteString("write this text");

            //do not call scope.complete for this test
        }

        Console.WriteLine(
            "FileTestRollback file exists: {0}",
                File.Exists(@"c:\DniTestFile2.txt"));
    }

    static void TwoFileRollback()
    {
        //use two files within the same transaction.
        //both should be rolled back

        TransactionScope scope = new TransactionScope();
        using (scope)
        {
            CommittableFile file3
                = new CommittableFile(@"c:\DniTestFile3.txt");
            file3.WriteString("write this text");
```

```
        CommittableFile file4
            = new CommittableFile(@"c:\DniTestFile4.txt");
        file4.WriteString("write this text");

        //do not call scope.complete for this test
    }

    Console.WriteLine(
        "TwoFileRollback files exist: {0}, {1}",
            File.Exists(@"c:\DniTestFile3.txt"),
            File.Exists(@"c:\DniTestFile4.txt"));
    }


}
}
```

The code runs a series of tests using these classes. The first test (NoTranFileTest) uses the CommittableFile class on its own without a transaction. The second test (FileTestCommit) uses a transaction and commits it. The third test (FileTestRollback) also uses a transaction but causes the transaction to fail. This should roll back changes to the file. The final test (TwoFileRollback) performs a rollback of two files by allowing the transactional code block to exit without calling Complete.

At the completion of each test, we check for the existence of the expected output file(s). When we execute this code, we see these results:

```
NoTranFileTest file exists: True
FileTestCommit file exists: True
FileTestRollback file exists: False
TwoFileRollback files exist: False, False
Press enter to continue
```

As expected, the first two tests successfully wrote the file. The last two tests did not, since they rolled back the transaction instead of committing it.

How It Works

In the implementation shown in the preceding section, the commit and rollback logic was placed in the resource class itself (CommittableFile). The resource manager class (FileResourceManager) was simply a pass-through to the methods in the resource.

This is just one way to implement these classes. We could just as easily push the commit and rollback logic into the resource manager. The resource class would then be greatly simplified, allowing it to focus on the job of writing a file without rollback and commit logic. What follows is an alternate implementation of these classes that demonstrates this second approach.

We start with a revised version of the CommittableFile class in C# that we name CommittableFileAlt:

```csharp
using System;
using System.IO;
using System.Transactions;

namespace DniScResourceAlternate
{
    /// <summary>
    /// Writes a file that can be under the control
    /// of a transaction
    /// </summary>
    public class CommittableFileAlt
    {
        private string        m_FilePath;
        private StreamWriter  m_Writer;
        private bool          m_WriterOpen;

        public CommittableFileAlt(string filepath)
        {
            //save the file path
            m_FilePath = filepath;

            if (Transaction.Current != null)
            {
                //create our resource manager and enlist
                //it in the current transaction
                FileResourceManagerAlt resourceMgr
                    = new FileResourceManagerAlt(this);
                Transaction.Current.EnlistVolatile(
                    resourceMgr, EnlistmentOptions.None);
            }

            //open the output streamwriter
            m_Writer = new StreamWriter(m_FilePath);
            m_WriterOpen = true;
        }

        public string FilePath
        {
            get { return m_FilePath; }
            set { m_FilePath = value; }
        }

        public void WriteString(string data)
        {
            m_Writer.Write(data);
            m_Writer.Flush();
        }
```

```csharp
        public void Close()
        {
            if (m_WriterOpen)
            {
                m_Writer.Close();
                m_WriterOpen = false;
            }
        }
    }
}
```

We have removed the Commit and Rollback methods from the class and exposed a public
Close method. We have also exposed a new property named FilePath that allows us to change
the path from our resource manager class.

The constructor still creates the resource manager (an alternate version of it) and enlists it
in the current transaction. Notice that this now takes place prior to creation of the StreamWriter.
This allows the resource manager constructor to change the file name to a temporary file. It
uses the FilePath property that we added to do this.

The revised resource manager class looks like this in C#:

```csharp
using System;
using System.IO;
using System.Transactions;

namespace DniScResourceAlternate
{
    public class FileResourceManagerAlt : IEnlistmentNotification
    {
        private CommittableFileAlt m_File;
        private string m_FilePath;
        private string m_TempFilePath;

        public FileResourceManagerAlt(CommittableFileAlt file)
        {
            //save the file object passed to us
            m_File = file;

            //save the original file path
            m_FilePath = m_File.FilePath;
            //create a temporary file path
            string path = Path.GetPathRoot(m_FilePath);
            string tempFileOnly
                = Path.GetFileName(Path.GetTempFileName());
            m_TempFilePath = Path.Combine(path, tempFileOnly);
            //tell the file object to use the temporary
            //file instead of the original file
            m_File.FilePath = m_TempFilePath;
        }
```

```csharp
        public void Commit(Enlistment enlistment)
        {
            //close the temporary file
            m_File.Close();
            //copy the temporary file to the real file name
            File.Copy(m_TempFilePath, m_FilePath, true);
            //delete the temporary file
            File.Delete(m_TempFilePath);
            //indicate that everything committed ok
            enlistment.Done();
        }

        public void InDoubt(Enlistment enlistment)
        {
            //the transaction is in doubt because one or more
            //resource managers cannot be contacted
            Rollback(enlistment);
        }

        public void Prepare(PreparingEnlistment preparingEnlistment)
        {
            //called when we are about to commit.
            //indicate that everything is ok to commit.
            preparingEnlistment.Prepared();
        }

        public void Rollback(Enlistment enlistment)
        {
            //the transaction is rolling back. We need
            //to clean up any temporary and permanent files
            m_File.Close();
            //delete the temporary file if it exists
            if (File.Exists(m_TempFilePath))
            {
                File.Delete(m_TempFilePath);
            }
            enlistment.Done();
        }
    }
}
```

During construction, a temporary file name is generated and used to set the FilePath property of the CommittableFileAlt object. This causes all writing to be done to the temporary file.

The Commit and Rollback methods now contain the logic that previously resided in the resource class.

We can revise our client test code to include these new tests:

```
static void AlternateNoTranFileTest()
{
    //use the file class without a transaction

    CommittableFileAlt file
        = new CommittableFileAlt(@"c:\DniAltTestFile0.txt");
    file.WriteString("write this text");
    file.Close();

    Console.WriteLine(
        "AlternateNoTranFileTest file exists: {0}",
            File.Exists(@"c:\DniAltTestFile0.txt"));
}

static void AlternateFileTestCommit()
{
    //use the file class within a transaction
    //and successfully commit it

    TransactionScope scope = new TransactionScope();
    using (scope)
    {
        CommittableFileAlt file
            = new CommittableFileAlt(@"c:\DniAltTestFile1.txt");
        file.WriteString("write this text");
        scope.Complete();
    }

    Console.WriteLine(
        "AlternateFileTestCommit file exists: {0}",
            File.Exists(@"c:\DniAltTestFile1.txt"));
}

static void AlternateFileTestRollback()
{
    //use the file class within a transaction
    //and successfully commit it

    TransactionScope scope = new TransactionScope();
    using (scope)
    {
        CommittableFileAlt file
            = new CommittableFileAlt(@"c:\DniAltTestFile2.txt");
        file.WriteString("write this text");
        //do not call scope.complete for this test
    }
```

```
    Console.WriteLine(
        "AlternateFileTestRollback file exists: {0}",
            File.Exists(@"c:\DniAltTestFile2.txt"));
}
```

We also need an additional using statement since we placed these new classes in a new namespace:

```
using DniScResourceAlternate;
```

Finally, we add code to execute the new test methods:

```
static void Main(string[] args)
{
    NoTranFileTest();
    FileTestCommit();
    FileTestRollback();
    TwoFileRollback();

    AlternateNoTranFileTest();
    AlternateFileTestCommit();
    AlternateFileTestRollback();

    Console.WriteLine("Press enter to continue");
    Console.Read();
}
```

The results now look like this:

```
NoTranFileTest file exists: True
FileTestCommit file exists: True
FileTestRollback file exists: False
TwoFileRollback files exist: False, False
AlternateNoTranFileTest file exists: True
AlternateFileTestCommit file exists: True
AlternateFileTestRollback file exists: False
Press enter to continue
```

The results show that this new approach works just as well as the original.

Regardless of the approach used, writing our own custom resource manager is actually a straightforward task. By doing this, we have the opportunity to place just about any task under transaction control. We can enlist our new resources in the same transaction with those that traditionally use transactions, such as databases.

Related Information

See recipe 9-7 (Implementing Transactional Code Blocks).

9-9. Using Services Without Components

Problem

Is there a way to access COM+ services without implementing a COM+ component? More specifically, can you use COM+ transactions without a component?

Solution

The traditional way to use the services provided by COM+ is to develop a COM+ component. To do that in .NET, you must implement a class that is derived from ServicedComponent. While this works in most situations, it is sometimes useful to use COM+ services without implementing a full COM+ component.

.NET provides two ways to use COM+ transactions without a COM+ component. Recipe 9-7 (Implementing Transactional Code Blocks) describes the use of the TransactionScope class that was added in the .NET Framework 2.0. This recipe describes the second way to do this: *services without components.*

▓Note The support for services without components was added with COM+ version 1.5 and was deployed with Windows XP and Windows 2003 Server. Because this support is lacking from earlier versions of COM+, the approach to COM+ services outlined in this recipe cannot be used when deploying to Windows 2000.

Services without components allows you to create a COM+ context directly anywhere in your code. A COM+ context is the runtime environment used to host COM+ components. When a COM+ component is activated, it lives in a new or existing context. The properties of the context determine the runtime characteristics of any components activated within the context.

By creating a context in code, you determine the block of code that executes within that context. Once the context is created, all code following that point is executed as if it were a method of a COM+ component. When you have finished with the context, you can exit it. To COM+, this appears just as if a method returned. At this point, any active transaction is either completed or aborted.

The ServiceDomain and ServiceConfig classes enable you to use these COM+ services from a .NET class. The ServiceConfig class is used to provide the configuration for the context. Think of this as the definition of the runtime environment for your code, for example:

```
ServiceConfig config            = new ServiceConfig();
config.Transaction              = TransactionOption.Required;
config.TrackingAppName          = "MyAppName";
config.TrackingComponentName    = "MyComponentName";
config.TrackingEnabled          = true;
```

The most important property that you set is Transaction, since this defines the kind of transaction support that you are requesting. In this example, we set this property to Required, which will ensure that we have a transaction. The other properties that we set here define an application and component name that are used for tracking of the context during execution.

■Note Setting the Tracking properties allows you to actually view your COM+ context within the Component Services Management Console plug-in. You can see the executing context by drilling down into the Running Processes tree. Once there, you should see a process with the application and component name that you specify here.

From this management tool, your context looks just like any other COM+ component. The reality is that it isn't; it's simply a block of code within a method that you chose to execute within a COM+ context.

Once you set the values in the ServiceConfig object, you can enter a COM+ context like this:

```
ServiceDomain.Enter(config);
```

The static Enter method requires an instance of the ServiceConfig class to be passed as a parameter.

You can execute this statement anywhere in your code. Any code that you execute after this statement is run within the context that you configured. If you requested a COM+ transaction by setting the Transaction property of the ServiceConfig object, you now have an active transaction. Any code that uses a resource manager, such as a database or queue, will be enlisted in that transaction.

When you have finished with your work in the context and wish to exit, you use the static Leave method like this:

```
ServiceDomain.Leave();
```

If you were in a transaction, you must remember to cast your vote for the transaction prior to leaving the COM+ context.

One you have left the domain, you are free to execute any other code in your method. The difference is that now you are executing code outside of a COM+ context. If a transaction was active while you were in the context, it has now either completed or aborted based on your vote.

How It Works

The C# code that follows demonstrates the use of the ServiceConfig and ServiceDomain classes to use COM+ services without a component:

```csharp
using System;
using System.EnterpriseServices;

using TransactionLogging;

namespace DniScServices
{
    public interface IServicesWithoutComponents
    {
        void UseComPlusServices(Boolean succeed);
    }
```

```
public class DniScServicesObj : IServicesWithoutComponents
{
    public void UseComPlusServices(Boolean succeed)
    {
        ServiceConfig config   = new ServiceConfig();
        config.Transaction     = TransactionOption.Required;
        config.TrackingAppName = "ServicesWithoutComponents";
        config.TrackingComponentName = "DniScServicesObj";
        config.TrackingEnabled = true;

        try
        {
            //enter a COM+ context
            ServiceDomain.Enter(config);

            //log the transaction
            TransactionLogger log
                = new TransactionLogger(this);

            //do work here involving one or more
            //resources such as a database or queue

            //complete or abort the transaction
            if (succeed)
            {
                ContextUtil.SetComplete();
            }
            else
            {
                ContextUtil.SetAbort();
            }
        }
        finally
        {
            //leave the COM+ context
            ServiceDomain.Leave();
        }
    }
}
```

We need to use the System.EnterpriseServices namespace, since it contains the classes that access COM+ services.

Notice that our class does not derive from ServicedComponent. We also do not need any of the EnterpriseServices attributes normally used when working with a COM+ component. Also missing are the assembly-level attributes that we normally use to register the assembly as a COM+ application. None of that is needed since this is ordinary C# code.

After setting up the properties of a ServiceConfig object, we call the static Enter method of ServiceDomain. At this point we are running within the context that COM+ created. If we were to view the Running Processes within the Component Services Management Console plug-in, we would see our process running as if it were a COM+ component.

Since we set the Transaction property of the ServiceConfig object to Required, we now have a transaction. To prove this, we use the TransactionLogger class that we developed in an earlier recipe. This logs the state of the transaction immediately upon construction as well as at completion of the transaction.

Depending on a parameter passed to the test method, we call either SetComplete or SetAbort using the ContextUtil class. This places our transaction vote within this COM+ context.

Finally, we call the static Leave method of the ServiceDomain class. This exits the context and also causes the transaction to be completed. Based on our vote, it will either be committed or aborted at this point.

Here is the same class implemented in Visual Basic .NET (VB.NET):

```vb
Imports System.EnterpriseServices
Imports DniScServicesVB.TransactionLogging

Public Interface IServicesWithoutComponents
    Sub UseComPlusServices(ByVal succeed As Boolean)
End Interface

Public Class DniScServicesObj
    Implements IServicesWithoutComponents

    Public Sub UseComPlusServices(ByVal succeed As Boolean) _
        Implements IServicesWithoutComponents.UseComPlusServices

        'configure the COM+ services
        Dim config As ServiceConfig _
            = New ServiceConfig()
        config.Transaction = TransactionOption.Required
        config.TrackingAppName = "ServicesWithoutComponents"
        config.TrackingComponentName = "DniScServicesObj"
        config.TrackingEnabled = True

        Try
            'enter a COM+ context
            ServiceDomain.Enter(config)

            'log the transaction
            Dim log As TransactionLogger _
                = New TransactionLogger(Me)

            'do work here involving one or more
            'resources such as a database or queue
```

```
            'complete or abort the transaction
            If succeed Then
                ContextUtil.SetComplete()
            Else
                ContextUtil.SetAbort()
            End If
        Finally
            'leave the COM+ context
            ServiceDomain.Leave()
        End Try

    End Sub
End Class
```

Here is the C# console application that executes the C# implementation of this test class. To use the VB.NET version instead, you reference the VB.NET project instead of the C# project and change the using DniScServices statement to using DniScServicesVB:

```csharp
using System;
using DniScServices;

namespace ScServicesWithoutComponents
{
    class Program
    {
        static void Main(string[] args)
        {
            IServicesWithoutComponents obj
                = new DniScServicesObj();

            //execute a test that completes the transaction
            obj.UseComPlusServices(true);

            //give the transaction logs time to clean up
            System.Threading.Thread.Sleep(200);

            //execute another test that aborts the transaction
            obj.UseComPlusServices(false);

            Console.WriteLine("Press enter to continue");
            Console.Read();
        }
    }
}
```

We call the UseComPlusServices test method twice. The first time we pass true, which results in a completed transaction. The second time, we pass false, and the transaction should be aborted.

After running this test, we can view the transaction log file that was created by the TransactionLogger class. For our test, the log looks like this:

```
------Starting method call------
*Transaction at start of method:
 IsInTransaction: True
 MyTransactionVote: Commit
 IsolationLevel: Serializable
 Tran start time: 01:15:51.7977
 DistId: 00000000-0000-0000-0000-000000000000
 TranId: a48a886f-7dc9-49b3-b9ee-cc9117f7b9c9:1
 Tran Status: Active
*Transaction at TransactionCompleted:
 IsInTransaction: False
 IsolationLevel: Serializable
 Tran start time: 01:15:51.7977
 DistId: 00000000-0000-0000-0000-000000000000
 TranId: a48a886f-7dc9-49b3-b9ee-cc9117f7b9c9:1
 Tran Status: Committed
------Starting method call------
*Transaction at start of method:
 IsInTransaction: True
 MyTransactionVote: Commit
 IsolationLevel: Serializable
 Tran start time: 01:15:52.0481
 DistId: 00000000-0000-0000-0000-000000000000
 TranId: a48a886f-7dc9-49b3-b9ee-cc9117f7b9c9:2
 Tran Status: Active
*Transaction at TransactionCompleted:
 IsInTransaction: False
 IsolationLevel: Serializable
 Tran start time: 01:15:52.0481
 DistId: 00000000-0000-0000-0000-000000000000
 TranId: a48a886f-7dc9-49b3-b9ee-cc9117f7b9c9:2
 Tran Status: Aborted
```

As expected, the logs show that the first transaction was committed and the second was aborted. We have successfully used COM+ transactions from outside of a COM+ component.

Related Information

See recipe 9-7 (Implementing Transactional Code Blocks) and 9-2 (Enabling Automatic Transactions).

Index

You Need the Companion eBook

Your purchase of this book entitles you to its companion eBook for only $10.

We believe this Apress title will prove so indispensable that you'll want to carry it with you everywhere, which is why we are offering the companion eBook for $10 to customers who purchase this book now. Convenient and fully searchable, the eBook version of any content-rich, page-heavy Apress book makes a valuable addition to your programming library. You can easily find, copy, and apply code—and then perform examples by quickly toggling between instructions and the application. Even simultaneously tackling a donut, diet soda, and complex code becomes simplified with hands-free eBooks!

Once you purchase this book, getting the $10 companion eBook is simple:

❶ Visit **www.apress.com/promo/tendollars/**.

❷ Complete a basic registration form to receive a randomly generated question about this title.

❸ Answer the question correctly in 60 seconds and you will receive a promotional code to redeem for the $10 eBook.

2560 Ninth Street • Suite 219 • Berkeley, CA 94710

Offer valid through 10/06.

Printed in the United States
By Bookmasters